MindTap™

QUICK START GUIDE

1. To get started, navigate to www.cengagebrain.com and select "Register a Product."

A new screen will appear prompting you to add a Course Key. A Course Key is a code given to you by your instructor — this is the first of two codes you will need to access MindTap. Every student in your course section should have the same Course Key.

2. Enter the Course Key and click "Register."

If you are accessing MindTap through your school's Learning Management System, such as BlackBoard or Desire2Learn, you may be redirected to use your Course Key/Access Code there. Follow the prompts you are given and feel free to contact support if you need assistance.

3. Confirm your course information above and proceed to the log in portion below.

If you have a CengageBrain username and password, enter it under "Returning Students" and click "Login." If this is your first time, register under "New Students" and click "Create a New Account."

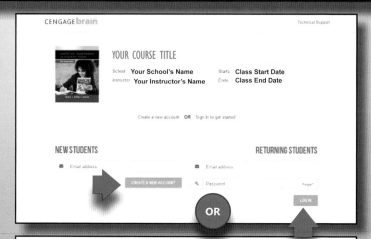

4. Now that you are logged in, you can access the course for free by selecting "Start Free Trial" for 20 days or enter in your Access Code.

Your Access Code is unique to you and acts as payment for MindTap. You may have received it with your book or purchased separately in the bookstore or at www.cengagebrain.com. Enter it and click "Register."

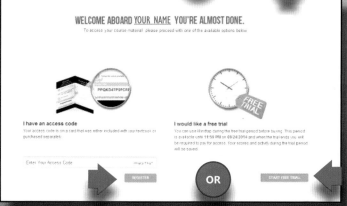

NEED HELP?

For CengageBrain Support: Login to **Support.Cengage.com**. Call **866-994-2427** or access our **24/7 Student Chat!** Or access the **First Day of School PowerPoint Presentation** found at **www.cengagebrain.com**.

THE
AMERICAN PAGEANT

A History of the American People

SIXTEENTH EDITION

VOLUME 1: TO 1877

David M. Kennedy

Stanford University

Lizabeth Cohen

Harvard University

CENGAGE
Learning·

Australia • Brazil • Mexico • Singapore • United Kingdom • United States

CENGAGE
Learning®

The American Pageant: A History of the American People, Vol 1: To 1877,
Sixteenth Edition
David M. Kennedy/Lizabeth Cohen

Product Manager: Clint Attebery

Senior Content Developer:
Margaret McAndrew Beasley

Associate Content Developer: Alison Levy

Product Assistant: Liz Fraser

Media Developer: Kate MacLean

Marketing Development Manager:
Kyle Zimmerman

Senior Content Project Manager:
Carol Newman

Senior Art Director: Cate Rickard Barr

Manufacturing Planner: Sandee Milewski

IP Project Manager: Alexandra Ricciardi

IP Analyst: Amber Hosea

Production Service/Compositor:
Cenveo Publisher Services

Text Designer: Liz Harasymczuk Design

Cover Designer: Wing Ngan, ink design, inc.

Part-opener design images: Rocky Mountain
Quilt Museum, PQ1991.001.022, photo by
Mellisa Karlin Mahoney

Chapter-opener design images: New England
Quilt Museum, 1991.24, photo by Ken Burris

Cover Image: "The Flag That Was Waved One
Hundred Years Ago," July 4, 1876, lithograph.
Mary Evans Picture Library/The Everett
Collection

For product information and technology assistance, contact us at
Cengage Learning Customer & Sales Support, 1-800-354-9706.

For permission to use material from this text or product,
submit all requests online at **www.cengage.com/permissions.**
Further permissions questions can be e-mailed to
permissionrequest@cengage.com.

Library of Congress Control Number: 2014936315

Student Edition:
ISBN: 978-1-305-07593-1

Cengage Learning
20 Channel Center Street
Boston, MA 02210
USA

Cengage Learning is a leading provider of customized learning solutions with
office locations around the globe, including Singapore, the United Kingdom,
Australia, Mexico, Brazil, and Japan. Locate your local office at
www.cengage.com/global.

Cengage Learning products are represented in Canada by
Nelson Education, Ltd.

To learn more about Cengage Learning Solutions, visit **www.cengage.com.**

Purchase any of our products at your local college store
or at our preferred online store **www.cengagebrain.com.**

Printed in the United States of America
Print Number: 01   Print Year: 2014

ABOUT THE AUTHORS

David M. Kennedy is the Donald J. McLachlan Professor of History Emeritus and Director Emeritus of The Bill Lane Center for the Study of the American West at Stanford University, where he has taught for more than four decades. Born and raised in Seattle, he received his undergraduate education at Stanford and did his graduate training at Yale in American Studies, combining the fields of history, economics, and literature. His first book, *Birth Control in America: The Career of Margaret Sanger* (1970), was honored with both the Bancroft Prize and the John Gilmary Shea Prize. His study of the World War I era, *Over Here: The First World War and American Society* (1980; rev. ed., 2005), was a Pulitzer Prize finalist. In 1999 he published *Freedom from Fear: The American People in Depression and War, 1929–1945*, which won the Pulitzer Prize for History, as well as the Francis Parkman Prize, the English-Speaking Union's Ambassador's Prize, and the Commonwealth Club of California's Gold Medal for Literature. At Stanford he has taught both undergraduate and graduate courses in American political, diplomatic, intellectual, and social history, as well as in American literature. He has received several teaching awards, including the Dean's Award for Distinguished Teaching and the Hoagland Prize for Excellence in Undergraduate Teaching. He has been a visiting professor at the University of Florence, Italy, and in 1995–1996 served as the Harmsworth Professor of American History at Oxford University. He has also served on the Advisory Board for the PBS television series, *The American Experience*, and as a consultant to several documentary films, including *The Great War*, *Cadillac Desert*, and *Woodrow Wilson*. From 1990 to 1995 he chaired the Test Development Committee for the Advanced Placement United States History examination. He is an elected Fellow of the American Academy of Arts and Sciences and of the American Philosophical Society and served from 2002 to 2011 on the board of the Pulitzer Prizes. Married and the father of two sons and a daughter, in his leisure time he enjoys hiking, bicycling, river-rafting, flying, sea-kayaking, and fly-fishing. His most recent book is *The Modern American Military* (2013).

Lizabeth Cohen is the Howard Mumford Jones Professor of American Studies in the history department and the Dean of the Radcliffe Institute for Advanced Study at Harvard University. In 2007–2008 she was the Harmsworth Professor of American History at Oxford University. Previously she taught at New York University (1992–1997) and Carnegie Mellon University (1986–1992). Born and raised in the New York metropolitan area, she received her A.B. from Princeton University and her M.A. and Ph.D. from the University of California at Berkeley. Her first book, *Making a New Deal: Industrial Workers in Chicago, 1919–1939* (1990), won the Bancroft Prize in American History and the Philip Taft Labor History Award and was a finalist for the Pulitzer Prize. In 2008 it was reissued in a second edition with a new introduction, and in 2014 it appeared in Cambridge University Press's Canto Classic Series. Her article "Encountering Mass Culture at the Grassroots: The Experience of Chicago Workers in the 1920s" (1989) was awarded the Constance Roarke Prize of the American Studies Association. Her next book, *A Consumers' Republic: The Politics of Mass Consumption in Postwar America* (2003), explored how an economy and culture built around mass consumption shaped social life and politics in post–World War II America. An article related to this book, "From Town Center to Shopping Center: The Reconfiguration of Community Marketplaces in Postwar America" (1996), was honored as the best article in urban history by the Urban History Association and received the ABC-CLIO, America: History and Life Award for the journal article that most advances previously unconsidered topics. She is currently writing a book, *Saving America's Cities: Ed Logue and the Struggle to Renew Urban America in the Suburban Age*, about the complexities of urban renewal in American cities after World War II. At Harvard, she has taught courses in twentieth-century American history, with particular attention to the intersection of social and cultural life and politics, and she now oversees the Radcliffe Institute, a major center for scholarly research, creative arts, and public programs. Before attending graduate school, she taught history at the secondary level and worked in history and art museums. She continues to help develop public history programs for general audiences through museums and documentary films. She is married to an historian of modern France, with whom she has two daughters. For leisure, she enjoys swimming and bicycling with her family, watching films, and reading fiction.

Thomas A. Bailey (1903–1983) was the original author of *The American Pageant* and saw it through its first seven editions. He taught history for nearly forty years at Stanford University, his alma mater. Long regarded as one of the nation's leading historians of American diplomacy, he was honored by his colleagues in 1968 with election to the presidencies of both the Organization of American Historians and the Society for Historians of American Foreign Relations. He was the author, editor, or co-editor of some twenty books, but the work in which he took most pride was *The American Pageant*, through which, he liked to say, he had taught American history to several million students.

BRIEF CONTENTS

CONTENTS

Part One
Founding the New Nation
CA. 33,000 B.C.E.–1783 C.E.

2

Part Two
Building the New Nation
1776–1860

158

Part Three
Testing the New Nation
1820–1877
338

MAPS

TABLES

FIGURES

PREFACE

This sixteenth edition of *The American Pageant* reflects our continuing collaboration to bring the most recent scholarship about American history to the broadest possible student audience, while preserving the readability that has long been the *Pageant's* hallmark. We are often told that the *Pageant* stands out as the only American history text with a distinctive personality, an observation that brings us considerable satisfaction. We define the *Pageant's* leading characteristics as clarity, concreteness, a strong emphasis on major themes, integration of a broad range of historical topics into a coherent and clutter-free narrative, attention to a variety of interpretive perspectives, and a colorful writing style leavened, as appropriate, with wit. That personality, we strongly believe, is what has made the *Pageant* both appealing and useful to countless students for more than six decades.

Our collaboration on the *Pageant* reflects our respective scholarly interests, which are complementary to a remarkable degree. While we share broad interests in the evolving character of American society and in its global role, David Kennedy is primarily a political and economic historian, while Lizabeth Cohen's work emphasizes social and cultural history. Together, we have once again revised the *Pageant* chapter by chapter, even paragraph by paragraph, guided by our shared commitment to tell the story of the American past as vividly and clearly as possible, without sacrificing a sense of the often sobering seriousness of history and of its sometimes challenging complexity.

Goals of *The American Pageant*

Like its predecessors, this edition of *The American Pageant* seeks to cultivate in its readers the critical thinking skills necessary for balanced judgment and informed understanding about American society by holding up to the present the mirror and measuring rod that is the past. The division of the book into six parts, each with an introductory essay, encourages students to understand that the study of history is not just a matter of piling up mountains of facts but is principally concerned with discovering complex patterns of change over time and organizing seemingly disparate events, actions, and ideas into meaningful chains of cause and consequence.

A strong narrative propels the story, reinforced in this edition by a new feature, "Contending Voices," that presents paired quotes from the past to encourage critical thinking about controversial issues. Still more highlighted quotes throughout the text help students hear the language of real people who shaped and experienced historical events. In addition, "Examining the Evidence" features enable students to deepen their understanding of the historical craft by conveying how historians develop interpretations of the past through research in many different kinds of primary sources. Here students learn to probe a wide range of historical documents and artifacts: correspondence between Abigail and John Adams in 1776, and what it reveals about women's place in the American Revolution; the Gettysburg Address and the light it sheds not only on President Lincoln's brilliant oratory but also on his vision of the American nation; a letter from a black freedman to his former master in 1865 that illuminates his family's experience in slavery as well as their hopes for a new life; the manuscript census of 1900 and what it teaches us about immigrant households on the Lower East Side of New York at the dawn of the twentieth century; a new kind of architectural structure—the shopping mall—and how it changed both consumers' behavior and politicians' campaign tactics after World War II; and a national security document that gives insight into the foreign policy-making process.

The *Pageant's* goal is not to teach the art of prophecy but the much subtler and more difficult arts of seeing things in context, of understanding the roots and direction and pace of change, and of distinguishing what is truly new under the sun from what is not. The study of history, it has been rightly said, does not make one smart for the next time, but wise forever.

We hope that the *Pageant* will help to develop the art of critical thinking in its readers and that those who use the book will take from it both a fresh appreciation of what has gone before and a seasoned perspective on what is to come. We hope, too, that readers will take as much pleasure in reading *The American Pageant* as we have had in writing it.

Changes in the Sixteenth Edition

As in past revisions, we have updated and streamlined the entire text narrative, while our main focus in this new edition is a major revision of Part Six, comprising the seven chapters covering 1945 to the present.

The Post–World War II Era

Making sense of the more recent past poses unique challenges, as scholars assessing events and personalities only just passing into the realm of "history" have had less time to develop an agreed master narrative. But we believe that sufficient time has passed for historians to have reached at least a tentative interpretative framework for understanding the post-1945 period of American history. Accordingly, we have been especially concerned to impart greater thematic coherence to this part of the text in this sixteenth edition.

Reflecting an emerging scholarly consensus, our framework for the post-1945 period roughly divides it into two eras, which can be summarized as follows: a midcentury era defined by sustained economic growth, broadly shared prosperity, and the international context of Cold War confrontation with the Soviet Union, followed by a new historical phase, originating in the pivotal decade of the 1970s, that has seen more fitful growth alongside both decreasing economic equality and increasing social inclusiveness, as well as a struggle to define America's international role after the collapse of the Soviet Union in 1991. The introductory essay to Part Six (Chapters 35–41) clarifies this interpretive scheme and directs students' attention to significant details in the extensively rewritten chapters that follow. Here, as throughout the text, we believe that anchoring the narrative of events in a coherent interpretive framework facilitates readers' acquisition of important historical thinking skills, including periodization, synthetic reasoning, and contextual and comparative analysis.

Additional revisions in this section further enhance the development of key historical thinking skills while incorporating the insights of newer scholarship. A new "Thinking Globally" essay, "The Global 1960s" (Chapter 37), places the youth politics of that era in an international and comparative context, while a new "Examining the Evidence" item on a George W. Bush–era national security document (Chapter 41) grapples explicitly with the task of crafting sound arguments from controversial historical evidence. The "Thinking Globally" essay on globalization (now in Chapter 38) has been substantially revised to emphasize the changing international economic context for domestic U.S. developments beginning in the 1970s. "Varying Viewpoints" essays on the 1960s (Chapter 37) and conservatism (Chapter 39) have also been updated extensively to incorporate new historiography and to emphasize the challenges of weighing differing historical interpretations. Finally, we have thoroughly revamped and updated the final chapter (41) to provide a coherent narrative of major events from 2001 through 2014.

"Contending Voices"

We have added a new feature to each chapter, designed to nurture students' historical thinking skills by exposing them to the contested nature of history as well as historical interpretation. "Contending Voices" offers paired quotes from original historical sources, accompanied by questions that ask students to assess conflicting perspectives on often hotly contested subjects. The feature complements the historiographical debates covered in the "Varying Viewpoints" essays by highlighting the ways in which historical actors themselves have debated the meaning of events in which they played roles.

Global Context

We have once again deepened the *Pageant*'s treatment of the global context of American history. Today, political leaders, capital investment, consumer products, rock bands, the Internet, and much else constantly traverse the globe. But even before sophisticated technology and mass communication, complex exchanges among peoples and nations around the world deeply shaped the course of American history. Students will frequently encounter in these pages the people, ideas, and events that crossed national borders to influence the experience of the United States. They will also be invited to compare salient aspects of American history with developments elsewhere in the world. We believe that a full understanding of what makes America exceptional requires knowing about other societies and knowing when and why America's path followed or departed from that taken by other nations.

Within each chapter, both text and graphics help students compare American developments to developments around the world. The frontier experience, railroad building, cotton production, city size and urban reform strategies, immigration, automobile ownership, the economic effects of the Great Depression, women's participation in voting and the work force, the cultural upheavals of the 1960s, and much more should now be understood as parts of world trends, not just as isolated American phenomena. New boxed quotes bring more international voices to the events chronicled in the *Pageant*'s historical narrative. Updated "Varying Viewpoints" essays reflect new interpretations of significant trends and events, emphasizing, when appropriate, their global contexts.

We have revised and expanded the "Thinking Globally" essays, which present different aspects of the American experience contextualized within world history. Readers learn how developments in North America were part of worldwide phenomena, be it the challenge to empire in the eighteenth century, the rise of socialist ideology in the nineteenth century, or the globalization that followed World War II in the twentieth century. Students also see how key aspects of American history—such as participating in the slave trade and its abolition, making a revolution for independence, creating an integrated national state in the mid-nineteenth century, and struggling to survive the Great Depression and World War II—were encountered by other nations but resolved in distinctive ways according to each country's history, cultural traditions, and political and economic structures.

This edition also gives renewed attention to teaching strategies and pedagogical materials aimed at helping students deepen their comprehension of American history. New visual materials—documentary images, graphs, and tables—illuminate complex and important historical ideas. Readers will also find redesigned maps with topographical detail and clear labeling to better communicate the text's analytical points. Key terms are printed in bold in each chapter and defined in a glossary at the end of the book. Every chapter concludes with an expanded chronology and a list of readable books to consult in order "To Learn More." In addition, a list of the chapter key terms and a list of "People to Know"—created to help students focus on the most significant people introduced in that chapter—appear at the end of each chapter to help students review chapter highlights. A revised Appendix contains annotated copies of the Declaration of Independence and Constitution and key historical events and dates, such as admission of the states and presidential elections.

See the Supplements section that follows for a complete description of the many materials found online. It is our hope that readers will view online resources such as MindTap and Aplia, as an exploratory laboratory enhancing *The American Pageant*'s text.

Notes on Content Revisions

Chapter 1: New World Beginnings 33,000 B.C.E.–1769 C.E.
• New Contending Voices: "Europeans and Indians" (Juan Ginés de Sepulveda, Bartolomé de las Casas)

Chapter 2: The Planting of English America 1500–1733
• New Contending Voices: "Old World Dreams and New World Realities" (Richard Hakluyt, George Percy)

Chapter 3: Settling the Northern Colonies 1619–1700
• New Contending Voices: "Anne Hutchinson Accused and Defended" (John Winthrop, Anne Hutchinson)

Chapter 4: American Life in the Seventeenth Century 1607–1692
• New Contending Voices: "Berkeley Versus Bacon" (Nathaniel Bacon, William Berkeley)

Chapter 5: Colonial Society on the Eve of Revolution 1700–1775
• New Contending Voices: "Race and Slavery" (Samuel Sewall, Virginia slave code of 1705)

Chapter 6: The Duel for North America 1608–1763
• New Contending Voices: "The Proclamation of 1763" (Royal Proclamation of 1763, George Washington)

Chapter 7: The Road to Revolution 1763–1775
• New Contending Voices: "Reconciliation or Independence?" (John Dickinson, Thomas Paine)

Chapter 8: America Secedes from the Empire 1775–1783
• New Contending Voices: "Two Revolutions: French and American" (Friedrich von Gentz, John Quincy Adams)

Chapter 9: The Confederation and the Constitution 1776–1790
• New Contending Voices: "Debating the New Constitution" (Jonathan Smith, Patrick Henry)

Chapter 10: Launching the New Ship of State 1789–1800
• New Contending Voices: "Human Nature and the Nature of Government" (Alexander Hamilton, Thomas Jefferson)

Chapter 11: The Triumphs and Travails of the Jeffersonian Republic 1800–1812
• New Contending Voices: "The Divisive Embargo" (Federalist pamphlet, W. B. Giles)

Chapter 12: The Second War for Independence and the Upsurge of Nationalism 1812–1824
• New Contending Voices: "Sizing Up the Monroe Doctrine" (Klemens von Metternich, Colombian newspaper)

Chapter 13: The Rise of a Mass Democracy 1824–1840
• New Contending Voices: "Taking the Measure of Andrew Jackson" (Maryland supporter, Thomas Jefferson)

Chapter 14: Forging the National Economy 1790–1860
• New Contending Voices: "Immigration, Pro and Con" (Know-Nothing party platform, Orestes Brownson)

Chapter 15: The Ferment of Reform and Culture 1790–1860
• Revised and expanded discussion of religion in the early Republic
• New Contending Voices: "The Role of Women" (differing newspaper commentaries on Seneca Falls)

Chapter 16: The South and the Slavery Controversy 1793–1860
- New Contending Voices: "Perspectives on Race and Slavery" (William A. Smith, American Anti-Slavery Society)

Chapter 17: Manifest Destiny and Its Legacy 1841–1848
- New Contending Voices: "Warring over the Mexican War" (*New York Evening Post*, Henry Clay)

Chapter 18: Renewing the Sectional Struggle 1848–1854
- New Contending Voices: "The Compromise of 1850" (John C. Calhoun, Daniel Webster)

Chapter 19: Drifting Toward Disunion 1854–1861
- New Contending Voices: "Judging John Brown" (Harriet Tubman, Abraham Lincoln)

Chapter 20: Girding for War: The North and the South 1861–1865
- New Contending Voices: "War Aims: Emancipation or Union?" (Horace Greeley, Abraham Lincoln)

Chapter 21: The Furnace of Civil War 1861–1865
- New Contending Voices: "The Controversy over Emancipation" (*Cincinnati Enquirer*, Abraham Lincoln)

Chapter 22: The Ordeal of Reconstruction 1865–1877
- New Contending Voices: "Radical Republicans and Southern Democrats" (Thaddeus Stephens, James Lawrence Orr)

Chapter 23: Political Paralysis in the Gilded Age 1869–1896
- New Contending Voices: "The Spoils System" (George Washington Plunkitt, Theodore Roosevelt)

Chapter 24: Industry Comes of Age 1865–1900
- New Contending Voices: "Class and the Gilded Age" (Populist platform, William Graham Sumner)

Chapter 25: America Moves to the City 1865–1900
- New Contending Voices: "The New Immigration" (Henry Cabot Lodge, Grover Cleveland)

Chapter 26: The Great West and the Agricultural Revolution 1865–1896
- New Contending Voices: "The Ghost Dance and the Wounded Knee Massacre" (James McLaughlin, Black Elk)

Chapter 27: Empire and Expansion 1890–1909
- New Contending Voices: "Debating Imperialism" (Albert Beveridge, George Hoar)

Chapter 28: Progressivism and the Republican Roosevelt 1901–1912
- New Contending Voices: "Debating the Muckrakers" (Theodore Roosevelt, Ida Tarbell)

Chapter 29: Wilsonian Progressivism in Peace and War 1913–1920
- Material on the Wilson presidency and World War I condensed and consolidated into this new single chapter

- New Contending Voices: "Battle of the Ballot" (Carrie Chapman Catt, Mrs. Barclay Hazard)

NOTE: Due to the consolidation of two chapters (fifteenth edition Chapters 29 and 30) into a single chapter (sixteenth edition Chapter 29), subsequent chapters have been renumbered for a total of 41 chapters in the sixteenth edition.

Chapter 30: American Life in the "Roaring Twenties" 1920–1929
- New Contending Voices: "All That Jazz" (Henry van Dyke, Duke Ellington)

Chapter 31: The Politics of Boom and Bust 1920–1932
- New Contending Voices: "Depression and Protection" (Willis Hawley, economists' petition)

Chapter 32: The Great Depression and the New Deal 1933–1939
- New Contending Voices: "The New Deal at High Tide" (Franklin Roosevelt, Herbert Hoover)

Chapter 33: Franklin D. Roosevelt and the Shadow of War 1933–1941
- New Contending Voices: "To Intervene or Not to Intervene" (Sterling Morton, Franklin Roosevelt)

Chapter 34: America in World War II 1941–1945
- New Contending Voices: "War and the Color Line" (Franklin Roosevelt, African American soldier)

Part Six
- Revised and updated introductory essay to Part Six to lay out the overarching framework

Chapter 35: The Cold War Begins 1945–1952
- Restructured the order of foreign-policy and domestic sections so that the global setting now provides a clearer context for domestic U.S. developments
- Revised text throughout, including new material on the Cold War's impact on religion, radical politics, and civil rights
- New Contending Voices: "Debating the Cold War" (George Kennan, Henry Wallace)

Chapter 36: American Zenith 1952–1963
- Retitled chapter, now covering both the Eisenhower and Kennedy presidencies
- Revised section on postwar culture to emphasize common characteristics across the arts
- Revised text throughout to emphasize the unifying theme of the long postwar boom and the international and national factors driving it
- New Contending Voices: "The 'Kitchen Debate'" (Richard Nixon, Nikita Khrushchev)

Chapter 37: The Stormy Sixties 1963–1973
- Shifted the time frame of the chapter from 1960–1968 in earlier editions to 1963–1973 for this edition
- Includes a new introduction to discuss periodizing "the sixties"

- Revised text throughout, including new material on postwar conservatism, party realignment, and party nomination reforms
- New "Thinking Globally" essay, "The Global 1960s"
- Revised and updated "Varying Viewpoints" essay on the 1960s that incorporates newer historiography on civil rights
- New Contending Voices: "Differing Visions of Black Freedom" (Martin Luther King, Jr., Malcolm X)

Chapter 38: Challenges to the Postwar Order 1973–1980
- Retitled chapter
- Includes a new introduction laying out the chapter's key theme: the 1970s as a pivotal, transformative decade for American politics and political economy
- A new section on "The Turn Toward the Market" in U.S. politics, economics, and intellectual currents in the 1970s
- Added material on the conservative movement as well as the cultural impact of second-wave feminism
- Revised "Thinking Globally" essay on globalization, which discusses the changing international economic context for U.S. developments in the 1970s
- New Contending Voices: "The Political Mobilization of Business" (Lewis Powell, Douglas Fraser)

Chapter 39: The Resurgence of Conservatism 1980–1992
- Revised and updated "Varying Viewpoints" essay on conservatism to incorporate the new historiography on the rise of the right
- Revised the text throughout, including new material on the religious right, supply-side economics, and the AIDS epidemic
- New Contending Voices: "Who Ended the Cold War?" (Margaret Thatcher, Mikhail Gorbachev)

Chapter 40: America Confronts the Post–Cold War Era 1992–2000
- Changed the time frame from 1992–2011 in earlier editions to 1992–2000 in this edition
- Includes a new introduction emphasizing the key themes of this 1990s chapter: the search for a post–Cold War global order and political conflict amidst prosperity
- Revised text throughout, including new material on the "Republican Revolution" of 1994, racial politics in the 1990s, globalization, financial deregulation, the computer revolution, and the emergence of anti-American Islamist terrorism
- Revised sections on multiculturalism and post-modernism to emphasize common sources and characteristics of late-twentieth-century cultural developments
- New Contending Voices: "Welfare Reform Divides the Democrats" (Joseph Lieberman, Marion Wright Edelman)

Chapter 41: The American People Face a New Century 2001–2014
- Changed this final chapter from the thematic overview found in previous editions to a narrative chapter in its own right, covering events from 2001 to 2014
- Includes a new introduction emphasizing deepening political polarization amidst post-9/11 international crises and, later, the global economic crisis of 2008
- New "Examining the Evidence" item on the National Security Strategy of 2002
- Revised, expanded, and updated narrative coverage of the Bush and Obama years, including new material on the politics of immigration reform during both presidencies; the Obama electoral coalition; the Supreme Court under John Roberts; the 2012 election; the budget and debt-ceiling showdowns of 2011 and 2013; and advances for gay rights
- New Contending Voices: "Populist Politics in a Polarized Age" (Tea Party activist, Occupy Wall Street activist)

Supplements Available with *The American Pageant*, Sixteenth Edition

Instructor Resources

MindTap™ MindTap for *The American Pageant: A History of the American People*, Sixteenth Edition, is a personalized, online digital learning platform providing students with an immersive learning experience that builds critical thinking skills. Through a carefully designed chapter-based learning path, MindTap allows students to easily identify the chapter's learning objectives, complete readings that are organized into short, manageable blocks, and test their content knowledge with Aplia™ Critical Thinking Activities developed for the most important concepts in each chapter (see Aplia description below).

- *Activator:* Each chapter of the MindTap begins with a brief video that introduces the chapter's major themes in a compelling, visual way that encourages students to think critically about the subject matter.
- *Aplia:* The Aplia Critical Thinking assignments include at least one map-based exercise, one primary source–based exercise, and an exercise summarizing the content and themes of the chapter.
- *Reflection Activity:* Every chapter ends with an assignable, gradable writing assignment, either an essay or discussion board, through which students can apply a theme or idea they've just studied.

MindTap also provides a set of web applications known as MindApps to help you create the most engaging course for your students. The MindApps range from ReadSpeaker (which reads the text out-loud to students) to Kaltura (allowing you to insert inline video and audio into your curriculum) to ConnectYard (allowing you to create digital "yards" through social media—all without "friending" your students). MindTap for *The American Pageant* goes well beyond an eBook, a homework solution/digital supplement, a resource center website, or a Learning Management System (LMS). It is truly a Personal Learning Experience that allows you to synchronize the text reading and engaging assignments. To learn more, ask your Cengage Learning sales representative to demo it for you—or go to www.Cengage.com/MindTap.

Aplia™ Aplia is an online interactive learning solution that improves comprehension and outcomes by increasing student effort and engagement. Founded by a professor to enhance his own courses, Aplia provides automatically graded assignments with detailed, immediate explanations on every question. The interactive assignments have been developed to address the major concepts covered in *The American Pageant* and are designed to promote critical thinking and engage students more fully in learning. Question types include questions built around animated maps, primary sources such as newspaper extracts, or imagined scenarios, like engaging in a conversation with a historical or finding a diary and being asked to fill in some blanks. More in-depth primary source question sets address a major topic with a number of related primary sources and questions that promote deeper analysis of historical evidence. Many of the questions incorporate images, video clips, or audio clips. Students get immediate feedback on their work (not only what they got right or wrong, but also why), and they can choose to see another set of related questions if they want more practice. A searchable eBook is available inside the course as well so that students can easily reference it as they work. Map-reading and writing tutorials are also available to get students off to a good start.

Aplia's simple-to-use course management interface allows instructors to post announcements, upload course materials, host student discussions, e-mail students, and manage the gradebook. A knowledgeable and friendly support team offers assistance and personalized support in customizing assignments to the instructor's course schedule. To learn more and view a demo for this book, visit www.aplia.com.

Instructor Companion Website This website is an all-in-one resource for class preparation, presentation, and testing for instructors. Accessible through Cengage.com/login with your faculty account, you will find an Instructor's Manual, PowerPoint presentations (descriptions below), and test bank files (please see Cognero description).

Instructor's Manual This manual contains for each chapter: focus questions, chapter themes, a chapter summary, suggested lecture topics, and discussion questions.

PowerPoint® Lecture Tools These presentations are ready-to-use, visual outlines of each chapter. They are easily customized for your lectures. There are presentations of only lectures or only images, as well as combined lecture and image presentations. Also available is a per-chapter JPEG library of images and maps.

Cengage Learning Testing Powered by Cognero® for *The American Pageant* and accessible through Cengage.com/login with your faculty account, this test bank contains multiple-choice and essay questions for each chapter. Cognero is a flexible, online system that allows you to author, edit, and manage test bank content. Create multiple test versions instantly and deliver them through your LMS from your classroom, or wherever you may be, with no special installs or downloads required.

The following format types are available for download from the Instructor Companion website: Blackboard, Angel, Moodle, Canvas, Desire2Learn. You can import these files directly into your LMS to edit, manage questions, and create tests. The test bank is also available in PDF format from the Instructor Companion website.

MindTap Reader MindTap Reader for *The American Pageant: A History of the American People*, Sixteenth Edition, is an eBook specifically designed to address the ways students assimilate content and media assets. MindTap Reader combines thoughtful navigation ergonomics; advanced student annotation, note-taking, and search tools; embedded media assets such as video and MP3 chapter summaries; primary source documents with critical thinking questions; and interactive (zoomable) maps. Students can use the eBook as their primary text or as a multimedia companion to their printed book. The MindTap Reader eBook is available within the MindTap found at www.cengagebrain.com.

CourseReader CourseReader is an online collection of primary and secondary sources that lets you create a customized electronic reader in minutes. With an easy-to-use interface and assessment tool, you can choose exactly what your students will be assigned—simply search or browse Cengage Learning's extensive document database to preview and select your customized collection of readings. In addition to print sources of all types (letters, diary entries, speeches, newspaper accounts, etc.), this collection includes a growing number of images and video and audio clips. Each primary source document includes a descriptive headnote that puts the reading into context and is further supported by both critical thinking and multiple-choice questions designed to reinforce key points. For more information, visit www.cengage.com/coursereader.

Reader Program Cengage Learning publishes a number of readers, some containing exclusively primary sources, others a combination of primary and secondary sources, and some designed to guide students through the process of historical inquiry. Visit Cengage.com/history for a complete list of readers.

Cengagebrain.com Save your students time and money. Direct them to www.cengagebrain.com for choice in formats and savings and a better chance to succeed in your class. Cengagebrain.com, Cengage Learning's online store, is a single destination for more than 10,000 new textbooks, eTextbooks, eChapters, study tools, and audio supplements. Students have the freedom to purchase à la carte exactly what they need when they need it. Students can save 50 percent on the electronic textbook and can pay as little as $1.99 for an individual eChapter.

Custom Options Nobody knows your students like you, so why not give them a text that is tailor-fit to their needs? Cengage Learning offers custom solutions for your course—whether it's making a small modification to *The American Pageant* to match your syllabus or combining multiple sources to create something truly unique. You can pick and choose chapters, include your own material, and insert additional exercises along with the Rand McNally Atlas to create a text that fits the way you teach. Ensure that your students get the most out of their textbook dollar by giving them exactly what they need. Contact your Cengage Learning representative to explore custom solutions for your course.

Student Resources

MindTap Reader MindTap Reader is an eBook specifically designed to address the ways students assimilate content and media assets. MindTap Reader combines thoughtful navigation ergonomics; advanced student annotation, note-taking, and search tools; embedded media assets such as video and MP3 chapter summaries; primary source documents with critical thinking questions; and interactive (zoomable) maps. Students can use the eBook as their primary text or as a multimedia companion to their printed book. The MindTap

Reader eBook is available within the MindTap found at www.cengagebrain.com.

Reader Program Cengage Learning publishes a number of readers, some containing exclusively primary sources, others a combination of primary and secondary sources, and some designed to guide students through the process of historical inquiry. Visit Cengage.com/history for a complete list of readers.

Cengagebrain.com Save time and money! Go to www.cengagebrain.com for choice in formats and savings and a better chance to succeed in your class. Cengagebrain.com, Cengage Learning's online store, is a single destination for more than 10,000 new textbooks, eTextbooks, eChapters, study tools, and audio supplements. Students have the freedom to purchase à la carte exactly what they need when they need it. Students can save 50 percent on the electronic textbook and can pay as little as $1.99 for an individual eChapter.

Writing for College History, 1e [ISBN: 9780618306039] Prepared by Robert M. Frakes, Clarion University, this brief handbook for survey courses in American history, Western civilization/European history, and world civilization guides students through the various types of writing assignments they encounter in a history class. Providing examples of student writing and candid assessments of student work, this text focuses on the rules and conventions of writing for the college history course.

The History Handbook, 2c [ISBN: 9780495906766] Prepared by Carol Berkin of Baruch College, City University of New York, and Betty Anderson of Boston University, this book teaches students both basic and history-specific study skills such as how to read primary sources, research historical topics, and correctly cite sources. Substantially less expensive than comparable skill-building texts, *The History Handbook* also offers tips for Internet research and evaluating online sources.

Doing History: Research and Writing in the Digital Age, 2e [ISBN: 9781133587880] *Doing History* was prepared by Michael J. Galgano, J. Chris Arndt, and Raymond M. Hyser of James Madison University. Whether you're starting down the path as a history major or simply looking for a straightforward and systematic guide to writing a successful paper, you'll find this text an indispensable handbook to historical research. Its "soup to nuts" approach to researching and writing about history addresses every step of the process, from locating your sources and gathering information to writing clearly and making proper use of various citation styles to avoid plagiarism. You'll also learn how to make the most of every tool available to you—especially the technology that helps you conduct the process efficiently and effectively.

The Modern Researcher, 6e [ISBN: 9780495318705]

Prepared by Jacques Barzun and Henry F. Graff of Columbia University, this classic introduction to the techniques of research and the art of expression is used widely in history courses, but it is also appropriate for writing and research methods courses in other departments. Barzun and Graff thoroughly cover every aspect of research, from the selection of a topic through the gathering, analysis, writing, revision, and publication of findings, presenting the process not as a set of rules but through actual cases that put the subtleties of research in a useful context. Part One covers the principles and methods of research; Part Two covers writing, speaking, and getting one's work published.

Rand McNally Historical Atlas of the World, 2e [ISBN: 9780618841912]

This valuable resource features more than 70 maps that portray the rich panoply of the world's history from preliterate times to the present. The maps show how cultures and civilization were linked and how they interacted, making it clear that history is not static but rather is about change and movement across time. The maps show change by presenting the dynamics of expansion, cooperation, and conflict. This atlas includes maps that display the world from the beginning of civilization; maps of the political development of all major areas of the world; expanded coverage of Africa, Latin America, and the Middle East; maps of the current Islamic world; and maps of world population changes in 1900 and 2000.

Acknowledgments

Many people have contributed to this revision of *The American Pageant*. Foremost among them are the countless students and teachers who have written unsolicited letters of comment or inquiry. We have learned from every one of them and encourage all readers to offer us suggestions for improving future editions.

Reviewers for the Sixteenth Edition

We are especially indebted to our colleagues who helped us think through the extensive revisions to Part Six: Mark Brilliant, University of California, Berkeley; Jennifer Burns, Stanford University; and Bruce Schulman, Boston University.

In addition, we owe a special thanks to Andy Hammann at Stanford University and Sam Rosenfeld at Harvard University for their invaluable assistance throughout the revision process.

We also appreciate feedback for this revision from the following reviewers: William Bolt, Francis Marion University; Curtis Burchfield, Itawamba Community College; and Ann Pond, Bishop State Community College.

In addition to the reviewers who helped shape this new edition, we also thank the following history instructors and publishing professionals who helped create a variety of useful, dynamic content that accompanies this book: Jennifer Black, Misericordia University; Barney Rickman, Valdosta State University; and Jeffrey Goldings.

David M. Kennedy
Lizabeth Cohen

Sail, sail thy best, ship of Democracy,
Of value is thy freight, 'tis not the Present only,
The Past is also stored in thee,
Thou holdest not the
   venture of thyself alone, not of
   the Western continent alone,
Earth's résumé entire floats on thy keel, O ship, is
   steadied by thy spars,
With thee Time voyages in trust, the antecedent
   nations sink or swim with thee,
With all their ancient struggles, martyrs, heroes, epics,
   wars, thou bear'st the other continents,
Theirs, theirs as much as thine, the destination-port
   triumphant....

Walt Whitman
"Thou Mother with Thy Equal Brood," 1872

THE AMERICAN PAGEANT

Part One

Founding the New Nation

ca. 33,000 B.C.E.–1783 C.E.

The European explorers who followed Christopher Columbus to North America in the sixteenth century had no notion of founding a new nation. Neither did the first European settlers who peopled the thirteen English colonies on the eastern shores of the continent in the seventeenth and eighteenth centuries. These original colonists may have fled poverty or religious persecution in the Old World, but they continued to view themselves as Europeans and as subjects of the English king. They regarded America as but the westernmost rim of a transatlantic European world.

Yet life in the New World gradually made the colonists different from their European cousins, and eventually, during the American Revolution, the Americans came to embrace a vision of their country as an independent nation. How did this epochal transformation come about? How did the colonists overcome the conflicts that divided them, unite against Britain, and declare themselves at great cost to be an "American" people?

They had much in common to begin with. Most were English-speaking. Most came determined to create an agricultural society modeled on English customs. Conditions in the New World deepened their common bonds. Most colonists strove to live lives unfettered by the tyrannies of royal authority, official religion, and social hierarchies that they had left behind. They grew to cherish ideals that became synonymous with American life—reverence for individual liberty, self-government, religious tolerance, and economic opportunity. They also commonly displayed a willingness to subjugate outsiders—first Indians, who were nearly annihilated through war and disease, and then Africans, who were brought in chains to serve as enslaved workers, especially on the tobacco, rice, and indigo plantations of the southern colonies.

But if the settlement experience gave people a common stock of values, both good and bad, it also divided them. The thirteen colonies were quite different from one another. Puritans carved tight, pious, and relatively democratic communities of small family farms out of rocky-soiled New England. Theirs was a close-knit, homogeneous world in comparison to most of the southern colonies,

The New York Public Library/Art Resource, NY

The Town of Secota, Engraving, by Theodore de Bry, 1590, after John White Painting John White was an English watercolorist who accompanied the first English expedition to Roanoke Island (later part of Virginia) in 1585. His paintings faithfully recorded the Indian way of life that was now imperiled by the arrival of the Europeans.

where large landholders, mostly Anglicans, built plantations along the coast from which they lorded over a labor force of enslaved blacks and looked down upon the poor white farmers who settled the backcountry. Different still were the middle colonies stretching from New York to Delaware. There diversity reigned. Well-to-do merchants put their stamp on New York City, as Quakers did on Philadelphia, while out in the countryside sprawling estates were interspersed with modest homesteads. Within individual colonies, conflicts festered over economic interests, ethnic rivalries, and religious practices. All those clashes long made it difficult for colonists to imagine that they were a single people with a common destiny, much less that they ought to break free from Britain.

The American colonists in fact had little reason to complain about Britain. Each of the thirteen colonies enjoyed a good deal of self-rule. Many colonists profited from trade within the British Empire. But by the 1760s, this stable arrangement began to crumble, a victim of the imperial rivalry between France and Britain. Their struggle for supremacy in North America began in the late seventeenth century and finally dragged in the colonists during the French and Indian War from 1756 to 1763. That war in one sense strengthened ties with Britain because colonial militias fought triumphantly alongside the British army against their mutual French and Indian enemies. But once the French were driven from the North American continent and new Anglo-Indian peace treaties were forged, the colonists no longer felt that they needed the British army for protection.

Indeed, they increasingly resented British efforts to prevent them from encroaching on Indian lands west of the Appalachians. More important still, after 1763 a financially overstretched British government made the fateful choice of imposing new taxes on colonies that had been accustomed to answering mainly to their own colonial assemblies. By the 1770s issues of taxation, self-rule, western expansion, and trade restrictions brought the crisis of imperial authority to a head. Although as late as 1775 most people in the colonies clung to the hope of some kind of accommodation short of outright independence, royal intransigence soon thrust the colonists into a war of independence that neither antagonist could have anticipated just a few years before.

Eight years of revolutionary war did more than anything in the colonial past to bring Americans together as a nation. Comradeship-in-arms and the struggle to shape a national government forced Americans to subdue their differences as best they could. But the spirit of national unity was hardly universal. One in five colonists sided with the British as "Loyalists," and a generation would pass before the wounds of this first American "civil war" fully healed. Yet in the end, Americans won the Revolution, with no small measure of help from the French, because in every colony people shared a firm belief that they were fighting for the "unalienable rights" of "life, liberty, and the pursuit of happiness," in the words of Thomas Jefferson's magnificent Declaration of Independence. Almost two hundred years of living a new life had prepared Americans to found a new nation.

Library of Congress Prints and Photographs Division[LC-USZC4-554]

Philadelphia, Corner of Second and High Streets Delegates to the Constitutional Convention in 1787 gathered in Philadelphia, the largest city in North America, a vivid symbol of the rise of American society from its precarious beginnings at Jamestown and Plymouth nearly two centuries earlier.

Chapter 1

New World Beginnings

33,000 B.C.E.–1769 C.E.

I have come to believe that this is a mighty continent which was hitherto unknown.... Your Highnesses have an Other World here.

CHRISTOPHER COLUMBUS, 1498

*S*everal billion years ago, that whirling speck of cosmic dust known as the earth, fifth in size among the planets, came into being.

About six thousand years ago—only a minute in geological time—recorded history of the Western world began. Certain peoples of the Middle East, developing a written culture, gradually emerged from the haze of the past.

Five hundred years ago—only a few seconds figuratively speaking—European explorers stumbled on the Americas. This dramatic accident forever altered the future of both the Old World and the New, and of Africa and Asia as well (see Figure 1.1).

✵ The Shaping of North America

Planet earth took on its present form slowly. Some 225 million years ago, a single supercontinent, called Pangaea by geologists, contained all the world's dry land. Then enormous chunks of terrain began to drift away from this colossal landmass, opening the Atlantic and Indian Oceans, narrowing the Pacific Ocean, and forming the great continents of Eurasia, Africa, Australia, Antarctica, and the Americas. The existence of a single original continent has been proved in part by the discovery of nearly identical species of fish that swim today in long-separated freshwater lakes throughout the world.

Continued shifting and folding of the earth's crust thrust up mountain ranges. The Appalachians were probably formed even before continental separation,

perhaps 350 million years ago. The majestic ranges of western North America—the Rockies, the Sierra Nevada, the Cascades, and the Coast Ranges—arose much more recently, geologically speaking, some 135 million to 25 million years ago. They are truly "American" mountains, born after the continent took on its own separate geological identity.

By about 10 million years ago, nature had sculpted the basic geological shape of North America. The continent was anchored in its northeastern corner by the massive **Canadian Shield**—a zone undergirded by ancient rock, probably the first part of what became the North American landmass to have emerged above sea level. A narrow eastern coastal plain, or "tidewater" region, creased by many river valleys, sloped gently upward to the timeworn ridges of the Appalachians. Those ancient mountains slanted away on their western side into the huge midcontinental basin that rolled downward to the Mississippi Valley bottom and then rose relentlessly to the towering peaks of the Rockies. From the Rocky Mountain crest—the "roof of America"—the land fell off jaggedly into the intermountain Great Basin, bounded by the Rockies on the east and the Sierra and Cascade ranges on the west. The valleys of the Sacramento and San Joaquin Rivers and the Willamette–Puget Sound trough seamed the interiors of present-day California, Oregon, and Washington. The land at last met the foaming Pacific, where the Coast Ranges rose steeply from the sea.

Nature laid a chill hand over much of this terrain in the Great Ice Age, beginning about 2 million years ago. Two-mile-thick ice sheets crept from the

FIGURE 1.1 The Arc of Time © 2016 Cengage Learning

polar regions to blanket parts of Europe, Asia, and the Americas. In North America the great glaciers carpeted most of present-day Canada and the United States as far southward as a line stretching from Pennsylvania through the Ohio Country and the Dakotas to the Pacific Northwest.

When the glaciers finally retreated about ten thousand years ago, they left the North American landscape transformed and much as we know it today. The weight of the gargantuan ice mantle had depressed the level of the Canadian Shield. The grinding and flushing action of the moving and melting ice had scoured away the shield's topsoil, pitting its rocky surface with thousands of shallow depressions into which the melting glaciers flowed to form lakes. The same glacial action scooped out and filled the Great Lakes. They originally drained southward through the Mississippi River system to the Gulf of Mexico. When the melting ice unblocked the Gulf of St. Lawrence, the lake water sought the St. Lawrence River outlet to the Atlantic Ocean, lowering the Great Lakes' level and leaving the Missouri-Mississippi-Ohio system to drain the enormous midcontinental basin between the Appalachians and the Rockies. Similarly, in the West, water from the melting glaciers filled sprawling Lake Bonneville, covering much of present-day Utah, Nevada, and Idaho. It drained to the Pacific Ocean through the Snake and Columbia River systems until diminishing rainfall from the ebbing ice cap lowered the water level, cutting off access to the Snake River outlet. Deprived of both inflow and drainage, the giant lake became a gradually shrinking inland sea. It grew increasingly saline, slowly evaporated, and left an arid, mineral-rich desert. Only the Great Salt Lake remains as a relic of Bonneville's former vastness. Today Lake Bonneville's ancient beaches are visible on

mountainsides up to 1,000 feet above the dry floor of the Great Basin.

✴ Peopling the Americas

The Great Ice Age shaped more than the geological history of North America. It also contributed to the origins of the continent's human history. Though recent (and still highly controversial) evidence suggests that some early peoples may have reached the Americas in crude boats, most probably came by land. Some thirty-five thousand years ago, the Ice Age congealed much of the world's oceans into massive ice-pack glaciers, lowering the level of the sea. As the sea level dropped, it exposed a land bridge connecting Eurasia with North America in the area of the present-day Bering Sea between Siberia and Alaska. Across that bridge, probably following migratory herds of game, ventured small bands of nomadic Asian hunters—the "immigrant" ancestors of the Native Americans. They continued to trek across the Bering isthmus for some 250 centuries, slowly peopling the American continents (see Map 1.1).

As the Ice Age ended and the glaciers melted, the sea level rose again, inundating the land bridge about ten thousand years ago. Nature thus barred the door to further immigration for many thousands of years, leaving this part of the human family marooned for millennia on the now-isolated American continents.

Time did not stand still for these original Americans. The same climatic warming that melted the ice and drowned the bridge to Eurasia gradually opened ice-free valleys through which vanguard bands groped their way southward and eastward across the Americas. Roaming slowly through this awesome wilderness, they eventually reached the far tip of South America, some

ARCTIC OCEAN

BERING
LAND BRIDGE

ATLANTIC
OCEAN

PACIFIC
OCEAN

Tropic of Cancer

Equator—0°

Tropic of Capricorn

MAP 1.1 The First Discoverers of America   The origins of the first Americans remain something of a mystery. According to the most plausible theory of how the Americas were populated, for some twenty-five thousand years people crossed the Bering land bridge from Eurasia to North America. Gradually they dispersed southward down ice-free valleys, populating both the American continents. © 2016 Cengage Learning

| 0 | 500 | 1000 Km. |
| 0 | 500 | 1000 Mi. |

Extent of land, ca. 33,000–10,500 B.C.E.
Glaciers, ca. 15,000 B.C.E.
Probable ancient shoreline
Probable migratory route
Selected Paleo-Indian site

fifteen thousand miles from Siberia. By the time Europeans arrived in America in 1492, perhaps 54 million people inhabited the two American continents.* Over the centuries they split into countless tribes, evolved more than two thousand separate languages, and developed many diverse religions, cultures, and ways of life.

Incas in Peru, Mayans in Central America, and **Aztecs** in Mexico shaped stunningly sophisticated civilizations. Their advanced agricultural practices, based primarily on the cultivation of maize, which is Indian corn, fed large populations, perhaps as many

*Much controversy surrounds estimates of the pre-Columbian Native American population. The figures here are from William M. Denevan, ed., *The Native Population of the Americas in 1492*, rev. ed. (Madison: University of Wisconsin Press, 1992).

Making Sense of the New World

This map from 1546 by Sebastian Münster represents one of the earliest efforts to make geographic sense out of the New World (*Nouus Orbis* and *Die Nüw Welt* on the map). The very phrase *New World* suggests just how staggering a blow to the European imagination was the discovery of the Americas. Europeans reached instinctively for the most expansive of all possible terms—*world*, not simply *places*, or even *continents*—to comprehend Columbus's startling report that lands and peoples previously unimagined lay beyond the horizon of Europe's western sea.

Gradually the immense implications of the New World's existence began to impress themselves on Europe, with consequences for literature, art, politics, the economy, and, of course, cartography. Maps can only be *representations* of reality and are therefore necessarily distortions. This map bears a recognizable resemblance to modern mapmakers' renderings of the American continents, but it also contains gross geographic inaccuracies (note the location of Japan—*Zipangri*—relative to the North American west coast) as well as telling commentaries on

what sixteenth-century Europeans found remarkable (note the Land of Giants—*Regio Gigantum*—and the indication of cannibals—*Canibali*—in present-day Argentina and Brazil, respectively). What further clues to the European mentality of the time does the map offer? In what ways might misconceptions about the geography of the Americas have influenced further exploration and settlement patterns?

National Archives of Canada

as 20 million in Mexico alone. Although without large draft animals such as horses and oxen, and lacking even the simple technology of the wheel, these peoples built elaborate cities and carried on far-flung commerce. Talented mathematicians, they made strikingly accurate astronomical observations. The Aztecs also routinely sought the favor of their gods by offering human sacrifices, cutting the hearts out of the chests of living victims, who were often captives conquered in battle. By some accounts more than five thousand people were ritually slaughtered to celebrate the crowning of one Aztec chieftain.

✴ The Earliest Americans

Agriculture, especially corn growing, accounted for the size and sophistication of the Native American civilizations in Mexico and South America. About 5000 B.C.E. hunter-gatherers in highland Mexico developed a wild grass into the staple crop of corn, which became their staff of life and the foundation of the complex, large-scale, centralized Aztec and Incan civilizations that eventually emerged. Cultivation of corn spread across the Americas from the Mexican heartland. Everywhere it was planted, corn began to transform nomadic hunting bands into settled agricultural villagers, but this process went forward slowly and unevenly.

Corn planting reached the present-day American Southwest as early as 2000 B.C.E. and powerfully molded Pueblo culture. The Pueblo peoples in the Rio Grande valley constructed intricate irrigation systems to water their cornfields. They were dwelling in villages of multistoried, terraced buildings when Spanish explorers made contact with them in the sixteenth century. (*Pueblo* means "village" in Spanish.)

Corn cultivation reached other parts of North America considerably later. The timing of its arrival in different localities explains much about the relative rates of development of different Native American peoples (see Map 1.2). Throughout the continent to the north and east of the land of the Pueblos, social life was less elaborately developed—indeed "societies" in the modern sense of the word scarcely existed. No dense concentrations of population or complex

Corn Culture   This statue of a corn goddess from the Moche culture of present-day coastal Peru, made between 200 and 600 B.C.E., vividly illustrates the centrality of corn to Native American peoples a thousand years before the rise of the great Incan and Aztec empires that the Europeans later encountered.

bpk, Berlin/Art Resource, NY

nation-states comparable to the Aztec empire existed in North America outside of Mexico at the time of the Europeans' arrival—one of the reasons for the relative ease with which the European colonizers subdued the native North Americans.

The Mound Builders of the Ohio River valley, the Mississippian culture of the lower Midwest, and the desert-dwelling Anasazi peoples of the Southwest did sustain some large settlements after the incorporation of corn planting into their ways of life during the first millennium C.E. The Mississippian settlement at **Cahokia**, near present-day East St. Louis, was at one time home to as many as twenty-five thousand people. The Anasazis built an elaborate pueblo of more than six hundred interconnected rooms at Chaco Canyon in modern-day New Mexico. But mysteriously, perhaps due to prolonged drought, all those ancient cultures fell into decline by about 1300 C.E.

The cultivation of maize, as well as of high-yielding strains of beans and squash, reached the southeastern Atlantic seaboard region of North America about 1000 C.E. These plants made possible **three-sister farming**, with beans growing on the trellis of the cornstalks and squash covering the planting mounds to retain moisture in the soil. The rich diet provided by this environmentally clever farming technique produced some of the highest population densities on the continent, among them the Creek, Choctaw, and Cherokee peoples.

The Iroquois in the northeastern woodlands, inspired by a legendary leader named Hiawatha, created in the sixteenth century perhaps the closest North American approximation to the great empires of Mexico and Peru. The Iroquois Confederacy developed the political and organizational skills to sustain a robust military alliance that menaced its neighbors, Native American and European alike, for well over a century (see "Makers of America: The Iroquois," pp. 38–39).

But for the most part, the native peoples of North America were living in small, scattered, and impermanent settlements on the eve of the Europeans' arrival. In more settled agricultural groups, women tended the crops while men hunted, fished, gathered fuel, and cleared fields for planting. This pattern of life frequently conferred substantial authority on women,

MAP 1.2 North American Indian Peoples at the Time of First Contact with Europeans   Because this map depicts the location of various Indian peoples *at the time of their first contact with Europeans*, and because initial contacts ranged from the sixteenth to the nineteenth centuries, it is necessarily subject to considerable chronological skewing and is only a crude approximation of the "original" territory of any given group. The map also cannot capture the fluidity and dynamism of Native American life even before Columbus's "discovery." For example, the Navajo and Apache peoples had migrated from present-day northern Canada only shortly before the Spanish first encountered them in the present-day American Southwest in the 1500s. The map also places the Sioux on the Great Plains, where Europeans met up with them in the early nineteenth century—but the Sioux had spilled onto the plains not long before then from the forests surrounding the Great Lakes. The indigenous populations of the southeastern and mid-Atlantic regions are especially difficult to represent accurately in a map like this because pre-Columbian intertribal conflicts had so scrambled the native inhabitants that it is virtually impossible to determine which groups were originally where. © 2016 Cengage Learning

and many North American native peoples, including the Iroquois, developed matrilineal cultures, in which power and possessions passed down the female side of the family line.

Unlike the Europeans, who would soon arrive with the presumption that humans had dominion over the earth and with the technologies to alter the very face of the land, the Native Americans had neither the desire nor the means to manipulate nature aggressively. They revered the physical world and endowed nature with spiritual properties. Yet they did sometimes ignite massive forest fires, deliberately torching thousands of acres of trees to create better hunting habitats, especially for deer. This practice accounted for the open, parklike appearance of the eastern woodlands that so amazed early European explorers.

But in a broad sense, the land did not feel the hand of the Native Americans heavy upon it, partly because they were so few in number. They were so thinly spread across the continent that vast areas were virtually untouched by a human presence. In the fateful year 1492, probably no more than 4 million Native Americans padded through the whispering, primeval forests and paddled across the sparkling, virgin waters of the continent north of Mexico. They were blissfully unaware that the historic isolation of the Americas was about to end forever, as the land and the native peoples alike felt the full shock of the European "discovery."

✴ Indirect Discoverers of the New World

Europeans, for their part, were equally unaware of the existence of the Americas. Blond-bearded Norse seafarers from Scandinavia had chanced upon the northeastern shoulder of North America about 1000 C.E. They landed at a place near L'Anse aux Meadows in present-day Newfoundland that abounded in wild grapes, which led them to name the spot Vinland. But no strong nation-state, yearning to expand, supported these venturesome voyagers. Their flimsy settlements consequently were soon abandoned, and their discovery was forgotten, except in Scandinavian saga and song.

For several centuries thereafter, other restless Europeans, with the growing power of ambitious governments behind them, sought contact with a wider world, whether for conquest or trade. They thus set in

Cahokia   Houses and mounds dot the landscape in an artist's rendering of ancient Cahokia circa 1150, when its population of twenty thousand exceeded London's.

Cahokia Mounds Historic Site, painting by William R. Iseminger

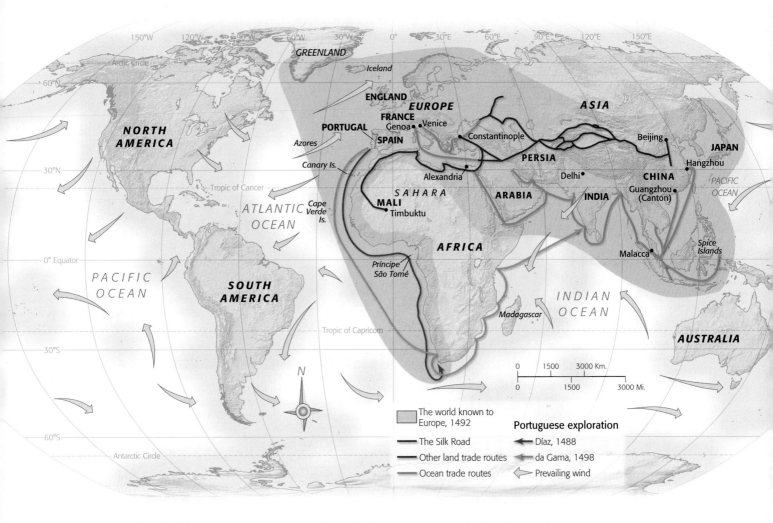

MAP 1.3 The World Known to Europe and Major Trade Routes with Asia, 1492 Goods on the early routes passed through so many hands along the way that their ultimate source remained mysterious to Europeans. © 2016 Cengage Learning

motion the chain of events that led to a drive toward Asia, the penetration of Africa, and the completely accidental discovery of the New World.

Christian crusaders must rank high among America's indirect discoverers. Clad in shining armor, tens of thousands of these European warriors tried from the eleventh to the fourteenth centuries to wrest the Holy Land from Muslim control. Foiled in their military assaults, the crusaders nevertheless acquired a taste for the exotic delights of Asia. Goods that had been virtually unknown in Europe now were craved—silk for clothing, drugs for aching flesh, perfumes for unbathed bodies, colorful draperies for gloomy castles, and spices—especially sugar, a rare luxury in Europe before the crusades—for preserving and flavoring food. Europe's developing sweet tooth would have momentous implications for world history.

The luxuries of the East were prohibitively expensive in Europe. They had to be transported enormous distances from the Spice Islands (Indonesia), China, and India, in creaking ships and on swaying camel back. The journey led across the Indian Ocean, the Persian Gulf, and the Red Sea or along the tortuous caravan routes of Asia or the Arabian Peninsula, ending at the ports of the eastern Mediterranean (see Map 1.3). Muslim **middlemen** exacted a heavy toll en route. By the time the strange-smelling goods reached Italian merchants at Venice and Genoa, they were so costly that purchasers and profits alike were narrowly limited. European consumers and distributors were naturally eager to find a less expensive route to the riches of Asia or to develop alternate sources of supply.

✦ Europeans Enter Africa

European appetites were further whetted when footloose Marco Polo, an Italian adventurer, returned to Europe in 1295 and began telling tales of his nearly

Marco Polo Passing Through the Strait of Hormuz This illustration, from the first printed edition of *The Travels of Marco Polo* in 1477, shows the traveler crossing the Persian Gulf between the Arabian Peninsula and Persia (present-day Iran).

twenty-year sojourn in China. Though he may in fact never have seen China (legend to the contrary, the hard evidence is sketchy), he must be regarded as an indirect discoverer of the New World, for his book, with its descriptions of rose-tinted pearls and golden pagodas, stimulated European desires for a cheaper route to the treasures of the East.

These accumulating pressures eventually brought a breakthrough for European expansion. Before the middle of the fifteenth century, European sailors refused to sail southward along the coast of West Africa because they could not beat their way home against the prevailing northerly winds and south-flowing currents. About 1450, Portuguese mariners overcame those obstacles. Not only had they developed the **caravel**, a ship that could sail more closely into the wind, but they had discovered that they could return to Europe by sailing northwesterly from the African coast toward the Azores, where the prevailing westward breezes would carry them home.

The new world of sub-Saharan Africa now came within the grasp of questing Europeans. The northern shore of Africa, as part of the Mediterranean world, had been known to Europe since antiquity. But because sea travel down the African coast had been virtually impossible, Africa south of the forbidding Sahara Desert barrier had remained remote and mysterious. African gold, perhaps two-thirds of Europe's

supply, crossed the Sahara on camelback, and shadowy tales may have reached Europe about the flourishing West African kingdom of Mali in the Niger River valley, with its impressive Islamic university at Timbuktu. But Europeans had no direct access to sub-Saharan Africa until the Portuguese navigators began to creep down the West African coast in the middle of the fifteenth century.

The Portuguese promptly set up trading posts along the African shore for the purchase of gold—and slaves. Arab flesh merchants and Africans themselves had traded slaves for centuries before the Europeans arrived. The slavers routinely charged higher prices for captives from distant sources because they could not easily flee to their native villages or be easily rescued by their kin. Slave brokers also deliberately separated persons from the same tribes and mixed unlike people together to frustrate organized resistance. Thus from its earliest days, slavery by its very nature disrupted African communities and inhibited the expression of regional African cultures and tribal identities.

The Portuguese adopted these Arab and African practices. They built up their own systematic traffic in slaves to work the sugar plantations that Portugal, and later Spain, established on the African coastal islands of Madeira, the Canaries, São Tomé, and Principe. The enormous Portuguese appetite for slaves dwarfed the modest scale of the pre-European traffic. Slave trading

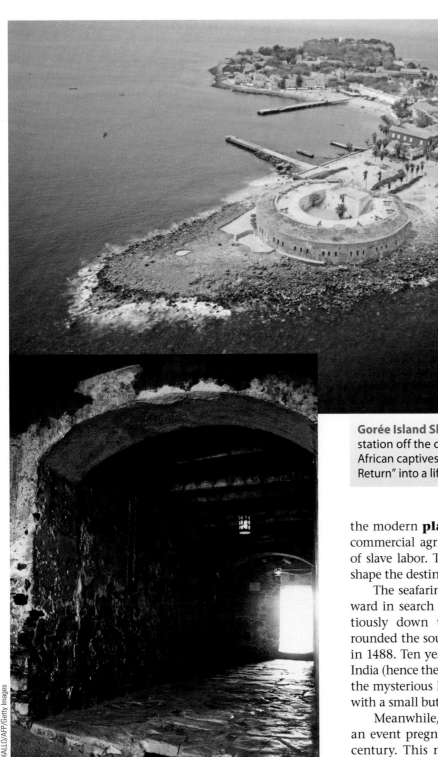

Gamma-Rapho via Getty Images

Gorée Island Slave Fortress From this holding station off the coast of Senegal, thousands of African captives passed through the "Door of No Return" into a lifetime of slavery in the New World.

SEYLLOU DIALLO/AFP/Getty Images

the modern **plantation** system, based on large-scale commercial agriculture and the wholesale exploitation of slave labor. This kind of plantation economy would shape the destiny of much of the New World.

The seafaring Portuguese pushed still farther southward in search of the water route to Asia. Edging cautiously down the African coast, Bartholomeu Dias rounded the southernmost tip of the "Dark Continent" in 1488. Ten years later Vasco da Gama finally reached India (hence the name "Indies," given by Europeans to all the mysterious lands of the Orient) and returned home with a small but tantalizing cargo of jewels and spices.

Meanwhile, the kingdom of Spain became united—an event pregnant with destiny—in the late fifteenth century. This new unity resulted primarily from the marriage of two sovereigns, Ferdinand of Aragon and Isabella of Castile, and from the brutal expulsion of the "infidel" Muslim Moors from Spain after centuries of Christian-Islamic warfare. Glorying in their sudden strength, the Spaniards were eager to outstrip their Portuguese rivals in the race to tap the wealth of the Indies. To the south and east, Portugal controlled the African coast and thus the gateway to the round-Africa water route to India. Of necessity, therefore, Spain looked westward.

became a big business. Some forty thousand Africans were carried away to the Atlantic sugar islands in the last half of the fifteenth century. Millions more were to be wrenched from their home continent after the discovery of the Americas. In these fifteenth-century Portuguese adventures in Africa were to be found the origins of

✦ Columbus Comes upon a New World

The stage was now set for a cataclysmic shift in the course of history—the history not only of Europe but of all the world. Europeans clamored for more and cheaper products from the lands beyond the Mediterranean. Africa had been established as a source of abundant slave labor for plantation agriculture. The Portuguese voyages had demonstrated the feasibility of long-range ocean navigation. In Spain a modern national state was taking shape, with the unity, wealth, and power to shoulder the formidable tasks of discovery, conquest, and colonization. The dawn of the Renaissance in the fourteenth century nurtured an ambitious spirit of optimism and adventure. Printing presses, introduced about 1450, facilitated the spread of scientific knowledge. The mariner's compass, possibly borrowed from the Arabs, eliminated some of the uncertainties of sea travel. Meanwhile, across the ocean, the unsuspecting New World innocently awaited its European "discoverers."

Onto this stage stepped Christopher Columbus. This skilled Italian seafarer persuaded the Spanish monarchs to outfit him with three tiny but seaworthy ships, manned by a motley crew. Daringly, he unfurled the sails of his cockleshell craft and headed westward. His superstitious sailors, fearful of venturing into the oceanic unknown, grew increasingly mutinous. After six weeks at sea, failure loomed until, on October 12, 1492, the crew sighted an island in the Bahamas. A new world thus swam within the vision of Europeans.

Columbus's sensational achievement obscures the fact that he was one of the most successful failures in history. Seeking a new water route to the fabled Indies, he in fact had bumped into an enormous land barrier blocking the ocean pathway. For decades thereafter explorers strove to get through it or around it. The truth gradually dawned that sprawling new continents had been discovered. Yet Columbus was at first so certain that he had skirted the rim of the "Indies" that he called the native peoples Indians, a gross geographical misnomer that somehow stuck.

Columbus's discovery would eventually convulse four continents—Europe, Africa, and the two Americas. Thanks to his epochal voyage, an interdependent global economic system emerged on a scale undreamed-of before he set sail. Its workings touched every shore washed by the Atlantic Ocean. Europe provided the markets, the capital, and the technology; Africa furnished the labor; and the New World offered its raw materials, especially its precious metals and its soil for the cultivation of sugar cane. For Europeans as well as for Africans and Native Americans, the world after 1492 would never be the same, for better or worse.

✦ When Worlds Collide

Two ecosystems—the fragile, naturally evolved networks of relations among organisms in a stable environment—commingled and clashed when Columbus waded ashore. The reverberations from that historic encounter—often called the **Columbian exchange** (see Figure 1.2)—echoed for centuries after 1492. The flora and fauna—as well as the peoples—of the Old and New Worlds had been separated for thousands of years. European explorers marveled at the strange sights that greeted them, including exotic beasts such as iguanas and "snakes with castanets" (rattlesnakes). Native New World plants such as tobacco, maize, beans, tomatoes, and especially the lowly potato eventually revolutionized the international economy as well as the European diet, feeding the rapid population growth of the Old World. These foodstuffs were among the most important Indian gifts to the Europeans and to the rest of the world. Perhaps three-fifths of the crops cultivated around the globe today originated in the Americas. Ironically, the introduction into Africa of New World foodstuffs like maize, manioc, and sweet potatoes may have fed an African population boom that numerically, though not morally, more than offset the losses inflicted by the slave trade.

In exchange the Europeans introduced Old World crops and animals to the Americas. Columbus returned to the Caribbean island of Hispaniola (present-day Haiti and the Dominican Republic) in 1493 with seventeen ships that unloaded twelve hundred men and a virtual Noah's Ark of cattle, swine, and horses. The horses soon reached the North American mainland through Mexico. Over the next two centuries, they spread as far as Canada. Southwestern Indian tribes like the Comanche, Apache, and Navajo swiftly adopted the horse; northern tribes like the Lakota, Shoshone, and Blackfeet somewhat later. Horses transformed newly mounted cultures into highly mobile, wide-ranging hunter-warrior societies that roamed the grassy Great Plains in pursuit of the shaggy buffalo and that suppressed unmounted peoples like the Paiute. Columbus also brought seedlings of sugar cane, which thrived in the warm Caribbean climate. A "sugar revolution" consequently took place in the European diet, fueled by the forced migration of millions of Africans to work the canefields and sugar mills of the New World.

Unwittingly, the Europeans also brought other organisms in the dirt on their boots and the dust on their clothes, such as the seeds of Kentucky bluegrass, dandelions, and daisies. Most ominous of all, in their bodies they carried the germs that caused smallpox, yellow fever, and malaria. Old World diseases quickly devastated the Native Americans. During the Indians'

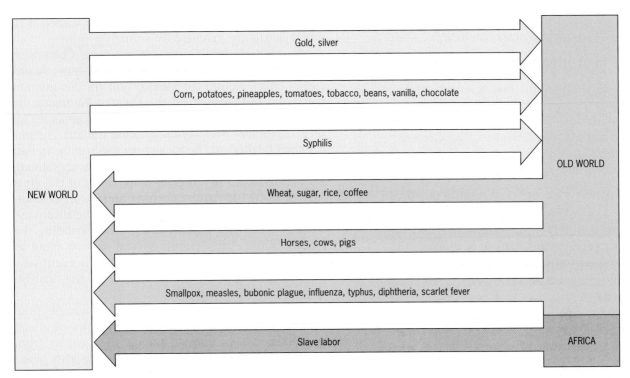

FIGURE 1.2 The Columbian Exchange
Columbus's discovery initiated the kind of explosion in international commerce that a later age would call "globalization." © 2016 Cengage Learning

millennia of isolation in the Americas, most of the Old World's killer maladies had disappeared from among them. But generations of freedom from those illnesses had also wiped out protective antibodies. Devoid of natural resistance to Old World sicknesses,

The Scourge of Smallpox These scenes of Aztec Indians afflicted with smallpox contracted from the Spaniards were drawn by a native artist to illustrate Father Bernardino de Sahagun's remarkable sixteenth-century treatise, "General History of the Things of New Spain," a pioneering work of ethnography and anthropology.

Indians died in droves. Within fifty years of the Spanish arrival, the population of the Taino natives in Hispaniola dwindled from some 1 million people to about 200. Enslavement and armed aggression took their toll, but the deadliest killers were microbes, not muskets. The lethal germs spread among the New World peoples with the speed and force of a hurricane, swiftly sweeping far ahead of the human invaders; most of those afflicted never laid eyes on a European. In the centuries after Columbus's landfall, as many as 90 percent of the Native Americans perished, a demographic catastrophe without parallel in human history. This depopulation was surely not intended by the Spanish, but it was nevertheless so severe that entire cultures and ancient ways of life were extinguished forever. Baffled, enraged, and vengeful, Indian slaves sometimes kneaded tainted blood into their masters' bread, to little effect. Perhaps it was poetic justice that the Indians unintentionally did take a kind of revenge by infecting the early explorers with syphilis, injecting that lethal sexually transmitted disease for the first time into Europe.

�֎ The Conquest of Mexico and Peru

Gradually, Europeans realized that the American continents held rich prizes, especially the gold and silver of the advanced Indian civilizations in Mexico and

Contending Voices
Europeans and Indians

In 1550–1551, two renowned scholars in Valladolid, Spain, formally debated whether the native peoples of the New World were "true men," capable of governing themselves and becoming Christians. Juan Ginés de Sepulveda (1489–1573), who had never seen the New World, believed that:

❝The Spanish have a perfect right to rule these barbarians of the New World and the adjacent islands, who in prudence, skill, virtues, and humanity are as inferior to the Spanish as children to adults, or women to men, for there exists between the two as great a difference as between...apes and men.❞

The Dominican friar Bartolomé de Las Casas (1484–1566), who had long labored among the Indians, replied:

❝I call the Spaniards who plunder that unhappy people torturers.... The Indians are our brothers, and Christ has given his life for them. Why, then, do we persecute them with such inhuman savagery when they do not deserve such treatment?❞

To what extent did attitudes like those persist over the next several centuries?

Peru. Spain secured its claim to Columbus's discovery in the **Treaty of Tordesillas** (1494), dividing with Portugal the "heathen lands" of the New World (see Map 1.4). The lion's share went to Spain, but Portugal received compensating territory in Africa and Asia, as well as title to lands that one day would be Brazil.

The islands of the Caribbean Sea—the West Indies as they came to be called, in yet another perpetuation of Columbus's geographic confusion—served as offshore bases for staging the Spanish invasion of the mainland Americas. Here supplies could be stored, and men and horses could be rested and acclimated, before proceeding to the conquest of the continents. The loosely organized and vulnerable native communities of the West Indies also provided laboratories for testing the techniques that would eventually subdue the advanced Indian civilizations of Mexico and Peru. The most important such technique was the institution known as the ***encomienda***. It allowed the government to "commend," or give, Indians to certain colonists in return for the promise to try to Christianize them. In all but name, it was slavery. Spanish missionary Bartolomé de Las Casas, appalled

by the *encomienda* system in Hispaniola, called it "a moral pestilence invented by Satan."

In 1519 Hernán Cortés set sail from Cuba with sixteen fresh horses and several hundred men aboard eleven ships, bound for Mexico and for destiny. On the island of Cozumel off the Yucatán Peninsula, he rescued a Spanish castaway who had been enslaved for several years by the Mayan-speaking Indians. A short distance farther on, he picked up the female Indian slave Malinche, who knew both Mayan and Nahuatl, the language of the powerful Aztec rulers of the great empire in the highlands of central Mexico. In addition to his superior firepower, Cortés now had the advantage, through these two interpreters, of understanding the speech of the native peoples whom he was about to encounter, including the Aztecs. Malinche eventually learned Spanish and was baptized with the Spanish name of Doña Marina.

Near present-day Veracruz, Cortés made his final landfall. Through his interpreters he learned of unrest within the Aztec empire among the peoples from whom the Aztecs demanded tribute. He also heard alluring tales of the gold and other wealth stored up in the legendary Aztec capital of Tenochtitlán. He lusted to tear open the coffers of the Aztec kingdom. To quell his mutinous troops, he boldly burned his ships, cutting off any hope of retreat. Gathering a force of some twenty thousand Indian allies, he marched on Tenochtitlán and toward one of history's most dramatic and fateful encounters.

As Cortés proceeded, the Aztec chieftain Moctezuma sent ambassadors bearing fabulous gifts to welcome the approaching Spaniards. These only whetted the *conquistador*'s appetite. "We Spanish suffer from a strange disease of the heart," Cortés allegedly informed the emissaries, "for which the only known remedy is gold." The ambassadors reported this comment to Moctezuma, along with the astonishing fact that the newcomers rode on the backs of "deer" (horses). The superstitious Moctezuma also believed that Cortés was the god Quetzalcoatl, whose return from the eastern sea was predicted in

Bartolomé de Las Casas (1484–1566), a reform-minded Dominican friar, wrote The Destruction of the Indies *in 1542 to chronicle the awful fate of the Native Americans and to protest Spanish policies in the New World. He was especially horrified at the catastrophic effects of disease on the native peoples:*

❝Who of those in future centuries will believe this? I myself who am writing this and saw it and know the most about it can hardly believe that such was possible.❞

MAP 1.4 Principal Voyages of Discovery Spain, Portugal, France, and England reaped the greatest advantages from the New World, but much of the earliest exploration was done by Italians, notably Christopher Columbus of Genoa. John Cabot, another native of Genoa (his original name was Giovanni Caboto), sailed for England's King Henry VII. Giovanni da Verrazano was a Florentine employed by France. © 2016 Cengage Learning

Aztec legends. Expectant yet apprehensive, Moctezuma allowed the *conquistadores* to approach his capital unopposed.

As the Spaniards entered the Valley of Mexico, the sight of the Aztec capital of Tenochtitlán amazed them. With 300,000 inhabitants spread over ten square miles, it rivaled in size and pomp any city in contemporary Europe. The Aztec metropolis rose from an island in the center of a lake, surrounded by floating gardens of extraordinary beauty. It was connected to the mainland by a series of causeways and supplied with fresh water by an artfully designed aqueduct.

Moctezuma treated Cortés hospitably at first, but soon the Spaniards' hunger for gold and power exhausted their welcome. "They thirsted mightily for gold; they stuffed themselves with it; they starved for it; they lusted for it like pigs," said one Aztec. On the **noche triste** (sad night) of June 30, 1520, the Aztecs attacked, driving the Spanish down the causeways from Tenochtitlán in a frantic, bloody retreat. Cortés then laid siege to the city, and it capitulated on August 13, 1521. That same year a smallpox epidemic burned through the Valley of Mexico. The combination of conquest and disease took a grisly toll. The Aztec empire gave way to three centuries of Spanish rule. The temples of Tenochtitlán were destroyed to make way for the Christian cathedrals of Mexico City, built on the site of the ruined Indian capital. And the native population of Mexico, winnowed mercilessly by the invaders' diseases, shrank from some 20 million to 2 million people in less than a century.

In 1492, the same year that Columbus sighted America, the great Moorish city of Granada, in Spain, fell after a ten-year siege. For five centuries the Christian kingdoms of Spain had been trying to drive the North African Muslim *Moors* ("the Dark Ones," in Spanish) off the Iberian Peninsula, and with the fall of Granada, they succeeded. But the lengthy *Reconquista* had left its mark on Spanish society. Centuries of military and religious confrontation nurtured an obsession with status and honor, bred religious zealotry and intolerance, and created a large class of men who regarded manual labor and commerce contemptuously. With the *Reconquista* ended, some of these men turned their restless gaze to Spain's New World frontier.

At first Spanish hopes for America focused on the Caribbean and on finding a sea route to Asia. Gradually, however, word filtered back of rich kingdoms on the mainland. Between 1519 and 1540, Spanish *conquistadores* swept across the Americas in two wide arcs of conquest—one driving from Cuba through Mexico into what is now the southwestern United States; the other starting from Panama and pushing south into Peru. Within half a century of Columbus's arrival in the Americas, the *conquistadores* had extinguished the great Aztec and Incan empires and claimed for church and crown a territory that extended from Colorado to Argentina, including much of what is now the continental United States.

The military conquest of this vast region was achieved by just ten thousand men, organized in a series of private expeditions. Hernán Cortés, Francisco Pizarro, and other aspiring conquerors signed contracts with the Spanish monarch, raised money from investors, and then went about recruiting an army. Only a small minority of the *conquistadores*—leaders or followers—were nobles. About half were professional soldiers and sailors; the rest comprised peasants, artisans, and members of the middling classes. Most were in their twenties and early thirties, and all knew how to wield a sword.

Diverse motives spurred these motley adventurers. Some hoped to win royal

Conquistadores, ca. 1534   This illustration for a book called the *Köhler Codex of Nuremberg* may be the earliest depiction of the *conquistadores* in the Americas. It portrays men and horses alike as steadfast and self-assured in their work of conquest.

Shortly thereafter in South America, the iron-fisted conqueror Francisco Pizarro crushed the Incas of Peru in 1532 and added a huge hoard of booty to Spanish coffers. By 1600 Spain was swimming in New World silver, mostly from the fabulously rich mines at Potosí in present-day Bolivia, as well as from Mexico. This flood of precious metal touched off a price revolution in Europe that increased consumer costs by as much as 500 percent in the hundred years

after the mid-sixteenth century. Some scholars see in this ballooning European money supply the fuel that fed the growth of the economic system known as **capitalism**. Certainly, New World bullion helped transform the world economy. It filled the vaults of bankers from Spain to Italy, laying the foundations of the modern banking system. It clinked in the purses of merchants in France and Holland, stimulating the spread of commerce and manufacturing. And it paid

Library of Congress Prints and Photographs Division

An Aztec View of the Conquest, 1531 Produced just a dozen years after Cortés's arrival in 1519, this drawing by an Aztec artist pictures the Indians rendering tribute to their conquerors. The inclusion of the banner showing the Madonna and child also illustrates the early incorporation of Christian beliefs by the Indians.

titles and favors by bringing new peoples under the Spanish flag. Others sought to ensure God's favor by spreading Christianity to the pagans. Some men hoped to escape dubious pasts, and others sought the kind of historical adventure experienced by heroes of classical antiquity. Nearly all shared a lust for gold. As one of Cortés's foot soldiers put it, "We came here to serve God and the king, and also to get rich." One historian adds that the *conquistadores* first fell on their knees and then fell upon the aborigines.

Armed with horses and gunpowder and preceded by disease, the *conquistadores* quickly overpowered the Indians. But most never achieved their dreams of glory. Few received titles of nobility, and many of the rank and file remained permanently indebted to the absentee investors who paid for their equipment. Even when an expedition captured exceptionally rich booty, the spoils

were unevenly divided: men from the commander's home region often received more, and men on horseback generally got two shares to the infantryman's one. The *conquistadores* lost still more power as the crown gradually tightened its control in the New World. By the 1530s in Mexico and the 1550s in Peru, colorless colonial administrators had replaced the freebooting *conquistadores*.

Nevertheless, the *conquistadores* achieved a kind of immortality. Because of a scarcity of Spanish women in the early days of the conquest, many of the *conquistadores* married Indian women. The soldiers who conquered Paraguay received three native women each, and Cortés's soldiers in Mexico—who were forbidden to consort with pagan women—quickly had their lovers baptized into the Catholic faith. Their offspring, the "new race" of *mestizos*, formed a cultural and a biological bridge between Latin America's European and Indian races.

for much of the burgeoning international trade with Asia, whose sellers had little use for any European good except silver.

Yet the invaders brought more than conquest and death. They brought crops and animals, language and laws, customs and religion, all of which proved adaptable to the peoples of the Americas. Especially in Mexico, they intermarried with the surviving Indians, creating a distinctive culture of **mestizos**,

people of mixed Indian and European heritage. To this day Mexico remains a unique blend of the Old World and the New, producing both ambivalence and pride among its people. Cortés's translator, Malinche, for example, has given her name to the Mexican language in the word *malinchista*, or "traitor." But Mexicans also celebrate Columbus Day as the *Dia de la Raza*—the birthday of a wholly new race of people.

19

Artist's Rendering of Tenochtitlán Amid tribal strife in the fourteenth century, the Aztecs built a capital on a small island in a lake in the central Valley of Mexico. From here they oversaw the most powerful empire yet to arise in Mesoamerica. Two main temples stood at the city's sacred center, one dedicated to Tlaloc, the ancient rain god, and the other to Huitzilopochtli, the tribal god, who was believed to require human hearts for sustenance.

Museo Nacional De Antropologia/INHA, Mexico, photo by Bob Schalkwijk

✴ Exploration and Imperial Rivalry

In the service of God, as well as in search of gold and glory, Spanish **conquistadores** (conquerors) continued to fan out across the New World and beyond (see "Makers of America: The Spanish *Conquistadores*," pp. 18–19). On Spain's long roster of notable deeds, two spectacular exploits must be headlined. Vasco Nuñez Balboa, hailed as the European discoverer of the Pacific Ocean, waded into the foaming waves off Panama in 1513 and boldly claimed for his king all the lands washed by that sea (see Map 1.5). Ferdinand Magellan started from Spain in 1519 with five tiny ships. After beating through the storm-lashed strait off the tip of South America that still bears his name, he was slain by the inhabitants of the Philippines. His one remaining vessel creaked home in 1522, completing the first circumnavigation of the globe.

Other ambitious Spaniards ventured into North America. In 1513 and 1521, Juan Ponce de León explored Florida, which he at first thought was an island. Seeking gold—and probably not the mythical "fountain of youth"—he instead met with death by an Indian arrow. In 1540–1542 Francisco Coronado, in quest of fabled golden cities that turned out to be adobe pueblos, wandered with a clanking cavalcade through Arizona and New Mexico, penetrating as far east as Kansas. En route his expedition discovered two awesome natural wonders: the Grand Canyon of the Colorado River and enormous herds of buffalo (bison). Hernando de Soto, with six hundred armored men,

undertook a fantastic gold-seeking expedition during 1539–1542. Floundering through marshes and pine barrens from Florida westward, he discovered and crossed the majestic Mississippi River just north of its junction with the Arkansas River. After brutally mistreating the Indians with iron collars and fierce dogs, he at length died of fever and wounds. His troops secretly disposed of his remains at night in the Mississippi, lest the Indians exhume and abuse their abuser's corpse.

Spain's colonial empire grew swiftly and impressively. Within about half a century of Columbus's landfall, hundreds of Spanish cities and towns flourished in the Americas, especially in the great silver-producing centers of Peru and Mexico. Some 160,000 Spaniards, mostly men, had subjugated millions of Indians. Majestic cathedrals dotted the land, printing presses turned out books, and scholars founded distinguished universities, including those at Mexico City and Lima, Peru, both established in 1551, eighty-five years before Harvard, the first college established in the English colonies.

But how secure were these imperial possessions? Other powers were already sniffing around the edges of the Spanish domain, eager to bite off their share of the promised wealth of the new lands. The upstart English sent Giovanni Caboto (known in English as John Cabot) to explore the northeastern coast of North America in 1497 and 1498. The French king dispatched another Italian mariner, Giovanni da Verrazano, to probe the eastern seaboard in 1524. Ten years later the Frenchman Jacques Cartier journeyed hundreds of miles up the St. Lawrence River.

MAP 1.5 Principal Early Spanish Explorations and Conquests Note that Coronado traversed northern Texas and Oklahoma. In present-day eastern Kansas, he found, instead of the great golden city he sought, a drab encampment, probably of Wichita Indians. © 2016 Cengage Learning

To safeguard the northern periphery of their New World domain against such encroachments and to convert more Indian souls to Christianity, the Spanish began to fortify and settle their North American borderlands. In a move to block French ambitions and to protect the sea-lanes to the Caribbean, the Spanish erected a fortress at St. Augustine, Florida, in 1565, thus founding the oldest continually inhabited European settlement in the future United States.

In Mexico the tales of Coronado's expedition of the 1540s to the upper Rio Grande and Colorado River regions continued to beckon the *conquistadores* northward. A dust-begrimed expeditionary column, with eighty-three rumbling wagons and hundreds of grumbling men, traversed the bare Sonora Desert from Mexico into the Rio Grande valley in 1598. Led by Don Juan de Oñate, the Spaniards cruelly abused the Pueblo peoples they encountered. In the **Battle of Acoma** in 1599, the victorious Spanish severed one foot of each surviving Indian. They proclaimed the area to be the province of New Mexico in 1609 and founded its capital at Santa Fé the following year (see Map 1.6).

The Spanish settlers in New Mexico found a few furs and precious little gold, but they did discover a wealth of souls to be harvested for the Christian religion. The Roman Catholic mission became the central institution in colonial New Mexico until the missionaries' efforts to suppress native religious customs provoked an Indian uprising called **Popé's Rebellion** in 1680. The Pueblo rebels destroyed every Catholic church in the province and killed a score of priests and hundreds of Spanish settlers. In a reversal of Cortés's treatment of the Aztec temples more than a century earlier, the Indians rebuilt a *kiva*, or ceremonial religious chamber,

on the ruins of the Spanish plaza at Santa Fé. It took nearly half a century for the Spanish fully to reclaim New Mexico from the insurrectionary Indians.

Meanwhile, as a further hedge against the ever-threatening French, who had sent an expedition under Robert de La Salle down the Mississippi River in the 1680s, the Spanish began around 1716 to establish settlements in Texas. Some refugees from the Pueblo uprising trickled into Texas, and a few missions were established there, including the one at San Antonio later known as the Alamo. But for at least another century, the Spanish presence remained weak in this distant northeastern outpost of Spain's Mexican empire.

To the west, in California, no serious foreign threat loomed, and Spain directed its attention there only belatedly. Juan Rodriguez Cabrillo had explored the California coast in 1542, but he failed to find San Francisco Bay or anything else of much interest. For some two centuries thereafter, California slumbered undisturbed by European intruders. Then in 1769 Spanish missionaries led by Father Junipero Serra founded at San Diego the first of a chain of twenty-one missions that wound up the coast as far as Sonoma, north of San Francisco Bay. Father Serra's brown-robed Franciscan friars toiled with zealous devotion to Christianize the 300,000 native Californians. They gathered the seminomadic Indians into fortified missions and taught them horticulture and basic crafts. These "mission Indians" did adopt Christianity, but they also lost contact with their native cultures and often lost their lives as well, as the white man's diseases doomed these biologically vulnerable peoples.

The misdeeds of the Spanish in the New World obscured their substantial achievements and helped

MAP 1.6 Spain's North American Frontier, 1542–1823

© 2016 Cengage Learning

give birth to the **Black Legend**. This false concept held that the conquerors merely tortured and butchered the Indians ("killing for Christ"), stole their gold, infected them with smallpox, and left little but misery behind. The Spanish invaders did indeed kill, enslave, and infect countless natives, but they also erected a colossal empire, sprawling from California and Florida to Tierra del Fuego. They grafted their culture, laws, religion, and language onto a wide array of native societies, laying the foundations for a score of Spanish-speaking nations.

Clearly, the Spaniards, who had more than a century's head start over the English, were genuine empire builders and cultural innovators in the New World. As compared with their Anglo-Saxon rivals, their colonial establishment was larger and richer, and it was destined to endure more than a quarter of a century longer. And in the last analysis, the Spanish paid the Native Americans the high compliment of

fusing with them through marriage and incorporating indigenous culture into their own, rather than shunning and eventually isolating the Indians as their English adversaries would do.

Arrival of Cortés, with Dona Marina, at Tenochtitlán in 1519 This painting by a Mexican artist depicts Cortés in the dress of a Spanish gentleman. His translator Malinche, whose Christian name was Marina, is given an honorable place at the front of the procession. She eventually married one of Cortés's soldiers, with whom she traveled to Spain and was received by the Spanish court.

Chapter Review

KEY TERMS

Canadian Shield (4)
Incas (6)
Aztecs (6)
nation-states (8)
Cahokia (8)
three-sister farming (8)
middlemen (11)
caravel (12)
plantation (13)
Columbian exchange (14)

Tordesillas, Treaty of (16)
encomienda (16)
noche triste (17)
capitalism (18)
mestizos (19)
conquistadores (20)
Battle of Acoma (21)
Popé's Rebellion (21)
Black Legend (22)

PEOPLE TO KNOW

Ferdinand of Aragon
Isabella of Castile
Christopher Columbus
Francisco Coronado
Francisco Pizarro
Bartolomé de Las Casas
Hernán Cortés

Malinche (Doña Marina)
Moctezuma
Giovanni Caboto (John Cabot)
Robert de La Salle
Father Junipero Serra

CHRONOLOGY

ca. 33,000–8000 B.C.E.	First humans cross into Americas from Asia
ca. 5000 B.C.E.	Corn is developed as a staple crop in highland Mexico
ca. 4000 B.C.E.	First civilized societies develop in the Middle East
ca. 2000 B.C.E.	Corn planting reaches present-day American Southwest
ca. 1000 C.E.	Norse voyagers discover and briefly settle in northeastern North America. Corn cultivation reaches Midwest and southeastern Atlantic seaboard
ca. 1100 C.E.	Height of Mississippian settlement at Cahokia
ca. 1100–1300 C.E.	Christian crusades arouse European interest in the East
1295	Marco Polo returns to Europe
late 1400s	Spain becomes united
1488	Dias rounds southern tip of Africa
1492	Columbus lands in the Bahamas
1494	Treaty of Tordesillas between Spain and Portugal
1498	Da Gama reaches India. Cabot explores northeastern coast of North America for England
1513	Balboa claims all lands touched by the Pacific Ocean for Spain
1513, 1521	Ponce de León explores Florida
1519–1521	Cortés conquers Mexico for Spain
1522	Magellan's vessel completes circumnavigation of the world
1524	Verrazano explores eastern seaboard of North America for France
1532	Pizarro crushes Incas
1534	Cartier journeys up the St. Lawrence River
1539–1542	De Soto explores the Southeast and discovers the Mississippi River
1540–1542	Coronado explores present-day Southwest
1542	Cabrillo explores California coast for Spain
1565	Spanish build fortress at St. Augustine
late 1500s	Iroquois Confederacy founded, according to Iroquois legend
ca. 1598–1609	Spanish under Oñate conquer Pueblo peoples of Rio Grande valley
1609	Spanish found New Mexico
1680	Popé's Rebellion in New Mexico
1680s	French expedition down Mississippi River under La Salle
1769	Serra founds first California mission, at San Diego

TO LEARN MORE

Mark A. Burkholder and Lyman L. Johnson, *Colonial Latin America* (2000)

Alfred W. Crosby, Jr., *The Columbian Exchange: Biological and Cultural Consequences of 1492* (1972)

Jared Diamond, *Guns, Germs, and Steel: The Fates of Human Societies* (1998)

Tom Dillehay, *The Settlement of the Americas: A New Prehistory* (2000)

J. H. Elliott, *Empires of the Atlantic World* (2006)

Steven W. Hackel, *Children of Coyote, Missionaries of Saint Francis: Indian-Spanish Relations in Colonial California, 1769–1850* (2005)

Hugh Honour, *The New Golden Land* (1975)

Alice Beck Keyhoe, *America Before the European Invasions* (2002)

Anthony Pagden, *Peoples and Empires: A Short History of European Migration, Exploration, and Conquest, from Greece to the Present* (2003)

Andrés Reséndez, *A Land So Strange: The Epic Journey of Cabeza de Vaca* (2007)

John Thornton, *Africa and Africans in the Making of the Atlantic World, 1400–1800* (1992)

David J. Weber, *Bárbaros: Spaniards and Their Savages in the Age of Enlightenment* (2005)

A complete, annotated bibliography for this chapter—along with brief descriptions of the People to Know—may be found on the *American Pageant* website. The key terms are defined in the glossary at the end of the text.

Chapter 2

The Planting of English America

1500–1733

...For I shall yet live to see it [Virginia] an Inglishe nation.

SIR WALTER RALEIGH, 1602

As the seventeenth century dawned, scarcely a hundred years after Columbus's momentous landfall, the face of much of the New World had already been profoundly transformed. European crops and livestock had begun to alter the very landscape, touching off an ecological revolution that would reverberate for centuries to come. From Tierra del Fuego in the south to Hudson Bay in the north, disease and armed conquest had cruelly winnowed and disrupted the native peoples. Several hundred thousand enslaved Africans toiled on Caribbean and Brazilian sugar plantations. From Florida and New Mexico southward, most of the New World lay firmly within the grip of imperial Spain.

But north of Mexico, America in 1600 remained largely unexplored and effectively unclaimed by Europeans. Then, as if to herald the coming century of colonization and conflict in the northern continent, three European powers planted three primitive outposts in three distant corners of the continent within three years of one another: the Spanish at Santa Fé in 1610, the French at Québec in 1608, and, most consequentially for the future United States, the English at Jamestown, Virginia, in 1607.

✦ England's Imperial Stirrings

Feeble indeed were England's efforts in the 1500s to compete with the sprawling Spanish Empire. As Spain's ally in the first half of the century, England took little interest in establishing its own overseas colonies. Religious conflict also disrupted England in midcentury, after King Henry VIII broke with the Roman Catholic Church in the 1530s, launching the English **Protestant Reformation**. Catholics battled Protestants for decades, and the religious balance of power seesawed. But after the Protestant Elizabeth ascended to the English throne in 1558, Protestantism became dominant in England, and rivalry with Catholic Spain intensified.

Ireland, which nominally had been under English rule since the twelfth century, became an early scene of that rivalry. The Catholic Irish sought help from Catholic Spain to throw off the yoke of the new Protestant English queen. But Spanish aid never amounted to much; in the 1570s and 1580s, Elizabeth's troops crushed the Irish uprising with terrible ferocity, inflicting unspeakable atrocities upon the native Irish people. The English crown confiscated Catholic Irish lands and "planted" them with new Protestant landlords from Scotland and England. This policy also planted the seeds of the centuries-old religious conflicts that persist in Ireland to the present day. Many English soldiers developed in Ireland a sneering contempt for the "savage" natives, an attitude that they brought with them to the New World.

✦ Elizabeth Energizes England

Encouraged by the ambitious Elizabeth I (see Table 2.1), hardy English buccaneers now swarmed out upon the shipping lanes. They sought to promote the twin goals of Protestantism and plunder by seizing Spanish treasure ships and raiding Spanish

25

TABLE 2.1 The Tudor Rulers of England*	
Name, Reign	**Relation to America**
Henry VII, 1485–1509	Cabot voyages, 1497, 1498
Henry VIII, 1509–1547	English Reformation began
Edward VI, 1547–1553	Strong Protestant tendencies
"Bloody" Mary, 1553–1558	Catholic reaction
Elizabeth I, 1558–1603	Break with Roman Catholic Church final; Drake; Spanish Armada defeated

*See Table 3.1, p. 50, for a continuation of the table.

settlements, even though England and Spain were technically at peace. The most famous of these semi-piratical "sea dogs" was the courtly Sir Francis Drake. He swashbuckled and looted his way around the planet, returning in 1580 with his ship heavily ballasted with Spanish booty. The venture netted profits of about 4,600 percent to his financial backers, among whom, in secret, was Queen Elizabeth. Defying Spanish protest, she brazenly knighted Drake on the deck of his barnacled ship.

The bleak coast of Newfoundland was the scene of the first English attempt at colonization. This effort collapsed when its promoter, Sir Humphrey Gilbert, lost his life at sea in 1583. Gilbert's ill-starred dream inspired his gallant half-brother Sir Walter Raleigh to try again in warmer climes. Raleigh organized an expedition that first landed in 1585 on North Carolina's **Roanoke Island**, off the coast of Virginia—a vaguely defined region named in honor of Elizabeth, the "Virgin Queen." After several false starts, the hapless Roanoke colony mysteriously vanished, swallowed up by the wilderness.

These pathetic English failures at colonization contrasted embarrassingly with the glories of the Spanish Empire, whose profits were fabulously enriching Spain. Philip II of Spain, self-anointed foe of the Protestant Reformation, used part of his imperial gains to amass an "Invincible Armada" of ships for an invasion of England. The showdown came in 1588 when the lumbering Spanish flotilla, 130 strong, hove into the English Channel. The English sea dogs fought back. Using craft that were swifter, more maneuverable, and more ably manned, they inflicted heavy damage on the cumbersome, overladen Spanish ships. Then a devastating storm arose (the "Protestant wind"), scattering the crippled Spanish fleet.

The rout of the **Spanish Armada** marked the beginning of the end of Spanish imperial dreams, though Spain's New World empire would not fully collapse for three more centuries. Within a few decades, the Spanish Netherlands (Holland) would secure its independence, and much of the Spanish Caribbean would slip from Spain's grasp. Bloated by Peruvian and Mexican silver and cockily convinced of its own invincibility, Spain had overreached itself, sowing the seeds of its own decline.

Elizabeth I (1533–1603), by George Gower, ca. 1588 In this "Armada Portrait" of Queen Elizabeth I, the artist proclaims her the Empress of the World. She was accused of being vain, fickle, prejudiced, and miserly, but Elizabeth proved to be an unusually successful ruler. She never married (hence, the "Virgin Queen"), although many romances were rumored and royal matches schemed.

The Gallery Collection/Corbis

Contending Voices
Old World Dreams and New World Realities

In the years immediately following the defeat of the Spanish Armada, the English writer Richard Hakluyt (1552?–1616)—a tireless promoter who never set foot in the Americas—extravagantly exhorted his countrymen to cast off their "sluggish security" and undertake the colonization of the New World:

❝There is under our noses the great and ample country of Virginia; the inland whereof is found of late to be so sweet and wholesome a climate, so rich and abundant in silver mines, a better and richer country than Mexico itself. If it shall please the Almighty to stir up Her Majesty's heart to continue with transporting one or two thousand of her people, she shall by God's assistance, in short space, increase her dominions, enrich her coffers, and reduce many pagans to the faith of Christ.❞

A few years later, George Percy (1580–1631) saw Virginia firsthand. He accompanied Captain John Smith on his expedition to Virginia in 1606–1607 and served as deputy governor of the colony in 1609–1610. He returned to England in 1612, where he wrote A Discourse of the Plantation of Virginia *about his experiences:*

❝Our men were destroyed with cruel diseases as swellings, burning fevers, and by wars, and some departed suddenly, but for the most part they died of mere famine. There were never Englishmen left in a foreign country in such misery as we were in this new discovered Virginia.❞

How does one account for the difference in these views—or were both accurate?

England's victory over the Spanish Armada also marked a red-letter day in American history. It dampened Spain's fighting spirit and helped ensure England's naval dominance in the North Atlantic. It started England on its way to becoming master of the world oceans—a fact of enormous importance to the American people. Indeed England now had many of the characteristics that Spain displayed on the eve of its colonizing adventure a century earlier: a strong, unified national state under a popular monarch; a measure of religious unity after a protracted struggle between Protestants and Catholics; and a vibrant sense of nationalism and national destiny.

A wondrous flowering of the English national spirit bloomed in the wake of the Spanish Armada's defeat. A golden age of literature dawned in this exhilarating atmosphere, with William Shakespeare, at its forefront, making occasional poetical references to England's American colonies. The English were seized with restlessness, with thirst for adventure, and with curiosity about the unknown. Everywhere there blossomed a new spirit of self-confidence, of vibrant patriotism, and of boundless faith in the future of the English nation. When England and Spain finally signed a treaty of peace in 1604, the English people were poised to plunge headlong into the planting of their own colonial empire in the New World.

✦ England on the Eve of Empire

England's scepter'd isle, as Shakespeare called it, throbbed with social and economic change as the seventeenth century opened. Its population was mushrooming, from some 3 million people in 1550 to about 4 million in 1600. In the ever-green English countryside, landlords were "enclosing" croplands for sheep grazing, forcing many small farmers into precarious tenancy or off the land altogether. It was no accident that the woolen districts of eastern and western England—where Puritanism had taken strong root—supplied many of the earliest immigrants to America. When economic depression hit the woolen trade in the late 1500s, thousands of footloose farmers took to the roads. They drifted about England, chronically unemployed, often ending up as beggars and paupers in cities like Bristol and London.

This remarkably mobile population alarmed many contemporaries. They concluded that England was burdened with a "surplus population," though present-day London holds twice as many people as did all of England in 1600.

At the same time, laws of **primogeniture** decreed that only eldest sons were eligible to inherit landed estates. Landholders' ambitious younger sons, among them Gilbert, Raleigh, and Drake, were forced to seek their fortunes elsewhere. Bad luck plagued their early, lone-wolf enterprises. But by the early 1600s, when the **joint-stock company**, forerunner of the modern corporation, was perfected, a considerable number of investors, called "adventurers," were able to pool their capital.

Peace with a chastened Spain provided the opportunity for English colonization. Population growth provided the workers. Unemployment, as well as a thirst for adventure, for markets, and for religious

Sir Walter Ralegh (Raleigh) (ca. 1552–1618), 1588 A dashing courtier who was one of Queen Elizabeth's favorites for his wit, good looks, and courtly manners, he launched important colonizing failures in the New World. For this portrait, Raleigh presented himself as the queen's devoted servant, wearing her colors of black and white and her emblem of a pearl in his left ear. After seducing (and secretly marrying) one of Queen Elizabeth's maids of honor, he fell out of favor but continued his colonial ventures in the hopes of challenging Catholic Spain's dominance in the Americas. He was ultimately beheaded for treason.

freedom, provided the motives. Joint-stock companies provided the financial means. The stage was now set for a historic effort to establish an English beachhead in the still uncharted North American wilderness.

✺ England Plants the Jamestown Seedling

In 1606, two years after peace with Spain, the hand of destiny beckoned toward Virginia. A joint-stock company, known as the **Virginia Company** of London, received a charter from King James I of England for a settlement in the New World. The main attraction was the promise of gold, combined with a strong desire to find a passage through America to the Indies. Like most joint-stock companies of the day, the Virginia Company was intended to endure for only a few years, after which its stockholders hoped to liquidate it for a profit. This arrangement put severe pressure on the luckless colonists, who were threatened with abandonment in the wilderness if they did not quickly strike it rich on the company's behalf. Few of the investors thought in terms of long-term colonization. Apparently no one even faintly suspected that the seeds of a mighty nation were being planted.

The **charter** of the Virginia Company is a significant document in American history. It guaranteed to the overseas settlers the same rights of Englishmen that they would have enjoyed if they had stayed at home. This precious boon was gradually extended to subsequent English colonies, helping to reinforce the colonists' sense that even on the far shores of the Atlantic, they remained comfortably within the embrace of traditional English institutions. But ironically, a century and a half later, their insistence on the "rights of Englishmen" fed hot resentment against an increasingly meddlesome mother country and nourished their appetite for independence.

Setting sail in late 1606, the Virginia Company's three ships landed near the mouth of Chesapeake Bay, where Indians attacked them. Pushing on up the bay, the tiny band of colonists eventually chose a location on the wooded and malarial banks of the James River, named in honor of King James I. The site was easy to defend, but it was mosquito-infested and devastatingly unhealthful. There, on May 24, 1607, about a hundred English settlers, all of them men, disembarked. They called the place **Jamestown** (see Map 2.1).

The early years of Jamestown proved a nightmare for all concerned—except the buzzards. Forty would-be colonists perished during the initial voyage in 1606–1607. Another expedition in 1609 lost its leaders and many of its precious supplies in a shipwreck off Bermuda. Once ashore in Virginia, the settlers died by the dozens from disease, malnutrition, and starvation. Ironically, the woods rustled with game and the rivers flopped with fish, but the greenhorn settlers, many of them self-styled "gentlemen" unaccustomed to fending for themselves, wasted valuable time grubbing for nonexistent gold when they should have been gathering provisions.

Virginia was saved from utter collapse at the start largely by the leadership and resourcefulness of an intrepid young adventurer, Captain John Smith. Taking over in 1608, he whipped the gold-hungry colonists into line with the rule "He who shall not work shall not eat." He had been kidnapped in December 1607 and subjected to a mock execution by the Indian

MAP 2.1 Early Maryland and Virginia © 2016 Cengage Learning

The authorities meted out harsh discipline in the young Virginia colony. One Jamestown settler who publicly criticized the governor was sentenced to

❝ be disarmed [and] have his arms broken and his tongue bored through with an awl [and] shall pass through a guard of 40 men and shall be butted [with muskets] by every one of them and at the head of the troop kicked down and footed out of the fort. **❞**

in the spring of 1610, only to be met at the mouth of the James River by a long-awaited relief party headed by a new governor, Lord De La Warr. He ordered the settlers back to Jamestown, imposed a harsh military regime on the colony, and soon undertook aggressive military action against the Indians.

Disease continued to reap a gruesome harvest among the Virginians. By 1625 Virginia contained only some twelve hundred hard-bitten survivors of the nearly eight thousand adventurers who had tried to start life anew in the ill-fated colony.

Pocahontas (ca. 1595–1617) Taken to England by her husband, she was received as a princess. She died when preparing to return, but her infant son ultimately reached Virginia, where hundreds of his descendants have lived, including the second Mrs. Woodrow Wilson.

chieftain Powhatan, whose daughter Pocahontas had "saved" Smith by dramatically interposing her head between his and the war clubs of his captors. The symbolism of this ritual was apparently intended to impress Smith with Powhatan's power and with the Indians' desire for peaceful relations with the Virginians. Pocahontas became an intermediary between the Indians and the settlers, helping to preserve a shaky peace and to provide needed foodstuffs.

Still, the colonists died in droves, and living skeletons were driven to desperate acts. They were reduced to eating "dogges, Catts, Ratts, and Myce" and even to digging up corpses for food. One hungry man killed, salted, and ate his wife, for which misbehavior he was executed. Of the four hundred settlers who managed to make it to Virginia by 1609, only sixty survived the "starving time" winter of 1609–1610.

Diseased and despairing, the remaining colonists dragged themselves aboard homeward-bound ships

✦ Cultural Clashes in the Chesapeake

When the English landed in 1607, the chieftain Powhatan dominated the native peoples living in the James River area. He had asserted supremacy over a few dozen small tribes, loosely affiliated in what somewhat grandly came to be called Powhatan's Confederacy. The English colonists dubbed all the local Indians, somewhat inaccurately, the Powhatans. Powhatan at first may have considered the English potential allies in his struggle to extend his power still further over his Indian rivals, and he tried to be conciliatory. But relations between the Indians and the English remained tense, especially as the starving colonists took to raiding Indian food supplies.

The atmosphere grew even more strained after Lord De La Warr arrived in 1610. He carried orders from the Virginia Company that amounted to a declaration of war against the Indians in the Jamestown region. A veteran of the vicious campaigns against the Irish, De La Warr now introduced "Irish tactics" against the Indians. His troops raided Indian villages, burned houses, confiscated provisions, and torched cornfields. A peace settlement ended this **First Anglo-Powhatan War** in 1614, sealed by the marriage of Pocahontas to the colonist John Rolfe—the first known interracial union in Virginia.

A fragile respite followed, which endured eight years. But the Indians, pressed by the land-hungry whites and ravaged by European diseases, struck back in 1622. A series of Indian attacks left 347 settlers dead, including John Rolfe. In response the Virginia Company issued new orders calling for "a perpetual war without peace or truce," one that would prevent the Indians "from being any longer a people." Periodic punitive raids systematically reduced the native population and drove the survivors ever farther westward.

In the **Second Anglo-Powhatan War** in 1644,

> *The wife of a Virginia governor wrote to her sister in England in 1623 of her voyage:*
>
> **"** For our Shippe was so pestered with people and goods that we were so full of infection that after a while we saw little but throwing folkes over board: It pleased god to send me my helth till I came to shoare and 3 dayes after I fell sick but I thank god I am well recovered. Few else are left alive that came in that Shippe. **"**

the Indians made one last effort to dislodge the Virginians. They were again defeated. The peace treaty of 1646 repudiated any thought of assimilating the native peoples into Virginia society or of peacefully coexisting with them. Instead it effectively banished the Chesapeake Indians from their ancestral lands and formally separated Indian from white areas of settlement—the origins of the later reservation system. By 1669 an official census revealed that only about two thousand Indians remained in Virginia, perhaps 10 percent of the population the original English settlers had encountered in 1607. By 1685 the English considered the Powhatan peoples extinct.

It had been the Powhatans' calamitous misfortune to fall victim to three Ds: disease, disorganization, and disposability. Like native peoples throughout the New World, they were extremely susceptible to European-borne maladies. Epidemics of smallpox and measles raced mercilessly through their villages. The Powhatans also—despite the apparent cohesiveness of "Powhatan's Confederacy"—lacked the unity with which to make effective opposition to the comparatively well-organized and militarily disciplined whites. Finally, unlike the Indians whom the Spaniards had encountered to the south, who could be put to work in the mines and had gold and silver to trade, the Powhatans served no economic

The Granger Collection, NYC

A Carolina Indian Woman and Child, by John White The artist was a member of the Raleigh expedition of 1585. Notice that the Indian girl carries a European doll, illustrating the mingling of cultures that had already begun.

function for the Virginia colonists. They provided no reliable labor source and, after the Virginians began growing their own food crops, had no valuable commodities to offer in commerce. The natives, as far as the Virginians were concerned, could be disposed of without harm to the colonial economy. Indeed the Indian presence frustrated the colonists' desire for a local commodity the Europeans desperately wanted: land.

✳ The Indians' New World

The fate of the Powhatans foreshadowed the destinies of indigenous peoples throughout the continent as the process of European settlement went forward. Native Americans, of course, had a history well before Columbus's arrival. They were no strangers to change, adaptation, and even catastrophe, as the rise and decline of civilizations such as the Mississippians and the Anasazis demonstrated. But the shock of large-scale European colonization disrupted Native American life on a vast scale, inducing unprecedented demographic and cultural transformations.

Some changes were fairly benign. Horses—stolen, strayed, or purchased from Spanish invaders—catalyzed a substantial Indian migration onto the Great Plains in the eighteenth century. Peoples such as the Lakotas (Sioux), who had previously been sedentary forest dwellers, now moved onto the wide-open plains.

Benjamin Franklin (1706–1790) in a 1753 letter to Peter Collinson commented on the attractiveness of Indian life to Europeans:

" When an Indian child has been brought up among us, taught our language and habituated to our customs, yet if he goes to see his relations and make one Indian ramble with them, there is no persuading him ever to return. [But] when white persons of either sex have been taken prisoners by the Indians, and lived awhile among them, though ransomed by their friends, and treated with all imaginable tenderness to prevail with them to stay among the English, yet in a short time they become disgusted with our manner of life, and the care and pains that are necessary to support it, and take the first good opportunity of escaping again into the woods, from whence there is no reclaiming them."

There they thrived impressively, adopting an entirely new way of life as mounted nomadic hunters. But the effects of contact with Europeans proved less salutary for most other native peoples.

Disease was by far the biggest disrupter, as Old World pathogens licked lethally through biologically defenseless Indian populations. Disease took more

Carolina Indians German painter Philip Georg Friedrich von Reck drew these Yuchi Indians in the 1730s. The blanket and rifle show that trade with the English settlers had already begun to transform Native American culture.

than human life; it extinguished entire cultures and occasionally helped shape new ones. Epidemics often robbed native peoples of the elders who preserved the oral traditions that held clans together. Devastated Indian bands then faced the daunting task of literally reinventing themselves without benefit of accumulated wisdom or kin networks. The decimation and forced migration of native peoples sometimes scrambled them together in wholly new ways. The Catawba nation of the southern Piedmont region, for example, was formed from splintered remnants of several different groups uprooted by the shock of the Europeans' arrival.

Trade also transformed Indian life, as traditional barter-and-exchange networks gave way to the temptations of European commerce. Firearms, for example, conferred enormous advantages on those who could purchase them from Europeans. The desire for firearms thus intensified competition among the tribes for access to prime hunting grounds that could supply the skins and pelts that the European arms traders wanted. The result was an escalating cycle of Indian-on-Indian violence, fueled by the lure and demands of European trade goods.

Native Americans were swept up in the expanding Atlantic economy, but they usually struggled in vain to control their own place in it. One desperate band of Virginia Indians, resentful at the prices offered by British traders for their deerskins, loaded a fleet of canoes with hides and tried to paddle to England to sell their goods directly. Not far from the Virginia shore, a storm swamped their frail craft. Their cargo lost, the few survivors were picked up by an English ship and sold into slavery in the West Indies.

Indians along the Atlantic seaboard felt the most ferocious effects of European contact. Farther inland, native peoples had the advantages of time, space, and numbers as they sought to adapt to the European incursion. The Algonquins in the Great Lakes area, for instance, became a substantial regional power. They bolstered their population by absorbing various surrounding bands and dealt from a position of strength with the few Europeans who managed to penetrate the interior. As a result, a British or French trader wanting to do

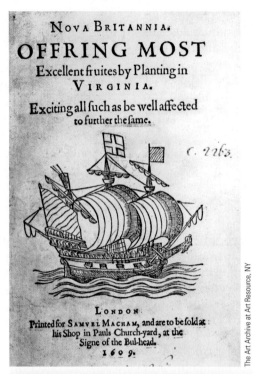

NOVA BRITANNIA.

OFFRING MOST

Excellent fruites by Planting in VIRGINIA.

Exciting all such as be well affected to further the same.

LONDON

Printed for SAMVEL MACHAM, and are to be sold at his Shop in Pauls Church-yard, at the Signe of the Bul-head. 1609.

The Art Archive at Art Resource, NY

Advertisement for a Voyage to America, 1609

business with the inland tribes had little choice but to conform to Indian ways, often taking an Indian wife. Thus was created a middle ground, a zone where both Europeans and Native Americans were compelled to accommodate to one another—at least until the Europeans began to arrive in large numbers.

✷ Virginia: Child of Tobacco

John Rolfe, the husband of Pocahontas, became father of the tobacco industry and an economic savior of the Virginia colony. By 1612 he had perfected methods of raising and curing the pungent weed, eliminating much of the bitter tang. Soon the European demand for tobacco was nearly insatiable. A tobacco rush swept over Virginia, as crops were planted in the streets of Jamestown and even between the numerous graves. So exclusively did the colonists concentrate on planting the yellow leaf that at first they had to import some of their foodstuffs. Colonists who had once hungered for food now hungered for land, ever more land on which to plant ever more tobacco. Relentlessly, they pressed the frontier of settlement up the river valleys to the west, abrasively edging against the Indians.

Virginia's prosperity was finally built on tobacco smoke. This "bewitching weed" played a vital role in putting the colony on firm economic foundations. But tobacco—King Nicotine—was something of a tyrant. It was ruinous to the soil when greedily planted in successive years, and it enchained the fortunes of Virginia to the fluctuating price of a single crop. Fatefully, tobacco also promoted the broad-acred plantation system and with it a brisk demand for fresh labor.

In 1619, the year before the Plymouth Pilgrims landed in New England, what was described as a Dutch warship appeared off Jamestown and sold some twenty Africans. The scanty record does not reveal whether they were purchased as lifelong slaves or as servants committed to limited years of servitude. However it transpired, this simple commercial transaction planted the seeds of the North American slave system. Yet blacks were too costly for most of the hard-pinched white colonists to acquire, and for decades few were brought to Virginia. In 1650 Virginia counted but three hundred blacks, although by the end of the century blacks, most of them enslaved, made up approximately 14 percent of the colony's population.

Representative self-government was also born in primitive Virginia, in the same cradle with slavery and in the same year—1619. The Virginia Company authorized the settlers to summon an assembly, known as the **House of Burgesses**. A momentous precedent was thus feebly established, for this assemblage was the first of many miniature parliaments to flourish in the soil of America.

As time passed, James I grew increasingly hostile to Virginia. He detested tobacco, and he distrusted the representative House of Burgesses, which he branded a "seminary of sedition." In 1624 he revoked the charter of the bankrupt and beleaguered Virginia Company, thus making Virginia a royal colony directly under his control.

✴ Maryland: Catholic Haven

Maryland—the second plantation colony but the fourth English colony to be planted—was founded in 1634 by Lord Baltimore of a prominent English Catholic family. He embarked upon the venture partly to reap financial profits and partly to create a refuge for his fellow Catholics. Protestant England was still persecuting Roman Catholics; among numerous discriminations, a couple seeking wedlock could not be legally married by a Catholic priest.

Absentee proprietor Lord Baltimore hoped that the two hundred settlers who founded Maryland at St. Marys, on Chesapeake Bay, would be the vanguard of a vast new feudal domain. Huge estates were to be awarded to his largely Catholic relatives, and gracious manor houses, modeled on those of England's aristocracy, were intended to arise amidst the fertile forests. As in Virginia, colonists proved willing to come only if offered the opportunity to acquire land of their own. Soon they were dispersed around the Chesapeake region on modest farms, and the haughty land barons, mostly Catholic, were surrounded by resentful backcountry planters, mostly Protestant. Resentment flared into open rebellion near the end of the century, and the Baltimore family for a time lost its proprietary rights.

Despite these tensions Maryland prospered. Like Virginia, it blossomed forth in acres of tobacco. Also like Virginia, it depended for labor in its early years mainly on white indentured servants—penniless persons who bound themselves to work for a number of years to pay their passage. In both colonies it was only in the later years of the seventeenth century that black slaves began to be imported in large numbers.

Lord Baltimore, a canny soul, permitted unusual freedom of worship at the outset. He hoped that he would thus purchase toleration for his own fellow worshipers. But the heavy tide of Protestants threatened to submerge the Catholics and place severe restrictions on them, as in England. Faced with disaster, the Catholics of Maryland threw their support behind the famed **Act of Toleration**, which was passed in 1649 by the local representative assembly.

Maryland's new religious statute guaranteed toleration to all Christians. But, less liberally, it decreed the death penalty for those, like Jews and atheists, who denied the divinity of Jesus. The law thus sanctioned less toleration than had previously existed in the settlement, but it did extend a temporary cloak of protection to the uneasy Catholic minority. One result was that when the colonial era ended, Maryland probably sheltered more Roman Catholics than any other English-speaking colony in the New World.

✴ The West Indies: Way Station to Mainland America

While the English were planting the first frail colonial shoots in the Chesapeake, they also were busily colonizing the islands of the West Indies. Spain, weakened by military overextension and distracted by its rebellious Dutch provinces, relaxed its grip on much of the Caribbean in the early 1600s. By the mid-seventeenth century, England had secured its claim to several West Indian islands, including the large prize of Jamaica in 1655.

Sugar formed the foundation of the West Indian economy. What tobacco was to the Chesapeake, sugar cane was to the Caribbean—with one crucial difference. Tobacco was a poor man's crop. It could be planted easily, it produced commercially marketable leaves within a year, and it required only simple processing. Sugar cane, in contrast, was a rich man's crop. It had to be planted

African slaves destined for the West Indian sugar plantations were bound and branded on West African beaches and ferried out in canoes to the waiting slave ships. An English sailor described the scene:

"The Negroes are so wilful and loth to leave their own country, that have often leap'd out of the canoes, boat and ship, into the sea, and kept under water till they were drowned, to avoid being taken up and saved by our boats, which pursued them; they having a more dreadful apprehension of Barbadoes than we can have of hell.**"**

The Granger Collection, NYC

Florilegius/SSPL/Getty Images

(above) Sugar Mill in Brazil, by Frans Post, ca. 1640; (left) *Saccharum Officinarum* (sugar cane)

1700, enslaved blacks outnumbered white settlers in the English West Indies by nearly four to one, and the region's population has remained predominantly black ever since. West Indians thus take their place among the numerous children of the African diaspora—the vast scattering of African peoples throughout the New World in the three and a half centuries following Columbus's discovery.

To control this large and potentially restive slave population, English authorities devised formal "codes"

The Barbados slave code (1661) declared,

"If any Negro or slave whatsoever shall offer any violence to any Christian by striking or the like, such Negro or slave shall for his or her first offence be severely whipped by the Constable. For his second offence of that nature he shall be severely whipped, his nose slit, and be burned in some part of his face with a hot iron. And being brutish slaves, [they] deserve not, for the baseness of their condition, to be tried by the legal trial of twelve men of their peers, as the subjects of England are. And it is further enacted and ordained that if any Negro or other slave under punishment by his master unfortunately shall suffer in life or member, which seldom happens, no person whatsoever shall be liable to any fine therefore."

extensively to yield commercially viable quantities of sugar. Extensive planting, in turn, required extensive and arduous land clearing. And the cane stalks yielded their sugar only after an elaborate process of refining in a sugar mill. The need for land and for the labor to clear it and to run the mills made sugar cultivation a capital-intensive business. Only wealthy growers with abundant capital to invest could succeed in sugar.

The sugar lords extended their dominion over the West Indies in the seventeenth century. To work their sprawling plantations, they imported enormous numbers of enslaved Africans—more than a quarter of a million in the five decades after 1640. By about that defined the slaves' legal status and their masters' prerogatives. The notorious **Barbados slave code** of 1661 denied even the most fundamental rights to slaves and gave masters virtually complete control over their laborers, including the right to inflict vicious punishments for even slight infractions.

The profitable sugar-plantation system soon crowded out almost all other forms of Caribbean agriculture. The West Indies increasingly depended on the North American mainland for foodstuffs and other basic supplies. And smaller English farmers, squeezed out by the greedy sugar barons, began to migrate to the newly founded southern mainland colonies. A group of displaced English settlers from Barbados arrived in Carolina in 1670. They brought with them a few enslaved Africans, as well as the model of the Barbados slave code, which eventually inspired statutes governing slavery throughout the mainland colonies. Carolina officially adopted a version of the Barbados slave code in 1696. Just as the West Indies had been a testing ground for the *encomienda* system that the Spanish had brought to Mexico and South America, so the Caribbean islands now served as a staging area for the slave system that would take root elsewhere in English North America.

�帶 Colonizing the Carolinas

Civil war convulsed England in the 1640s. King Charles I had dismissed Parliament in 1629, and when he eventually recalled it in 1640, the members were mutinous. Finding their great champion in the Puritan-soldier Oliver Cromwell, they ultimately beheaded Charles in 1649, and Cromwell ruled England for nearly a decade. Finally, Charles II, son of the decapitated king, was restored to the throne in 1660.

Colonization had been interrupted during this period of bloody unrest. Now, in the so-called Restoration period, empire building resumed with even greater intensity—and royal involvement (see Table 2.2). Carolina, named for Charles II, was formally created in 1670, after the king granted to eight of his court favorites, the Lords Proprietors, an expanse of wilderness ribboning across the continent to the Pacific. These aristocratic founders hoped to grow foodstuffs to provision the sugar plantations in Barbados and to export non-English products like wine, silk, and olive oil.

Carolina prospered by developing close economic ties with the flourishing sugar islands of the English West Indies. In a broad sense, the mainland colony was

TABLE 2.2 The Thirteen Original Colonies

Name	Founded by	Year	Charter	Made Royal	1775 Status
1. Virginia	London Co.	1607	1606 1609 1612	1624	Royal (under the crown)
2. New Hampshire	John Mason and others	1623	1679	1679	Royal (absorbed by Mass., 1641–1679)
3. Massachusetts	Puritans	ca. 1628	1629	1691	Royal
Plymouth	Separatists	1620	None		(Merged with Mass., 1691)
Maine	F. Gorges	1623	1639		(Bought by Mass., 1677)
4. Maryland	Lord Baltimore	1634	1632	____	Proprietary (controlled by proprietor)
5. Connecticut	Mass. emigrants	1635	1662	____	Self-governing (under local control)
New Haven	Mass. emigrants	1638	None		(Merged with Conn., 1662)
6. Rhode Island	R. Williams	1636	1644 1663	____	Self-governing
7. Delaware	Swedes	1638	None	____	Proprietary (merged with Pa., 1682; same governor, but separate assembly, granted 1703)
8. N. Carolina	Virginians	1653	1663	1729	Royal (separated informally from S.C., 1691)
9. New York	Dutch	ca. 1613			
	Duke of York	1664	1664	1685	Royal
10. New Jersey	Berkeley and Carteret	1664	None	1702	Royal
11. Carolina	Eight nobles	1670	1663	1729	Royal (separated formally from N.C., 1712)
12. Pennsylvania	William Penn	1681	1681	____	Proprietary
13. Georgia	Oglethorpe and others	1733	1732	1752	Royal

but the most northerly of those outposts. Many original Carolina settlers, in fact, had emigrated from Barbados, bringing that island's slave system with them. They also established a vigorous slave trade in Carolina itself. Enlisting the aid of the coastal Savannah Indians, they forayed into the interior in search of captives. The Lords Proprietors in London protested against Indian slave trading in their colony, but to no avail. Manacled Indians soon were among the young colony's major exports. As many as ten thousand Indians were dispatched to lifelong labor in the West Indian canefields and sugar mills. Others were sent to New England. One Rhode Island town in 1730 counted more than two hundred enslaved Carolina Indians in its midst.

In 1707 the Savannah Indians decided to end their alliance with the Carolinians and to migrate to the backcountry of Maryland and Pennsylvania, where a new colony founded by Quakers under William Penn promised better relations between whites and Indians. But the Carolinians determined to "thin" the Savannahs before they could depart. A series of bloody raids all but annihilated the Indian tribes of coastal Carolina by 1710.

After much experimentation, rice emerged as the principal export crop in Carolina. Rice was then an exotic food in England; no rice seeds were sent out from London in the first supply ships to Carolina. But rice was grown in Africa, and the Carolinians were soon paying premium prices for West African slaves experienced in rice cultivation. The Africans' agricultural skill and their relative immunity to malaria (thanks to a genetic trait that also, unfortunately, made them and their descendants susceptible to sickle-cell anemia) made them ideal laborers on the hot and swampy rice plantations. By 1710 they constituted a majority of Carolinians.

Moss-festooned Charles Town—also named for the king—rapidly became the busiest seaport in the South. Many high-spirited sons of English landed families, deprived of an inheritance, came to the Charleston area and gave it a rich aristocratic flavor. The village became a colorfully diverse community, to which French Protestant refugees, Jews, and others were attracted by religious toleration.

Nearby, in Florida, the Catholic Spaniards abhorred the intrusion of these Protestant heretics. Carolina's frontier was often aflame. Spanish-incited Indians brandished their tomahawks, and armor-clad warriors of Spain frequently unsheathed their swords during the successive Anglo-Spanish wars. But by 1700 Carolina was too strong to be wiped out.

✹ The Emergence of North Carolina

The wild northern expanse of the huge Carolina grant bordered on Virginia. From the older colony there drifted down a ragtag group of poverty-stricken outcasts and religious dissenters. Many of them had

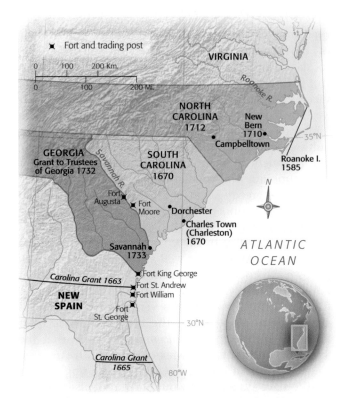

MAP 2.2 Early Carolina and Georgia Settlements
© 2016 Cengage Learning

been repelled by the rarefied atmosphere of Virginia, dominated as it was by big-plantation gentry belonging to the Church of England. North Carolinians, as a result, have been called "the quintessence of Virginia's discontent." The newcomers, who frequently were **"squatters"** without legal right to the soil, raised their tobacco and other crops on small farms, with little need for slaves.

Distinctive traits developed rapidly in North Carolina. The poor but sturdy inhabitants, regarded as riffraff by their snobbish neighbors, earned a reputation for being irreligious and hospitable to pirates. Isolated from neighbors by raw wilderness and stormy Cape Hatteras, "graveyard of the Atlantic," the North Carolinians developed a strong spirit of resistance to authority. Their location between aristocratic Virginia and aristocratic South Carolina caused the area to be dubbed "a vale of humility between two mountains of conceit." Following much friction with governors, North Carolina was officially separated from South Carolina in 1712, and subsequently each segment became a royal colony (see Map 2.2).

North Carolina shares with tiny Rhode Island several distinctions. These two outposts were the most democratic, the most independent-minded, and the least aristocratic of the original thirteen English colonies.

Although northern Carolina, unlike the colony's southern reaches, did not at first import large numbers of African slaves, both regions shared in the ongoing tragedy of bloody relations between Indians and Europeans. Tuscarora Indians fell upon the fledgling settlement at New Bern in 1711. The North Carolinians, aided by their heavily armed brothers from the south, retaliated by crushing the Indians in the **Tuscarora War**, selling hundreds of them into slavery and leaving the survivors to wander northward to seek the protection of the Iroquois. The Tuscaroras eventually became the Sixth Nation of the Iroquois Confederacy. In another ferocious encounter four years later, the South Carolinians defeated and dispersed the **Yamasee Indians**.

With the conquest of the Yamasees, virtually all the coastal Indian tribes in the southern colonies had been utterly devastated by about 1720. Yet in the interior, in the hills and valleys of the Appalachian Mountains, the powerful Cherokees, Creeks, and Iroquois (see "Makers of America: The Iroquois," pp. 38–39) remained. Stronger and more numerous than their coastal cousins, they managed for half a century more to contain British settlement to the coastal plain east of the mountains.

� Late-Coming Georgia: The Buffer Colony

Pine-forested Georgia, with the harbor of Savannah nourishing its chief settlement, was formally founded in 1733. It proved to be the last of the thirteen colonies to be planted—126 years after the first, Virginia, and 52 years after the twelfth, Pennsylvania. Chronologically Georgia belongs elsewhere, but geographically it may be grouped with its southern neighbors.

The English crown intended Georgia to serve chiefly as a **buffer**. It would protect the more valuable Carolinas against vengeful Spaniards from Florida and against the hostile French from Louisiana. Georgia indeed suffered much buffeting, especially when wars broke out between Spain and England in the European arena. As a vital link in imperial defense, the exposed colony received monetary subsidies from the British government at the outset—the only one of the "original thirteen" to enjoy this benefit in its founding stage.

Named in honor of King George II of England, Georgia was launched by a high-minded group of philanthropists. In addition to protecting their neighboring northern colonies and producing silk and wine, they were determined to carve out a haven for wretched souls imprisoned for debt. They were also determined, at least at first, to keep slavery out of Georgia. The ablest of the founders was the dynamic soldier-statesman James Oglethorpe, who became keenly interested in prison reform after one of his friends died in a debtors' jail. As a competent military leader, Oglethorpe repelled Spanish attacks. As an imperialist and a philanthropist, he saved "the Charity Colony" by his energetic leadership and by heavily mortgaging his own personal fortune.

The hamlet of Savannah, like Charleston, was a melting-pot community. German Lutherans and kilted Scots Highlanders, among others, added color to the pattern. All Christian worshipers except Catholics enjoyed religious toleration. Many missionaries armed with Bibles and hope arrived in Savannah to work among debtors and Indians. Prominent among them was young John Wesley, who later returned to England and founded the Methodist Church.

Georgia grew with painful slowness and at the end of the colonial era was perhaps the least populous of the colonies. The development of a plantation economy was thwarted by an unhealthy climate, by early restrictions on black slavery, and by demoralizing Spanish attacks.

✩ The Plantation Colonies

Certain distinctive features were shared by England's southern mainland colonies: Maryland, Virginia, North Carolina, South Carolina, and Georgia. Broadacred, these outposts of empire were all in some degree devoted to exporting commercial agricultural products. Profitable staple crops were the rule, notably tobacco and rice, though to a lesser extent in small-farm North Carolina. Slavery was found in all the plantation colonies, though only after 1750 in reform-minded Georgia. Immense acreage in the hands of a favored few fostered a strong aristocratic atmosphere, except in North Carolina and to some extent in debtor-tinged Georgia. The wide scattering of plantations and farms, often along stately rivers, retarded the growth of cities and made the establishment of churches and schools both difficult and expensive. In 1671 the governor of Virginia actually thanked God that no free schools or printing presses existed in his colony.

All the plantation colonies permitted some religious toleration. The tax-supported Church of England became the dominant faith, though it was weakest of all in nonconformist North Carolina.

These colonies were in some degree expansionary. "Soil butchery" by excessive tobacco growing drove settlers westward, and the long, lazy rivers invited penetration of the continent—and continuing confrontation with Native Americans.

Well before the crowned heads of Europe turned their eyes and their dreams of empire toward North America, a great military power had emerged in the Mohawk Valley of what is now New York State. The **Iroquois Confederacy**, dubbed by whites the "League of the Iroquois," bound together five Indian nations—the Mohawks, the Oneidas, the Onondagas, the Cayugas, and the Senecas (see Map 2.3). According to Iroquois legend, it was founded in the late 1500s by two leaders, Deganawidah and Hiawatha. This proud and potent league vied initially with neighboring Indians for territorial supremacy, then with the French, English, and Dutch for control of the fur trade. Ultimately, infected by the white man's diseases, intoxicated by his whiskey, and intimidated by his muskets, the Iroquois struggled for their very survival as a people.

The building block of Iroquois society was the longhouse. This wooden structure deserved its descriptive name. Only twenty-five feet in breadth, the longhouse stretched from eight to two hundred feet in length. Each building contained three to five fireplaces, around which gathered two nuclear families consisting of parents and children. All families residing in the longhouse were related, their connections of blood running exclusively through the maternal line. A single longhouse might shelter a woman's family and those of her mother, sisters, and daughters—with the oldest woman being the honored matriarch. When a man married, he left his childhood hearth in the home of his mother to join the longhouse of his wife. Men dominated in Iroquois society, but they owed their positions of prominence to their mothers' families.

As if sharing one great longhouse, the five nations joined in the Iroquois Confederacy but kept their own separate fires. Although they celebrated together and shared a common policy toward outsiders, they remained essentially independent of one another. On the eastern flank of the league, the Mohawks, known as the Keepers of the Eastern Fire, specialized as

MAP 2.3 Iroquois Lands and European Trade Centers, ca. 1590–1650 © 2016 Cengage Learning

*Map labels:* Fort · MONTAGNAIS · Québec · ALGONQUIN · NEW FRANCE · 75°W · Montréal · ABENAKI · St. Lawrence R. · Lake Champlain · NEW ENGLAND · HURON · IROQUOIS CONFEDERACY · MOHAWK · Lake Ontario · SENECA · CAYUGA · ONONDAGA · ONEIDA · Mohawk R. · MAHICAN · Connecticut R. · NEW NETHERLAND · Fort Orange · Hudson R. · L. Erie · Susquehanna R. · Delaware R. · New Amsterdam · 40°N

An Iroquois Canoe In frail but artfully constructed craft like this, the Iroquois traversed the abundant waters of their confederacy and traded with their neighbors, Indians as well as whites.

Peabody Essex Museum, Salem, MA

The Longhouse (Reconstruction) This photo shows a modern-day reconstruction of an Iroquois Indian longhouse typical of the kind built by many tribes in the northeastern United States and parts of Canada. Bent saplings and sheets of elm bark made for sturdy, weathertight shelters. Longhouses were typically furnished with deerskin-covered bunks and shelves for storing baskets, pots, fur pelts, and corn.

middlemen with European traders, whereas the outlying Senecas, the Keepers of the Western Fire, became fur suppliers.

After banding together to end generations of violent warfare among themselves, the Five Nations vanquished their rivals, the neighboring Hurons, Eries, and Petuns. Some other tribes, such as the Tuscaroras from the Carolina region, sought peaceful absorption into the Iroquois Confederacy. The Iroquois further expanded their numbers by means of periodic "mourning wars," whose objective was the large-scale adoption of captives and refugees. But the arrival of gun-toting Europeans threatened Iroquois supremacy and enmeshed the confederacy in a tangled web of diplomatic intrigues. Throughout the seventeenth and eighteenth centuries, they allied alternately with the English against the French and vice versa, for a time successfully working this perpetual rivalry to their own advantage. But when the American Revolution broke out, the confederacy could reach no consensus

on which side to support. Each tribe was left to decide independently; most, though not all, sided with the British. The ultimate British defeat left the confederacy in tatters. Many Iroquois, especially the Mohawks, moved to new lands in British Canada; others were relegated to reservations in western New York.

Reservation life proved unbearable for a proud people accustomed to domination over a vast territory. Morale sank; brawling, feuding, and alcoholism became rampant. Out of this morass arose a prophet, an Iroquois called Handsome Lake. In 1799 angelic figures clothed in traditional Iroquois garb appeared to Handsome Lake in a vision and warned him that the moral decline of his people must end if they were to endure. He awoke from his vision to warn his tribespeople to mend their ways. His socially oriented gospel inspired many Iroquois to forsake alcohol, to affirm family values, and to revive old Iroquois customs. Handsome Lake died in 1815, but his teachings, in the form of the Longhouse religion, survive to this day.

Chapter Review

KEY TERMS

Protestant Reformation (25)
Roanoke Island (26)
Spanish Armada (26)
primogeniture (27)
joint-stock company (27)
Virginia Company (28)
charter (28)
Jamestown (28)
First Anglo-Powhatan War (30)

Second Anglo-Powhatan War (30)
House of Burgesses (33)
Act of Toleration (33)
Barbados slave code (35)
squatters (36)
Iroquois Confederacy (38)
Tuscarora War (37)
Yamasee Indians (37)
buffer (37)

PEOPLE TO KNOW

Henry VIII
Elizabeth I
Sir Francis Drake
Sir Walter Raleigh
James I
Captain John Smith
Powhatan

Pocahontas
Lord De La Warr
John Rolfe
Lord Baltimore
Oliver Cromwell
James Oglethorpe
Hiawatha

CHRONOLOGY

1558	Elizabeth I becomes queen of England
ca. 1565–1590	English crush Irish uprising
1577	Drake circumnavigates the globe
1585	Raleigh founds "lost colony" at Roanoke Island
1588	England defeats Spanish Armada
1603	James I becomes king of England
1604	Spain and England sign peace treaty
1607	Virginia colony founded at Jamestown
1612	Rolfe perfects tobacco culture in Virginia
1614	First Anglo-Powhatan War ends
1619	First Africans arrive in Jamestown Virginia House of Burgesses established
1624	Virginia becomes royal colony
1634	Maryland colony founded
1640s	Large-scale slave-labor system established in English West Indies
1644	Second Anglo-Powhatan War
1649	Act of Toleration in Maryland Charles I beheaded; Cromwell rules England
1660	Charles II restored to English throne
1661	Barbados slave code adopted
1670	Carolina colony created
1711–1713	Tuscarora War in North Carolina
1712	North Carolina formally separates from South Carolina
1715–1716	Yamasee War in South Carolina
1733	Georgia colony founded

TO LEARN MORE

Ira Berlin, *Generations of Captivity: A History of African American Slaves* (2003)

——, *Many Thousands Gone: The First Two Centuries of Slavery in North America* (1998)

Kathleen Brown, *Good Wives, Nasty Wenches, and Anxious Patriarchs: Gender, Race, and Power in Colonial Virginia* (1996)

Colin G. Calloway, *New Worlds for All: Indians, Europeans, and the Remaking of America* (1997)

Ralph Davis, *The Rise of the Atlantic Economies* (1973)

Jack P. Greene, *Pursuits of Happiness: The Social Development of Early Modern British Colonies and the Formation of American Culture* (1988)

April Lee Hatfield, *Atlantic Virginia: Intercolonial Relations in the Seventeenth Century* (2004)

Edmund S. Morgan, *American Slavery, American Freedom* (1975)

David B. Quinn, *England and the Discovery of America, 1481–1620* (1974)

Daniel K. Richter, *Facing East from Indian Country: A Native History of Early America* (2003)

Nancy Shoemaker, *A Strange Likeness: Becoming Red and White in Eighteenth-Century North America* (2004)

Alan Taylor, *American Colonies: The Settling of North America* (2001)

Camilla Townsend, *Pocahontas and the Powhatan Dilemma* (2004)

A complete, annotated bibliography for this chapter—along with brief descriptions of the People to Know—may be found on the *American Pageant* website. The key terms are defined in the glossary at the end of the text.

Chapter 3

Settling the Northern Colonies

1619–1700

God hath sifted a nation that he might send Choice Grain into this Wilderness.

WILLIAM STOUGHTON [OF MASSACHUSETTS BAY], 1699

Although colonists both north and south were bound together by a common language and a common allegiance to Mother England, they established different patterns of settlement, different economies, different political systems, and even different sets of values—defining distinctive regional characteristics that would persist for generations. The promise of riches—especially from golden-leaved tobacco—drew the first settlers to the southern colonies. But to the north, in the fertile valleys of the middle Atlantic region and especially along the rocky shores of New England, it was not worldly wealth but religious devotion that principally shaped the earliest settlements.

✴ The Protestant Reformation Produces Puritanism

Little did the German friar Martin Luther suspect, when he nailed his protests against Catholic doctrines to the door of Wittenberg's cathedral in 1517, that he was shaping the destiny of a yet unknown nation. Denouncing the authority of priests and popes, Luther declared that the Bible alone was the source of God's word. He ignited a fire of religious reform (the "Protestant Reformation") that licked its way across Europe for more than a century, dividing peoples, toppling sovereigns, and kindling the spiritual fervor of millions of men and women—some of whom helped to found America.

The reforming flame burned especially brightly in the bosom of John Calvin of Geneva. This somber and severe religious leader elaborated Martin Luther's ideas in ways that profoundly affected the thought and character of generations of Americans yet unborn. **Calvinism** became the dominant theological credo not only of the New England Puritans but of other American settlers as well, including the Scottish Presbyterians, French Huguenots, and communicants of the Dutch Reformed Church.

Calvin spelled out his basic doctrine in a learned Latin tome of 1536, entitled *Institutes of the Christian Religion.* God, Calvin argued, was all-powerful and all-good. Humans, because of the corrupting effect of original sin, were weak and wicked. God was also all-knowing—and he knew who was going to heaven and who was going to hell. Since the first moment of creation, some souls—the elect—had been destined for eternal bliss and others for eternal torment. Good works could not save those whom **predestination** had marked for the infernal fires.

But neither could the elect count on their predetermined salvation and lead lives of wild, immoral abandon. For one thing, no one could be certain of his or her status in the heavenly ledger. Gnawing doubts about their eternal fate plagued Calvinists. They constantly sought, in themselves and others, signs of **conversion**, or the receipt of God's free gift of saving grace. Conversion was thought to be an intense, identifiable personal experience in which God revealed to the elect their heavenly destiny. Thereafter they were expected to lead "sanctified" lives, demonstrating

42

by their holy behavior that they were among the "visible saints."

These doctrines swept into England just as King Henry VIII was breaking his ties with the Roman Catholic Church in the 1530s, making himself the head of the Church of England. Henry would have been content to retain Roman rituals and creeds, but his action powerfully stimulated some English religious reformers to undertake a total purification of English Christianity. Many of these **Puritans**, as it happened, came from the commercially depressed woolen districts (see "England on the Eve of Empire" in Chapter 2, p. 27). Calvinism, with its message of stark but reassuring order in the divine plan, fed on this social unrest and provided spiritual comfort to the economically disadvantaged. As time went on, Puritans grew increasingly unhappy over the snail-like progress of the Protestant Reformation in England. They burned with pious zeal to see the Church of England wholly de-catholicized.

The most devout Puritans, including those who eventually settled New England, believed that only "visible saints" (that is, persons who felt the stirrings of grace in their souls and could demonstrate its presence to their fellow Puritans) should be admitted to church membership. But the Church of England enrolled all the king's subjects, which meant that the "saints" had to share pews and communion rails with the "damned." Appalled by this unholy fraternizing, a tiny group of dedicated Puritans, known as **Separatists**, vowed to break away entirely from the Church of England.

King James I, a shrewd Scotsman, was head of both the state and the church in England from 1603 to 1625. He quickly perceived that if his subjects could defy him as their spiritual leader, they might one day defy him as their political leader (as in fact they would later defy and behead his son, Charles I). He therefore threatened to harass the more bothersome Separatists out of the land.

✴ The Pilgrims End Their Pilgrimage at Plymouth

The most famous congregation of Separatists, fleeing royal wrath, departed for Holland in 1608. During the ensuing twelve years of toil and poverty, they were increasingly distressed by the "Dutchification" of their children. They longed to find a haven where they could live and die as English men and women—and as purified Protestants. America was the logical refuge, despite the early ordeals of Jamestown and despite tales of New World cannibals roasting steaks from their white victims over open fires.

A group of the Separatists in Holland, after negotiating with the Virginia Company, at length secured rights to settle under its jurisdiction. But their crowded *Mayflower*, sixty-five days at sea, missed its destination and arrived off the stony coast of New England in 1620 with a total of 102 persons. One had died en route—an unusually short casualty list—and one had been born and appropriately named Oceanus. Fewer than half of the entire party were Separatists. Prominent among the nonbelongers was a peppery and stocky soldier of

Picture Research Consultants & Archives

Plymouth Plantation
Carefully restored, the modest village at Plymouth looks today much as it did nearly four hundred years ago.

fortune, Captain Myles Standish, dubbed by one of his critics "Captain Shrimp." He later rendered indispensable service as an Indian fighter and negotiator.

The Pilgrims did not make their initial landing at Plymouth Rock, as commonly supposed, but undertook a number of preliminary surveys. They finally chose for their site the shore of inhospitable Plymouth Bay. This area was outside the domain of the Virginia Company, and consequently the settlers became squatters. They were without legal right to the land and without specific authority to establish a government.

Before disembarking, the Pilgrim leaders drew up and signed the brief **Mayflower Compact**. Although setting an invaluable precedent for later written constitutions, this document was not a constitution at all. It was a simple agreement to form a crude government and to submit to the will of the majority under the regulations agreed upon. The compact was signed by forty-one adult males, eleven of them with the exalted rank of "mister," though not by the servants and two seamen. The pact was a promising step toward genuine self-government, for soon the adult male settlers were assembling to make their own laws in open-discussion town meetings—a vital laboratory of liberty.

The Pilgrims' first winter of 1620–1621 took a grisly toll. Only 44 out of the 102 survived. At one time only 7 were well enough to lay the dead in their frosty graves. Yet when the *Mayflower* sailed back to England in the spring, not a single one of the courageous band of Separatists left. As one of them wrote, "It is not with us as with other men, whom small things can discourage."

God made his children prosperous, so the Pilgrims believed. The next autumn, that of 1621, brought bountiful harvests and with them the first Thanksgiving Day in New England. In time the frail colony found sound economic legs in fur, fish, and lumber. The beaver and the Bible were the early mainstays: the one for the sustenance of the body, the other for the sustenance of the soul. Plymouth proved that the English could maintain themselves in this uninviting region.

William Bradford (1590–1657) wrote in Of Plymouth Plantation,

❝Thus out of small beginnings greater things have been produced by His hand that made all things of nothing, and gives being to all things that are; and, as one small candle may light a thousand, so the light here kindled hath shone unto many, yea in some sort to our whole nation.**❞**

The Pilgrims were extremely fortunate in their leaders. Prominent among them was the cultured William Bradford, a self-taught scholar who read Hebrew, Greek, Latin, French, and Dutch. He was chosen governor thirty times in the annual elections. Among his major worries was his fear that independent, non-Puritan settlers "on their particular" might corrupt his godly experiment in the wilderness. Bustling fishing villages and other settlements did sprout to the north of Plymouth, on the storm-lashed shores of Massachusetts Bay, where many people were as much interested in cod as God.

Quiet and quaint, the little colony of Plymouth was never important economically or numerically. Its population numbered only seven thousand by 1691, when, still charterless, it merged with its giant neighbor, the Massachusetts Bay Colony. But the tiny settlement of Pilgrims was big both morally and spiritually.

✴ The Bay Colony Bible Commonwealth

The Separatist Pilgrims were dedicated extremists—the purest Puritans. More moderate Puritans sought to reform the Church of England from within. Though resented by bishops and monarchs, they slowly gathered support, especially in Parliament. But when Charles I dismissed Parliament in 1629 and sanctioned the anti-Puritan persecutions of the reactionary Archbishop William Laud, many Puritans saw catastrophe in the making.

In 1629 an energetic group of non-Separatist Puritans, fearing for their faith and for England's future, secured a royal charter to form the Massachusetts Bay Company. They proposed to establish a sizable settlement in the infertile Massachusetts area, with Boston soon becoming its hub. Stealing a march on both king and church, the newcomers brought their charter with them. For many years they used it as a kind of constitution, out of easy reach of royal authority. They steadfastly denied that they wanted to separate from the Church of England, only from its impurities. But back in England, the highly orthodox Archbishop Laud snorted that the Bay Colony Puritans were "swine which rooted in God's vineyard."

The **Massachusetts Bay Colony** was singularly blessed. The well-equipped expedition of 1630, with eleven vessels carrying nearly a thousand immigrants, started the colony off on a larger scale than any of the other English settlements. Continuing turmoil in England tossed up additional enriching waves of Puritans on the shores of Massachusetts in the following decade. During the **Great English Migration** of the 1630s, about seventy thousand refugees left England

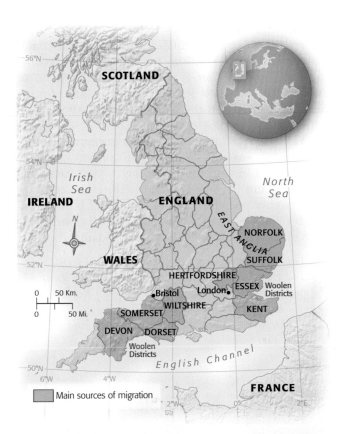

MAP 3.1A Sources of the Puritan "Great English Migration" to New England, c. 1620–1640 The shaded areas indicate the main sources of the migration. © 2016 Cengage Learning

MAP 3.1B The Great English Migration, ca. 1630–1642 Much of the early history of the United States was written by New Englanders, who were not disposed to emphasize the larger exodus of English migrants to the Caribbean islands. When the mainland colonists declared independence in 1776, they hoped that these island outposts would join them, but the existence of the British navy had a dissuading effect. © 2016 Cengage Learning

colonists believed that they had a covenant with God, an agreement to build a holy society that would be a model for humankind.

★ Building the Bay Colony

These common convictions deeply shaped the infant colony's life. Soon after the colonists' arrival, the franchise was extended to all "freemen"—adult males who belonged to the Puritan congregations, which in time came to be called collectively the Congregational Church. Unchurched men remained voteless in provincial elections, as did all women. On this basis about two-fifths of adult males enjoyed the franchise in provincial affairs, a far larger proportion than in contemporary England. Town governments, which conducted much important business, were even more inclusive. There all male property holders, and in some cases other residents as well, enjoyed the priceless boon of publicly discussing local issues, often with much heat, and of voting on them by a majority-rule show of hands.

Yet the provincial government, liberal by the standards of the time, was not a democracy. The able Governor Winthrop feared and distrusted the "commons" as the "meaner sort" and thought that democracy was the "meanest and worst" of all forms of government. "If the people be governors," asked one Puritan

(see Map 3.1). But not all of them were Puritans, and only about twenty thousand came to Massachusetts. Many were attracted to the warm and fertile West Indies, especially the sugar-rich island of Barbados. More Puritans came to this Caribbean islet than to all of Massachusetts.

Many fairly prosperous, educated persons immigrated to the Bay Colony, including John Winthrop, a well-to-do pillar of English society, who became the colony's first governor. A successful attorney and manor lord in England, Winthrop eagerly accepted the offer to become governor of the Massachusetts Bay Colony, believing that he had a "calling" from God to lead the new religious experiment. He served as governor or deputy governor for nineteen years. The resources and skills of talented settlers like Winthrop helped Massachusetts prosper, as fur trading, fishing, and shipbuilding blossomed into important industries, especially fish and ships. The Massachusetts Bay Colony rapidly shot to the fore as both the biggest and the most influential of the New England outposts.

Massachusetts also benefited from a shared sense of purpose among most of the first settlers. "We shall be as a city upon a hill," a beacon to humanity, declared Governor Winthrop. The Puritan bay clergyman, "who shall be governed?" True, the freemen annually elected the governor and his assistants, as well as a representative assembly called the General Court. But only Puritans—the "visible saints" who alone were eligible for church membership—could be freemen. And according to the doctrine of the covenant, the whole purpose of government was to enforce God's laws—which applied to believers and nonbelievers alike. Moreover, nonbelievers as well as believers paid taxes for the government-supported church.

Religious leaders thus wielded enormous influence in the Massachusetts "Bible Commonwealth." They powerfully influenced admission to church membership by conducting public interrogations of persons claiming to have experienced conversion. Prominent among the early clergy was fiery John Cotton. Educated at England's Cambridge University, a Puritan citadel, he immigrated to Massachusetts to avoid persecution for his criticism of the Church of England. In the Bay Colony, he devoted his considerable learning to defending the government's duty to enforce religious rules. Profoundly pious, he sometimes preached and prayed up to six hours in a single day.

But the power of the preachers was not absolute. A congregation had the right to hire and fire its minister and to set his salary. Clergymen were also barred from holding formal political office. Puritans in England had suffered too much at the hands of a "political" Anglican clergy to permit in the New World another unholy union of religious and government power. In a limited way, the bay colonists thus endorsed the idea of the separation of church and state.

The Puritans were a worldly lot, despite—or even because of—their spiritual intensity. Like John Winthrop, they believed in the doctrine of a "calling" to do God's work on earth. They shared in what was later called the "Protestant ethic," which involved serious commitment to work and to engagement in worldly pursuits. Legend to the contrary, they also enjoyed simple pleasures: they ate plentifully, drank heartily, sang songs occasionally, and made love mostly monogamously. Like other peoples of their time in both America and Europe, they passed laws aimed at making sure these pleasures

Anne Hutchinson, Dissenter Mistress Hutchinson (1591–1643) held unorthodox views that challenged the authority of the clergy and the very integrity of the Puritan experiment in the Massachusetts Bay Colony. An outcast in her day, she has been judged a heroine in the eye of history. This statue in her honor, erected in the nineteenth century, now graces the front of the Boston, Massachusetts, Statehouse.

Picture Research Consultants & Archives

stayed simple by repressing certain human instincts. In New Haven, for example, a young married couple was fined twenty shillings for the crime of kissing in public, and in later years Connecticut came to be dubbed "the Blue Law State." (It was so named for the blue paper on which the repressive laws—also known as "sumptuary laws"—were printed.)

Yet, to the Puritans, life was serious business, and hellfire was real—a hell where sinners shriveled and shrieked in vain for divine mercy. An immensely popular poem in New England, selling one copy for every twenty people, was clergyman Michael Wigglesworth's "Day of Doom" (1662). Especially horrifying were his descriptions of the fate of the damned:

They cry, they roar for anguish sore,
and gnaw their tongues for horrour. But get away
without delay,
*   Christ pitties not your cry:*
*   Depart to Hell, there may you yell, and roar*
*   Eternally.*

✴ Trouble in the Bible Commonwealth

The Bay Colony enjoyed a high degree of social harmony, stemming from common beliefs, in its early years. But even in this tightly knit community, dissension soon appeared. Quakers, who flouted the authority of the Puritan clergy, were persecuted with fines, floggings, and banishment. In one extreme case, four Quakers who defied expulsion, one of them a woman, were hanged on the Boston Common.

A sharp challenge to Puritan orthodoxy came from Anne Hutchinson. She was an exceptionally intelligent, strong-willed, and talkative woman, ultimately the mother of fourteen children. Swift and sharp in theological argument, she carried to logical extremes the Puritan doctrine of predestination. She claimed that a holy life was no sure sign of salvation and that the truly saved need not bother to obey the law of either God or man. This assertion, known as **antinomianism** (from the Greek, "against the law"), was high heresy.

Brought to trial in 1638, the quick-witted Hutchinson bamboozled her clerical inquisitors for days, until she eventually boasted that she had come by her beliefs through a direct revelation from God. This was even higher heresy. The Puritan magistrates had little choice but to banish her, lest she pollute the entire Puritan experiment. With her family, she set out on foot for Rhode Island, though pregnant. She finally moved to New York, where she and all but one of her household were killed by Indians. Back in the Bay Colony, the pious John Winthrop saw "God's hand" in her fate.

More threatening to the Puritan leaders was a personable and popular Salem minister, Roger Williams. Williams was a young man with radical ideas and an unrestrained tongue. An extreme Separatist, he hounded his fellow clergymen to make a clean break with the corrupt Church of England. He also challenged the legality of the Bay Colony's charter, which he condemned for expropriating the land from the Indians without fair compensation. As if all this were not enough, he went on to deny the authority of civil government to regulate religious behavior—a seditious blow at the Puritan idea of government's very purpose.

Their patience exhausted by 1635, the Bay Colony authorities found Williams guilty of disseminating "newe & dangerous opinions" and ordered him banished. He was permitted to remain several months longer because of illness, but he kept up his criticisms. The outraged magistrates, fearing that he might organize a rival colony of malcontents, made plans to exile him to England. But Williams foiled them.

✳ The Rhode Island "Sewer"

Aided by friendly Indians, Roger Williams fled to the Rhode Island area in 1636, in the midst of a bitter winter. At Providence the courageous and far-visioned Williams built a Baptist church, probably the first in America. He established complete freedom of religion, even for Jews and Catholics. He demanded no oaths regarding religious beliefs, no compulsory attendance at worship, no taxes to support a state church. He even sheltered the abused Quakers, although disagreeing sharply with their views. Williams's endorsement of religious tolerance made Rhode Island more liberal than any of the other English settlements in the New World and more advanced than most Old World communities as well.

Those outcasts who clustered about Roger Williams enjoyed additional blessings. They exercised simple manhood suffrage from the start, though this broadminded practice was later narrowed by a property qualification. Opposed to special privilege of any sort, the intrepid Rhode Islanders managed to achieve remarkable freedom of opportunity.

Other scattered settlements soon dotted Rhode Island. They consisted largely of malcontents and exiles, some of whom could not bear the stifling theological atmosphere of the Bay Colony. Many of these restless souls in "Rogues' Island," including Anne Hutchinson, had little in common with Roger Williams—except being unwelcome anywhere else. The Puritan clergy back in Boston sneered at Rhode Island as "that sewer" in which the "Lord's debris" had collected and rotted.

Planted by dissenters and exiles, Rhode Island became strongly individualistic and stubbornly independent. With good reason "Little Rhody" was later known as "the traditional home of the otherwise minded." Begun as a squatter colony in 1636 without legal standing, it finally established rights to the soil when it secured a charter from Parliament in 1644. A huge bronze statue of the "Independent Man" appropriately stands today on the dome of the statehouse in Providence.

✳ New England Spreads Out

The smiling valley of the Connecticut River, one of the few highly fertile expanses of any size in all New England, had meanwhile attracted a sprinkling of Dutch and English settlers. Hartford was founded in 1635 (see Map 3.2). The next year witnessed a

---

Contending Voices
Anne Hutchinson Accused and Defended

In his opening remarks at the examination of Anne Hutchinson in 1637, Governor John Winthrop (1587–1649) declared:

❝ …you have spoken diverse things…very prejudicial to the honour of the churches…and you have maintained a meeting and an assembly in your house that hath been condemned by the general assembly as a thing not tolerable…nor fitting for your sex.… ❞

Hutchinson (1591–1643) defended herself as follows:

❝ Will it please you to answer me this and to give me a rule for then I will willingly submit to any truth. If any come to my house to be instructed in the ways of God what rule have I to put them away? ❞

In what ways did the accusations against Anne Hutchinson go beyond doctrinal heresy?

MAP 3.2 Seventeenth-Century New England Settlements
The Massachusetts Bay Colony was the hub of New England. All earlier colonies grew into it; all later colonies grew out of it. © 2016 Cengage Learning

spectacular beginning of the centuries-long westward movement across the continent. An energetic group of Boston Puritans, led by the Reverend Thomas Hooker, swarmed as a body into the Hartford area, with the ailing Mrs. Hooker carried on a horse litter.

Three years later, in 1639, the settlers of the new Connecticut River colony drafted in open meeting a trailblazing document known as the **Fundamental Orders**. It was in effect a modern constitution, which established a regime democratically controlled by the "substantial" citizens. Essential features of the Fundamental Orders were later borrowed by Connecticut for its colonial charter and ultimately for its state constitution.

Another flourishing Connecticut settlement began to spring up at New Haven in 1638. It was a prosperous community, founded by Puritans who contrived to set up an even closer church-government alliance than in Massachusetts. Although only squatters without a charter, the colonists dreamed of making New Haven a bustling seaport. But they fell into disfavor with Charles II as a result of having sheltered two of the judges who had condemned his father, Charles I, to death. In 1662, to the acute distress of the New Havenites, the crown granted a charter to

Connecticut that merged New Haven with the more democratic settlements in the Connecticut Valley.

Far to the north, enterprising fishermen and fur-traders had been active on the coast of Maine for a dozen or so years before the founding of Plymouth. After disheartening attempts at colonization in 1623 by Sir Ferdinando Gorges, this land of lakes and forests was absorbed by Massachusetts Bay after a formal purchase in 1677 from the Gorges heirs. It remained a part of Massachusetts for nearly a century and a half before becoming a separate state.

Granite-ribbed New Hampshire also sprang from the fishing and trading activities along its narrow coast. It was absorbed in 1641 by the grasping Bay Colony, under a strained interpretation of the Massachusetts charter. The king, annoyed by this display of greed, arbitrarily separated New Hampshire from Massachusetts in 1679 and made it a royal colony.

✦ Puritans Versus Indians

The spread of English settlements inevitably led to clashes with the Indians, who were particularly weak in New England. Shortly before the Pilgrims had arrived at Plymouth in 1620, an epidemic, probably triggered by contact with English fishermen, had swept through the coastal tribes and killed more than three-quarters of the native people. Deserted Indian fields, ready for tillage, greeted the Plymouth settlers, and scattered skulls and bones provided grim evidence of the impact of the disease.

In no position to resist the English incursion, the local Wampanoag Indians at first befriended the settlers. Cultural accommodation was facilitated by Squanto, a Wampanoag who had learned English from a ship's captain who had kidnapped him some years earlier. The Wampanoag chieftain Massasoit signed a treaty with the Plymouth Pilgrims in 1621 and helped them celebrate the first Thanksgiving after the autumn harvests that same year.

As more English settlers arrived and pushed inland into the Connecticut River valley, confrontations between Indians and whites ruptured these peaceful relations. Hostilities exploded in 1637 between the English settlers and the powerful Pequot tribe. Besieging a Pequot village on Connecticut's Mystic River, English militiamen and their Narragansett Indian allies set fire to the Indian wigwams and shot the fleeing survivors. The slaughter wrote a brutal finish to the **Pequot War**, virtually annihilated the Pequot tribe, and inaugurated four decades of uneasy peace between Puritans and Indians.

Lashed by critics in England, the Puritans made some feeble efforts at converting the remaining

Attack on a Pequot Fort During the Pequot War of 1637, engraving by J. W. Barber, 1830 This was the first war between natives and Europeans in British North America. It culminated in the Puritan militia's vicious burning out and slaughtering of nearly three hundred Pequot men, women, and children. The defeat of the Pequots eliminated armed resistance to the new settlements of New Haven and Guildford. The Connecticut Valley would not see significant "Indian troubles" again for forty years, when the Indians of New England united in their final stand against the encroachments of English settlers, King Philip's War.

Indians to Christianity, although Puritan missionary zeal never equaled that of the Catholic Spanish and French. A mere handful of Indians were gathered into Puritan "praying towns" to make the acquaintance of the English God and to learn the ways of English culture.

The Indians' only hope for resisting English encroachment lay in intertribal unity—a pan-Indian alliance against the swiftly spreading English settlements. In 1675 Massasoit's son, Metacom, called King Philip by the English, forged such an alliance and mounted a series of coordinated assaults on English villages throughout New England. Frontier settlements were especially hard hit, and refugees fell back toward the relative safety of Boston. When the war ended in 1676, fifty-two Puritan towns had been attacked, and twelve destroyed entirely. Hundreds of colonists and many more Indians lay dead. Metacom's wife and son were sold into slavery; he himself was captured, beheaded, and drawn and quartered. His head was carried on a pike back to Plymouth, where it was mounted on grisly display for years.

King Philip's War slowed the westward march of English settlement in New England for several decades. But the war inflicted a lasting defeat on New England's Indians. Drastically reduced in numbers, dispirited, and disbanded, they thereafter posed only sporadic threats to the New England colonists.

✴ Seeds of Colonial Unity and Independence

A path-breaking experiment in union was launched in 1643, when four colonies banded together to form the **New England Confederation**. The **English Civil War** was then deeply distracting old England, throwing the colonists upon their own resources. The primary purpose of the confederation was defense against foes or potential foes, notably the Indians, the French, and the Dutch. Purely intercolonial problems, such as runaway servants and criminals who had fled from one colony to another, also came within the jurisdiction of the confederation. Each member colony, regardless of size, wielded two votes—an arrangement highly displeasing to the most populous colony, Massachusetts Bay.

The confederation was essentially an exclusive Puritan club. It consisted of the two Massachusetts colonies (the Bay Colony and bantam-sized Plymouth) and the two Connecticut colonies (New Haven and the scattered valley settlements). The Puritan leaders blackballed Rhode Island as well as the Maine outposts. These places, it was charged, harbored too many heretical or otherwise undesirable characters. Shockingly, one of the Maine towns had made a tailor its mayor and had even sheltered an excommunicated minister of the gospel.

Weak though it was, the confederation was the first notable milestone on the long and rocky road toward colonial unity. The delegates took tottering but long-overdue steps toward acting together on matters of intercolonial importance. Rank-and-file colonists, for their part, received valuable experience in delegating their votes to properly chosen representatives.

Back in England the king had paid little attention to the American colonies during the early years of their planting. They were allowed, in effect, to become semiautonomous commonwealths. This era of benign neglect was prolonged when the crown, struggling to retain its power, became enmeshed during the 1640s in civil wars with the parliamentarians.

But when Charles II was restored to the English throne in 1660 (see Table 3.1), the royalists and their Church of England allies were once more firmly in the saddle. Puritan hopes of eventually purifying the old English church withered. Worse, Charles II was determined to take an active, aggressive hand in the management of the colonies. His plans ran headlong against the habits that decades of relative independence had bred in the colonists.

Deepening colonial defiance was nowhere more glaringly revealed than in Massachusetts. One of the king's agents in Boston was mortified to find that royal orders had no more effect than old issues of the London *Gazette*. Punishment was soon forthcoming. As a slap at Massachusetts, Charles II gave rival Connecticut in 1662 a sea-to-sea charter grant, which legalized the squatter settlements. The very next year, the outcasts in Rhode Island received a new charter, which gave kingly sanction to the most religiously tolerant government yet devised in America. A final and crushing blow fell on the stiff-necked Bay Colony in 1684, when its precious charter was revoked by the London authorities.

✹ Andros Promotes the First American Revolution

Massachusetts suffered further humiliation in 1686, when the **Dominion of New England** was created by royal authority (see Map 3.3). Unlike the homegrown New England Confederation, it was imposed from London. Embracing at first all of New England, it was expanded two years later to include New York and East and West Jersey. The dominion also aimed at bolstering colonial defense in the event of war with the Indians and hence, from the imperial viewpoint of Parliament, was a statesman-like move.

More importantly, the Dominion of New England was designed to promote urgently needed efficiency in

TABLE 3.1 The Stuart Dynasty in England*

Name, Reign	Relation to America
James I, 1603–1625	Va., Plymouth founded; Separatists persecuted
Charles I, 1625–1649	Civil wars, 1642–1649; Mass., Md. founded
(Interregnum, 1649–1660)	Commonwealth; Protectorate (Oliver Cromwell)
Charles II, 1660–1685	The Restoration; Carolinas, Pa., N.Y. founded; Conn. chartered
James II, 1685–1688	Catholic trend; Glorious Revolution, 1688
William & Mary, 1689–1702 (Mary died 1694)	King William's War, 1689–1697

*See p. 26 for predecessors; p. 104 for successors.

the administration of the English **Navigation Laws**. Those laws reflected the intensifying colonial rivalries of the seventeenth century. They sought to stitch England's overseas possessions more tightly to the motherland by throttling American trade with countries not ruled by the English crown. Like colonial peoples everywhere, the Americans chafed at such confinements, and smuggling became an increasingly common and honorable occupation.

At the head of the new dominion stood autocratic Sir Edmund Andros, an able English military man, conscientious but tactless. Establishing headquarters in puritanical Boston, he generated much hostility by his open affiliation with the despised Church of England. The colonists were also outraged by his noisy and Sabbath-profaning soldiers, who were accused of teaching the people "to drink, blaspheme, curse, and damn."

Andros was prompt to use the mailed fist. He ruthlessly curbed the cherished town meetings; laid heavy restrictions on the courts, the press, and the schools; and revoked all land titles. Dispensing with the popular assemblies, he taxed the people without the consent of their duly elected representatives. He also strove to enforce the unpopular Navigation Laws and suppress smuggling. Liberty-loving colonists, accustomed to unusual privileges during long decades of neglect, were goaded to the verge of revolt.

The people of old England soon taught the people of New England a few lessons in resisting oppression. In 1688–1689 the English engineered the memorable **Glorious (or Bloodless) Revolution**. Dethroning the despotic and unpopular Catholic James II, they enthroned the Protestant rulers of the Netherlands,

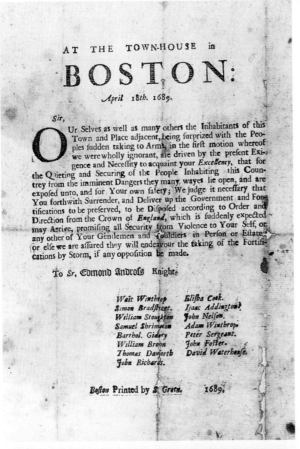

Sir Edmund Andros (1637–1714); a Boston Broadside Urging Him to Surrender, 1689 After being expelled from New England, Andros eventually returned to the New World as governor of Virginia (1692–1697). (left) Massachusetts Historical Society; (right) Private Collection/© Look and Learn/The Bridgeman Art Library

MAP 3.3 Andros's Dominion of New England © 2016 Cengage Learning

the Dutch-born William III and his English wife, Mary II, daughter of James II.

When the news of the Glorious Revolution reached America, the ramshackle Dominion of New England collapsed like a house of cards. A Boston mob, catching the fever, rose against the existing regime. Sir Edmund Andros attempted to flee in women's clothing but was betrayed by boots protruding beneath his dress. He was hastily shipped off to England.

Massachusetts, though rid of the despotic Andros, did not gain as much from the upheaval as it had hoped. In 1691 it was arbitrarily made a royal colony, with a new charter and a new royal governor. The permanent loss of the ancient charter was a staggering blow to the proud Puritans, who never fully recovered. Worst of all, the privilege of voting, once a monopoly of church members, was now to be enjoyed by all qualified male property holders.

England's Glorious Revolution reverberated throughout the colonies from New England to the Chesapeake. Inspired by the challenge to the crown in old England, many colonists seized the occasion to strike against royal authority in America. Unrest rocked both New York and Maryland from 1689 to 1691, until newly appointed royal governors restored a semblance of order. Most importantly, the new monarchs relaxed the royal grip on colonial trade, inaugurating a period of **"salutary neglect"** when the much-resented Navigation Laws were only weakly enforced.

Yet residues remained of Charles II's effort to assert tighter administrative control over his empire. More English officials—judges, clerks, customs officials—now staffed the courts and strolled the wharves of English America. Many were incompetent, corrupt hacks who knew little and cared less about American affairs. Appointed by influential patrons in far-off England, they blocked the rise of local leaders to positions of political power by their very presence. Aggrieved Americans viewed them with mounting contempt and resentment as the eighteenth century wore on.

✵ Old Netherlanders at New Netherland

Late in the sixteenth century, the oppressed people of the Netherlands unfurled the standard of rebellion against Catholic Spain. After bloody and protracted fighting, they finally succeeded, with the aid of Protestant England, in winning their independence.

The seventeenth century—the era of Rembrandt and other famous artists—was a golden age in Dutch history. This vigorous little lowland nation finally emerged as a major commercial and naval power, and then it ungratefully challenged the supremacy of its former benefactor, England. Three great Anglo-Dutch naval wars were fought in the seventeenth century, with as many as a hundred ships on each side. The sturdy Dutch dealt blows about as heavy as they received.

The Dutch republic also became a leading colonial power, with by far its greatest activity in the East Indies. There it maintained an enormous and profitable empire for over three hundred years. The Dutch East India Company was virtually a state within a state and at one time supported an army of 10,000 men and a fleet of 190 ships, 40 of them men-of-war.

Seeking greater riches, this enterprising company employed an English explorer, Henry Hudson. Disregarding orders to sail northeast, he ventured into Delaware Bay and New York Bay in 1609 and then ascended the Hudson River, hoping that at last he had chanced upon the coveted shortcut through the continent. But, as the event proved, he merely filed a Dutch claim to a magnificently wooded and watered area.

Much less powerful than the mighty Dutch East India Company was the Dutch West India Company, which maintained profitable enterprises in the Caribbean. At times it was less interested in trading than in raiding and at one fell swoop in 1628 captured a fleet of Spanish treasure ships laden with loot worth $15 million. The company also established outposts in Africa and a thriving sugar industry in Brazil, which for several decades was its principal center of activity in the New World.

New Netherland, in the beautiful Hudson River area, was planted in 1623–1624 on a permanent basis (see Map 3.4). Established by the Dutch West India Company for its quick-profit fur trade, it was never more than a secondary interest of the founders. The company's most brilliant stroke was to buy Manhattan Island from the Indians (who did not actually "own" it) for virtually worthless trinkets—twenty-two thousand acres of what is now perhaps the most valuable real estate in the world for pennies per acre.

MAP 3.4 Early Settlements in the Middle Colonies, with Founding Dates © 2016 Cengage Learning

New Amsterdam—later New York City—was a company town. It was run by and for the Dutch company, in the interests of the stockholders. The investors had no enthusiasm for religious toleration, free speech, or democratic practices; and the governors appointed by the company as directors-general were usually harsh and despotic. Religious dissenters who opposed the official Dutch Reformed Church were regarded with suspicion, and for a while Quakers were savagely abused. In response to repeated protests by the aggravated colonists, a local body with limited lawmaking power was finally established.

This picturesque Dutch colony took on a strongly aristocratic tint and retained it for generations. Vast feudal estates fronting the Hudson River, known

A Woman, by Gerret Duyckinck This portrait, painted between 1690 and 1710, depicts a prosperous woman in colonial New York. Her elegant dress of silk and lace, coral jewelry, and Chinese fan, and the Turkish rug beneath her arm, testify to the luxurious tastes and ties to international markets common among the "Hudson River lords."

Courtesy, The Henry Francis du Pont Winterthur Museum

dividends, even at the expense of the colony's welfare. The Indians, infuriated by Dutch cruelties, retaliated with horrible massacres. As a defense measure, the hard-pressed settlers on Manhattan Island erected a stout wall, from which Wall Street derives its name.

New England was hostile to the growth of its Dutch neighbor, and the people of Connecticut finally ejected intruding Hollanders from their verdant valley. The Swedes also trespassed on Dutch preserves, from 1638 to 1655, by planting the anemic colony of New Sweden on the Delaware River (see Map 3.4). This was the golden age of Sweden, during and following the Thirty Years' War of 1618–1648, in which its brilliant King Gustavus Adolphus had carried the torch for Protestantism. This outburst of energy in Sweden caused it to enter the costly colonial game in America, though on something of a shoestring.

Resenting the Swedish intrusion on the Delaware, the Dutch dispatched a small military expedition in 1655. It was led by the ablest of the directors-general, Peter Stuyvesant, who had lost a leg while soldiering in the West Indies and was dubbed "Father Wooden Leg" by the Indians. The main fort fell after a bloodless siege, whereupon Swedish rule came to an abrupt end. The colonists were absorbed by New Netherland.

New Sweden, never important, soon faded away, leaving behind in later Delaware a sprinkling of Swedish place names and Swedish log cabins (the first in America), as well as an admixture of Swedish blood.

✴ Dutch Residues in New York

Lacking vitality, and representing only a secondary commercial interest of the Dutch, New Netherland lay under the menacing shadow of the vigorous English colonies to the north. In addition, it was honeycombed with New England immigrants. Numbering about one-half of New Netherland's ten thousand souls in 1664, they might in time have seized control from within.

The days of the Dutch on the Hudson were numbered, for the English regarded them as intruders. In 1664, after the imperially ambitious Charles II had granted the area to his brother, the Duke of York, a strong English squadron appeared off the decrepit defenses of New Amsterdam. A fuming Peter Stuyvesant, short of all munitions except courage, was forced to surrender without firing a shot. New Amsterdam was thereupon renamed New York, in honor of the Duke of York. England won a splendid harbor, strategically located in the middle of the mainland colonies, and the stately Hudson River penetrating the interior. With the removal of this foreign wedge, the English banner now waved triumphantly over a solid stretch of territory from Maine to the Carolinas.

as **patroonships**, were granted to promoters who agreed to settle fifty people on them. One patroonship in the Albany area was slightly larger than the later state of Rhode Island.

Colorful little New Amsterdam attracted a cosmopolitan population, as is common in seaport towns. Twenty-three Jews arrived in 1654, refugees from religious persecution in Catholic Brazil—a harbinger of the city's later reputation as a haven for the homeless and the harried. A French Jesuit missionary, visiting in the 1640s, noted that eighteen different languages were being spoken in the streets. New York's later babel of immigrant tongues was thus foreshadowed.

✴ Friction with English and Swedish Neighbors

Vexations beset the Dutch company-colony from the beginning. The directors-general were largely incompetent. Company shareholders demanded their

New Amsterdam, 1664
The future metropolis, already a bustling port, is shown here as it was in the year that the English took over New Netherland and renamed it New York.

© Collection of the New-York Historical Society

The conquered Dutch province tenaciously retained many of the illiberal features of earlier days. An autocratic spirit survived, and the aristocratic element gained strength when certain corrupt English governors granted immense acreage to their favorites. Influential landowning families—such as the Livingstons and the De Lanceys—wielded disproportionate power in the affairs of colonial New York. These monopolistic land policies, combined with the lordly atmosphere, discouraged many European immigrants from coming. The physical growth of New York was correspondingly retarded.

The Dutch peppered place names over the land, including Harlem (Haarlem), Brooklyn (Breuckelen), and Hell Gate (Hellegat). They likewise left their imprint on the gambrel-roofed architecture. As for social customs and folkways, no other foreign group of comparable size has made so colorful a contribution. Noteworthy are Easter eggs, Santa Claus, waffles, sauerkraut, bowling, sleighing, skating, and *kolf* (golf)—a dangerous game played with heavy clubs and forbidden in settled areas.

✵ Penn's Holy Experiment in Pennsylvania

A remarkable group of dissenters, commonly known as **Quakers**, arose in England during the mid-1600s. Their name derived from the report that they "quaked"

when under deep religious emotion. Officially they were known as the Religious Society of Friends.

Quakers were especially offensive to the authorities, both religious and civil. They refused to support the established Church of England with taxes. They built simple meetinghouses, congregated without a paid clergy, and "spoke up" themselves in meetings when moved. Believing that they were all children in the sight of God, they kept their broad-brimmed hats on in the presence of their "betters" and addressed others with simple "thee"s and "thou"s, rather than with conventional titles. They would take no oaths because Jesus had commanded, "Swear not at all." This peculiarity often embroiled them with government officials, for "test oaths" were still required to establish the fact that a person was not a Roman Catholic.

The Quakers, beyond a doubt, were a people of deep conviction. They abhorred strife and warfare and refused military service. As advocates of passive resistance, they would turn the other cheek and rebuild their meetinghouse on the site where their enemies had torn it down. Their courage and devotion to principle finally triumphed. Although at times they seemed stubborn and unreasonable, they were a simple, devoted, democratic people, contending in their own high-minded way for religious and civic freedom.

William Penn, a wellborn and athletic young Englishman, was attracted to the Quaker faith in 1660, when only sixteen years old. His father, disapproving,

Quakers in the Colonial Era   Quakers, or Friends, were renowned for their simplicity of architecture, dress, manner, and speech. They also distinguished themselves from most other Protestant denominations by allowing women to speak in Quaker meetings and to share in making decisions for the church and the family.

administered a sound flogging. After various adventures in the army (the best portrait of the peaceful Quaker has him in armor), the youth firmly embraced the despised faith and suffered much persecution. The courts branded him a "saucy" and "impertinent" fellow. Several hundred of his less fortunate fellow Quakers died of cruel treatment, and thousands more were fined, flogged, or cast into dank prisons.

Penn's thoughts naturally turned to the New World, where a sprinkling of Quakers had already fled, notably to Rhode Island, North Carolina, and New Jersey. Eager to establish an asylum for his people, he also hoped to experiment with liberal ideas in government and at the same time make a profit. Finally, in 1681, he managed to secure from the king an immense grant of fertile land, in consideration of a monetary debt owed to his deceased father by the crown. The king called the area Pennsylvania ("Penn's Woodland") in honor of the sire. The modest son, fearing that critics would accuse him of naming it after himself, sought unsuccessfully to change the name.

Pennsylvania was by far the best advertised of all the colonies. Its founder—the "first American advertising man"—sent out paid agents and distributed countless pamphlets printed in English, Dutch, French, and German. Unlike the lures of many other American real estate promoters, then and later, Penn's inducements were generally truthful. He especially welcomed forward-looking spirits and substantial citizens, including industrious carpenters, masons, shoemakers, and other manual workers. His liberal land policy, which

encouraged substantial holdings, was instrumental in attracting a heavy inflow of immigrants.

✴ Quaker Pennsylvania and Its Neighbors

Penn formally launched his colony in 1681. His task was simplified by the presence of several thousand "squatters"—Dutch, Swedish, English, Welsh—who were already scattered along the banks of the Delaware River. Philadelphia, meaning "brotherly love" in Greek, was more carefully planned than most colonial cities and consequently enjoyed wide and attractive streets.

Penn farsightedly bought land from the Indians, including Chief Tammany, later patron saint of New York's political Tammany Hall. His treatment of the native peoples was so fair that the Quaker "broad brims" went among them unarmed and even employed them as baby-sitters. For a brief period, Pennsylvania seemed the promised land of amicable Indian–white relations. Some southern tribes even migrated to Pennsylvania, seeking the Quaker haven. But ironically, Quaker tolerance proved the undoing of Quaker Indian policy. As non-Quaker European immigrants flooded into the province, they undermined the Quakers' own benevolent policy toward the Indians. The feisty Scots-Irish were particularly unpersuaded by Quaker idealism.

Penn's new proprietary regime was unusually liberal and included a representative assembly elected by the landowners. No tax-supported state church drained coffers or demanded allegiance. Freedom of worship was guaranteed to all residents, although Penn, under pressure from London, was forced to deny Catholics and Jews the privilege of voting or holding office. The death penalty was imposed only for treason and murder, as compared with some two hundred capital crimes in England.

Among other noteworthy features, no provision was made by the peace-loving Quakers of Pennsylvania for a military defense. No restrictions were placed on immigration, and naturalization was made easy. The humane Quakers early developed a strong dislike of black slavery, and in the genial glow of Pennsylvania some progress was made toward social reform.

With its many liberal features, Pennsylvania attracted a rich mix of ethnic groups. They included numerous religious misfits who were repelled by the harsh practices of neighboring colonies. This Quaker refuge boasted a surprisingly modern atmosphere in an unmodern age and to an unusual degree afforded economic opportunity, civil liberty, and religious freedom. Even so, **"blue laws"** prohibited "ungodly revelers," stage plays, playing cards, dice, games, and excessive hilarity.

Under such generally happy auspices, Penn's brainchild grew lustily. The Quakers were shrewd businesspeople, and in a short time the settlers were exporting grain and other foodstuffs. Within two years Philadelphia claimed three hundred houses and twenty-five hundred people. Within nineteen years—by 1700—the colony was surpassed in population and wealth only by long-established Virginia and Massachusetts.

William Penn, who altogether spent about four years in Pennsylvania, was never fully appreciated by his colonists. His governors, some of them incompetent and tactless, quarreled bitterly with the people, who were constantly demanding greater political control. Penn himself became too friendly with James II, the deposed Catholic king. Thrice arrested for treason, thrust for a time into a debtors' prison, and afflicted by a paralytic stroke, he died full of sorrows. His enduring monument was not only a noble experiment

Penn's Treaty, by Edward Hicks The peace-loving Quaker founder of Pennsylvania made a serious effort to live in harmony with the Indians, as this treaty-signing scene illustrates. But the westward thrust of white settlement eventually caused friction between the two groups, as in other colonies.

in government but also a new commonwealth. Based on civil and religious liberty, and dedicated to freedom of conscience and worship, it held aloft a hopeful torch in a world of semidarkness.

Small Quaker settlements flourished next door to Pennsylvania. New Jersey was started in 1664 when two noble proprietors received the area from the Duke of York. A substantial number of New Englanders, including many whose weary soil had petered out, flocked to the new colony. One of the proprietors sold West New Jersey in 1674 to a group of Quakers, who here set up a sanctuary even before Pennsylvania was launched. East New Jersey was also acquired in later years by the Quakers, whose wings were clipped in 1702 when the crown combined the two Jerseys in a royal colony.

Swedish-tinged Delaware consisted of only three counties—two at high tide, the witticism goes—and was named after Lord De La Warr, the harsh military governor who had arrived in Virginia in 1610. Harboring some Quakers, and closely associated with Penn's prosperous colony, Delaware was granted its own assembly in 1703. But until the American Revolution, it remained under the governor of Pennsylvania.

✴ The Middle Way in the Middle Colonies

The middle colonies—New York, New Jersey, Delaware, and Pennsylvania—enjoyed certain features in common.

In general, the soil was fertile and the expanse of land was broad, unlike rock-bestrewn New England. Pennsylvania, New York, and New Jersey came to be known as the "bread colonies," by virtue of their heavy exports of grain.

Rivers also played a vital role. Broad, languid streams—notably the Susquehanna, the Delaware, and the Hudson—tapped the fur trade of the interior and beckoned adventuresome spirits into the backcountry. The rivers had few cascading waterfalls, unlike New England's, and hence presented little inducement to milling or manufacturing with water-wheel power.

A surprising amount of industry nonetheless hummed in the middle colonies. Virginal forests abounded for lumbering and shipbuilding. The presence of deep river estuaries and landlocked harbors stimulated both commerce and the growth of seaports, such as New York and Philadelphia.

Even Albany, more than a hundred miles up the Hudson, was a port of some consequence in colonial days.

The middle colonies were in many respects midway between New England and the southern plantation group. Except in aristocratic New York, the landholdings were generally intermediate in size—smaller than in the plantation South but larger than in small-farm New England. Local government lay somewhere between the personalized town meeting of New England and the diffused county government of the South. There were fewer industries in the middle colonies than in New England, more than in the South.

Yet the middle colonies, which in some ways were the most American part of America, could claim certain distinctions in their own right. Generally speaking, the population was more ethnically mixed than that of other settlements. The people were blessed with an unusual degree of religious toleration and democratic control. Earnest and devout Quakers, in particular, made a compassionate contribution to human freedom out of all proportion to their numbers. Desirable land was more easily acquired in the middle colonies than in New England or in the tidewater South. One result was that a considerable amount of economic and social democracy prevailed, though less so in aristocratic New York.

Modern-minded Benjamin Franklin, often regarded as the most representative American personality of his era, was a child of the middle colonies. Although it is true that Franklin was born a Yankee in puritanical Boston, he entered Philadelphia as a seventeen-year-old in 1720 with a loaf of bread under each arm and immediately found a congenial home in the urbane, open atmosphere of what was then North America's biggest city. One Pennsylvanian later boasted that Franklin "came to life at seventeen, in Philadelphia."

By the time Franklin arrived in the City of Brotherly Love, the American colonies were themselves "coming to life." Population was growing robustly. Transportation and communication were gradually improving. The British, for the most part, continued their hands-off policies, leaving the colonists to fashion their own local governments, run their own churches, and develop networks of intercolonial trade. As people and products crisscrossed the colonies with increasing frequency and in increasing volume, Americans began to realize that—far removed from Mother England—they were not merely surviving, but truly thriving.

Examining the Evidence

A Seventeenth-Century Valuables Cabinet

In 1999 a boatyard worker on Cape Cod and his sister, a New Hampshire teacher, inherited a small (20-pound, 16½-inch-high) chest that had always stood on their grandmother's hall table, known in the family as the "Franklin chest." Eager to learn more about it, they set out to discover the original owner, tracing their family genealogy and consulting with furniture experts. In January 2000 this rare seventeenth-century cabinet, its full provenance now known, appeared on the auction block and sold for a record $2.4 million to the Peabody Essex Museum in Salem, Massachusetts. No less extraordinary

than the price was the history of its creator and its owners embodied in the piece. Salem cabinetmaker James Symonds (1636–1726) had made the chest for his relatives Joseph Pope (1650–1712) and Bathsheba Folger (1652–1726) to commemorate their 1679 marriage. Symonds carved the Popes' initials and the date on the door of the cabinet. He also put elaborate S curves on the sides remarkably similar to the Mannerist carved oak paneling produced in Norfolk, England, from which his own cabinetmaker father had emigrated. Behind the chest's door are ten drawers where the Popes would

have kept jewelry, money, deeds, and writing materials. Surely they prized the chest as a sign of refinement to be shown off in their best room, a sentiment passed down through the next thirteen generations even as the Popes' identities were lost. The chest may have become known as the "Franklin chest" because Bathsheba was Benjamin Franklin's aunt, but also because that identification appealed more to descendants ashamed that the Quaker Popes, whose own parents had been persecuted for their faith, were virulent accusers during the Salem witch trials of 1692.

Christie's Images/The Bridgeman Art Library

Europeanizing America or Americanizing Europe?

The history of discovery and colonization raises perhaps the most fundamental question about all American history. Should it be understood as the extension of European civilization into the two continents of the New World or as the gradual development of uniquely "American" cultures? An older school of thought tended to emphasize the Europeanization of America. Historians of that persuasion paid close attention to the situation in Europe, particularly England and Spain, in the fifteenth and sixteenth centuries. They also focused on the exportation of the values and institutions of the mother countries to the new lands in the western sea. Although some historians also examined the transforming effect of America on Europe, this approach, too, remained essentially Eurocentric.

More recently, historians have concentrated on the distinctiveness of America. The concern with European origins has evolved into a comparative treatment of European settlements in the New World. England, Spain, Holland, and France now attract more attention for the divergent kinds of societies they fostered in America than for the way they commonly pursued Old World ambitions in the New. The newest trend to emerge is a transatlantic history that views European empires and their American colonies as part of a process of cultural cross-fertilization affecting not only the colonies but Europe and Africa as well.

This less Eurocentric approach has also changed the way historians explain the colonial development of America. Rather than telling the story of colonization as the imposition of European ways of life through "discovery" and "conquest," historians increasingly view the colonial period as one of "contact" and "adaptation" between European, African, and Native American ways of life. Scholars, including Richard White, Alfred Crosby, William Cronon, Karen Kupperman, and Timothy Silver, have enhanced understanding of the cultural as well as the physical transformations that resulted from contact. An environment of forests and meadows, for example, gave way to a landscape of fields and fences as Europeans sought to replicate the agricultural villages they had known in Europe. Aggressive deforestation even produced climatic changes, as treeless tracts made for colder winters, hotter summers, and earth-gouging floods. Ramon Gutierrez's *When Jesus Came, the Corn Mothers Went Away* (1991) has expanded the colonial stage to include interactions between Spanish settlers and Native Americans in the Southwest.

J. H. Elliott's magisterial work *Empires of the Atlantic World* (2006) makes brilliant use of the comparative approach to illuminate the worlds of the British and Spanish Empires. Spain had a grand imperial plan that it pursued with notable consistency: exclude Jews and Moors (Muslims) from its domains, convert the native peoples to Catholicism, follow military conquest with military rule, and eventually defer to colonial elites for the orderly administration of its possessions. Britain had no comparably systematic plan. It showed relatively little interest in converting the Indians, tolerated all kinds of immigrants to its colonies, long left them alone to cultivate institutions of self-government and representative democracy, and when it eventually tried to tighten its imperial grip, pressured local elites into open revolt. The two empires left consequential and contrasting legacies of political stability in the United States and chronic political turmoil in Latin America. As one reviewer summarized the argument, "George Washington could draw on an inherited political culture, whereas [the great Latin American liberator] Simón Bolívar had to invent one."

The variety of American societies that emerged out of the interaction of Europeans, Africans, and Native Americans is now well appreciated. Early histories by esteemed historians like Perry Miller exaggerated the extent to which the New England Puritan experience defined the essence of America. Not only did these historians overlook non-English experiences, but they failed to recognize the diversity in motives, methods, and consequences that existed even within English colonization. The numbers alone tell an interesting story. By 1700 about 220,000 English colonists had immigrated to the Caribbean, about 120,000 to the southern mainland colonies, and only about 40,000 to the middle Atlantic and New England colonies (although by the mid-eighteenth century, those headed for the latter destination would account for more than half of the total).

Studies such as Richard S. Dunn's *Sugar and Slaves* (1972) emphasize the importance of the Caribbean in early English colonization efforts and make clear that the desire for economic gain, more than the quest for religious freedom, fueled the migration to the Caribbean islands. Similarly, Edmund S. Morgan's *American Slavery, American Freedom* (1975) stresses the role of economic ambition in explaining the English peopling of the Chesapeake and the eventual importation of enslaved Africans to that region. Studies by Bernard Bailyn and David Hackett Fischer demonstrate that there was scarcely a "typical" English migrant to the New World. English colonists migrated both singly and in families, and for economic, social, political, and religious reasons.

Recent studies have also paid more attention to the conflicts that emerged out of this diversity in settler populations and colonial societies. This perspective emphasizes the contests for economic and political supremacy within the colonies, such as the efforts of the Massachusetts Bay elite to ward off the challenges of religious "heretics" and the pressures that an increasingly restless lower class put on wealthy merchants and large landowners. Nowhere was internal conflict so prevalent as in the ethnically diverse middle colonies, where factional antagonisms became the defining feature of public life.

The picture of British colonial North America that is emerging from all this new scholarship is of a society unique—and diverse—from inception. No longer simply Europe transplanted, British America by 1700 is now viewed as an outgrowth of many intertwining roots—of different European and African heritages, of varied encounters with native peoples and a wilderness environment, and of complicated mixtures of settler populations, each with its own distinctive set of ambitions.

Chapter Review

KEY TERMS

Calvinism (42)
predestination (42)
conversion (42)
Puritans (43)
Separatists (43)
Mayflower Compact (44)
Massachusetts Bay Colony (44)
Great English Migration (44)
antinomianism (46)
Fundamental Orders (48)
Pequot War (48)
King Philip's War (49)
New England Confederation (49)
English Civil War (49)
Dominion of New England (50)
Navigation Laws (50)
Glorious (or Bloodless) Revolution (50)
salutary neglect (51)
patroonships (53)
Quakers (54)
blue laws (56)

PEOPLE TO KNOW

Martin Luther
John Calvin
William Bradford
John Winthrop
Anne Hutchinson
Roger Williams
Massasoit
Metacom (King Philip)
Charles II
Sir Edmund Andros
William III
Mary II
Henry Hudson
Peter Stuyvesant
Duke of York
William Penn

CHRONOLOGY

1517	Martin Luther begins Protestant Reformation
1536	John Calvin of Geneva publishes *Institutes of the Christian Religion*
1620	Pilgrims sail on the *Mayflower* to Plymouth Bay
1624	Dutch found New Netherland
1629	Charles I dismisses Parliament and persecutes Puritans
1630	Puritans found Massachusetts Bay Colony
1635–1636	Roger Williams convicted of heresy and founds Rhode Island colony
1635–1638	Connecticut and New Haven colonies founded
1636–1638	Pequot War
1638	Anne Hutchinson banished from Massachusetts colony
1639	Connecticut's Fundamental Orders drafted
1642–1651	English Civil War
1643	New England Confederation formed
1650	William Bradford completes *Of Plymouth Plantation*
1655	New Netherland conquers New Sweden
1664	England seizes New Netherland from Dutch East and West Jersey colonies founded
1675–1676	King Philip's War
1681	William Penn founds Pennsylvania colony
1686	Royal authority creates Dominion of New England
1688–1689	Glorious Revolution overthrows Stuarts and Dominion of New England

TO LEARN MORE

Patricia Bonomi, *A Factious People: Politics and Society in Colonial New York* (1971)

Timothy H. Breen, *Puritans and Adventurers* (1980)

Jon Butler, *Awash in a Sea of Faith: Christianizing the American People* (1990)

John Demos, *The Unredeemed Captive: A Family Story from Early America* (1994)

David Hall, *Worlds of Wonder, Days of Judgment: Popular Religious Belief in Early New England* (1989)

Japp Jacobs, *The Colony of New Netherland: A Dutch Settlement in Seventeenth-Century America* (2009)

Donna Merwick, *The Shame and the Sorrow: Dutch-Amerindian Encounters in New Netherland* (2006)

Edmund S. Morgan, *Roger Williams: The Church and State* (1967)

Jenny Hale Pulsipher, *Subjects unto the Same King: Indians, English, and the Contest for Authority in Colonial New England* (2005)

Christina Snyder, *Slavery in Indian Country: The Changing Face of Captivity in Early America* (2010)

Harry Stout, *The New England Soul: Preaching and Culture in Colonial New England* (1986)

A complete, annotated bibliography for this chapter—along with brief descriptions of the People to Know—may be found on the *American Pageant* website. The key terms are defined in the glossary at the end of the text.

Chapter 4

American Life in the Seventeenth Century

1607–1692

*Being thus passed the vast ocean, and a sea of troubles before in their preparation . . . ,
they had now no friends to wellcome them, nor inns to entertaine or refresh their
weatherbeaten bodys, no houses or much less towns to repaire too, to seeke for succore.*

WILLIAM BRADFORD, OF PLYMOUTH PLANTATION, CA. 1630

As the seventeenth century unfolded, the crude encampments of the first colonists slowly gave way to permanent settlements. Durable and distinctive ways of life emerged as Europeans and Africans adapted to the New World and as Native Americans adapted to the newcomers. Even the rigid doctrines of Puritanism softened somewhat in response to the circumstances of life in America. And though all the colonies remained tied to England, and all were stitched tightly into the fabric of an Atlantic economy, regional differences continued to crystallize, notably the increasing importance of slave labor to the southern way of life.

✴ The Unhealthy Chesapeake

Life in the American wilderness was nasty, brutish, and short for the earliest Chesapeake settlers. Malaria, dysentery, and typhoid took a cruel toll, cutting ten years off the life expectancy of newcomers from England. Half the people born in early Virginia and Maryland did not survive to celebrate their twentieth birthdays. Few of the remaining half lived to see their fiftieth—or even their fortieth, if they were women.

The disease-ravaged settlements of the Chesapeake grew only slowly in the seventeenth century, mostly through fresh immigration from England.

The great majority of immigrants were single men in their late teens and early twenties, and most perished soon after arrival. Surviving males competed for the affections of the extremely scarce women, whom they outnumbered nearly six to one in 1650 and still outnumbered by three to two at the end of the century. Eligible women did not remain single for long.

Families were both few and fragile in this ferocious environment. Most men could not find mates. Most marriages were destroyed by the death of a partner within seven years. Scarcely any children reached adulthood under the care of two parents, and almost no one knew a grandparent. Weak family ties were reflected in the many pregnancies among unmarried young girls. In one Maryland county, more than a third of all brides were already pregnant when they wed.

Yet despite these hardships, the Chesapeake colonies struggled on. The native-born inhabitants eventually acquired immunity to the killer diseases that had ravaged the original immigrants. The presence of more women allowed more families to form, and by the end of the seventeenth century, the white population of the Chesapeake was growing on the basis of its own birthrate. As the eighteenth century opened, Virginia, with some fifty-nine thousand people, was the most populous colony. Maryland, with about thirty thousand, was the third largest (after Massachusetts).

✪ The Tobacco Economy

Although unhealthy for human life, the Chesapeake was immensely hospitable to tobacco cultivation. Profit-hungry settlers often planted tobacco to sell before they planted corn to eat. But intense tobacco cultivation quickly exhausted the soil, creating a nearly insatiable demand for new land. Relentlessly seeking fresh fields to plant in tobacco, commercial growers plunged ever farther up the river valleys, provoking ever more Indian attacks.

Leaf-laden ships annually hauled some 1.5 million pounds of tobacco out of Chesapeake Bay by the 1630s and almost 40 million pounds a year by the end of the century. This enormous production depressed prices, but colonial Chesapeake tobacco growers responded to falling prices in the familiar way of farmers: by planting still more acres to tobacco and bringing still more product to market.

More tobacco meant more labor, but where was it to come from? Families procreated too slowly to provide it by natural population increase. Indians died too quickly on contact with whites to be a reliable labor force. African slaves were expensive, and the Chesapeake's high mortality rates made the investment too risky. But England still had a "surplus" of displaced workers and farmers, desperate for employment. Many of them were young men who had fled the disastrous slump in the cloth trades that hit England in the early seventeenth century. Others were tenants who had been forced from their modest farms when landlords "enclosed" ever more acreage for sheep grazing. Making their way from town to town in search of wages, they eventually drifted into port cities like Bristol and London. There they boarded ship for America as **indentured servants**, voluntarily mortgaging the sweat of their bodies for several years (usually four to seven) to Chesapeake masters. In exchange they received transatlantic passage and eventual "freedom dues," including an ax and a hoe, a few barrels of corn, a suit of clothes, and perhaps a small parcel of land.

Both Virginia and Maryland employed the **headright system** to encourage the importation of servant workers. Under its terms, whoever paid the passage of a laborer received the right to acquire fifty acres of land. Masters—not the servants themselves—thus reaped the benefits of landownership from the headright system. Some masters, men who already had at least modest financial means, soon parlayed their investments in servants into vast holdings in real estate. They became the great merchant-planters, lords of sprawling riverfront estates that came to dominate the agriculture and commerce of the southern colonies. Ravenous for both labor and land,

Early Tobacco Advertising Crude woodcuts like this one were used to identify various "brands" of tobacco— one of the first products to be sold by brand-name advertising.

Chesapeake planters brought some 100,000 indentured servants to the region by 1700. These "white slaves" represented more than three-quarters of all European immigrants to Virginia and Maryland in the seventeenth century.

Indentured servants led a hard but hopeful life in the early days of the Chesapeake settlements. They looked forward to becoming free and acquiring land of their own after completing their term of

An agent for the Virginia Company in London submitted the following description of the Virginia colony in 1622:

❝I found the plantations generally seated upon mere salt marshes full of infectious bogs and muddy creeks and lakes, and thereby subjected to all those inconveniences and diseases which are so commonly found in the most unsound and most unhealthy parts of England.❞

servitude. But as prime land became scarcer, masters became increasingly resistant to including land grants in "freedom dues." The servants' lot grew harsher as the seventeenth century wore on. Misbehaving servants, such as a housemaid who became pregnant or a laborer who killed a hog, might be punished with an extended term of service. Even after formal freedom was granted, penniless freed workers often had little choice but to hire themselves out for pitifully low wages to their former masters.

✦ Frustrated Freemen and Bacon's Rebellion

An accumulating mass of footloose, impoverished freemen drifted discontentedly about the Chesapeake region by the late seventeenth century. Mostly single young white men, they were frustrated by their broken hopes of acquiring land, as well as by their gnawing failure to find single women to marry.

The swelling numbers of these wretched bachelors rattled the established planters. The Virginia assembly in 1670 disfranchised most of the landless knockabouts, accusing them of "having little interest in the country" and causing "tumults at the election to the disturbance of his majesty's peace." Virginia's Governor William Berkeley lamented his lot as ruler of this rabble: "How miserable that man is that governs a people where six parts of seven at least are poor, endebted, discontented, and armed."

Berkeley's misery soon increased. About a thousand Virginians broke out of control in 1676, led by a twenty-nine-year-old planter, Nathaniel Bacon. Many of the rebels were frontiersmen who had been forced into the untamed backcountry in search of arable land. They fiercely resented Berkeley's friendly policies toward the Indians, whose thriving fur trade the governor monopolized. When Berkeley refused to retaliate against a series of brutal Indian attacks on frontier settlements, Bacon and his followers took matters into their own hands. They fell murderously upon the Indians, friendly and hostile alike, chased Berkeley from Jamestown, and put the torch to the capital. Chaos swept the raw colony, as frustrated freemen and resentful servants—described as "a rabble of the basest sort of people"—went on a rampage of plundering and pilfering.

As this civil war in Virginia ground on, Bacon suddenly died of disease, like so many of his fellow colonists. Berkeley thereupon crushed the uprising with brutal cruelty, hanging more than twenty rebels. Back in England Charles II complained, "That old fool has put to death more people in that naked country than I did here for the murder of my father."

The distant English king could scarcely imagine the depths of passion and fear that **Bacon's Rebellion** excited in Virginia. Bacon had ignited the smoldering resentments of landless former servants, and he had pitted the hardscrabble backcountry frontiersmen against the haughty gentry of the tidewater plantations. The rebellion was now suppressed, but these tensions remained. Lordly planters, surrounded by a still-seething sea of malcontents, anxiously looked about for less troublesome laborers to toil in the restless tobacco kingdom. Their eyes soon lit on Africa.

✦ Colonial Slavery

More than 7 million Africans were carried in chains to the New World in the three centuries or so following Columbus's landing (see "Thinking Globally: The Atlantic Slave Trade, 1500–1860," pp. 66–67). Only about 400,000 of them ended up in North America, the great majority arriving after 1700. Most of the early human cargoes were hauled to Spanish

Examining the Evidence

An Indentured Servant's Contract, 1746

Legal documents, such as this contract signed in Virginia in 1746, not only provide evidence about the ever-changing rules by which societies have regulated their affairs, but also furnish rich information about the conditions of life and the terms of human relationships in the past. This agreement between Thomas Clayton and James Griffin provides a reminder that not all indentured servants in early America came from abroad. Indentured servitude could be equivalent to an apprenticeship, in which a young person traded several years of service to a master in exchange for instruction in the master's craft. Here Clayton pledges himself to five years in Griffin's employ in return for a promise to initiate the young man into the "Mystery" of the master's craft. Why might the master's trade be described as a "mystery"? From the evidence of this contract, what are the principal objectives of each of the parties to it? What problems does each anticipate? What obligations does each assume? What does the consent of Clayton's mother to the contract suggest about the young man's situation?

Special Collections, John D. Rockefeller, Jr. Library, The Colonial Williamsburg Foundation

Special Collections, John D. Rockefeller, Jr. Library, The Colonial Williamsburg Foundation

The Atlantic Slave Trade, 1500–1860

For more than three centuries following Columbus's discovery, slave merchants crammed some 11 million African men, women, and children into the holds of ships and carried them like common cargo to the New World. Roughly 2 million souls perished midvoyage before confronting the agonies and indignities of slavery in the Americas. As Map 4.1 shows, some 400,000 enslaved Africans came ashore in North America, while the overwhelming majority were destined for South America and the Caribbean.

European and American slave traders reaped enormous profits from this human trafficking, as did the African warlords who sold their hapless captives into lifelong bondage. British, French, Portuguese, Dutch, and New England slavers stuffed their ships to capacity with little regard for the health or comfort of their suffering cargo. One enslaved boy, Olaudah Equiano, later wrote of his constant fear during the voyage that his tormenting captors would murder him, as they did several others before his young eyes. Equiano survived, but the hideous conditions aboard those floating hells killed countless Africans and deeply traumatized many others.

Slave trading fed off the insatiable European appetite for sugar, as well as for tobacco, cotton, and other New World products that both Europeans and Americans craved. Marketing human beings on such a vast scale required the complicity not only of warlords and sailors but also of bankers and stevedores, planters and tailors, shopkeepers and bakers, and finally tea drinkers, smokers, and a host of middlemen on four continents.

Once purchased by their New World masters, slaves faced a life of ceaseless, unpaid toil. Though conditions varied across the vast slave dominion that stretched from Brazil to North America, most slaves had few if any legal rights. The Caribbean and Deep South sugar plantations in particular demanded notoriously man-killing, backbreaking labor.

Slavery in the Americas continued to gain importance, and human imports from Africa peaked in the late eighteenth century. Only in the nineteenth century, beginning with Britain in 1807, did nations in Europe and the Americas begin to outlaw the

The Granger Collection, NYC

An African Slave Coffle   Yoked and bound, these men, women, and children were on their way to a coastal slave market, where they would be herded aboard ship for the Americas.

MAP 4.1 Main Sources and Destinations of African Slaves, ca. 1500–1860 More than three centuries of the "African Diaspora" scattered blacks throughout the New World. Britain's North American colonies (the future United States) constituted the extreme northern periphery of this system, receiving about 400,000 of the nearly 10 million arrivals, the great majority of whom ended up in the West Indies and Brazil. © 2016 Cengage Learning

international slave trade (see "The Struggle to Abolish Slavery" in Chapter 16, pp. XXX–XXX). After Congress banned further slave importations to the United States in 1808, a flourishing internal market developed. Masters in the upper South bred slaves for sale on the rapidly expanding cotton frontier in the Old Southwest. Europeans, as well as Americans in the "free states," lent indirect support to that domestic slave trade as they continued to consume slave-produced goods. Slavery would not finally be abolished in the United States until 1863.

The "Middle Passage" The "middle passage" referred to the transatlantic sea voyage that brought slaves to the New World—the long and hazardous "middle" segment of a journey that began with a forced march to the African coast and ended with a trek into the American interior.

and Portuguese South America or to the sugar-rich West Indies.

Africans had been brought to Jamestown as early as 1619, but as late as 1670 they numbered only about 2,000 in Virginia (out of a total population of some 35,000 persons) and about 7 percent of the 50,000 people in the southern plantation colonies as a whole. Hard-pinched white colonists, struggling to stay alive and to hack crude clearings out of the forests, could not afford to pay high prices for slaves who might die soon after arrival. White servants might die, too, but they were far less costly.

Drastic changes came in the closing years of the seventeenth century. Rising wages in England shrank the pool of penniless folk willing to gamble on a new life or an early death as indentured servants in America. Gradually improving mortality rates made an investment in slaves somewhat less risky. West Indian planters brought new rice and indigo planting to the Carolinas, swelling the demand for labor. And in the wake of Bacon's Rebellion, the large planters were growing increasingly fearful of the multitudes of potentially mutinous former servants in their midst. By the mid-1680s, for the first time, black slaves outnumbered white servants among the plantation colonies' new arrivals. In 1698 the **Royal African Company**, first chartered in 1672, lost its crown-granted monopoly on carrying slaves to the colonies.

Enterprising Americans, especially Rhode Islanders, rushed to cash in on the lucrative slave trade, and the supply of slaves rose steeply. More than ten thousand Africans were pushed ashore in America in the decade after 1700, and tens of thousands more in the next half-century. By 1700, enslaved blacks already made up more than one-third the population of South Carolina; twenty years later they outnumbered whites by two to one. Blacks accounted for nearly half the population of Virginia by 1750.

Most of the slaves who reached North America came from the west coast of Africa, especially the area stretching from present-day Senegal to Angola. They were originally captured by African coastal tribes, who traded them in crude markets on the shimmering tropical beaches to itinerant European—and American—flesh merchants. Usually branded and bound, the captives were herded aboard sweltering ships for the gruesome **middle passage**, on which death rates ran as high as 20 percent. Terrified survivors were eventually shoved onto auction blocks in New World ports like Newport, Rhode Island, or Charleston, South Carolina, where a giant slave market traded in human misery for more than a century.

A few of the earliest African immigrants gained their freedom, and some even became slaveowners themselves. But as the number of Africans in their midst increased dramatically toward the end of the

The Slave Ship *Albatross*, 1846 This eyewitness painting captures the dankness, gloom, and despair that reigned in the slaver's cargo hold.

The Mennonites of Germantown, Pennsylvania, recorded the earliest known protest against slavery in America in 1688:

"There is a saying, that we should do to all men like as we will be done ourselves....But to bring men hither, or to rob and sell them against their will, we stand against....Pray, what thing in the world can be done worse towards us, than if men should rob or steal us away, and sell us for slaves to strange countries, separating husbands from their wives and children?**"**

seventeenth century, white colonists reacted remorselessly to this supposed racial threat.

Earlier in the century, the legal difference between a slave and a servant was unclear. But now the law began to make sharp distinctions between the two—largely on the basis of race. Beginning in Virginia in 1662, statutes appeared that formally decreed the iron conditions of slavery for blacks. These earliest **"slave codes"** made blacks *and their children* the property (or "chattels") for life of their white masters. Some colonies made it a crime to teach a slave to read or write. Not even conversion to Christianity could qualify a slave for freedom. Thus did the God-fearing whites put the fear of God into their hapless black laborers. Slavery might have begun in America for economic reasons, but by the end of the seventeenth century, it was clear that racial discrimination also powerfully molded the

American slave system. And just as race shaped slavery, so did slavery shape the entire spectrum of race relations, as both law and custom increasingly circumscribed the lives of enslaved and free blacks alike, in the North as well as in the South. From this time forward, the boundary between freedom and unfreedom in America ran along the color line.

✴ Southern Society

As slavery spread, the gaps in the South's social structure widened. The rough equality of poverty and disease of the early days was giving way to a defined hierarchy of wealth and status in the early eighteenth century. At the top of this southern social ladder perched a small but powerful covey of great planters. Owning gangs of slaves and vast domains of land, the planters ruled the region's economy and virtually monopolized political power. A clutch of extended clans—such as the Fitzhughs, the Lees, and the Washingtons—possessed among them horizonless tracts of Virginia real estate, and together they dominated the House of Burgesses. Just before the Revolutionary War, 70 percent of the leaders of the Virginia legislature came from families established in Virginia before 1690—the famed "first families of Virginia," or "FFVs."

Yet, legend to the contrary, these great seventeenth-century merchant-planters were not silk-swathed cavaliers gallantly imitating the ways of English country gentlemen. They did eventually build stately riverfront manors, occasionally rode to the hounds, and

The Granger Collection, NYC

RICE CULTURE ON THE OGEECHEE, NEAR SAVANNAH, GEORGIA.—SKETCHED BY A. R. WAUD.—[SEE PAGE 5.]

Rice Cultivation in the Colonial South Rice growing, imported from Africa along with enslaved Africans to work the swampy rice fields, made South Carolina the rice basket of the British Empire.

Charleston, South Carolina   Founded in 1680, Charleston grew to become the bustling seaport pictured in this drawing done in the 1730s. Charleston was by then the largest city in the mostly rural southern colonies. It flourished as a seaport for the shipment to England of slave-grown Carolina rice.

The Colonial Williamsburg Foundation. Museum Purchase.

some of them even cultivated the arts and accumulated distinguished libraries. But for the most part, they were a hard-working, businesslike lot, laboring long hours over the problems of plantation management. Few problems were more vexatious than the unruly, often surly, servants. One Virginia governor had such difficulty keeping his servants sober that he struck a deal allowing them to get drunk the next day if they would only lay off the liquor long enough to look after his guests at a celebration of the queen's birthday in 1711.

Beneath the planters—far beneath them in wealth, prestige, and political power—were the small farmers, the largest social group. They tilled their modest plots and might own one or two slaves, but they lived a ragged, hand-to-mouth existence. Still lower on the social scale were the landless whites, most of them luckless former indentured servants. Beneath them were those persons still serving out the term of their indenture. Their numbers gradually diminished as black slaves increasingly replaced white indentured servants toward the end of the seventeenth century. The oppressed black slaves, of course, remained enchained in society's basement.

Few cities sprouted in the colonial South, and consequently an urban professional class, including lawyers and financiers, was slow to emerge. Southern life revolved around the great plantations, distantly isolated from one another. Waterways provided the principal means of transportation. Roads were so wretched that in bad weather funeral parties could not reach church burial grounds—an obstacle that accounts for

the development of family burial plots in the South, a practice unlike anything in old England or New England.

✦ The New England Family

Nature smiled more benignly on pioneer New Englanders than on their disease-plagued fellow colonists to the south. Clean water and cool temperatures retarded the spread of killer microbes. In stark contrast to the fate of Chesapeake immigrants, settlers in seventeenth-century New England *added* ten years to their life spans by migrating from the Old World. One settler claimed that "a sip of New England's air is better than a whole draft of old England's ale." The first generations of Puritan colonists enjoyed, on the average, about seventy years on this earth—not very different from the life expectancy of present-day Americans.

In further contrast with the Chesapeake, New Englanders tended to migrate not as single individuals but as families, and the family remained at the center of New England life. Almost from the outset, New England's population grew from natural reproductive increase. The people were remarkably fertile, even if the soil was not.

Early marriage encouraged the booming birthrate. Women typically wed by their early twenties and produced babies about every two years thereafter until menopause. Ceaseless childbearing drained the vitality of many pioneer women, as the weather-eroded colonial tombstones eloquently reveal. A number of the largest families were borne by several mothers, though claims about the frequency of death in childbirth have probably been exaggerated. But the dread of death in the birthing bed haunted many women, and it was small wonder that they came to fear pregnancy. A married woman could expect to experience up to ten pregnancies and rear as many as eight surviving children. Massachusetts governor William Phips was one of twenty-seven children, all by the same mother. A New England woman might well have dependent children living in her household from the earliest days of her marriage up until the day of her death, and child raising became in essence her full-time occupation.

The longevity of the New Englanders contributed to family stability. Children grew up in nurturing environments where they were expected to learn habits of obedience, above all. They received guidance not only from their parents but from their grandparents as well. This novel intergenerational continuity has inspired the observation that New England "invented" grandparents. Family stability was reflected in low premarital pregnancy rates (again in contrast with the Chesapeake) and in the generally strong, tranquil social structure characteristic of colonial New England.

New England early acquired a reputation as a healthy environment. Urging his fellow Englishmen to emigrate to the Massachusetts Bay Colony in 1630, the Reverend John White described New England (somewhat fancifully) as follows:

❝ No country yields a more propitious air for our temper than New England.... Many of our people that have found themselves always weak and sickly at home, have become strong and healthy there: perhaps by the dryness of the air and constant temper[ature] of it, which seldom varies from cold to heat, as it does with us.... Neither are the natives at any time troubled with pain of teeth, soreness of eyes, or ache in their limbs.**❞**

Still other contrasts came to differentiate the southern and New England ways of life. Oddly enough, the fragility of southern families advanced the economic security of southern women, especially of women's property rights. Because southern men frequently died young, leaving widows with small children to support, the southern colonies generally allowed married women to retain separate title to their property and gave widows the right to inherit their husbands' estates. But in New England, Puritan lawmakers worried that recognizing women's separate property rights would undercut the unity of married persons by acknowledging conflicting interests between husband and wife. New England women, therefore, usually gave up their property rights when they married. Yet in contrast to old England, the laws of New England made secure provision for the property rights of widows—and even extended important protections to women within marriage.

"A true wife accounts subjection her honor," one Massachusetts Puritan leader declared, expressing a sentiment then common in Europe as well as America. But in the New World, a rudimentary conception of women's rights as individuals was beginning to appear in the seventeenth century. Women still could not vote, and the popular attitude persisted that they were morally weaker than men—a belief rooted in the biblical tale of Eve's treachery in the Garden of Eden. But a husband's power over his wife was not absolute. The New England authorities could and did intervene to restrain abusive spouses. One man was punished for kicking his wife off a stool; another was disciplined for drawing an "uncivil" portrait of his mate in the snow. Women also had some spheres of autonomy. Midwifery—assisting with childbirths—was a virtual female monopoly, and midwives often fostered

Mrs. Elizabeth Freake and Baby Mary   This portrait of a Boston mother and child in about 1674 suggests the strong family ties that characterized early New England society.

Freake-Gibbs Painter (American, active about 1670), "Elizabeth Clarke Freake (Mrs. John Freake) and Baby Mary," about 1671–1674, oil on canvas, 42 1/2 x 36 3/4 in., Worchester Art Museum (MA), Gift of Mr. and Mrs. Albert W. Rice, 1963.134

Courtesy of the Massachusetts Historical Society

Mary Mirick Davie (1635–1752)   This woman exemplified the longevity of New Englanders. She bore nine children, buried three husbands, and was still performing household tasks past the age of one hundred.

networks of women bonded by the common travails of motherhood. One Boston midwife alone delivered over three thousand babies.

Above all, the laws of Puritan New England sought to defend the integrity of marriages. Divorce was exceedingly rare, and the authorities commonly ordered separated couples to reunite. Outright abandonment was among the very few permissible grounds for divorce. Adultery was another. Convicted adulterers—especially if they were women—were whipped in public and forced forever after to wear the capital letter "A" cut out in cloth and sewed on their outer garments—the basis for Nathaniel Hawthorne's famous 1850 tale *The Scarlet Letter*.

✶ Life in the New England Towns

Sturdy New Englanders evolved a tightly knit society, the basis of which was small villages and farms. This development was natural in a people anchored by geography and hemmed in by the Indians, the French, and the Dutch. Puritanism likewise made for unity of purpose—and for concern about the moral health of the whole community. It was no accident that the nineteenth-century crusade for abolishing black

slavery—with Massachusetts agitators at the forefront—sprang in some degree from the New England conscience with its Puritan roots.

In the Chesapeake region, the expansion of settlement was somewhat random and was usually undertaken by lone-wolf planters on their own initiative, but New England society grew in a more orderly fashion. New towns were legally chartered by the colonial authorities, and the distribution of land was entrusted to the steady hands of sober-minded town fathers, or "proprietors." After receiving a grant of land from the colonial legislature, the proprietors moved themselves and their families to the designated place and laid out their town. It usually consisted of a meetinghouse, which served as both the place of worship and the town hall, surrounded by houses. Also marked out was a village green, where the militia could drill. Each family received several parcels of land, including a woodlot for fuel, a tract suitable for growing crops, and another for pasturing animals.

Towns of more than fifty families were required to provide elementary education, and roughly half of the adults knew how to read and write. As early as 1636, just six years after the colony's founding, the Massachusetts Puritans established Harvard College, today the oldest corporation in America, to train local boys for the ministry. Only in 1693, eighty-six years after staking out Jamestown, did the Virginians establish their first college, William and Mary.

Puritans ran their own churches, and democracy in **Congregational Church** government led logically to democracy in political government. The town meeting, in which the adult males met together and each man voted, was a showcase and a classroom for democracy. New England villagers from the outset gathered regularly in their meetinghouses to elect their officials, appoint schoolmasters, and discuss such mundane matters as road repairs. The town

The Massachusetts School Law of 1647 stated,

❝ It being one chief project of the old deluder, Satan, to keep men from the knowledge of the Scriptures, as in former times by keeping them in an unknown tongue, it is therefore ordered that every township in this jurisdiction, after the Lord has increased them [in] number to fifty householders, shall then forthwith appoint one within their town to teach all such children as shall resort to him to write and read, whose wages shall be paid either by the parents or masters of such children, or by the inhabitants in general. **❞**

meeting, observed Thomas Jefferson, was "the best school of political liberty the world ever saw."

✦ The Half-Way Covenant and the Salem Witch Trials

Yet worries plagued the God-fearing pioneers of these tidy New England settlements. The pressure of a growing population was gradually dispersing the Puritans onto outlying farms, far from the control of church and neighbors. And although the core of Puritan belief still burned brightly, the passage of time was dampening the first generation's flaming religious zeal. About the middle of the seventeenth century, a new form of sermon began to be heard from Puritan pulpits—the **jeremiad**. Taking their cue from the doom-saying Old Testament prophet Jeremiah, earnest preachers scolded parishioners for their waning piety. Especially alarming was the apparent decline in conversions—testimonials by individuals that they had received God's grace and therefore deserved to be admitted to the church as members of the elect.

A Colonial Primer   Religious instruction loomed large in early colonial schools. This textbook taught lessons of social duty and Christian faith, as well as reading and writing.

Library of Congress

Troubled ministers in 1662 announced a new formula for church membership, the **Half-Way Covenant**. This new arrangement modified the "covenant," or the agreement between the church and its adherents, to admit to baptism—but not "full communion"—the children of baptized but not-yet-converted existing members. (On "conversion," see p. 42.) By conferring partial membership rights in the once-exclusive Puritan congregations, the Half-Way Covenant weakened the distinction between the "elect" and others, further diluting the spiritual purity of the original settlers' godly community.

The Half-Way Covenant dramatized the difficulty of maintaining at fever pitch the religious devotion of the founding generation. Jeremiads continued to thunder from the pulpits, but as time went on, the doors of the Puritan churches swung fully open to all comers, whether converted or not. This widening of church membership gradually blurred the distinction between the "elect" and other members of society. In effect, strict religious purity was sacrificed somewhat to the cause of wider religious participation. Interestingly, from this time onward, women, always pillars of the Puritan congregations, came to make up the majority of churchgoers.

Women also played a prominent role in one of New England's most frightening religious episodes. A group of adolescent girls in Salem, Massachusetts, claimed to have been bewitched by certain older women. An hysterical "witch hunt" ensued, leading to the legal lynching in 1692 of twenty individuals, nineteen of whom were hanged and one of whom was pressed to death. Two dogs were also hanged.

Larger-scale witchcraft persecutions were then common in Europe, and several outbreaks had already flared forth in the colonies—often directed at property-owning women. But the reign of horror in Salem grew not only from the superstitions and prejudices of the age but also from the turmoil of the wars with the Indians, as well as the unsettled social and religious conditions of the rapidly evolving Massachusetts village. Most of the accused witches came from families associated with Salem's burgeoning market economy; their accusers came largely from subsistence farming families in Salem's hinterland. The **Salem witch trials** thus reflected the widening social stratification of New England, as well as the fear of many religious traditionalists that the Puritan heritage was being eclipsed by Yankee commercialism.

The witchcraft hysteria eventually ended in 1693 when the governor, alarmed by an accusation against his own wife and supported by the more responsible members of the clergy, prohibited any further trials and pardoned those already convicted. Twenty years later a penitent Massachusetts legislature annulled the "convictions" of the "witches" and made reparations

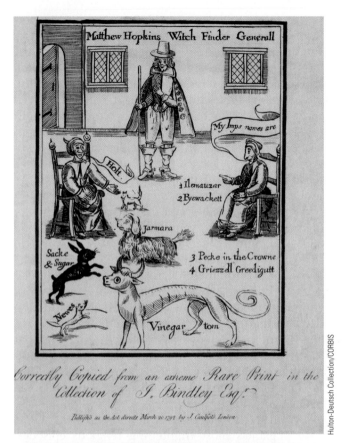

Correctly Copied from an extreme Rare Print in the Collection of J. Bindley Esq.

Published as the Act directs March 26 1792 by J. Caulfield London

Hutton-Deutsch Collection/CORBIS

Matthew Hopkins's Witch Finder   Hopkins was a seventeenth-century English witch-hunter whose techniques included watching suspects to see if diabolical creatures, in the form of common animals, fed on the alleged witch's blood. He also urged that suspected witches be bound hand and foot and tossed in a pond. The innocent, he claimed, would sink (and often drown), while the guilty would float to the surface. His methods brought death to hundreds of women, men, and children in eastern England in the 1640s.

to their heirs. The Salem witchcraft delusion marked an all-time high in the American experience of popular passions run wild. "Witch-hunting" passed into the American vocabulary as a metaphor for the often dangerously irrational urge to find a scapegoat for social resentments.

✴ The New England Way of Life

Oddly enough, the story of New England was largely written by rocks. The heavily glaciated soil was strewn with countless stones, many of which were forced to the surface after a winter freeze. In a sense the Puritans did not possess the soil; it possessed them by shaping their character. Scratching a living from the protesting earth was an early American success story. Back-bending toil

put a premium on industry and penny-pinching frugality, for which New Englanders became famous. Traditionally sharp Yankee traders, some of them palming off wooden nutmegs for real nutmegs, made their mark. Connecticut came in time to be called good-humoredly "the Nutmeg State." Cynics exaggerated when they said that the three stages of progress in New England were "to get on, to get honor, to get honest."

The grudging land also left colonial New England less ethnically mixed than its southern neighbors. Non-English immigrants were less attracted to a site where the soil was so stony—and the sermons so sulfurous.

Climate likewise molded New England, where the summers were often uncomfortably hot and the winters cruelly cold. Many early immigrants complained of the region's extremes of weather. Yet the soil and climate of New England eventually encouraged a diversified economy. Staple products like tobacco did not flourish, as in the South. Black slavery, although employed on a modest scale, could not exist profitably on small farms, especially where the surest crop was stones. No broad, fertile expanses comparable to those in the tidewater South beckoned people inland. The mountains ran fairly close to the shore, and the rivers were generally short and rapid.

And just as the land shaped New Englanders, so they shaped the land. The Native Americans had left an early imprint on the New England earth. They traditionally beat trails through the woods as they migrated seasonally for hunting and fishing. They periodically burned the woodlands to restore leafy first-growth forests that would sustain the deer population. The Indians recognized the right to use the land, but the concept of exclusive, individual *ownership* of the land was alien to them.

The English settlers had a different philosophy. They condemned the Indians for "wasting" the earth by underutilizing its bounty and used this logic to justify their own expropriation of the land from the native inhabitants. Consistent with this outlook, the Europeans felt a virtual duty to "improve" the land by clearing woodlands for pasturage and tillage, building roads and fences, and laying out permanent settlements.

Some of the greatest changes resulted from the introduction of livestock. The English brought pigs, horses, sheep, and cattle from Europe to the settlements. Because the growing herds needed ever more pastureland, the colonists were continually clearing forests. The animals' voracious appetites and heavy hooves compacted the soil, speeding erosion and flooding. In some cases the combined effect of these developments actually may have changed local climates and made some areas even more susceptible to extremes of heat and cold.

Repelled by the rocks, the hardy New Englanders turned instinctively to their fine natural harbors. Hacking timber from their dense forests, they became experts in shipbuilding and commerce. They also ceaselessly exploited the self-perpetuating codfish lode off the coast of Newfoundland—the fishy "gold mines of New England," which have yielded more wealth than all the treasure chests of the Aztecs. During colonial days the wayfarer seldom got far from the sound of the ax and hammer, or the swift rush of the ship down the ways to the sea, or the smell of rotting fish. As a reminder of the importance of fishing, a handsome replica of the "sacred cod" is proudly displayed to this day in the Massachusetts Statehouse in Boston.

The combination of Calvinism, soil, and climate in New England made for energy, purposefulness, sternness, stubbornness, self-reliance, and resourcefulness. Righteous New Englanders prided themselves on being God's chosen people. They long boasted that Boston was "the hub of the universe"—at least in spirit. A famous jingle of later days ran,

> I come from the city of Boston
> The home of the bean and the cod
> Where the Cabots speak only to Lowells
> And the Lowells speak only to God.

New England has had an incalculable impact on the rest of the nation. Ousted by their sterile soil, thousands of New Englanders scattered from Ohio to Oregon and even Hawaii. They sprinkled the land with new communities modeled on the orderly New England town, with its central green and tidy schoolhouse, and its simple town-meeting democracy. "Yankee ingenuity," originally fostered by the flinty fields and comfortless climate of New England, came to be claimed by all Americans as a proud national trait. And the fabled "New England conscience," born of the steadfast Puritan heritage, left a legacy of high idealism in the national character and inspired many later reformers.

✴ The Early Settlers' Days and Ways

The cycles of the seasons and the sun set the schedules of all the earliest American colonists, men as well as women, northerners as well as southerners, blacks as well as whites. The overwhelming majority of colonists were farmers. They planted in the spring, tended their crops in the summer, harvested in the fall, and prepared in the winter to begin the cycle anew. They usually rose at dawn and went to bed at dusk. Chores might be performed after nightfall only if they were "worth the candle," a phrase that has persisted in American speech.

Women, enslaved or free, on southern plantations or northern farms, wove, cooked, cleaned, and cared for children. Men cleared land; fenced, planted, and cropped it; cut firewood; and butchered livestock as needed. Children helped with all these tasks, while picking up such schooling as they could.

Life was humble but comfortable by contemporary standards. Compared to most seventeenth-century Europeans, Americans lived in affluent abundance.

Gift of Newton C. Brainard, The Connecticut Historical Society

Life and Death in Colonial America, by Prudence Punderson Note the artist's initials, "P.P.," on the coffin. This embroidery suggests the stoic resolve of a colonial woman, calmly depicting the inevitable progression of her own life from the cradle to the grave.

Land was relatively cheap, though somewhat less available in the planter-dominated South than elsewhere. In the northern and middle colonies, an acre of virgin soil cost about what American carpenters could earn in one day as wages, which were roughly three times those of their English counterparts.

"Dukes don't emigrate," the saying goes, for if people enjoy wealth and security, they are not likely to risk exposing their lives in the wilderness. Similarly, the very poorest members of a society may not possess even the modest means needed to pull up stakes and seek a fresh start in life. Accordingly, most white migrants to early colonial America came neither from the aristocracy nor from the dregs of European society—with the partial exception of the impoverished indentured servants.

Crude frontier life did not in any case permit the flagrant display of class distinctions, and seventeenth-century society in all the colonies had a certain simple sameness to it, especially in the more egalitarian New England and middle colonies. Yet many settlers, who considered themselves to be of the "better sort," tried to recreate on a modified scale the social structure they had known in the Old World. To some extent they succeeded, though yeasty democratic forces frustrated their full triumph. Resentment against upper-class pretensions helped to spark outbursts like Bacon's Rebellion of 1676 in Virginia and the uprising of Maryland's Protestants toward the end of the seventeenth century. In New York animosity between lordly landholders and aspiring merchants fueled **Leisler's Rebellion**, an ill-starred and bloody insurgence that rocked New York City from 1689 to 1691.

For their part, would-be American blue bloods resented the pretensions of the "meaner sort" and passed laws to try to keep them in their place. Massachusetts in 1651 prohibited poorer folk from "wearing gold or silver lace," and in eighteenth-century Virginia a tailor was fined and jailed for arranging to race his horse—"a sport only for gentlemen." But these efforts to reproduce the finely stratified societies of Europe proved feeble in the early American wilderness, where equality and democracy found fertile soil—at least for white people.

Chapter Review

KEY TERMS

indentured servants (63)

headright system (63)

Bacon's Rebellion (64)

Royal African Company (68)

middle passage (68)

slave codes (69)

Congregational Church (72)

jeremiad (73)

Half-Way Covenant (73)

Salem witch trials (73)

Leisler's Rebellion (76)

PEOPLE TO KNOW

William Berkeley

Nathaniel Bacon

CHRONOLOGY

1619	First Africans arrive in Virginia
1625	Population of English colonies in America about 2,000
1636	Harvard College founded
1662	Half-Way Covenant for Congregational Church membership established
1670	Virginia assembly disfranchises landless freemen
1676	Bacon's Rebellion in Virginia
1680s	Mass expansion of slavery in colonies
1689–1691	Leisler's Rebellion in New York
1692	Salem witch trials in Massachusetts
1693	College of William and Mary founded
1698	Royal African Company slave trade monopoly ended
1700	Population of English colonies in America about 250,000

TO LEARN MORE

Virginia DeJohn Anderson, *Creatures of Empire: How Domestic Animals Transformed America* (2004)

Bernard Bailyn, *The Barbarous Years* (2012)

Ira Berlin, *Many Thousands Gone: The First Two Centuries of Slavery in North America* (1998)

William Cronon, *Changes in the Land* (1983)

John Demos, *Entertaining Satan* (1982)

David Hackett Fischer, *Albion's Seed: Four British Folkways in America* (1989)

Patrick Griffin, *The People with No Name: Ireland's Ulster Scots, America's Scots Irish, and the Creation of a British Atlantic World, 1689–1764* (2001)

Mary Beth Norton, *In the Devil's Snare: The Salem Witchcraft Crisis of 1692* (2002)

Daniel Blake Smith, *Inside the Great House: Planter Family Life in Eighteenth-Century Chesapeake Society* (1980)

Laurel T. Ulrich, *Good Wives: Image and Reality in the Lives of Women in Northern New England, 1650–1750* (1982)

Daniel Vickers, *Farmers and Fishermen: Two Centuries of Work in Essex County, Massachusetts, 1630–1850* (1994)

A complete, annotated bibliography for this chapter—along with brief descriptions of the People to Know—may be found on the *American Pageant* website. The key terms are defined in the glossary at the end of the text.

Chapter 5

Colonial Society on the Eve of Revolution

1700–1775

Driven from every other corner of the earth, freedom of thought and the right of private judgment in matters of conscience direct their course to this happy country as their last asylum.

SAMUEL ADAMS, 1776

The common term thirteen original colonies is misleading. Britain ruled thirty-two colonies in North America by 1775, including Canada, the Floridas, and various Caribbean islands. But only thirteen of them unfurled the standard of rebellion. A few of the nonrebels, such as Canada and Jamaica, were larger, wealthier, or more populous than some of the revolting thirteen. Why, then, did some British colonies eventually strike for their independence, while others did not? Part of the answer is to be found in the distinctive social, economic, and political structures of the thirteen Atlantic seaboard colonies—and in the halting, gradual appearance of a recognizably *American* way of life.

✸ Conquest by the Cradle

Among the distinguishing characteristics that the eventually rebellious settlements shared was lusty population growth. In 1700 they contained fewer than 300,000 souls, about 20,000 of whom were black. By 1775, 2.5 million people inhabited the thirteen colonies, of whom about half a million were black. White immigrants made up nearly 400,000 of the increased number, and black "forced immigrants" accounted for almost as many again. But most of the spurt stemmed from the remarkable natural fertility of all Americans, white and black. To the amazement and dismay of Europeans, the colonists were doubling their numbers every twenty-five years. Unfriendly Dr. Samuel Johnson, back in England, growled that

the Americans were multiplying like their own rattlesnakes. They were also a youthful people, whose average age in 1775 was about sixteen.

This population boom had political consequences. In 1700 there were twenty English subjects for each American colonist. By 1775 the English advantage in numbers had fallen to three to one—setting the stage for a momentous shift in the balance of power between the colonies and Britain.

The bulk of the population was cooped up east of the Alleghenies, although by 1775 a vanguard of pioneers had trickled into the stump-studded clearings of Tennessee and Kentucky. The most populous colonies in 1775 were Virginia, Massachusetts, Pennsylvania, North Carolina, and Maryland—in that order. Only four communities could properly be called cities: Philadelphia, including suburbs, was first with about 34,000 residents, trailed by New York, Boston, and Charleston. About 90 percent of the people lived in rural areas.

✸ A Mingling of the Races

Colonial America was a melting pot and had been from the outset. The population, although basically English in stock and language, was picturesquely mottled with numerous foreign groups (see Map 5.1).

Heavy-accented Germans constituted about 6 percent of the total population, or 150,000, by 1775. Fleeing religious persecution, economic oppression, and the ravages of war, they had flocked to America in the early 1700s and had settled chiefly in Pennsylvania. They belonged to several different Protestant sects—primarily Lutheran—and thus further enhanced the religious diversity of the colony. Known popularly but erroneously as the Pennsylvania Dutch (a corruption of the German word *Deutsch*, for "German"), they totaled about one-third of the colony's population. In parts of Philadelphia, the street signs were painted in both German and English.

These German newcomers moved into the backcountry of Pennsylvania, where their splendid stone barns gave—and still give—mute evidence of industry and prosperity. Not having been brought up English, they had no deep-rooted loyalty to the British crown, and they clung tenaciously to their German language and customs.

The Scots-Irish, who in 1775 numbered around 175,000, or 7 percent of the population, were an important non-English group, although they spoke English. They were not Irish at all, but turbulent Scots Lowlanders. Over many decades, they had been transplanted to northern Ireland, where they had not prospered. The Irish Catholics already there, hating Scottish Presbyterianism, resented the intruders and still do—the source of many of the modern-day "troubles" in the Northern Ireland province of Ulster. The economic life of the Scots-Irish was severely hampered, especially when the English government placed burdensome restrictions on their production of linens and woolens.

Early in the 1700s, tens of thousands of embittered Scots-Irish finally abandoned Ireland and came to America, chiefly to tolerant and deep-soiled Pennsylvania. Finding the best acres already taken by Germans and Quakers, they pushed out onto the frontier, making them among the first settlers of the American West. There many of them illegally but defiantly squatted on unoccupied lands and quarreled with both Indian and white owners. When the westward-flowing Scots-Irish tide lapped up against the Allegheny barrier, it was deflected southward into the backcountry of Maryland, down Virginia's Shenandoah Valley, and into the western Carolinas. Their often rickety settlements bore the marks of Scots-Irish restlessness. Whereas their German neighbors typically erected sturdy homes and cleared their fields meticulously, the Scots-Irish satisfied themselves with floorless, flimsy log cabins. As befitted an uprooted, questing people, they chopped down trees, planted crops between the stumps, exhausted the soil swiftly, and moved on.

Already experienced colonizers and agitators in Ireland, the Scots-Irish proved to be superb frontiersmen, though their readiness to visit violence on the Indians repeatedly inflamed the western districts. By the mid-eighteenth century, a chain of Scots-Irish

MAP 5.1 Immigrant Groups in 1775 America was already a nation of diverse nationalities in the colonial period. This map shows the great variety of immigrant groups, especially in Pennsylvania and New York. It also illustrates the tendency of later arrivals, particularly the Scots-Irish, to push into the backcountry. © 2016 Cengage Learning

settlements lay scattered along the "great wagon road," which hugged the eastern Appalachian foothills from Pennsylvania to Georgia.

It was said, somewhat unfairly, that the Scots-Irish kept the Sabbath—and all else they could lay

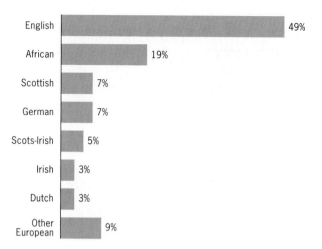

FIGURE 5.1 Ethnic and Racial Composition of the American People, 1790

Based on surnames. *Adapted from the American Council of Learned Societies, "Report of Committee on Linguistic and National Stocks in the Population of the United States," 1932. Percentages total more than 100 percent due to rounding.*) © 2016 Cengage Learning

their hands on. Pugnacious, lawless, and individual-istic, they brought with them the Scottish secrets of whiskey distilling and dotted the Appalachian hills and hollows with their stills. They cherished no love for the British government that had uprooted them and still lorded over them—or for any other govern-ment, it seemed. They led the armed march of the **Paxton Boys** on Philadelphia in 1764, protesting the Quaker oligarchy's lenient policy toward the Indi-ans, and a few years later spearheaded the **Regulator movement** in North Carolina, a small but nasty insurrection against eastern domination of the colo-ny's affairs. Many of these hotheads—including the young Andrew Jackson—eventually joined the embat-tled American revolutionaries. All told, about a dozen future presidents were of Scots-Irish descent.

The young Frenchman Michel-Guillaume Jean de Crèvecoeur (1735–1813) wrote of the diverse population in about 1770,

❝They are a mixture of English, Scotch, Irish, French, Dutch, Germans, and Swedes. From this promiscuous breed, that race now called Americans have arisen.... I could point out to you a family whose grandfather was an Englishman, whose wife was Dutch, whose son married a French woman, and whose present four sons have now four wives of different nations.**❞**

Approximately 5 percent of the multicolored colo-nial population consisted of other European groups. These embraced French Huguenots, Welsh, Dutch, Swedes, Jews, Irish, Swiss, and Scots Highlanders—as distinguished from the Scots-Irish. Except for the Scots Highlanders, such hodgepodge elements felt little loyalty to the British crown. By far the largest single non-English group was African, accounting for nearly 20 percent of the colonial population in 1775 and heavily concentrated in the South.

The population of the thirteen colonies, though mainly Anglo-Saxon, was perhaps the most mixed to be found anywhere in the world (see Figure 5.1). The South, holding about 90 percent of the slaves, already displayed its historic black-and-white racial composi-tion. New England, mostly staked out by the original Puritan migrants, showed the least ethnic diversity. The middle colonies, especially Pennsylvania, received the bulk of later white immigrants and boasted an astonishing variety of peoples. Outside of New Eng-land, about one-half the population was non-English in 1775. Of the fifty-six signers of the Declaration of Independence in 1776, eighteen were non-English and eight had not been born in the colonies.

As these various immigrant groups mingled and intermarried, they laid the foundations for a new mul-ticultural American national identity unlike anything known in Europe. The French settler Michel-Guillaume Jean de Crèvecoeur saw in America in the 1770s a "strange mixture of blood, which you will find in no other country," and he posed his classic question, "What then is the American, this new man?" Nor were white colonists alone in creating new societies out of diverse ethnic groups. The African slave trade long had mixed peoples from many different tribal backgrounds, giving birth to an African *American* community far more variegated in its cultural origins than anything to be found in Africa itself. Similarly, in the New England "praying towns," where Indians were gathered to be Christianized, and in Great Lakes villages such as Detroit, home to dozens of different displaced indigenous peoples, polyglot Native Ameri-can communities emerged, blurring the boundaries of individual tribal identities.

✦ Africans in America

Slavery exploded in the North American colonies dur-ing the eighteenth century. Life for slaves was every-where terrible, though not everywhere the same. In the deepest South, slave life was especially severe. The climate was hostile to health, and the labor was life-draining. The widely scattered South Carolina rice and indigo plantations were lonely hells on earth where gangs of mostly male Africans toiled and perished.

Only fresh imports could sustain the slave population under these loathsome conditions.

Blacks in the tobacco-growing Chesapeake region had a somewhat easier lot. Tobacco was a less physically demanding crop than those of the deeper South, and tobacco plantations were larger and closer to one another than rice plantations. The size and proximity of these tobacco farms permitted the slaves more frequent contact with friends and relatives. By about 1720 the proportion of females in the Chesapeake slave population had begun to rise, making family life possible. The captive black population of the Chesapeake area soon began to grow through its own fertility—making it one of the few slave societies in history to perpetuate itself by its own natural reproduction. From this point forward, slave imports to the Chesapeake from the West Indies and Africa dropped significantly, while the deeper South remained heavily dependent on the continuing transatlantic slave trade.

Slavery in the colonies north of the Chesapeake, though smaller in overall magnitude, grew as well. By the eve of the Revolutionary War, the northern colonies counted some forty-eight thousand slaves. Many of these men, women, and children toiled in cities, often for artisans. But many labored like their southern brethren in agricultural gangs in New York's Hudson River valley or in northern New Jersey.

As the ratio of native-born blacks to imported Africans grew during the 1700s, a distinctive African American culture began to flourish throughout the colonies that was a mixture of African and American elements of speech, religion, and folkways (see "Makers of America: From African to African American," pp. 82–83). On the sea islands off South Carolina's coast, blacks evolved a unique language, *Gullah* (probably a corruption of *Angola*, the African region from which many of them had come), that blended English with several African languages, including Yoruba, Igbo, and Hausa. Through it many African words have passed into American speech—such as *goober* (peanut), *gumbo* (okra), and *voodoo* (witchcraft). The ringshout, a West African religious dance performed by shuffling in a circle while answering a preacher's shouts, was brought to colonial America by Africans and eventually contributed to the development of jazz. The banjo and the bongo drum were other African contributions to American culture.

Enslaved Africans also helped mightily to build the country with their labor. A few became skilled artisans—carpenters, bricklayers, and tanners. But chiefly they performed the sweaty toil of clearing swamps, grubbing out trees, and doing other menial tasks. Condemned to life under the lash, slaves naturally pined for freedom. The **New York slave revolt** that erupted in 1712 cost the lives of nine whites and

caused the execution of twenty-one blacks, some of them burned at the stake over a slow fire. A **South Carolina slave revolt** erupted in 1739 when more than fifty resentful blacks along the **Stono River** tried to march to Spanish Florida, only to be stopped by the local militia. But in the end, enslaved Africans in the South proved to be a more tightly controlled labor force than the white indentured servants they gradually replaced. No slave uprising in American history matched the scale of Bacon's Rebellion in 1676 (see "Frustrated Freemen and Bacon's Rebellion" in Chapter 4, p. 64).

Contending Voices
Race and Slavery

Samuel Sewall (1652–1730), a Massachusetts judge and one of the magistrates at the Salem witch trials, was among the earliest critics of slavery in the colonies. In 1700 he advised:

"And seeing GOD hath said, He that stealeth a man and selleth him…he shall surely be put to death.…What louder cry can there be made of the celebrated warning, Caveat Emptor!…It would conduce more to the welfare of the province, to have white servants for a term of years, than to have slaves for life. Few can endure to hear of a Negro's being made free; and…there is such a disparity in their conditions, color & hair, that they can never embody with us…and grow up into orderly families, to the peopling of the land.**"**

Meanwhile, colonial legislatures were beginning to define the legal status of slavery. The Virginia slave code of 1705 declared that

"if any [runaway] slave resist his master…and shall happen to be killed [during his punishment]…the master…shall be free and acquit[ted] of all punishment…as if such accident had never happened…baptism of slaves doth not exempt them from bondage…whatsoever English, or other white man or woman, being free, shall intermarry with a negro or mulatto man or woman, bond or free, shall, by judgment of the county court, be committed to prison.**"**

What attitudes about race were shared by pro- and antislavery advocates alike?

Dragged in chains from West African shores, the first African Americans struggled to preserve their diverse heritages from the ravages of slavery. Their children, the first generation of American-born slaves, melded these various African traditions—Guinean, Igbo, Yoruba, Angolan—into a distinctive African American culture. Their achievement sustained them during the cruelties of enslavement and has endured to enrich American life to this day.

With the arrival of the first Africans in the seventeenth century, a cornucopia of African traditions poured into the New World: handicrafts and skills in numerous trades; a plethora of languages, styles of music, and cuisines; even rice-planting techniques that conquered the inhospitable soil of South Carolina. It was North America's rice paddies, tilled by experienced West Africans, that introduced rice into the English diet and furnished so many English tables with the sticky staple.

These first American slaves were mostly males. Upon arrival they were sent off to small isolated farms, where social contact with other Africans, especially women, was an unheard-of luxury. Yet their legal status was at first uncertain. A few slaves were able to buy their freedom in the seventeenth century. One,

Anthony Johnson of Northampton County, Virginia, actually became a slaveholder himself.

But by the beginning of the eighteenth century, a settled slave society was emerging in the southern colonies. Laws tightened; slave traders stepped up their deliveries of human cargo; large plantations formed. Most significantly, a new generation of American-born slaves joined their forebears at labor in the fields. By 1740 large groups of slaves lived together on sprawling plantations, the American-born outnumbered the African-born, and importations from African slowed.

Forging a common culture and finding a psychological weapon with which to resist their masters and preserve their dignity were daunting challenges for American-born slaves. Plantation life was beastly, an endless cycle of miserable toil in the field or foundry from sunup to sundown. Enslaved females were forced to perform double duty. After a day's backbreaking work, women were expected to sit up for hours spinning, weaving, or sewing to clothe themselves and their families. Enslaved women also lived in constant fear of sexual exploitation by predatory masters.

Yet eventually a vibrant slave culture began to flower. And precisely because of the diversity of African peoples represented in America, the culture

(above) Africans Destined for Slavery   This engraving from 1830 is an example of antislavery propaganda in the pre-Civil War era. It shows hapless Africans being brought ashore in America under the whips of slave traders and, ironically, under the figurative shadow of the national Capitol.

(right) Advertisements for Slave Sales in Charleston, South Carolina, 1753   Charleston had the largest slave market in the colonies.

Yarrow Mamout, by Charles Willson Peale, 1819 When Peale painted this portrait, Mamout was over one hundred years old. A devout Muslim brought to Maryland as a slave, he eventually bought his freedom and settled in Georgetown.

The Emergence of an African American Culture In this scene from the mid-nineteenth century, African Americans play musical instruments of European derivation, like the fiddle, as well as instruments of African origin, like the bones and banjo—a vivid illustration of the blending of the two cultures in the crucible of the New World.

that emerged was a uniquely New World creation. It derived from no single African model and incorporated many Western elements, though often with significant modifications.

Slave religion illustrates this pattern. Cut off from their native African religions, most slaves became Christians but fused elements of African and Western traditions and drew their own conclusions from Scripture. White Christians might point to Christ's teachings of humility and obedience to encourage slaves to "stay in their place," but black Christians emphasized God's role in freeing the Hebrews from slavery and saw Jesus as the Messiah who would deliver them from bondage. They also often retained an African definition of heaven as a place where they would be reunited with their ancestors.

At their Sunday and evening-time prayer meetings, slaves also patched African remnants onto conventional Christian ritual. Black Methodists, for example, ingeniously evaded the traditional Methodist ban on dancing as sinful: three or four people would stand still in a ring, clapping hands and beating time

with their feet (but never crossing their legs, thus not officially "dancing"), while others walked around the ring, singing in unison. This "ringshout" derived from African practices; modern American dances, including the Charleston, in turn derived from this African American hybrid.

Christian slaves also often used outwardly religious songs as encoded messages about escape or rebellion. "Good News, the Chariot's Comin'" might sound like an innocent hymn about divine deliverance, but it could also announce the arrival of a guide to lead fugitives safely to the North. Similarly, "Wade in the Water" taught fleeing slaves one way of covering their trail. The "Negro spirituals" that took shape as a distinctive form of American music thus had their origins in *both* Christianity and slavery.

Indeed much American music was born in the slave quarters from African importations. Jazz, with its meandering improvisations and complex syncopations and rhythms, constitutes the most famous example. But this rich cultural harvest came at the cost of generations of human agony.

✦ The Structure of Colonial Society

In comparison to contemporary Europe, eighteenth-century America seemed like a shining land of equality and opportunity—with the notorious exception of slavery. No titled nobility dominated society from on high, and no pauperized underclass threatened it from below. Most white Americans, and even a handful of free blacks, were small farmers. Clad in buckskin breeches, they owned modest holdings and tilled them with their own hands and horses. The cities contained a small class of skilled artisans, with their well-greased leather aprons, as well as shopkeepers, tradespeople, and some unskilled day laborers. The most remarkable feature of the social ladder was its openness. An ambitious colonist, even a former indentured servant, could rise from a lower rung to a higher one, a rare step in old England.

Yet in contrast with seventeenth-century America, colonial society on the eve of the Revolution was beginning to show signs of stratification and barriers to mobility that raised worries about the "Europeanization" of America. The gods of war contributed to these developments. The armed conflicts of the 1690s and early 1700s had allowed a number of merchant princes in the New England and middle colonies to lay the foundations of their fortunes with profits made as military suppliers. Roosting regally atop the social ladder, these elites now feathered their nests more finely, sporting imported clothing and dining at tables laid with English china and gleaming silverware. Prominent individuals came to be seated in churches and schools according to their social rank. By midcentury the richest 10 percent of Bostonians and Philadelphians owned nearly two-thirds of the taxable wealth in their cities.

The plague of war also created a class of widows and orphans, who became dependent for their survival on charity. Both Philadelphia and New York built almshouses in the 1730s to care for the destitute. Yet the numbers of poor people remained tiny compared to the numbers in England, where about a third of the population lived in impoverished squalor.

In the New England countryside, the descendants of the original settlers faced more limited prospects than had their pioneering forebears. As the supply of unclaimed soil dwindled and families grew, existing landholdings were repeatedly subdivided. The average size of farms shrank drastically. Younger sons, as well as daughters, were forced to hire out as wage laborers, or eventually to seek virgin tracts of land beyond the Alleghenies. By 1750 Boston contained a large number of homeless poor, who were supported by public charity and compelled to wear a large red "P" on their clothing.

In the South the power of the great planters continued to be bolstered by their disproportionate

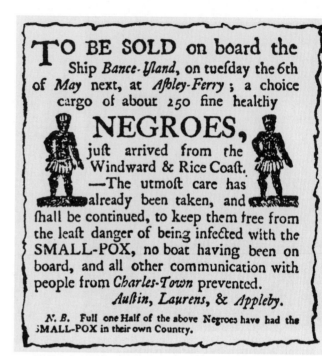

A South Carolina Advertisement for Slaves in the 1760s   Note the reference to these slaves' origin on West Africa's "Rice Coast," a reminder of South Carolina's reliance on African skill and labor for rice cultivation. Note, too, that half the slaves were said to have survived smallpox and thus acquired immunity from further infection—and that care had been taken to insulate the others from a smallpox epidemic apparently then raging in Charleston.

Schomburg Center, NYPL/Art Resource, NY

ownership of slaves. The riches created by the growing slave population in the eighteenth century were not distributed evenly among the whites. Wealth was concentrated in the hands of the largest slaveowners, widening the gap between the prosperous gentry and the "poor whites," who were more and more likely to become tenant farmers.

In all the colonies, the ranks of the lower classes were further swelled by the continuing stream of indentured servants, many of whom ultimately achieved prosperity and prestige. Two became signers of the Declaration of Independence.

Far less fortunate than the voluntary indentured servants were the paupers and convicts involuntarily shipped to America. Altogether, about fifty thousand "jayle birds" were dumped on the colonies by the London authorities. This riffraff crowd—including robbers, rapists, and murderers—was generally sullen and undesirable and not bubbling over with goodwill for the king's government. But many convicts were the unfortunate victims of circumstances and of a viciously unfair English penal code that included about two hundred capital crimes. Some of the deportees, in fact, came to be highly respectable citizens.

Least fortunate of all, of course, were the enslaved blacks. They enjoyed no equality with whites and dared not even dream of ascending, or even approaching, the ladder of opportunity. Oppressed and downtrodden, the slaves were America's closest approximation to Europe's volatile lower classes, and fears of black rebellion plagued the white colonists. Some colonial legislatures, notably South Carolina's in 1760, sensed the dangers present in a heavy concentration of resentful slaves and attempted to restrict or halt their importation. But the British authorities, seeking to preserve the supply of cheap labor for the colonies, especially the West Indies sugar plantations, repeatedly vetoed all efforts to stem the transatlantic traffic in slaves. Many North American colonists condemned these vetoes as morally callous, although New England slave traders benefited handsomely from the British policy. The cruel complexity of the slavery issue was further revealed when Thomas Jefferson, himself a slaveholder, assailed the British vetoes in an early draft of the Declaration of Independence but was forced to withdraw the proposed clause by a torrent of protest from southern slavemasters.

✸ Clerics, Physicians, and Jurists

Most honored of the professions was the Christian ministry. In 1775 the clergy wielded less influence than in the early days of Massachusetts, when piety had burned more warmly. But they still occupied a position of high prestige.

Most physicians, on the other hand, were poorly trained and not highly esteemed. Not until 1765 was the first medical school established, although European centers attracted some students. Aspiring young doctors served for a while as apprentices to older practitioners and were then turned loose on their "victims." Bleeding was a favorite and frequently fatal remedy; when the physician was not available, a barber was often summoned.

Epidemics were a constant nightmare. Especially dreaded was smallpox, which afflicted one out of five persons, including the heavily pockmarked George Washington. A crude form of inoculation was introduced in 1721, despite the objections of many physicians and some of the clergy, who opposed tampering with the will of God. Powdered dried toad was a favorite prescription for smallpox. Diphtheria was also a deadly killer, especially of young people. One epidemic in the 1730s took the lives of thousands. This grim reminder of their mortality may have helped to prepare many colonists in their hearts and minds for the religious revival that was soon to sweep them up.

At first the law profession was not favorably regarded. In this pioneering society, which required much honest manual labor, the parties to a dispute often presented their own cases in court. Lawyers were commonly regarded as noisy windbags or troublemaking rogues; an early Connecticut law classed them with drunkards and brothel keepers. When future president John Adams was a young law student, the father of his wife-to-be frowned upon him as a suitor because of his chosen profession.

✸ Workaday America

Agriculture was the leading industry, involving about 90 percent of the people. Tobacco continued to be the staple crop in Maryland and Virginia, though wheat cultivation also spread through the Chesapeake, often on lands depleted by the overgrowth of tobacco. The fertile middle ("bread") colonies produced large quantities of grain, and by 1759 New York alone was exporting eighty thousand barrels of flour a year. Seemingly the farmer had only to tickle the soil with a hoe, and it would laugh with a harvest. Overall, Americans probably enjoyed a higher standard of living than the masses of any country in history up to that time.

Fishing (including whaling), though ranking far below agriculture, was rewarding. Pursued in all the American colonies, this harvesting of the sea was a major industry in New England, which exported smelly shiploads of dried cod to the Catholic countries of Europe. The fishing fleet also stimulated shipbuilding and served as a nursery for the seamen who manned the navy and merchant marine. A bustling commerce, both coastwise and overseas, enriched all the colonies, especially the New England group, New York, and Pennsylvania (see Map 5.2). Commercial ventures and land speculation, in the absence of later get-rich-quick schemes, were the surest avenues to speedy wealth. Yankee seamen were famous in many climes not only as skilled mariners but also

Cotton Mather (1663–1728), Puritan clergyman and avid scientist, became frustrated with Boston residents' opposition to inoculation during the Boston smallpox epidemic of 1721. He wrote to a doctor friend,

❝Never till now was that rule contested, of two evils, choose the least.... I would ask them whether it be not a most criminal ingratitude unto the God of Health, when He has acquainted us with a most invaluable method of the saving of our lives from so great a death, to treat with neglect and contempt, and multiply abuses on them who thankfully and in a spirit of obedience to Him, embrace His blessings?**❞**

Codfishing in Newfoundland, 1738 Early European explorers were awed by the enormous schools of cod on the Grand Banks off Newfoundland. Fish were so numerous that they sometimes impeded the progress of sailing vessels. By the eighteenth century, New Englanders were aggressively exploiting the apparently limitless Grand Banks fishery, drying and salting huge catches for export to Europe and the West Indies. Some three centuries later, the accumulated predation of generations has depleted the once-fabulous Grand Banks cod population.

as tightfisted traders. They provisioned the Caribbean sugar islands with food and forest products. They also hauled Spanish and Portuguese gold, wine, and oranges to London, to be exchanged for industrial goods, which were then sold for a juicy profit in America.

The so-called **triangular trade** was infamously profitable, though small in relation to total colonial commerce (see Map 5.3). A skipper, for example, would leave a New England port with a cargo of rum and sail to the Gold Coast of Africa. Bartering the fiery liquor with African chiefs for captured African slaves, he would proceed to the West Indies with his sobbing and suffocating cargo sardined below deck. There he would exchange the survivors for molasses, which he would then carry to New England, where it would be distilled into rum. He would then repeat the trip, making a handsome profit on each leg of the triangle.

Manufacturing in the colonies was of only secondary importance, although there was a surprising variety of small enterprises. As a rule, workers could get ahead faster in soil-rich America by tilling the land. Huge quantities of "kill devil" rum were distilled in Rhode Island and Massachusetts, and even some of the "elect of the Lord" developed an overfondness for it. Handsome beaver hats were manufactured in

MAP 5.2 The Colonial Economy By the eighteenth century, the various colonial regions had distinct economic identities. The northern colonies grew grain and raised cattle, harvested timber and fish, and built ships. The Chesapeake colonies and North Carolina were still heavily dependent on tobacco, whereas the southernmost colonies grew mostly rice and indigo. Cotton, so important to the southern economy in the nineteenth century, had not yet emerged as a major crop. © 2016 Cengage Learning

quantity, despite British restrictions. Smoking iron forges, including Pennsylvania's Valley Forge, likewise dotted the land and in fact were more numerous in 1775, though generally smaller, than those of England. In addition, household manufacturing, including spinning and weaving by women, added up to an impressive output. As in all pioneering countries, strong-backed laborers and skilled craftspeople were scarce and highly prized. In early Virginia a carpenter who had committed a murder was freed because his woodworking skills were needed.

Lumbering was perhaps the most important single manufacturing activity. Countless cartloads of fresh-felled timber were consumed by shipbuilders, at first chiefly in New England and then elsewhere in the colonies. By 1770 about four hundred vessels of assorted sizes were splashing down the ways each year, and about one-third of the British merchant marine was American-built.

Colonial naval stores—such as tar, pitch, rosin, and turpentine—were highly valued, for Britain was anxious to gain and retain a mastery of the seas. London offered generous bounties to stimulate production of these items; otherwise Britain would have had to turn to the uncertain and possibly hostile Baltic areas. Towering trees, ideal as masts for His Majesty's

navy, were marked with the king's broad arrow for future use. The luckless colonist who was caught cutting down this reserved timber was subject to a fine. Even though there were countless unreserved trees and the blazed ones were being saved for the common defense, this shackle on free enterprise engendered considerable bitterness.

Americans held an important flank of a thriving, many-sided Atlantic economy by the dawn of the eighteenth century. Yet strains appeared in this complex network as early as the 1730s. While the fast-breeding Americans demanded more and more British products, the slow-growing British population early reached the saturation point for absorbing imports from America. This trade imbalance raised a question: how could the colonists sell the goods to make the money to buy what they wanted in Britain? The answer was obvious: by seeking foreign (non-British) markets.

By the eve of the Revolution, the bulk of Chesapeake tobacco was filling pipes in France and in other

MAP 5.3 Colonial Trade Patterns, ca. 1770 Future president John Adams noted about this time that "the commerce of the West Indies is a part of the American system of commerce. They can neither do without us, nor we without them. The Creator has placed us upon the globe in such a situation that we have occasion for each other." © 2016 Cengage Learning

European countries, though it passed through the hands of British re-exporters, who took a slice of the profits for themselves. More important was the trade with the West Indies, especially the French islands. West Indian purchases of North American timber and foodstuffs provided the crucial cash for the colonists to continue to make their own purchases from Britain. But in 1733, bowing to pressure from influential *British* West Indian planters, Parliament passed the **Molasses Act**, aimed at squelching North American trade with the *French* West Indies. If successful, this scheme would have struck a crippling blow to American international trade and to the colonists' standard of living. American merchants responded to the act by bribing and smuggling their way around the law. Thus was foreshadowed the impending imperial crisis, when headstrong Americans would revolt rather than submit to the dictates of the far-off Parliament, apparently bent on destroying their very livelihood.

✶ Horsepower and Sailpower

All sprawling and sparsely populated pioneer communities are cursed with oppressive problems of transportation. America, with a scarcity of both money and workers, was no exception.

Not until the 1700s did roads connect even the major cities, and these dirt thoroughfares were treacherously deficient. A wayfarer could have rumbled along more rapidly over the Roman highways in the days of Julius Caesar, nearly two thousand years earlier. It took young Benjamin Franklin nine long, rain-drenched days in 1720 to journey from Boston to Philadelphia, traveling by sailing sloop, rowboat, and foot. News of the Declaration of Independence in 1776 reached Charleston from Philadelphia twenty-nine days after the Fourth of July.

Roads were often clouds of dust in the summer and quagmires of mud in the winter. Stagecoach travelers braved such additional dangers as tree-strewn roads, rickety bridges, carriage overturns, and runaway horses. A traveler venturesome enough to journey from Philadelphia to New York, for example, would not think it amiss to make a will and pray with the family before departing.

Where man-made roads were wretched, heavy reliance was placed on God-grooved waterways. Population tended to cluster along the banks of navigable rivers. There was also much coastwise traffic, and although it was slow and undependable, it was relatively cheap and pleasant, at least in fair weather.

Taverns sprang up along the main routes of travel, as well as in the cities. Their attractions customarily included such amusements as bowling alleys, pool tables, bars, and gambling equipment. Before a

Collection of Morgan B. Brainard; Gift of Mrs. Morgan Brainard, The Connecticut Historical Society

Sign of the Pine Tree Inn, 1768 Inns like Joseph Read III's in Lisbon, Connecticut, not only provided food, drink, shelter, and entertainment for colonial Americans but also were raucous arenas for debating political issues. This sign, with its circular yellow orb (sun) over a pine tree, may have been intended as a veiled reference to the Sons of Liberty, an extralegal resistance organization that had adopted as its symbol the Liberty Tree. The date of 1768 coincided with the British enactment of the Townshend Acts, which ignited a new wave of colonial resistance to British rule.

cheerful, roaring log fire, all social classes would mingle, including the village loafers and drunks. The tavern was yet another cradle of democracy.

TABLE 5.1 Established (Tax-Supported) Churches in the Colonies, 1775*

Colonies	Churches	Year Disestablished
Massachusetts (incl. Maine)	Congregational	1833
Connecticut		1818
New Hampshire		1819
New York	Anglican (in New York City and three neighboring counties)	1777
Maryland	Anglican	1777
Virginia		1786
North Carolina		1776
South Carolina		1778
Georgia		1777
Rhode Island	None	
New Jersey		
Delaware		
Pennsylvania		

*Note the persistence of the Congregational establishment in New England.

TABLE 5.2 Estimated Religious Census, 1775

Name	Number	Chief Locale
Congregationalists	575,000	New England
Anglicans	500,000	N.Y., South
Presbyterians	410,000	Frontier
German churches (incl. Lutheran)	200,000	Pa.
Dutch Reformed	75,000	N.Y., N.J.
Quakers	40,000	Pa., N.J., Del.
Baptists	25,000	R.I., Pa., N.J., Del.
Roman Catholics	25,000	Md., Pa.
Methodists	5,000	Scattered
Jews	2,000	N.Y., R.I.
EST. TOTAL MEMBERSHIP	1,857,000	
EST. TOTAL POPULATION	2,493,000	
PERCENTAGE CHURCH MEMBERS	74%	

Gossips also gathered at the taverns, which were clearinghouses of information, misinformation, and rumor—frequently stimulated by alcoholic refreshment and impassioned political talk. A successful politician, like the wire-pulling Samuel Adams, was often a man who had a large alehouse fraternity in places like Boston's Green Dragon Tavern. Taverns were important in crystallizing public opinion and proved to be hotbeds of agitation as the revolutionary movement gathered momentum.

An intercolonial postal system was established by the mid-1700s, although private couriers remained. Some mail was handled on credit. Service was slow and infrequent, and secrecy was problematic. Mail carriers, serving long routes, would sometimes pass the time by reading the letters entrusted to their care.

Dominant Denominations

Two "established," or tax-supported, churches were conspicuous in 1775 (see Table 5.1): the Anglican and the Congregational. A considerable segment of the population, surprisingly enough, did not worship in any church. And in those colonies that maintained an "established" religion, only a minority of the people belonged to it (see Table 5.2).

The Church of England, whose members were commonly called Anglicans, became the official faith in Georgia, North and South Carolina, Virginia, Maryland, and a part of New York. Established also in England, it served in America as a major prop of kingly authority. British officials naturally made vigorous attempts to impose it on additional colonies, but they ran into a stone wall of opposition.

In America the Anglican Church fell distressingly short of its promise. Secure and self-satisfied, like its parent in England, it clung to a faith that was less fierce and more worldly than the religion of Puritanical New England. Sermons were shorter; hell was less scorching; and amusements, like Virginia fox hunting, were less scorned. So dismal was the reputation of the Anglican clergy in seventeenth-century Virginia that the College of William and Mary was founded in 1693 to train a better class of clerics.

The influential Congregational Church, which had grown out of the Puritan Church, was formally established in all the New England colonies, except independent-minded Rhode Island. At first Massachusetts taxed all residents to support Congregationalism but later relented and exempted members of other well-known denominations. Presbyterianism, though closely associated with Congregationalism, was never made official in any colonies.

Ministers of the gospel, turning from the Bible to this sinful world, increasingly grappled with burning

Benjamin Franklin's (1706–1790) Poor Richard's Almanack contained such thoughts on religion as these:

"A good example is the best sermon."

"Many have quarreled about religion that never practiced it."

"Serving God is doing good to man, but praying is thought an easier service, and therefore more generally chosen."

"How many observe Christ's birthday; how few his precepts! O! 'tis easier to keep holidays than commandments."

political issues. As the early rumblings of revolution against the British crown could be heard, sedition flowed freely from pulpits. Presbyterianism, Congregationalism, and rebellion became a neo-trinity. Many leading Anglican clergymen, aware of which side their tax-provided bread was buttered on, naturally supported their king.

Anglicans in the New World were seriously handicapped by not having a resident bishop, whose presence would be convenient for the ordination of young ministers. American students of Anglican theology had to travel to England to be ordained. On the eve of the Revolution, there was serious talk of creating an American bishopric, but the scheme was violently opposed by many non-Anglicans, who feared a tightening of the royal reins. This controversy poured holy oil on the smoldering fires of rebellion.

Religious toleration had indeed made enormous strides in America, at least when compared with its halting steps abroad. Roman Catholics were still generally discriminated against, as in England, even in officeholding. But there were fewer Catholics in America, and hence the anti-papist laws were less severe and less strictly enforced. In general, people could worship—or not worship—as they pleased.

✷ The Great Awakening

In all the colonial churches, religion was less fervid in the early eighteenth century than it had been a century earlier, when the colonies were first planted. The Puritan churches in particular sagged under the weight of two burdens: their elaborate theological doctrines and their compromising efforts to liberalize membership requirements. Churchgoers increasingly complained about the "dead dogs" who droned out tedious, overly erudite sermons from Puritan pulpits. Some ministers, on the other hand, worried

that many of their parishioners had gone soft and that their souls were no longer kindled by the hellfire of orthodox Calvinism. Liberal ideas began to challenge the old-time religion. Some worshipers now proclaimed that human beings were not necessarily predestined to damnation and might save themselves by leading a life of good works. Most threatening to the Calvinist doctrine of predestination was **Arminianism**, named after the Dutch theologian Jacobus Arminius, who preached that individual free will, not divine decree, determined a person's eternal fate, and that *all* humans, not just the "elect," could be saved if they freely accepted God's grace. Pressured by these "heresies," a few churches grudgingly conceded that spiritual conversion was not necessary for church membership. Together, these twin trends toward clerical intellectualism and lay liberalism were sapping doctrinal rigor from many denominations—though Americans remained a remarkably religious people.

The stage was thus set for a rousing religious revival. Known as the **Great Awakening**, it exploded in the 1730s and 1740s and swept through the colonies like a fire through prairie grass. The Awakening was first ignited in Northampton, Massachusetts, by a tall, delicate, and intellectual pastor, Jonathan Edwards. Perhaps the deepest theological mind ever nurtured in America, Edwards proclaimed with burning righteousness the folly of believing in salvation through good works and affirmed the need for complete dependence on God's grace. Warming to his subject, he painted in lurid detail the landscape of hell and the eternal torments of the damned. "Sinners in the Hands of an Angry God" was the title of one of his most famous sermons. He believed that hell was "paved with the skulls of unbaptized children."

Edwards's preaching style was learned and closely reasoned, but his stark doctrines sparked a warmly sympathetic reaction among his parishioners in 1734. Four years later the itinerant English parson George Whitefield loosed a different style of evangelical preaching on America and touched off a conflagration of religious ardor that revolutionized the spiritual life of the colonies. A former alehouse attendant, Whitefield was an orator of rare gifts. His magnificent voice boomed sonorously over thousands of enthralled listeners in an open field. One of England's greatest actors of the day commented enviously that Whitefield could make audiences weep merely by pronouncing the word *Mesopotamia* and that he would "give a hundred guineas if I could only say 'O!' like Mr. Whitefield."

Triumphantly touring the colonies, Whitefield trumpeted his message of human helplessness and divine omnipotence. His eloquence reduced Jonathan Edwards to tears and even caused the skeptical and thrifty Benjamin Franklin to empty his pockets into the collection plate. During these roaring revival meetings, countless sinners professed conversion, and hundreds of the "saved" groaned, shrieked, or rolled in the snow from religious excitation. Whitefield soon inspired American imitators. Taking up his electrifying new style of preaching, they heaped abuse on sinners and shook enormous audiences with emotional appeals. One preacher cackled hideously in the face of hapless wrongdoers. Another, naked to the waist, leapt frantically about in the light of flickering torches.

Orthodox clergymen, known as **old lights**, were deeply skeptical of the emotionalism and the theatrical antics of the revivalists. **New lights**, on the other hand, defended the Awakening for its role in revitalizing American religion. Congregationalists and Presbyterians split over this issue, and many of the believers in religious conversion went over to the Baptists, Methodists, and other sects more prepared to make room for emotion in religion. The Awakening left many lasting effects. Its emphasis on direct, emotive spirituality seriously undermined the older clergy, whose authority had derived from their education and erudition. The schisms it set off in many denominations greatly increased the number and the competitiveness

Jonathan Edwards (1703–1758) preached hellfire, notably in one famous sermon:

❝The God that holds you over the pit of hell, much as one holds a spider or some loathsome insect over the fire, abhors you, and is dreadfully provoked. His wrath toward you burns like fire; he looks upon you as worthy of nothing else but to be cast into the fire.**❞**

of American churches. It encouraged a fresh wave of missionary work among the Indians and even among black slaves, many of whom also attended the mass open-air revivals. It led to the founding of "new light" centers of higher learning such as Princeton, Brown, Rutgers, and Dartmouth. Perhaps most significant, the Great Awakening was the first spontaneous mass movement of the American people. It tended to break down sectional boundaries as well as denominational lines and contributed to the growing sense that Americans were a single people, united by a common history and shared experiences.

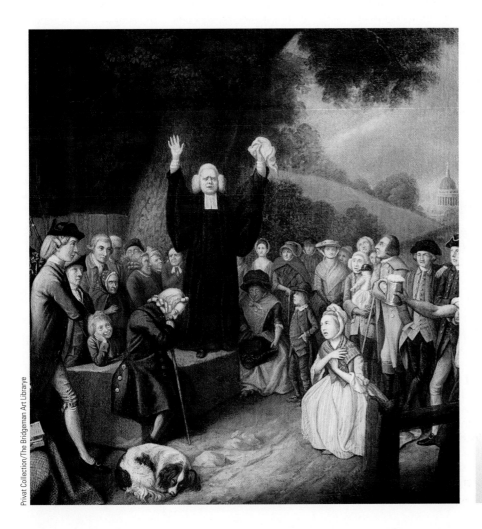

George Whitefield Preaching
Americans of both genders and all races and regions were spellbound by Whitefield's emotive oratory.

✦ Schools and Colleges

A time-honored English idea regarded education as a blessing reserved for the aristocratic few, not for the unwashed many. Education should be for leadership, not citizenship, and primarily for males. Only slowly and painfully did the colonists break the chains of these ancient restrictions.

Puritan New England, largely for religious reasons, was more zealously interested in education than any other section. Dominated by the Congregational Church, it stressed the need for Bible reading by the individual worshiper. The primary goal of the clergy was to make good Christians rather than good citizens. A more secular approach was evident late in the eighteenth century, when some children were warned in the following verse:

> He who ne'er learns his A.B.C.
> Forever will a blockhead be.
> But he who learns his letters fair
> Shall have a coach to take the air.

Education, principally for boys, flourished almost from the outset in New England. This densely populated region boasted an impressive number of graduates from the English universities, especially Cambridge, the intellectual center of England's Puritanism. New Englanders, at a relatively early date, established primary and secondary schools, which varied widely in the quality of instruction and in the length of time that their doors remained open each year. Back-straining farm labor drained much of a youth's time and energy.

Fairly adequate elementary schools were also hammering knowledge into the heads of reluctant "scholars" in the middle colonies and in the South. Some of these institutions were tax-supported; others were privately operated. The South, with its white and black population diffused over wide areas, was severely handicapped by geography in attempting to establish an effective school system. Wealthy families leaned heavily on private tutors.

The general atmosphere in the colonial schools and colleges continued grim and gloomy. Most of the emphasis was placed on religion and on the classical languages, Latin and Greek. The focus was not on experiment and reason, but on doctrine and dogma. The age was one of orthodoxy, and independence of

The College of New Jersey at Princeton, 1764 Later known as Princeton University, it was chartered in 1746 by the Presbyterian Synod, though open to students of all religious persuasions. The fourth college to be founded in British North America, it met in Elizabeth and Newark, New Jersey, until a gift of ten acres of land precipitated a move to Princeton in 1756. All classes were held in the large building, Nassau Hall. Here the Continental Congress met for three months during the summer of 1783, making Princeton for a short time the capital of the nation. This copper engraving, based on a drawing by one of Princeton's earliest students, was part of a series of college views that reflected colonial Americans' growing pride in institutions of higher learning.

TABLE 5.3 Colonial Colleges

Name	Original Name (if Different)	Location	Opened or Founded	Denomination
1. Harvard		Cambridge, Mass.	1636	Congregational
2. William and Mary		Williamsburg, Va.	1693	Anglican
3. Yale		New Haven, Conn.	1701	Congregational
4. Princeton	College of New Jersey	Princeton, N.J.	1746	Presbyterian
5. Pennsylvania	The Academy	Philadelphia, Pa.	1751	Nonsectarian
6. Columbia	King's College	New York, N.Y.	1754	Anglican
7. Brown	Rhode Island College	Providence, R.I.	1764	Baptist
8. Rutgers	Queen's College	New Brunswick, N.J.	1766	Dutch Reformed
9. Dartmouth (begun as an Indian missionary school)		Hanover, N.H.	1769	Congregational

thinking was discouraged. Discipline was quite severe, with many a mischievous child being sadistically "birched" with a switch cut from a birch tree. Sometimes punishment was inflicted by indentured-servant teachers, who could themselves be whipped for their failures as workers and who therefore were not inclined to spare the rod.

College education—at least at first in New England—was geared toward preparing men for the ministry. After all, churches would wither if a new crop of ministers was not adequately trained to lead the region's spiritual flocks. Annoyed by this exclusively religious emphasis, many well-to-do families, especially in the South, sent their boys abroad to acquire a "real"—meaning a refined and philosophical—education in elite English institutions.

For purposes of convenience and economy, nine local colleges were established during the colonial era (see Table 5.3). Student enrollments were small, numbering about two hundred boys at the most; and at one time a few lads as young as eleven were admitted to Harvard. Instruction was poor by present-day standards. The curriculum was still heavily loaded with theology and the "dead" languages, although by 1750 there was a distinct trend toward "live" languages and other modern subjects. A significant contribution was made by Benjamin Franklin. He had never attended college but played a major role in launching what became the University of Pennsylvania, the first American college free from denominational control.

✴ A Provincial Culture

When it came to art and culture, colonial Americans were still in thrall to European tastes, especially British. The simplicity of pioneering life had not yet bred many homespun patrons of the arts. One

John Adams (ca. 1736–1826), the future second president, wrote to his wife,

❝The education of our children is never out of my mind.... I must study politics and war that my sons may have the liberty to study mathematics and philosophy. My sons ought to study mathematics and philosophy, geography, natural history, naval architecture, navigation, commerce, and agriculture, in order to give their children a right to study painting, poetry, music, architecture, statuary, tapestry, and porcelain.**❞**

Colonial Craftsmanship   In the "Pennsylvania Dutch" country, parents gave daughters painted wooden chests to hold their precious dowry linens at marriage. The horsemen, unicorns, and flower patterns on this dower chest confirm its origins in Berks County, Pennsylvania. The Granger Collection, NYC

The Magnetic Dispensary, ca. 1790 This British painting made sport of the era's faddish preoccupations with electricity. Following Franklin's experiments, static electricity, generated here by the machine on the right, was employed for "medicinal" purposes as well as for tingling entertainments.

The Library Company of Philadelphia

aspiring painter, John Trumbull (1756–1843) of Connecticut, was discouraged in his youth by his father's chilling remark, "Connecticut is not Athens." Like so many of his talented artistic contemporaries, Trumbull was forced to travel to London to pursue his ambitions. Charles Willson Peale (1741–1827), best known for his portraits of George Washington, ran a museum, stuffed birds, and practiced dentistry. Gifted Benjamin West (1738–1820) and precocious John Singleton Copley (1738–1815) succeeded in their ambitions to become famous painters, but like Trumbull they had to go to England to complete their training. Only abroad could they find subjects who had the leisure to sit for their portraits and the money to pay handsomely for them. Copley was regarded as a Loyalist during the Revolutionary War, and West, a close friend of George III and official court painter, was buried in London's St. Paul's Cathedral.

Architecture was largely imported from the Old World and modified to meet the peculiar climatic and religious conditions of the New World. Even the lowly log cabin was apparently borrowed from Sweden. The red-bricked Georgian style, so common in the pre-Revolutionary decades, was introduced around 1720 and is best exemplified by the beauty of now-restored Williamsburg, Virginia.

Colonial literature, like art, was generally undistinguished and for many of the same reasons. One noteworthy exception was the precocious poet Phillis Wheatley (ca. 1753–1784), an enslaved girl brought to Boston at age eight and never formally educated.

Taken to England when twenty years of age, she published a book of verse and subsequently wrote other polished poems that revealed the influence of Alexander Pope. Her verse compares favorably with the best of the poetry-poor colonial period, but the remarkable fact is that she could overcome her severely disadvantaged background and write any poetry at all.

Versatile Benjamin Franklin, often called "the first civilized American," also shone as a literary light. Although his autobiography is now a classic, he was best known to his contemporaries for ***Poor Richard's Almanack***, which he edited from 1732 to 1758. This famous publication, containing many pithy sayings culled from the thinkers of the ages, emphasized such homespun virtues as thrift, industry, morality, and common sense. Examples are "What maintains one vice would bring up two children"; "Plough deep while sluggards sleep"; "Honesty is the best policy"; and "Fish and visitors stink in three days." *Poor Richard's* was well known in Europe and was more widely read in America than anything except the Bible. Dispensing witty advice to old and young alike, Franklin had an incalculable influence in shaping the American character.

Science, rising above the shackles of superstition, was making some progress, though lagging behind that of the Old World. A few botanists, mathematicians, and astronomers had won some repute, but Benjamin Franklin was perhaps the only first-rank scientist produced in the American colonies. Franklin's spectacular but dangerous experiments, including the famous kite-flying episode proving that lightning was a form of electricity, won him numerous honors in Europe. But his mind also had a practical turn. Among his numerous inventions were bifocal spectacles and the highly efficient Franklin stove. His lightning rod, perhaps not surprisingly, was condemned by some stodgy clergymen who felt it was "presuming on God" by attempting to control the "artillery of the heavens."

⭐ Pioneer Presses

Stump-grubbing Americans were generally too poor to buy quantities of books and too busy to read them. A South Carolina merchant in 1744 advertised the arrival of a shipment of "printed books, Pictures, Maps, and Pickles." A few private libraries of fair size could be found, especially among the clergy. The Byrd family of Virginia enjoyed perhaps the largest collection in the colonies, consisting of about four thousand volumes. Bustling Benjamin Franklin established in Philadelphia the first privately supported circulating library in America, and by 1776 there were about fifty public libraries and collections supported by subscription.

Hand-operated printing presses cranked out pamphlets, leaflets, and journals. On the eve of the Revolution, there were about forty colonial newspapers, chiefly weeklies that consisted of a single large sheet folded once. Columns ran heavily to somber essays, frequently signed with such pseudonyms as *Cicero*, *Philosophicus*, and *Pro Bono Publico* ("For the Public Good"). The "news" often lagged many weeks behind the event, especially in the case of overseas happenings, in which the colonists were deeply interested. Newspapers proved to be a powerful agency for airing colonial grievances and rallying opposition to British control.

A celebrated legal case, in 1734–1735, involved John Peter Zenger, a newspaper printer. Significantly, the **Zenger trial** arose in New York, reflecting the tumultuous give-and-take of politics in the middle colonies, where so many different ethnic groups jostled against one another. Zenger's newspaper had assailed the corrupt royal governor. Charged with seditious libel, the accused was hauled into court, where he was defended by a former indentured servant, now a distinguished Philadelphia lawyer, Andrew Hamilton. Zenger argued that he had printed the truth, but the bewigged royal chief justice instructed the jury not to consider the truth or falsity of Zenger's statements; the mere fact of printing, irrespective of the truth, was enough to convict. Hamilton countered that "the very liberty of both exposing and opposing arbitrary power" was at stake. Swayed by his eloquence, the jurors defied the bewigged judges and daringly returned a verdict of not guilty. Cheers burst from the spectators.

The Zenger decision was a banner achievement for freedom of the press and for the health of democracy. It pointed the way to the kind of open public discussion required by the diverse society that colonial New York already was and that all America was to become. Although contrary to existing law and not immediately accepted by other judges and juries, in time it helped establish the doctrine that true statements about public officials could not be prosecuted as libel. Newspapers were thus eventually free to print responsible criticisms of powerful officials, though full freedom of the press was unknown during the pre-Revolutionary era.

⭐ The Great Game of Politics

American colonists may have been backward in natural or physical science, but they were making noteworthy contributions to political science.

The thirteen colonial governments took a variety of forms. By 1775 eight of the colonies had royal governors, who were appointed by the king. Three—Maryland, Pennsylvania, and Delaware—were under proprietors who themselves chose the governors. And two—Connecticut and Rhode Island—elected their own governors under self-governing charters.

Practically every colony utilized a two-house legislative body. The upper house, or council, was normally appointed by the crown in the **royal colonies** and by the proprietor in the **proprietary colonies**.

Andrew Hamilton (ca. 1676–1741) concluded his eloquent plea in the Zenger case with these words:

❝The question before the court and you, gentlemen of the jury, is not of small nor private concern. It is not the cause of a poor printer, nor of New York alone, which you are now trying. No! It may, in its consequence, affect every freeman that lives under a British government on the main [land] of America. It is the best cause. It is the cause of liberty.❞

Junius, the pseudonym for a critic (or critics) of the British government from 1768 to 1772, published a pointed barb in criticizing one new appointee:

❝It was not Virginia that wanted a governor but a court favorite that wanted a salary.❞

The Hunting Party, New Jersey Fox hunting began as a necessity in the colonies, where farmers on foot tried to keep foxes from overrunning the countryside. By the eighteenth century it had become an organized sport among the well-to-do, mounted on horseback. George Washington was famed as an ardent fox hunter, breeding his own hounds and importing a fine hunting wardrobe from England. Huntsmen wore scarlet coats to be easily visible, even in the depths of the forest, and cork-lined black hats for protection from low-hanging branches or a fall.

The Metropolitan Museum of Art/Art Resource, NY

It was chosen by the voters in the self-governing colonies. The lower house, as the popular branch, was elected by the people—or rather by those who owned enough property to qualify as voters. In several of the colonies, the backcountry elements were seriously underrepresented, and they hated the ruling colonial clique perhaps more than they did kingly authority. Legislatures, in which the people enjoyed direct representation, voted such taxes as they chose for the necessary expenses of colonial government. Self-taxation through representation was a precious privilege that Americans had come to cherish above most others.

Governors appointed by the king were generally able men, sometimes outstanding figures. Some, unfortunately, were incompetent or corrupt—brokendown politicians badly in need of jobs. The worst of the group was probably impoverished Lord Cornbury, first cousin of Queen Anne, who was made governor of New York and New Jersey in 1702. He proved to be a drunkard, a spendthrift, a grafter, an embezzler, a religious bigot, and a vain fool, who was accused (probably inaccurately) of dressing like a woman. Even the best appointees had trouble with the colonial legislatures, basically because the royal governor embodied a bothersome transatlantic authority some three thousand miles away.

The colonial assemblies found various ways to assert their authority and independence. Some of them employed the trick of withholding the governor's salary unless he yielded to their wishes. He was normally in need of money—otherwise he would not have come to this godforsaken country—so the power of the purse usually forced him to terms. But one governor of North Carolina died with his salary eleven years in arrears.

The London government, in leaving the colonial governor to the tender mercies of the legislature, was guilty of poor administration. In the interests of simple efficiency, the British authorities should have arranged to pay him from independent sources. As events turned out, control over the purse by the colonial legislatures led to prolonged bickering, which proved to be one of the persistent irritants that generated a spirit of revolt.*

Administration at the local level was also varied. County government remained the rule in the plantation South; town-meeting government predominated

---

*Parliament finally arranged for separate payment of the governors through the Townshend taxes of 1767, but by then the colonists were in such an ugly mood over taxation that this innovation only added fresh fuel to the flames.

in New England; and a modification of the two developed in the middle colonies. In the town meeting, with its open discussion and open voting, direct democracy functioned at its best. In this unrivaled cradle of self-government, Americans learned to cherish their privileges and exercise their duties as citizens of the New World commonwealths.

Yet the ballot was by no means a birthright. Religious or property qualifications for voting, with even stiffer qualifications for officeholding, existed in all the colonies in 1775. The privileged upper classes, fearful of democratic excesses, were unwilling to grant the ballot to every "biped of the forest." Perhaps half of the adult white males were thus disfranchised. But because of the ease of acquiring land and thus satisfying property requirements, the right to vote was not beyond the reach of most industrious and enterprising colonists. Yet somewhat surprisingly, eligible voters often did not exercise this precious privilege. They frequently acquiesced in the leadership of their "betters," who ran colonial affairs—though always reserving the right to vote misbehaving rascals out of office.

By 1775 America was not yet a true democracy—socially, economically, or politically. But it was far more democratic than England and the European continent. Colonial institutions were giving freer rein to the democratic ideals of tolerance, educational advantages, equality of economic opportunity, freedom of speech, freedom of the press, freedom of assembly, and representative government. And these democratic seeds, planted in rich soil, were to bring forth a lush harvest in later years.

✶ Colonial Folkways

Everyday life in the colonies may now seem glamorous, especially as reflected in antique shops. But judged by modern standards, it was drab and tedious. For most people the labor was heavy and constant—from "can see" to "can't see."

Food was plentiful, though the diet could be coarse and monotonous. Americans probably ate more bountifully, especially of meat, than any people in the Old World. Lazy or sickly was the person whose stomach was empty.

Basic comforts now taken for granted were lacking. Churches were not heated at all, except for charcoal foot-warmers that the women carried. During the frigid New England winters, the preaching of hellfire may not have seemed altogether unattractive. Drafty homes were poorly heated, chiefly by inefficient fireplaces. There was no running water in the houses, no indoor plumbing, and probably not a single bathtub in all of colonial America. Candles and whale-oil lamps provided faint and flickering illumination. Garbage disposal was primitive. Long-snouted hogs customarily ranged the streets to consume refuse, while buzzards, protected by law, flapped greedily over tidbits of waste.

Library of Congress Prints and Photographs Division[LC-US262- 20404]

The Popular Game of Billiards Most likely brought over by Dutch and English settlers, billiards provided amusement in local taverns throughout the colonies. By the nineteenth century, Americans, like the British and French who had long dominated the sport, had become obsessed with these games of cues and balls. The most popular form of pool, eight ball, was not invented until 1900.

Amusement was eagerly pursued where time and custom permitted. The militia assembled periodically for "musters," which consisted of several days of drilling, liberally interspersed with merrymaking and flirting. On the frontier, pleasure was often combined with work at house-raisings, quilting bees, husking bees, and apple parings. Funerals and weddings everywhere afforded opportunities for social gatherings, which customarily involved the swilling of much strong liquor.

Winter sports were common in the North, whereas in the South card playing, horse racing, cockfighting, and fox hunting were favorite pastimes. George Washington, not surprisingly, was a superb rider. In the non-puritanical South, dancing was the rage—jigs, square dances, the Virginia reel—and the agile Washington could swing his fair partner with the best of them.

Other diversions beckoned. Lotteries were universally approved, even by the clergy, and were used to raise money for churches and colleges, including Harvard. Stage plays became popular in the South but were frowned upon in Quaker and Puritan colonies and in some places forbidden by law. Many of the New England clergy saw playacting as time-consuming and immoral; they preferred religious lectures, from which their flocks derived much spiritual satisfaction.

Holidays were everywhere celebrated in the American colonies, but Christmas was frowned upon in New England as an offensive reminder of "Popery." "Yuletide is fooltide" was a common Puritan sneer. Thanksgiving Day came to be a truly American festival, for it combined thanks to God with an opportunity for jollification, gorging, and guzzling.

By the mid-eighteenth century, Britain's several North American colonies, despite their differences, revealed some striking similarities. All were basically English in language and customs and Protestant in religion, while the widespread presence of other peoples and faiths compelled every colony to cede at least some degree of ethnic and religious toleration. Compared with contemporary Europe, they all afforded to enterprising individuals unusual opportunities for social mobility. They all possessed some measure of self-government, though by no means complete democracy. Communication and transportation among the colonies were improving. British North America by 1775 looked like a patchwork quilt—each part slightly different but stitched together by common origins, common ways of life, and common beliefs in toleration, economic development, and, above all, self-rule. Fatefully, all the colonies were also separated from the seat of imperial authority by a vast ocean moat some three thousand miles wide. These simple facts of shared history, culture, and geography set the stage for the colonists' struggle to unite as an independent people.

[*Varying Viewpoints*]
Colonial America: Communities of Conflict or Consensus?

The earliest historians of colonial society portrayed close-knit, homogeneous, and hierarchical communities. Richard Bushman's *From Puritan to Yankee* (1967) challenged that traditional view when he described colonial New England as an expanding, opening society. In this view the colonists gradually lost the religious discipline and social structure of the founding generations as they poured out onto the frontier or sailed the seas in search of fortune and adventure. Rhys Isaac viewed the Great Awakening in the South as similar evidence of the erosion of the social constraints and deference that once held colonial society together. Unbridled religious enthusiasm, directed by itinerant preachers both North and South, encouraged the sort of quest for personal autonomy that eventually led Americans to demand national independence.

Other scholars have focused on the negative aspects of this alleged breakdown in the traditional order, particularly on the rise of new social inequalities. Social historians like Kenneth Lockridge have argued that the decline of cohesive communities, population pressure on the land, and continued dominance of church and parental authority gave rise to a landless class, forced to till tenant plots in the countryside or find work as manual laborers in the cities. Gary Nash, in *The Urban Crucible* (1979), likewise traced the rise of a competitive, individualistic social order in colonial cities, marking the end of the patronage and paternalism that had once bound communities together. Increasingly, Nash contended, class antagonisms split communities. The wealthy abandoned their traditional obligations toward the poor for more selfish capitalistic social relations that favored their class peers. The consequent politicization of the laboring classes helped motivate their participation in the American Revolution.

Some scholars have disputed that "declension" undermined colonial communities. Christine Heyrman, in particular, has argued in *Commerce and Culture* (1984) that the decline of traditional mores has been overstated; religious beliefs and commercial activities coexisted throughout the late seventeenth and early eighteenth centuries. Similarly, Jack Greene has suggested that the obsession with the decline of deference has obscured the fact that colonies outside of New England, like Virginia and Maryland, actually experienced a consolidation of religious and social authority throughout the seventeenth and eighteenth centuries, becoming more hierarchical and paternalistic.

Like Greene, many historians have focused on sectional differences between the colonies and the peculiar nature of social equality and inequality in each. Much of the impetus for this inquiry stems from an issue that has long perplexed students of early America: the simultaneous evolution of a rigid racial caste system alongside democratic political institutions. Decades ago, when most historians came from Yankee stock, they resolved the apparent paradox by locating the seeds of democracy in New England. The aggressive independence of the people, best expressed by the boisterous town meetings, spawned the American obsession with freedom. On the other hand, this view holds, the slave societies of the South were hierarchical, aristocratic communities under the sway of a few powerful planters.

More recently some historians have attacked this simple dichotomy, noting many undemocratic features in colonial New England and arguing that while the South may have been the site of tremendous inequality, it also produced most of the Founding Fathers. Washington, Jefferson, and Madison—the architects of American government with its foundation in liberty—all hailed from slaveholding Virginia. In fact, nowhere were republican principles stronger than in Virginia. Some scholars, notably Edmund S. Morgan in *American Slavery, American Freedom* (1975), consider the willingness of wealthy planters to concede the equality and freedom of all white males a device to ensure racial solidarity and to mute class conflict. In this view the concurrent emergence of slavery and democracy was no paradox. White racial solidarity muffled animosity between rich and poor and fostered the devotion to equality among whites that became a hallmark of American democracy. Historians of Latin America point out that other New World societies, like Brazil and Mexico, had far sharper class divisions than the British colonies, with lasting consequences for their social integrity and political stability.

Few historians still argue that the colonies offered boundless opportunities for inhabitants, white or black. But scholars disagree vigorously over what kinds of inequalities and social tensions most shaped eighteenth-century society and contributed to the revolutionary agitation that eventually consumed—and transformed—colonial America. Even so, whether one accepts Morgan's argument that "Americans bought their independence with slave labor" or those interpretations that point to rising social conflict between whites as the salient characteristic of colonial society on the eve of the Revolution, the once-common assumption that America was a world of equality and consensus no longer reigns undisputed. Yet because one's life chances were still unquestionably better in America than in Europe, immigrants continued to pour in, imbued with high expectations about America as a land of opportunity.

Chapter Review

KEY TERMS

Paxton Boys (80)

Regulator movement (80)

New York slave revolt (81)

South Carolina slave revolt (Stono River) (81)

triangular trade (86)

Molasses Act (88)

Arminianism (90)

Great Awakening (90)

old lights (91)

new lights (91)

Poor Richard's Almanack (94)

Zenger trial (95)

royal colonies (95)

proprietary colonies (95)

PEOPLE TO KNOW

Michel-Guillaume Jean de Crèvecoeur

Jacobus Arminius

Jonathan Edwards

George Whitefield

John Trumbull

John Singleton Copley

Phillis Wheatley

John Peter Zenger

CHRONOLOGY

1693	College of William and Mary founded
1701	Yale College founded
1712	New York Slave Revolt
1721	Smallpox inoculation introduced
1732	First edition of Franklin's *Poor Richard's Almanack*
1734	Jonathan Edwards begins Great Awakening
1734–1735	Zenger free-press trial in New York
1738	George Whitefield spreads Great Awakening

1739	South Carolina slave revolt
1746	Princeton College founded
1760	Britain vetoes South Carolina anti–slave trade measures
1764	Paxton Boys march on Philadelphia Brown College founded
1766	Rutgers College founded
1768–1771	Regulator protests
1769	Dartmouth College founded

TO LEARN MORE

Bernard Bailyn, *The Peopling of British North America* (1986)

Ira Berlin, *Many Thousands Gone: The First Two Centuries of Slavery in North America* (1998)

———, *King and People in Provincial Massachusetts* (1985)

John Butler, *Becoming America: The Revolution Before 1776* (2000)

Olaudah Equiano, *Equinao's Travels* (1789)

Benjamin Franklin, *Autobiography* (1868)

James Henretta, *The Evolution of American Society, 1700–1815* (1973)

Rhys Isaac, *Landon Carter's Uneasy Kingdom: Revolution and Rebellion on a Virginia Plantation* (2004)

Jill Lepore, *New York Burning* (2005)

Marcus Rediker, *Between the Devil and the Deep Blue Sea: Merchant Seamen, Pirates, and the Anglo-American Maritime World, 1700–1750* (1987)

Gordon Wood, *The Americanization of Benjamin Franklin* (2004)

A complete, annotated bibliography for this chapter—along with brief descriptions of the People to Know—may be found on the *American Pageant* website. The key terms are defined in the glossary at the end of the text.

Chapter 6

The Duel for North America

1608–1763

A torch lighted in the forests of America set all Europe in conflagration.

VOLTAIRE, CA. 1756

As the seventeenth century neared its sunset, a titanic struggle was shaping up for mastery of the North American continent. The contest involved three Old World nations—England,* France, and Spain—and it unavoidably swept up Native American peoples as well. From 1688 to 1763, four bitter wars convulsed Europe. All four of those conflicts were world wars. They amounted to a death struggle for domination in Europe as well as in the New World, and they were fought on the waters and soil of two hemispheres. Counting these first four clashes, nine world wars have been waged since 1688. The American people, whether as British subjects or as American citizens, proved unable to stay out of a single one of them. And one of those wars—known as the Seven Years' War in Europe and sometimes as the French and Indian War in America—set the stage for America's independence.

✴ France Finds a Foothold in Canada

Like England and Holland, France was a latecomer in the scramble for New World real estate and for basically the same reasons. It was convulsed during the 1500s by foreign wars and domestic strife, including the frightful clashes between Roman Catholics and Protestant **Huguenots**. On St. Bartholomew's Day, 1572, more than ten thousand Huguenots—men, women, and children—were butchered in cold blood.

A new era dawned in 1598 when the **Edict of Nantes**, issued by the crown, granted limited toleration to French Protestants. Religious wars ceased, and in the new century France blossomed into the mightiest and most feared nation on the European continent, led by a series of brilliant ministers and by the vainglorious King Louis XIV. Enthroned as a five-year-old boy, he reigned for no less than seventy-two years (1643–1715), surrounded by a glittering court and scheming ministers and mistresses. Fatefully for North America, Louis XIV also took a deep interest in overseas colonies.

After rocky beginnings, success finally rewarded the exertions of France in the New World. In 1608, the year after the founding of Jamestown, the permanent beginnings of a vast empire (see Map 6.1) were established at Québec, a granite sentinel commanding the St. Lawrence River. The leading figure was Samuel de Champlain, an intrepid soldier and explorer whose energy and leadership fairly earned him the title "Father of New France."

Champlain entered into friendly relations—a fateful friendship—with the nearby Huron Indian tribes. At their request, he joined them in battle against their foes, the federated Iroquois tribes of the upper New York area. Two volleys from the "lightning sticks" of the whites routed the terrified Iroquois, who left behind three dead and one wounded. France, to its sorrow, thus earned the lasting enmity of the Iroquois tribes. They thereafter hampered French penetration of the Ohio Valley, sometimes ravaging French settlements and frequently serving as allies of the British in the prolonged struggle for supremacy on the continent.

*After the union of England and Scotland in 1707, the nation's official name became "Great Britain."

MAP 6.1 France's American Empire at Its Greatest Extent, 1700 © 2016 Cengage Learning

The government of New France (Canada) finally fell under the direct control of the king after various commercial companies had faltered or failed. This royal regime was almost completely autocratic. The people elected no representative assemblies, nor did they enjoy the right to trial by jury, as in the English colonies.

The population of Catholic New France grew at a listless pace. As late as 1750, only sixty thousand or so whites inhabited New France. Landowning French peasants, unlike the dispossessed English tenant farmers who embarked for the British colonies, had little economic motive to move. Protestant Huguenots, who might have had a religious motive to migrate, were denied a refuge in this raw colony. The French government, in any case, favored its Caribbean island colonies, rich in sugar and rum, over the snow-cloaked wilderness of Canada.

✴ New France Fans Out

New France did contain one valuable resource: the beaver. European fashion-setters valued beaver-pelt hats for their warmth and opulent appearance. To adorn the heads of Europeans, French fur-trappers ranged over the woods and waterways of North America in pursuit of beaver. These colorful **coureurs de bois** ("runners of the woods") were also runners of risks—two-fisted drinkers, free spenders, free livers and lovers. They littered the land with scores of place names, including Baton Rouge (red stick), Terre Haute (high land), Des Moines (some monks), and Grand Teton (big breast).

Singing, paddle-swinging French **voyageurs** also recruited Indians into the fur business. The Indian fur flotilla arriving in Montréal in 1693 numbered four hundred canoes. But the fur trade had some disastrous drawbacks. Indians recruited into the fur business were decimated by the white man's diseases and debauched by his alcohol. Slaughtering beaver by the boatload also violated many Indians' religious beliefs and sadly demonstrated the shattering effect that contact with Europeans wreaked on traditional Indian ways of life.

Pursuing the sharp-toothed beaver ever deeper into the heart of the continent, the French trappers and their Indian partners hiked, rode, snowshoed, sailed, and paddled across amazing distances. They trekked in a huge arc across the Great Lakes, into present-day Saskatchewan and Manitoba; along the valleys of the Platte, the Arkansas, and the Missouri; west to the Rockies; and south to the border of Spanish Texas (see Map 6.2). In the process they all but extinguished the beaver population in many areas, inflicting incalculable ecological damage.

French Catholic missionaries, notably the Jesuits, labored zealously to save the Indians for Christ and from the fur-trappers. Some of the Jesuit missionaries, their efforts scorned, suffered unspeakable tortures at the hands of the Indians. But though they made few permanent converts, the Jesuits played a vital role as explorers and geographers.

Other explorers sought neither souls nor fur, but empire. To thwart English settlers pushing into the

Québec Scene, by Jean-Baptiste-Louis Franquelin, ca. 1699 (detail) The metal cooking pot and the Indians' clothing and blankets show the Native Americans' growing reliance on European trade goods.

- ● French trading post (1604–1760)
- ▲ Hudson's Bay Company (1670–1869)
- ■ Montréal-based fur trade (1763–1784)
- ▲ North West Company (1784–1821)
- ■ Spain and New Mexico (1598–1821)

0   200   400 Km.
0   200   400 Mi.

MAP 6.2 Fur-Trading Posts   To serve the needs of European fashion, fur-traders pursued the beaver for more than two centuries over the entire continent of North America. They brought many Indians for the first time into contact with white culture. © 2016 Cengage Learning

Ohio Valley, Antoine Cadillac founded Detroit, "the City of Straits," in 1701. To check Spanish penetration into the region of the Gulf of Mexico, ambitious Robert de La Salle floated down the Mississippi in 1682 to the point where it mingles with the Gulf. He named the great interior basin "Louisiana," in honor of his sovereign, Louis XIV. Dreaming of empire, he returned to the Gulf three years later with a colonizing expedition of four ships. But he failed to find the Mississippi delta, landed in Spanish Texas, and in 1687 was murdered by his mutinous men.

Undismayed, French officials persisted in their efforts to block Spain on the Gulf of Mexico. They planted several fortified posts in what is now Mississippi and Louisiana, the most important of which was New Orleans (1718). Commanding the mouth of the Mississippi River, this strategic semitropical outpost also tapped the fur trade of the huge interior valley. The fertile Illinois country—where the French established forts and trading posts at Kaskaskia, Cahokia, and Vincennes—became the garden of France's North American empire. Surprising amounts of grain were floated down the Mississippi for transshipment to the West Indies and to Europe.

✴ The Clash of Empires

The earliest contests among the European powers for control of North America, known to the British colonists as **King William's War** (1689–1697) and **Queen Anne's War** (1702–1713) (see Table 6.1), mostly pitted British colonists against the French *coureurs de bois*, with both sides recruiting whatever Indian allies they could. Neither France nor Britain at this stage considered America worth the commitment of large detachments of regular troops, so the combatants waged a kind of primitive guerrilla warfare. Indian allies of the French ravaged with torch and tomahawk the British colonial frontiers, visiting especially bloody violence on the villages of Schenectady,

TABLE 6.1 Later English Monarchs*

Name, Reign	Relation to America
William III, 1689–1702	Collapse of Dominion of New England; King William's War
Anne, 1702–1714	Queen Anne's War, 1702–1713
George I, 1714–1727	Navigation Laws laxly enforced ("salutary neglect")
George II, 1727–1760	Ga. founded; King George's War; Seven Years' War
George III, 1760–1820	American Revolution, 1775–1783

*See pp. 26 and 50 for earlier monarchs.

New York, and Deerfield, Massachusetts (see Map 6.3). Spain, eventually allied with France, probed from its Florida base at outlying South Carolina settlements. For their part the British colonists failed miserably in sallies against Québec and Montréal but scored a signal victory when they temporarily seized the stronghold of Port Royal in Acadia (present-day Nova Scotia).

Peace terms, signed at Utrecht in 1713, revealed how badly France and its Spanish ally had been beaten (see Map 6.4). Britain was rewarded with French-populated Acadia (which the British renamed Nova Scotia, or New Scotland) and the wintry wastes of Newfoundland and Hudson Bay. These immense tracts pinched the St. Lawrence settlements of France, foreshadowing their ultimate doom. A generation of peace ensued, during which Britain provided its American colonies with decades of "salutary neglect"—fertile soil for the roots of independence.

By the treaty of 1713, the British also won limited trading rights in Spanish America, but these rights later fostered much friction over smuggling. Ill feeling flared up when the British captain Robert Jenkins, encountering Spanish revenue authorities, had one ear sliced off by a sword. The Spanish commander reportedly sneered, "Carry this home to the King, your master, whom, if he were present, I would serve in like fashion." The victim, with a tale of woe on his tongue and a shriveled ear in his hand, aroused furious resentment when he returned home to Britain.

MAP 6.3 Scenes of the French Wars The arrows indicate French-Indian attacks. Schenectady was burned to the ground in the raid of 1690. At Deerfield, site of one of the New England frontier's bloodiest confrontations, invaders killed fifty inhabitants and sent more than a hundred others fleeing for their lives into the winter wilderness. The Indian attackers also took over one hundred Deerfield residents captive, including the child Titus King. He later wrote, "Captivity is an awful school for children, when we see how quick they will fall in with the Indian ways. Nothing seems to be more taking [appealing]. In six months' time they forsake father and mother, forget their own land, refuse to speak their own tongue, and seemingly be wholly swallowed up with the Indians." © 2016 Cengage Learning

Chief of the Taensa Indians Receiving La Salle, March 20, 1682, by George Catlin, 1847–1848
Driven by the dream of a vast North American empire for France, La Salle spent years exploring the Great Lakes region and the valleys of the Illinois and Mississippi Rivers. This scene of his encounter with an Indian chieftain was imaginatively recreated by the nineteenth-century artist George Catlin.

The **War of Jenkins's Ear**, curiously but aptly named, broke out in 1739 between the British and the Spaniards. It was confined to the Caribbean Sea and to the much-buffeted buffer colony of Georgia, where philanthropist-soldier James Oglethorpe fought his Spanish foe to a standstill.

This small-scale scuffle with Spain in America soon merged with the large-scale War of Austrian Succession in Europe (see Table 6.2) and came to be called **King George's War** in America. Once again, France allied itself with Spain. And once again, a rustic force of New Englanders invaded New France. With help from a British fleet and with a great deal of good luck, the raw and sometimes drunken recruits captured the reputedly impregnable French fortress of Louisbourg, which was on Cape Breton Island and commanded the approaches to the St. Lawrence River (see Map 6.3).

When the peace treaty of 1748 handed Louisbourg back to their French foe, the victorious New Englanders were outraged. The glory of their arms—never terribly lustrous in any event—seemed tarnished by the wiles of Old World diplomats. Worse, Louisbourg was still a cocked pistol pointed at the heart of the American continent. France, powerful and unappeased, still clung to its vast holdings in North America.

✴ George Washington Inaugurates War with France

As the dogfight intensified in the New World, the Ohio Valley became the chief bone of contention between the French and British. The Ohio Country was the critical area into which the westward-pushing British colonists would inevitably penetrate. For France it was also the key to the continent that the French had to retain, particularly if they were going to link their Canadian holdings with those of the lower Mississippi Valley. By the

Territorial claims
- British
- French
- Spanish

0 500 1000 Km.
0 500 1000 Mi.

MAP 6.4 North America After Two Wars, 1713 © 2016 Cengage Learning

TABLE 6.2 The Nine World Wars

Dates	In Europe	In America
1688–1697	War of the League of Augsburg	King William's War, 1689–1697
1701–1713	War of Spanish Succession	Queen Anne's War, 1702–1713
1740–1748	War of Austrian Succession	King George's War, 1744–1748
1756–1763	Seven Years' War	French and Indian War, 1754–1763
1778–1783	War of the American Revolution	American Revolution, 1775–1783
1793–1802	Wars of the French Revolution	Undeclared French War, 1798–1800
1803–1815	Napoleonic Wars	War of 1812, 1812–1814
1914–1918	World War I	World War I, 1917–1918
1939–1945	World War II	World War II, 1941–1945

mid-1700s, the British colonists, painfully aware of these basic truths, were no longer so reluctant to bear the burdens of empire. Alarmed by French land-grabbing and cutthroat fur-trade competition in the Ohio Valley, they were determined to fight for their economic security and for the supremacy of their way of life in North America.

Rivalry for the lush lands of the upper Ohio Valley brought tensions to the snapping point. In 1749 a group of British colonial speculators, chiefly influential Virginians, including the Washington family, had secured shaky legal "rights" to some 500,000 acres in this region. In the same disputed wilderness, the French were in the process of erecting a chain of forts commanding the strategic Ohio River. Especially formidable was Fort Duquesne at the pivotal point where the Monongahela and Allegheny Rivers join to form the Ohio—the later site of Pittsburgh.

In 1754 the governor of Virginia ushered George Washington, a twenty-one-year-old surveyor and fellow Virginian, onto the stage of history. To secure the Virginians' claims, Washington was sent to the Ohio Country as a lieutenant colonel in command of about 150 Virginia militiamen. Encountering a small detachment of French troops in the forest

New Englanders Capture Louisbourg, 1745 When the final peace settlement of 1748 returned this fortress to France, the American colonists felt betrayed by their British masters.

about forty miles from Fort Duquesne (see Map 6.5), the Virginians fired the first shots of the globe-girdling new war. The French leader was killed, and his men retreated. An exultant Washington wrote, "I heard the bullets whistle, and believe me, there is something charming in the sound." It soon lost its charm.

The French promptly returned with reinforcements, who surrounded Washington in his hastily constructed breastworks, Fort Necessity. After a ten-hour siege, he was forced to surrender his entire command in July 1754—ironically the fourth of July. But he was permitted to march his men away with the full honors of war.

With the shooting already started and in danger of spreading, the British authorities in Nova Scotia took vigorous action. Understandably fearing a stab in the back from the French **Acadians**, whom Britain had conquered in 1713, the British brutally uprooted some four thousand of them in 1755. These unhappy French deportees were scattered as far south as Louisiana, where the descendants of the French-speaking Acadians are now called "Cajuns" and number nearly a million.

✦ Global War and Colonial Disunity

The first three Anglo-French colonial wars had all started in Europe, but the tables were now reversed. The fourth struggle, sometimes known as the **French and Indian War**, began in America. Touched off by George Washington in the wilds of the Ohio Valley in 1754, it rocked along on an undeclared basis for two years and then widened into the most far-flung conflict the world had yet seen—the **Seven Years' War**. It was fought not only in America but also in Europe, in the West Indies, in the Philippines, in Africa, and on the ocean. The Seven Years' War was a seven-seas war (see Map 6.6).

In Europe the principal adversaries were Britain and Prussia on one side, arrayed against France, Spain, Austria, and Russia on the other. The bloodiest theater was in Germany, where Frederick the Great deservedly won the title of "Great" by repelling French, Austrian, and Russian armies, often with the opposing forces

MAP 6.5 The French and Indian War in North America, 1754–1760 © 2016 Cengage Learning

Events of the Seven Years' War

1. Virginia-Pennsylvania-Ohio, 1753–1764
2. Nova Scotia, 1754
3. Hudson River-Lake Champlain, 1755–1760
4. Minorca, 1756
5. Central Europe, 1756–1762
6. Bengal, 1757
7. Louisbourg, 1758
8. West Africa, 1758
9. Madras, 1758–1759
10. Québec and Upper St. Lawrence, 1759–1760
11. Eastern Caribbean, 1759–1762
12. Iberian Coast, 1759
13. French Coast, 1759–1761
14. Upper Great Lakes, 1759–1764
15. Pondicherry, 1760–1762
16. Spain, 1762
17. Newfoundland, 1762
18. Havana, 1762
19. Manila, 1762
20. Pontiac's Rebellion, 1763–1764

Territorial claims, ca. 1750
- British
- French
- Netherlands
- Portuguese
- Spanish

MAP 6.6 Global Scale of the Seven Years' War   Among the first of the truly "world wars" of the modern era, the Seven Years' War sucked in several nations who did battle around the globe. © 2016 Cengage Learning

outnumbering his own three to one. The London government, unable to send him effective troop reinforcements, liberally subsidized him with gold. Luckily for the British colonists, the French wasted so much strength in this European bloodbath that they were unable to throw an adequate force into the New World. "America was conquered in Germany," declared Britain's great statesman William Pitt.

In previous colonial clashes, the Americans had revealed an astonishing lack of unity. Colonists who were nearest the shooting had responded much more generously with volunteers and money than those enjoying the safety of remoteness. Even the Indians had laughed at the inability of the colonists to pull together. Now, with musketballs already splitting the air in Ohio, the crisis demanded concerted action.

Library of Congress Prints & Photographs Division, [LC-USZC4-5315]

Famous Cartoon by Benjamin Franklin Delaware and Georgia were omitted.

In 1754 the British government summoned an intercolonial congress to Albany, New York, near the Iroquois Indian country. Travel-weary delegates from only seven of the thirteen colonies showed up. The immediate purpose was to keep the scalping knives of the Iroquois tribes loyal to the British in the spreading war. The chiefs were harangued at length and then presented with thirty wagonloads of gifts, including guns.

The longer-range purpose at Albany was to achieve greater colonial unity and thus bolster the common defense against France. A month before the congress assembled, ingenious Benjamin Franklin published in his *Pennsylvania Gazette* the most famous cartoon of the colonial era. Showing the separate colonies as parts of a disjointed snake, it broadcast the slogan "Join, or Die."

Franklin himself, a wise and witty counselor, was the leading spirit of the **Albany Congress**. His outstanding contribution was a well-devised but premature scheme for colonial home rule. The Albany delegates unanimously adopted the plan, but the individual colonies spurned it, as did the London regime. To the colonists, it did not seem to give enough independence; to the British officials, it seemed to give too much. The disappointing result confirmed one of Franklin's sage observations: all people agreed on the need for union, but their "weak noddles" were "perfectly distracted" when they attempted to agree on details.

� Braddock's Blundering and Its Aftermath

The opening clashes of the French and Indian War went badly for the British colonists. Haughty and bull-headed General Edward Braddock, a sixty-year-old officer experienced in European warfare, was sent to Virginia with a strong detachment of British **regulars**. After foraging scanty supplies from the reluctant colonists, he set out in 1755 with some two thousand men to capture Fort Duquesne. A considerable part of his force consisted of ill-disciplined colonial militiamen ("buckskins"), whose behind-the-tree methods of fighting Indians won "Bulldog" Braddock's professional contempt.

Braddock's expedition, dragging heavy artillery, moved slowly. Axmen laboriously hacked a path through the dense forest, thus opening a road that was later to be an important artery to the West. A few miles from Fort Duquesne, Braddock encountered a much smaller French and Indian army. At first the enemy force was repulsed, but it quickly melted into the thickets and poured a murderous fire into the ranks of the redcoats. In the ensuing battle, George Washington, an energetic and fearless aide to Braddock, had two horses shot from under him, and four bullets pierced his coat. Braddock himself was mortally wounded. The entire British force was routed after appalling losses.

Inflamed by this easy victory, the Indians took to a wider warpath. The whole frontier from Pennsylvania to North Carolina, left virtually naked by Braddock's bloody defeat, felt their fury. Scalping forays occurred within eighty miles of Philadelphia, and in desperation the local authorities offered bounties for Indian scalps: $50 for a woman's and $130 for a warrior's. George Washington, with only three hundred men, tried desperately to defend the scorched frontier.

The British launched a full-scale invasion of Canada in 1756, now that the undeclared war in America had at last merged into a world conflict. But they unwisely tried to attack a number of exposed wilderness posts simultaneously, instead of throwing all their strength at Québec and Montréal. If these strongholds had fallen, all the smaller outposts to the west would have withered for lack of riverborne supplies. But the British ignored such sound strategy, and defeat after defeat tarnished their arms, both in America and in Europe.

✰ Pitt's Palms of Victory

In the hour of crisis, Britain brought forth, as it repeatedly has, a superlative leader—William Pitt. A tall and imposing figure, whose flashing eyes were set in a hawklike face, he was popularly known as the "Great Commoner." Pitt drew much of his strength from the common people, who admired him so greatly that on occasion they kissed his horses. A splendid orator endowed with a majestic voice, he believed passionately in his cause, in his country, and in himself.

View of the Taking of Québec, 1759 On the night of September 13, British forces scaled the rocky cliffs of Québec and defeated the French army defending the city. The following year, Montréal, France's last bastion in North America, surrendered. Fighting continued in the Caribbean, Europe, and the Philippines for two more years, until the Treaty of Paris was signed in 1763, eliminating France as a colonial power in North America.

In 1757 Pitt became a foremost leader in the London government. Throwing himself headlong into his task, he soon earned the title "Organizer of Victory." He wisely decided to soft-pedal assaults on the French West Indies, which had been bleeding away much British strength, and to concentrate on the vitals of Canada—the Québec-Montréal area. He also picked young and energetic leaders, thus bypassing incompetent and cautious old generals.

Pitt first dispatched a powerful expedition in 1758 against Louisbourg. The frowning fortress, though it had been greatly strengthened, fell after a blistering siege. Wild rejoicing swept Britain, for this was the first significant British victory of the entire war.

Québec was next on Pitt's list. For this crucial expedition, he chose the thirty-two-year-old James Wolfe, who had been an officer since the age of fourteen. Though slight and sickly, Wolfe combined a mixture of dash with painstaking attention to detail. The British attackers were making woeful progress when Wolfe, in a daring night move, sent a detachment up a poorly guarded part of the rocky eminence protecting Québec. This vanguard scaled the cliff, pulling itself upward by the bushes and showing the way for the others. In the morning the two armies faced each other on the Plains of Abraham on the outskirts of Québec, the British under Wolfe and the French under the Marquis de Montcalm. Both commanders fell, fatally wounded, but the French were defeated, and the city surrendered.

The **Battle of Québec** in 1759 ranks as one of the most significant engagements in British and American history. When Montréal fell in 1760, the French flag had fluttered in Canada for the last time. By the peace settlement at Paris (1763), French power was thrown completely off the continent of North America, leaving behind a fertile French population that is to this day a strong minority in Canada. This bitter pill was sweetened somewhat when the French were allowed to retain several small but valuable sugar islands in the West Indies and two never-to-be-fortified islets in the Gulf of St. Lawrence for fishing stations. A final blow came when the French, to compensate their luckless Spanish ally for its losses, ceded to Spain all trans-Mississippi Louisiana, plus the outlet of New Orleans. Spain, for its part, turned Florida over to Britain in

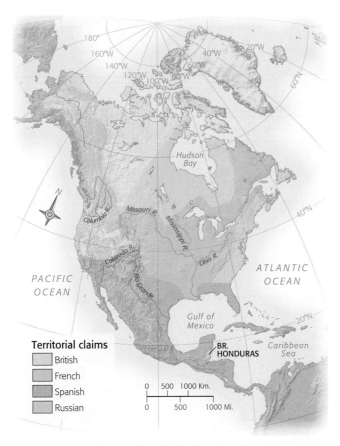

MAP 6.7A North America Before 1754
© 2016 Cengage Learning

MAP 6.7B North America After 1763 (after **French losses**) © 2016 Cengage Learning

return for Cuba, where Havana had fallen to British arms (see Map 6.7).

Great Britain thus emerged as the dominant power in North America while taking its place as the leading naval power of the world.

★ Restless Colonists

Britain's colonists, baptized by fire, emerged with increased confidence in their military strength. They had borne the brunt of battle at first; they had fought bravely alongside the crack British regulars; and they had gained valuable experience, officers and men alike. In the closing days of the conflict, some twenty thousand American recruits were under arms.

The French and Indian War, while bolstering colonial self-esteem, simultaneously shattered the myth of British invincibility. On Braddock's bloody field, the "buckskin" militia had seen the demoralized regulars huddling helplessly together or fleeing their unseen enemy.

Ominously, friction had developed during the war between arrogant British officers and the raw colonial

"boors." Displaying the contempt of the professional soldier for amateurs, the British refused to recognize any American militia commission above the rank of captain—a demotion humiliating to "Colonel" George Washington. They also showed the usual condescension of snobs from the civilized Old Country toward the "scum" who had confessed failure by fleeing to the

The Reverend Andrew Burnaby, an observant Church of England clergyman who visited the colonies in the closing months of the Seven Years' War, scoffed at any possibility of unification (1760):

❝ ...for fire and water are not more heterogeneous than the different colonies in North America. Nothing can exceed the jealousy and emulation which they possess in regard to each other....In short...were they left to themselves there would soon be a civil war from one end of the continent to the other, while the Indians and Negros would... impatiently watch the opportunity of exterminating them all together.**❞**

Detroit, 1794   A key French outpost from 1701 to 1760, Detroit fell to Britain during the Seven Years' War. The British remained at Detroit even after the American War of Independence, exciting bitter resentment in the infant American Republic (see "The World's Ugly Duckling," p. 167).

"outhouses of civilization." General Wolfe referred to the colonial militia, with exaggeration, as "in general the dirtiest, most contemptible, cowardly dogs that you can conceive." Energetic and hard-working American settlers, in contrast, believed themselves to be the cutting edge of British civilization. They felt that they deserved credit rather than contempt for risking their lives to secure a New World empire.

British officials were further distressed by the reluctance of the colonists to support the common cause wholeheartedly. American shippers, using fraudulent papers, developed a golden traffic with the enemy ports of the Spanish and French West Indies. This treasonable trade in foodstuffs actually kept some of the hostile islands from starving at the very time when the British navy was trying to subdue them. In the final year of the war, the British authorities, forced to resort to drastic measures, forbade the export of all supplies from New England and the middle colonies.

Other colonists, self-centered and alienated by distance from the war, refused to provide troops and money for the conflict. They demanded the rights and privileges of Englishmen, without the duties and responsibilities of Englishmen. Not until Pitt had offered to reimburse the colonies for a substantial part of their expenditures—some £900,000—did they move with some enthusiasm. If the Americans had to be bribed to defend themselves against a relentless and savage foe, would they ever unite to strike the mother country?

The curse of intercolonial disunity, present from early days, had continued throughout the recent hostilities. It had been caused mainly by enormous distances; by geographical barriers like rivers; by conflicting religions, from Catholic to Quaker; by varied nationalities, from German to Irish; by differing types of colonial governments; by many boundary disputes; and by the resentment of the crude backcountry settlers against the aristocratic bigwigs.

Yet unity received some encouragement during the French and Indian War. When soldiers and statesmen from widely separated colonies met around common campfires and council tables, they were often agreeably surprised by what they found. Despite deep-seated jealousy and suspicion, they discovered that they were all fellow Americans who generally spoke the same language and shared common ideals. Barriers of disunity began to melt, although a long and rugged road lay ahead before a coherent nation would emerge.

✦ War's Fateful Aftermath

The removal of the French menace in Canada profoundly affected American attitudes. While the French hawk had been hovering in the North and West, the colonial chicks had been forced to cling close to the wings of their British mother hen. Now that the hawk was killed, they could range far afield with a new spirit of independence.

The French, humiliated by the British and saddened by the fate of Canada, consoled themselves with one wishful thought. Perhaps the loss of their American empire would one day result in Britain's loss of its American empire. In a sense the history of the United States began with the fall of Québec and Montréal; the infant Republic was cradled on the Plains of Abraham.

The Spanish and Indian menaces were also now substantially reduced. Spain was (temporarily) eliminated from Florida, although entrenched in Louisiana and New Orleans, and was still securely in possession of much of western North America, including the vast territory from present-day Texas to California. As for the Indians, the Treaty of Paris that ended the Seven Years' War dealt a harsh blow to the Iroquois, Creeks, and other interior tribes. The Spanish removal from Florida and the French removal from Canada deprived the Indians of their most powerful diplomatic weapon—the ability to play off the rival European powers against one another. In the future the Indians would have to negotiate exclusively with the British.

Sensing the newly precarious position of the Indian peoples, the Ottawa chief Pontiac in 1763 led several tribes, aided by a handful of French traders who remained in the region, in a violent campaign to drive the British out of the Ohio Country. **Pontiac's uprising** laid siege to Detroit in the spring of 1763 and eventually overran all but three British posts west of the Appalachians, killing some two thousand soldiers and settlers.

The British retaliated swiftly and cruelly. Waging a primitive version of biological warfare, one British commander ordered blankets infected with small-pox to be distributed among the Indians. Such tactics crushed the uprising and brought an uneasy truce to the frontier. His bold plan frustrated, Pontiac himself perished in 1769 at the hands of a rival chieftain. As for the British, the bloody episode convinced them of

the need to stabilize relations with the western Indians and to keep regular troops stationed along the restless frontier, a measure for which they soon asked the colonists to foot the bill.

Land-hungry American colonists were now free to burst over the dam of the Appalachian Mountains and flood out over the verdant western lands. A tiny rivulet of pioneers had already trickled into Tennessee and Kentucky; other courageous settlers made their preparations for the long, dangerous trek over the mountains.

Then, out of a clear sky, the London government issued its **Proclamation of 1763**. It flatly prohibited settlement in the area beyond the Appalachians, pending further adjustments (see Map 6.8). The truth is that this hastily drawn document was not designed to oppress the colonists at all, but to work out the Indian problem fairly and prevent another bloody eruption like Pontiac's uprising.

But countless Americans, especially land speculators, were dismayed and angered. Was not the land

---

Contending Voices
The Proclamation of 1763

The Royal Proclamation of 1763 explicitly forbade the acquisition of western lands by individual colonists:

❝We do, with the advice of our Privy Council strictly enjoin and require, that no private person do presume to make any purchase from the said Indians of any lands reserved to the said Indians... but that, if at any time any of the said Indians should be inclined to dispose of the said lands, the same shall be purchased only for us [the British Crown], in our name....❞

In 1767, George Washington (1732–1799) wrote in confidence to a friend:

❝I can never look upon that Proclamation in any other light (but this I say between ourselves) than as a temporary expedient to quiet the minds of the Indians....Any person therefore who neglects the present opportunity of hunting out good lands and in some measure marking and distinguishing them for their own (in order to keep others from settling them) will never regain it....❞

> Were the colonists justified in their resentment of the Proclamation?

Legend:
- European settlement before 1700
- European settlement 1700–1763
- Frontier, 1763
- Proclamation Line of 1763
- Pontiac's uprising, 1763

MAP 6.8 British Colonies at End of the Seven Years' War, 1763 This map, showing the colonies thirteen years before the Declaration of Independence, helps to explain why the British would be unable to conquer their offspring. The colonists were spreading rapidly into the backcountry, where the powerful British navy could not flush them out. During the Revolutionary War, the British at one time or another captured the leading colonial cities—Boston, New York, Philadelphia, and Charleston—but the more remote interior remained a sanctuary for rebels. © 2016 Cengage Learning beyond the mountains their birthright? Had they not, in addition, purchased it with their blood in the recent war? In complete defiance of the proclamation, they clogged the westward trails. In 1765 an estimated one thousand wagons rolled through the town of Salisbury, North Carolina, on their way "up west." This wholesale flouting of royal authority boded ill for the longevity of British rule in America.

The Seven Years' War also caused the colonists to develop a new vision of their destiny. With the path cleared for the conquest of a continent, with their birthrate high and their energy boundless, they sensed that they were a potent people on the march. And they were in no mood to be restrained.

Lordly Britons, whose suddenly swollen empire had tended to produce swollen heads, were in no mood for back talk. Puffed up over their recent victories, they were already annoyed with their unruly colonial subjects. The stage was set for a violent family quarrel.

Chapter Review

KEY TERMS

Huguenots (101)
Edict of Nantes (101)
coureurs de bois (102)
voyageurs (102)
King William's War (103)
Queen Anne's War (103)
War of Jenkins's Ear (105)
King George's War (105)
Acadians (107)
French and Indian War (Seven Years' War) (107)
Albany Congress (109)
regulars (109)
Québec, Battle of (110)
Pontiac's uprising (113)
Proclamation of 1763 (113)

PEOPLE TO KNOW

Louis XIV
Samuel de Champlain
Edward Braddock
William Pitt
James Wolfe
Pontiac

CHRONOLOGY

1598	Edict of Nantes (repealed in 1685)
1608	Champlain colonizes Québec for France
1643	Louis XIV becomes king of France
1682	La Salle explores Mississippi River to the Gulf of Mexico
1689–1697	King William's War (War of the League of Augsburg)
1702–1713	Queen Anne's War (War of Spanish Succession)
1718	French found New Orleans
1739	War of Jenkins's Ear
1744–1748	King George's War (War of Austrian Succession)
1754	Washington battles French on frontier Albany Congress
1756–1763	Seven Years' War (French and Indian War)
1755	Braddock's defeat
1757	Pitt emerges as leader of British government
1759	Battle of Québec
1763	Peace of Paris Pontiac's uprising Proclamation of 1763

TO LEARN MORE

Fred Anderson, *Crucible of War: The Seven Years' War and the Fate of Empire in British North America, 1754–1766* (2001)

David Armitage, ed., *The British Atlantic World, 1500–1800* (2002)

Colin G. Calloway, *The Scratch of a Pen: 1763 and the Transformation of America* (2006)

David Dixon, *Never Come to Peace Again: Pontiac's Uprising and the Fate of the British Empire in North America* (2005)

Elizabeth Mancke and Carole Shammas, eds., *The Creation of the British Atlantic World* (2005)

Jane T. Merrit, *At the Crossroads: Indians and Empires on a Mid-Atlantic Frontier, 1700–1763* (2007)

Paul David Nelson, *William Tryon and the Course of Empire: A Life in British Imperial Service* (1990)

Carolyn Podruchny, *Making the Voyageur World: Travelers and Traders in the North American Fur Trade* (2006)

James Pritchard, *In Search of Empire: The French in the Americas, 1670–1730* (2004)

Peter Silver, *Our Savage Neighbors: How Indian War Transformed Early America* (2007)

A complete, annotated bibliography for this chapter—along with brief descriptions of the People to Know—may be found on the *American Pageant* website. The key terms are defined in the glossary at the end of the text.

Chapter 7

The Road to Revolution

1763–1775

The Revolution was effected before the war commenced.
The Revolution was in the minds and hearts of the people.

JOHN ADAMS, 1818

Victory in the Seven Years' War made Britain the master of a vastly enlarged imperial domain in North America. But victory—including the subsequent need to garrison ten thousand troops along the sprawling American frontier—was painfully costly. The London government therefore struggled after 1763 to compel the American colonists to shoulder some of the financial costs of empire. This change in British colonial policy reinforced an emerging sense of American political identity and helped to precipitate the American Revolution.

The eventual conflict was by no means inevitable. Indeed, given the tightening commercial, military, and cultural bonds between colonies and mother country since the first crude settlements a century and a half earlier, it might be considered remarkable that the Revolution happened at all. The truth is that Americans were reluctant revolutionaries. Until late in the day, they sought only to claim the "rights of Englishmen," not to separate from the mother country. But what began as a squabble about economic policies soon exposed irreconcilable differences between Americans and Britons over cherished political principles. The ensuing clash gave birth to a new nation.

✷ The Deep Roots of Revolution

In a broad sense, America was a revolutionary force from the day of its discovery by Europeans. The New World nurtured new ideas about the nature of society, citizen, and government. In the Old World, many humble folk had long lived in the shadow of graveyards that contained the bones of their ancestors for a thousand years past. Few people born into such changeless surroundings dared to question their social status. But European immigrants in the New World were not so easily subdued by the scowl of their superiors. In the American wilderness, they encountered a world that was theirs to make afresh.

Two ideas in particular had taken root in the minds of the American colonists by the mid-eighteenth century: one was what historians call **republicanism**. Looking to the models of the ancient Greek and Roman republics, exponents of republicanism defined a just society as one in which all citizens willingly subordinated their private, selfish interests to the common good. Both the stability of society and the authority of government thus depended on the virtue of the citizenry—its capacity for selflessness, self-sufficiency, and courage, and especially its appetite for civic involvement. By its very nature, republicanism was opposed to hierarchical and authoritarian institutions such as aristocracy and monarchy.

A second idea that fundamentally shaped American political thought derived from a group of British political commentators known as **radical Whigs**. Widely read by the colonists, the Whigs feared the threat to liberty posed by the arbitrary power of the monarch and his ministers relative to elected representatives in Parliament. The Whigs mounted withering attacks on the use of patronage and bribes by the king's ministers—symptoms of a wider moral failure in society that they called "corruption," in the sense of rot or decay. The Whigs warned citizens to be on guard against corruption and to be eternally vigilant against possible conspiracies to denude them of their hard-won liberties. Together, republican and Whig ideas predisposed the American colonists to be on hair-trigger alert against any threat to their rights.

The circumstances of colonial life had done much to bolster those attitudes. Dukes and princes, barons and bishops were unknown in the colonies, while property ownership and political participation were relatively accessible. The Americans had also grown accustomed to running their own affairs, largely unmolested by remote officials in London. Distance weakens authority; great distance weakens authority greatly. So it came as an especially jolting shock when Britain after 1763 tried to enclose its American colonists more snugly in its grip.

✴ Mercantilism and Colonial Grievances

Britain's empire was acquired in a "fit of absentmindedness," an old saying goes, and there is much truth in the jest. Not one of the original thirteen colonies except Georgia was formally planted by the British government. All the others were haphazardly founded by trading companies, religious groups, or land speculators.

The Female Combatants, 1776 Britain is symbolized as a lady of fashion; her rebellious daughter, America, as an Indian princess. Their shields of Obedience and Liberty seem mutually exclusive standards. Compare this cartoon with the one on p. 155.

The British authorities nevertheless embraced a theory, called **mercantilism**, that justified their control over the colonies. Mercantilists believed that wealth was power and that a country's economic wealth (and hence its military and political power) could be measured by the amount of gold or silver in its treasury. To amass gold or silver, a country needed to export more than it imported. Possessing colonies thus conferred distinct advantages because the colonies could both supply raw materials to the mother country (thereby reducing the need for foreign imports) and provide a guaranteed market for exports.

The London government looked on the American colonists more or less as tenants. They were expected to furnish products needed in the mother country, such as tobacco, sugar, and ships' masts; to refrain from making for export certain products, such as woolen cloth or beaver hats; to buy imported manufactured goods exclusively from Britain; and not to indulge in bothersome dreams of economic self-sufficiency or, worse, self-government.

From time to time, Parliament passed laws to regulate the mercantilist system. The first of these, the Navigation Law of 1650, was aimed at rival Dutch shippers trying to elbow their way into the American carrying trade. Thereafter all commerce flowing to and from the colonies could be transported only in British (including colonial) vessels. Subsequent laws required that European goods destined for America first had to be landed in Britain, where tariff duties could be collected and British middlemen could take a slice of the profits. Other laws stipulated that American merchants must ship certain "enumerated" products, notably tobacco, exclusively to Britain, even though prices might be better elsewhere.

British policy also inflicted a currency shortage on the colonies. Because the colonists regularly bought more from Britain than they sold there, the difference had to be made up in hard cash. Every year gold and silver coins, mostly earned in illicit trade with the Spanish and French West Indies, drained out of the colonies, creating an acute money shortage. To facilitate everyday purchases, the colonists resorted to butter, nails, pitch, and feathers for purposes of exchange.

Currency issues came to a boil when dire financial need forced many of the colonies to issue paper money, which swiftly depreciated. British merchants and creditors squawked so loudly that Parliament prohibited the colonial legislatures from printing paper currency and from passing indulgent bankruptcy laws—practices that might harm British merchants. The Americans grumbled that their welfare was being sacrificed for the well-being of British commercial interests.

The British crown also reserved the right to nullify any legislation passed by the colonial assemblies if such laws worked mischief with the mercantilist

Paul Revere, by John Singleton Copley, ca. 1768 This painting of the famed silversmith-horseman challenged convention—but reflected the new democratic spirit of the age—by portraying an artisan in working clothes. Note how Copley depicted the serene confidence of the master craftsman and Revere's quiet pride in his work.

Photograph © 2011 Museum of Fine Arts, Boston, 30.781

system. This royal veto was used rather sparingly—just 469 times in connection with 8,563 laws. But the colonists fiercely resented its very existence—another example of how principle could weigh more heavily than practice in fueling colonial grievances.

✶ The Merits and Menace of Mercantilism

In theory the British mercantile system seemed thoroughly selfish and deliberately oppressive. But the truth is that until 1763, the various Navigation Laws imposed no intolerable burden, mainly because they were only loosely enforced. Enterprising colonial merchants learned early to disregard or evade troublesome restrictions. Some of the first American fortunes, like that of John Hancock, were amassed by wholesale smuggling.

Americans also reaped direct benefits from the mercantile system. If the colonies existed for the benefit of the mother country, it was hardly less true that Britain existed for the benefit of the colonies. London paid liberal bounties to colonial producers of ship parts, over the protests of British competitors. Virginia

tobacco planters enjoyed a monopoly in the British market, snuffing out the tiny British tobacco industry. The colonists also benefited from the protection of the world's mightiest navy and a strong, seasoned army of redcoats—all without a penny of cost.

But even when painted in its rosiest colors, the mercantile system burdened the colonists with annoying liabilities. Mercantilism stifled economic initiative and imposed a rankling dependency on British agents and creditors. Most grievously, many Americans simply found the mercantilist system debasing. They felt used, kept in a state of perpetual economic adolescence, and never allowed to come of age. As Benjamin Franklin wrote in 1775,

We have an old mother that peevish is grown;
She snubs us like children that scarce walk alone;
She forgets we're grown up and have sense of our own.

Revolution broke out, as Theodore Roosevelt later remarked, because Britain failed to recognize an emerging nation when it saw one.

✶ The Stamp Tax Uproar

Victory-flushed Britain emerged from the Seven Years' War holding one of the biggest empires in the world—and also, less happily, the biggest debt, some £140 million, about half of which had been incurred defending the American colonies. To justify and service that debt, British officials now moved to redefine their relationship with their North American colonies.

Prime Minister George Grenville first aroused the resentment of the colonists in 1763 by ordering the British navy to begin strictly enforcing the Navigation Laws. He also secured from Parliament the so-called **Sugar Act** of 1764, the first law ever passed by that body for raising tax revenue in the colonies for the crown. Among various provisions, it increased the duty on foreign sugar imported from the West Indies. After bitter protests from the colonists, the duties were lowered substantially, and the agitation died down. But resentment was kept burning by the **Quartering Act** of 1765. This measure required certain colonies to provide food and quarters for British troops.

The Boston Gazette *declared in 1765,*

❝A colonist cannot make a button, a horseshoe, nor a hobnail, but some snooty ironmonger or respectable buttonmaker of Britain shall bawl and squall that his honor's worship is most egregiously maltreated, injured, cheated, and robbed by the rascally American republicans.**❞**

Then in the same year, 1765, Grenville imposed the most odious measure of all: a **stamp tax**, to raise revenues to support the new military force. The Stamp Act mandated the use of stamped paper or the affixing of stamps, certifying payment of tax. Stamps were required on bills of sale for about fifty trade items as well as on certain types of commercial and legal documents, including playing cards, pamphlets, newspapers, diplomas, bills of lading, and marriage licenses.

Grenville regarded all of these measures as reasonable and just. He was simply asking the Americans to pay a fair share of the costs for their own defense, through taxes that were already familiar in Britain. In fact, the British people for two generations had endured a stamp tax far heavier than that passed for the colonies.

Yet the Americans were angrily aroused at what they regarded as Grenville's fiscal aggression. The new laws did not merely pinch their pocketbooks. Far more ominously, Grenville also seemed to be striking at the local liberties they had come to assume as a matter of right. Thus some colonial assemblies defiantly refused to comply with the Quartering Act or voted only a fraction of the supplies that it called for.

Worst of all, Grenville's noxious legislation seemed to jeopardize the basic rights of the colonists as Englishmen. Both the Sugar Act and the Stamp Act provided for trying offenders in the hated **admiralty courts**, where juries were not allowed. The burden of proof was on the defendants, who were assumed to be guilty unless they could prove themselves innocent. Trial by jury and the precept of "innocent until proved guilty" were ancient privileges that British people everywhere, including the American colonists, held most dear.

And why was a British army needed at all in the colonies, now that the French were expelled from the continent and Pontiac's warriors crushed? Could its real purpose be to whip rebellious colonists into line? Many Americans, weaned on radical Whig suspicion of all authority, began to sniff the strong scent of a conspiracy to strip them of their historic liberties. They lashed back violently, and the Stamp Act became the target that drew their most ferocious fire.

Angry throats raised the cry "No taxation without representation." There was some irony in the slogan because the seaports and tidewater towns that were most wrathful against the Stamp Act had long denied full representation to their own backcountry pioneers. But now the aggravated colonists took the high ground of principle.

The Americans made a distinction between "legislation" and "taxation." They conceded the right of Parliament to legislate about matters that affected the entire empire, including the regulation of trade. But they steadfastly denied the right of Parliament, in which no Americans were seated, to impose taxes on Americans. Only their own elected colonial legislatures, the Americans insisted, could legally tax them. Taxes levied by the distant British Parliament amounted to robbery, a piratical assault on the sacred rights of property.

Grenville dismissed these American protests as hairsplitting absurdities. The power of Parliament was supreme and undivided, he asserted, and in any case the Americans *were* represented in Parliament. Elaborating the theory of "virtual representation," Grenville claimed that every member of Parliament represented all British subjects, even those Americans in Boston or Charleston who had never voted for a member of Parliament.

The Americans scoffed at the notion of virtual representation. And truthfully, they did not really want direct representation in Parliament, which might have seemed like a sensible compromise. If they had obtained it, any gouty member of the House of Commons could have proposed an oppressive tax bill for the colonies, and the outvoted American representatives, few in number, would have stood bereft of a principle with which to resist.

Thus the principle of no taxation without representation was supremely important, and the colonists clung to it with tenacious consistency. When the British replied that the sovereign power of government could not be divided between "legislative" authority in London and "taxing" authority in the colonies, they forced the Americans to deny the authority of Parliament altogether and to begin to consider their own political independence. This chain of logic eventually led, link by link, to revolutionary consequences.

✦ Forced Repeal of the Stamp Act

Colonial outcries against the hated stamp tax took various forms. The most conspicuous assemblage was the **Stamp Act Congress** of 1765, which brought together in New York City twenty-seven distinguished delegates from nine colonies. After dignified debate the members drew up a statement of their rights and grievances and beseeched the king and Parliament to repeal the repugnant legislation.

The Stamp Act Congress, which was largely ignored in England, made little splash at the time in

English statesman Edmund Burke (1729–1797) warned in 1775,

❝Young man, there is America—which at this day serves for little more than to amuse you with stories of savage men and uncouth manners; yet shall, before you taste of death, show itself equal to the whole of that commerce which now attracts the envy of the world.❞

America. Its ripples, however, began to erode sectional suspicions, for it brought together around the same table leaders from the different and rival colonies. It was one more halting but significant step toward intercolonial unity.

More effective than the congress was the widespread adoption of **nonimportation agreements** against British goods. Woolen garments of homespun became fashionable, and the eating of lamb chops was discouraged so that the wool-bearing sheep would be allowed to mature. Nonimportation agreements were in fact a promising stride toward union; they spontaneously united the American people for the first time in common action.

Mobilizing in support of nonimportation gave ordinary American men and women new opportunities to participate in colonial protests. Many people who had previously stood on the sidelines now signed petitions swearing to uphold the terms of the consumer boycotts. Groups of women assembled in public to hold spinning bees and make homespun cloth as a replacement for shunned British textiles. Such public defiance helped spread angry resistance throughout American colonial society.

Sometimes violence accompanied colonial protests. Groups of ardent spirits, known as **Sons of Liberty** and **Daughters of Liberty**, took the law into their own hands. Crying "Liberty, Property, and No Stamps," they enforced the nonimportation agreements against violators, often with a generous coat of tar and feathers. Patriotic mobs ransacked the houses of unpopular officials, confiscated their money, and hanged effigies of stamp agents on liberty poles.

Shaken by colonial commotion, the machinery for collecting the tax broke down. On that dismal day in 1765 when the new act was to go into effect, the stamp agents had all been forced to resign, and there was no one to sell the stamps. While flags flapped at

Contending Voices
Reconciliation or Independence?

John Dickinson (1732–1808), a lawyer and popular essayist, advocated a middle-of-the-road response to the new British revenue acts of the 1760s that appealed to most colonists at the time:

"The constitutional modes of obtaining relief are those which I wish to see pursued on the present occasion.... We have an excellent prince, in whose good disposition we may confide.... Let us behave like dutiful children who have received unmerited blows from a beloved parent. Let us complain to our parent; but let our complaint speak at the same time the language of affliction and veneration."

Thomas Paine (1737–1809), a radical English propagandist who emigrated to America in 1774 with the help of Benjamin Franklin, argued in his famous tract of 1776, Common Sense, *that separation from England was the only logical course for the rebellious colonists:*

"Everything that is right or reasonable pleads for separation. The blood of the slain, the weeping face of nature, cries, 'tis time to part.... [T]here is something absurd in supposing a continent to be perpetually governed by an island. In no instance hath nature made the satellite larger than its primary planet; and as England and America, with respect to each other, reverse the common order of nature, it is evident that they belong to different systems. England to Europe: America to itself...."

Why did Paine's advice prevail over Dickinson's?

Protesting the Stamp Act   Even common household wares in the 1760s testified to the colonists' mounting rage against the Stamp Act. Many people in Britain sympathized with the Americans—and sought to profit from their anger, as this English-made teapot demonstrates. (left) The Colonial Williamsburg Foundation; (right) Courtesy of the Peabody Essex Museum, Salem, MA half-mast, the law was openly and flagrantly defied—or, rather, nullified.

England was hard hit. America then bought about one-quarter of all British exports, and about one-half of British shipping was devoted to the American trade. Merchants, manufacturers, and shippers suffered from the colonial nonimportation agreements, and hundreds of laborers were thrown out of work. Loud demands converged on Parliament for repeal of the Stamp Act. But many of the members could not understand why 7.5 million Britons had to pay heavy taxes to protect the colonies, whereas some 2 million colonists refused to pay for only one-third of the cost of their own defense.

After a stormy debate, Parliament in 1766 grudgingly repealed the Stamp Act. Grateful residents of New York erected a leaden statue to King George III. But American rejoicing was premature. Having withdrawn the Stamp Act, Parliament in virtually the same breath provocatively passed the **Declaratory Act**, reaffirming Parliament's right "to bind" the colonies

"in all cases whatsoever." The British government thereby drew its line in the sand. It defined the constitutional principle it would not yield: absolute and unqualified sovereignty over its North American colonies. The colonists had already drawn their own battle line by making it clear that they wanted a measure of sovereignty of their own and would undertake drastic action to secure it. The stage was set for a continuing confrontation. Within a few years, that statue of King George would be melted into thousands of bullets to be fired at his troops.

✦ The Townshend Tea Tax and the Boston "Massacre"

Control of the British ministry was now seized by the gifted but erratic Charles ("Champagne Charley") Townshend, a man who could deliver brilliant speeches in Parliament even while drunk. Rashly promising to pluck feathers from the colonial goose with a minimum of squawking, he persuaded Parliament in 1767 to pass the **Townshend Acts**. The most important of these new regulations was a light import duty on glass, white lead, paper, paint, and tea. Townshend, seizing on a dubious distinction between internal and external taxes, made this tax, unlike the stamp tax, an indirect customs duty payable at American ports. But to the increasingly restless colonists, this was a phantom distinction. For them the real difficulty remained taxes—in any form—without representation.

Flushed with their recent victory over the stamp tax, the colonists were in a rebellious mood. The impost on tea was especially irksome, for an estimated 1 million people drank the refreshing brew twice a day.

The new Townshend revenues, worse yet, were to be earmarked to pay the salaries of the royal governors and judges in America. From the standpoint of efficient administration by London, this was a reform long overdue. But the ultrasuspicious Americans, who had beaten the royal governors into line by controlling the purse, regarded Townshend's tax as another attempt to enchain them. Their worst fears took on greater reality when the London government, after passing the Townshend taxes, suspended the legislature of New York in 1767 for failure to comply with the Quartering Act.

Nonimportation agreements, previously potent, were quickly revived against the Townshend Acts. But they proved less effective than those devised against the Stamp Act. The colonists, again enjoying prosperity, took the new tax less seriously than might have been expected, largely because it was light and indirect. They found, moreover, that they could secure smuggled tea at a cheap price, and consequently smugglers increased their activities, especially in Massachusetts.

Public Punishment for the Excise Man, 1774 This popular rendering of the punishment of Commissioner of Customs John Malcomb shows him tarred and feathered and forcibly "paid" with great quantities of tea. From the Liberty Tree in the background dangles the threat of hanging, all for attempting to collect duties in Boston.

Fotosearch/Archive Photos/Getty Images

Two Views of the Boston Massacre, 1770 and 1856   Both of these prints of the Boston Massacre were art as well as propaganda. Paul Revere's engraving (left) began circulating within three weeks of the event in March 1770, depicting not a clash of brawlers but armed soldiers taking aim at peaceful citizens. Absent also was any evidence of the mulatto ringleader, Crispus Attucks. Revere wanted his print to convince viewers of the indisputable justice of the colonists' cause. By the mid-1850s, when the chromolithograph (right) circulated, it served a new political purpose. In the era of the abolitionist movement, freedman Crispus Attucks held center place in the print, which portrayed his death as an American martyr in the revolutionary struggle for freedom.

British officials, faced with a breakdown of law and order, landed two regiments of troops in Boston in 1768. Many of the soldiers were drunken and profane characters. Liberty-loving colonists, resenting the presence of the red-coated "ruffians," taunted the "bloody backs" unmercifully.

A clash soon erupted. On the evening of March 5, 1770, a crowd of some sixty townspeople began taunting and throwing snowballs at a squad of ten redcoats. The Bostonians were still angry over the death of an eleven-year-old boy, shot ten days earlier during a protest against a merchant who had defied the colonial boycott of British goods. Acting apparently without orders, but nervous and provoked by the jeering crowd, the troops opened fire and killed or wounded eleven citizens, an event that became known as the **Boston Massacre**. One of the first to die was Crispus Attucks, described by contemporaries as a powerfully built runaway "mulatto" and a leader of the mob. Both sides were in some degree to blame, and in the subsequent trial (in which future president John Adams served as defense attorney for the soldiers), only two of the redcoats were found guilty of manslaughter. The soldiers were released after being branded on the hand.

✴ The Seditious Committees of Correspondence

By 1770 King George III, then only thirty-two years old, was strenuously attempting to assert the power of the British monarchy. He was a good man in his private morals, but he proved to be a bad ruler. Earnest, industrious, stubborn, and lustful for power, he surrounded himself with cooperative "yes men," notably his corpulent prime minister, Lord North.

The ill-timed Townshend Acts had failed to produce revenue, though they did produce near-rebellion. Net proceeds from the tax in one year were a paltry £295, while in that same year Britain's military costs in the colonies had mounted to £170,000. Nonimportation agreements, though feebly enforced, were pinching

Giving new meaning to the proverbial tempest in a teapot, a group of 126 Boston women signed an agreement, or "subscription list," that announced,

❝We the Daughters of those Patriots who have and now do appear for the public interest…do with Pleasure engage with them in denying ourselves the drinking of Foreign Tea, in hopes to frustrate a Plan that tends to deprive the whole Community of…all that is valuable in Life.❞

Samuel Adams (1722–1803) A second cousin of John Adams, he contributed a potent pen and tongue to the American Revolution as a political agitator and organizer of rebellion. He was the leading spirit in hosting the Boston Tea Party. A failure in the brewing business, he was sent by Massachusetts to the First Continental Congress of 1774. He signed the Declaration of Independence and served in Congress until 1781.

Portrait Traditionally Said to Be That of Abigail Adams (1744–1818) The wife of Revolutionary War leader and future president John Adams, she was a prominent Patriot in her own right. She was also among the first Americans to see, however faintly, the implications of revolutionary ideas for changing the status of women.

British manufacturers. The government of Lord North, bowing to various pressures, finally persuaded Parliament to repeal the Townshend revenue duties. But the three-pence toll on tea, the tax the colonists found most offensive, was retained to keep alive the principle of Parliament's right to tax the colonies.

Flames of discontent in America continued to be fanned by numerous incidents, including the redoubled efforts of the British officials to enforce the Navigation Laws. Resistance was further kindled by a master propagandist and engineer of rebellion, Samuel Adams of Boston, a cousin of John Adams. Unimpressive in appearance (his hands trembled), he lived and breathed only for politics. His friends had to buy him a presentable suit of clothes when he left Massachusetts on intercolonial business. Zealous, tenacious, and courageous, he was ultrasensitive to infractions of colonial rights. Cherishing a deep faith in the common people, he appealed effectively to what was called his "trained mob."

Samuel Adams's signal contribution was to organize in Massachusetts the local **committees of correspondence**. After he had formed the first one in Boston during 1772, some eighty towns in the colony speedily set up similar organizations. Their chief function was to spread the spirit of resistance by exchanging letters and thus keep alive opposition to British policy. One critic referred to the committees as "the foulest, subtlest, and most venomous serpent ever issued from the egg of sedition."

Intercolonial committees of correspondence were the next logical step. Virginia led the way in 1773 by creating such a body as a standing committee of the House of Burgesses. Within a short time, every colony had established a central committee through which it could exchange ideas and information with other colonies. These intercolonial groups were supremely significant in stimulating and disseminating sentiment in favor of united action. They evolved directly into the first American congresses.

✯ Tea Brewing in Boston

Thus far—that is, by 1773—nothing had happened to make rebellion inevitable. Nonimportation was weakening. Increasing numbers of colonists were reluctantly paying the tea tax because the legal tea was now cheaper than the smuggled tea, even cheaper than tea in England.

A new ogre entered the picture in 1773. The powerful British East India Company, overburdened with 17 million pounds of unsold tea, was facing bankruptcy. If it collapsed, the London government would lose heavily in tax revenue. The ministry therefore decided to assist the company by awarding it a complete monopoly of the American tea business. The giant corporation would now be able to sell the coveted leaves more cheaply than ever before, even with the three-pence tax tacked on. But many American tea drinkers, rather than rejoicing at the lower prices, cried foul. They saw this British move as a shabby attempt to trick the Americans, with the bait of cheaper tea, into swallowing the principle of the detested tax. For the determined Americans, principle remained far more important than price.

If the British officials insisted on the letter of the law, violence was highly likely. Fatefully, the British colonial authorities decided to enforce the law. Once more, the colonists rose up in wrath to defy it. Not a single one of the several thousand chests of tea shipped by the East India Company ever reached the hands of the consignees. In Philadelphia and New York, mass demonstrations forced the tea-bearing ships to return to England with their cargo holds still full. At Annapolis, Marylanders burned both cargo and vessel, while proclaiming "liberty and Independence or death in pursuit of it." In Charleston, South Carolina, officials seized the tea for nonpayment of duties after intimidated local merchants refused to accept delivery. (Ironically, the confiscated Charleston tea was later auctioned to raise money for the Revolutionary army.)

Only in Boston did a British official stubbornly refuse to be cowed. Massachusetts governor Thomas Hutchinson had already felt the fury of the mob, when Stamp Act protesters had destroyed his home in 1765. This time he was determined not to budge. Ironically, Hutchinson agreed that the tea tax was unjust, but he believed even more strongly that the colonists had no right to flout the law. Hutchinson infuriated Boston's radicals when he ordered the tea ships not to clear Boston harbor until they had unloaded their cargoes. Sentiment against him was further inflamed when Hutchinson's enemies published one of his private letters in which he declared that "an abridgement of what are called English liberties" was necessary for the preservation of law and order in the colonies—apparently confirming the darkest conspiracy theories of the American radicals.

On December 16, 1773, roughly a hundred Bostonians, loosely disguised as Indians, boarded the docked ships, smashed open 342 chests of tea, and dumped their contents into the Atlantic, an action that came to be known as the **Boston Tea Party**. A crowd of several hundred watched approvingly from the shore as Boston harbor became a vast teapot. Donning Indian disguise provided protesters with a threatening image—and a convenient way of avoiding detection. Tea was the perfect symbol to rally around as almost every colonist, rich or poor, consumed this imported, caffeinated beverage.

Reactions varied. All up and down the eastern seaboard, sympathetic colonists applauded. Referring to tea as "a badge of slavery," they burned the hated leaves in solidarity with Boston. But conservatives complained that the destruction of private property violated the law and threatened anarchy and the breakdown of civil decorum. Hutchinson, chastened and disgusted with the colonies, retreated to Britain, never to return. The British authorities, meanwhile,

The Boston Tea Party, December 16, 1773 Crying "Boston harbor a teapot this night," Sons of Liberty disguised as Indians hurled chests of tea into the sea to protest the tax on tea and to make sure that its cheap price did not prove an "invincible temptation" to the people.

Ann Hulton (d. 1779?), a Loyalist, described colonial political divisions and her hopes and fears for her own future in a letter she sent to a friend in England in 1774:

"Those who are well disposed towards Government are termed Tories. They daily increase & have made some efforts to take the power out of the hands of the Patriots, but they are intimidated & overpowered by Numbers.... However I don't despair of seeing Peace & tranquility in America, tho' they talk very high & furious at present."

saw little alternative to whipping the upstart colonists into shape. The granting of some measure of home rule to the Americans might at this stage still have prevented rebellion, but few British politicians were willing to swallow their pride and take the high road. The perilous path they chose instead led only to reprisals, bitterness, and escalating conflict.

✵ Parliament Passes the "Intolerable Acts"

An irate Parliament responded speedily to the Boston Tea Party with measures that brewed a revolution. By huge majorities in 1774, it passed a series of acts designed to chastise Boston in particular and Massachusetts in general. They were branded in America as "the massacre of American Liberty."

Most drastic of all was the Boston Port Act. It closed the tea-stained harbor until damages were paid and order could be ensured. By other **"Intolerable Acts"**—as they were called in America—many of the chartered rights of colonial Massachusetts were swept away. Restrictions were likewise placed on the precious town meetings. Contrary to previous practice, enforcing officials who killed colonists in the line of duty could now be sent to Britain for trial. There, suspicious Americans assumed, the officials would be likely to get off scot-free. Particularly intolerable to Bostonians was a new Quartering Act, which gave local authorities the power to lodge British soldiers anywhere, even in private homes.

By a fateful coincidence, the "Intolerable Acts" were accompanied in 1774 by the **Quebec Act**. Passed at the same time, it was erroneously regarded in English-speaking America as part of the British reaction to the turbulence in Boston. Actually, the Quebec Act was a good law in bad company. For many years the British government had debated how it should administer the sixty thousand or so conquered French subjects in Canada, and it had finally framed this farsighted and statesmanlike measure. The French were guaranteed

their Catholic religion. They were also permitted to retain many of their old customs and institutions, which did not include a representative assembly or trial by jury in civil cases. In addition, the old boundaries of the province of Québec were now extended southward all the way to the Ohio River.

The Quebec Act, from the viewpoint of the French Canadians, was a shrewd and conciliatory measure. If Britain had only shown as much foresight in dealing with its English-speaking colonies, it might not have lost them.

But from the viewpoint of the American colonists as a whole, the Quebec Act was especially noxious. All the other "Intolerable Acts" slapped directly at Massachusetts, but this one had a much wider range. By sustaining unrepresentative assemblies and denials of jury trials, it seemed to set a dangerous precedent in America. It alarmed land speculators, who were distressed to see the huge trans-Allegheny area snatched from their grasp (see Map 7.1). It aroused anti-Catholics, who were shocked by the extension of Roman Catholic jurisdiction southward into a huge region that had once been earmarked for Protestantism—a region about as large as the thirteen original colonies. One angry Protestant cried that there ought to be a "jubilee in hell" over this enormous gain for "Popery."

✵ Bloodshed

American dissenters responded sympathetically to the plight of Massachusetts. It had put itself in the wrong by the violent destruction of the tea cargoes; now Britain had put itself in the wrong by brutal punishment that seemed far too cruel for the crime. Flags were flown at half-mast throughout the colonies on the day that the Boston Port Act went into effect, and sister colonies rallied to send food to the stricken city. Rice was shipped even from faraway South Carolina.

Most memorable of the responses to the "Intolerable Acts" was the summoning of the **First Continental Congress** in 1774. It was to meet in Philadelphia to consider ways of redressing colonial grievances. Twelve of the thirteen colonies, with Georgia alone missing, sent fifty-five well-respected men, among them Samuel Adams, John Adams, George Washington, and Patrick Henry. Intercolonial frictions were partially melted away by social activity after working hours; in fifty-four days George Washington dined at his own lodgings only nine times.

The First Continental Congress deliberated for seven weeks, from September 5 to October 26, 1774. It was not a legislative but a consultative body—a convention rather than a congress. John Adams played a stellar role. Eloquently swaying his colleagues to a

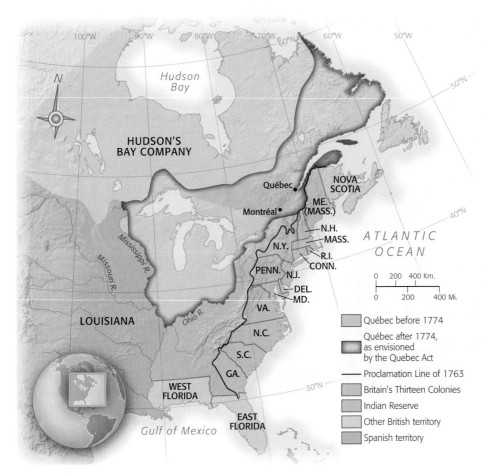

MAP 7.1 Québec Before and After 1774   Young Alexander Hamilton voiced the fears of many colonists when he warned that the Quebec Act of 1774 would introduce "priestly tyranny" into Canada, making that country another Spain or Portugal. "Does not your blood run cold," he asked, "to think that an English Parliament should pass an act for the establishment of arbitrary power and Popery in such a country?" © 2016 Cengage Learning

revolutionary course, he helped defeat by the narrowest of margins a proposal by the moderates for a species of American home rule under British direction. After prolonged argument the Congress drew up several dignified papers. These included a ringing Declaration of Rights, as well as solemn appeals to other British American colonies, to the king, and to the British people.

The most significant action of the Congress was the creation of **The Association**. Unlike previous nonimportation agreements, The Association called for a complete boycott of British goods: nonimportation, nonexportation, and nonconsumption. Yet it is important to note that the delegates were not yet calling for independence. They sought merely to repeal the offensive legislation and return to the happy days before parliamentary taxation. If colonial grievances were redressed, well and good; if not, the Congress

was to meet again in May 1775. Resistance had not yet ripened into open rebellion.

But the fatal drift toward war continued. Parliament rejected the Congress's petitions. In America chickens squawked and tar kettles bubbled as violators of The Association were tarred and feathered. Muskets were gathered, men began to drill openly, and a clash seemed imminent.

In April 1775 the British commander in Boston sent a detachment of troops to nearby **Lexington and Concord**. They were to seize stores of colonial gunpowder and also to bag the "rebel" ringleaders, Samuel Adams and John Hancock. At Lexington the colonial "Minute Men" refused to disperse rapidly enough, and shots were fired that killed eight Americans and wounded several more. The affair was more the "Lexington Massacre" than a battle. The redcoats pushed on to Concord, whence they were forced to

A View of the Town of Concord, ca. 1775 Redcoats here drill on the Concord Green, near where colonial militiamen would soon repel their advance on stores of rebel gunpowder.

retreat by the rough and ready Americans, whom Emerson immortalized:

> *By the rude bridge that arched the flood,*
> *Their flag to April's breeze unfurled,*
> *Here once the embattled farmers stood,*
> *And fired the shot heard round the world.**

The bewildered British, fighting off murderous fire from militiamen crouched behind thick stone walls, finally regained the sanctuary of Boston. Licking their wounds, they could count about three hundred casualties, including some seventy killed. Britain now had a war on its hands.

★ Imperial Strength and Weakness

Aroused Americans had brashly rebelled against a mighty empire (see "Thinking Globally: Imperial Rivalry and Colonial Revolt," pp. 130–131). The population odds were about three to one against the rebels— some 7.5 million Britons to 2.5 million colonists. The odds in monetary wealth and naval power overwhelmingly favored the mother country.

*Ralph Waldo Emerson, "Concord Hymn."

The great conservative political theorist and champion of the American cause Edmund Burke made a stirring speech in Britain's House of Commons in 1775, pleading in vain for reconciliation with the colonies:

❝As long as you have the wisdom to keep the sovereign authority of this country as the sanctuary of liberty...they will turn their faces towards you.... Slavery they can have anywhere; freedom they can have from none but you. This is the commodity of price, of which you have the monopoly. This is the true Act of Navigation, which binds to you the commerce of the colonies, and through them secures to you the wealth of the world. Deny them this participation of freedom, and you break that sole bond which originally made, and must still preserve, the unity of the empire.❞

Britain then boasted a professional army of some fifty thousand men, as compared with the numerous but wretchedly trained American militia. George III, in addition, had the treasury to hire foreign soldiers, and some thirty thousand Germans—so-called

Hessians—were ultimately employed. The British enrolled about fifty thousand American Loyalists and enlisted the services of many Indians, who though unreliable fair-weather fighters, inflamed long stretches of the frontier. One British officer boasted that the war would offer no problems that could not be solved by an "experienced sheep herder."

Yet Britain was weaker than it seemed at first glance. Oppressed Ireland was a smoking volcano, and British troops had to be detached to watch it. France, bitter from its recent defeat, was awaiting an opportunity to stab Britain in the back. The London government was confused and inept. There was no William Pitt, "Organizer of Victory," only the stubborn George III and his pliant Tory prime minister, Lord North.

Many earnest and God-fearing Britons had no desire whatever to kill their American cousins. William Pitt withdrew a son from the army rather than see him thrust his sword into fellow Anglo-Saxons struggling for liberty. The English Whig factions, opposed to Lord North's Tory wing, openly cheered American victories—at least at the outset. Aside from trying to embarrass the Tories politically, many Whigs believed that the battle for British freedom was being fought in America. If George III triumphed, his rule at home might become tyrannical. This outspoken sympathy in Britain, though plainly a minority voice, greatly encouraged the Americans. If they continued their resistance long enough, the Whigs might come into power and deal generously with them.

Britain's army in America had to operate under endless difficulties. The generals were second-rate; the soldiers, though on the whole capable, were brutally treated. There was one extreme case of eight hundred lashes on the bare back for striking an officer. Provisions were often scarce, rancid, and wormy. On one occasion a supply of biscuits, captured some fifteen years earlier from the French, was softened by dropping cannonballs on them.

Other handicaps loomed. The redcoats had to conquer the Americans; restoring the pre-1763 status quo would be a victory for the colonists. Britain was operating some three thousand miles from its home base, and distance added greatly to the delays and uncertainties arising from storms and other mishaps. Military orders were issued in London that, when received months later, would not fit the changing situation.

America's geographical expanse was enormous: roughly 1,000 by 600 miles. The united colonies had no urban nerve center, like France's Paris, whose capture would cripple the country as a whole. British armies took every city of any size, yet like a boxer punching a feather pillow, they made little more than a dent in the entire country. The Americans wisely traded space for time. Benjamin Franklin calculated that during the prolonged campaign in which the redcoats captured Bunker Hill and killed some 150 Patriots, about 60,000 American babies were born.

✦ American Pluses and Minuses

The revolutionaries were blessed with outstanding leadership. George Washington was a giant among men; Benjamin Franklin was a master among diplomats. Open foreign aid, theoretically possible from the start, eventually came from France. Numerous European officers, many of them unemployed and impoverished, volunteered their swords for pay. In a class by himself was a wealthy young French nobleman, the Marquis de Lafayette. Fleeing from boredom, loving glory and ultimately liberty, the "French gamecock" was made a major general in the colonial army at age nineteen. His commission was largely a recognition of his family influence and political connections, but the services of this teenage general in securing further aid from France were invaluable.

Other conditions aided the Americans. They were fighting defensively, with the odds, all things considered, favoring the defender. In agriculture, the colonies were mainly self-sustaining, like a kind of Robinson Crusoe's island. The Americans also enjoyed the moral advantage that came from belief in a just cause. The historical odds were not impossible. Other peoples had triumphed in the face of greater obstacles: Greeks against Persians, Swiss against Austrians, Dutch against Spaniards.

Yet the American rebels were badly organized for war. From the earliest days, they had been almost fatally lacking in unity, and the new nation lurched forward uncertainly like an uncoordinated centipede. Even the Continental Congress, which directed the conflict, was hardly more than a debating society, and it grew feebler as the struggle dragged on. "Their Congress now is quite disjoint'd," gibed an English satirist, "Since Gibbits (gallows) [are] for them appointed." The disorganized colonists fought almost the entire war before adopting a written constitution—the Articles of Confederation—in 1781.

General Washington's (1732–1799) disgust with his countrymen is reflected in a diary entry for 1776:

❝Chimney corner patriots abound; venality, corruption, prostitution of office for selfish ends, abuse of trust, perversion of funds from a national to a private use, and speculations upon the necessities of the times pervade all interests.**❞**

Imperial Rivalry and Colonial Revolt

In 1765 tax revolts exploded almost simultaneously in both Britain's and Spain's New World empires. In Boston the hated Stamp Act sparked riots and inspired a campaign to boycott British goods. At virtually the same moment in Quito (in present-day Ecuador), a two-mile-high Spanish colonial city nearly twice the size of Boston, surging crowds ransacked the local tax collector's office. Among other demands, they insisted that "pure" Spaniards leave Quito unless they had married into the native Creole (New World–born white) or indigenous Indian communities. Spanish officials restored order by force of arms, but antitax agitation continued to smolder everywhere in Spanish America. "There is no American," a Quito lawyer remarked, "who does not reject any novelty whatsoever in the management of taxation"—a sentiment that resonated as strongly in Philadelphia as in Mexico City.

Things soon got worse. Madrid's New World imperial authority was shaken to the core in 1781 when another tax revolt erupted in New Granada (present-day Colombia). By that time, the British colonials' War of Independence in North America was in its fifth year.

Intensifying imperial rivalry fueled events on both the American continents. Until the mid-seventeenth century, the three great Old World powers—England, France, and Spain—had largely confined their competition to struggles over boundaries and religious affiliation on the European continent. But after the Treaty of Westphalia in 1648 brought a truce to the wars of religion that had racked Europe for decades (the Thirty Years' War), great-power competition began to shift overseas. The faraway New World imperial outposts of Britain, Spain, and France now became pawns in a global struggle for mastery in Europe.

The Seven Years' War (1756–1763) ushered in a still more ferocious cycle of imperial conflict. Britain succeeded in expelling France from North America, but victory brought the burdens of managing vast new territories as well as the prospect of fresh confrontations with Native Americans threatened by westward expansion. Spain, France's erstwhile ally, grew increasingly wary of the newly invigorated and ambitious British Empire, which threatened Spanish interests at sea and along the sketchy borderlands that separated the two powers' imperial domains. As the risks and costs of imperial competition soared, London and Madrid adopted the same strategy: pressure the colonies to pay their share. New taxes and customs duties followed, along with more energetic efforts to collect them. To imperial officials like Britain's Prime Minister George Grenville or Madrid's "visitor general" to New

Tupac Amaru II A Peruvian national hero, Tupac Amaru II is memorialized to this day with his portrait on the nation's currency.

De Español y Mestiza Castiza

Couple with Child by Miguel Cabrera   This eighteenth-century portrait of a Mexican family illustrates the common intermarriage of Europeans and Indians in the Spanish New World. The ethnic complexity of Spanish America kept colonists there from uniting against imperial authorities as successfully as their northern neighbors.

Scala/Art Resource, NY

the answer. Spanish America was badly riven by sharp ethnic and racial divisions. The Spanish court had long encouraged the relatively few Spaniards who settled in the New World to intermarry with the local inhabitants. By the eighteenth century, the Spanish colonies had become a complex, tension-ridden mosaic of European, Creole, *mestizo*, and Indian peoples and cultures. When in 1780 the self-proclaimed Incan royal descendant Tupac Amaru II rebelled against Spanish rule, he at first attracted Creoles, but they bolted as the movement radicalized, and his rebellion was soon cruelly crushed.

To be sure, the British North American colonists had their ethnic differences, too, but many fewer. They had nurtured a culture of exclusion, rejecting intermarriage with Indians and blacks and banishing Indians to the wilderness. And they faced no Indian threat on the scale of Tupac Amaru II's uprising.

Inherited political traditions also played different roles. British settlers enjoyed long-standing institutions of political representation. They had brought with them from the mother country devotion to individual rights and the privilege of legal assembly that, when revolution came, gave their cause the kind of legitimacy that comes from time-honored habits. It was precisely the violation of those rights and privileges that "taxation without representation" seemed to threaten. Spanish colonists had representative institutions, too, but in Spain's much more autocratic imperial scheme, local assemblies lacked the authority, autonomy, and legitimacy they had come to enjoy in the British domains. North American colonists asserted their right to self-government on the basis of their historic rights as British subjects, a claim that was much more difficult to make in the absolutist monarchy of the Spanish Empire.

Spain, José Gálvez, such reforms seemed not only reasonable but in tune with Enlightenment ideas about efficient administration. To colonial subjects these new policies were an anathema, a flagrant offense to their fundamental rights as colonial subjects.

But why did revolts against these new imperial policies kindle a full-fledged war for independence in the British colonies but not in Spanish America—at least not until Napoleon's invasion of Spain in 1808 hurled the Spanish Empire into tumult?

The role of rich and powerful allies provides part of the answer. The North American rebels could count on Britain's French and Spanish enemies to tender financial as well as military support. Spanish American anticolonial rebels had no such allies in London or Paris, which saw little prospect of unraveling the Spanish Empire and were already fully engaged on opposite sides of the American War of Independence.

The demographic composition of the two empires furnishes another part of

Gilbert du Motier, Marquis de Lafayette (1757–1834), by Joseph Boze, 1790 This youthful French officer gave to America not only military service but some $200,000 of his private funds. He returned to France after the American Revolution to play a conspicuous role in the French Revolution.

Jealousy everywhere raised its hideous head. Individual states, proudly regarding themselves as sovereign, resented the attempts of Congress to exercise its flimsy powers. Sectional jealousy boiled up over the appointment of military leaders; some distrustful New Englanders almost preferred British officers to Americans from other sections.

Economic difficulties were nearly insuperable. Metallic money had already been heavily drained away. A cautious Continental Congress, unwilling to raise anew the explosive issue of taxation, was forced to print "Continental" paper money in great amounts. As this currency poured from the presses, it depreciated until the expression "not worth a Continental" became current. One barber contemptuously papered his shop with the near-worthless dollars. The confusion proliferated when the individual states were compelled to issue depreciated paper money of their own.

Inflation of the currency inevitably skyrocketed prices. Families of the soldiers at the fighting front were hard hit, and hundreds of anxious husbands and fathers deserted. Debtors easily acquired handfuls of the quasi-worthless money and gleefully paid their debts "without mercy"—sometimes with the bayonets of the authorities to back them up.

✷ A Thin Line of Heroes

Basic military supplies in the colonies were dangerously scanty. While many families and towns did own firearms—widespread militia service meant men needed weapons for training—the colonists had long relied heavily on Britain for troops, armaments, and military subsidies during expensive wars against Indians, France, and Spain. The rebels were caught in an unavoidable trap: at the very moment that the supply of British funds and war materiel evaporated, the cost of home defense mounted. Sufficient stores of gunpowder, cannon, and other armaments (let alone ships to transport them) could not be found. Among the reasons for the eventual alliance with France was the need for a reliable source of essential military supplies.

Other shortages bedeviled the rebels. At **Valley Forge**, Pennsylvania, shivering American soldiers went without bread for three successive days in the cruel winter of 1777–1778. In one southern campaign, some men fainted for lack of food. Manufactured goods also were generally in short supply in agricultural America, and clothing and shoes were appallingly scarce. The path of the Patriot fighting men was often marked by bloody snow. At frigid Valley Forge, during one anxious period, twenty-eight hundred men were barefooted or nearly naked. Woolens were desperately needed against the wintry blasts, and in general the only real uniform of the colonial army was uniform raggedness. During a grand parade at Valley Forge, some of the officers appeared wrapped in woolen bedcovers. One Rhode Island unit was known as the "Ragged, Lousy, Naked Regiment."

American militiamen were numerous but also highly unreliable. Able-bodied American males—perhaps several hundred thousand of them—had received rudimentary training. But poorly trained plowboys could not stand up in the open field against professional British troops advancing with bare bayonets. Many of these undisciplined warriors would, in the words of Washington, "fly from their own shadows." At the same time, deadly smallpox outbreaks ravaged the army, further weakening forces.

Women played a significant part in the Revolution. Many maintained farms and businesses while their fathers and husbands fought. Large numbers of female **camp followers** accompanied the American army, cooking and sewing for the troops in return for money and rations. One Massachusetts woman dressed in men's clothing and served in the army for seventeen months.

A few thousand regulars—perhaps seven or eight thousand at the war's end—were finally whipped into

Massachusetts Historical Society

Courtesy of Mae Theresa Bonitto/Picture Research Consultants & Archives

The Flutist, by Brazilla Lew This portrait is believed to be that of an African American fifer in the Revolutionary War. Lew was a veteran of the Seven Years' War who had marched to Ticonderoga and served in the army a full seven years as frontline soldier, fifer, and drummer. In 1775, at the age of thirty-two, he fought at Bunker Hill as an enlistee in the 27th Massachusetts Regiment. A resident of Chelmsford, Massachusetts, he was said to have taught all twelve of his children to play musical instruments.

Enslaved blacks hoped that the Revolutionary crisis would make it possible for them to secure their own liberty. On the eve of the war in South Carolina, merchant Josiah Smith, Jr., noted such a rumor among the slaves:

❝ [Freedom] is their common Talk throughout the Province, and has occasioned impertinent behavior in many of them, insomuch that our Provincial Congress now sitting hath voted the immediate raising of Two Thousand Men Horse and food, to keep those mistaken creatures in awe. **❞**

Despite such repressive measures, slave uprisings continued to plague the southern colonies through 1775 and 1776.

shape by stern drillmasters. Notable among them was an organizational genius, the salty German Baron von Steuben. He spoke no English when he reached America, but he soon taught his men that bayonets were not for broiling beefsteaks over open fires. As they gained experience, these soldiers of the Continental line more than held their own against crack British troops.

Blacks also fought and died for the American cause. Although many states initially barred them from militia service, by war's end more than five thousand blacks had enlisted in the American armed forces. The largest contingents came from the northern states with substantial numbers of free blacks.

Blacks fought at Trenton, Brandywine, Saratoga, and other important battles. Some, including Prince Whipple—later immortalized in Emanuel Leutze's famous painting "Washington Crossing the Delaware" (see p. 147)—became military heroes. Others served as cooks, guides, spies, drivers, and road builders.

African Americans also served on the British side. In November 1775 Lord Dunmore, royal governor of Virginia, issued a proclamation promising freedom for any enslaved black in Virginia who joined the British army. News of Dunmore's decree traveled swiftly. Virginia and Maryland tightened slave patrols, but within one month, three hundred slaves had joined what came to be called "Lord Dunmore's Ethiopian Regiment." In time thousands of blacks fled plantations for British promises of emancipation. When one of James Madison's slaves was caught trying to escape to the British lines, Madison refused to punish him for "coveting that liberty" that white Americans proclaimed the "right & worthy pursuit of every human being." At war's end the British kept their word, to some at least, and evacuated as many as fourteen thousand "Black Loyalists" to Nova Scotia, Jamaica, and England.

Morale in the Revolutionary army was badly undermined by American profiteers. Putting profits before patriotism, they sold to the British because the invader could pay in gold. Speculators forced prices sky-high, and some Bostonians made profits of 50 to 200 percent on army garb while the American army was freezing at Valley Forge. Washington never had as many as twenty thousand effective troops in one place at one time, despite bounties of land and other inducements. Yet if the rebels had thrown themselves into the struggle with zeal, they could easily have raised many times that number.

The brutal truth is that only a select minority of the American colonists attached themselves to the cause of independence with a spirit of selfless devotion. These were the dedicated souls who bore the burden of battle and the risks of defeat. Seldom have so few done so much for so many.

Chapter Review

KEY TERMS

republicanism (117)
radical Whigs (117)
mercantilism (118)
Sugar Act (119)
Quartering Act (119)
stamp tax (120)
admiralty courts (120)
Stamp Act Congress (120)
nonimportation agreements (121)
Sons of Liberty (121)
Daughters of Liberty (121)
Declaratory Act (122)
Townshend Acts (122)
Boston Massacre (123)
committees of correspondence (124)
Boston Tea Party (125)
"Intolerable Acts" (126)
Quebec Act (126)
First Continental Congress (126)
The Association (127)
Lexington and Concord (127)
Valley Forge (132)
camp followers (132)

PEOPLE TO KNOW

John Hancock
George Grenville
Charles ("Champagne Charley") Townshend
Crispus Attucks
George III
Lord North
Samuel Adams
Thomas Hutchinson
Marquis de Lafayette
Baron von Steuben
Lord Dunmore

CHRONOLOGY

1650 First Navigation Laws to control colonial commerce

1763 Seven Years' War (French and Indian War) ends

1764 Sugar Act

1765 Quartering Act
Stamp Act
Stamp Act Congress

1766 Declaratory Act

1767 Townshend Acts
New York legislature suspended by Parliament

1768 British troops occupy Boston

1770 Boston Massacre
All Townshend Acts except tea tax repealed

1772 Committees of correspondence formed

1773 British East India Company granted tea monopoly
Governor Hutchinson's actions provoke Boston Tea Party

1774 "Intolerable Acts"
Quebec Act
First Continental Congress
The Association boycotts British goods

1775 Battles of Lexington and Concord

TO LEARN MORE

R. B. Bernstein, *Thomas Jefferson* (2003)
Timothy H. Breen, *The Marketplace of Revolution: How Consumer Politics Shaped American Independence* (2004)
David Hackett Fischer, *Paul Revere's Ride* (1994)
Sylvia R. Frey, *Water from the Rock: Black Resistance in a Revolutionary Age* (1991)
Woody Holton, *Forced Founders: Indians, Debtors, Slaves, and the Making of the American Revolution in Virginia* (1999)
Pauline Maier, *From Resistance to Revolution: Colonial Radicals and the Development of American Opposition to Britain, 1765–1776* (1972)
David McCullough, *John Adams* (2001)
Robert Middlekauff, *The Glorious Cause: The American Revolution, 1763–1789* (2005)
Edmund S. Morgan and Helen M. Morgan, *The Stamp Act Crisis* (1953)
Joseph C. Morton, *The American Revolution* (2003)
Ray Raphael, *A People's History of the American Revolution* (2001)
Walter Stahr, *John Jay: Founding Father* (2005)
Alfred F. Young, *The Shoemaker and the Tea Party* (1999)

A complete, annotated bibliography for this chapter—along with brief descriptions of the People to Know—may be found on the *American Pageant* website. The key terms are defined in the glossary at the end of the text.

Chapter 8

America Secedes from the Empire

1775–1783

These are the times that try men's souls. The summer soldier and the sunshine patriot will, in this crisis, shrink from the service of their country; but he that stands it now, deserves the love and thanks of man and woman.

THOMAS PAINE, DECEMBER 1776

*B*loodshed at Lexington and Concord in April of 1775 was a clarion call to arms. About twenty thousand musket-bearing "Minute Men" swarmed around Boston, there to entrap the outnumbered British.

The **Second Continental Congress** met in Philadelphia the next month, on May 10, 1775, and this time the full slate of thirteen colonies was represented. The conservative element in Congress was still strong, despite the shooting in Massachusetts. There was still no well-defined sentiment for independence—merely a desire to continue fighting in the hope that the king and Parliament would consent to a redress of grievances. Congress hopefully drafted new appeals to the British people and king—appeals that were spurned. Anticipating a possible rebuff, the delegates also adopted measures to raise money and to create an army and a navy. The British and the Americans now teetered on the brink of all-out warfare.

✦ Congress Drafts George Washington

Perhaps the most important single action of the Congress was to select George Washington, one of its members already in an officer's uniform, to head the hastily improvised army besieging Boston. This choice was made with considerable misgivings. The tall, powerfully built, dignified Virginia planter, then forty-three, had never risen above the rank of a colonel in the militia. His largest command had numbered only twelve hundred men, and that had been some twenty years earlier. Falling short of true military genius, Washington would actually lose more pitched battles than he won.

But the distinguished Virginian was gifted with outstanding powers of leadership and immense strength of character. He radiated patience, courage, self-discipline, and a sense of justice. He was a great moral force rather than a great military mind—a symbol and a rallying point. People instinctively trusted him; they sensed that when he put himself at the head of a cause, he was prepared, if necessary, to go down with the ship. He insisted on serving without pay, though he kept a careful expense account amounting to more than $100,000. Later he sternly reprimanded his steward at Mount Vernon for providing the enemy, under duress, with supplies. He would have preferred to see the enemy put the torch to his mansion.

The Continental Congress, though dimly perceiving Washington's qualities of leadership, chose more wisely than it knew. His selection, in truth, was largely political. Americans in other sections of the colonies, already jealous, were beginning to distrust the large New England army being collected around Boston. Prudence suggested a commander from Virginia, the largest and most populous of the colonies. As a man of wealth, both by inheritance and by marriage, Washington could not be accused of being a fortune-seeker. As an aristocrat, he could be counted on by his peers to check "the excesses of the masses."

Washington at Verplanck's Point, New York, 1782, Reviewing the French Troops After the Victory at Yorktown, by John Trumbull, 1790 This noted American artist accentuated Washington's already imposing height (six feet two inches) by showing him towering over his horse. Washington so appreciated this portrait of himself that he hung it in the dining room of his home at Mount Vernon, Virginia.

De Agostini/Getty Images

✵ Bunker Hill and Hessian Hirelings

The clash of arms continued on a strangely contradictory basis. On the one hand, the Americans were emphatically affirming their loyalty to the king and earnestly voicing their desire to patch up difficulties. On the other hand, they were raising armies and shooting down His Majesty's soldiers. This curious war of inconsistency was fought for fourteen long months—from April 1775 to July 1776—before the fateful plunge into independence was taken.

Gradually the tempo of warfare increased. In May 1775 a tiny American force under Ethan Allen and Benedict Arnold surprised and captured the British garrisons at Ticonderoga and Crown Point, on the scenic lakes of upper New York. A priceless store of gunpowder and artillery for the siege of Boston was thus secured. In June 1775 the colonists seized a hill, now known as **Bunker Hill** (actually Breed's Hill), from which they menaced the enemy in Boston. The British, instead of cutting off the retreat of their foes by flanking them, blundered bloodily when they launched a frontal attack with three thousand men. Sharpshooting Americans, numbering fifteen hundred and strongly entrenched, mowed down the advancing redcoats with frightful slaughter. But the colonists' scanty store of gunpowder finally gave out, and they were forced to abandon the hill in disorder. With two more such victories, remarked the French foreign minister, the British would have no army left in America.

Even at this late date, in July 1775, the Continental Congress adopted the **Olive Branch Petition**, professing American loyalty to the crown and begging the king to prevent further hostilities. But following Bunker Hill, King George III slammed the door on all hope of reconciliation. In August 1775 he formally proclaimed the colonies in rebellion; the skirmishes were now out-and-out treason, a hanging crime. The next month he widened the chasm when he sealed arrangements for hiring thousands of German troops to help crush his rebellious subjects. Six German princes involved in the transaction needed the money (one reputedly had seventy-four children); George III needed the men. Because most of these soldiers-for-hire came from the German principality of Hesse, the Americans called all the European mercenaries **Hessians**.

News of the Hessian deal shocked the colonists. The quarrel, they felt, was within the family. Why bring in outside mercenaries, especially foreigners who had an exaggerated reputation for butchery?

Hessian hirelings proved to be good soldiers in a mechanical sense, but many of them were more interested in booty than in duty. For good reason they were dubbed "Hessian flies." Seduced by American promises of land, hundreds of them finally deserted and remained in America to become respected citizens.

✵ The Abortive Conquest of Canada

The unsheathed sword continued to take its toll. In October 1775, on the eve of a cruel winter, the British burned Falmouth (Portland), Maine. In that same autumn, the rebels daringly undertook a two-pronged invasion of Canada. American leaders believed, erroneously, that the conquered French were explosively restive under the British yoke. A successful assault on Canada would add a fourteenth colony, while depriving Britain of a valuable base for striking at the colonies in revolt. But this large-scale

Battle of Bunker Hill, June 17, 1775 This British engraving conveys the vulnerability of the British regulars to attacks by the American militiamen. Although a defeat for the colonists, the battle quickly proved a moral victory for the Patriots. Outnumbered and outgunned, they held their own against the British and suffered many fewer casualties.

attack, involving some two thousand American troops, contradicted the claim of the colonists that they were merely fighting defensively for a redress of grievances. Invasion northward was undisguised offensive warfare.

This bold stroke for Canada narrowly missed success (see Map 8.1). One invading column under the Irish-born General Richard Montgomery, formerly of the British army, pushed up the Lake Champlain route and captured Montréal. He was joined at Québec by the bedraggled army of General Benedict Arnold, whose men had been reduced to eating dogs and shoe leather during their grueling march through the Maine woods. An assault on Québec, launched on the last day of 1775, was beaten off. The able Montgomery was killed; the dashing Arnold was wounded in one leg. Scattered remnants under his command retreated up the St. Lawrence River, reversing the way Montgomery had come. French Canadian leaders, who had been generously treated by the British in the Quebec Act of 1774, showed no real desire to welcome the plundering anti-Catholic invaders.

Bitter fighting persisted in the colonies, though most Americans continued to disclaim a desire for independence. In January 1776 the British set fire to the Virginia town of Norfolk. In March the British were finally forced to evacuate Boston, taking with them the leading friends of the king. (Evacuation Day is still celebrated annually in Boston.) In the South the rebellious colonists won two victories in 1776—one in February against some fifteen hundred Loyalists at Moore's Creek Bridge in North Carolina, and the other in June against an invading British fleet at Charleston harbor.

✯ Thomas Paine Preaches Common Sense

Why did Americans continue to deny any intention of independence? Loyalty to the empire was deeply ingrained; many Americans continued to consider themselves part of a transatlantic community in which

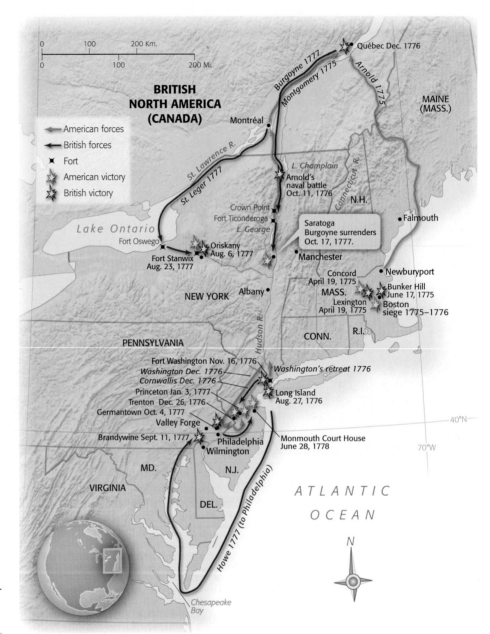

MAP 8.1 Revolution in the North, 1775–1776 Benedict Arnold's troops were described as "pretty young men" when they sailed from Massachusetts. They were considerably less pretty on their arrival in Québec, after eight weeks of struggling through wet and frigid forests, often without food. "No one can imagine," one of them wrote, "the sweetness of a roasted shot-pouch [ammunition bag] to the famished appetite." © 2016 Cengage Learning

the mother country of Britain played a leading role; colonial unity was growing but far from robust; and open rebellion was dangerous, especially against a formidable Britain. Irish rebels of that day were customarily hanged, drawn, and quartered. American rebels might have fared no better. As late as January 1776—five months before independence was declared—the king's health was being toasted by the officers of Washington's mess near Boston. "God save the king" had not yet been replaced by "God save the Congress."

Gradually the Americans were shocked into recognizing the necessity of separating from the crown. Their eyes were jolted open by harsh British acts like the burning of Falmouth and Norfolk and especially by the hiring of the Hessians.

Then in 1776 came the publication of ***Common Sense***, one of the most influential pamphlets ever written. Its author was the radical Thomas Paine, once an impoverished corset-maker's apprentice, who had come over from Britain a year earlier. He began his incendiary tract with a treatise on the nature of government and eloquently anticipated Thomas Jefferson's declaration that the only lawful states were those that derive "their just powers from the consent of the governed." As for the king, whom the Americans professed to revere, he was nothing but "the Royal Brute

In Common Sense, *Thomas Paine (1737–1809) argued for the superiority of a republic over a monarchy:*

❝The nearer any government approaches to a republic the less business there is for a king. It is somewhat difficult to find a proper name for the government of England. Sir William Meredith calls it a republic; but in its present state it is unworthy of the name, because the corrupt influence of the crown, by having all the places in its disposal, hath so effectively swallowed up the power, and eaten out the virtue of the house of commons (the republican part of the constitution) that the government of England is nearly as monarchical as that of France or Spain.**❞**

Thomas Paine, by Auguste Millière

of Great Britain." *Common Sense* became a whirlwind best seller. Within a few months the astonishing total of 120,000 copies were sold.

Paine flatly branded the shilly-shallying of the colonists as contrary to "common sense." Nowhere in the physical universe did the smaller heavenly body control the larger one. So why should the tiny island of Britain control the vast continent of America? Paine's pen went a long way toward convincing the American colonists that their true cause was independence rather than reconciliation with Britain—not least because without independence, they could not hope for foreign assistance. Paine could thus be said to have drafted the foundational document not only of American independence, but of American foreign policy as well.

✦ Paine and the Idea of "Republicanism"

Paine's passionate protest was as compelling as it was eloquent and radical—even doubly radical. It called not simply for independence, but for the creation of a new kind of political society, a *republic*, where power flowed from the people themselves, not from a corrupt and despotic monarch. In language laced with biblical imagery familiar to common folk, he argued that all government officials—governors, senators, and judges—not just representatives in a house of commons, should derive their authority from popular consent.

Paine was hardly the first person to champion a republican form of government. Political philosophers

had advanced the idea since the days of classical Greece and Rome. Revived in the Renaissance and in seventeenth-century England, republican ideals had uneasily survived within the British "mixed government," with its delicate balance of king, nobility, and commons. Republicanism particularly appealed to British politicians critical of excessive power in the hands of the king and his advisers. Their writings found a responsive audience among the American colonists, who interpreted the vengeful royal acts of the previous decade as part of a monarchical conspiracy to strip them of their liberties as British subjects. Paine's radical prescription for the colonies—to reject

The French philosopher Abbé Raynal (1713–1796) wrote in 1770,

❝If any fortunate revolution should take place in the world, it will begin in America.... It will become the asylum of our people who have been oppressed by political establishments, or driven away by war.**❞**

monarchy and empire and embrace an independent republic—fell on receptive ears.

The colonists' experience with governance had prepared them well for Paine's summons to create a republic. Many settlers, particularly New Englanders, had practiced a kind of republicanism in their democratic town meetings and annual elections, while the popularly elected committees of correspondence during 1774 and 1775 had demonstrated the feasibility of republican government. The absence of a hereditary aristocracy and the relative equality of condition enjoyed by landowning farmers meshed well with the republican repudiation of a fixed hierarchy of power.

Most Americans considered citizen "virtue" fundamental to any successful republican government. Because political power no longer rested with the central, all-powerful authority of the king, individuals in a republic needed to sacrifice their personal self-interest to the public good. The collective good of "the people" mattered more than the private rights and interests of individuals. Paine inspired his contemporaries to view America as fertile ground for the cultivation of such civic virtue.

Yet not all Patriots agreed with Paine's ultrademocratic approach to republicanism. Some favored a republic ruled by a "natural aristocracy" of talent. Republicanism for them meant an end to hereditary aristocracy, but not an end to all social hierarchy. These more conservative republicans feared that the fervor for liberty would overwhelm the stability of the social order. They watched with trepidation as the "lower orders" of society—poorer farmers, tenants, and laboring classes in towns and cities—seemed to embrace a kind of runaway republicanism that amounted to radical "leveling." The contest to define the nature of American republicanism would noisily continue for at least the next hundred years.

✦ Jefferson's "Explanation" of Independence

Members of the Philadelphia Congress, instructed by their respective colonies, gradually edged toward a clean break. On June 7, 1776, fiery Richard Henry Lee of Virginia moved that "these United Colonies are, and of right ought to be, free and independent states." After considerable debate, the motion was adopted nearly a month later, on July 2, 1776.

The passing of Lee's resolution was the formal "declaration" of independence by the American colonies, and technically this was all that was needed to cut the British tie. John Adams wrote confidently that ever thereafter, July 2 would be celebrated annually with fireworks. But something more was required. An

The American signers of the Declaration of Independence had reason to fear for their necks. In 1802, twenty-six years later, George III (1738–1820) approved this death sentence for seven Irish rebels:

" … [You] are to be hanged by the neck, but not until you are dead; for while you are still living your bodies are to be taken down, your bowels torn out and burned before your faces, your heads then cut off, and your bodies divided each into four quarters, and your heads and quarters to be then at the King's disposal; and may the Almighty God have mercy on your souls. "

epochal rupture of this kind called for some formal explanation. An inspirational appeal was also needed to enlist other British colonies in the Americas, to invite assistance from foreign nations, and to rally resistance at home.

Shortly after Lee made his memorable motion on June 7, Congress appointed a committee to prepare a more formal statement of separation. The task of drafting it fell to Thomas Jefferson, a tall, freckled, sandy-haired Virginia lawyer of thirty-three. Despite his youth, he was already recognized as a brilliant writer, and he measured up splendidly to the awesome assignment. After some debate and amendment, the **Declaration of Independence** was formally approved by the Congress on July 4, 1776. It might better have been called "the Explanation of Independence" or, as one contemporary described it, "Mr. Jefferson's advertisement of Mr. Lee's resolution."

Jefferson's pronouncement, couched in a lofty style, was magnificent. He gave his appeal universality by invoking the "natural rights" of humankind—not just British rights. He argued persuasively that because the king had flouted these rights, the colonists were justified in cutting their connection. He then set forth a long list of the presumably tyrannous misdeeds of George III. The overdrawn bill of indictment included imposing taxes without consent, dispensing with trial by jury, abolishing valued laws, establishing a military dictatorship, maintaining standing armies in peacetime, cutting off trade, burning towns, hiring mercenaries, and inciting hostility among the Indians.*

Jefferson's withering blast was admittedly one-sided. He acted, in effect, as a prosecuting attorney, and he took certain liberties with historical truth. He was not writing history; he was making it through what

---

*For an annotated text of the Declaration of Independence, see the Appendix.

has been called "the world's greatest editorial." He owned many slaves, and his affirmation that "all men are created equal" was to haunt him and his fellow citizens for generations.

The formal Declaration of Independence cleared the air as a thundershower does on a muggy day. As Paine had predicted, and as events were to prove, foreign assistance could now be solicited with greater hope of success. Those Patriots who defied the king were now rebels, not loving subjects shooting their way into reconciliation. They must all hang together, Franklin is said to have grimly remarked, or they would all hang separately. Or, in the eloquent language of the great Declaration, "We mutually pledge to each other our lives, our fortunes and our sacred honor."

The Granger Collection, New York

King George III of England (1738–1820), by Johann Zoffany, 1771 America's last king, he was a good man, unlike some of his scandal-tainted brothers and sons, but a bad king. Doggedly determined to regain arbitrary power for the crown, he antagonized and then lost the thirteen American colonies. During much of his sixty-year reign, he seemed to be insane, but recently medical science has found that he was suffering from a rare metabolic and hereditary disease called porphyria.

Jefferson's defiant Declaration of Independence had a universal impact unmatched by any other American document. This "shout heard round the world" has been a source of inspiration to countless revolutionary movements against arbitrary authority. Lafayette hung a copy on a wall in his home, leaving beside it room for a future French **Declaration of the Rights of Man**—a declaration that was officially born thirteen years later.

✦ Patriots and Loyalists

The War of Independence, strictly speaking, was a war within a war. Colonials loyal to the king (**Loyalists**) fought the American rebels (**Patriots**), while the rebels also fought the British redcoats (see "Makers of America: The Loyalists," pp. 144–145). Loyalists were derisively called "Tories," after the dominant political factions in Britain, whereas Patriots were called "Whigs," after the opposition factions in Britain. A popular definition of a Tory among the Patriots betrayed bitterness: "A Tory is a thing whose head is in England, and its body in America, and its neck ought to be stretched."

Like many revolutions, the American Revolution was a minority movement. Many colonists were apathetic or neutral, including the Byrds of Virginia, who sat on the fence. The opposing forces contended not only against each other but also for the allegiance and support of the civilian population. In this struggle for the hearts and minds of the people, the British proved fatally inept, and the Patriot militias played a crucial role. The British military proved able to control only those areas where it could maintain a massive military presence. Elsewhere, as soon as the redcoats had marched on, the rebel militiamen appeared and took up the task of "political education"—sometimes by coercive means. Often lacking bayonets but always loaded with political zeal, the ragtag militia units served as remarkably effective agents of Revolutionary ideas. They convinced many colonists, even those indifferent to independence, that the British army was an unreliable friend and that they had better throw in their lot with the Patriot cause. They also mercilessly harassed small British detachments and occupation forces. One British officer ruefully observed that "the Americans would be less dangerous if they had a regular army."

Loyalists, numbering perhaps 16 percent of the American people, remained true to their king. Families often split over the issue of independence: Benjamin Franklin supported the Patriot side, whereas his handsome illegitimate son, William Franklin (the last royal governor of New Jersey), upheld the Loyalist cause. The Loyalists were tragic figures. For generations the

A Revolution for Women? Abigail Adams Chides Her Husband, 1776

In the midst of the revolutionary fervor of 1776, at least one woman—Abigail Adams, wife of noted Massachusetts Patriot (and future president) John Adams—raised her voice on behalf of women. Yet she apparently raised it only in private—in this personal letter to her husband. Private documents like the correspondence and diaries of individuals both prominent and ordinary offer invaluable sources for the historian seeking to discover sentiments, opinions, and perspectives that are often difficult to discern in the official public record. What might it suggest about the historical circumstances of the 1770s that Abigail Adams confined her claim for women's equality to this confidential exchange with her spouse? What might have inspired the arguments she employed? Despite her privileged position and persuasive power, and despite her threat to "foment a rebellion," Abigail Adams's plea went largely unheeded in the Revolutionary era—as did comparable pleadings to extend the revolutionary principle of equality to blacks. What might have accounted for this limited application of the ideas of liberty and equality in the midst of a supposedly democratic revolution?

Massachusetts Historical Society

Massachusetts Historical Society

British in the New World had been taught fidelity to the crown. Loyalty is ordinarily regarded as a major virtue—loyalty to one's family, one's friends, one's country. If the king had triumphed, as he seemed likely to do, the Loyalists would have been acclaimed patriots, and defeated rebels like Washington would have been disgraced, severely punished, and probably forgotten.

Many people of education and wealth, of culture and caution, remained loyal. These wary souls were satisfied with their lot and believed that any violent change would only be for the worse. Loyalists were also more numerous among the older generation. Young people make revolutions, and from the outset energetic, purposeful, and militant young people surged forward—figures like the sleeplessly scheming Samuel Adams and the impassioned Patrick Henry, whose flaming outcry before the Virginia Assembly— "Give me liberty or give me death!"—still quickens patriotic pulses.

Loyalists also included the king's officers and other beneficiaries of the crown—people who knew from which side their daily bread came. The same was generally true of the Anglican clergy and a large portion of their congregations, all of whom had long been taught submission to the king.

Usually the Loyalists were most numerous where the Anglican Church was strongest. A notable exception was Virginia, where the debt-burdened Anglican aristocrats flocked into the rebel camp. The king's followers were well entrenched in aristocratic New York City and Charleston and also in Quaker Pennsylvania and New Jersey, where General Washington felt that he was fighting in "the enemy's country." While his men were starving at Valley Forge, nearby Pennsylvania farmers were selling their produce to the British for the king's gold.

Loyalists were least numerous in New England, where self-government was especially strong and mercantilism was especially weak. Rebels were the most numerous where Presbyterianism and Congregationalism flourished, notably in New England. Invading British armies vented their contempt and anger by using Yankee churches for pigsties.

✦ The Loyalist Exodus

Before the Declaration of Independence in 1776, persecution of the Loyalists was relatively mild. Yet they were subjected to some brutality, including tarring and feathering and riding astride fence rails.

After the Declaration of Independence, which sharply separated Loyalists from Patriots, harsher methods prevailed. The rebels naturally desired a united front. Putting loyalty to the colonies first, they regarded their opponents, not themselves, as traitors. Loyalists were roughly handled, hundreds were imprisoned, and a few noncombatants were hanged. But there was no wholesale reign of terror comparable to that which later bloodied both France and Russia during their revolutions. For one thing, the colonists reflected Anglo-Saxon regard for order; for another, the leading Loyalists were prudent enough to flee to the British lines.

About eighty thousand loyal supporters of George III were driven out or fled, but several hundred thousand or so of the mild Loyalists were permitted to stay. The estates of many of the fugitives were confiscated and sold—a relatively painless way to help finance the war. Confiscation often worked great hardship, as, for example, when two aristocratic women were forced to live in their former chicken house for leaning Toryward.

Some fifty thousand Loyalist volunteers at one time or another bore arms for the British. They also helped the king's cause by serving as spies, by inciting the Indians, and by keeping Patriot soldiers at home to protect their families. Ardent Loyalists had their hearts in their cause, and a major blunder of the haughty British was not to make full use of them in the fighting.

✦ General Washington at Bay

With Boston evacuated in March 1776, the British concentrated on New York as a base of operations. Here was a splendid seaport, centrally located, where the king could count on cooperation from the numerous Loyalists. An awe-inspiring British fleet appeared off New York in July 1776. It consisted of some five hundred ships and thirty-five thousand men—the largest armed force to be seen in America until the Civil War. General Washington, dangerously outnumbered, could muster only eighteen thousand ill-trained troops with which to meet the crack army of the invader.

Disaster befell the Americans in the summer and fall of 1776. Outgeneraled and outmaneuvered, they were routed at the **Battle of Long Island**, where panic seized the raw recruits. By the narrowest of margins, and thanks to a favoring wind and fog, Washington escaped to Manhattan Island. Retreating northward, he crossed the Hudson River to New Jersey and finally reached the Delaware River with the British close at his heels. Tauntingly, enemy buglers sounded the fox-hunting call, so familiar to Virginians of Washington's day. The Patriot cause was at low ebb when the rebel remnants fled across the river after collecting all available boats to forestall pursuit.

The wonder is that Washington's adversary, General William Howe, did not speedily crush the

In late 1776 Catherine Van Cortlandt wrote to her husband, a New Jersey merchant fighting in a Loyalist brigade, about the Patriot troops who had quartered themselves in her house. "They were the most disorderly of species," she complained, "and their officers were from the dregs of the people."

Like the Van Cortlandts, many Loyalists thought of themselves as the "better sort of people." They viewed their adversaries as "lawless mobs" and "brutes." Conservative, wealthy, and well educated, Loyalists of this breed thought a break with Britain would invite anarchy. Loyalism made sense to them, too, for practical reasons. Viewing colonial militias as no match for His Majesty's army, Loyalist pamphleteer Daniel Leonard warned his Patriot enemies in 1775 that "nothing short of a miracle could gain you one battle."

But Loyalism was hardly confined to the well-to-do. It also appealed to many people of modest means who identified strongly with Britain or who had reason to fear a Patriot victory. Thousands of British veterans of the Seven Years' War, for example, had settled in the colonies after 1763. Many of them took up farming on two-hundred-acre land grants in New York. They were loath to turn their backs on the crown. So, too, were recent immigrants from non-English regions of the British Isles, especially from Scotland and Ireland, who had settled in Georgia or the backcountry of North and South Carolina. Many of these newcomers, resenting the plantation elite who ran these colonies, filled the ranks of Tory brigades such as the Volunteers of Ireland and the North Carolina Highlanders, organized by the British army to galvanize Loyalist support.

Other ethnic minorities found their own reasons to support the British. Some members of Dutch, German, and French religious sects believed that religious tolerance would be greater under the British than under the Americans, whose prejudices they had already encountered. Though Native American groups had varied responses to the war, many fought on the side of the British, expecting that their treaties with the empire would protect their land claims.

Thousands of African Americans also joined Loyalist ranks in the hope that service to the British might offer an escape from bondage. British officials encouraged that belief. Throughout the war and in every colony, some African Americans fled to British lines, where they served as soldiers, servants, laborers, and spies. Many of them joined black regiments that specialized in making small sorties against Patriot militias. In Monmouth, New Jersey, the black Loyalist Colonel Tye and his band of raiders became legendary for capturing Patriots and their supplies.

As the war drew to an end in 1783, the fate of black Loyalists varied

Tough Times for Loyalists Under the shadow of the tar bucket and bag of feathers shown in the upper right background, these Virginia Loyalists were roughly handled by a club-wielding crowd of Patriots.

Library of Congress Prints and Photographs Division, [LC-USZC4-5280]

Loyalists Through British Eyes   This British cartoon depicts the Loyalists as doubly victimized—by Americans caricatured as "savage" Indians and by the British prime minister, the Earl of Shelburne, for offering little protection to Britain's defenders.

enormously. Many thousands who came to Loyalism as fugitive slaves managed to find a way to freedom, most notably the large group who won British passage from the port of New York to Nova Scotia. Other African American Loyalists suffered betrayal. British general Lord Charles Cornwallis abandoned more than four thousand former slaves in Virginia, and many black Loyalists who boarded ships from British-controlled ports expecting to embark for freedom instead found themselves sold back into slavery in the West Indies.

White Loyalists faced no threat of enslavement, but they did suffer travails beyond mere disgrace: arrest, exile, confiscation of property, and loss of legal rights. Faced with such retribution, some eighty thousand Loyalists fled abroad, mostly to Britain and the maritime provinces of Canada, where they became known as the United Empire Loyalists. Some settled contentedly as exiles, but many, especially those who went to Britain, where they had difficulty becoming

accepted, lived diminished and lonely lives—"cut off," as Loyalist Thomas Danforth put it, "from every hope of importance in life…[and] in a station much inferior to that of a menial servant."

But most Loyalists remained in America, where they faced the special burdens of reestablishing themselves in a society that viewed them as traitors. Some succeeded remarkably despite the odds, such as Hugh Gaine, a printer in New York City who eventually reopened a business and even won contracts from the new government. Ironically, this former Loyalist soldier published the new national army regulations authored by the Revolutionary hero Baron von Steuben. Like many former Loyalists, Gaine reintegrated himself into public life by siding with the Federalist call for a strong central government and powerful executive. When New York ratified the Constitution in 1788, Gaine rode the float at the head of the city's celebration parade. He had, like many other former Loyalists, become an American.

New York Patriots Pull Down the Statue of King George III   Erected after the repeal of the Stamp Act in 1766, this statue was melted down by the revolutionaries into bullets to be used against the king's troops.

demoralized American forces. But he was no military genius, and he well remembered the horrible slaughter at Bunker Hill, where he had commanded. The country was rough, supplies were slow in coming, and as a professional soldier, Howe did not relish the rigors of winter campaigning. He evidently found more agreeable the bedtime company of his mistress, the wife of one of his subordinates—a scandal with which American satirists had a good deal of ribald fun.

Washington, who was now almost counted out, stealthily recrossed the ice-clogged Delaware River. At **Trenton**, on December 26, 1776, he surprised and captured a thousand Hessians who were sleeping off the effects of their Christmas celebration. A week later, leaving his campfires burning as a ruse, he slipped away and inflicted a sharp defeat on a smaller British detachment at Princeton. This brilliant New Jersey campaign, crowned by these two life-saving victories, revealed "Old Fox" Washington at his military best.

✴ Burgoyne's Blundering Invasion

In 1777 London officials adopted an intricate scheme for capturing the vital Hudson River valley. If successful, the British would sever New England from the rest of the states and paralyze the American cause.

The main invading force, under an actor-playwright-soldier, General John ("Gentleman Johnny") Burgoyne, would push down the Lake Champlain route from Canada. General Howe's troops in New York, if needed, could advance up the Hudson River to meet Burgoyne near Albany. A third and much smaller British force, commanded by Colonel Barry St. Leger, would come in from the west by way of Lake Ontario and the Mohawk Valley.

In this sermon, published in the Pennsylvania Gazette *on April 18, 1778, a minister decried the brutality of the British army:*

❝The waste and ravage produced by this unhappy war are every where felt. Wherever our foes pervade, ruin and devastation follow after them; or rather, they march in their front, and on their right, and on their left, and in their rear they rage without controul. No house is sacred; no person secure. Age or sex, from blooming youth to decrepit age, they regard or spare not. And in the field, how many of our countrymen and friends have fallen?❞

Washington Crossing the Delaware, by Emanuel Gottlieb Leutze, 1851 On Christmas Day, 1776, George Washington set out from Pennsylvania with twenty-four hundred men to surprise the British forces, chiefly Hessians, in their quarters across the river in New Jersey. The subsequent British defeat proved to be a turning point in the Revolution, as it checked the British advance toward Philadelphia and restored American morale. Seventy-five years later, Leutze, a German American immigrant who had returned to Germany, mythologized the heroic campaign in this painting. Imbued with the liberal democratic principles of the American Revolution, Leutze intended his painting to inspire Europeans in their revolutions of 1848. To that end, he ignored the fact that the Stars and Stripes held by Lieutenant James Monroe was not adopted until 1777; that Washington could not possibly have stood so long on one leg; that the colonists crossed the Delaware at night, not during the day; and that no African American would have been present. What Leutze did capture was the importance of ordinary men in the Revolutionary struggle and the tremendous urgency they felt at this particular moment in 1776, when victory seemed so elusive.

British planners did not reckon with General Benedict Arnold. After his repulse at Québec in 1775, he had retreated slowly along the St. Lawrence River back to the Lake Champlain area, by heroic efforts keeping an army in the field. The British had pursued his tattered force to Lake Champlain in 1776. But they could not move farther south until they had won control of the lake, which, in the absence of roads, was indispensable for carrying their supplies.

While the British stopped to construct a sizable fleet, the tireless Arnold assembled and fitted out every floatable vessel. His tiny flotilla was finally destroyed after desperate fighting, but time, if not the battle, had been won. Winter was descending, and the British were forced to retire to Canada. General Burgoyne had to start anew from this base the following year. If Arnold had not contributed his daring and skill, the British invaders of 1776 almost certainly would have recaptured Fort Ticonderoga. If Burgoyne had started

from this springboard in 1777, instead of from Montréal, he almost certainly would have succeeded in his venture. (At last the apparently futile American invasion of Canada in 1775 was beginning to pay rich dividends.)

General Burgoyne began his fateful invasion with seven thousand regular troops. He was encumbered by a heavy baggage train and a considerable number of women, many of whom were wives of his officers. Progress was painfully slow, for sweaty axmen had to chop a path through the forest, while American militiamen began to gather like hornets on Burgoyne's flanks.

General Howe, meanwhile, was causing astonished eyebrows to rise. At a time when it seemed obvious that he should be starting up the Hudson River from New York to join his slowly advancing colleague, he deliberately embarked with the main British army for an attack on Philadelphia, the rebel capital.

As scholars now know, he wanted to force a general engagement with Washington's army, destroy it, and leave the path wide-open for Burgoyne's thrust. Howe apparently assumed that he had ample time to assist Burgoyne directly, should he be needed.

General Washington, keeping a wary eye on the British in New York, hastily transferred his army to the vicinity of Philadelphia. There, late in 1777, he was defeated in two pitched battles, at Brandywine Creek and Germantown. Pleasure-loving General Howe then settled down comfortably in the lively capital, leaving Burgoyne to flounder through the wilds of upper New York. Benjamin Franklin, recently sent to Paris as an envoy, truthfully jested that Howe had not captured Philadelphia but that Philadelphia had captured Howe. Washington finally retired to winter quarters at Valley Forge, a strong, hilly position some twenty miles northwest of Philadelphia. There his frostbitten and hungry men were short of about everything except misery. This rabble was nevertheless whipped into a professional army by the recently arrived Prussian drillmaster, the profane but patient Baron von Steuben.

Burgoyne meanwhile had begun to bog down north of Albany, while a host of American militiamen, scenting the kill, swarmed about him. In a series of sharp engagements, in which General Arnold was again shot in the leg at Québec, the British army was trapped. Meanwhile, the Americans had driven back St. Leger's force at Oriskany. Unable to advance or retreat, Burgoyne was forced to surrender his entire command at **Saratoga** on October 17, 1777, to the American general Horatio Gates.

Saratoga ranks high among the decisive battles of both American and world history. The victory immensely revived the faltering colonial cause. Even more important, it made possible the urgently needed foreign aid from France, which in turn helped ensure American independence.

� Revolution in Diplomacy?

France, thirsting for revenge against Britain, was eager to inflame the quarrel that had broken out in America. Stripped of its North American colonies, Britain would presumably cease to be a front-rank power. France might then regain its former position and prestige, the loss of which in the recent Seven Years' War rankled deeply. For their part, the American revolutionaries badly needed help in the struggle to throw off the British yoke. The stage seemed set for the embattled new nation to make its diplomatic debut by sealing an alliance with France against the common British foe.

After concluding the alliance, France sent a minister to America, to the delight of one Patriot journalist:

"Who would have thought that the American colonies, imperfectly known in Europe a few years ago and claimed by every pettifogging lawyer in the House of Commons, every cobbler in the beer-houses of London, as a part of their property, should to-day receive an ambassador from the most powerful monarchy in Europe."

Yet just as they stood for revolutionary political ideas at home, the rebellious Americans also harbored revolutionary ideas about international affairs. They wanted an end to colonialism and mercantilism. They strongly supported free trade and freedom of the seas. They hoped to substitute the rule of law for the ancient reliance on raw power to arbitrate the affairs of nations. (When the new Republic's great seal proclaimed "a new order for the ages"—*novus ordo seculorum* in Latin—the sentiment was meant to apply to international as well as domestic affairs.) The Continental Congress in the summer of 1776 had accordingly drafted a **Model Treaty** to guide the American commissioners it was about to dispatch to the French court. One of the treaty's chief authors, John Adams, described its basic principles: "1. No political connection.... 2. No military connection.... 3. Only a commercial connection."

For a nascent nation struggling to secure its very existence, these were remarkably self-denying restrictions. Yet they represented an emerging school of thought, popular among enlightened figures in both Europe and America, that deemed history to have reached a momentous turning point when military conflict would be abandoned and the bonds of mutual commercial interest would guarantee peaceful relations among states. Many critics then and later have derided this dream of an imminent golden age as hopelessly naive and impractically utopian; yet it infused an element of idealism into American attitudes toward international affairs that has proved stubbornly persistent.

When wily old Benjamin Franklin arrived in Paris to negotiate the treaty with France, he was determined that his very appearance should herald the diplomatic revolution the Americans hoped to achieve. In his clothing and demeanor, he affected a persona that deliberately violated every norm of diplomatic behavior. Instead of the customary ceremonial sword, he toted only a plain white walking stick. Forsaking ermined robes and fancy wigs, he sported homespun garments and a simple cap of marten fur. "Figure me,"

RMN-Grand Palais/Art Resource, NY

Benjamin Franklin in His Fabled Cap He left school at age ten and became a wealthy businessman, a journalist, an inventor, a scientist, a legislator, and preeminently a statesman-diplomat. He was sent to France in 1776 as the American envoy at age seventy, and he remained there until 1785, negotiating the alliance with the French and helping to negotiate the treaty of peace. His fame had preceded him, and when he discarded his wig for the fur cap of a simple "American agriculturist," he took French society by storm. French aristocratic women, with whom he was a great favorite, honored him by adopting the high *coiffure à la Franklin* in imitation of his cap.

he wrote to a friend, "very plainly dress'd, wearing my thin grey strait Hair, that peeps out under my only Coiffure, a fine Fur Cap, which comes down my Forehead almost to my Spectacles. Think how this must appear among the Powder'd Heads of Paris." He shocked the royal court, besotted as it was with pomp and protocol. But ordinary Parisians adored him as a specimen of a new democratic social order, devoid of pretense and ornament. When Franklin embraced and kissed the famed French philosopher Voltaire in a Paris theater, the spectators applauded wildly. Meanwhile, the diplomatic game intensified.

After the humiliation at Saratoga in 1777, the British Parliament belatedly passed a measure that in effect offered the Americans home rule within the empire. This was essentially all that the colonials had ever asked for—except independence. If the French were going to break up the British Empire, they would have to bestir themselves. Franklin now played skillfully on French fears of Anglo-American reconciliation. On February 6, 1778, France offered the Americans a treaty of alliance. It did not conform

exactly to the terms of the Model Treaty Franklin had brought with him—an early example of practical self-interest trumping abstract idealism in America's conduct of foreign affairs. Against its better judgment, the young Republic concluded its first entangling military alliance and would soon regret it. But the treaty with France also constituted an official recognition of America's independence and lent powerful military heft to the Patriot cause. Both allies bound themselves to wage war until the United States had fully secured its freedom and until both agreed to terms with the common enemy. With those pledges, the American Revolutionary War now became a world war.

✦ The Colonial War Becomes a Wider War

England and France thus came to blows in 1778, and the shot fired at Lexington rapidly widened into a global conflagration. Spain entered the fray against Britain in 1779, as did Holland. Combined Spanish and French fleets outnumbered those of Britain, and on two occasions the British Isles seemed to be at the mercy of hostile warships.

The weak maritime neutrals of Europe, who had suffered from Britain's dominance over the seas, now began to demand more respect for their rights (see Table 8.1). In 1780 the imperious Catherine the Great of Russia took the lead in organizing the **Armed Neutrality**, a lineup of almost all the remaining European neutrals in an attitude of passive hostility toward Britain. She later sneeringly called this the "Armed Nullity." The war was now being fought not only in Europe and North America, but also in South America, the Caribbean, and Asia.

To say that America, with some French aid, defeated Britain is like saying "Daddy and I killed the bear." To Britain, struggling for its very life, the scuffle in the New World became secondary. The Americans deserve credit for having kept the war going until 1778, with secret French aid. But they did not achieve their independence until the conflict erupted into a multipower world war that was too big for Britain to handle. From 1778 to 1783, France provided the rebels with guns, money, immense amounts of equipment, about one-half of America's regular armed forces, and practically all of the new nation's naval strength.

France's entrance into the conflict forced the British to change their basic strategy in America. Hitherto they could count on blockading the colonial coast and commanding the seas. Now the French had powerful fleets in American waters, chiefly to protect their own valuable West Indies islands, but in a position to jeopardize Britain's blockade and lines of supply.

TABLE 8.1 Britain Against the World

Britain and Allies	Enemy or Unfriendly Powers	
Great Britain Some Loyalists and Indians 30,000 hired Hessians *(Total population on Britain's side: ca. 8 million)*	Belligerents *(Total population: ca. 39.5 million)*	United States, 1775–1783 France, 1778–1783 Spain, 1779–1783 Holland, 1779–1783
		Ireland (restive)
	Members of the Armed Neutrality (with dates of joining)	Russia, 1780 Denmark-Norway, 1780 Sweden, 1780 Holy Roman Empire, 1781 Prussia, 1782 Portugal, 1782 Two Sicilies, 1783 (after peace signed)

The British, therefore, decided to evacuate Philadelphia and concentrate their strength in New York City.

In June 1778 the withdrawing redcoats were attacked by General Washington at Monmouth, New Jersey, on a blisteringly hot day. Scores of men collapsed or died from sunstroke. But the battle was indecisive, and the British escaped to New York, although about one-third of their Hessians deserted. Henceforth, except for the Yorktown interlude of 1781, Washington remained in the New York area hemming in the British.

✦ Blow and Counterblow

In the summer of 1780, a powerful French army of six thousand regular troops, commanded by the Comte de Rochambeau, arrived in Newport, Rhode Island. The Americans were somewhat suspicious of their former enemies; in fact, several ugly flare-ups, involving minor bloodshed, had already occurred between the new allies. But French gold and goodwill melted hard hearts. Dancing parties were arranged with the prim Puritan maidens; one French officer related, doubtless with exaggeration, "The simple innocence of the Garden of Eden prevailed." No real military advantage came immediately from this French reinforcement, although preparations were made for a Franco-American attack on New York.

Improving American morale was staggered later in 1780 when General Benedict Arnold turned traitor.

A leader of undoubted dash and brilliance, he was ambitious, greedy, unscrupulous, and suffering from a well-grounded but petulant feeling that his valuable services were not fully appreciated. He plotted with the British to sell out the key stronghold of West Point, which commanded the Hudson River, for £6,300 and an officer's commission. By the sheerest accident, the plot was detected in the nick of time, and Arnold fled to the British. "Whom can we trust now?" cried General Washington in anguish.

The British meanwhile had devised a plan to roll up the colonies, beginning with the South, where the Loyalists were numerous (see Map 8.2). The colony of Georgia was ruthlessly overrun in 1778–1779; Charleston, South Carolina, fell in 1780. The surrender of the city to the British involved the capture of five thousand men and four hundred cannon and was a heavier loss to the Americans, in relation to existing strength, than that of Burgoyne was to the British.

Warfare now intensified in the Carolinas, where Patriots bitterly fought their Loyalist neighbors. It was not uncommon for prisoners on both sides to be butchered in cold blood after they had thrown down their arms. The tide turned later in 1780 and early in 1781, when American riflemen wiped out a British detachment at King's Mountain and then defeated a smaller force at Cowpens. In the Carolina campaign of 1781, General Nathanael Greene, a Quaker-reared tactician, distinguished himself by his strategy of delay. Standing and then retreating, he exhausted his

MAP 8.2 War in the South, 1780–1781 © 2016 Cengage Learning

foe, General Charles Cornwallis, in vain pursuit. By losing battles but winning campaigns, the "Fighting Quaker" finally succeeded in clearing most of Georgia and South Carolina of British troops.

✹ The Land Frontier and the Sea Frontier

The West was ablaze during much of the war. Indian allies of George III, hoping to protect their land, were busy with torch and tomahawk; they were egged on by British agents branded as "hair buyers" because they paid bounties for American scalps. Fateful 1777 was known as "the bloody year" on the frontier. Although two nations of the Iroquois Confederacy, the Oneidas and the Tuscaroras, sided with the Americans, the Senecas, Mohawks, Cayugas, and Onondagas joined the British. They were urged on by Mohawk chief Joseph Brant, a convert to Anglicanism who believed, not without reason, that a victorious Britain would restrain American expansion into the West.

Joseph Brant, by Gilbert Stuart, 1786 Siding with the British, this Mohawk chief led Indian frontier raids so ferocious that he was dubbed "monster Brant." When he later met King George III, he declined to kiss the king's hand but asked instead to kiss the hand of the queen.

MAP 8.3 George Rogers Clark's Campaign, 1778–1779
© 2016 Cengage Learning

Brant and the British ravaged large areas of backcountry Pennsylvania and New York until checked by an American force in 1779. In 1784 the pro-British Iroquois were forced to sign the **Treaty of Fort Stanwix**, the first treaty between the United States and an Indian nation. Under its terms the Indians ceded most of their land.

Yet even in wartime, the human tide of westward-moving pioneers did not halt its flow. Eloquent testimony is provided by place names in Kentucky, such as Lexington (named after the battle) and Louisville (named after America's new ally, Louis XVI).

In the wild Illinois country, the British were especially vulnerable to attack, for they held only scattered posts that they had captured from the French. An audacious frontiersman, George Rogers Clark, conceived the idea of seizing these forts by surprise. In 1778–1779 he floated down the Ohio River with about 175 men and captured in quick succession the forts Kaskaskia, Cahokia, and Vincennes (see Map 8.3). Clark's admirers have argued, without positive proof, that his success forced the British to cede the region north of the Ohio River to the United States at the peace table in Paris.

America's infant navy had meanwhile been laying the foundations of a brilliant tradition. The naval establishment consisted of only a handful of nondescript ships, commanded by daring officers, the most famous of whom was a hard-fighting young Scotsman, John Paul Jones. As events turned out, this tiny naval force never made a real dent in Britain's thunderous fleets. Its chief contribution was in destroying British merchant shipping and thus carrying the war into the waters around the British Isles.

More numerous and damaging than ships of the regular American navy were swift **privateers**. These craft were privately owned armed ships—legalized pirates in a sense—specifically authorized by Congress to prey on enemy shipping. Altogether over a thousand American privateers, responding to the call of patriotism and profit, sallied forth with about seventy thousand men ("sailors of fortune"). They captured some six hundred British prizes, while British warships captured about as many American merchantmen and privateers.

Baron von Steuben (1730–1794), a Prussian general who helped train the Continental Army, found the Americans to be very different from other soldiers he had known. As von Steuben explained to a fellow European,

❝The genius of this nation is not in the least to be compared with that of the Prussians, Austrians, or French. You say to your soldier, 'Do this' and he doeth it; but I am obliged to say, 'This is the reason why you ought to do that,' and then he does it.**❞**

Privateering was not an unalloyed asset. It had the unfortunate effect of diverting manpower from the main war effort and involving Americans, including Benedict Arnold, in speculation and graft. But the privateers brought in urgently needed gold, harassed the enemy, and raised American morale by providing victories at a time when victories were few. British shipping was so badly riddled by privateers and by the regular American navy that insurance rates skyrocketed. Merchant ships were compelled to sail in convoy, and British shippers and manufacturers brought increasing pressure on Parliament to end the war on honorable terms.

✸ Yorktown and the Final Curtain

One of the darkest periods of the war was 1780–1781, before the last decisive victory. Inflation of the currency continued at full gallop. The government, virtually bankrupt, declared that it would repay many of its debts at the rate of only 2.5 cents on the dollar. Despair prevailed, the sense of unity withered, and mutinous sentiments infected the army.

Meanwhile, the British general Cornwallis was blundering into a trap. After futile operations in

Virginia, he had fallen back to Chesapeake Bay at **Yorktown** to await seaborne supplies and reinforcements. He assumed Britain would continue to control the sea. But these few fateful weeks happened to be one of the brief periods during the war when British naval superiority slipped away.

The French were now prepared to cooperate energetically in a brilliant stroke. Admiral de Grasse, operating with a powerful fleet in the West Indies, advised the Americans that he was free to join with them in an assault on Cornwallis at Yorktown. Quick to seize this opportunity, General Washington made a swift march of more than three hundred miles to the Chesapeake from the New York area. Accompanied by Rochambeau's French army, Washington beset the British by land, while de Grasse blockaded them by sea after beating off the British fleet. Completely cornered, Cornwallis surrendered his entire force of seven thousand men on October 19, 1781, as his band appropriately played "The World Turn'd Upside Down." The triumph was no less French than American: the French provided essentially all the sea power and about half of the regular troops in the besieging army of some sixteen thousand men.

Stunned by news of the disaster, Prime Minister Lord North cried, "Oh God! It's all over! It's all over!"

Battle of the Chesapeake Capes, 1781 A young French naval officer, Pierre Joseph Jennot, sketched what is probably the only depiction of the epochal sea battle by a participant. The British and French fleets first engaged on September 5 and for two days chased each other while drifting one hundred miles south. On September 8 the French turned back northward and occupied Chesapeake Bay, cutting off General Cornwallis, ashore in Yorktown, from support and escape by sea. When General Washington, with more French help, blocked any British retreat by land, a doomed Cornwallis surrendered.

But it was not. George III stubbornly planned to continue the struggle, for Britain was far from being crushed. It still had fifty-four thousand troops in North America, including thirty-two thousand in the United States. Washington returned with his army to New York, there to continue keeping a vigilant eye on the British force of ten thousand men.

Fighting actually continued for more than a year after Yorktown, with Patriot–Loyalist warfare in the South especially savage. "No quarter for Tories" was the common battle cry. One of Washington's most valuable contributions was to keep the languishing cause alive, the army in the field, and the states together during these critical months. Otherwise a satisfactory peace treaty might never have been signed.

✷ Peace at Paris

After Yorktown, despite George III's obstinate eagerness to continue fighting, many Britons were weary of war and increasingly ready to come to terms. They had suffered heavy reverses in India and in the West Indies. The island of Minorca in the Mediterranean had fallen; the Rock of Gibraltar was tottering. Lord North's ministry collapsed in March 1782, temporarily ending the personal rule of George III. A Whig ministry, rather favorable to the Americans, replaced the Tory regime of Lord North.

Three American peace negotiators had meanwhile gathered at Paris: the aging but astute Benjamin Franklin; the flinty John Adams, vigilant for New England interests; and the impulsive John Jay of New York, deeply suspicious of Old World intrigue. The three envoys had explicit instructions from Congress to make no separate peace and to consult with their French allies at all stages of the negotiations. But the American representatives chafed under this directive. They well knew that it had been written by a subservient Congress, with the French Foreign Office indirectly guiding the pen.

France was in a painful position. It had induced Spain to enter the war on its side, in part by promising to deliver British-held Gibraltar. Yet the towering

Blundering George III, a poor loser, wrote this of America:

❝ Knavery seems to be so much the striking feature of its inhabitants that it may not in the end be an evil that they become aliens to this Kingdom. **❞**

Contending Voices
Two Revolutions: French and American

The French Revolution broke out in the decade following America's own revolution, which partly inspired it. Yet the French upheaval swiftly descended into mob violence and soon led to Napoleon Bonaparte's wars, which convulsed Europe for a decade before the French monarchy was restored in 1814. Then and later, scholars have tried to understand the relation between the two revolutions. In 1800 the Prussian statesman Friedrich von Gentz (1764–1832) published an essay titled "Origins and Principles of the American Revolution, Compared with the French." In it he argued that

❝ the Americans escaped the most dangerous of all the rocks, which in our times threatens the founders of any revolution: the deadly passion for making political experiments with abstract theories and untried systems. **❞**

Future American Secretary of State and President John Quincy Adams (1767–1848) translated von Gentz's work into English, because, he said,

❝ it rescues [the American] revolution from the disgraceful imputation of having proceeded from the same principles as the French. **❞**

According to von Gentz and Adams, what part of the American experience before 1776 accounted for the major differences between the revolutions in France and America?

rock was defying frantic joint assaults by French and Spanish troops. Spain also coveted the immense trans-Allegheny area, on which restless American pioneers were already settling.

France, ever eager to smash Britain's empire, desired an independent United States, but one independent in the abstract, not in action. It therefore schemed to keep the new Republic cooped up east of the Allegheny Mountains. A weak America—like a horse sturdy enough to plow but not vigorous enough to kick—would be easier to manage in promoting French interests and policy. France was paying a heavy price in men and treasure to win America's independence, and it wanted to get its money's worth.

But John Jay was unwilling to play France's game. Suspiciously alert, he perceived that the French could not satisfy the conflicting ambitions of both Americans and Spaniards. He saw signs—or thought he did—indicating that the Paris Foreign Office was about to betray America's trans-Appalachian interests to satisfy those of Spain. He therefore secretly made separate overtures to London, contrary to his instructions from Congress. The hard-pressed British, eager to entice one of their enemies from the alliance, speedily came to terms with the Americans. A preliminary treaty of peace was signed in 1782; the final peace, the next year.

By the **Treaty of Paris** of 1783, the British formally recognized the independence of the United States. In addition, they granted generous boundaries, stretching majestically to the Mississippi on the west, to the Great Lakes on the north, and to Spanish Florida on the south. (Spain had recently captured Florida from Britain.) The Yankees, though now divorced from the empire, were to retain a share in the priceless fisheries of Newfoundland. The Canadians, of course, were profoundly displeased.

The Americans, on their part, had to yield important concessions. Loyalists were not to be further persecuted, and Congress was to *recommend* to the state legislatures that confiscated Loyalist property be restored. As for the debts long owed to British creditors, the states vowed to put no lawful obstacles in the way of their collection. Unhappily for future harmony, the assurances regarding both Loyalists and debts were not carried out in the manner hoped for by London.

As for Britain, its acceptance of defeat in North America eventually paid enormous strategic dividends. Persisting in the colonial conflict might well have bled Britain dry. But shutting down the war against the Americans enabled London to rebuild its army and navy and eventually prevail in its titanic struggle with Napoleon—and to become the preeminent world power in the nineteenth century.

✶ A New Nation Legitimized

Britain's terms were liberal almost beyond belief. The enormous trans-Appalachian area was thrown in as a virtual gift, for George Rogers Clark had captured only a small segment of it. Why the generosity? Had the United States beaten Britain to its knees?

The key to the riddle may be found in the Old World. At the time the peace terms were drafted, Britain was trying to seduce America from its French alliance, so it made the terms as alluring as possible. The shaky Whig ministry, hanging on by its fingernails for only a few months, was more friendly to the

The Reconciliation Between Britannia and Her Daughter America (detail) America (represented by an Indian) is invited to buss (kiss) her mother. Compare this cartoon with the one on p. 118.

Americans than were the Tories. It was determined, by a policy of liberality, to salve recent wounds, reopen old trade channels, and prevent future wars over the coveted trans-Appalachian region. This farsighted policy was regrettably not followed by the successors of the Whigs.

In spirit, the Americans made a separate peace—contrary to the French alliance. In fact, they did not. The Paris Foreign Office formally approved the terms of peace, though disturbed by the lone-wolf course of its American ally. France was immensely relieved by the prospect of bringing the costly conflict to an end and of freeing itself from its embarrassing promises to the Spanish crown.

America alone gained from the world-girdling war. The British, though soon to stage a comeback, were battered and beaten. The French savored sweet revenge but plunged headlong down the slippery slope to bankruptcy and revolution. The Americans fared much better. Snatching their independence from the furnace of world conflict, they began their national career with a splendid territorial birthright and a priceless heritage of freedom. Seldom, if ever, have any people been so favored.

Whose Revolution?

Historians once assumed that the Revolution was just another chapter in the unfolding story of human liberty—an important way station on a divinely ordained pathway toward moral perfection in human affairs. This approach, often labeled the "Whig view of history," was best expressed in George Bancroft's ten-volume *History of the United States of America*, published between the 1830s and 1870s.

By the end of the nineteenth century, a group of historians known as the "imperial school" challenged Bancroft, arguing that the Revolution was best understood not as the fulfillment of national destiny, but as a constitutional conflict within the British Empire. For historians like George Beer, Charles Andrews, and Lawrence Gipson, the Revolution was the product of a collision between two different views of empire. While the Americans were moving steadily toward more self-government, Britain increasingly tightened its grip, threatening a stranglehold that eventually led to wrenching revolution.

By the early twentieth century, these approaches were in turn challenged by the so-called progressive historians, who argued that neither divine destiny nor constitutional quibbles had much to do with the Revolution. Rather, the Revolution stemmed from deep-seated class tensions within American society. Once released by revolt, those tensions produced a truly transformed social order. Living themselves in a reform age when entrenched economic interests cowered under heavy attack, progressive historians like Carl Becker insisted that the Revolution was not just about "home rule" within the British Empire, but also about "who should rule at home" in America, the upper or lower classes. J. Franklin Jameson took Becker's analysis one step further in his influential *The American Revolution Considered as a Social Movement* (1926). He claimed that the Revolution not only grew out of intense struggles between social groups but also inspired many ordinary Americans to seek greater economic and political power, fundamentally democratizing society in its wake.

In the 1950s the progressive historians fell out of favor as the political climate became more conservative. Interpretations of the American Revolution as a class struggle did not play well in a country obsessed with the spread of communism, and in its place arose the so-called consensus view. Historians such as Robert Brown and Edmund Morgan downplayed the role of class conflict in the Revolutionary era but emphasized that colonists of all ranks shared a commitment to certain fundamental political principles of self-government. The unifying power of ideas was now back in fashion almost a hundred years after Bancroft.

Since the 1950s two broad interpretations have contended with each other and perpetuated the controversy over whether political ideals or economic and social realities were most responsible for the Revolution. The first, articulated most prominently by Bernard Bailyn, has emphasized ideological and psychological factors. Focusing on the power of ideas to foment revolution, Bailyn argued that the colonists, incited by their reading of seventeenth-century and early-eighteenth-century English political theorists, grew extraordinarily (perhaps even exaggeratedly) suspicious of any attempts to tighten the imperial reins on the colonies. When confronted with new taxes and commercial regulations, these hypersensitive colonists screamed "conspiracy against liberty" and "corrupt ministerial plot." In time they took up armed insurrection in defense of their intellectual commitment to liberty.

A second school of historians, inspired by the social movements of the 1960s and 1970s, revived the progressive interpretation of the Revolution. Gary Nash, in *The Urban Crucible* (1979), and Edward Countryman, in *A People in Revolution* (1981), pointed to the increasing social and economic divisions among Americans in both the urban seaports and the isolated countryside in the years leading up to the Revolution. Attacks by laborers on political elites and expressions of resentment toward wealth were taken as evidence of a society that was breeding revolutionary change from within, quite aside from British provocations. Some of these arguments have continued into more recent scholarship; Woody Holton, in *Forced Founders* (1999), argues that pressures exerted by the presence of Indians, slaves, and poor whites forced the Virginia elite onto the road toward independence.

While the concerns of the progressive historians echo in these socioeconomic interpretations of the Revolution, the neoprogressives have been more careful not to reduce the issues simplistically to the one-ring arena of economic self-interest. Instead, they have argued that the varying material circumstances of American participants led them to hold distinctive versions of republicanism, giving the Revolution a less unified and more complex ideological underpinning than the idealistic historians had previously suggested. The dialogue between proponents of "ideas" and "interests" has gradually led to a more nuanced meeting of the two views.

In another recent trend, scholars have taken a more transatlantic view of the Revolution's origins, asking when and how colonists shifted from identifying as "British" to viewing themselves as "American." Fred Anderson has argued that long before rebellion, the Seven Years' War (1756–1763) helped create a sense of American identity apart from Britain. Still other historians, such as T. H. Breen, argue that British nationalism actually intensified in the colonies over the course of the eighteenth century, as economic and cultural ties between Britain and North America strengthened through increased trade and the migration of ideas with the growth of print culture. Only when colonists realized that the British did not see them as equal imperial citizens, entitled to the same rights as Englishmen, did American nationalism emerge and Americans rebel. Taking a broader global view, David Armitage has argued that the American Declaration of Independence had an impact far beyond the British Atlantic world, shaping the rhetoric of countries claiming their independence into the following century and beyond.

Chapter Review

KEY TERMS

Second Continental
Congress (135)

Bunker Hill, Battle of (136)

Olive Branch Petition (136)

Hessians (136)

Common Sense (138)

Declaration of
Independence (140)

Declaration of the Rights
of Man (141)

Loyalists (141)

Patriots (141)

Long Island, Battle of (143)

Trenton, Battle of (146)

Saratoga, Battle of (148)

Model Treaty (148)

Armed Neutrality (149)

Fort Stanwix,
Treaty of (152)

privateers (152)

Yorktown, Battle of (153)

Paris, Treaty of (155)

PEOPLE TO KNOW

Ethan Allen

Benedict Arnold

Richard Montgomery

Thomas Paine

Abigail Adams

Richard Henry Lee

Lord Charles Cornwallis

William Howe

John ("Gentleman
Johnny") Burgoyne

Benjamin Franklin

Comte de Rochambeau

Nathanael Greene

Joseph Brant

George Rogers Clark

Admiral de Grasse

CHRONOLOGY

1775	Battles of Lexington and Concord
	Second Continental Congress
	Americans capture British garrisons at Ticonderoga and Crown Point
	Battle of Bunker Hill
	King George III formally proclaims colonies in rebellion
	Failed invasion of Canada
1776	Paine's *Common Sense*
	Declaration of Independence
	Battle of Trenton
1777	Battle of Brandywine
	Battle of Germantown
	Battle of Saratoga

1778	Formation of French-American alliance
	Battle of Monmouth
1778–1779	Clark's victories in the West
1781	Battle of King's Mountain
	Battle of Cowpens
	Greene leads Carolina campaign
	French and Americans force Cornwallis to surrender at Yorktown
1782	North's ministry collapses in Britain
1783	Treaty of Paris
1784	Treaty of Fort Stanwix

TO LEARN MORE

David Armitage, *The Declaration of Independence: A Global History* (2007)

T. H. Breen, *American Insurgents, American Patriots: The Revolution of the People* (2010)

Robert M. Calhoon, *The Loyalists in Revolutionary America* (1973)

Caroline Cox, *A Proper Sense of Honor: Service and Sacrifice in George Washington's Army* (2004)

Joseph J. Ellis, *His Excellency: George Washington* (2004)

David Hackett Fischer, *Washington's Crossing* (2004)

James H. Hutson, *John Adams and the Diplomacy of the American Revolution* (1980)

Linda K. Kerber, *Women of the Republic: Intellect and Ideology in Revolutionary America* (1980)

Wim Klooster, *Revolutions in the Atlantic World: A Comparative History* (2005)

Mary Beth Norton, *The British-Americans: The Loyalist Exiles in England* (1972)

——, *Liberty's Daughters: The Revolutionary Experience of American Women* (1980)

Cassandra Pybus, *Epic Journeys of Freedom: Runaway Slaves of the American Revolution and Their Global Quest for Liberty* (2006)

Alan Taylor, *The Divided Ground: Indians, Settlers, and the Northern Borderland of the American Revolution* (2006)

——, *The Internal Enemy: Slavery and War in Virginia, 1772–1832* (2013)

A complete, annotated bibliography for this chapter—along with brief descriptions of the People to Know—may be found on the *American Pageant* website. The key terms are defined in the glossary at the end of the text.

Part Two

Building the New Nation

1776–1860

By 1783 Americans had won their freedom. Now they had to build their country. They were blessed with a vast and fertile land, and they inherited from their colonial experience a proud legacy of self-rule. But history provided scant precedent for erecting a republic on a national scale. No law of nature guaranteed that the thirteen rebellious colonies would stay glued together as a single nation, or that they would preserve, not to mention expand, their democratic way of life. New institutions had to be created, new habits of thought cultivated. Who could predict whether the American experiment in government by the people would succeed?

The feeble national government cobbled together under the Articles of Confederation during the Revolutionary War soon proved woefully inadequate to the task of nation building. In less than ten years after the Revolutionary War's conclusion, the Articles were replaced by a new Constitution, but even its adoption did not end the debate over just what form American government should take. Would the president, the Congress, or the courts be the dominant branch? What should be the proper division of authority between the federal government and the states? How could the rights of individuals be protected against a potentially powerful government? What economic policies would best serve the infant Republic? How should the nation defend itself against foreign foes? What principles should guide foreign policy? Was America a nation at all, or was it merely a geographic expression, destined to splinter into several bitterly quarreling sections, as had happened to so many other would-be countries?

After a shaky start under George Washington and John Adams in the 1790s, buffeted by foreign troubles and domestic crises, the new Republic passed a major test when power was peacefully transferred from the conservative Federalists to the more liberal Jeffersonians in the election of 1800. A confident President Jefferson proceeded boldly to expand the national territory with the landmark Louisiana Purchase in 1803. But before long Jefferson, and then his successor, James Madison, were embroiled in what eventually proved to be a fruitless effort to spare the United States from the ravages of the war then raging in Europe.

The Verdict of the People (detail) This election-day crowd exudes the exuberant spirit of the era of Andrew Jackson, when the advent of universal white male suffrage made the United States the modern world's first mass participatory democracy. Yet the black man with the wheelbarrow, literally pushing his way into the painting, is a pointed reminder that the curse of slavery still blighted this happy scene.

Saint Louis Art Museum, Missouri, USA/Gift of Bank of America/The Bridgeman Art Library

Art Resource, NY

Women Weavers at Work (detail) These simple cotton looms heralded the dawn of the Industrial Revolution, which transformed the lives of Americans even more radically than the events of 1776.

America was dangerously divided during the War of 1812 and suffered a humiliating defeat. But a new sense of national unity and purpose was unleashed in the land thereafter. President Monroe, presiding over this "Era of Good Feelings," proclaimed in the Monroe Doctrine of 1823 that both of the American continents were off-limits to further European intervention. The foundations of a continental-scale economy were laid, as a "transportation revolution" stitched the country together with canals and railroads and turnpikes. Settlers flooded over those new arteries into the burgeoning West, often brusquely shouldering aside the native peoples. Immigrants, especially from Ireland and Germany, flocked to American shores. The combination of new lands, new labor, and revolutionary new technologies like the telegraph and the railroad fed the growth of a market economy, including the commercialization of agriculture and the beginnings of the factory system of production. Old ways of life withered as the market economy drew women as well as men, children as well as adults, blacks as well as whites, into its embrace. Ominously, the slave system grew robustly as the production of cotton, mostly for sale on European markets, exploded into the booming Southwest.

Meanwhile, the United States in the era of Andrew Jackson gave the world an impressive lesson in political science. Between roughly 1820 and 1840, Americans virtually invented mass democracy, creating huge political parties and enormously expanding political participation by enfranchising nearly all adult white males. Nor was the spirit of innovation confined to the political realm. A wave of reform and cultural vitality swept through many sectors of American society. Utopian experiments proliferated. Religious revivals and even new religions, like Mormonism, flourished. A national literature blossomed. Crusades were launched for temperance, prison reform, women's rights, and the abolition of slavery.

By the second quarter of the nineteenth century, the outlines of a distinctive American national character had begun to emerge. Americans were a diverse, restless people, tramping steadily westward, eagerly forging their own nascent Industrial Revolution, proudly exercising their democratic political rights, impatient with the old, in love with the new, testily asserting their superiority over all other peoples—and increasingly divided, in heart, in conscience, and in politics, over the single greatest blight on their record of nation making and democracy building: slavery.

Chapter 9

The Confederation and the Constitution

1776–1790

The example of changing a constitution by assembling the wise men of the State instead
of assembling armies will be worth as much to the world as the former examples we had given them.

THOMAS JEFFERSON, 1789

The American Revolution was not a revolution in the sense of a radical or total change. It did not suddenly and violently overturn the entire political and social framework, as later occurred in the French and Russian Revolutions. What happened was accelerated evolution rather than outright revolution. During the conflict itself, people went on working and praying, marrying and playing. Many of them were not seriously disturbed by the actual fighting, and the most isolated communities scarcely knew that a war was on. But at war's end, all Americans faced a great question: what would be done with the independence that had been so dearly won?

✦ A Shaky Start Toward Union

Prospects for erecting a lasting regime were far from bright. It is always difficult to set up a new government and doubly difficult to set up a new *type* of government. Disruptive forces stalked the land. The departure of some eighty thousand Loyalists left the new ship of state without conservative ballast, fostering sometimes unsound experimentation and innovation. Patriots had fought the war with a high degree of disunity, but they had at least concurred on allegiance to a common cause. Now even that was gone. It would have been almost a miracle if any government fashioned in all this confusion had long endured.

Hard times, the bane of all regimes, set in shortly after the war and hit bottom in 1786. As if other troubles were not enough, British manufacturers, with dammed-up surpluses, began flooding the American market with cut-rate goods. War-baby American industries, in particular, suffered industrial colic from such ruthless competition. One Philadelphia newspaper in 1783 urged readers to don home-stitched garments of homespun cloth:

> *Of foreign gewgaws let's be free,*
> *And wear the webs of liberty.*

Yet hopeful signs could be discerned. The thirteen sovereign states were basically alike in governmental structure and functioned under similar constitutions. Americans enjoyed a rich political inheritance, derived partly from Britain and partly from their own homegrown devices for self-government. Finally, they were blessed with political leaders of a high order in men like George Washington, James Madison, John Adams, Thomas Jefferson, and Alexander Hamilton. Ultimately, this formative moment, while more evolution than revolution, did usher in some striking changes—changes in social structures and customs, economic practices, and political institutions—as well as ideas about race, class, and gender.

✦ Constitution Making in the States

The Continental Congress in 1776 called upon the colonies to draft new constitutions. In effect, the Continental Congress was actually asking the colonies to summon themselves into being as new states. The sovereignty of these new states, according to the theory of republicanism, would rest on the authority of the people. For a time the manufacture of governments was even more pressing than the manufacture of gunpowder. Although the states of Connecticut and Rhode Island merely retouched their colonial charters, constitution writers elsewhere worked tirelessly to capture on black-inked parchment the republican spirit of the age.

Massachusetts contributed one especially noteworthy innovation when it called a special convention to draft its constitution and then submitted the final draft directly to the people for ratification. Once adopted in 1780, the Massachusetts constitution could be changed only by another specially called constitutional convention. This procedure was later imitated in the drafting and ratification of the federal Constitution. Adopted almost a decade before the federal Constitution, the Massachusetts constitution remains the longest-lived constitution in the world.

The newly penned state constitutions had many features in common. Their similarity, as it turned out, made easier the drafting of a workable federal charter when the time was ripe. In the British tradition, a "constitution" was not a written document, but rather an accumulation of laws, customs, and precedents. Americans invented something different. The documents they drafted were contracts that defined the powers of government, as did the old colonial charters, but they drew their authority from the people, not from the royal seal of a distant king. As *written* documents the state constitutions were intended to represent a *fundamental* law, superior to the transient whims of ordinary legislation. Most of these documents included bills of rights, specifically guaranteeing long-prized liberties against later legislative encroachment. Most of them required the annual election of legislators, who were thus forced to stay in touch with the mood of the people. All of them deliberately created weak executive and judicial branches, at least by present-day standards. A generation of quarreling with His Majesty's officials had implanted a deep distrust of despotic governors and arbitrary judges.

In all the new state governments, the legislatures, as presumably the most democratic branch of government, were given sweeping powers. But as Thomas Jefferson warned, "173 despots [in a legislature] would surely be as oppressive as one." Many Americans soon came to agree with him.

The democratic character of the new state legislatures was vividly reflected by the presence of many members from the recently enfranchised poorer western districts. Their influence was powerfully felt in their several successful movements to relocate state capitals from the haughty eastern seaports into the less pretentious interior. In the Revolutionary era, the capitals of New Hampshire, New York, Virginia,

North Carolina, South Carolina, and Georgia were all moved westward. These geographical shifts portended political shifts that deeply discomfited many more conservative Americans.

✵ Economic Crosscurrents

Economic changes begotten by the war were likewise noteworthy, but not overwhelming. States seized control of former crown lands, and although rich speculators had their day, many of the large Loyalist holdings were confiscated and eventually cut up into small farms. Roger Morris's huge estate in New York, for example, was sliced into 250 parcels—thus accelerating the spread of economic democracy. The frightful excesses of the French Revolution were avoided, partly because cheap land was easily available and because America had so few deeply entrenched landed aristocrats to be overthrown. It is highly significant that in the United States, economic democracy, broadly speaking, preceded political democracy.

A sharp stimulus was given to manufacturing by the prewar nonimportation agreements and later by the war itself. Goods that had formerly been imported from Britain were mostly cut off, and the ingenious Yankees were forced to make their own. Ten years after the Revolution, busy Brandywine Creek, south of Philadelphia, was turning the water wheels of numerous mills along an eight-mile stretch. Yet America remained overwhelmingly a nation of soil-tillers.

Economically speaking, independence had drawbacks. Much of the coveted commerce of Britain was still reserved for the loyal parts of the empire. American ships were now barred from British and British West Indies harbors. Fisheries were disrupted, and bounties for ships' stores had abruptly ended. In some respects the hated British Navigation Laws were more disagreeable after independence than before.

New commercial outlets, fortunately, compensated partially for the loss of old ones. Americans could now trade freely with foreign nations, subject to local restrictions—a boon they had not enjoyed in the days of mercantilism. Enterprising Yankee shippers ventured boldly—and profitably—into the Baltic and China Seas. In 1784 the *Empress of China*, carrying a valuable weed (ginseng) that was highly prized by Chinese herb doctors as a cure for impotence, led the way into the East Asian markets.

Yet the general economic picture was far from rosy. War had spawned demoralizing extravagance, speculation, and profiteering, with profits for some as indecently high as 300 percent. State governments

Copley Family Portrait, ca. 1776–1777

A portrait painting like this one by John Singleton Copley (1738–1815) documents physical likenesses, clothing styles, and other material possessions typical of an era. But it can do more than that. In the execution of the painting itself, the preeminent portrait painter of colonial America revealed important values of his time. Copley's composition and use of light emphasized the importance of the mother in the family. Mrs. Copley is the visual center of the painting: the light falls predominantly on her, and she provides the focus of activity for the family group. Although Copley had moved to England in 1774 to avoid the disruptions of war, he had made radical friends in his hometown of Boston and surely had imbibed the sentiment of the age about "republican motherhood"—a sentiment that revered women as homemakers and mothers, the cultivators of good republican values in young citizens. What other prevailing attitudes, about gender and age, for example, might this painting reveal?

John Singleton Copley, The Copley Family, Andrew W. Mellon Fund, image courtesy of the Board of Trustees, National Gallery of Art, Washington, D.C.

had borrowed more during the war than they could ever hope to repay. Runaway inflation had been ruinous to many citizens, and Congress had failed in its feeble attempts to curb economic laws. The average citizen was probably worse off financially at the end of the shooting than at the start.

The whole economic and social atmosphere was unhealthy. A newly rich class of profiteers was noisily conspicuous, whereas many once-wealthy people were left destitute. The controversy leading to the Revolutionary War had bred a keen distaste for taxes and encouraged disrespect for the majesty of the law generally. John Adams had been shocked when gleefully told by a horse-jockey neighbor that the courts of justice were all closed—a plight that proved to be only temporary.

✦ Creating a Confederation

The Second Continental Congress of Revolutionary days was little more than a conference of ambassadors from the thirteen states. It was totally without constitutional authority and in general did only what it

Western Merchants Negotiating for Tea in Hong Kong, ca. 1800 Yankee merchants and shippers figured prominently in the booming trade with China in the late eighteenth century. Among the American entrepreneurs who prospered in the China trade was Warren Delano, ancestor of President Franklin Delano Roosevelt.

dared to do, though it asserted some control over military affairs and foreign policy. In nearly all respects, the thirteen states were sovereign, for they coined money, raised armies and navies, and erected tariff barriers. The legislature of Virginia even ratified separately the treaty of alliance of 1778 with France.

Shortly before declaring independence in 1776, Congress appointed a committee to draft a written constitution for the new nation. The finished product was the **Articles of Confederation**. Adopted by Congress in 1777, it was translated into French after the Battle of Saratoga so as to convince France that America had a genuine government in the making. The Articles were not ratified by all thirteen states until 1781, less than eight months before the victory at Yorktown.

The chief apple of discord was western lands. Six of the jealous states, including Pennsylvania and Maryland, had no holdings beyond the Allegheny Mountains. Seven, notably New York and Virginia, were favored with enormous acreage, in most cases on the basis of earlier charter grants. The six land-hungry states argued that the more fortunate states would not have retained possession of this splendid prize if all the other states had not fought for it also.

A major complaint was that the land-rich states could sell their trans-Allegheny tracts and thus pay off pensions and other debts incurred in the common cause. States without such holdings would have to tax themselves heavily to defray these obligations. Why not turn the whole western area over to the central government?

Unanimous approval of the Articles of Confederation by the thirteen states was required, and land-starved Maryland stubbornly held out until March 1, 1781. Maryland at length gave in when New York surrendered its western claims and Virginia seemed about to do so. To sweeten the pill, Congress pledged itself to dispose of these vast areas for the "common benefit." It further agreed to carve from the new public domain not colonies, but a number of "republican" states, which in time would be admitted to the Union on terms of complete equality with all the others. This extraordinary commitment faithfully reflected the anticolonial spirit of the Revolution, and the pledge was later fully redeemed in the famed Northwest Ordinance of 1787 (see Map 9.1).

Fertile public lands thus transferred to the central government proved to be an invaluable bond of union.

MAP 9.1 Western Land Cessions to the United States, 1782–1802 © 2016 Cengage Learning

The states that had thrown their heritage into the common pot had to remain in the Union if they were to reap their share of the advantages from the land sales. An army of westward-moving pioneers purchased their farms from the federal government, directly or indirectly, and they learned to look to the national capital, rather than to the state capitals—with a consequent weakening of local influence. Finally, a uniform national land policy was made possible.

✦ The Articles of Confederation: America's First Constitution

The Articles of Confederation—some have said "Articles of Confusion"—provided for a loose confederation or "firm league of friendship." Thirteen independent states were thus linked together for joint action in dealing with common problems, such as foreign affairs. A clumsy Congress was to be the chief agency of government. There was no executive branch—George III had left a bad taste—and the vital judicial arm was left almost exclusively to the states.

Congress, though dominant, was severely hobbled. Each state had a single vote, so that some sixty-eight thousand Rhode Islanders had the same voice as more than ten times that many Virginians. All bills dealing with subjects of importance required the support of nine states; any amendment of the Articles themselves required unanimous ratification. Unanimity was almost impossible, and this meant that the amending process, perhaps fortunately, was unworkable. If it had been workable, the Republic might have struggled along with a patched-up Articles of Confederation rather than replace it with an effective Constitution.

The shackled Congress was weak—and was purposely designed to be weak. Suspicious states, having just won control over taxation and commerce from Britain, had no desire to yield their newly acquired privileges to an American parliament—even one of their own making.

Two handicaps of Congress were crippling. It had no power to regulate commerce, and this loophole left the states free to establish different, and often conflicting, laws regarding tariffs and navigation. Nor could Congress enforce its tax-collection program. It established a tax quota for each of the states and then asked them please

Picture Research Consultants & Archives

Independence Hall, Philadelphia, 1776 Originally built in the 1730s as a meeting place for the Pennsylvania colonial assembly, this building witnessed much history: here Washington was given command of the Continental Army, the Declaration of Independence was signed, and the Constitution was hammered out. The building began to be called "Independence Hall" in the 1820s and is today a major tourist destination in Philadelphia.

to contribute their share on a voluntary basis. The central authority—a "government by supplication"—was lucky if in any year it received one-fourth of its requests.

The feeble national government in Philadelphia could advise and advocate and appeal. But in dealing with the independent states, it could not command or coerce or control. It could not act directly upon the individual citizens of a sovereign state; it could not even protect itself against gross indignities. In 1783 a group of mutinous Pennsylvania soldiers, whose pay was in arrears, marched to Philadelphia and made a threatening demonstration in front of Independence Hall. After Congress appealed in vain to the state for protection, its members fled to safety at Princeton College in New Jersey. The new Congress, with all its paper powers, was even less effective than the old Continental Congress, which had wielded no constitutional powers at all.

Yet the Articles of Confederation, weak though they were, proved to be a landmark in government. They were for those days a model of what a loose confederation could be. Thomas Jefferson enthusiastically hailed the new structure as the best one "existing or that ever did exist." To compare it with the European governments, he thought, was like comparing "heaven and hell." But although the Confederation was praiseworthy as confederations went, the troubled times demanded not a loosely woven *con*federation but a

tightly knit federation. This involved the yielding by the states of their sovereignty to a completely recast federal government, which in turn would leave them free to control their local affairs.

In spite of their defects, the anemic Articles of Confederation were a significant stepping stone toward the present Constitution. They clearly outlined the general powers that were to be exercised by the central government, such as making treaties and establishing a postal service. As the first written constitution of the Republic, the Articles kept alive the flickering ideal of union and held the states together—until such time as they were ripe for the establishment of a strong constitution by peaceful, evolutionary methods. Without this intermediary jump, the states probably would never have consented to the breathtaking leap from the old boycott Association of 1774 to the Constitution of the United States.

✸ Landmarks in Land Laws

Handcuffed though the Congress of the Confederation was, it succeeded in passing supremely farsighted pieces of legislation. These related to an immense part of the public domain recently acquired from the states and commonly known as the **Old Northwest**. This

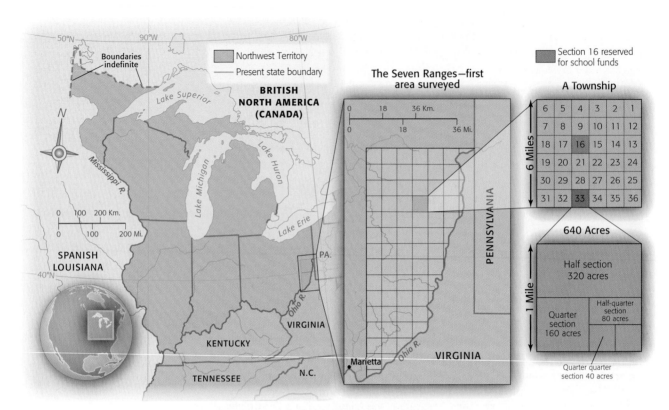

MAP 9.2 Surveying the Old Northwest Under the Land Ordinance of 1785   Sections of a township under the Land Ordinance of 1785. © 2016 Cengage Learning

area of land lay northwest of the Ohio River, east of the Mississippi River, and south of the Great Lakes.

The first of these red-letter laws was the **Land Ordinance of 1785** (see Map 9.2). It provided that the acreage of the Old Northwest should be sold and that the proceeds should be used to help pay off the national debt. The vast area was to be surveyed before sale and settlement, thus forestalling endless confusion and lawsuits. It was to be divided into townships six miles square, each of which in turn was to be split into thirty-six sections of one square mile each. The sixteenth section of each township was set aside to be sold for the benefit of the public schools—a priceless gift to education in the Northwest. The orderly settlement of the Northwest Territory, where the land was methodically surveyed and titles duly recorded, contrasted sharply with the chaos south of the Ohio River, where uncertain ownership was the norm and fraud was rampant.

Even more noteworthy was the **Northwest Ordinance** of 1787, which related to the governing of the Old Northwest. This law came to grips with the problem of how a nation should deal with its colonies—the same problem that had bedeviled the king and Parliament in London. The solution provided by the Northwest Ordinance was a judicious compromise: temporary tutelage, then permanent equality. First,

there would be two evolutionary territorial stages, during which the area would be subordinate to the federal government. Then, when a territory could boast sixty thousand inhabitants, it might be admitted by Congress as a state, with all the privileges of the thirteen charter members. (This is precisely what the Continental Congress had promised the states when they surrendered their lands in 1781.) The ordinance also forbade slavery in the Old Northwest—a path-breaking step, though it exempted slaves already present.

The wisdom of Congress in handling this explosive problem deserves warm praise. If it had attempted to chain the new territories in permanent subordination, a second American Revolution almost certainly would have erupted in later years, fought this time by the West against the East. Congress thus neatly solved the seemingly insoluble problem of empire. The scheme worked so well that its basic principles were ultimately carried over from the Old Northwest to other frontier areas.

✦ The World's Ugly Duckling

Foreign relations, especially with London, remained troubled during these anxious years of the Confederation. Britain resented the stab in the back from its rebellious offspring and for eight years refused to send a minister to America's "backwoods" capital. London suggested, with barbed irony, that if it sent one, it would have to send thirteen.

Britain flatly declined to make a commercial treaty or to repeal its ancient Navigation Laws. Lord Sheffield, whose ungenerous views prevailed, argued persuasively in a widely sold pamphlet that Britain would win back America's trade anyhow. Commerce, he insisted, would naturally follow old channels. So why go to the Americans hat in hand? The British also officially closed their profitable West Indies trade to the United States, though the Yankees, with their time-tested skill in smuggling, illegally partook nonetheless.

Scheming British agents were also active along the far-flung northern frontier. They intrigued with the disgruntled Allen brothers of Vermont and sought to annex that rebellious area to Britain. Along the northern border, the redcoats continued to hold a chain of trading posts on U.S. soil, and there they maintained their fur trade with the Indians. One plausible excuse for remaining was the failure of the American states to honor the treaty of peace in regard to debts and Loyalists. But the main purpose of Britain in hanging on was probably to curry favor with the Indians and keep their tomahawks lined up on the side of the king as a barrier against future American attacks on Canada.

All these grievances against Britain were maddening to patriotic Americans. Some citizens demanded, with more heat than wisdom, that the United States force the British into line by imposing restrictions on their imports to America. But Congress could not control commerce, and the states refused to adopt a uniform tariff policy. Some "easy states" deliberately lowered their tariffs in order to attract an unfair share of trade.

Spain, though recently an enemy of Britain, was openly unfriendly to the new Republic. It controlled the mouth of the all-important Mississippi, down which the pioneers of Tennessee and Kentucky were forced to float their produce. In 1784 Spain closed the river to American commerce, threatening the West with strangulation. Spain likewise claimed a large area north of the Gulf of Mexico, including a part of West Florida, granted to the United States by the British in 1783. At Natchez, on disputed soil, it held an important fort. It also schemed with the neighboring Indians, grievously antagonized by the rapacious land policies of Georgia and North Carolina, to hem in the Americans east of the Appalachians. Spain and Britain together, radiating their influence out among resentful Indian tribes, prevented America from exercising effective control over about half of its total territory (see Map 9.3).

MAP 9.3 Main Centers of Spanish and British Influence After 1783 This map shows graphically that the United States in 1783 achieved complete independence in name only, particularly in the area west of the Appalachian Mountains. Not until twenty years had passed did the new Republic, with the purchase of Louisiana from France in 1803, eliminate foreign influence from the east bank of the Mississippi River. Much of Florida remained in Spanish hands until the Adams-Onís Treaty of 1819 (see Chapter 12 p. 242). © 2016 Cengage Learning

Even France, America's comrade-in-arms, cooled off now that it had humbled Britain. The French demanded the repayment of money loaned during the war and restricted trade with their bustling West Indies and other ports.

Pirates of the North African states, including the arrogant Dey of Algiers, were ravaging America's Mediterranean commerce and enslaving Yankee sailors. The British purchased protection for their own subjects, and as colonists the Americans had enjoyed this shield. But as an independent nation, the United States was too weak to fight and too poor to bribe. A few Yankee shippers engaged in the Mediterranean trade with forged British protection papers, but not all were so bold or so lucky.

John Jay, secretary for foreign affairs, derived some hollow satisfaction from these insults. He hoped they would at least humiliate the American people into framing a new government at home that would be strong enough to command respect abroad.

⭐ The Horrid Specter of Anarchy

Economic storm clouds continued to loom in the mid-1780s. The requisition system of raising money was breaking down; some of the states refused to pay anything, while complaining bitterly about the tyranny of "King Congress." Interest on the public debt was piling up at home, and the nation's credit was evaporating abroad.

Individual states were getting out of hand. Quarrels over boundaries generated numerous minor pitched battles. Some of the states were levying duties on goods from their neighbors; New York, for example, taxed firewood from Connecticut and cabbages from New Jersey. A number of the states were again starting to grind out depreciated paper currency, and a few of them had passed laws sanctioning the semiworthless "rag money." As a contemporary rhymester put it,

> *Bankrupts their creditors with rage pursue;*
> *No stop, no mercy from the debtor crew.*

An alarming uprising, known as **Shays's Rebellion**, flared up in western Massachusetts in 1786. Impoverished backcountry farmers, many of them Revolutionary War veterans, were losing their farms through mortgage foreclosures and tax delinquencies. Led by Captain Daniel Shays, a veteran of the Revolution, these desperate debtors demanded that the state issue paper money, lighten taxes, and suspend property takeovers. Hundreds of angry agitators, again seizing their muskets, attempted to enforce their demands.

Massachusetts authorities responded with drastic action. Supported partly by contributions from wealthy citizens, they raised a small army. Several skirmishes occurred—at Springfield three Shaysites were killed, and one was wounded—and the movement collapsed. Daniel Shays, who believed that he was fighting anew against tyranny, was condemned to death but was later pardoned.

Shays's followers were crushed, but the nightmarish memory lingered on. The Massachusetts legislature soon passed debtor-relief laws of the kind Shays had championed, seemingly confirming Thomas Jefferson's fear of "democratic despotism." "An elective despotism was not the government we fought for," Jefferson wrote. The outbursts of Shays and other distressed debtors struck fear in the hearts of the propertied class, who began to suspect that the Revolution had created a monster of "mobocracy." Unbridled republicanism, it seemed to many of the elite, had fed an insatiable appetite for liberty that was fast becoming license. In this state of affairs, many citizens feared that civic virtue, the bedrock of republican government, was insufficient to rein in self-interest and greed. It had become "undeniably evident," one skeptic sorrowfully lamented, "that some malignant

Debtors Protest, 1787 This drawing done on the eve of the writing of the U.S. Constitution features a farmer with a plow, a rake, and a bottle complaining, "Takes all to pay taxes." The discontent of debt-rich and currency-poor farmers alarmed republican leaders and helped persuade them that the Articles of Confederation needed to be replaced with a new constitution.

disorder has seized upon our body politic." The antidote, a growing minority argued, was stronger central government. A few panicky citizens even talked of importing a European monarch to carry on where George III had failed.

How critical were conditions under the Confederation? Conservatives, anxious to safeguard their wealth and position, naturally exaggerated the seriousness of the nation's plight. They were eager to persuade their fellow citizens to amend the Articles of Confederation in favor of a muscular central government. But the poorer states' rights people pooh-poohed the talk of anarchy. Many were debtors who feared that a powerful federal government would force them to pay their creditors.

Yet friends and critics of the Confederation agreed that it needed some strengthening. Popular toasts were "Cement to the Union" and "A hoop to the barrel." The chief differences arose over how this goal should be attained and how a maximum degree of states' rights could be reconciled with a strong central government. America probably could have muddled through somehow with amended Articles of Confederation. But the adoption of a completely new constitution certainly spared the Republic much costly indecision, uncertainty, and turmoil.

The nationwide picture was actually brightening before the Constitution was drafted. Nearly half the states had not issued semiworthless paper currency, and some of the monetary black sheep showed signs of returning to the sound-money fold. Prosperity was beginning to emerge from the fog of depression. By 1789 overseas shipping had largely regained its place in the commercial world. If conditions had been as grim in 1787 as painted by foes of the Articles of Confederation, the move for a new constitution would hardly have encountered such heated opposition.

✦ A Convention of "Demigods"

Control of commerce, more than any other problem, touched off the chain reaction that led to a constitutional convention. Interstate squabbling over this issue had become so alarming by 1786 that Virginia, taking the lead, issued a call for a convention at Annapolis, Maryland. Nine states appointed delegates, but only five were finally represented. With so laughable a showing, nothing could be done about the ticklish question of commerce. A charismatic New Yorker, thirty-one-year-old Alexander Hamilton, brilliantly saved the convention from complete failure by engineering the adoption of his report. It called upon Congress to summon a convention to meet in Philadelphia the next year, not to deal with commerce alone, but to bolster the entire fabric of the Articles of Confederation.

Congress, though slowly and certainly dying in New York City, was reluctant to take a step that might hasten its day of reckoning. But after six of the states had seized the bit in their teeth and appointed delegates anyhow, Congress belatedly issued the call for a convention *"for the sole and express purpose of revising"* the Articles of Confederation.

Every state chose representatives, except for independent-minded Rhode Island (still "Rogues' Island"), a stronghold of paper-moneyites. These leaders were all appointed by the state legislatures, whose members had been elected by voters who could qualify as property holders. This double distillation inevitably brought together a select group of propertied men—though the once-popular idea that they shaped the Constitution primarily to protect their personal financial interests no longer holds sway among historians.

When one of them did suggest restricting federal office to major property owners, he was promptly denounced for the unwisdom of "interweaving into a republican constitution a veneration for wealth."

A quorum of the fifty-five emissaries from twelve states finally convened at Philadelphia on May 25, 1787, in the imposing red-brick statehouse. The smallness of the assemblage facilitated intimate acquaintance and hence compromise. Sessions were held in complete secrecy, with armed sentinels posted at the doors. Delegates knew that they would generate heated differences, and they did not want to advertise their own dissensions or put the ammunition of harmful arguments into the mouths of the opposition.

The caliber of the participants was extraordinarily high—"demigods," Jefferson called them. The urgency of the crisis induced the ablest men to drop their personal pursuits and come to the aid of their country. Most of the members were lawyers, and most of them fortunately were old hands at constitution making in their own states.

George Washington, towering, austere, and aloof among the "demigods," was unanimously elected chairman. His enormous prestige, as "the Sword of the Revolution," served to quiet overheated tempers. Benjamin Franklin, then eighty-one, added the urbanity of an elder statesman, though he was inclined to be indiscreetly talkative in his declining years. Concerned for the secrecy of their deliberations, the convention assigned chaperones to accompany Franklin to dinner parties and make sure he held his tongue. James Madison, then thirty-six and a profound student of government, made contributions so notable that he has been dubbed "the Father of the Constitution." Alexander Hamilton, then only thirty-two, was present as an advocate of a super-powerful central government. His five-hour speech in behalf of his plan, though the most eloquent of the convention, left only one delegate convinced—himself.

Rising Sun Symbol at the Top of Washington's Chair   This brass sun adorned the chair in which George Washington sat during the Constitutional Convention. Pondering the symbol, Benjamin Franklin observed, "I have the happiness to know it is a rising and not a setting sun." Henry Groskinsky/Time Life Pictures/Getty Images

Thomas Jefferson (1743–1826), despite his high regard for the leaders at the Philadelphia convention, still was not unduly concerned about Shaysite rebellions. He wrote in November 1787,

"What country before ever existed a century and a half without a rebellion?...The tree of liberty must be refreshed from time to time with the blood of patriots and tyrants. It is its natural manure.**"**

Most of the fiery Revolutionary leaders of 1776 were absent. Thomas Jefferson, John Adams, and Thomas Paine were in Europe; Samuel Adams and John Hancock were not elected by Massachusetts. Patrick Henry, ardent champion of states' rights, was chosen as a delegate from Virginia but declined to serve, declaring that he "smelled a rat." It was perhaps well that these architects of revolution were absent. The time had come to yield the stage to leaders interested in fashioning solid political systems.

✦ Patriots in Philadelphia

The fifty-five delegates were a conservative, well-to-do body: lawyers, merchants, shippers, land speculators, and moneylenders. Not a single spokesperson was present from the poorer debtor groups. Nineteen of the fifty-five owned slaves. They were young (the average age was about forty-two) but experienced statesmen. Above all, they were nationalists, more interested in preserving and strengthening the young Republic than in further stirring the roiling cauldron of popular democracy.

The delegates hoped to crystallize the last evaporating pools of Revolutionary idealism into a stable political structure that would endure. They strongly desired a firm, dignified, and respected government. They believed in republicanism but sought to protect the American experiment from its excesses at home and its weaknesses abroad. In a broad sense, the piratical Dey of Algiers, who highlighted the need for centralized authority in foreign-policymaking, was a Founding Father. They aimed to clothe the central authority with genuine power, especially in controlling tariffs, so that the United States could wrest satisfactory commercial

treaties from foreign nations. The shortsighted hostility of the British mercantilists spurred the constitution framers to their task, and in this sense the illiberal Lord Sheffield was also a Founding Father.

Other motives hovered in the Philadelphia hall. Delegates were determined to preserve the union, forestall anarchy, and ensure security of life and property against dangerous uprisings by the "mobocracy." Above all, they sought to curb the unrestrained democracy rampant in the various states. "We have, probably, had too good an opinion of human nature in forming our confederation," Washington concluded. The specter of the recent outburst in Massachusetts was especially alarming, and in this sense Daniel Shays was yet another Founding Father. Grinding necessity extorted the Constitution from a reluctant nation. Fear occupied the fifty-sixth chair.

✦ Hammering Out a Bundle of Compromises

Some of the travel-stained delegates, when they first reached Philadelphia, decided upon a daring step. They would completely *scrap* the old Articles of Confederation, despite explicit instructions from Congress to *revise*. Technically, these bolder spirits were determined to overthrow the existing government of the United States (see Table 9.1) by peaceful means.

A scheme proposed by populous Virginia, and known as "the large-state plan," was first pushed forward as the framework of the Constitution. The **Virginia Plan**'s essence was that representation in both houses of a bicameral Congress should be based on population—an arrangement that would naturally give the larger states an advantage.

Tiny New Jersey, suspicious of brawny Virginia, countered with "the small-state plan." The **New Jersey Plan** provided for equal representation in a unicameral Congress by states, regardless of size and population, as under the existing Articles of Confederation. The weaker states feared that under the Virginia scheme, the stronger states would band together and lord it over the rest. Angry debate, heightened by a stifling heat wave, led to deadlock. The danger

TABLE 9.1 Evolution of Federal Union		
Years	**Attempts at Union**	**Participants**
1643–1684	New England Confederation	4 colonies
1686–1689	Dominion of New England	7 colonies
1754	Albany Congress	7 colonies
1765	Stamp Act Congress	9 colonies
1772–1776	Committees of Correspondence	13 colonies
1774	First Continental Congress (adopts The Association)	12 colonies
1775–1781	Second Continental Congress	13 colonies
1781–1789	Articles of Confederation	13 states
1789–1790	Federal Constitution	13 states

loomed that the convention would unravel in complete failure. Even skeptical old Benjamin Franklin seriously proposed that the daily sessions be opened with a prayer by a local clergyman.

After bitter and prolonged debate, the **Great Compromise** of the convention was hammered out and agreed upon. A cooling of tempers came coincidentally with a cooling of the temperature. The larger states were conceded representation by population in the House of Representatives (Art. I, Sec. II, para. 3; see the Appendix), and the smaller states were appeased by equal representation in the Senate (see Art. I, Sec. III, para. 1). Each state, no matter how poor or small, would have two senators. The big states obviously yielded more. As a sop to them, the delegates agreed that every tax bill or revenue measure must originate in the House, where population counted more heavily (see Art. I, Sec. VII, para. 1). This critical compromise broke the logjam, and from then on success seemed within reach.

The final Constitution was short, not least because it grew out of the Anglo-American **common law** legal tradition, which made it unnecessary to be specific about every conceivable detail. It mostly provided a flexible guide to broad rules of procedure, rather than a fixed set of detailed laws. The original (unamended) Constitution contained just seven articles and ran to about ten printed pages. Elsewhere, where **civil law** traditions prevailed, constitutions took the form of elaborate legal codes and were often strikingly lengthy. India's constitution, for example, which came into force in 1950, contains almost four hundred articles and runs to nearly two hundred pages.

In a significant reversal of the arrangement most state constitutions had embodied, the new Constitution provided for a robust—though still legally restrained—executive in the presidency. The framers were here partly inspired by the example of Massachusetts, where a vigorous, popularly elected governor had suppressed Shays's Rebellion. The president was to have broad authority to make appointments to domestic offices—including judgeships—as well as veto power over legislation. Yet presidential power was far from absolute. The president, as commander in chief, was granted the power to wage war, but Congress retained the crucial right to *declare* war—a division of responsibilities that has been an invitation to conflict between president and Congress ever since.

The Constitution as drafted was a bundle of compromises; they stand out in every section. A key compromise was the method of electing the president indirectly by the Electoral College, rather than by direct means. While the large states would have the advantage in the first round of popular voting, as a state's share of electors was based on the total of its senators and representatives in Congress, the small states would gain a larger voice if no candidate got a majority of electoral votes and the election was thrown to the House of Representatives, where each state would have, for this purpose only, just a single vote (see Art. II, Sec. I, para. 2). Although the framers of the Constitution expected election by the House to occur frequently, it has happened just twice, in 1800 and in 1824.

Dr. James McHenry (1753–1816), a delegate from Maryland to the Constitutional Convention of 1787, took notes on the arguments made for and against the drafting of a new constitution:

❝Gov. Randolph observed that the confederation is incompetent to any one object for which it was instituted. The framers of it wise and great men; but human rights were the chief knowle[d]ge of the times when it was framed so far as they applied to oppose Great Britain. Requisitions for men and money had never offered their form to our assemblies. None of those vices that have since discovered themselves were apprehended.❞

Signing of the Constitution of the United States, 1787 George Washington presided from the dais as the Constitutional Convention's president. At a table in the front row sat James Madison, later called the Father of the Constitution, who recorded the proceedings in shorthand. Daily from 10 A.M. to 3 P.M., from late May through mid-September 1787, the fifty-five delegates wrangled over ideas for a new federal government.

Sectional jealousy also intruded. Should the vote-less slave of the southern states count as a person in apportioning direct taxes and in according representation in the House of Representatives? The South, not wishing to be deprived of influence, answered "yes." The North replied "no," arguing that, as slaves were not citizens, the North might as logically demand additional representation based on its horses. As a compromise between total representation and none at all, it was decided that a slave might count as three-fifths of a person. Hence the memorable, if arbitrary, **three-fifths compromise** (see Art. I, Sec. II, para. 3).

Other items dealing with slavery appeared in the final signed draft, although, as with the three-fifths clause, the word *slave* was carefully avoided (see Table 9.2). The most notable of these constitutional elements touched the issue of slave trading. Building on a sentiment expressed in the First Continental Congress, most states wanted to shut down the importation of human souls. But South Carolina and Georgia, requiring slave labor in their rice paddies and malarial swamps, raised vehement protests. By way of compromise, the convention stipulated that Americans could import slaves until the end of 1807, at which time Congress would have the authority to turn off the spigot (see Art. I, Sec. IX, para. 1). It did so as soon as the prescribed interval had elapsed. Meanwhile, all the new state constitutions except Georgia's forbade overseas slave trade.

✴ Safeguards for Conservatism

Heated clashes among the delegates have been over-played. The area of agreement was actually large; otherwise the convention would have speedily disbanded. Economically, the members of the Constitutional Convention generally saw eye-to-eye; they demanded sound money and the protection of private property. Politically, they were in basic agreement; they favored a stronger government, with three branches and with checks and balances among them—what critics branded a "triple-headed monster." Finally, the convention was virtually unanimous in believing that manhood-suffrage democracy—government by "democratick babblers"—was something to be feared and fought.

Daniel Shays, the prime bogeyman, still frightened the conservative-minded delegates. They deliberately erected safeguards against the excesses of the "mob," and they made these barriers as strong as they dared. The awesome federal judges were to be appointed for life. The powerful president was to be elected *indirectly* by the Electoral College; the lordly senators were to be chosen *indirectly* by state legislatures (see Art. I, Sec. III, para. 1). Only in the case of one-half of one of the three great branches—the House of Representatives—were qualified (propertied) citizens permitted to choose their officials by *direct* vote (see Art. I, Sec. II, para. 1).

Yet the new charter also contained democratic elements. Above all, it stood foursquare on the two great

TABLE 9.2 Slavery and the Constitution

Section	Issue	Effect/Implication
Article 1, Section 2	Apportionment of direct taxes and representation in the House and Electoral College	Prescribed that federal representation be made proportionate to state populations of free people, plus 3/5 of the number of "other Persons" (slaves and Indians) in each state. It boosted the South's influence in Congress and the Electoral College.
Article 1, Section 9	Slave importation	Prohibited Congress, for a period of twenty years, from banning the "importation of such persons as any of the states now existing shall think proper to admit" (African and West Indian slaves).
Article 4, Section 1	States must respect laws of other states	Implied that states that did not legally sanction slavery must nonetheless respect the laws of states that did.
Article 4, Section 2	Runaway slaves and indentured servants	Stipulated that "no person held to service or labor in one state…escaping into another" (runaway slaves) could thereby achieve freedom. The basis for the Fugitive Slave Act of 1793.
Article 4, Section 4	Federal defense and protection of states	Guaranteed federal intervention on behalf of states dealing with "domestic violence" (such as slave uprisings).

Note: Although the word *slavery* does not appear in the Constitution, the document nevertheless contained several provisions that the framers well understood to address slavery.

principles of republicanism: that the only legitimate government was one based on the consent of the governed, and that the powers of government should be limited—in this case specifically limited by a written constitution. The virtue of the people, not the authority of the state, was to be the ultimate guarantor of liberty, justice, and order. "We the people," the preamble began, in a ringing affirmation of these republican doctrines.

At the end of seventeen muggy weeks—May 25 to September 17, 1787—only forty-two of the original fifty-five members remained to sign the Constitution. Three of the forty-two, refusing to do so, returned to their states to resist ratification. The remainder, adjourning to the City Tavern, celebrated the toast-worthy occasion. But no members of the convention were completely happy about the result. They were too near their work—and too weary. Whatever their personal desires, they finally had to compromise and adopt what was acceptable to the entire body, and what presumably would be acceptable to the entire country.

One of the Philadelphia delegates recorded in his journal a brief episode involving Benjamin Franklin, who was asked by a woman when the convention ended,

❝Well, Doctor, what have we got, a republic or a monarchy?❞

The elder statesman answered,

❝A republic, if you can keep it.❞

✵ The Clash of Federalists and Antifederalists

The Framing Fathers early foresaw that nationwide acceptance of the Constitution would not be easy to obtain. A formidable barrier was unanimous ratification by all thirteen states, as required for amendment by the still-standing Articles of Confederation. But since absent Rhode Island was certain to veto the Constitution, the delegates boldly adopted a different scheme. They stipulated that when nine states had registered their approval through specially elected conventions, the Constitution would become the supreme law of the land in those states ratifying (see Art. VII).

This was extraordinary, even revolutionary. It was in effect an appeal over the heads of the Congress that had called the convention, and over the heads of the legislatures that had chosen its members, to the people—or those of the people who could vote. In this way the framers could claim greater popular sanction for their handiwork. A divided Congress submitted the document to the states on this basis, without recommendation of any kind.

The American people were somewhat astonished, so well had the secrets of the convention been concealed. The public had expected the old Articles of Confederation to be patched up; now it was handed a startling new document in which, many thought, the precious jewel of state sovereignty was swallowed up (see Table 9.3). One of the hottest debates of American history forthwith erupted. The **antifederalists**, who

TABLE 9.3 Strengthening the Central Government	
Under Articles of Confederation	**Under Federal Constitution**
A loose confederation of states	A firm union of people
One vote in Congress for each state	Two votes in Senate for each state; representation by population in House (see Art. I, Secs. II, III)
Vote of nine states in Congress for all important measures	Simple majority vote in Congress, subject to presidential veto (see Art. I, Sec. VII, para. 2)
Laws administered loosely by committees of Congress	Laws executed by powerful president (see Art. II, Secs. II, III)
No congressional power over commerce	Congress to regulate both foreign and interstate commerce (see Art. I, Sec. VIII, para. 3)
No congressional power to levy taxes	Extensive power in Congress to levy taxes (see Art. I, Sec. VIII, para. 1)
Limited federal courts	Federal courts, capped by Supreme Court (see Art. III)
Unanimity of states for amendment	Amendment less difficult (see Art. V)
No authority to act directly upon individuals and no power to coerce states	Ample power to enforce laws by coercion of individuals and to some extent of states

opposed the stronger federal government, were arrayed against the **federalists**, who obviously favored it.

A motley crew gathered in the antifederalist camp. Its leaders included prominent revolutionaries like Samuel Adams, Patrick Henry, and Richard Henry Lee. Their followers consisted primarily, though not exclusively, of states' rights devotees, backcountry dwellers, and one-horse farmers—in general, the poorest classes (see Map 9.4). They were joined by paper-moneyites and debtors, many of whom feared that a potent central government would force them to pay off their debts—and at full value. Large numbers of antifederalists saw in the Constitution a plot by the upper crust to steal power back from the common folk.

Silver-buckled federalists had power and influence on their side. They enjoyed the support of such commanding figures as George Washington and Benjamin Franklin. Most of them lived in the settled areas along the seaboard, not in the raw backcountry. Overall, they were wealthier than the antifederalists, more educated, and better organized. They also controlled the press. More than a hundred newspapers were published in America in the 1780s; only a dozen supported the antifederalist cause.

Antifederalists voiced vehement objections to the "gilded trap" known as the Constitution. They cried with much truth that it had been drawn up by the aristocratic elements and hence was antidemocratic. They likewise charged that the sovereignty of the states was being submerged and that the freedoms of the individual were jeopardized by the absence of a bill of rights. They decried the dropping of annual elections for congressional representatives, the erecting of a federal stronghold ten miles square (later the District of Columbia), the creation of a standing army, the omission of any reference to God, and the highly

questionable procedure of ratifying with only two-thirds of the states. A Philadelphia newspaper added that Benjamin Franklin was "a fool from age" and George Washington "a fool from nature."

✦ The Great Debate in the States

Special elections, some apathetic but others hotly contested, were held in the various states for members of the ratifying conventions (see Table 9.4). The candidates—federalist or antifederalist—were elected on the basis of their pledges for or against the Constitution.

With the ink barely dry on the parchment, four small states quickly accepted the Constitution, for they had come off much better than they expected. Pennsylvania, number two on the list of ratifiers, was the first large state to act, but not until high-handed irregularities had been employed by the federalist legislature in calling a convention. These included the forcible seating of two antifederalist members, their clothes torn and their faces red with rage, in order to complete a quorum.

Massachusetts, the second most populous state, provided an acid test. If the Constitution had failed in Massachusetts, the entire movement might easily have bogged down. The Boston ratifying convention at first contained an antifederalist majority. It included grudging Shaysites and the aging Samuel Adams, as suspicious of government power in 1787 as he had been in 1776. The assembly buzzed with dismaying talk of summoning another constitutional convention, as though the nation had not already shot its bolt. Clearly the choice was not between this Constitution and a better one, but between this Constitution and the creaking Articles of Confederation. The absence of a bill of rights alarmed the antifederalists. But the

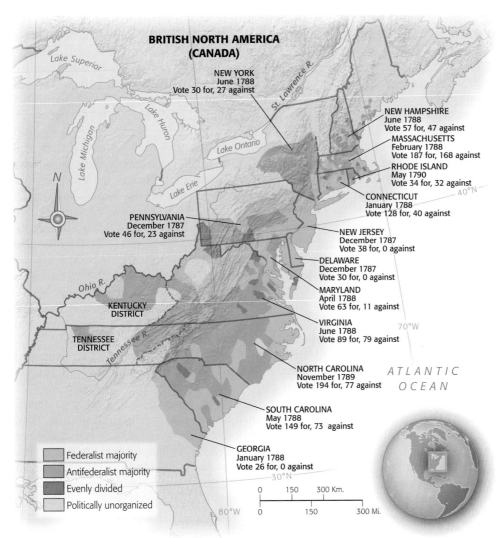

MAP 9.4 The Struggle over Ratification This mottled map shows that federalist support tended to cluster around the coastal areas, which had enjoyed profitable commerce with the outside world, including the export of grain and tobacco. Impoverished frontiersmen, suspicious of a powerful new central government under the Constitution, were generally antifederalists. © 2016 Cengage Learning

TABLE 9.4 Ratification of the Constitution

State	Date	Vote in Convention	Rank in Population	1790 Population
1. Delaware	Dec. 7, 1787	Unanimous	13	59,096
2. Pennsylvania	Dec. 12, 1787	46 to 23	3	433,611
3. New Jersey	Dec. 18, 1787	Unanimous	9	184,139
4. Georgia	Jan. 2, 1788	Unanimous	11	82,548
5. Connecticut	Jan. 9, 1788	128 to 40	8	237,655
6. Massachusetts (incl. Maine)	Feb. 7, 1788	187 to 168	2	475,199
7. Maryland	Apr. 28, 1788	63 to 11	6	319,728
8. South Carolina	May 23, 1788	149 to 73	7	249,073
9. New Hampshire	June 21, 1788	57 to 46	10	141,899
10. Virginia	June 26, 1788	89 to 79	1	747,610
11. New York	July 26, 1788	30 to 27	5	340,241
12. North Carolina	Nov. 21, 1789	195 to 77	4	395,005
13. Rhode Island	May 29, 1790	34 to 32	12	69,112

federalists gave them solemn assurances that the first Congress would add such a safeguard by amendment, and ratification was then secured in Massachusetts by the rather narrow margin of 187 to 168.

Three more states fell into line. The last of these was New Hampshire, whose convention at first had contained a strong antifederalist majority. The federalists cleverly arranged a prompt adjournment and then won over enough waverers to secure ratification. Nine states—all but Virginia, New York, North Carolina, and Rhode Island—had now taken shelter under the "new federal roof," and the document was officially adopted on June 21, 1788. Francis Hopkinson exulted in his song "The New Roof":

> *Huzza! my brave boys, our work is complete;*
> *The world shall admire Columbia's fair seat.*

But such rejoicing was premature so long as the four dissenters, conspicuously New York and Virginia, dug in their heels.

✴ The Four Laggard States

Proud Virginia, the biggest and most populous state, provided fierce antifederalist opposition. There the college-bred federalist orators, for once, encountered worthy antagonists, including the fiery Patrick Henry. He professed to see in the fearsome document the death warrant of liberty. George Washington, James Madison, and John Marshall, on the federalist side, lent influential support. With New Hampshire about to ratify, the new Union was going to be formed anyhow, and Virginia could not very well continue comfortably as an independent state. After exciting debate in the state convention, ratification carried, 89 to 79.

New York also experienced an uphill struggle, burdened as it was with its own heavily antifederalist state convention. Alexander Hamilton at heart favored a much stronger central government than that under debate, but he contributed his sparkling personality and persuasive eloquence to whipping up support for federalism as framed. He also joined John Jay and James Madison in penning a masterly series of articles for the New York newspapers. Though designed as propaganda, these essays remain the most penetrating commentary ever written on the Constitution and are still widely sold in book form as ***The Federalist***. Probably the most famous of these is Madison's *Federalist* No. 10, which brilliantly refuted the conventional wisdom of the day that it was impossible to extend a republican form of government over a large territory.

New York finally yielded. Realizing that the state could not prosper apart from the Union, the convention ratified the document by the close count of 30 to 27. At the same time, it approved thirty-two proposed amendments and—vain hope—issued a call for yet another convention to modify the Constitution.

Last-ditch dissent developed in only two states. A hostile convention met in North Carolina, then adjourned without taking a vote. Rhode Island did not even summon a ratifying convention, rejecting the Constitution by popular referendum. The two most ruggedly individualist centers of the colonial era—homes of the "otherwise minded"—thus ran true to form. They were to change their course, albeit unwillingly, only after the new government had been in operation for some months.

Banner Paraded by the Society of Pewterers in New York City, 1788   This silk banner was carried by members of the Society of Pewterers in a parade in New York City, on July 23, 1788, to celebrate the impending ratification of the United States Constitution by New York State. The enthusiasm of these craftsmen for the Constitution confirms that not all federalists were well-to-do.

REDEUNT SATURNIA REGNA.

On the erection of the Eleventh PILLAR of the great National DOME, we beg leave most sincerely to felicitate " OUR DEAR COUNTRY."

Rise it will

The foundation good—it may yet be SAVED.

The FEDERAL EDIFICE.

A Triumphant Cartoon
This cartoon appeared in the *Massachusetts Centinel* on August 2, 1788. Note the two laggards, especially the sorry condition of Rhode Island.

The race for ratification, despite much apathy, was close and quite bitter in some localities. No lives were lost, but riotous disturbances broke out in New York and Pennsylvania, involving bruises and bloodshed. There was much behind-the-scenes pressure on delegates who had promised their constituents to vote against the Constitution. The last four states ratified, not because they wanted to but because they had to. They could not safely exist outside the fold.

✴ A Conservative Triumph

The minority had triumphed—twice. A militant minority of American radicals had engineered the military Revolution that cast off the unwritten British constitution. A militant minority of conservatives—now embracing many of the earlier radicals—had engineered the peaceful revolution that overthrew the inadequate constitution known as the Articles of Confederation. Eleven states, in effect, had seceded from the Confederation, leaving the two still in, actually out in the cold.

A majority had not spoken. Only about one-fourth of the adult white males in the country, chiefly the propertied people, had voted for delegates to the ratifying conventions. Careful estimates indicate that if the new Constitution had been submitted to a manhood-suffrage vote, as in New York, it would have encountered much more opposition, probably defeat.

Conservatism was victorious. Safeguards had been erected against mob-rule excesses, while the republican gains of the Revolution were conserved. Radicals such as Patrick Henry, who had ousted British rule, saw themselves in turn upended by American conservatives. The federalists were convinced that by setting the drifting ship of state on a steady course, they could restore economic and political stability.

Yet if the architects of the Constitution were conservative, it is worth emphasizing that they conserved the principle of republican government through a redefinition of popular sovereignty. Unlike the antifederalists, who believed that the sovereignty of the people resided in a single branch of government—the legislature—the

---

Contending Voices
Debating the New Constitution

The Constitution drafted at Philadelphia in 1787 was hotly contested at the time and has been both warmly revered and sharply criticized ever since. Jonathan Smith, a Massachusetts farmer unsympathetic to Shays's Rebellion of 1787, wrote approvingly of the new federal constitution:

❝ I am a plain man, and I get my living by the plow. I have lived in a part of the country where I have known the worth of good government by the want of it. The black cloud of Shays rebellion rose last winter in my area. It brought on a state of anarchy that led to tyranny.... When I saw this Constitution I found that it was a cure for these disorders. I got a copy of it and read it over and over.... I don't think the worse of the Constitution because lawyers, and men of learning, and moneyed men are fond of it. [They] are all embarked in the same cause with us, and we must all swim or sink together. **❞**

Yet prominent Virginia Patriot Patrick Henry (1736–1799) countered in 1788 that the proposed constitution endangered everything the Revolution had sought to protect:

❝ This constitution is said to have beautiful features; but when I come to examine these features, Sir, they appear to me horridly frightful: Among other deformities, it has an awful squinting; it squints towards monarchy: And does not this raise indignation in the breast of every American? Your President may easily become King: Your Senate is so imperfectly constructed that your dearest rights may be sacrificed by what may be a small minority; ... Where are your checks in this Government? **❞**

In what ways did the positions of Smith and Henry foreshadow debates about the Constitution over the next two centuries?

federalists contended that every branch—executive, judiciary, and legislature—effectively represented the people. By ingeniously embedding the doctrine of self-rule in a self-limiting system of checks and balances among these branches, the Constitution reconciled the potentially conflicting principles of liberty and order. It represented a marvelous achievement, one that elevated the ideals of the Revolution even while setting boundaries to them. One of the distinctive—and enduring—paradoxes of American history was thus revealed: in the United States, conservatives and radicals alike have championed the heritage of republican revolution.

✴ The Pursuit of Equality

"All men are created equal," the Declaration of Independence had proclaimed, and equality was everywhere the watchword during this formative and tumultuous period. Most states reduced (but usually did not eliminate altogether) property-holding requirements for voting. Ordinary men and women demanded to be addressed as "Mr." and "Mrs."—titles once reserved for the wealthy and highborn. Employers were now called "boss," not "master." In 1784 New Yorkers released a shipload of freshly arrived indentured servants, on the grounds that their status violated democratic ideals; by 1800 this kind of bonded labor was virtually unknown. Most Americans ridiculed the lordly pretensions of Continental Army officers who formed an exclusive hereditary order, the **Society of the Cincinnati**. Social democracy was further stimulated by the growth of trade organizations for artisans and laborers. Citizens

in several states, flushed with republican fervor, also sawed off the remaining shackles of medieval inheritance laws, such as primogeniture, which awarded all of a father's property to the eldest son.

A protracted fight for separation of church and state resulted in notable gains. Although the well-entrenched Congregational Church continued to be legally established in some New England states, the Anglican Church, tainted by association with the British crown, was humbled. De-anglicized, it re-formed as the Protestant Episcopal Church and was everywhere **disestablished**. The struggle for divorce between religion and government proved fiercest in Virginia. It was prolonged to 1786, when freethinking Thomas Jefferson and his co-reformers, including the Baptists, won a complete victory with the passage of the **Virginia Statute for Religious Freedom**. (See Table 5.1, on established churches, on p. 89.)

The egalitarian sentiments unleashed by the war likewise challenged the institution of slavery. Philadelphia Quakers in 1775 founded the world's first antislavery society. Several northern states either abolished slavery outright or legislated a phased elimination of the institution. In certain parts of the plantation South, mostly in middle states like Virginia and Maryland, a small but notable population of idealistic masters made personal decisions to free their human chattels—the first frail sprouts of the later abolitionist movement.

But this revolution of sentiments was sadly incomplete. Despite opposition to further slave importations, the *domestic* trade in slaves continued to have legal sanction and, in fact, grew dramatically during the

Membership Certificate for the General Society of Mechanics & Tradesmen, 1786 Thirteen artisans gathered in New York on November 17, 1785, to establish the General Society of Mechanics & Tradesmen, a craftsmen's mutual aid organization intended to assist brethren in need and promote the significance of manufacturing to the local economy.

The impact of the American Revolution was worldwide. About 1783 a British ship stopped at some islands off the East African coast, where the natives were revolting against their Arab masters. When asked why they were fighting, they replied,

" America is free, Could not we be? **"**

nineteenth century. It became a great financial boon for upper-South states whose profit from tobacco cultivation was on the decline. And most of the emancipation laws passed throughout the North removed the institution only gradually, leaving hundreds if not thousands of northern blacks in chains until well into the nineteenth century—some until the end of the Civil War. Finally, no states south of Pennsylvania abolished slavery, and in both North and South, the law discriminated harshly against freed blacks and enslaved blacks alike. Emancipated African Americans could be barred from purchasing property, holding certain jobs, and educating their children. Laws against interracial marriage also sprang up at this time.

Why, in this dawning democratic age, did abolition not go further and cleanly blot the evil of slavery from the fresh face of the new nation? The sorry truth is that the fledgling idealism of the Founding Fathers was sacrificed to political expediency. A fight over slavery would have fractured the fragile national unity that was so desperately needed. "Great as the evil [of slavery] is," the young Virginian James Madison wrote in 1787, "a dismemberment of the union would be worse." Nearly a century later, the slavery issue did wreck the Union—temporarily.

Likewise incomplete was the extension of the doctrine of equality to women. Some women did serve (disguised as men) in the military, and New Jersey's new constitution in 1776 even, for a time, enabled

Elizabeth "Mumbet" Freeman (ca. 1744–1829), by Susan Anne Livingston Ridley Sedgwick, 1811   In 1781, having overheard Revolutionary-era talk about the "rights of man," Mumbet sued her Massachusetts master for her freedom from slavery. She won her suit and lived the rest of her life as a paid domestic servant in the home of the lawyer who had pleaded her case.

Massachusetts Historical Society, Boston, MA, USA/The Bridgeman Art Library

The Revolution enhanced the expectations and power of women as wives and mothers. As one "matrimonial republican" wrote in 1792,

" I object to the word 'obey' in the marriage-service because it is a general word, without limitations or definition.... The obedience between man and wife, I conceive, is, or ought to be mutual.... Marriage ought never to be considered a contract between a superior and an inferior, but a reciprocal union of interest, an implied partnership of interests, where all differences are accommodated by conference; and where the decision admits of no retrospect. **"**

women to vote. But though Abigail Adams teased her husband, John, in 1776 that "the Ladies" were determined "to foment a rebellion" of their own if they were not given political rights, the civil status of women did not change meaningfully.

Yet women did not go untouched by Revolutionary ideals. Central to republican ideology was the concept of **civic virtue**—the notion that democracy depended on the unselfish commitment of each citizen to the public good. And who could better cultivate the habits of a virtuous citizenry than mothers, to whom society entrusted the moral education of the young? Indeed the selfless devotion of a mother to her family was often cited as the very model of proper republican behavior. The idea of "**republican motherhood**" thus took root, elevating women to a newly prestigious role as the special keepers of the nation's conscience. Educational opportunities for women expanded, in the expectation that educated wives and mothers could better cultivate the virtues demanded by the Republic in their husbands, daughters, and sons. Republican women now bore crucial responsibility for the survival of the nation.

The Constitution: Revolutionary or Counterrevolutionary?

Although the Constitution has endured for over two centuries as the basis of American government, historians have differed sharply over how to interpret its origins and meaning. The so-called Nationalist School of historians, writing in the late nineteenth century, viewed the Constitution as the logical culmination of the Revolution and, more generally, as a crucial step in the God-given progress of Anglo-Saxon peoples. As described in John Fiske's *The Critical Period of American History* (1888), the young nation, buffeted by foreign threats and growing internal chaos, with only a weak central government to lean on, was saved by the adoption of a more rigorous Constitution, the ultimate fulfillment of republican ideals.

By the early twentieth century, however, the progressive historians had turned a more critical eye to the Constitution. Having observed the Supreme Court of their own day repeatedly overrule legislation designed to better social conditions for the masses, they began to view the original document as an instrument created by elite conservatives to wrest political power away from the common people. For historians like Carl Becker and Charles Beard, the Constitution was part of the Revolutionary struggle between the lower classes (small farmers, debtors, and laborers) and the upper classes (merchants, financiers, and manufacturers).

Beard's *An Economic Interpretation of the Constitution of the United States* (1913) argued that the Articles of Confederation had protected debtors and small property owners and displeased wealthy elites heavily invested in trade, the public debt, and the promotion of manufacturing. Only a stronger, more centralized government could protect their extensive property interests. Reviewing the economic holdings of the Founding Fathers, Beard determined that most of those men were indeed deeply involved in investments that would increase in value under the Constitution. In effect, Beard argued, the Constitution represented a successful attempt by conservative elites to buttress their own economic supremacy at the expense of less fortunate Americans. He further contended that the Constitution was ratified by default because the people most disadvantaged by the new government did not possess the property qualifications needed to vote—more evidence of the class conflict underlying the struggle between the federalists and the antifederalists.

Beard's economic interpretation of the Constitution held sway through the 1940s. In the 1950s, however, this analysis fell victim to the attacks of the "consensus" historians, who sought explanations for the Constitution in factors other than class interest. Scholars such as Robert Brown and Forrest McDonald convincingly disputed Beard's evidence about delegates' property ownership and refuted his portrayal of the masses as propertyless and disfranchised. They argued that the Constitution derived from an emerging consensus that the country needed a stronger central government.

Scholars since the 1950s have searched for new ways to understand the origins of the Constitution. The most influential work has been Gordon Wood's *Creation of the American Republic* (1969). Wood reinterpreted the ratification controversy as a struggle to define the true essence of republicanism. Antifederalists so feared human inclination toward corruption that they shuddered at the prospect of putting powerful political weapons in the hands of a central government. They saw small governments susceptible to local control as the only safeguard against tyranny. Federalists, on the other hand, believed that a strong, balanced national government would rein in selfish human instincts and channel them toward the pursuit of the common good. Alarmed by the indulgences of the state governments, the federalists, James Madison in particular (especially in *Federalist* No. 10), developed the novel ideal of an "extensive republic," a polity that would achieve stability by virtue of its great size and diversity. This conception challenged the conventional wisdom that a republic could survive only if it extended over a small area with a homogeneous population. In this sense, Wood argued, the Constitution represented a bold experiment—the fulfillment, rather than the repudiation, of the most advanced ideas of the Revolutionary era—even though it emanated from traditional elites determined to curtail dangerous disruptions to the social order.

Several recent studies have revived the progressive approach, focusing on the turmoil of the period. David Waldstreicher's *Slavery's Constitution* (2009) argues for the importance of slavery in the creation of the Constitution, even though it was not addressed by name in the text. Another recent treatment, Woody Holton's *Unruly Americans* (2008), argues that despite the antidemocratic tendencies of the framers, they were forced to create what was ultimately a radical document due to pressures from nonelites.

Chapter Review

KEY TERMS

Articles of
 Confederation (163)
Old Northwest (165)
Land Ordinanceof
 1785 (166)
Northwest
 Ordinance (166)
Shays's Rebellion (168)
Virginia Plan (170)
New Jersey Plan (170)
Great Compromise (171)
common law (171)
civil law (171)

three-fifths
 compromise (172)
antifederalists (173)
federalists (174)
The Federalist (176)
Society of the
 Cincinnati (178)
disestablished (178)
Virginia Statute for
 Religious Freedom (178)
civic virtue (179)
republican
 motherhood (179)

PEOPLE TO KNOW

Lord Sheffield
Daniel Shays
Patrick Henry

CHRONOLOGY

1774	First Continental Congress calls for abolition of slave trade
1775	Philadelphia Quakers found world's first antislavery society
1776	New Jersey constitution temporarily gives women the vote
1777	Articles of Confederation adopted by Second Continental Congress
1780	Massachusetts adopts first constitution drafted in convention and ratified by popular vote
1781	Articles of Confederation put into effect
1783	Military officers form Society of the Cincinnati
1785	Land Ordinance of 1785
1786	Virginia Statute for Religious Freedom Shays's Rebellion Meeting of five states to discuss revision of the Articles of Confederation
1787	Northwest Ordinance Constitutional Convention in Philadelphia
1788	Ratification by nine states guarantees a new government under the Constitution

TO LEARN MORE

Richard Bushman, *The Refinement of America: Persons, Houses, Cities* (1992)

Ron Chernow, *Alexander Hamilton* (2004)

Joseph Ellis, *Founding Brothers: The Revolutionary Generation* (2001)

Joanne Pope Melish, *Disowning Slavery: Gradual Emancipation and "Race" in New England, 1780–1860* (1998)

John Ragosta, *Wellspring of Liberty: How Virginia's Religious Dissenters Helped Win the American Revolution and Secured Religious Liberty* (2010)

Jack Rakove, *James Madison and the Creation of the American Republic* (2002)

———, ed., *The Federalist: The Essential Essays, by Alexander Hamilton, James Madison, and John Jay* (2003)

David Szatmary, *Shays' Rebellion* (1980)

David Waldstreicher, *Slavery's Constitution: From Revolution to Ratification* (2009)

Gordon S. Wood, *The Radicalism of the American Revolution* (1991)

A complete, annotated bibliography for this chapter—along with brief descriptions of the People to Know—may be found on the *American Pageant* website. The key terms are defined in the glossary at the end of the text.

Chapter 10

Launching the New Ship of State

1789–1800

I shall only say that I hold with Montesquieu, that a government must be fitted to a nation, as much as a coat to the individual; and, consequently, that what may be good at Philadelphia may be bad at Paris, and ridiculous at Petersburg [Russia].

ALEXANDER HAMILTON, 1799

America's new ship of state did not spread its sails to the most favorable breezes. Within twelve troubled years, the American people had risen up and thrown overboard both the British yoke and the Articles of Confederation. A decade of lawbreaking and constitution smashing was not the best training for government making. Americans had come to regard a central authority, replacing that of George III, as necessary, but also something to be distrusted, watched, and curbed.

The finances of the infant government were likewise precarious. The revenue had declined to a trickle, whereas the public debt, with interest heavily in arrears, was mountainous. Worthless paper money, both state and national, was as plentiful as metallic money was scarce. America's precarious national security was also threatened by the wars that rocked Europe in the wake of the French Revolution of 1789—an event that also roiled domestic politics in the fledgling United States. In the face of all those difficulties, the Americans were brashly trying to erect a republic on an immense scale, something that no other people had attempted and that traditional political theory deemed impossible. The eyes of a skeptical world were on the upstart United States.

Even after the battles over adoption of the Constitution, conflict continued to rage about the nature of government. Some, such as Thomas Jefferson and James Madison, supported a limited government. Others, such as George Washington and Alexander Hamilton, hoped to extend the powers of the government in order to create institutions that could strengthen the new country. The political fights of the Washington and Adams years made for a contentious start to the early Republic.

✦ Growing Pains

When the Constitution was launched in 1789, the Republic was continuing to grow at an amazing rate. Population was doubling about every twenty-five years, and the first official census of 1790 recorded almost 4 million people. Cities had blossomed proportionately: Philadelphia numbered 42,000, New York 33,000, Boston 18,000, Charleston 16,000, and Baltimore 13,000.

America's population was still about 90 percent rural, despite the flourishing cities. All but 5 percent of the people lived east of the Appalachian Mountains. The trans-Appalachian overflow was concentrated chiefly in Kentucky, Tennessee, and Ohio, all of which were welcomed as states within fourteen years.

The French statesman Anne Robert Jacques Turgot (1727–1781) had high expectations for a united America:

❝ This people is the hope of the human race.... The Americans should be an example of political, religious, commercial and industrial liberty.... But to obtain these ends for us, America...must not become...a mass of divided powers, contending for territory and trade. **❞**

(Vermont preceded them, becoming the fourteenth state in 1791.) Foreign visitors to America looked down their noses at the roughness and crudity resulting from ax-and-rifle pioneering life.

People of the western waters—in the stump-studded clearings of Kentucky, Tennessee, and Ohio—were particularly restive and dubiously loyal. The mouth of the Mississippi, their life-giving outlet, lay in the hands of unfriendly Spaniards. Smooth-talking Spanish and British agents, jingling gold, moved freely among the settlers and held out seductive promises of independence. Many observers wondered whether the emerging United States would ever grow to maturity.

✪ Washington for President

George Washington, the esteemed war hero, was unanimously drafted as president by the Electoral College in 1789—the only presidential nominee ever to be honored by unanimity. His presence was imposing: 6 feet 2 inches, 175 pounds, broad and sloping shoulders, strongly pointed chin, and pockmarks (from smallpox) on nose and cheeks. Much preferring the quiet of Mount Vernon to the turmoil of politics, he was perhaps the only president who did not in some way angle for this exalted office. Balanced rather than brilliant, he commanded his followers by strength of character rather than by the arts of the politician.

Washington's long journey from Mount Vernon to New York City, the temporary capital, was a triumphal procession. He was greeted by roaring cannon, pealing bells, flower-carpeted roads, and singing and shouting citizens. With appropriate ceremony, he solemnly and somewhat nervously took the oath of office on April 30, 1789, on a crowded balcony overlooking Wall Street, which some have regarded as a bad omen.

Washington soon put his stamp on the new government, especially by establishing the cabinet. The Constitution does not mention a cabinet (see Table 10.1); it merely provides that the president "may require" written opinions of the heads of the executive-branch departments (see Art. II, Sec. II, para. 1 in the Appendix). But this system proved so cumbersome, and involved so much homework, that cabinet meetings gradually evolved in the Washington administration.

TABLE 10.1 Evolution of the Cabinet		
Position	Date Established	Comments
Secretary of state	1789	
Secretary of treasury	1789	
Secretary of war	1789	Loses cabinet status, 1947
Attorney general	1789	Not head of Justice Dept. until 1870
Secretary of navy	1798	Loses cabinet status, 1947
Postmaster general	1829	Loses cabinet status, 1970
Secretary of interior	1849	
Secretary of agriculture	1889	
Secretary of commerce and labor	1903	Office divided, 1913
Secretary of commerce	1913	
Secretary of labor	1913	
Secretary of defense	1947	Subordinate to this secretary, without cabinet rank, are secretaries of army, navy, and air force
Secretary of health, education, and welfare	1953	Office divided, 1979
Secretary of housing and urban development	1965	
Secretary of transportation	1966	
Secretary of energy	1977	
Secretary of health and human services	1979	
Secretary of education	1979	
Secretary of veterans' affairs	1989	
Secretary of homeland security	2002	

Washington Honored   This idealized portrait symbolizes the reverential awe in which Americans held "the Father of His Country."

At first only three full-fledged department heads served under the president: Secretary of State Thomas Jefferson, Secretary of the Treasury Alexander Hamilton, and Secretary of War Henry Knox.

✖ The Bill of Rights

The new nation faced some unfinished business. Many antifederalists had sharply criticized the Constitution drafted at Philadelphia for its failure to provide guarantees of individual rights such as freedom of religion and trial by jury. Many states had ratified the federal Constitution on the understanding that it would soon be amended to include such guarantees. Drawing up a bill of rights headed the list of imperatives facing the new government.

Amendments to the Constitution could be proposed in either of two ways—by a new constitutional convention requested by two-thirds of the states or by a two-thirds vote of both houses of Congress. Fearing that a new convention might unravel the narrow federalist victory in the ratification struggle, James Madison determined to draft the amendments himself. He then guided them through Congress, where his

intellectual and political skills were quickly making him the leading figure.

Adopted by the necessary number of states in 1791, the first ten amendments to the Constitution, popularly known as the **Bill of Rights**, safeguard some of the most precious American principles. Among these are protections for freedom of religion, speech, and the press; the right to bear arms and to be tried by a jury; and the right to assemble and petition the government for redress of grievances. The Bill of Rights also prohibits cruel and unusual punishments and arbitrary government seizure of private property.

To guard against the danger that enumerating such rights might lead to the conclusion that they were the only ones protected, Madison inserted the crucial Ninth Amendment. It declares that specifying certain rights "shall not be construed to deny or disparage others retained by the people." In a gesture of reassurance to the states' righters, he included the equally significant Tenth Amendment, which reserves all rights not explicitly delegated or prohibited by the federal Constitution "to the States respectively, or to the people." By preserving a strong central government while specifying protections for minority and individual liberties, Madison's amendments partially swung the federalist pendulum back in an antifederalist direction. (See Amendments I–X.)

The first Congress also nailed other newly sawed government planks into place. It created effective federal courts under the **Judiciary Act of 1789**. The act organized the Supreme Court, with a chief justice and five associates, as well as federal district and circuit courts, and established the office of attorney general. New Yorker John Jay, Madison's collaborator on *The Federalist* papers and one of the young Republic's most seasoned diplomats, became the first chief justice of the United States.

✖ Hamilton Revives the Corpse of Public Credit

The key figure in the new government was still smooth-faced Treasury Secretary Alexander Hamilton, a native of the British West Indies. Hamilton's genius was unquestioned, but critics claimed he loved his adopted country more than he loved his countrymen. Doubts about his character and his loyalty to the republican experiment always swirled about his head. Hamilton regarded himself as a kind of prime minister in Washington's cabinet and on occasion thrust his hands into the affairs of other departments, including that of his archrival, Thomas Jefferson, who served as secretary of state.

A financial wizard, Hamilton set out immediately to correct the economic vexations that had crippled

The text in the cartoon reads:

"This will make the 'Squire ... me our fill at grog."

"come friend bum, I'll take thee to thy master."

"Lo these are our old friend the long nosed gentleman."

"My poor Humphrey,"

"Let us tar and feather the rascal."

AN EXCISEMAN. Carrying off two Kegs of Whiskey, is pursued by two farmers, intending to tar and feather him. he runs for 'Squire Vultures to divide with him; but is met on the way by his evil genius who claps an hook in his nose, leads him off to a Gallows, where he is immediately hanged.

The Whiskey Boys The cartoonist clearly favored the Pennsylvania rebels who resisted Hamilton's imposition of an excise tax on whiskey.

out these basic functions, Hamilton argued, a national bank would be not only "proper" but "necessary." By inference or implication—that is, by virtue of "implied powers"—Congress would be fully justified in establishing the Bank of the United States. In short, Hamilton contended for a "loose" or "broad" interpretation of the Constitution. He and his federalist followers thus evolved the theory of "loose construction" by invoking the "elastic clause" of the Constitution—a precedent for enormous federal powers.

Hamilton's financial views prevailed. His eloquent and realistic arguments were accepted by Washington, who reluctantly signed the bank measure into law. This explosive issue had been debated with much heat in Congress, where the old North-South cleavage still lurked ominously. The most enthusiastic support for the bank naturally came from the commercial and financial centers of the North, whereas the strongest opposition arose from the agricultural South.

The **Bank of the United States**, as created by Congress in 1791, was chartered for twenty years. Located in Philadelphia, it was to have a capital of $10 million, one-fifth of it owned by the federal government. Stock was thrown open to public sale. To the agreeable surprise of Hamilton, a milling crowd oversubscribed in less than two hours, pushing aside many would-be purchasers.

✶ Mutinous Moonshiners in Pennsylvania

The **Whiskey Rebellion**, which flared up in southwestern Pennsylvania in 1794, sharply challenged the new national government. Hamilton's high excise tax bore harshly on these homespun pioneer folk. They regarded it not as a tax on a frivolous luxury but as a burden on an economic necessity and a medium of exchange. Even preachers of the gospel were paid in "Old Monongahela rye." Rye and corn crops distilled into alcohol were more cheaply transported to eastern markets than bales of grain. Defiant distillers finally erected whiskey poles, similar to the liberty poles of anti–stamp tax days in 1765, and raised the cry "Liberty and No Excise." Boldly tarring and feathering revenue officers, they brought collections to a halt.

Contending Voices
Human Nature and the Nature of Government

Alexander Hamilton and Thomas Jefferson were adversaries in the realms of politics and ideas alike. Underlying their differences about the role of government were radically different assessments of human nature.

Hamilton: **❝**Your people, sir, is a great beast.... The people are turbulent and changing; they seldom judge or determine the right.**❞**

Jefferson: **❝**I have great confidence in the common sense of mankind in general.**❞**

How did Hamilton's and Jefferson's differing perspectives on human psychology affect their political views?

Attorney Hugh Henry Brackenridge (1748–1816) mediated between the Whiskey Rebels and the town of Pittsburgh. He later wrote of the hated excise tax,

❝ I saw the operation to be unequal in this country.... It is true that the excise paid by the country would be that only on spirits consumed in it. But even in the case of exports, the excise must be advanced in the first instance by the distiller and this would prevent effectually all the poorer part from carrying on the business. I...would have preferred a direct tax with a view to reach unsettled lands which all around us have been purchased by speculating men. **❞**

President Washington, once a revolutionary, was alarmed by what he called these "self-created societies." With the hearty encouragement of Hamilton, he summoned the militias of several states. Anxious moments followed the call, for there was much doubt as to whether men in other states would muster to crush a rebellion in a fellow state. Despite some opposition, an army of about thirteen thousand rallied to the colors, and two widely separated columns marched briskly forth in a gorgeous, leaf-tinted Indian summer, until knee-deep mud slowed their progress.

When the troops reached the hills of western Pennsylvania, they found no insurrection. The "Whiskey Boys" were overawed, dispersed, or captured. Washington, with an eye to healing old sores, pardoned the two small-fry convicted culprits.

The Whiskey Rebellion was minuscule—some three rebels were killed—but its consequences were mighty. George Washington's government, now substantially strengthened, commanded a new respect. Yet the foes of the administration condemned its brutal display of force—for having used a sledgehammer to crush a gnat.

✴ The Emergence of Political Parties

Almost overnight, Hamilton's fiscal feats had established the government's sound credit rating. The Treasury could now borrow needed funds in the Netherlands on favorable terms.

But Hamilton's financial successes—funding, assumption, the excise tax, the bank, the suppression of the Whiskey Rebellion—created some political liabilities. All these schemes encroached sharply upon states' rights. Many Americans, dubious about the new Constitution in the first place, might never have approved it if they had foreseen how the states

were going to be overshadowed by the federal colossus. Now, out of resentment against Hamilton's revenue-raising and centralizing policies, an organized opposition began to build. What once was a personal feud between Hamilton and Jefferson developed into a full-blown and frequently bitter political rivalry.

National political parties, in the modern sense, were unknown in America when George Washington took his inaugural oath. There had been Whigs and Tories, federalists and antifederalists, but these groups were factions rather than parties. They had sprung into existence over hotly contested special issues; they had faded away when their cause had triumphed or fizzled.

The Founders at Philadelphia had not envisioned the existence of permanent political parties. Organized opposition to the government—especially a democratic government based on popular consent—seemed tainted by disloyalty. Opposition to the government affronted the spirit of national unity that the glorious cause of the Revolution had inspired. The notion of a formal party apparatus was thus a novelty in the 1790s, and when Jefferson and Madison first organized their opposition to the Hamiltonian program, they confined their activities to Congress and did not anticipate creating a long-lived and popular party. But as their antagonism to Hamilton stiffened, and as the amazingly boisterous and widely read newspapers of the day spread their political message, and Hamilton's, among the people, primitive semblances of political parties began to emerge.

The two-party system has existed in the United States since that time (see Table 10.2). Ironically, in light of early suspicions about the very legitimacy of parties, their competition for power has actually proved to be among the indispensable ingredients of a sound democracy. The party out of power—"the loyal opposition"—traditionally plays the invaluable role of the balance wheel on the machinery of government, ensuring that politics never drifts too far out of kilter with the wishes of the people.

✴ The Impact of the French Revolution

When Washington's first administration ended in early 1793, Hamilton's domestic policies had already stimulated the formation of two political camps—Jeffersonian Democratic-Republicans and Hamiltonian Federalists. As Washington's second term began, foreign-policy issues brought the differences between them to a fever pitch.

Only a few weeks after Washington's inauguration in 1789, the curtain had risen on the first act of the French Revolution. (See "Thinking Globally: Two Revolutions," pp. 190–191.) Twenty-six years were

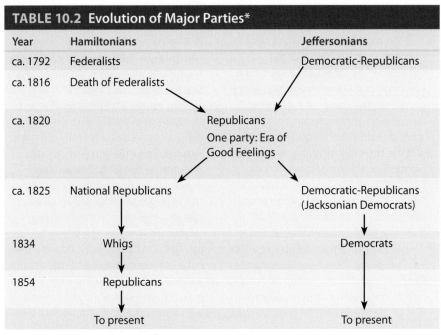

TABLE 10.2 Evolution of Major Parties*

Year	Hamiltonians	Jeffersonians
ca. 1792	Federalists	Democratic-Republicans
ca. 1816	Death of Federalists	
ca. 1820		Republicans One party: Era of Good Feelings
ca. 1825	National Republicans	Democratic-Republicans (Jacksonian Democrats)
1834	Whigs	Democrats
1854	Republicans	
	To present	To present

*See the Appendix (Presidential Elections) for third parties

sent tremors through much of the Western world and beyond.

In its early stages, the upheaval was surprisingly peaceful, involving as it did a successful attempt to impose constitutional shackles on Louis XVI. The American people, loving liberty and deploring despotism, cheered. They were flattered to think that the outburst in France was but the second chapter of their own glorious Revolution, as to some extent it was. Only a few ultraconservative Federalists—fearing change, reform, and "leveling" principles—were from the outset dubious or outspokenly hostile to the "despicable mobocracy." The more ardent Jeffersonians were overjoyed.

The French Revolution entered a more ominous phase in 1792, when France declared war on hostile Austria. Powerful ideals and powerful armies alike were on the march. Late in that year, the electrifying news reached America that French citizen armies had hurled back the invading foreigners and that France had proclaimed itself a republic.

to pass before the seething continent of Europe collapsed into a peace of exhaustion. Few non-American events have left a deeper scar on American political and social life. In a sense the French Revolution was misnamed: it was a historic, global revolution that

The Execution of Queen Marie Antoinette, 1793 The bloody excesses of the notorious guillotine disgusted many Americans and soured them on the promises of the French Revolution.

On July 14, 1789, a howling mob stormed the Bastille—a dank Parisian prison described by the Marquis de Lafayette as France's "fortress of despotism"—killed half a dozen soldiers, and paraded the severed heads of its commanding officer and the mayor of Paris throughout the city. The French Revolution was thus bloodily launched. Bastille Day is still celebrated as France's national birthday, just as Americans celebrate the Fourth of July.

The roots of the two Revolutions were thickly intertwined. To defray the cost of the war that had ousted France from North America in 1763, Britain had levied new taxes on its colonists, provoking them to revolt in 1776. In turn, aiding the rebellious Americans forced the French government to seek new revenues, lighting the fuse that led to the political explosion in Paris in 1789.

Even more notable was the intellectual commonality between the upheavals. The ideas that inspired the American and French revolutionaries grew from the common heritage of radical eighteenth-century Enlightenment thinking about equality, freedom, and the sovereignty of the people. The French Declaration of the Rights of Man (1789) deliberately echoed Thomas Jefferson's Declaration of Independence (1776) when it said that "men are born and remain free and equal in rights," among which were "liberty, property, security, and resistance to oppression." Many French thinkers openly credited the American Revolution as the inspiration for their own. As the American revolutionary Thomas Paine remarked to George Washington, "The principles of America opened the Bastille." Indeed, in many ways the French were even more radical than

the Americans; their Revolution abolished slavery (temporarily), something the Americans failed to do for almost one hundred years more.

And yet the American and French Revolutions unfolded in dramatically different ways and left vastly different legacies. The Americans largely disarmed after winning their independence; allowed some eighty thousand hard-core Loyalists to depart without suffering grievous retribution (see "Makers of America: The Loyalists," pp. 144–145); peacefully resumed their habits of worship, toil, and governance; and proceeded to draft the U.S. Constitution, under which they have lived, with amendments, for more than two centuries. The American revolutionaries, in short, secured the fruits of their Revolution fairly easily, while the French struggled through ghastly bloodshed to ultimate failure—an

Storming the Bastille, 1789   This event signaled the outbreak of the French Revolution.

RMN-Grand Palais/Art Resource, NY

outcome that haunted European politics for at least a century thereafter.

Revolutionaries in France had to grapple with the constant threats of counterrevolution at home and armed intervention from abroad. As a result, they soon descended into grisly violence, including the execution of some forty thousand Frenchmen in the notorious Reign of Terror of 1793–1794, the guillotining of the king and queen, and preemptive attacks on neighboring countries. They stripped the Catholic Church of its property and privileges, briefly experimented with a new state religion called the Cult of Reason, and eventually conceded supreme power to a brash young general, Napoleon Bonaparte, who convulsed all of Europe in the name of "liberty, equality, and fraternity." Napoleon was finally defeated at the Battle of Waterloo in 1815, after which the Bourbon monarchy was restored to the throne.

Why did these two great eruptions, sprung from a shared chain of events and espousing almost identical political philosophies, fare so differently? Many scholars have found the answer in the countries' markedly different pre-Revolutionary histories. France's Revolution confronted implacably entrenched adversaries in the landed nobility and the clergy. Those two "estates," as they were called, clung tenaciously to their ancient privileges, as did the princes and potentates who ruled in all the countries on France's borders. To succeed, the French Revolution had to concentrate power in the hands of a state powerful enough to extinguish its internal enemies and to forestall foreign intervention as well. Those stark necessities help account for the fact that down to the present day, central governments are stronger in almost all European societies than in the United States.

The Americans faced no such obstacles. They had no aristocracy worthy of the name, no church with the kind of influence that the Catholic Church commanded in France, and no menacing neighbors to fear. They had

the luxury of being able to focus on limiting the power of the state, not enlarging it. Theirs was largely a *colonial* conflict, whereas France had to endure a *class* conflict. Not until Reconstruction following the Civil War would Americans confront a comparable task of mustering sufficient power to uproot and permanently extinguish an entire social order.

It has been said that to mount a revolution is "to murder and create." What was exceptional about the American

revolutionaries was that they were spared the necessity to murder. The American Revolution grew not from abstract ideas, but from the preceding two centuries of American experience. It was less a revolution in the usual sense than a consolidation of already well-established norms, values, and behaviors. Alexander Hamilton understood that crucial point when he wrote to the Marquis de Lafayette in 1789, "I dread the reveries of your *philosophic* politicians."

The Key to the Bastille, Mount Vernon, Virginia The Marquis de Lafayette instructed Thomas Paine, his American Revolutionary War comrade, to deliver the key to the liberated Bastille to George Washington. It hangs to this day in the entry hall of Washington's home at Mount Vernon, Virginia, a lasting symbol of the deep affinity between the French and American Revolutions. Fotosearch RM/AGE Fotostock

British political observer William Cobbett (1763–1835) wrote of the frenzied reaction in America to the death of Louis XVI,

"Never was the memory of a man so cruelly insulted as that of this mild and humane monarch. He was guillotined in effigy, in the capital of the Union [Philadelphia], twenty or thirty times every day, during one whole winter and part of the summer. Men, women and children flocked to the tragical exhibition, and not a single paragraph appeared in the papers to shame them from it.**"**

Americans enthusiastically sang "The Marseillaise" and other rousing French Revolutionary songs, and they renamed thoroughfares with democratic flair. King Street in New York, for example, became Liberty Street, and in Boston, Royal Exchange Alley became Equality Lane.

But centuries of pent-up poison could not be purged without baleful results. The guillotine was set up, the king was beheaded in 1793, the church was attacked, and the head-rolling **Reign of Terror** was begun. Back in America, God-fearing Federalist aristocrats nervously fingered their tender white necks and eyed the Jeffersonian masses apprehensively. Lukewarm Federalist approval of the early Revolution turned, almost overnight, to heated talk of "blood-drinking cannibals."

Sober-minded Jeffersonians regretted the bloodshed. But they felt, with Jefferson, that one could not expect to be carried from "despotism to liberty in a feather bed" and that a few thousand aristocratic heads were a cheap price to pay for human freedom.

Such approbation was shortsighted, for dire peril loomed ahead. The earlier battles of the French Revolution had not hurt America directly, but now Britain was sucked into the contagious conflict. The conflagration speedily spread to the New World, where it vividly affected the expanding young American Republic. Thus was repeated the familiar story of every major European war, beginning with 1688, that involved a watery duel for control of the Atlantic Ocean. (See Table 6.2 on p. 106.)

✹ Washington's Neutrality Proclamation

Ominously, the Franco-American alliance of 1778 was still on the books. By its own terms, it was to last "forever." It bound the United States to help the French defend their West Indies against future foes, and the booming British fleets were certain to attack these strategic islands.

Many Jeffersonian Democratic-Republicans favored honoring the alliance. Aflame with the liberal ideals of the French Revolution, red-blooded Jeffersonians were eager to enter the conflict against Britain, the recent foe, at the side of France, the recent friend. America owed France its freedom, they argued, and now was the time to pay the debt of gratitude.

But President George Washington, level-headed as usual, was not swayed by the clamor of the crowd. Backed by Hamilton, he believed that war had to be avoided at all costs. Washington was coolly playing for enormous stakes. The nation in 1793 was militarily feeble, economically wobbly, and politically disunited. But solid foundations were being laid, and American cradles were continuing to rock a bumper crop of babies. Washington wisely reasoned that if America could avoid the broils of Europe for a generation or so, it would then be populous enough and powerful enough to assert its maritime rights with strength and success. Otherwise it might invite catastrophe. The strategy of delay—of playing for time while the birthrate fought America's battles—was a cardinal policy of the Founding Fathers. This principle of strategic patience was based on a shrewd assessment of American strengths and weaknesses at this critical moment in the young Republic's history. Hamilton and Jefferson, often poles apart on other issues, were in broad agreement here.

Accordingly, Washington boldly issued his **Neutrality Proclamation** in 1793, shortly after the outbreak of war between Britain and France. This epochal document not only proclaimed the government's official neutrality in the widening conflict but also sternly warned American citizens to be impartial toward both armed camps. As America's first formal declaration of aloofness from Old World quarrels, Washington's Neutrality Proclamation proved to be a major prop of the spreading isolationist tradition. It also proved to be enormously controversial. Many zealously pro-French Jeffersonians were enraged by the Neutrality Proclamation, especially by Washington's method of announcing it unilaterally, without consulting Congress. The pro-British Federalists were heartened.

Debate soon intensified. An impetuous, thirty-year-old representative of the French Republic, Citizen Edmond Genêt, had landed at Charleston, South Carolina. With unrestrained zeal he undertook to fit out privateers and otherwise take advantage of the existing Franco-American alliance. The giddy-headed envoy—all sail and no anchor—was soon swept away by his enthusiastic reception by the Jeffersonian Republicans. He foolishly came to believe that the Neutrality Proclamation did not reflect the true wishes of the American people, and he consequently embarked upon unneutral activity not authorized by the French alliance—including the recruitment of armies to invade Spanish Florida and Louisiana,

MAP 10.1 American Posts Held by the British and British-American Clashes After 1783 © 2016 Cengage Learning

as well as British Canada. Even Madison and Jefferson were soon disillusioned by his conduct. After he threatened to appeal over the head of "Old Washington" to the sovereign voters, the president demanded Genêt's withdrawal, and the Frenchman was replaced by a less impulsive emissary.

Washington's Neutrality Proclamation clearly illustrates the truism that self-interest is the basic cement of alliances. In 1778 both France and America stood to gain; in 1793 only France. Technically, the Americans did not flout their obligation because France never officially called upon them to honor it. American neutrality in fact favored France. The French West Indies urgently needed Yankee foodstuffs. If the Americans had entered the war at France's side, the British fleets would have blockaded the American coast and cut off those essential supplies. America was thus much more useful to France as a reliable neutral provider than as a blockaded partner-in-arms.

★ Embroilments with Britain

President Washington's far-visioned policy of neutrality was sorely tried by the British. For ten long years, they had been retaining the chain of northern frontier posts on U.S. soil, all in defiance of the peace treaty of 1783 (see Map 10.1). The London government was reluctant to abandon the lucrative fur trade in the Great Lakes region and also hoped to build up an Indian buffer state to contain the ambitious Americans. British agents openly sold firearms and firewater to the Indians of the Miami Confederacy, an alliance of eight Indian nations who terrorized Americans invading their lands. Little Turtle, war chief of the Miamis, gave notice that the confederacy regarded the Ohio River as the United States' northwestern, and their own southeastern, border. In 1790 and 1791, Little Turtle's braves defeated armies led by Generals Josiah Harmar and Arthur St. Clair, killing hundreds of soldiers and handing the United States what remains one of its worst defeats in the history of the frontier.

But in 1794, when a new army under General "Mad Anthony" Wayne routed the Miamis at the **Battle of Fallen Timbers**, the British refused to shelter Indians fleeing from the battle. Abandoned when it counted by their red-coated friends, the Indians soon offered Wayne the peace pipe. In the **Treaty of Greenville**, signed in August 1795, the confederacy gave up vast tracts of the Old Northwest, including most ofpresent-day Indiana and Ohio. In exchange the Indians received a lump-sum payment of $20,000, an annual annuity of $9,000, the right to hunt the lands they had ceded, and, most important, what they hoped

Signing the Treaty of Greenville, 1795 Following General Wayne's victory at the Battle of Fallen Timbers in 1794, the Miami Indians surrendered their claims to much of the Old Northwest.

© Chicago History Museum, USA/The Bridgeman Art Library

was recognition of their sovereign status. Although the treaty codified an unequal relationship, the Indians felt that it put some limits on the ability of the United States to decide the fate of Indian peoples.

On the sea frontier, the British were eager to starve out the French West Indies and naturally expected the United States to defend them under the Franco-American alliance. Hard-boiled commanders of the Royal Navy, ignoring America's rights as a neutral, struck savagely. They seized about three hundred American merchant ships in the West Indies, impressed scores of seamen into service on British vessels, and threw hundreds of others into foul dungeons.

These actions, especially impressment, incensed patriotic Americans. A mighty outcry arose, chiefly from Jeffersonians, that America should once again fight George III in defense of its liberties. At the very least,

it should cut off all supplies to its oppressor through a nationwide embargo. But the Federalists stoutly resisted all demands for drastic action. Hamilton's high hopes for economic development depended on trade with Britain. War with the world's mightiest commercial empire would pierce the heart of the Hamiltonian financial system.

✦ Jay's Treaty and Washington's Farewell

President Washington, in a last desperate gamble to avert war, decided to send Chief Justice John Jay to London in 1794. The Jeffersonians were acutely unhappy over the choice, partly because they feared that so notorious a Federalist and Anglophile would sell out his country. Arriving in London, Jay gave the Jeffersonians further cause for alarm when, at the presentation ceremony, he routinely kissed the queen's hand.

Unhappily, Jay entered the negotiations with weak cards, which were further sabotaged by Hamilton. The latter, fearful of war with Britain, secretly supplied the British with the details of America's bargaining strategy. Not surprisingly, Jay won few concessions. The British did promise to evacuate the chain of posts on U.S. soil—a pledge that inspired little confidence, since it had been made before in Paris (to the same John Jay!) in 1783. In addition, Britain consented to pay damages for the recent seizures of American ships. But the British stopped short of pledging anything about future maritime seizures and impressments or

Thomas Paine (1737–1809), then in France and resenting George Washington's anti-French policies, addressed the president in an open letter (1796) that reveals his bitterness:

❝And as to you, sir, treacherous in private friendship (for so you have been to me, and that in the day of danger) and a hypocrite in public life, the world will be puzzled to decide, whether you are an apostate or an imposter; whether you have abandoned good principles, or whether you ever had any.**❞**

about supplying arms to Indians. And they forced Jay to give ground by binding the United States to pay the debts still owed to British merchants on pre-Revolutionary accounts.

Jay's unpopular pact, more than any other issue, vitalized the newborn Democratic-Republican party of Thomas Jefferson. When the Jeffersonians learned of Jay's concessions, their rage was fearful to behold. The treaty seemed like an abject surrender to Britain, as well as a betrayal of the Jeffersonian South. Southern planters would have to pay the major share of the pre-Revolutionary debts, while rich Federalist shippers were collecting damages for recent British seizures. Jeffersonian mobs hanged, burned, and guillotined in effigy that "damn'd archtraitor, Sir John Jay." Even George Washington's huge popularity was compromised by the controversy over the treaty.

Jay's Treaty had other unforeseen consequences. Fearing that the treaty foreshadowed an Anglo-American alliance, Spain moved hastily to strike a deal with the United States. **Pinckney's Treaty** of 1795 with Spain granted the Americans virtually everything they demanded, including free navigation of the Mississippi, the right of deposit (warehouse rights) at New Orleans, and the large disputed territory of western Florida. (See Map 9.3 on p. 168.)

Exhausted after the diplomatic and partisan battles of his second term, President Washington decided to retire. His choice contributed powerfully to establishing a two-term tradition for American presidents.* In his **Farewell Address** to the nation in 1796 (never delivered orally but printed in the newspapers), Washington strongly advised the avoidance of "permanent alliances" like the still-vexatious Franco-American Treaty of 1778. Contrary to general misunderstanding, Washington did not oppose all alliances, but favored only "temporary alliances" for "extraordinary emergencies." This was admirable advice for a weak and divided nation in 1796. But what is sound counsel for a young stripling may not apply later to a mature and muscular giant.

Washington's contributions as president were enormous, even though the sparkling Hamilton at times seemed to outshine him. The central government, its fiscal feet now under it, was solidly established. The West was expanding. The merchant marine was plowing the seas. Above all, Washington had kept the nation out of both overseas entanglements and foreign wars. The experimental stage had passed, and the presidential chair could now be turned over to a less impressive figure. But republics are notoriously ungrateful. When Washington left office in 1797, he was showered with the brickbats of partisan abuse, quite in contrast with the bouquets that had greeted his arrival.

---

*Not broken until 1940 by Franklin D. Roosevelt and made a part of the Constitution in 1951 by the Twenty-second Amendment. (See the Appendix.)

✵ John Adams Becomes President

Who should succeed the exalted "Father of His Country"? Alexander Hamilton was the best-known member of the Federalist party, now that Washington had bowed out. But his financial policies, some of which had fattened the speculators, had made him so unpopular that he could not hope to be elected president. The Federalists were forced to turn to Washington's vice president, the experienced but ungracious John Adams,

John Adams, by John Singleton Copley, 1783   When he entered Harvard College in 1751, Adams intended to prepare for the ministry, but four absorbing years of study excited him about other intellectual and career possibilities: "I was a mighty metaphysician, at least I thought myself such." Adams also tried his hand at being a mighty scientist, doctor, and orator. Upon graduation he became a schoolmaster but soon decided to take up the law.

Although Thomas Jefferson (1743–1826) and John Adams hardly saw eye-to-eye, Jefferson displayed grudging respect for Adams in a piece of private correspondence in 1787:

❝ He is vain, irritable, and a bad calculator of the force and probable effect of the motives which govern men. This is all the ill which can possibly be said of him. He is as disinterested as the Being who made him. **❞**

a rugged chip off old Plymouth Rock. The Democratic-Republicans naturally rallied behind their master organizer and leader, Thomas Jefferson.

Political passions ran feverishly high in the presidential campaign of 1796. The lofty presence of Washington had hitherto imposed some restraints; now the lid was off. Cultured Federalists like Fisher Ames referred to the Jeffersonians as "fire-eating salamanders, poison-sucking toads." Federalists and Democratic-Republicans even drank their ale in separate taverns. The issues of the campaign, as it turned out, focused heavily on personalities. But the Jeffersonians again assailed the too-forceful crushing of the Whiskey Rebellion and, above all, the negotiation of Jay's hated treaty.

John Adams, with most of his support in New England, squeezed through by the narrow margin of 71 votes to 68 in the Electoral College. Jefferson, as runner-up, became vice president.* One of the ablest statesmen of his day, Adams at sixty-two was a stuffy figure. Sharp-featured, bald, relatively short (five feet seven inches), and thickset ("His Rotundity"),

---

*The possibility of such an inharmonious two-party combination in the future was removed by the Twelfth Amendment to the Constitution in 1804. (See the Appendix.)

he impressed observers as a man of stern principles who did his duty with stubborn devotion. Although learned and upright, he was a tactless and prickly intellectual aristocrat, with no appeal to the masses and with no desire to cultivate any. Many citizens regarded him with "respectful irritation."

The crusty New Englander suffered from other handicaps. He had stepped into Washington's shoes, which no successor could hope to fill. In addition, Adams was hated by Hamilton, who had resigned from the Treasury in 1795 and who now headed the war faction of the Federalist party, known as the "High Federalists." The famed financier even secretly plotted with certain members of the cabinet against the president, who had a conspiracy rather than a cabinet on his hands. Adams regarded Hamilton as "the most ruthless, impatient, artful, indefatigable and unprincipled intriguer in the United States, if not in the world." Most ominous of all, Adams inherited a violent quarrel with France—a quarrel whose gunpowder lacked only a spark.

✵ Unofficial Fighting with France

The French were infuriated by Jay's Treaty. They condemned it as the initial step toward an alliance with Britain, their perpetual foe. They further assailed the pact as a flagrant violation of the Franco-American Treaty of 1778. French warships, in retaliation, began to seize defenseless American merchant vessels, altogether about three hundred by mid-1797. Adding insult to outrage, the Paris regime haughtily refused to receive America's newly appointed envoy and even threatened him with arrest.

President Adams kept his head, temporarily, even though the nation was mightily aroused. True to Washington's policy of steering clear of war at all costs, he tried again to reach an agreement with the French

The XYZ Affair When President Adams's envoys to Paris were asked to pay a huge bribe as the price of doing diplomatic business, humiliated Americans rose up in wrath against France. Here an innocent young America is being plundered by Frenchmen as John Bull looks on in amusement from across the English Channel.

Preparation for War to Defend Commerce: The Building of the Frigate *Philadelphia* In 1803 this frigate ran onto the rocks near Tripoli harbor, and about three hundred officers and men were imprisoned by the Tripolitans (see Map 11.2 on p. 212). The ship was refloated for service against the Americans, but Stephen Decatur led a party of men that set it afire.

Free Library, Philadelphia, PA, USA/The Bridgeman Art Library

and appointed a diplomatic commission of three men, including John Marshall, the future chief justice.

Adams's envoys, reaching Paris in 1797, hoped to meet with Charles Maurice de Talleyrand, the crafty French foreign minister. They were secretly approached by three go-betweens, later referred to as X, Y, and Z in the published dispatches. The French spokesmen, among other concessions, demanded an unneutral loan of 32 million florins, plus what amounted to a bribe of $250,000, for the privilege of merely talking with Talleyrand.

These terms were intolerable. The American trio knew that bribes were standard diplomatic devices in Europe, but they gagged at paying a quarter of a million dollars for mere talk, without any assurances of a settlement. Negotiations quickly broke down, and John Marshall, on reaching New York in 1798, was hailed as a conquering hero for his steadfastness.

The **XYZ Affair** sent a wave of war hysteria sweeping through the United States, catching up even President Adams. The slogan of the hour became "Millions for defense, but not one cent for tribute." The Federalists were delighted at this unexpected turn of affairs, whereas all except the most rabid Jeffersonians hung their heads in shame over the misbehavior of their French friends.

War preparations in the United States were pushed along at a feverish pace, despite considerable Jeffersonian opposition in Congress. The Navy Department was created; the three-ship navy was expanded; the United States Marine Corps was reestablished (originally created in 1775, the Marine Corps had been disbanded at the end of the Revolutionary War). A new army of ten thousand men was authorized (but not fully raised).

Bloodshed was confined to the sea, and principally to the West Indies. In two and a half years of undeclared hostilities (1798–1800), American privateers and men-of-war of the new navy captured over eighty armed vessels flying the French colors, though several hundred Yankee merchant ships were lost to the enemy. Only a slight push, it seemed, might plunge both nations into a full-dress war.

✫ Adams Puts Patriotism Above Party

Embattled France, its hands full in Europe, wanted no war. An outwitted Talleyrand realized that to fight the United States would merely add one more foe to his enemy roster. The British, who were lending the Americans cannon and other war supplies, were actually driven closer to their wayward cousins than they were to be again for many years. Talleyrand therefore let it be known, through roundabout channels, that if the Americans would send a new minister, he would be received with proper respect.

This French furor brought to Adams a degree of personal acclaim that he had never known before—and was never to know again. He doubtless perceived that a full-fledged war, crowned by the conquest of the Floridas and Louisiana, would bring new plaudits to the Federalist party—and perhaps a second term to himself. But the heady wine of popularity did not sway his final judgment. He, like other Founding Fathers, realized full well that war must be avoided while the country was relatively weak.

Adams unexpectedly exploded a bombshell when, early in 1799, he submitted to the Senate the name of

The firmness of President John Adams (1735–1826) was revealed in his message to Congress (June 1798):

❝ I will never send another minister to France without assurances that he will be received, respected, and honored as the representative of a great, free, powerful, and independent nation. **❞**

a new minister to France. Hamilton and his war-hawk faction were enraged. But public opinion—Jeffersonian and reasonable Federalist alike—was favorable to one last try for peace.

America's envoys (now three) found the political skies brightening when they reached Paris early in 1800. The ambitious "Little Corporal," the Corsican Napoleon Bonaparte, had recently seized dictatorial power. He was eager to free his hands of the American squabble so that he might continue to redraw the map of Europe and perhaps create a New World empire in Louisiana. The afflictions and ambitions of the Old World were again working to America's advantage.

After a great deal of haggling, a memorable treaty known as the **Convention of 1800** was signed in Paris. France agreed to annul the twenty-two-year-old marriage of (in)convenience, but as a kind of alimony the United States agreed to pay the damage claims of American shippers. So ended the nation's only peacetime military alliance for a century and a half. Its troubled history does much to explain the traditional antipathy of the American people to foreign entanglements.

John Adams, flinty to the end, deserves immense credit for his belated push for peace, even though he was moved in part by jealousy of Hamilton. Adams not only avoided the hazards of war, but also unwittingly smoothed the path for the peaceful purchase of Louisiana three years later. He should indeed rank high among the forgotten purchasers of this vast domain. If America had drifted into a full-blown war with France in 1800, Napoleon would not have sold Louisiana to Jefferson on any terms in 1803.

President Adams, the bubble of his popularity pricked by peace, was aware of his signal contribution to the nation. He later suggested as the epitaph for his tombstone (not used), "Here lies John Adams, who took upon himself the responsibility of peace with France in the year 1800."

✪ The Federalist Witch Hunt

Exulting Federalists had meanwhile capitalized on the anti-French frenzy to drive through Congress in 1798 a sheaf of laws designed to muffle or minimize their Jeffersonian foes.

The first of these oppressive laws was aimed at supposedly pro-Jeffersonian "aliens." Most European immigrants, lacking wealth, were scorned by the aristocratic Federalist party. But they were welcomed as voters by the less prosperous and more democratic Jeffersonians. The Federalist Congress, hoping to discourage the "dregs" of Europe, erected a disheartening barrier. They raised the residence requirements for aliens who desired to become citizens from a tolerable five years to an intolerable fourteen. This drastic new law violated the traditional American policy of open-door hospitality and speedy assimilation.

Two additional **Alien Laws** struck heavily at undesirable immigrants. The president was empowered to deport dangerous foreigners in time of peace and to deport or imprison them in time of hostilities. Though defensible as a war measure—and an officially declared war with France seemed imminent—this was an arbitrary grant of executive power contrary to American tradition and to the spirit of the Constitution, even though the stringent Alien Laws were never enforced.

The "lockjaw" **Sedition Act**, the last measure of the Federalist clampdown, was a direct slap at two priceless freedoms guaranteed in the Constitution by the Bill of Rights—freedom of speech and freedom of the press (First Amendment). This law provided that anyone who impeded the policies of the government or falsely defamed its officials, including the president, would be liable to a heavy fine and imprisonment. Severe though the measure was, the Federalists believed that it was justified. The verbal violence of the day was unrestrained, and foul-penned editors, some of them exiled aliens, vilified Adams's anti-French policy in vicious terms.

Many outspoken Jeffersonian editors were indicted under the Sedition Act, and ten were brought to trial. All of them were convicted, often by packed juries swayed by prejudiced Federalist judges. Some of the victims were harmless partisans, who should have been spared the notoriety of martyrdom. Among them was Congressman Matthew Lyon (the "Spitting Lion"), who had earlier gained fame by spitting in the face of a Federalist. He was sentenced to four months in jail for writing of President Adams's "unbounded thirst for ridiculous pomp, foolish adulation, and selfish avarice." Another culprit was lucky to get off with a fine of $100 after he had expressed the wish that the wad of a cannon fired in honor of Adams had landed in the seat of the president's breeches.

The Sedition Act seemed to be in direct conflict with the Constitution. But the Supreme Court, dominated by Federalists, was of no mind to declare this Federalist law unconstitutional. (The Federalists intentionally wrote the law to expire in 1801, so that it could not be used against them if they lost the next

Congressional Pugilists
Satirical representation of Matthew Lyon's fight in Congress with the Federalist representative Roger Griswold.

election.) This attempt by the Federalists to crush free speech and silence the opposition party, high-handed as it was, undoubtedly made many converts for the Jeffersonians.

Yet the Alien and Sedition Acts, despite pained outcries from the Jeffersonians they muzzled, commanded widespread popular support. Anti-French hysteria played directly into the hands of witch-hunting conservatives. In the congressional elections of 1798–1799, the Federalists, riding a wave of popularity, scored the most sweeping victory of their entire history.

In 1800 James Callender (1758–1803) published a pamphlet that assailed the president in strong language. For blasts like the following tirade, Callender was prosecuted under the Sedition Act, fined $250, and sentenced to prison for nine months:

"The reign of Mr. Adams has, hitherto, been one continued tempest of *malignant* passions. As president, he has never opened his lips, or lifted his pen, without threatening and scolding. The grand object of his administration has been to exasperate the rage of contending parties, to calumniate and destroy every man who differs from his opinions.... Every person holding an office must either quit it, or think and vote exactly with Mr. Adams."

✴ The Virginia (Madison) and Kentucky (Jefferson) Resolutions

Resentful Jeffersonians naturally refused to take the Alien and Sedition Acts lying down. Jefferson himself feared that if the Federalists managed to choke free speech and free press, they would then wipe out other precious constitutional guarantees. His own fledgling political party might even be stamped out of existence. If this had happened, the country might have slid into a dangerous one-party dictatorship.

Fearing prosecution for sedition, Jefferson secretly penned a series of resolutions, which the Kentucky legislature approved in 1798 and 1799. His friend and fellow Virginian James Madison drafted a similar but less extreme statement, which was adopted by the legislature of Virginia in 1798.

Both Jefferson and Madison stressed the compact theory—a theory popular among English political philosophers in the seventeenth and eighteenth centuries. As applied to America by the Jeffersonians, this concept meant that the thirteen sovereign states, in creating the federal government, had entered into a "compact," or contract, regarding its jurisdiction. The national government was consequently the agent or creation of the states. Since water can rise no higher than its source, the individual states were the final judges of whether their agent had broken the "compact" by overstepping the authority originally granted. Invoking this logic, Jefferson's

Kentucky resolutions concluded that the federal regime *had* exceeded its constitutional powers and that with regard to the Alien and Sedition Acts, "nullification"—a refusal to accept them—was the "rightful remedy."

No other state legislatures, despite Jefferson's hopes, fell into line. Some of them flatly refused to endorse the Virginia and Kentucky resolutions. Others, chiefly in Federalist states, added ringing condemnations. Many Federalists argued that the people, not the states, had made the original compact, and that it was up to the Supreme Court—not the states—to nullify unconstitutional legislation passed by Congress. This practice, though not specifically authorized by the Constitution, was finally adopted by the Supreme Court in 1803 (see "The 'Dead Clutch' of the Judiciary" in Chapter 11, pp. 210–212).

The **Virginia and Kentucky resolutions** were a brilliant formulation of the extreme states' rights view regarding the Union—indeed more sweeping in their implications than their authors had intended. They were later used by southerners to support nullification—and ultimately secession. Yet neither Jefferson nor Madison, as Founding Fathers of the Union, had any intention of breaking it up; they were groping for ways to preserve it. Their resolutions were basically campaign documents designed to crystallize opposition to the Federalist party and to unseat it in the upcoming presidential election of 1800. The only real nullification that Jefferson had in view was the nullification of Federalist abuses.

✦ Federalists Versus Democratic-Republicans

As the presidential contest of 1800 approached, the differences between Federalists and Democratic-Republicans were sharply etched (see Table 10.3). As might be expected, most federalists of the pre-Constitution period (1787–1789) became Federalists in the 1790s. Largely welded by Hamilton into an effective group by 1793, they openly advocated rule by the "best people." "Those who own the country," remarked Federalist John Jay, "ought to govern it." With their intellectual arrogance and Tory tastes, Hamiltonians distrusted full-blown democracy as the fountain of all mischiefs and feared the "swayability" of the untutored common folk.

Hamiltonian Federalists also advocated a strong central government with the power to crush democratic excesses like Shays's Rebellion, protect the lives and estates of the wealthy, subordinate the sovereignty-loving states, and promote foreign trade. They believed that government should support private enterprise but not interfere with it. This attitude came naturally to the merchants, manufacturers, and shippers along the Atlantic seaboard, who made up the majority of Federalist support. Farther inland, few Hamiltonians dwelled.

The hinterland was largely anti-Federalist territory. Leading the anti-Federalists, who came eventually to be known as Democratic-Republicans or

TABLE 10.3 The Two Political Parties, 1793–1800	
Federalist Features	**Democratic-Republican (Jeffersonian) Features**
Rule by the "best people"	Rule by the informed masses
Hostility to extension of democracy	Friendliness toward extension of democracy
A powerful central government at the expense of states' rights	A weak central government so as to preserve states' rights
Loose interpretation of Constitution	Strict interpretation of Constitution
Government to foster business; concentration of wealth in interests of capitalistic enterprise	No special favors for business; agriculture preferred
A protective tariff	No special favors for manufacturers
Pro-British (conservative Tory tradition)	Pro-French (radical revolutionary tradition)
National debt a blessing, if properly funded	National debt a bane; rigid economy
An expanding bureaucracy	Reduction of federal officeholders
A powerful central bank	Encouragement to state banks
Restrictions on free speech and press	Relatively free speech and press
Concentration in seacoast area	Concentration in South and Southwest; in agricultural areas and backcountry
A strong navy to protect shippers	A minimal navy for coastal defense

Art Gallery, Williams Center, Lafayette College

Thomas Jefferson at Natural Bridge, by Caleb Boyle, ca. 1801 A great statesman, Jefferson wrote his own epitaph: "Here was buried Thomas Jefferson, Author of the Declaration of Independence, of the Statute of Virginia for Religious Freedom, and Father of the University of Virginia."

sometimes simply Republicans, was Thomas Jefferson. His rivalry with Hamilton defined the archetypal conflict in American political history. The two leaders appealed to different constituencies and expressed different theories of society, politics, and diplomacy.

Lanky and relaxed in appearance, lacking personal aggressiveness, weak-voiced, and unable to deliver a rabble-rousing speech, Jefferson became a master political organizer through his ability to lead people rather than drive them. His strongest appeal was to the middle class and to the underprivileged—the "dirt" farmers, the laborers, the artisans, and the small shopkeepers.

Liberal-thinking Jefferson, with his aristocratic head set on a farmer's frame, was a bundle of inconsistencies. By one set of tests, he should have been a Federalist, for he was a Virginia aristocrat and slaveowner who lived in an imposing hilltop mansion at Monticello. A so-called traitor to his own upper class, Jefferson cherished uncommon sympathy for the common people, especially the downtrodden, the oppressed, and the persecuted. As he wrote in 1800, "I have sworn upon the altar of God eternal hostility against every form of tyranny over the mind of man."

Jeffersonian Republicans demanded a weak central regime. They believed that the best government was the one that governed least. The bulk of the power, Jefferson argued, should be retained by the states. There the people, in intimate contact with local affairs, could keep a more vigilant eye on their public servants. Otherwise a dictatorship might develop. Central authority—a kind of necessary evil—was to be kept at a minimum through a strict interpretation of the Constitution. The national debt, which he saw as a curse illegitimately bequeathed to later generations, was to be paid off.

Jeffersonian Republicans, themselves primarily agrarians, insisted that there should be no special privileges for special classes, particularly manufacturers. Agriculture, to Jefferson, was the favored branch of the economy and formed the foundation of his political thought. "Those who labor in the earth are the chosen people of God," he said. Most of his followers naturally came from the agricultural South and Southwest.

Above all, Jefferson advocated the rule of the people. But he did not propose thrusting the ballot into the hands of every adult white male. He favored government *for* the people, but not by *all* the people—only by those white men who were literate enough to inform themselves and wear the mantle of American citizenship worthily. Universal education would have to precede universal suffrage. The ignorant, he argued, were incapable of self-government. But he had profound faith in the reasonableness and teachableness of the masses and in their collective wisdom when taught.

Thomas Jefferson's vision of a republican America was peopled with virtuous farmers, not factory hands. As early as 1784, he wrote,

❝ While we have land to labor then, let us never wish to see our citizens occupied at a work-bench, or twirling a distaff.... For the general operations of manufacture, let our workshops remain in Europe.... The mobs of great cities add just so much to the support of pure government, as sores do to the strength of the human body. **❞**

Landlessness among American citizens threatened popular democracy as much as illiteracy, in Jefferson's eyes. He feared that propertyless dependents would be political pawns in the hands of their landowning superiors. How could the emergence of a landless class of voters be avoided? The answer, in part, was by slavery. A system of black slave labor in the South ensured that white yeoman farmers could remain independent landowners. Without slavery, poor whites would have to provide the cheap labor so necessary for the cultivation of tobacco and rice, and their low wages would preclude their ever owning property. Jefferson thus tortuously reconciled slaveholding—his own included—with his more democratic impulses.

Yet for his time, Jefferson's confidence that white, free men could become responsible and knowledgeable citizens was open-minded. He championed their freedom of speech, for without free speech, the misdeeds of tyranny could not be exposed. Jefferson even dared to say that given the choice of "a government without newspapers" and "newspapers without a government," he would opt for the latter. Yet no other American leader, except perhaps Abraham Lincoln, ever suffered more foul abuse from editorial pens; Jefferson might well have prayed for freedom from the Federalist press.

Differences over foreign policy defined another sharp distinction between Hamilton and Jefferson. Hamilton looked outward and eastward. He sought to build a strong national state that would assert and expand America's commercial interests. "No Government could give us tranquility and happiness at home," he declared, "which did not possess sufficient stability and strength to make us respectable abroad." Foreign trade, especially with Britain, was a key cog in Hamilton's fiscal machinery, and friendship with Britain was thus indispensable. Jeffersonian Republicans, unlike the Federalist "British boot-lickers," were basically pro-French. They earnestly believed that it was to America's advantage to support the liberal ideals of the French Revolution, rather than applaud the reaction of the British Tories. Jefferson, in effect, faced inward and westward. His priorities were to protect and strengthen democracy at home, especially in the frontier regions beyond the Appalachians, rather than flex America's muscles abroad.

So as the young Republic's first full decade of nationhood came to a close, the Founders' hopes seemed already imperiled. Conflicts over domestic politics and foreign policy undermined the unity of the Revolutionary era and called into question the very viability of the American experiment in democracy. As the presidential election of 1800 approached, the danger loomed that the fragile and battered American ship of state, like many another before it and after it, would founder on the rocks of controversy. The shores of history are littered with the wreckage of nascent nations torn asunder before they could grow to a stable maturity. Why should the United States expect to enjoy a happier fate?

Chapter Review

KEY TERMS

Bill of Rights (184)
Judiciary Act of 1789 (184)
funding at par (185)
assumption (185)
tariff (186)
excise tax (186)
Bank of the United States (187)
Whiskey Rebellion (187)
Reign of Terror (192)
Neutrality Proclamation (192)
Fallen Timbers, Battle of (193)
Greenville, Treaty of (193)
Jay's Treaty (195)
Pinckney's Treaty (195)
Farewell Address (195)
XYZ Affair (197)
Convention of 1800 (198)
Alien Laws (198)
Sedition Act (198)
Virginia and Kentucky resolutions (200)

PEOPLE TO KNOW

George Washington
Alexander Hamilton
Louis XVI
Edmond Genêt
Little Turtle
"Mad Anthony" Wayne
John Jay
John Adams
Charles Maurice de Talleyrand

CHRONOLOGY

1789   Constitution formally put into effect
Judiciary Act of 1789
Washington elected president
French Revolution begins
Declaration of the Rights of Man (France)

1790   First official census

1791   Bill of Rights adopted
Vermont becomes fourteenth state
Bank of the United States created
Excise tax passed

1792   Washington reelected president

1792–1793   Federalist and Democratic-Republican parties formed

1793   Louis XVI beheaded; radical phase of French Revolution
France declares war on Britain and Spain
Washington's Neutrality Proclamation
Citizen Genêt affair

1794   Whiskey Rebellion
Battle of Fallen Timbers
Jay's Treaty with Britain

1795   Treaty of Greenville: Indians cede Ohio
Pinckney's Treaty with Spain

1796   Washington's Farewell Address

1797   Adams becomes president
XYZ Affair

1798   Alien and Sedition Acts

1798–1799   Virginia and Kentucky resolutions

1798–1800   Undeclared war with France

1800   Convention of 1800: peace with France

TO LEARN MORE

Joanne Freeman, *Affairs of Honor: National Politics in the New Republic* (2001)

Francois Furstenberg, *In the Name of the Father: Washington's Legacy, Slavery, and the Making of a Nation* (2006)

Frank Lambert, *The Barbary Wars: American Independence in the Atlantic World* (2005)

Michael Merrill and Sean Wilentz, eds., *The Key of Liberty: The Life and Democratic Writings of William Manning, "A Laborer," 1747–1814* (1992)

Jeffrey L. Pasley, *"The Tyranny of Printers": Newspaper Politics in the Early American Republic* (2001)

Jeffrey L. Pasley, Andrew W. Robertson, and David Waldstreicher, eds., *Beyond the Founders: New Approaches to the Political History of the Early American Republic* (2004)

Bernard Schwartz, *The Great Rights of Mankind: A History of the American Bill of Rights* (1991)

Thomas P. Slaughter, *The Whiskey Rebellion: Frontier Epilogue to the American Revolution* (1986)

Robert W. Smith, *Keeping the Republic: Ideology and Early American Diplomacy* (2004)

Alan Taylor, *William Cooper's Town: Power and Persuasion on the Frontier of the Early American Republic* (1995)

Gordon Wood, *Empire of Liberty: A History of the Early Republic, 1789–1815* (2009)

Robert E. Wright, *Hamilton Unbound: Finance and the Creation of the American Republic* (2002)

A complete, annotated bibliography for this chapter—along with brief descriptions of the People to Know—may be found on the *American Pageant* website. The key terms are defined in the glossary at the end of the text.

Chapter 11

The Triumphs and Travails of the Jeffersonian Republic

1800–1812

Timid men … prefer the calm of despotism to the boisterous sea of liberty.

THOMAS JEFFERSON, 1796

In the critical presidential contest of 1800, the first in which Federalists and Democratic-Republicans functioned as two national political parties, John Adams and Thomas Jefferson again squared off against each other. The choice seemed clear and dramatic: Adams's Federalists waged a defensive struggle for strong central government and public order. Their Jeffersonian opponents presented themselves as the guardians of agrarian purity, liberty, and states' rights. The next dozen years, however, would turn what seemed like a clear-cut choice in 1800 into a messier reality, as conflicts over foreign policy confronted the Jeffersonians with a series of opportunities and crises requiring the assertion of federal authority. As the first challengers to rout a reigning party, the Republicans were the first to learn that it is far easier to condemn from the stump than to govern consistently.

★ Federalist and Republican Mudslingers

In fighting for survival, the Federalists labored under heavy handicaps. Their Alien and Sedition Acts had aroused a host of enemies, although most of these critics were dyed-in-the-wool Jeffersonians anyhow. The Hamiltonian wing of the Federalist party, robbed of its glorious war with France, split openly with President Adams. Hamilton, a victim of arrogance, was so indiscreet as to attack the president in a privately printed pamphlet. Jeffersonians soon got hold of the pamphlet and gleefully published it.

The most damaging blow to the Federalists was the refusal of Adams to give them a rousing fight with France. Their feverish war preparations had swelled the public debt and had required disagreeable new taxes, including a stamp tax. After all these unpopular measures, the war scare had petered out, and the country was left with an all-dressed-up-but-no-place-to-go feeling. The military preparations now seemed not only unnecessary but also extravagant, as seamen for the "new navy" were called "John Adams's Jackasses." Adams himself was known, somewhat ironically, as "the Father of the American Navy."

Thrown on the defensive, the Federalists concentrated their fire on Jefferson himself, who became the victim of one of America's earliest "whispering campaigns." He was accused of having robbed a widow and her children of a trust fund and of having fathered numerous mulatto children by his own enslaved women. (Jefferson's long-rumored intimacy with one of his slaves, Sally Hemings, has been

The Reverend Timothy Dwight (1752–1817), president of Yale College, predicted that in the event of Jefferson's election,

❝the Bible would be cast into a bonfire, our holy worship changed into a dance of [French] Jacobin phrensy, our wives and daughters dishonored, and our sons converted into the disciples of Voltaire and the dragoons of Marat.❞

LOOK ON THIS PICTURE, AND ON THIS.

HERE IS____

THIS WAS____

New-York, June, 1807.

Washington and Jefferson Compared, 1807 This pro-Federalist, anti-Jefferson cartoon accuses Jefferson of sympathizing with French Revolutionary despotism.

confirmed through DNA testing. See "Examining the Evidence," p. 207.) As a liberal in religion, Jefferson had earlier incurred the wrath of the orthodox clergy, largely through his successful struggle to separate church and state in his native Virginia. Although Jefferson did believe in God, preachers throughout New England, stronghold of Federalism and Congregationalism, thundered against his alleged atheism. Old ladies of Federalist families, fearing Jefferson's election, even buried their Bibles or hung them in wells.

✷ The Jeffersonian "Revolution of 1800"

Jefferson won by a majority of seventy-three electoral votes to sixty-five (see Map 11.1). In defeat, the colorless and presumably unpopular Adams polled more electoral strength than he had gained four years earlier—except for New York. The Empire State fell into the Jeffersonian basket, and with it the election, largely because Aaron Burr, a master wire-puller, turned New York to Jefferson by the narrowest of margins. The Virginian polled the bulk of his strength in the South and West, particularly in those states where universal white manhood suffrage had been adopted.

Decisive in Jefferson's victory was the three-fifths clause of the Constitution. By counting three-fifths of the enslaved population for the purposes of congressional and Electoral College representation, the Constitution gave white southern voters a bonus that helped Jefferson win the White House. Northern critics fumed that Jefferson was a "Negro President" and an illegitimate embodiment of the "slave power" that the southern states wielded in the nation.

Jeffersonian joy was dampened by an unexpected deadlock. Through a technicality Jefferson, the presidential candidate, and Burr, his vice-presidential running mate, received the same number of electoral votes for the presidency. Under the Constitution the tie could be broken only by the House of Representatives (see Art. II, Sec. I, para. 2). This body was controlled for several more months by the lame-duck Federalists, who preferred Burr to the hated Jefferson.* Voting in the House moved slowly to a climax, as exhausted representatives snored in their seats.

---

*A "lame duck" has been humorously defined as a politician whose political goose has been cooked in the recent elections. The possibility of another such tie was removed by the Twelfth Amendment in 1804 (see the Appendix). Before then, each elector had two votes, with the second-place finisher becoming vice president.

1800

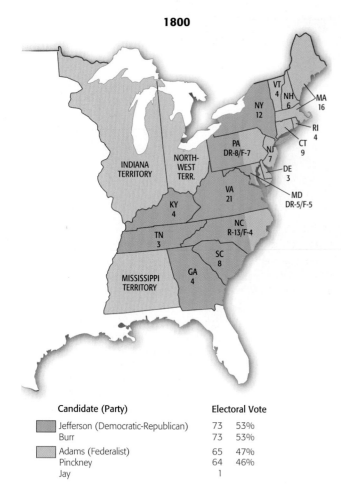

Candidate (Party)		Electoral Vote	
Jefferson (Democratic-Republican)		73	53%
Burr		73	53%
Adams (Federalist)		65	47%
Pinckney		64	46%
Jay		1	

MAP 11.1 Presidential Election of 1800 (with electoral vote by state) New York was the key state in this election, and Aaron Burr helped swing it away from the Federalists with tactics that anticipated the political "machines" of a later day. Federalists complained that Burr "travels every night from one meeting of Republicans to another, haranguing... them to the most zealous exertions. [He] can stoop so low as to visit every low tavern that may happen to be crowded with his dear fellow citizens." But Burr proved that the price was worth it. "We have beat you," Burr told kid-gloved Federalists after the election, "by superior *Management.*"

© 2016 Cengage Learning

❝ I have this morning witnessed one of the most interesting scenes a free people can ever witness. The changes of administration, which in every government and in every age have most generally been epochs of confusion, villainy and bloodshed, in this our happy country take place without any species of distraction, or disorder.**❞**

But the election was no revolution in the sense of a massive popular upheaval or an upending of the political system. In truth, Jefferson had narrowly squeaked through to victory. A switch of some 250 votes in New York would have thrown the election to Adams. Jefferson meant that his election represented a return to what he considered the original spirit of the Revolution. In his eyes Hamilton and Adams had betrayed the ideals of 1776 and 1787. Jefferson's mission, as he saw it, was to restore the republican experiment, to check the growth of government power, and to halt the decay of virtue that had set in under Federalist rule.

No less "revolutionary" was the peaceful and orderly transfer of power on the basis of an election whose results all parties accepted. This was a remarkable achievement for a raw young nation, especially after all the partisan bitterness that had agitated the country during Adams's presidency. It was particularly remarkable in that age; comparable successions would not take place in Britain for another generation. After a decade of division and doubt, Americans could take justifiable pride in the vigor of their experiment in democracy.

✦ Responsibility Breeds Moderation

"Long Tom" Jefferson was inaugurated president on March 4, 1801, in the swampy village of Washington, the crude new national capital. Tall (six feet two and a half inches), with large hands and feet, red hair ("the Red Fox"), and prominent cheekbones and chin, he was an arresting figure. Having spent five years as U.S. minister to France (1784–1789), he was fluent in French and was a sophisticated, cosmopolitan "citizen of the world," yet he never lost the common touch. Believing that the customary pomp did not befit his democratic ideals, he spurned a horse-drawn coach and strode by foot to the Capitol from his boardinghouse.

Jefferson's inaugural address, beautifully phrased, was a classic statement of democratic principles. "The will of the majority is in all cases to prevail," Jefferson

The agonizing deadlock was broken at last when a few Federalists, despairing of electing Burr and hoping for moderation from Jefferson, refrained from voting. The election then went to the rightful candidate.

John Adams, as fate would have it, was the last Federalist president of the United States. His party sank slowly into political oblivion and ultimately disappeared completely in the days of Andrew Jackson.

Jefferson later claimed that the election of 1800 was a "revolution" comparable to that of 1776, and historians have sometimes referred to the **Revolution of 1800**.

The Thomas Jefferson–Sally Hemings Controversy

In the aftermath of the rumor-fueled election of 1800, the firebrand journalist and political *provocateur* James Callender asserted in print that Thomas Jefferson had engaged in sexual relations with his Monticello slave, Sally Hemings. Promptly and gleefully, Federalist newspapers broadcast this ripe gossip across the country. This print, titled "A Philosophic Cock," attacked Jefferson by depicting him as a rooster and Hemings as a hen. The rooster, or cock, was also a symbol of Revolutionary France. Jefferson's enemies sought to discredit him for personal indiscretions as well as radical sympathies. Although he resolutely denied having an affair with Hemings, the charge that at first seemed to be only a politically motivated defamation refused to go away. In the 1870s two new oral sources of evidence came to light. Madison Hemings, Sally's next-to-last child, claimed that his mother had identified Jefferson as the father of all five of her children. Soon thereafter James Parton's biography of Jefferson revealed that among Jefferson's white descendants, it was said that his nephew had fathered all or most of Sally's children. In the 1950s several large publishing projects on Jefferson's life and writings uncovered new evidence and inspired renewed debate. Most convincing was Dumas Malone's calculation that Jefferson had been present at Monticello nine months prior to the birth of each of Sally's children. Speculation continued throughout the rest of the century, with little new evidence, until scientific advances made possible DNA testing of the remains of Jefferson's white and possible black descendants to determine paternity. Two centuries after Callender first cast aspersions on Jefferson's morality, cutting-edge science helped establish the high probability that Jefferson had fathered Sally's youngest son and the likelihood that he was the father of all of her children.

A PHILOSOPHIC COCK

Courtesy, American Antiquarian Society

Litchfield Historical Society

Litchfield Historical Society

Mrs. Benjamin Tallmadge and Son Henry Floyd and Daughter Maria Jones; Colonel Benjamin Tallmadge and Son William Tallmadge, by Ralph Earl, 1790 The Tallmadges were among the leading citizens of Litchfield, a Federalist stronghold in the heavily Federalist state of Connecticut. Colonel Benjamin Tallmadge served with distinction in the Revolutionary War, became a wealthy merchant and banker, and represented his state in Congress from 1801 to 1817. Mary Floyd Tallmadge, like her husband, came from a prominent Long Island family. The opulence of the Tallmadges' clothing and surroundings in these paintings abundantly testifies to the wealth, and the social pretensions, of the Federalist elite. Note the toy carriage near the feet of the Tallmadge daughter—a replica of the actual, and elegant, carriage owned by the Tallmadge family.

declared. But, he added, "that will to be rightful must be reasonable; the minority possess their equal rights, which equal law must protect, and to violate would be oppression." Seeking to allay Federalist fears of a bull-in-the-china-closet overturn, Jefferson ingratiatingly intoned, "We are all Republicans, we are all Federalists." As for foreign affairs, he pledged "honest friendship with all nations, entangling alliances with none."

With its rustic setting, Washington lent itself admirably to the simplicity and frugality of the Jeffersonian Republicans. In this respect it contrasted sharply with the elegant atmosphere of Federalist Philadelphia, the former temporary capital. Extending democratic principles to etiquette, Jefferson established the rule of pell-mell at official dinners—that is, seating without regard to rank. The resplendent British minister, who had

enjoyed precedence among the pro-British Federalists, was insulted.

As president, Jefferson could be shockingly unconventional. He would receive callers in sloppy attire—once in a dressing gown and heel-less slippers. He started the precedent, unbroken until Woodrow Wilson's presidency 112 years later, of sending messages to Congress to be read by a clerk. Personal appearances, in the Federalist manner, suggested too strongly a monarchical speech from the throne. Besides, Jefferson was painfully conscious of his weak voice and unimpressive platform presence.

As if compelled by an evil twin, Jefferson was forced to reverse many of the political principles he had so vigorously championed. There were in fact two Thomas Jeffersons. One was the scholarly private citizen, who

Jefferson Inaugural Pitcher, 1801 This memento from the election of 1800 immortalized President Thomas Jefferson's words, "We are all Republicans, we are all Federalists," which turned out to be more hopeful than true. Jefferson was portrayed in the plain attire he favored, shunning the sartorial pretensions affected by many Federalists, such as the elegantly dressed Tallmadges shown on p. 208. Collection of Janice L. and David J. Frent

Thomas Jefferson's Polygraph, 1806 Jefferson's study reflected his fondness for ideas and inventions. One of his favorite devices was this polygraph, which Jefferson used to make copies of the letters he penned. It was patented in London in 1803. Jefferson acquired one the following year. "From sun-rise to one or two o'clock," he noted, "I am drudging at the writing table." Jefferson wrote almost 20,000 letters in his lifetime. He told John Adams that he suffered "under the persecution of letters," calculating that he received 1,267 letters in the year 1820, "many of them requiring answers of elaborate research, and all to be answered with due attention and consideration." The polygraph allowed him to keep duplicates of his letters, which he tied into bundles organized alphabetically and chronologically. Jefferson was thereby able to locate any given letter and even send for a particular one when he was away from his Monticello home.

philosophized in his study. The other was the harassed public official, who made the disturbing discovery that bookish theories worked out differently in the noisy arena of practical politics. The open-minded Virginian was therefore consistently inconsistent; it is easy to quote one Jefferson to refute the other.

The triumph of Thomas Jefferson's Democratic-Republicans and the eviction of the Federalists marked the first party overturn in American history. The vanquished naturally feared that the victors would grab all the spoils of office for themselves. But Jefferson, in keeping with his conciliatory inaugural address, showed unexpected moderation. To the dismay of his office-seeking friends, the new president dismissed few public servants for political reasons. Patronage-hungry Jeffersonians watched the Federalist appointees grow old in office and grumbled that "few die, none resign."

Jefferson quickly proved an able politician. He was especially effective in the informal atmosphere of a dinner party. There he wooed congressional representatives while personally pouring imported wines and serving the tasty dishes of his French cook. In part Jefferson had to rely on his personal charm because his party was so weak-jointed. Denied the power to dispense patronage, the Democratic-Republicans could not build a loyal

President John F. Kennedy (1917–1963) once greeted a large group of Nobel Prize winners as

❝the most extraordinary collection of talent, of human knowledge, that has ever been gathered together at the White House, with the possible exception of when Thomas Jefferson dined alone.❞

The toleration of Thomas Jefferson (1743–1826) was reflected in his inaugural address:

❝If there be any among us who would wish to dissolve this Union or to change its republican form, let them stand undisturbed as monuments of the safety with which error of opinion may be tolerated where reason is left free to combat it.❞

political following. Opposition to the Federalists was the chief glue holding them together, and as the Federalists faded, so did Democratic-Republican unity. The era of well-developed, well-disciplined political parties still lay in the future.

✴ Jeffersonian Restraint

At the outset Jefferson was determined to undo the Federalist abuses begotten by the anti-French hysteria. The hated Alien and Sedition Acts had already expired. The incoming president speedily pardoned the "martyrs" who were serving sentences under the Sedition Act, and the government remitted many fines. Shortly after the Congress met, the Jeffersonians enacted the new naturalization law of 1802. This act reduced the unreasonable requirement of fourteen years of residence to the previous and more reasonable requirement of five years.

Jefferson actually kicked away only one substantial prop of the Hamiltonian system. He hated the excise tax, which bred bureaucrats and bore heavily on his farmer following, and he early persuaded Congress to repeal it. His devotion to principle thus cost the federal government about a million dollars a year in urgently needed revenue.

Swiss-born and French-accented Albert Gallatin, "Watchdog of the Treasury," proved to be as able a secretary of the Treasury as Hamilton. Gallatin agreed with Jefferson that a national debt was a bane rather than a blessing and by strict economy succeeded in reducing it substantially while balancing the budget.

Except for excising the excise tax, the Jeffersonians left the Hamiltonian framework essentially intact. They did not tamper with the Federalist programs for funding the national debt at par and assuming the Revolutionary War debts of the states. They launched no attack on the Bank of the United States, nor did they repeal the mildly protective Federalist tariff. In later years they embraced Federalism to such a degree as to recharter a bigger bank and to boost the protective tariff to higher levels.

Paradoxically, Jefferson's moderation thus further cemented the gains of the "Revolution of 1800." By shrewdly absorbing the major Federalist programs, Jefferson showed that a change of regime need not be disastrous for the defeated group. His restraint pointed the way toward the two-party system that was later to become a characteristic feature of American politics.

✴ The "Dead Clutch" of the Judiciary

The "deathbed" **Judiciary Act of 1801** was one of the last important laws passed by the expiring Federalist Congress. It created sixteen new federal judgeships and other judicial offices. President Adams remained at his desk until nine o'clock in the evening of his last day in office, supposedly signing the commissions of the Federalist **"midnight judges."** (Actually only three commissions were signed on his last day.)

This Federalist-sponsored Judiciary Act, though a long-overdue reform, aroused bitter resentment. "Packing" these lifetime posts with anti-Jeffersonian partisans was, in Republican eyes, a brazen attempt by the ousted party to entrench itself in one of the three powerful branches of government. Jeffersonians condemned the last-minute appointees in violent language, denouncing the trickery of the Federalists as open defiance of the people's will, expressed emphatically at the polls.

The newly elected Republican Congress bestirred itself to repeal the Judiciary Act of 1801 the year after its passage. Jeffersonians thus swept sixteen benches from under the recently seated "midnight judges." Jeffersonians likewise had their knives sharpened for the scalp of Chief Justice John Marshall, whom Adams had appointed to the Supreme Court (as a fourth choice) in the dying days of his term. The strong-willed Marshall, with his rasping voice and steel-trap mind, was a cousin of Thomas Jefferson. Marshall's formal legal schooling had lasted only six weeks, but he dominated the Supreme Court with his powerful intellect and commanding personality. He shaped the American legal tradition more profoundly than any other single figure.

Marshall had served at Valley Forge during the Revolution. While suffering there from cold and hunger, he had been painfully impressed with the drawbacks of feeble central authority. The experience made him a lifelong Federalist, committed above all else to strengthening the power of the federal government. States' rights Jeffersonians condemned the crafty judge's "twistifications," but Marshall pushed ahead inflexibly on his Federalist course. He served for about thirty days under a Federalist administration and thirty-four years under the administrations of Jefferson and subsequent presidents. The Federalist party died out, but Marshall lived on, handing down Federalist decisions serenely for many more years. For over three decades, the ghost of Alexander Hamilton spoke through the lanky, black-robed judge.

One of the "midnight judges" of 1801 presented John Marshall with a historic opportunity. He was obscure William Marbury, whom President Adams had named a justice of the peace for the District of Columbia. When Marbury learned that his commission was being shelved by the new secretary of state, James Madison, he sued for its delivery. Chief Justice Marshall knew that his Jeffersonian rivals, entrenched in the executive branch, would hardly spring forward to enforce a writ to deliver the commission to his fellow Federalist Marbury. He therefore dismissed Marbury's suit, avoiding a direct political showdown. But the wily

John Marshall, Chief Justice, 1808   Depicted here as a young man, Marshall was destined to serve on the Supreme Court for thirty-four years (1801–1835) and deeply molded constitutional law. Born in a log cabin on the Virginia frontier, he attended law lectures for just a few weeks at the College of William and Mary—his only formal education. Yet Marshall would go on to prove himself a brilliant chief justice. One admiring lawyer wrote of him, "His black eyes…possess an irradiating spirit, which proclaims the imperial powers of the mind that sits enthroned therein."

In his decision in Marbury v. Madison, Chief Justice John Marshall (1755–1835) vigorously asserted his view that the Constitution embodied a "higher" law than ordinary legislation and that the Court must interpret the Constitution:

❝The Constitution is either a superior paramount law, unchangeable by ordinary means, or it is on a level with ordinary legislative acts, and like other acts, is alterable when the legislature shall please to alter it.

"If the former part of the alternative be true, then a legislative act contrary to the constitution is not law; if the latter part be true, then written constitutions are absurd attempts, on the part of the people, to limit a power in its own nature illimitable….

"It is emphatically the province and duty of the judicial department to say what the law is….

"If, then, the courts are to regard the Constitution, and the Constitution is superior to any ordinary act of the legislature, the Constitution, and not such ordinary act, must govern the case to which they are both applicable.❞

Marshall snatched a victory from the jaws of this judicial defeat. In explaining his ruling, Marshall said that the part of the Judiciary Act of 1789 on which Marbury tried to base his appeal was unconstitutional. The act had attempted to assign to the Supreme Court powers that the Constitution had not foreseen.

In this self-denying opinion, Marshall greatly magnified the authority of the Court—and slapped at the Jeffersonians. Until the case of **Marbury v. Madison** (1803), controversy had clouded the question of who had the final authority to determine the meaning of the Constitution. Jefferson in the Kentucky resolutions (1798) had tried to allot that right to the individual states. But now his cousin on the Court had cleverly promoted the contrary principle of "judicial

review"—the idea that the Supreme Court alone had the last word on the question of constitutionality. In this landmark case, Marshall inserted the keystone into the arch that supports the tremendous power of the Supreme Court in American life.*

Marshall's decision regarding Marbury spurred the Jeffersonians to seek revenge. Jefferson urged the impeachment of an arrogant and tart-tongued Supreme Court justice, Samuel Chase, who was so unpopular that Republicans named vicious dogs after him. Early in 1804 impeachment charges against Chase were voted by the House of Representatives, which then passed the question of guilt or innocence on to the Senate. The indictment by the House was based on "high crimes, and misdemeanors," as specified in the Constitution.†

Yet the evidence was plain that the intemperate judge had not been guilty of "high crimes," but only of unrestrained partisanship and a big mouth. The Senate failed to muster enough votes to convict and remove Chase. The precedent thus established was fortunate. From that day to this, no really serious attempt

---

*The next invalidation of a federal law by the Supreme Court came fifty-four years later, with the explosive *Dred Scott* decision (see "The Dred Scott Bombshell" on pp. 406–407).
†For impeachment, see Art. I, Sec. II, para.5; Art.I, Sec. III, paras.6, 7; Art. II, Sec. IV in the Appendix.

MAP 11.2 The Barbary States of North Africa and the Burning of the Frigate *Philadelphia*, 1804 The Tripolitan pirates had captured the U.S. ship *Philadelphia* (see also illustration on p. 197) and were preparing to use it against the Americans. In a daring exploit that ensured his lasting fame, twenty-four-year-old U.S. naval officer Stephen Decatur slipped into the harbor of Tripoli and burned the frigate to the waterline, denying it to the pirates. © 2016 Cengage Learning

The Burning of the Frigate Philadelphia in Tripoli Harbor by Nicolino Calyo (detail) The Mariners Museum, Newport News, Virginia

money than about republican ideals. Among his fondest hopes for America was that it might transcend the bloody wars and entangling alliances of Europe. The United States would set an example for the world, forswearing military force and winning friends through "peaceful coercion." Also, the Republicans distrusted large standing armies as standing invitations to dictatorship. Navies were less to be feared, as they could not march inland and endanger liberties. Still, the farm-loving Jeffersonians saw little point in building a fleet that might only embroil the Republic in costly and corrupting wars far from America's shores.

But harsh realities forced Jefferson's principles to bend. Pirates of the North African Barbary States (see Map 11.2) had long made a national industry of blackmailing and plundering merchant ships that ventured into the Mediterranean. Preceding Federalist administrations, in fact, had been forced to buy protection. At the time of the French crisis of 1798, when Americans were shouting, "Millions for defense but not one cent for tribute," twenty-six barrels of blackmail dollars were being shipped to piratical Algiers.

War across the Atlantic was not part of the Jeffersonian vision—but neither was paying tribute to a pack of pirate states. The showdown came in 1801. The pasha of Tripoli, dissatisfied with his share of protection money, informally declared war on the United States by cutting down the flagstaff of the American consulate. A gauntlet was thus thrown squarely into the face of Jefferson—the noninterventionist, the pacifist, the critic of a big-ship navy, and the political foe of Federalist shippers. He reluctantly rose to the challenge by dispatching the infant navy to the "shores of Tripoli," as related in the song of the U.S. Marine Corps. After four years of intermittent fighting, marked by spine-tingling exploits, Jefferson succeeded in extorting a treaty of peace from Tripoli in 1805. It was secured at the bargain price of only

has been made to reshape the Supreme Court by the impeachment weapon. Jefferson's ill-advised attempt at "judge breaking" was a reassuring victory for the independence of the judiciary and for the separation of powers among the three branches of the federal government.

✹ Jefferson, a Reluctant Warrior

One of Jefferson's first actions as president was to reduce the military establishment to a mere police force of twenty-five hundred officers and men. Critics called it penny-pinching, but Jefferson's reluctance to invest in soldiers and ships was less about

$60,000—a sum representing ransom payments for captured Americans.

Small gunboats, which the navy had used with some success in the **Tripolitan War**, fascinated Jefferson. Pledged to tax reduction, he advocated a large number of little coastal craft—"Jeffs" or the "mosquito fleet," as they were contemptuously called. He believed these fast but frail vessels would prove valuable in guarding American shores and need not embroil the Republic in diplomatic incidents on the high seas.

About two hundred tiny gunboats were constructed, democratically in small shipyards where votes could be made for Jefferson. Often mounting only one unwieldy gun, they were sometimes more of a menace to the crew than to the prospective enemy. During a hurricane and tidal wave at Savannah, Georgia, one of them was deposited eight miles inland in a cornfield, to the derisive glee of the Federalists. They drank toasts to American gunboats as the best in the world—on land.

★ The Louisiana Godsend

A secret pact, fraught with peril for America, was signed in 1800. Napoleon Bonaparte induced the king of Spain to cede to France, for attractive considerations, the immense trans-Mississippi region of Louisiana, which included the New Orleans area.

Rumors of the transfer were partially confirmed in 1802, when the Spaniards at New Orleans withdrew the right of deposit guaranteed America by Pinckney's Treaty of 1795 (see p. 195). Deposit (warehouse) privileges were vital to frontier farmers who floated their produce down the Mississippi to its mouth, there to await oceangoing vessels. A roar of anger rolled up the mighty river and into its tributary valleys. American pioneers talked wildly of descending upon New Orleans, rifles in hand. Had they done so, the nation probably would have been engulfed in war with both Spain and France.

Thomas Jefferson, both pacifist and anti-entanglement, was again on the griddle. Louisiana in the senile grip of Spain posed no real threat; America could seize the territory when the time was ripe. But Louisiana in the iron fist of Napoleon, the preeminent military genius of his age, foreshadowed a dark and blood-drenched future. The United States would probably have to fight to dislodge him; and because it alone was not strong enough to defeat his armies, it would have to seek allies, contrary to the deepening anti-alliance policy.

Hoping to quiet the clamor of the West, Jefferson moved decisively. Early in 1803 he sent James Monroe to Paris to join forces with the regular minister there, Robert R. Livingston. The two envoys were instructed to buy New Orleans and as much land to its east as they could get for a maximum of $10 million. If these proposals should fail and the situation became critical, negotiations were to be opened with Britain for an alliance. "The day that France takes possession of New Orleans," Jefferson wrote, "we must marry ourselves to the British fleet and nation." That remark dramatically demonstrated Jefferson's dilemma. Though a passionate hater of war and an enemy of entangling alliances, he was proposing to make an alliance with his old foe, Britain, against his old friend, France, in order to secure New Orleans.

At this critical juncture, Napoleon suddenly decided to sell all of Louisiana and abandon his dream of a New World empire. Two developments prompted his change of mind. First, he had failed in his efforts to reconquer the sugar-rich island of Santo Domingo (Haiti), for which Louisiana was to serve as a source of foodstuffs. Rebellious enslaved Africans, inspired by the French Revolution's promises of equality, and ably led by the gifted Toussaint L'Ouverture ("The Opener"), had struck for their freedom in 1791. Their revolt was ultimately broken. But then the island's second line of defense—mosquitoes carrying yellow fever—had swept away thousands of crack French troops. After the **Haitian Revolution**, Santo Domingo could not be had, except perhaps at a staggering cost; hence, there was no need for Louisiana's food supplies. "Damn sugar, damn coffee, damn colonies!" burst out Napoleon. Second, Bonaparte was about to end the twenty-month lull in his deadly conflict with Britain. Because the British controlled the seas, he feared that he might be forced to make them a gift of Louisiana. Rather than drive America into the arms of Britain by attempting to hold the area, he decided to sell the huge wilderness to the Americans and pocket the money for his schemes nearer home. Napoleon hoped that the United States, strengthened by Louisiana, would one day be a military and naval power that would thwart the ambitions of the lordly British in the New World. The predicaments of France in Europe were again paving the way for America's diplomatic successes.

Events now unrolled dizzily. The American minister, Robert Livingston, pending the arrival of Monroe, was busily negotiating in Paris for a window on the Gulf of Mexico at New Orleans. Suddenly, out of a clear sky, the French foreign minister asked him how much he would give for all of Louisiana. Scarcely able to believe his ears (he was partially deaf anyhow), Livingston nervously entered upon the negotiations. After about a week of haggling, while the fate of North America trembled in the balance, treaties were signed on April 30, 1803, ceding Louisiana to the United States for about $15 million.

When news of the bargain reached America, Jefferson was startled. He had authorized his envoys to

The Granger Collection, NYC

Toussaint L'Ouverture (ca. 1743–1803) A self-educated ex-slave and military genius, L'Ouverture was finally betrayed by the French, who imprisoned him in a chilly dungeon in France, where he coughed his life away. Indirectly, he did much to set up the sale of Louisiana to the United States. His slave rebellion in Haiti also (briefly) established the first black government in the New World, striking fear into the hearts of slaveowners throughout the Western Hemisphere.

In accepting the Louisiana Purchase, Jefferson thus compromised with conscience in a private letter:

❝It is the case of a guardian, investing the money of his ward in purchasing an important adjacent territory; and saying to him when of age, I did this for your good; I pretend to no right to bind you; you may disavow me, and I must get out of the scrape as I can; I thought it my duty to risk myself for you.**❞**

was no such clause. Yet Jefferson also perceived that the vast domain now within his reach could form a sprawling "empire of liberty" that would ensure the health and long life of America's experiment in democracy.

Conscience-stricken, Jefferson privately proposed that a constitutional amendment be passed. But his friends pointed out in alarm that in the interval Napoleon, for whom thought was action, might suddenly withdraw the offer. So Jefferson shamefacedly submitted the treaties to the Senate, while admitting to his associates that the purchase was unconstitutional.

The senators were less finicky than Jefferson. Reflecting enthusiastic public support, they registered their prompt approval of the transaction. Land-hungry Americans were not disposed to split constitutional hairs when confronted with perhaps the most magnificent real estate bargain in history—828,000 square miles at about three cents an acre.

✦ Louisiana in the Long View

Jefferson's bargain with Napoleon was epochal. Overnight he had avoided a possible rupture with France and the consequent entangling alliance with England. With the **Louisiana Purchase**, America secured at one bloodless stroke the western half of the richest river valley in the world and further laid the foundations of a future major power. The ideal of a great agrarian republic, as envisioned by Jefferson, could now be realized in the vast "Valley of Democracy." At the same time, the transfer established valuable precedents for future expansion: the acquisition of foreign territory and peoples by purchase and their incorporation into the Union not as vassal states but on a basis of equal membership. This was imperialism with a new and democratic face, as French Louisianans learned when the Washington government agreed to accept their legal code based on French civil law, rather than English common law. To this day Louisiana state law,

offer not more than $10 million for New Orleans and as much to the east in the Floridas as they could get. Instead they had signed three treaties that pledged $15 million for New Orleans, plus an immeasurable tract entirely to the west—an area that would more than double the size of the United States. They had bought a wilderness to get a city.

Once again the two Jeffersons wrestled with each other: the theorist and former strict constructionist versus the democratic visionary. Where in his beloved Constitution was the president authorized to negotiate treaties incorporating a huge new expanse into the Union—an expanse containing tens of thousands of Indian, French, Spanish, and black inhabitants? There uniquely in the American system, retains vestiges of its French origins.

Indian peoples within the purchase area would not prove so fortunate. In subsequent decades, they would be forcibly removed from their ancestral homes on the basis of questionably valid treaties, in order to open lands for the cotton boom—and for the expansion of slavery.

The purchase also contributed to making operational the isolationist principles of Washington's Farewell Address. Avoiding entangling alliances had been only an ideal to be pursued, rather than a realistic policy, so long as America had potentially hostile and powerful neighbors. By removing virtually the last remnant of significant European power from the North American continent, the United States was now at liberty to disengage almost entirely from the ancient system of Old World rivalries.

The enormous extent of the new area was more fully unveiled by a series of explorations under Jefferson's direction. In the spring of 1804, Jefferson sent his personal secretary, Meriwether Lewis, and a young army officer named William Clark to explore the northern part of the Louisiana Purchase. Lewis and Clark's **Corps of Discovery** ascended the "Great Muddy" (Missouri River) from St. Louis and spent the winter of 1804–1805 with the Mandan Indians in present-day North Dakota. Then, aided by the Shoshone woman Sacajawea, the thirty-three adventurers (one had died from illness in Iowa, the group's only casualty) struggled across the northern prairies and through the Rockies, finally descending the Columbia River to the Pacific coast.

Lewis and Clark's two-and-one-half-year expedition yielded a rich harvest of scientific observations, maps, knowledge of the Indians in the region, and hair-raising wilderness adventure stories. On the Great Plains, they marveled at the "immense herds of buffalo, elk, deer, and antelope feeding in one common and boundless pasture." Lewis was lucky to come back alive. When he and three other men left the expedition to explore the Marias River in present-day western Montana, a band of teenage Blackfoot Indians, armed with crude muskets by British fur-traders operating out of Canada, stole their horses. Lewis foolishly pursued the horse thieves on foot. He shot one marauder through the belly, but the Indian returned the fire. "Being bareheaded," Lewis later wrote, "I felt the wind of his bullet very distinctly." After killing another Blackfoot and hanging one of the expedition's "peace and friendship" medals around the dead man's neck as a warning to other Indians, Lewis and his terrified companions beat it out of the Marias country to rejoin the main party on the Missouri River.

Meriwether Lewis   Lewis is portrayed in this painting as he looked on his return from the great expedition through the Louisiana Purchase and the West.

The explorers also demonstrated the viability of an overland trail to the Pacific. Down the dusty track thousands of missionaries, fur-traders, and pioneering settlers would wend their way in the ensuing decades, bolstering America's claim to the Oregon Country. Other explorers also pushed into the uncharted West. Zebulon M. Pike trekked to the headwaters of the Mississippi River in 1805–1806. The next year Pike ventured into the southern portion of Louisiana Territory, where he sighted the Colorado peak that bears his name.

✵ The Aaron Burr Conspiracies

In the long run, the Louisiana Purchase greatly expanded the fortunes of the United States and the power of the federal government. In the short term, the vast expanse of territory and the feeble reach of

Chinook Indians, ca. 1805 William Clark served as the artist and cartographer of the Lewis and Clark expedition. Here he sketched the skull-molding practice that inspired Lewis and Clark to call these Indians "Flatheads." These people were distinct from the present-day Flathead Indians of Montana, who got their name from the French.

Gifts from the Great White Chief Among the objectives of the Lewis and Clark expedition was to establish good relations with the Indians in the newly acquired Louisiana Purchase. The American explorers presented all chiefs with copies of these medals, showing President Jefferson on one side and the hands of an Indian and a white man clasped in "peace and friendship" under a crossed "peace pipe" and hatchet on the other. All chiefs also received an American flag and a military uniform jacket, hat, and feather. Courtesy, The American Numismatic Society

the government obliged to control it raised fears of secession and foreign intrigue (see Map 11.3).

Aaron Burr, Jefferson's first-term vice president, played no small part in provoking—and justifying—such fears. Dropped from the cabinet in Jefferson's second term, Burr joined with a group of Federalist extremists to plot the secession of New England and New York. Alexander Hamilton, though no friend of Jefferson, exposed and foiled the conspiracy. Incensed, Burr challenged Hamilton to a duel. Hamilton deplored the practice of dueling, by that date illegal in several states, but felt his honor was at stake. He met Burr's challenge at the appointed hour but refused to fire. Burr killed Hamilton with one shot. Burr's pistol blew the brightest brain out of the Federalist party and destroyed its one remaining hope of effective leadership.

His political career as dead as Hamilton's, Burr turned his disunionist plottings to the trans-Mississippi West. There he struck up an allegiance with General James Wilkinson, the unscrupulous military governor of Louisiana Territory and a sometime secret agent in the pay of the Spanish crown. Burr's schemes are still shrouded in mystery, but he and Wilkinson apparently planned to separate the western part of the United States from the East and expand their new confederacy with invasions of Spanish-controlled Mexico and Florida. In the fall of 1806, Burr and sixty followers floated in flatboats down the Mississippi River to meet Wilkinson's army at Natchez. But when the general learned that Jefferson had gotten wind of the plot, he betrayed Burr and fled to New Orleans.

Burr was arrested and tried for treason. In what seemed to the Jeffersonians to be bias in favor of the accused, Chief Justice John Marshall, strictly hewing to the Constitution, insisted that a guilty verdict required proof of overt acts of treason, not merely treasonous intentions (see Art. III, Sec. III). Burr was acquitted and fled to Europe, where he urged Napoleon to make peace with Britain and launch a joint invasion of America. Burr's insurrectionary brashness demonstrated that it was one thing for the United States to purchase large expanses of western territory but quite another for it to govern them effectively.

MAP 11.3 Exploring the Louisiana Purchase and the West Seeking to avert friction with France by purchasing all of Louisiana, Jefferson bought trouble because of the vagueness of the boundaries. Among the disputants were Spain in the Floridas, Spain and Mexico in the Southwest, and Great Britain in Canada. © 2016 Cengage Learning

✴ A Precarious Neutrality

Jefferson was triumphantly reelected in 1804, with 162 electoral votes to only 14 votes for his Federalist opponent. But the laurels of Jefferson's first administration soon withered under the blasts of the new storm that broke in Europe. After unloading Louisiana in 1803, Napoleon deliberately provoked a renewal of his war with Britain—an awesome conflict that raged on for eleven long years.

For the first two years of war a maritime United States—the number one neutral carrier since 1793—enjoyed juicy commercial pickings. But a setback came in 1805. At the Battle of Trafalgar, one-eyed Horatio Lord Nelson achieved immortality by smashing the combined French and Spanish fleets off the coast of Spain, thereby ensuring Britain's supremacy on the seas. At the Battle of Austerlitz in Austria—the Battle of the Three Emperors—Napoleon crushed the combined Austrian and Russian armies, thereby ensuring his mastery of the land. Like the tiger and the shark, France and Britain now reigned supreme in their chosen elements.

Unable to hurt each other directly, the two antagonists were forced to strike indirect blows. Britain ruled the waves and waived the rules. The London government, beginning in 1806, issued a series of **Orders in Council**. These edicts closed the European ports under French control to foreign shipping, including American, unless the vessels first stopped at a British port. Napoleon struck back, ordering the seizure of all merchant ships, including American, that entered British ports. There was no way to trade with either nation without facing the other's guns. American vessels were, quite literally, caught between the Devil and the deep blue sea.

Even more galling to American pride than the seizure of wooden ships was the seizure of flesh-and-blood American seamen. **Impressment**—the forcible enlistment of sailors—was a crude form of conscription that the British, among others, had employed for over four centuries. Clubs and stretchers (for men knocked unconscious) were standard equipment of press gangs from His Majesty's man-hungry ships. Some six thousand bona fide U.S. citizens were impressed by the "piratical man-stealers" of Britain from 1808 to 1811 alone. A number of these luckless souls died or were killed in His Majesty's service, leaving their kinfolk and friends bereaved and embittered.

Britain's determination was spectacularly highlighted in 1807, in what came to be known as the

The Prairie Dog Sickened at the Sting of the Hornet, 1806 In this anti-Jefferson satire criticizing his negotiations for the purchase of West Florida in 1804, Napoleon, in the form of a hornet, stings Jefferson and makes him "cough up" $2 million in gold coins—the amount of the secret appropriation that Jefferson sought from Congress. The negotiations eventually failed.

Chesapeake **affair**. A royal frigate overhauled a U.S. frigate, the *Chesapeake*, about ten miles off the coast of Virginia. The British captain bluntly demanded the surrender of four alleged deserters. London had never claimed the right to seize sailors from a foreign warship, and the American commander, though totally unprepared to fight, refused the request. The British warship thereupon fired three devastating broadsides at close range, killing three Americans and wounding eighteen. Four deserters were dragged away, and the bloody hulk called the *Chesapeake* limped back to port.

Britain was clearly in the wrong, as the London Foreign Office admitted. But London's contrition availed little; a roar of national wrath went up from infuriated Americans. Jefferson, the peace lover, could easily have had war if he had wanted it.

✦ The Hated Embargo

National honor would not permit a slavish submission to British and French mistreatment. Yet a large-scale foreign war was contrary to the settled policy of the new Republic—and in addition it would be futile. The navy was weak, thanks largely to Jefferson's

antinavalism, and the army was even weaker. A disastrous defeat would not improve America's plight.

The warring nations in Europe depended heavily upon the United States for raw materials and foodstuffs. In his eager search for an alternative to war, Jefferson seized upon this essential fact. He reasoned that if America voluntarily cut off its exports, the offending powers would be forced to bow, hat in hand, and agree to respect its rights.

Responding to the presidential lash, Congress hastily passed the **Embargo Act** late in 1807. This rigorous law forbade the export of all goods from the United States, whether in American or foreign ships. More than just a compromise between submission and shooting, the embargo embodied Jefferson's idea of "peaceful coercion." If it worked, the embargo would vindicate the rights of neutral nations and point to a new way of conducting foreign affairs. If it failed, Jefferson feared the Republic would perish, subjugated to the European powers or sucked into their ferocious war.

The American economy staggered under the effect of the embargo long before Britain or France began to bend. Forests of dead masts gradually filled New England's once-bustling harbors; docks that had once rumbled were deserted (except for illegal trade); and soup kitchens cared for some of the hungry unemployed.

Launching of the Ship *Fame*, by George Ropes, Jr., 1802   Jefferson's embargo throttled thriving New England shipyards like this one, stirring bitter resentment.

Jeffersonian Republicans probably hurt the commerce of New England, which they avowedly were trying to protect, far more than Britain and France together were doing. Farmers of the South and West, the strongholds of Jefferson, suffered no less disastrously than New England. They were alarmed by the mounting piles of unexportable cotton, grain, and tobacco. Jefferson seemed to be waging war on his fellow citizens rather than on the offending foreign powers.

An enormous illicit trade mushroomed in 1808, especially along the Canadian border, where bands of armed Americans on loaded rafts overawed or overpowered federal agents. Irate citizens cynically transposed the letters of "Embargo" to read "O Grab Me," "Go Bar 'Em," and "Mobrage," while heartily cursing the "Dambargo."

Jefferson nonetheless induced Congress to pass iron-toothed enforcing legislation. It was so inquisitorial and tyrannical as to cause some Americans to think more kindly of George III, whom Jefferson had berated in the Declaration of Independence. One indignant New Hampshirite denounced the president with this ditty:

> *Our ships all in motion,*
> *Once whiten'd the ocean; They sail'd and return'd*
> *with a Cargo;*
> *Now doom'd to decay*
> *They are fallen a prey, To Jefferson, worms, and*
> *EMBARGO.*

The embargo even had the effect of reviving the moribund Federalist party. Gaining new converts, its leaders hurled their nullification of the embargo into the teeth of the "Virginia lordlings" in Washington. In 1804 the discredited Federalists had polled only 14 electoral

Contending Voices
The Divisive Embargo

The Embargo Act of 1807 provoked bitter divisions— divisions that foreshadowed the sectional conflict that would one day erupt into civil war. A Federalist circular in Massachusetts against the embargo cried out:

❝Let every man who holds the name of America dear to him, stretch forth his hands and put this accursed thing, this Embargo from him. Be resolute, act like sons of liberty, of God, and your country; nerve your arm with vengeance against the Despot [Jefferson] who would wrest the inestimable germ of your Independence from you—and you shall be *Conquerors!!!*❞

Virginia Senator W.B. Giles (1762–1830) offered this defense of Jefferson's embargo:

❝The first effect of the embargo upon the aggressing belligerents was to lessen their inducements to war, by keeping out of their way the rich spoils of our commerce, which had invited their cupidity, and which was saved by those laws.... The second effect which the embargo laws have had on the aggressing belligerents is to enhance the prices of all American produce.❞

Why might Massachusetts and Virginia have had different perspectives on the embargo?

votes out of 176; in 1808, the embargo year, the figure rose to 47 out of 175. New England seethed with talk of secession, and Jefferson later admitted that he felt the foundations of government tremble under his feet.

An alarmed Congress, yielding to the storm of public anger, finally repealed the embargo on March 1, 1809, three days before Jefferson's retirement. A half-loaf substitute was provided by the **Non-Intercourse Act**. This measure formally reopened trade with all the nations of the world, except the two most important, Britain and France. Though thus watered down, economic coercion continued to be the policy of the Jeffersonians from 1809 to 1812, when the nation finally plunged into war.

Why did the embargo, Jefferson's most daring act of statesmanship, collapse after fifteen dismal months? First of all, he underestimated the bulldog determination of the British, as others have, and overestimated the dependence of both belligerents on America's trade. Bumper grain crops blessed the British Isles during these years, and the revolutionary Latin American republics unexpectedly threw open their ports for compensating commerce. With most of Europe under his control, Napoleon could afford to tighten his belt and go without American trade. The French continued to seize American ships and steal their cargoes, while their emperor mocked the United States by claiming that he was simply helping them enforce the embargo.

More critically, perhaps, Jefferson miscalculated the unpopularity of such a self-crucifying weapon and the difficulty of enforcing it. The hated embargo was not continued long enough or tightly enough to achieve the desired results—and a leaky embargo was perhaps more costly than none at all.

Curiously enough, New England plucked a new prosperity from the ugly jaws of the embargo. With shipping tied up and imported goods scarce, the resourceful Yankees reopened old factories and erected new ones. The real foundations of modern America's industrial might were laid behind the protective wall of the embargo, followed by nonintercourse and the War of 1812. Jefferson, the avowed critic of factories, may have unwittingly done more for American manufacturing than Alexander Hamilton, industry's outspoken friend.

✵ Madison's Gamble

Following Washington's precedent, Jefferson left the presidency after two terms, happy to escape what he called the "splendid misery" of the highest office in the land. He strongly favored the nomination and election of a kindred spirit as his successor—his friend and fellow Virginian, the quiet, intellectual, and unassuming James Madison.

Madison took the presidential oath on March 4, 1809, as the awesome conflict in Europe was roaring to its climax. The scholarly Madison was small of stature, light of weight, bald of head, and weak of voice. Despite a distinguished career as a legislator, he was crippled as president by factions within his party and his cabinet. Unable to dominate Congress as Jefferson had done, Madison often found himself holding the bag for risky foreign policies not of his own making.

The Non-Intercourse Act of 1809—a watered-down version of Jefferson's embargo aimed solely at Britain and France—was due to expire in 1810. To Madison's dismay, Congress dismantled the embargo completely with a bargaining measure known as **Macon's Bill No. 2**. While reopening American trade with all the world, Macon's Bill dangled what Congress hoped was an attractive lure. If either Britain or France repealed its commercial restrictions, America would restore its embargo against the non-repealing nation. To Madison the bill was a shameful capitulation. It practically admitted that the United States could not survive without one of the belligerents as a commercial ally, but it left determination of who that ally would be to the potentates of London and Paris.

The crafty Napoleon saw his chance. Since 1806 Britain had justified its Orders in Council as retaliation for Napoleon's actions—implying, without promising outright, that trade restrictions would be lifted if the French decrees disappeared. Now the French held out the same half-promise. In August 1810 word came from Napoleon's foreign minister that the French decrees might be repealed if Britain also lifted its Orders in Council. The minister's message was deliberately

Rivals for the presidency, and for the soul of the young Republic, Thomas Jefferson and John Adams died on the same day—the Fourth of July, 1826—fifty years to the day after both men had signed the Declaration of Independence. Adams's last words were

❝Thomas Jefferson still survives.**❞**

But he was wrong, for three hours earlier, Jefferson had drawn his last breath.

Insisted the editor of Niles' Weekly Register *(June 27, 1812),*

❝The injuries received from France do not lessen the enormity of those heaped upon us by *England*....In this 'straight betwixt two' we had an unquestionable right to select our enemy. We have given the preference to *Great Britain*...on account of her more flagrant wrongs.**❞**

The Plumb-pudding in danger :— or State Epicures taking un Petit Souper.
"— the great Globe itself, and all which it inherit," is too small to satisfy such insatiable appetites

Britain and France Divide Up the World, 1805 The great-power rivalry symbolized here by British prime minister William Pitt and French emperor Napoleon wreathed the planet in years of warfare. When it ended with Napoleon's final defeat in 1815, Britain was the unchallenged mistress of the world's oceans.

ambiguous. Napoleon had no intention of permitting unrestricted trade between America and Britain. Rather, he hoped to maneuver the United States into resuming its embargo against the British, thus creating a partial blockade against his enemy that he would not have to raise a finger to enforce.

Madison knew better than to trust Napoleon, but he gambled that the threat of seeing the United States trade exclusively with France would lead the British to repeal their restrictions—and vice versa. Closing his eyes to the emperor's obvious subterfuge, he accepted the French offer as evidence of repeal. The terms of Macon's Bill gave the British three months to live up to their implied promise by revoking the Orders in Council and reopening the Atlantic to neutral trade.

They did not. In firm control of the seas, London saw little need to bargain. As long as the war with Napoleon went on, they decided, America could trade exclusively with the British Empire—or with nobody at all. Madison's gamble failed. The president saw no choice but to reestablish the embargo against Britain alone—a decision that he knew meant the end of American neutrality and that he feared was the final step toward war.

✦ Tecumseh and the Prophet

Not all of Madison's party was reluctant to fight. The complexion of the Twelfth Congress, which met late in 1811, differed markedly from that of its predecessor. Recent elections had swept away many of the older "submission men" and replaced them with young hotheads, many from the South and West. Dubbed **war hawks** by their Federalist opponents, the newcomers were indeed on fire for a new war with the old enemy. The war hawks were weary of hearing how their fathers had "whipped" the British single-handedly, and they detested the manhandling of American sailors and the British Orders in Council that dammed the flow of American trade, especially western farm products headed for Europe.

Western war hawks also yearned to wipe out a renewed Indian threat to the pioneer settlers who were streaming into the trans-Allegheny wilderness. As this white flood washed through the green forests, more and more Indians were pushed toward the setting sun.

Two remarkable Shawnee brothers, Tecumseh and Tenskwatawa, known to non-Indians as "the Prophet," concluded that the time had come to stem this

The Battle of the Thames, 1813   Here the Shawnee leader Tecumseh stood his ground against the superior American force and died. A gifted organizer and military chieftain, he had denounced the tribal custom of torturing prisoners and opposed the practice of allowing any one tribe to sell land that, he believed, belonged to all Indians.

onrushing tide. They began to weld together a far-flung confederacy of all the tribes east of the Mississippi, inspiring a vibrant movement of Indian unity and cultural renewal. Their followers gave up textile clothing for traditional buckskin garments. Their warriors forswore alcohol, the better to fight a last-ditch battle with the "paleface" invaders. Rejecting whites' concept of "ownership," Tecumseh urged his supporters never to cede land to whites unless all Indians agreed.

Meanwhile, frontiersmen and their war-hawk spokesmen in Congress became convinced that British "scalp buyers" in Canada were nourishing the Indians' growing strength. In the fall of 1811, William Henry Harrison, governor of Indiana Territory, gathered an army and advanced on Tecumseh's headquarters at the junction of the Wabash and Tippecanoe Rivers in present-day Indiana. Tecumseh was absent, recruiting supporters in the South, but the Prophet attacked Harrison's army—foolishly, in Tecumseh's eyes—with a small force of Shawnees. The Shawnees were routed and their settlement burned.

The **Battle of Tippecanoe** made Harrison a national hero. It also discredited the Prophet and drove Tecumseh into an alliance with the British. When America's war with Britain came, Tecumseh fought fiercely for the redcoats until his death in 1813 at the Battle of the Thames. With him perished the dream of an Indian confederacy.

★ Mr. Madison's War

By the spring of 1812, Madison believed war with Britain to be inevitable. The British arming of hostile Indians pushed him toward this decision, as did the

---

When the war hawks won control of the House of Representatives, they elevated to the Speakership thirty-four-year-old Henry Clay of Kentucky (1777–1852), the eloquent and magnetic "Harry of the West." Clamoring for war, he thundered,

❝ I prefer the troubled sea of war, demanded by the honor and independence of this country, with all its calamities and desolation, to the tranquil and putrescent pool of ignominious peace. **❞**

In a speech at Vincennes, Indiana Territory, Tecumseh (1768?–1813) said,

❝ Sell a country! Why not sell the air, the clouds, and the great sea, as well as the earth? Did not the Great Spirit make them all for the use of his children? **❞**

William Henry Harrison (1773–1841), Indian fighter and later president, called Tecumseh

❝one of those uncommon geniuses who spring up occasionally to produce revolutions and overturn the established order of things. If it were not for the vicinity of the United States, he would perhaps be founder of an Empire that would rival in glory that of Mexico or Peru.**❞**

whoops of the war hawks in his own party. People like Representative Felix Grundy of Tennessee, three of whose brothers had been killed in clashes with Indians, cried that there was only one way to remove the menace of the Indians: wipe out their Canadian base. "On to Canada, on to Canada" was the war hawks' chant. Southern expansionists, less vocal, cast a covetous eye on Florida, then weakly held by Britain's ally Spain.

Above all, Madison turned to war to restore confidence in the republican experiment. For five years the Republicans had tried to steer between the warring European powers, to set a course between submission and battle. Theirs had been a noble vision, but it had brought them only international derision and internal strife. Madison and the Republicans came to believe that only a vigorous assertion of American rights could demonstrate the viability of American nationhood—and of democracy as a form of government. If America could not fight to protect itself, its experiment in republicanism would be discredited in the eyes of a scoffing world. One prominent Republican called the war a test "to determine whether the republican system adopted by the people is imbecile and transient, or whether it has force and duration worthy of the enterprise." Thus, not for the last time, did war fever and democratic idealism make common cause.

Madison asked Congress to declare war on June 1, 1812. Congress obliged him two weeks later—the first of just five times in all of American history that Congress has formally exercised its constitutional power to declare war (see Art. I, Sec. VIII, para.11). The vote in the House was 79 to 49 for war, in the Senate 19 to 13. The close tally revealed deep divisions over the wisdom of fighting. The split was both sectional and partisan. Support for war came from the South and West, but also from Republicans in populous middle states such as Pennsylvania and Virginia. Federalists in both North and South damned the conflict, but their stronghold was New England, which greeted the declaration of war with muffled bells, flags at half-mast, and public fasting.

Why should seafaring New England oppose the war for a free sea? The answer is that pro-British Federalists in the Northeast sympathized with Britain and resented the Republicans' sympathy with Napoleon, whom they regarded as the "Corsican butcher" and the "anti-Christ of the age." The Federalists also opposed the acquisition of Canada, which would merely add more agrarian states from the wild Northwest. This, in turn, would increase the voting strength of the Jeffersonian Republicans.

The Present State of Our Country Partisan disunity over the War of 1812 threatened the nation's very existence. The prowar Jeffersonian at the left is attacking the pillar of federalism; the antiwar Federalist at the right is trying to pull down democracy. The spirit of Washington warns that the country's welfare depends on all three pillars, including republicanism.

The bitterness of New England Federalists against "Mr. Madison's War" led them to treason or near-treason. They were determined, wrote one Republican versifier,

> To rule the nation if they could,
> But see it damned if others should.

New England gold holders probably lent more dollars to the British Exchequer than to the federal Treasury. Federalist farmers sent huge quantities of supplies and foodstuffs to Canada, enabling British armies to invade New York. New England governors stubbornly refused to permit their militias to serve outside their own states. In a sense America had to fight two enemies simultaneously: old England and New England.

Thus perilously divided, the barely United States plunged into armed conflict against Britain, then the world's most powerful empire. No sober American could have much reasonable hope of victory, but by 1812 the Jeffersonian Republicans saw no other choice.

Chapter Review

KEY TERMS

Revolution of 1800 (206)

Judiciary Act of 1801 (210)

midnight judges (210)

Marbury v. *Madison* (211)

Tripolitan War (213)

Haitian Revolution (213)

Louisiana Purchase (214)

Corps of Discovery (215)

Orders in Council (217)

Impressment (217)

Chesapeake affair (218)

Embargo Act (218)

Non-Intercourse Act (220)

Macon's Bill No. 2 (220)

war hawks (221)

Tippecanoe, Battle of (222)

PEOPLE TO KNOW

Thomas Jefferson

Sally Hemings

Albert Gallatin

John Marshall

Samuel Chase

Napoleon Bonaparte

Robert R. Livingston

Toussaint L'Ouverture

Meriwether Lewis

William Clark

Sacajawea

Aaron Burr

James Wilkinson

James Madison

Tecumseh

Tenskwatawa ("the Prophet")

CHRONOLOGY

1791	Toussaint L'Ouverture launches Haitian Revolution
1800	Jefferson defeats Adams for presidency
1801	Judiciary Act of 1801
1801–1805	Naval war with Tripoli
1802	Revised naturalization law Judiciary Act of 1801 repealed
1803	*Marbury v. Madison* Louisiana Purchase
1804	Haiti emerges as first independent black republic Jefferson reelected president Impeachment of Justice Chase
1804–1806	Lewis and Clark expedition

1805	Peace treaty with Tripoli Battle of Trafalgar Battle of Austerlitz
1805–1807	Pike's explorations
1806	Burr treason trial
1807	*Chesapeake* affair Embargo Act
1808	Madison elected president
1809	Non-Intercourse Act replaces Embargo Act
1810	Macon's Bill No. 2 Napoleon announces (falsely) repeal of blockade decrees Madison reestablishes nonimportation against Britain
1811	Battle of Tippecanoe
1812	United States declares war on Britain

TO LEARN MORE

Catherine Allgor, *Parlor Politics* (2000)

Stephen E. Ambrose, *Undaunted Courage* (1996)

Joseph Ellis, *American Sphinx: The Character of Thomas Jefferson* (1997)

John Ferling, *Adams vs. Jefferson: The Tumultuous Election of 1800* (2004)

Thomas Fleming, *The Louisiana Purchase* (2003)

Donald R. Hickey, *Don't Give Up the Ship! Myths of the War of 1812* (2006)

Peter P. Hill, *Napoleon's Troublesome Americans: Franco-American Relations, 1804–1815* (2005)

Donald Jackson, *Thomas Jefferson and the Stony Mountain: Exploring the West from Monticello* (1981)

Jon Kukla, *A Wilderness So Immense* (2003)

Marshall Smelser, *The Democratic Republic, 1801–1815* (1968)

Anthony Wallace, *Jefferson and the Indians* (1999)

Gary Wills, *Negro President: Thomas Jefferson and the Slave Power* (2003)

A complete, annotated bibliography for this chapter—along with brief descriptions of the People to Know—may be found on the *American Pageant* website. The key terms are defined in the glossary at the end of the text.

Chapter 12

The Second War for Independence and the Upsurge of Nationalism

1812–1824

The American continents … are henceforth not to be considered as subjects for future colonization by any European powers.

PRESIDENT JAMES MONROE, DECEMBER 2, 1823

*T*he *War of 1812* was an especially divisive and ill-fought war. There was no burning national anger, as there had been in 1807 following the *Chesapeake* outrage. The supreme lesson of the conflict was the folly of leading a divided and apathetic people into war. And yet, despite the unimpressive military outcome and even less decisive negotiated peace, Americans came out of the war with a renewed sense of nationhood. For the next dozen years, an awakened spirit of nationalism would inspire activities ranging from protecting manufacturing to building roads to defending the authority of the federal government over the states.

✴ On to Canada over Land and Lakes

On the eve of the **War of 1812**, the regular army was ill-trained, ill-disciplined, and widely scattered. It had to be supplemented by the even more poorly trained militias, which were sometimes distinguished by their speed of foot in leaving the battlefield. Some of the ranking generals were semi-senile heirlooms from the Revolutionary War, rusting on their laurels and lacking in vigor and vision.

Canada became an important battleground in the War of 1812 because British forces were weakest there (see Map 12.1). A successful American offensive might have quashed British influence among the Indians and garnered new land for settlers. But the Americans' offensive strategy was poorly conceived. Had the Americans captured Montreal, the center of population and transportation, everything to the west might have died, just as the leaves of a tree wither when the trunk is girdled. But instead of laying ax to the trunk, the Americans frittered away their strength in the three-pronged invasion of 1812. The trio of invading forces that set out from Detroit, Niagara, and Lake Champlain were all beaten back shortly after they had crossed the Canadian border.

By contrast, the British and Canadians displayed energy from the outset. Early in the war, they captured the American fort of Michilimackinac, which commanded the upper Great Lakes and the Indian-inhabited area to the south and west. Their brilliant defensive operations were led by the inspired British general Isaac Brock and assisted (in the American camp) by "General Mud" and "General Confusion."

When several American land invasions of Canada were again hurled back in 1813, Americans looked for success on the water. Man for man and ship for ship, the American navy did much better than the army. In comparison to British ships, American craft on the

MAP 12.1 Battles in the War of 1812 © 2016 Cengage Learning

Map legend:
- American advances, 1812
- American advances, 1813
- American advances, 1814
- British advances, 1814
- American victory
- British victory
- Fort
- Annexed from Spain, 1812

Map labels: L. Superior; BRITISH NORTH AMERICA (CANADA); Sorel; Montréal; MAINE (MASS.); INDIANA TERR.; Michilimackinac July 17, 1812; Dearborn approaches Montreal but then retreats, Nov. 1812.; Plattsburgh; VT.; Lake Huron; L. Ontario; N.H.; Tecumseh killed in battle; pan-Indian alliance collapses.; Thames River Oct. 5, 1813; Fort Niagara; NEW YORK; MASS.; Lake Michigan; MICHIGAN TERR.; L. Erie; Perry 1813; CONN.; R.I.; Detroit Aug. 16, 1812; Put-in-Bay Sept. 10, 1813; Fort Meigs; PENNSYLVANIA; Baltimore Sept. 13, 1814; N.J.; The American capital falls to a British amphibious force. The government escapes, but the British occupation force plunders and then burns Washington, D.C.; Illinois R.; Wabash R.; Harrison 1813; OHIO; Ohio R.; Washington, D.C. Aug. 24–25, 1814; DELAWARE; MARYLAND; Ross 1814; Missouri R.; ILLINOIS TERR.; INDIANA TERR.; VIRGINIA; UNORGANIZED TERRITORY; KENTUCKY; NORTH CAROLINA; Arkansas R.; Mississippi R.; TENNESSEE; Tennessee R.; Andrew Jackson's combined Cherokee Indian and Tennessee militia massacre the Red Stick Creeks at Horseshoe Bend, March 27, 1814.; British naval blockade 1814–1815; Red R.; SOUTH CAROLINA; ATLANTIC OCEAN; MISSISSIPPI TERRITORY; Fort Jackson; GEORGIA; LOUISIANA; New Orleans Jan. 8, 1815; Mobile; Pensacola; SPANISH FLORIDA; Gulf of Mexico; 0 150 300 Km.; 0 150 300 Mi.

whole were more skillfully handled, had better gunners, and were manned by non-press-gang crews who were burning to avenge numerous indignities. Similarly, the American frigates, notably the *Constitution* ("Old Ironsides"), had thicker sides, heavier firepower, and larger crews, of which one sailor in six was a free black.

Control of the Great Lakes was vital, and an energetic American naval officer, Oliver Hazard Perry, managed to build a fleet of green-timbered ships on the shores of Lake Erie, manned by even greener seamen. When he captured a British fleet in a furious engagement on the lake, he reported to his superior, "We have met the enemy and they are ours." Perry's victory and his slogan infused new life into the drooping American cause. Forced to withdraw from Detroit and Fort Malden, the retreating redcoats were overtaken by General Harrison's army and beaten at the Battle of the Thames in October 1813.

Despite these successes, the Americans by late 1814, far from invading Canada, were grimly defending their own soil against the invading British. Napoleon's European adversaries had vanquished him—temporarily, as it turned out—in mid-1814 and had exiled the dangerous despot to the Mediterranean isle of Elba. The United States, which had so brashly provoked war behind the protective skirts of Napoleon, was now left to face the music alone. Thousands of Britain's victorious veteran redcoats began to pour into Canada from the Continent.

Assembling some ten thousand crack troops, the British prepared in 1814 for a crushing blow into New York along the familiar lake-river route. In the absence

Constitution and Guerrière, 1812   The *Guerrière* was heavily outweighed and out-gunned, yet its British captain eagerly—and foolishly—sought combat. His ship was destroyed. Historian Henry Adams later concluded that this duel "raised the United States in one half hour to the rank of a first-class Power in the world." Today the *Constitution*, berthed in Boston harbor, remains the oldest actively commissioned ship in the U.S. Navy.

of roads, the invader was forced to bring supplies over the Lake Champlain waterway. A weaker American fleet, commanded by the thirty-year-old Thomas Macdonough, challenged the British. The ensuing battle was desperately fought near Plattsburgh on September 11, 1814, on floating slaughterhouses. The American flagship at one point was in grave trouble. But Macdonough, unexpectedly turning his ship about with cables, confronted the enemy with a fresh broadside and snatched victory from the fangs of defeat.

The results of this heroic naval battle were momentous. The invading British army was forced to retreat. Macdonough thus saved at least upper New York from conquest, New England from further disaffection, and the Union from possible dissolution. He also profoundly affected the concurrent negotiations of the Anglo-American peace treaty in Europe.

✦ Washington Burned and New Orleans Defended

A second formidable British force, numbering about four thousand, landed in the Chesapeake Bay area in August 1814. Advancing rapidly on Washington, it easily dispersed some six thousand panicky militiamen at Bladensburg ("the Bladensburg races"). The invaders then entered the capital and set fire to most of the public buildings, including the Capitol and the White House. But while Washington burned, the Americans at Baltimore held firm. The British fleet hammered Fort McHenry with their cannon but could not capture the city. Francis Scott Key, a detained American

anxiously watching the bombardment from a British ship, was inspired by the doughty defenders to write the words of "The Star-Spangled Banner." Set to the tune of a saucy English tavern refrain, the song quickly attained popularity.

A third British blow of 1814, aimed at New Orleans, menaced the entire Mississippi Valley. Gaunt and hawk-faced Andrew Jackson, fresh from crushing the southwest Indians at the Battle of Horseshoe Bend, was placed in command (see Map 12.5 on p. 242). His hodgepodge force consisted of seven thousand sailors, regulars, pirates, and Frenchmen, as well as militiamen from Louisiana, Kentucky, and Tennessee. Among the defenders were two Louisiana regiments of free black volunteers, numbering about four hundred men. The Americans threw up their entrenchment, and in the words of a popular song,

Behind it stood our little force—
None wished it to be greater;
For ev'ry man was half a horse,
And half an alligator.

The overconfident British, numbering some eight thousand battle-seasoned veterans, blundered badly. They made the mistake of launching a frontal assault, on January 8, 1815, on the entrenched American riflemen and cannoneers. The attackers suffered the most devastating defeat of the entire war, losing over two thousand, killed and wounded, in half an hour, as compared with some seventy for the Americans. It was an astonishing victory for Jackson and his men.

News of the American victory in the **Battle of New Orleans** struck the country "like a clap of

The Fall of Washington, or Maddy in Full Flight President Madison ("Maddy") was forced into humiliating withdrawal from the capital in 1814, when British forces put the torch to Washington, D.C.

thunder," according to one contemporary. Andrew Jackson became a national hero as poets and politicians lined up to sing the praises of the defenders of New Orleans. It hardly mattered when word arrived that a peace treaty had been signed at Ghent, Belgium, ending the war two weeks before the battle. The United States had fought for honor as much as material gain. The Battle of New Orleans restored that honor, at least in American eyes, and unleashed a wave of nationalism and self-confidence.

Its wrath aroused, the Royal Navy had finally retaliated by throwing a ruinous naval blockade along America's coast and by landing raiding parties almost at will. American economic life, including fishing, was crippled. Customs revenues were choked off, and near the end of the war, the bankrupt Treasury was unable to meet its maturing obligations.

Andrew Jackson (1767–1845) appealed to the governor of Louisiana for help recruiting free blacks to defend New Orleans in 1814:

❝ The free men of colour in [your] city are inured to the Southern climate and would make excellent Soldiers.... They must be for or against us— distrust them, and you make them your enemies, place confidence in them, and you engage them by every dear and honorable tie to the interest of the country, who extends to them equal rights and [privileges] with white men. **❞**

✦ The Treaty of Ghent

Tsar Alexander I of Russia, feeling hard-pressed by Napoleon's army and not wanting his British ally to fritter away its strength in America, had proposed mediation between the clashing Anglo-Saxon cousins as early as 1812. The tsar's feeler eventually set in motion the machinery that brought five American peacemakers to the quaint Belgian city of Ghent in 1814. The bickering group was headed by early rising, puritanical John Quincy Adams, son of John Adams, who deplored the late-hour card playing of his high-living colleague Henry Clay.

Confident after their military successes, the British envoys made sweeping demands for a neutralized Indian buffer state in the Great Lakes region, control of the Great Lakes, and a substantial part of conquered Maine. The Americans flatly rejected these terms, and the talks appeared stalemated. But news of British reverses in upper New York and at Baltimore, and increasing war-weariness in Britain, made London more willing to compromise. Preoccupied with redrafting Napoleon's map of Europe at the **Congress of Vienna** (1814–1815) and eyeing still-dangerous France, the British lion resigned itself to licking its wounds.

The **Treaty of Ghent**, signed on Christmas Eve, 1814, was essentially an armistice. Both sides simply agreed to stop fighting and to restore conquered territory. No mention was made of those grievances for which America had ostensibly fought: the Indian menace, search and seizure, Orders in Council, impressment, and confiscations. These discreet omissions have often been cited as further evidence of the insincerity of the

Massachusetts, Connecticut, and Rhode Island Contemplate Abandoning the Union, engraving by William Charles, 1814   This anti-Federalist cartoon shows Great Britain welcoming back its "Yankee boys" with open arms, promising them "plenty molasses and codfish, plenty of goods to smuggle, honours, titles, and nobility into the bargain."

war hawks. Rather, they are proof that the Americans had not managed to defeat the British. With neither side able to impose its will, the treaty negotiations—like the war itself—ended as a virtual draw. Relieved Americans boasted "Not One Inch of Territory Ceded or Lost"—a phrase that contrasted strangely with the "On to Canada" rallying cry at the war's outset.

✴ Federalist Grievances and the Hartford Convention

Defiant New England remained a problem. It prospered during the conflict, owing largely to illicit trade with the enemy in Canada and to the absence of a British blockade until 1814. But the embittered opposition of the Federalists to the war continued unabated.

In a letter to her friend Mercy Otis Warren, Abigail Adams (1744–1818) fretted that the British were taking advantage of Americans' disagreement over the War of 1812:

❝We have our firesides, our comfortable habitations, our cities, our churches and our country to defend, our rights, privileges and independence to preserve. And for these are we not justly contending? Thus it appears to me. Yet I hear from our pulpits, and read from our presses, that it is an unjust, a wicked, a ruinous, and unnecessary war.... A house divided upon itself—and upon that foundation do our enemies build their hopes of subduing us.**❞**

As the war dragged on, New England extremists became more vocal. A small minority of them proposed secession from the Union, or at least a separate peace with Britain. Ugly rumors were afloat about "Blue Light" Federalists—treacherous New Englanders who supposedly flashed lanterns on the shore so that blockading British cruisers would be alerted to the attempted escape of American ships.

The most spectacular manifestation of Federalist discontent was the ill-omened **Hartford Convention**. Late in 1814, when the capture of New Orleans seemed imminent, Massachusetts issued a call for a convention at Hartford, Connecticut. The states of Massachusetts, Connecticut, and Rhode Island dispatched full delegations; neighboring New Hampshire and Vermont sent partial representation. This group of prominent men, twenty-six in all, met in complete secrecy for about three weeks—December 15, 1814, to January 5, 1815—to discuss their grievances and to seek redress for their wrongs.

In truth, the Hartford Convention was actually less radical than the alarmists supposed. Though a minority of delegates gave vent to wild talk of secession, the convention's final report was quite moderate. It demanded financial assistance from Washington to compensate for lost trade and proposed constitutional amendments requiring a two-thirds vote in Congress before an embargo could be imposed, new states admitted, or war declared. Most of the demands reflected Federalist fears that a once-proud New England was falling subservient to an agrarian South and West. Delegates sought to abolish the three-fifths clause of the Constitution (which allowed the South to count a portion of its slaves in calculating proportional representation), to limit presidents to a single term, and to prohibit the election of two successive presidents from the same state. This last clause was aimed at the much-resented "Virginia dynasty"—by 1814 a Virginian had been president for all but four years in the Republic's quarter-century of life.

Three special envoys from Massachusetts carried these demands to the burned-out capital of Washington. The trio arrived just in time to be overwhelmed by the glorious news from New Orleans, followed by that from Ghent. As the rest of the nation congratulated itself on a glorious victory, New England's wartime complaints seemed petty at best and treasonous at worst. Pursued by the sneers and jeers of the press, the envoys sank away in disgrace and into obscurity.

The Hartford resolutions, as it turned out, were the death dirge of the Federalist party. The Federalists were never again to mount a successful presidential campaign (see Map 12.2).

The War of 1812 won a new respect for America among many Britons. Michael Scott, a young lieutenant in the British navy, wrote,

❝ I don't like Americans; I never did, and never shall like them....I have no wish to eat with them, drink with them, deal with, or consort with them in any way; but let me tell the whole truth, nor fight with them, were it not for the laurels to be acquired, by overcoming an enemy so brave, determined, and alert, and in every way so worthy of one's steel, as they have always proved.**❞**

Federalist doctrines of disunity, which long survived the party, blazed a portentous trail. Until 1815 there was far more talk of nullification and secession in New England than in any other section, including the South. The outright flouting of the Jeffersonian embargo and the later crippling of the war effort were the two most damaging acts of nullification in America prior to the events leading to the Civil War.

✦ The Second War for American Independence

The War of 1812 was a small war, involving about 6,000 Americans killed or wounded. It was but a footnote to the mighty European conflagration that had been ignited by the French Revolution and Napoleon's imperial ambitions. In 1812, when Napoleon invaded Russia with about 500,000 men, Madison tried to invade Canada with about 5,000 men. But if the American conflict was globally unimportant, it had huge consequences for the United States.

The Republic had shown that it would take sword in hand to resist what it regarded as grievous wrongs. Other nations developed a new respect for America's fighting prowess. Naval officers like Perry and Macdonough were the most effective type of negotiators; the hot breath of their broadsides spoke the most eloquent diplomatic language. America's emissaries abroad were henceforth treated with less scorn. In a diplomatic sense, if not in a military sense, the conflict could be called the Second War for American Independence.

A new nation, moreover, was welded in the roaring furnace of armed conflict. Sectionalism, now identified with discredited New England Federalists, was dealt a black eye. The painful events of the war glaringly revealed, as perhaps nothing else could have done, the folly of sectional disunity. In a sense the most conspicuous casualty of the war was the Federalist party.

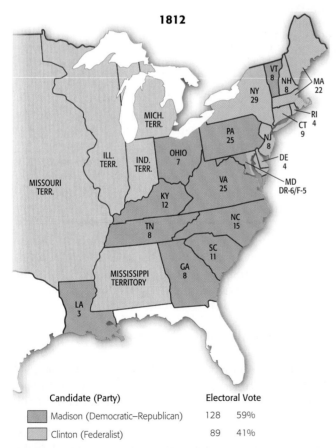

1812

Candidate (Party)   Electoral Vote

■ Madison (Democratic–Republican)   128   59%

■ Clinton (Federalist)   89   41%

MAP 12.2 Presidential Election of 1812 (with electoral vote by state) The Federalists showed impressive strength in the North, and their presidential candidate, DeWitt Clinton, the future "Father of the Erie Canal," almost won. If the 25 electoral votes of Pennsylvania had gone to the New Yorker, he would have won, 114 to 103. © 2016 Cengage Learning

The White House and Capitol, by Anthony St. John Baker, 1826 This watercolor painting reveals the rustic conditions of the early days in the nation's capital. The President's House (now called the White House), on the left, was designed by Irish-born James Hoban and built between 1792 and 1800 in the neoclassical style. It has been the residence of every president since John Adams. When Thomas Jefferson moved into the house in 1801, he worked with architect Benjamin Henry Latrobe to expand it, creating two colonnades that were meant to conceal stables and storage. In 1814, during the War of 1812, the British army set the President's House ablaze, destroying the interior and charring much of the exterior. Reconstruction began almost immediately, and President James Monroe moved into a partially finished house in 1817. The Capital dome is visible in the background on the right. It, too, burned in 1814. Its rebuilding, not completed until 1830, was overseen by Boston's Charles Bulfinch.

War heroes emerged, especially the two Indian-fighters Andrew Jackson and William Henry Harrison. Both of them were to become president. Left in the lurch by their British friends at Ghent, the Indians were forced to make such terms as they could. They reluctantly consented, in a series of treaties, to relinquish vast areas of forested land north of the Ohio River.

Manufacturing prospered behind the wooden wall of the British blockade. In both an economic and a diplomatic sense, the War of 1812 bred greater American independence. The industries that were thus stimulated by the fighting rendered America less dependent on Europe's workshops.

Canadian patriotism and nationalism also received a powerful stimulus from the clash. Many Canadians felt betrayed by the Treaty of Ghent. They were especially aggrieved by the failure to secure an Indian buffer state or even mastery of the Great Lakes. Canadians fully expected the frustrated Yankees to return, and for a time the Americans and British engaged in a floating arms race on the Great Lakes. But in 1817 the **Rush-Bagot agreement** between Britain and the United States severely limited naval armament on the lakes. Better relations brought the last border fortifications down in the 1870s, with the happy result that the United States and Canada came to share the world's longest unfortified boundary—5,527 miles long.

After Napoleon's final defeat at Waterloo in June 1815, Europe slumped into a peace of exhaustion. Deposed monarchs returned to battered thrones, as the Old World took the rutted road back to conservatism, illiberalism, and reaction. But the American people were largely unaffected by these European developments. Turning their backs on the Old World, they faced resolutely toward the untamed West—and toward the task of building their democracy.

✹ Nascent Nationalism

The most impressive by-product of the War of 1812 was a heightened nationalism—the spirit of nation-consciousness or national oneness. America may not have fought the war as one nation, but it emerged as one nation. The changed mood even manifested itself in the birth of a distinctively national literature. Washington Irving and James Fenimore Cooper attained international recognition in the 1820s, significantly as the nation's first writers of importance to use American scenes and themes. School textbooks, often British in an earlier era, were now being written by Americans for Americans. In the world of magazines, the highly intellectual *North American Review* began publication in 1815—the year of the triumph at New Orleans. Even American painters increasingly celebrated their native landscapes on their canvases.

A fresh nationalistic spirit could be recognized in many other areas as well. The rising tide of nation-consciousness even touched finance. A revived Bank of the United States was voted by Congress in 1816. A more handsome national capital began to rise from the ashes of Washington. The army was expanded to ten thousand men. The navy further covered itself with glory in 1815 when it administered a thorough beating to the piratical plunderers of North Africa. Stephen Decatur, naval hero of the War of 1812 and of the Barbary Coast expeditions, pungently captured the country's nationalist mood in a famous toast made on his return from the Mediterranean campaigns: "Our country! In her intercourse with foreign nations may she always be in the right; but our country, right or wrong!"

✹ "The American System"

Nationalism likewise manifested itself in manufacturing. Patriotic Americans took pride in the factories that had recently mushroomed forth, largely as a result of the self-imposed embargoes and the war.

When hostilities ended in 1815, British competitors undertook to recover lost ground. They began to dump the contents of their bulging warehouses on the United States, often cutting their prices below cost in an effort to strangle the American war-baby factories in the cradle. The infant industries bawled lustily for protection. To many red-blooded Americans, it seemed as though the British, having failed to crush Yankee fighters on the battlefield, were now seeking to crush Yankee factories in the marketplace.

A nationalist Congress, out-Federalizing the old Federalists, responded by passing the path-breaking **Tariff of 1816**—the first tariff in American history instituted primarily for protection, not revenue. Its rates—roughly 20 to 25 percent on the value of dutiable imports—were not high enough to provide completely adequate safeguards, but the law was a bold beginning. A strongly protective trend was started that stimulated the appetites of the protected for more protection.

Nationalism was further highlighted by a grandiose plan of Henry Clay for developing a profitable home market. Still radiating the nationalism of war-hawk days, he threw himself behind an elaborate scheme known by 1824 as the **American System**. This system had three main parts. It began with a strong banking system, which would provide easy and abundant credit. Clay also advocated a protective tariff, behind which eastern manufacturing would flourish. Revenues gushing from the tariff would provide funds for the third component of the American System—a network of roads and canals, especially in the burgeoning Ohio Valley. Through these new arteries of transportation would flow foodstuffs and raw materials from the South and West to the North and East. In exchange, a stream of manufactured goods would flow in the return direction, knitting the country together economically and politically.

Henry Clay (1777–1852), by John Neagle, 1843 This painting hangs in the corridors of the House of Representatives, where Clay worked as a glamorous, eloquent, and ambitious congressman for many years. Best known for promoting his nationalistic "American System" of protective tariffs for eastern manufactures and federally financed canals and highways to benefit the West, Clay is surrounded here by symbols of flourishing agriculture and burgeoning industries in the new nation.

Architect of the Capitol

Persistent and eloquent demands by Henry Clay and others for better transportation struck a responsive chord with the public. The recent attempts to invade Canada had all failed partly because of oath-provoking roads—or no roads at all. People who have dug wagons out of hub-deep mud do not quickly forget their blisters and backaches. An outcry for better transportation, rising most noisily in the road-poor West, was one of the most striking aspects of the nationalism inspired by the War of 1812.

But attempts to secure federal funding for roads and canals stumbled on Republican constitutional scruples. Congress voted in 1817 to distribute $1.5 million to the states for internal improvements, but President Madison sternly vetoed this handout measure as unconstitutional. The individual states were thus forced to venture ahead with construction programs of their own, including the Erie Canal, triumphantly completed by New York in 1825. Jeffersonian Republicans, who had gulped down Hamiltonian loose construction-ism on other important problems, choked on the idea of direct federal support of intrastate internal improvements. New England, in particular, strongly opposed federally constructed roads and canals because such outlets would further drain away population and create competing states beyond the mountains.

Nationalist Pride, ca. 1820 Nationalist sentiments swelled in the wake of the War of 1812, as Americans defined their country's very identity with reference to its antimonarchical origins.

Picture Research Consultants & Archives

★ The So-Called Era of Good Feelings

James Monroe—six feet tall, somewhat stooped, courtly, and mild-mannered—was nominated for the presidency in 1816 by the Republicans. They thus undertook to continue the so-called Virginia dynasty of Washington, Jefferson, and Madison. The fading Federalists ran a candidate for the last time in their checkered history, and he was crushed by 183 electoral votes to 34. The vanquished Federalist party was gasping its dying breaths, leaving the field to the triumphant Republicans and one-party rule.

In James Monroe, the man and the times auspiciously met. As the last president to wear an old-style cocked hat, he straddled two generations: the bygone age of the Founding Fathers and the emergent age of nationalism. Never brilliant, and perhaps not great, the serene Virginian with gray-blue eyes was in intellect and personal force the least distinguished of the first eight presidents. But the times called for sober administration, not dashing heroics. And Monroe was an experienced, levelheaded executive, with an ear-to-the-ground talent for interpreting popular rumblings.

Emerging nationalism was further cemented by a goodwill tour Monroe undertook early in 1817, ostensibly to inspect military defenses. He pushed northward deep into New England and then westward to Detroit, viewing en route Niagara Falls. Even in Federalist New England, "the enemy's country," he received a heartwarming welcome; a Boston newspaper was so far carried away as to announce that an "Era of Good Feelings" had been ushered in. This happy phrase has been commonly used since then to describe the administrations of Monroe.

The **Era of Good Feelings**, unfortunately, was something of a misnomer. Considerable tranquility and prosperity did in fact smile upon the early years of Monroe, but the period was a troubled one. The acute issues of the tariff, the bank, internal improvements,

> *Boston's* Columbian Centinel *was not the only newspaper to regard President Monroe's early months as the Era of Good Feelings. Washington's* National Intelligencer *observed in July 1817,*
>
> **❝**Never before, perhaps, since the institution of civil government, did the same harmony, the same absence of party spirit, the same national feeling, pervade a community. The result is too consoling to dispute too nicely about the cause.**❞**

Fairview Inn or Three Mile House on Old Frederick Road, by Thomas Coke Ruckle, ca. 1829 This busy scene on the Frederick Road, leading westward from Baltimore, was typical as pioneers flooded into the newly secured West in the early 1800s.

and the sale of public lands were being hotly contested. Sectionalism was crystallizing, and the conflict over slavery was beginning to raise its hideous head.

✷ The Panic of 1819 and the Curse of Hard Times

Much of the goodness went out of the good feelings in 1819, when a paralyzing economic panic descended. It brought deflation, depression, bankruptcies, bank failures, unemployment, soup kitchens, and overcrowded pesthouses known as debtors' prisons.

This was the first national financial panic since President Washington took office. Many factors contributed to the catastrophe of 1819, but looming large was overspeculation in frontier lands. The Bank of the United States, through its western branches, had become deeply involved in this popular type of outdoor gambling.

Financial paralysis from the panic, which lasted in some degree for several years, gave a rude setback to the nationalistic ardor. The West was especially hard hit. When the pinch came, the Bank of the United States forced the speculative ("wildcat") western banks to the wall and foreclosed mortgages on countless farms. All this was technically legal but politically unwise. In the eyes of the western debtor, the nationalist Bank of the United States soon became a kind of financial devil.

The **panic of 1819** also created backwashes in the political and social world. The poorer classes—the one-suspender men and their families—were severely strapped, and in their troubles was sown the seed of Jacksonian democracy. Hard times also directed attention to the inhumanity of imprisoning debtors. In extreme cases, often overplayed, mothers were torn from their infants for owing a few dollars. Mounting agitation against imprisonment for debt bore fruit in remedial legislation in an increasing number of states.

✷ Growing Pains of the West

The onward march of the West continued; nine frontier states had joined the original thirteen between 1791 and 1819. With an eye to preserving the North-South sectional balance, most of these commonwealths had been admitted alternately, free or slave. (See Admission of States in the Appendix.)

Why this explosive expansion? In part it was simply a continuation of the generations-old westward movement, which had been going on since early colonial days. In addition, the siren song of cheap land— "the Ohio fever"—had a special appeal to European immigrants. Eager newcomers from abroad were beginning to stream down the gangplanks in impressive numbers, especially after the war of boycotts and bullets. Land exhaustion in the older tobacco states, where the soil was "mined" rather than cultivated, likewise drove people westward. Glib speculators accepted small down payments, making it easier to buy new holdings.

The western boom was stimulated by additional developments. Acute economic distress during the embargo years turned many pinched faces toward the setting sun. The crushing of the Indians in the Northwest and South by Generals Harrison and Jackson pacified the frontier and opened up vast virgin tracts of land. The building of highways improved the land routes to the Ohio Valley. Noteworthy was the Cumberland Road, begun in 1811, which ran ultimately from western Maryland to Illinois. The use of the first steamboat on western waters, also in 1811, heralded a new era of upstream navigation.

But the West, despite the inflow of settlers, was still weak in population and influence. Not potent enough politically to make its voice heard, it was forced to ally itself with other sections. Thus strengthened, it demanded cheap acreage and partially achieved its goal in the **Land Act of 1820**, which authorized a buyer to purchase eighty virgin acres at a minimum of $1.25 an acre in cash. The West also demanded cheap transportation and slowly got it, despite the constitutional qualms of the presidents and the hostility of easterners. Finally, the West demanded cheap money, issued by its own "wildcat" banks, and fought the powerful Bank of the United States to attain its goal (see "Makers of America: Settlers of the Old Northwest," pp. 238–239).

✷ Slavery and the Sectional Balance

Sectional tensions, involving rivalry between the slave South and the free North over control of the beckoning West, were stunningly underscored in 1819. In that year the territory of Missouri knocked on the doors of Congress for admission as a slave state. This fertile and well-watered area contained sufficient population to warrant statehood. But the House of Representatives stymied the plans of the Missourians by passing the incendiary **Tallmadge amendment**. It stipulated that no more slaves should be brought into Missouri and also provided for the gradual emancipation of children born

Antislavery Propaganda in the 1820s These drawstring bags are made of silk and transfer-printed with "before" and "after" scenes of slavery. On the left bag, an African woman cradles her baby; on the right one, the grieving mother is childless and in chains, while slaves are being whipped in the background. These bags were purchased at an abolitionist fair, held to raise money for the antislavery movement. Purses and the like sold well at these events because women were prominent in the movement.

The Daughters of the American Revolution Museum, Washington, D.C. Gift of Mrs. Erwin L. Broecker; Photo by Mark Gulezian

to enslaved parents already there. A roar of anger burst from slaveholding southerners. They were joined by many depression-cursed pioneers who favored unhampered expansion of the West and by many northerners, especially diehard Federalists, who were eager to use the issue to break the back of the "Virginia dynasty."

Southerners saw in the Tallmadge amendment, which they eventually managed to defeat in the Senate, an ominous threat to sectional balance. When the Constitution was adopted in 1788, the North and South were running neck and neck in wealth and population. But with every passing decade, the North was becoming wealthier and also more thickly settled—an advantage reflected in an increasing northern majority in the House of Representatives. Yet in the Senate, each state had two votes, regardless of size. With eleven states free and eleven slave, the southerners had maintained equality. They were therefore in a good position to thwart any northern effort to interfere with the expansion of slavery, and they did not want to lose this veto.

The future of the slave system caused southerners profound concern. Missouri was the first state entirely west of the Mississippi River to be carved out of the Louisiana Purchase, and the Missouri emancipation amendment might set a damaging precedent for all the rest of the area. Even more disquieting was another possibility. If Congress could abolish the **peculiar institution** in Missouri, might it not attempt to do likewise in the older states of the South? The wounds of the Constitutional Convention of 1787 were once more ripped open.

Burning moral questions also protruded, even though the main issue was political and economic balance. A small but growing group of antislavery agitators in the North seized the occasion to raise an outcry against the evils of slavery. They were determined that the plague of human bondage should not spread further into the untainted territories.

✷ The Uneasy Missouri Compromise

Deadlock in Washington was at length broken in 1820 by the time-honored American solution of compromise—actually a bundle of three compromises. Courtly Henry Clay of Kentucky, gifted conciliator, played a leading role. Congress, despite abolitionist pleas, agreed to admit Missouri as a slave state. But at the same time, free-soil Maine, which until then had been a part of Massachusetts, was admitted as a separate state. The balance between North and South was thus kept at twelve states each and remained there for fifteen years. Although Missouri was permitted to retain slaves, all future bondage was prohibited in the remainder of the Louisiana Purchase north of the line of 36° 30'—the southern boundary of Missouri (see Map 12.3).

MAP 12.3 The Missouri Compromise and Slavery, 1820–1821 Note the 36° 30' line. In the 1780s Thomas Jefferson had written of slavery in America, "Indeed I tremble for my country when I reflect that God is just; that his justice cannot sleep forever; that…the Almighty has no attribute which can take side with us in such a contest." Now, at the time of the Missouri Compromise, Jefferson feared that his worst forebodings were coming to pass. "I considered it at once," he said of the Missouri question, "as the knell of the Union." © 2016 Cengage Learning

This horse-trading adjustment was politically evenhanded, though denounced by extremists on each side as a "dirty bargain." Both North and South yielded something; both gained something. The South won the prize of Missouri as an unrestricted slave state. The North won the concession that Congress could forbid slavery in the remaining territories. More gratifying to many northerners was the fact that the immense area north of 36° 30', except Missouri, was forever closed to the blight of slavery. Yet the restriction on future slavery in the territories was not unduly offensive to the slaveowners, partly because the northern prairie land did not seem suited to slave labor. Even so, a majority of southern congressmen still voted against the compromise.

Neither North nor South was acutely displeased, although neither was completely happy. The **Missouri Compromise** lasted thirty-four years—a vital formative period in the life of the young Republic—and during that time it preserved the shaky compact of the states. Yet the embittered dispute over slavery heralded the future breakup of the Union. Ever after, the morality of the South's "peculiar institution" was an issue that could not be swept under the rug. The Missouri Compromise only ducked the question—it did not

resolve it. Sooner or later, Thomas Jefferson predicted, it will "burst on us as a tornado."

The Missouri Compromise and the concurrent panic of 1819 should have dimmed the political star of President Monroe. Certainly both unhappy events

While the debate over Missouri was raging, Thomas Jefferson (1743–1826) wrote to a correspondent,

❝The Missouri question…is the most portentous one which ever yet threatened our Union. In the gloomiest moment of the revolutionary war I never had any apprehensions equal to what I feel from this source.…[The] question, like a firebell in the night, awakened and filled me with terror.…[With slavery] we have a wolf by the ears, and we can neither hold him nor safely let him go.**❞**

John Quincy Adams (1767–1848) confided to his diary,

❝I take it for granted that the present question is a mere preamble—a title-page to a great, tragic volume.**❞**

Settlers of the Old Northwest

The Old Northwest beckoned to settlers after the War of 1812. The withdrawal of the British protector weakened the Indians' grip on the territory. Then the transportation boom of the 1820s—steamboats on the Ohio, the National Highway stretching from Pennsylvania, the Erie Canal—opened broad arteries along which the westward movement flowed.

The first wave of newcomers came mainly from Kentucky, Tennessee, and the upland regions of Virginia and the Carolinas. Most migrants were rough-hewn white farmers who had been pushed from good land to bad by an expanding plantation economy. Like Joseph Cress of North Carolina, they were relieved to relinquish "them old red filds" where you "get nothing," in return for acres of new soil that "is as black and rich you wold want it." Some settlers acquired land for the first time. John Palmer, whose family left Kentucky for Illinois in 1831, recalled his father telling him "of land so cheap that we could all be landholders, where men were all equal." Migrants from the South settled mainly in the southern portions of Ohio, Indiana, and Illinois.

As Palmer testified, the Old Northwest offered southern farmers an escape from the lowly social position they had endured as nonslaveholders in a slave society. Not that they objected to slavery or sympathized with blacks. Far from it: by enacting Black Codes in their new territories, they tried to prevent blacks from following them to paradise. They wanted their own democratic community, free of rich planters and African Americans alike.

If southern "Butternuts," as these settlers were called, dominated settlement in the 1820s, the next decade brought Yankees from the Northeast. They were as land-starved as their southern counterparts. A growing population had gobbled up most of the good land east of the Appalachians. Yankee settlers came to the Old Northwest, especially to the northern parts of Ohio, Indiana, and Illinois, eager to make the region a profitable breadbasket for the Atlantic seaboard. Unlike the Butternuts, who wanted to quit forever the imposing framework of southern society, northerners hoped to re-create the world they had left behind.

Conflict soon emerged between Yankees and southerners. As self-sufficient farmers with little interest in producing for the market, the southerners viewed the northern newcomers as inhospitable, greedy, and excessively ambitious. "Yankee" became a term of reproach;

From the collections of Dayton History

Newcom Tavern, Dayton, Ohio Built in 1796, Newcom Tavern was a typical way station for the pioneers flowing into the newly secured Old Northwest in the early 1800s. Today it is Dayton's oldest building.

Building the Erie Canal A major engineering feat, the Erie Canal created an artificial waterway through upstate New York from the Hudson River to the Great Lakes, allowing people and goods to move to and from the Old Northwest more quickly and cheaply.

a person who was cheated was said to have been "Yankeed." Northerners, in turn, viewed the southerners as uncivilized, a "coon dog and butcher knife tribe" with no interest in education, self-improvement, or agricultural innovation. Yankees, eager to tame both the land and its people, wanted to establish public schools and build roads, canals, and railroads—and they advocated taxes to fund such progress. Southerners opposed all these reforms, especially public schooling, which they regarded as an attempt to northernize their children.

Religion divided settlers as well. Northerners, typically Congregationalists and Presbyterians, wanted their ministers to be educated in seminaries. Southerners embraced the more revivalist Baptist and Methodist denominations. They preferred humble preacher-farmers to professionally trained clergymen, whom they viewed as too distant from the Lord and the people. As the preacher Alexander Campbell, a founder of the Disciples of Christ, put it, "The scheme of a learned priesthood...has long since proved itself to be a grand device to keep men in ignorance and bondage."

Not everyone, of course, fitted neatly into these molds. Abraham Lincoln, with roots in Kentucky, came to adopt views more akin to those of the Yankees than the southerners, whereas his New England–born

archrival, Stephen Douglas, carefully cultivated the Butternut vote for the Illinois Democratic party.

As the population swelled and the region acquired its own character, the stark contrasts between northerners and southerners started to fade. By the 1850s northerners dominated numerically, and they succeeded in establishing public schools and fashioning internal improvements. Railroads and Great Lakes shipping tied the region ever more tightly to the Northeast. Yankees and southerners sometimes allied as new kinds of cleavages emerged—between rich and poor, between city dwellers and farmers, and, once Irish and German immigrants started pouring into the region, between native Protestants and newcomer Catholics. Still, echoes of the clash between Yankees and Butternuts persisted. During the Civil War, the southern counties of Ohio, Indiana, and Illinois, where southerners had first settled, harbored sympathizers with the South and served as a key area for Confederate military infiltration into the North. Decades later these same counties became a stronghold of the Ku Klux Klan. The Old Northwest may have become firmly anchored economically to the Northeast, but vestiges of its early dual personality persisted.

had a dampening effect on the Era of Good Feelings. But smooth-spoken James Monroe was so popular, and the Federalist opposition so weak, that in the presidential election of 1820 he received every electoral vote except one. Unanimity was an honor reserved for George Washington. Monroe, as it turned out, was the only president in American history to be reelected after a term in which a major financial panic began.

✦ John Marshall and Judicial Nationalism

The upsurging nationalism of the post-Ghent years, despite the ominous setbacks concerning slavery, was further reflected and reinforced by the Supreme Court. The high tribunal continued to be dominated by the tall, thin, and aggressive Chief Justice John Marshall. One group of his decisions—perhaps the most famous—bolstered the power of the federal government at the expense of the states. A notable case in this category was *McCulloch v. Maryland* (1819). The suit involved an attempt by the State of Maryland to destroy a branch of the Bank of the United States by imposing a tax on its notes. John Marshall, speaking for the Court, declared the bank constitutional by invoking the Hamiltonian doctrine of implied powers (see p. 186). At the same time, he strengthened federal authority and slapped at state infringements when he denied the right of Maryland to tax the bank. With ringing emphasis, he affirmed "that the power to tax involves the power to destroy" and "that a power to create implies a power to preserve."

Marshall's ruling in this case gave the doctrine of **loose construction** its most famous formulation. The Constitution, he said, derived from the consent of the people and thus permitted the government to act for their benefit. He further argued that the Constitution was "intended to endure for ages to come and, consequently, to be adapted to the various crises of human affairs." Finally, he declared, "Let the end be legitimate, let it be within the scope of the Constitution, and all means which are appropriate, which are plainly adapted to that end, which are not prohibited, but consist with the letter and spirit of the Constitution, are constitutional."

Two years later (1821) the case of *Cohens v. Virginia* gave Marshall one of his greatest opportunities to defend the federal power. The Cohen brothers, found guilty by the Virginia courts of illegally selling lottery tickets, appealed to the highest tribunal. Virginia "won," in the sense that the conviction of the Cohens was upheld. But in fact Virginia and all the individual states lost because Marshall resoundingly asserted the right of the Supreme Court to review the decisions of the state supreme courts in all questions involving powers of the federal government. The states' rights proponents were aghast.

Hardly less significant was the celebrated "steamboat case," *Gibbons v. Ogden* (1824). The suit grew out of an attempt by the State of New York to grant to a private concern a monopoly of waterborne commerce between New York and New Jersey. Marshall sternly reminded the upstart state that the Constitution conferred on Congress alone the control of interstate commerce (see Art. I, Sec. VIII, para. 3). He thus struck with one hand another blow at states' rights, while upholding with the other the sovereign powers of the federal government. Interstate streams were cleared of this judicial snag; the departed spirit of Hamilton may well have applauded.

✦ Judicial Dikes Against Democratic Excesses

Another sheaf of Marshall's decisions bolstered judicial barriers against democratic or demagogic attacks on property rights.

The notorious case of *Fletcher v. Peck* (1810) arose when a Georgia legislature, swayed by bribery, granted 35 million acres in the Yazoo River country (Mississippi) to private speculators. The next legislature, yielding to an angry public outcry, canceled the crooked transaction. But the Supreme Court, with Marshall presiding, decreed that the legislative grant was a contract (even though fraudulently secured) and that the Constitution forbids state laws "impairing" contracts (Art. I, Sec. X, para. 1). The decision was perhaps most noteworthy as further protecting property rights against popular pressures. It was also one of the earliest clear assertions of the right of the Supreme Court to invalidate state laws conflicting with the federal Constitution.

A similar principle was upheld in the case of *Dartmouth College v. Woodward* (1819), among the best remembered of Marshall's cases. The college had been granted a charter by King George III in 1769, but the democratic New Hampshire state legislature had seen fit to change it. Dartmouth appealed the case, employing as counsel its most distinguished alumnus, Daniel Webster (Class of '01). The "Godlike Daniel" reportedly pulled out all the stops of his tear-inducing eloquence when he declaimed, "It is, sir, as I have said, a small college. And yet there are those who love it."

When Supreme Court chief justice John Marshall died, a New York newspaper rejoiced:

❝ The chief place in the supreme tribunal of the Union will no longer be filled by a man whose political doctrines led him always...to strengthen government at the expense of the people. **❞**

© The Metropolitan Museum of Art/Art Resource, NY

Daguerreotype of Daniel Webster (1782–1852), by Southworth and Hawes Premier orator and statesman, Webster served many years in both houses of Congress and also as secretary of state. Often regarded as presidential timber, he was somewhat handicapped by an overfondness for good food and drink and was frequently in financial difficulties. His devotion to the Union was inflexible. "One country, one constitution, and one destiny," he proclaimed in 1837.

Marshall needed no dramatics in the *Dartmouth* case. He put the states firmly in their place when he ruled that the original charter must stand. It was a contract—and the Constitution protected contracts against state encroachments. The *Dartmouth* decision had the fortunate effect of safeguarding business enterprise from domination by the state governments. But it had the unfortunate effect of creating a precedent that enabled chartered corporations, in later years, to escape the handcuffs of needed public control.

If John Marshall was a Molding Father of the Constitution, Daniel Webster was an Expounding Father. Time and again he left his seat in the Senate, stepped downstairs to the Supreme Court chamber (then located in the Capitol building), and there expounded his Federalistic and nationalistic philosophy before the supreme bench. The eminent chief justice, so Webster reported, approvingly drank in the familiar arguments as a baby sucks in its mother's milk. The two men dovetailed strikingly with each other. Webster's classic speeches in the Senate, challenging states' rights and nullification, were largely repetitious of the arguments that he had earlier presented before a sympathetic Supreme Court.

Marshall's decisions are felt even today. In this sense his nationalism was the most tenaciously

enduring of the era. He buttressed the federal Union and helped to create a stable, nationally uniform environment for business. At the same time, Marshall checked the excesses of popularly elected state legislatures. In an age when white manhood suffrage was flowering and America was veering toward stronger popular control, Marshall almost single-handedly shaped the Constitution along conservative, centralizing lines that ran somewhat counter to the dominant spirit of the new country. Through him the conservative Hamiltonians partly triumphed from the tomb.

Sharing Oregon and Acquiring Florida

The robust nationalism of the years after the War of 1812 was likewise reflected in the shaping of foreign policy. To this end, the nationalistic President Monroe teamed with his nationalistic secretary of state, John Quincy Adams, the cold and scholarly son of the frosty and bookish ex-president. The younger Adams, a statesman of the first rank, happily rose above the ingrown Federalist sectionalism of his native New England and proved to be one of the great secretaries of state.

To its credit, the Monroe administration negotiated the much-underrated **Anglo-American Convention** of 1818 with Britain. This pact permitted Americans to share the coveted Newfoundland fisheries with their Canadian cousins. This multisided agreement also fixed the vague northern limits of Louisiana along the forty-ninth parallel from the Lake of the Woods (Minnesota) to the Rocky Mountains (see Map 12.4). The treaty further provided for a ten-year joint occupation of the untamed Oregon Country, without a surrender of the rights or claims of either America or Britain.

To the south lay semitropical Spanish Florida, which many Americans believed geography and providence had destined to become part of the United States. Americans already claimed West Florida, where uninvited American settlers had torn down the hated Spanish flag in 1810. Congress ratified this grab in 1812, and during the War of 1812 against Spain's ally, Britain, a small American army seized the Mobile region. But the bulk of Florida remained, tauntingly, under Spanish rule (see Map 12.5).

An epidemic of revolutions now broke out in South America, notably in Chile (1810), Venezuela (1811), and Argentina (1816), and Americans instinctively cheered the birth of these sister republics, though the checkered histories of the Latin democracies soon provided grounds for disappointment. But the upheavals in the southern continent forced Spain to denude Florida of troops in a vain effort to squelch the rebels. General Andrew Jackson, idol of the West and scourge of the Indians, saw opportunity in the

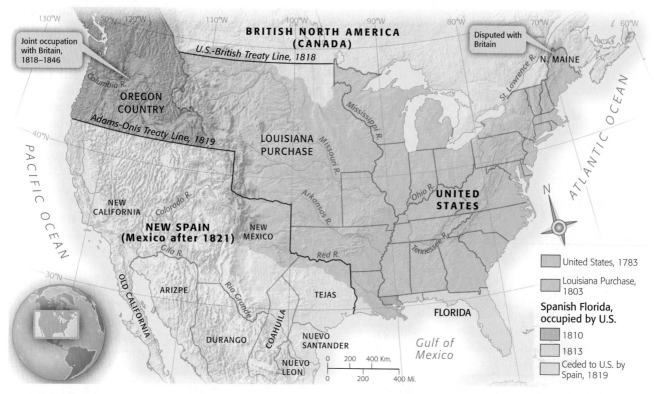

MAP 12.4 U.S.-British Boundary Settlement, 1818 Note that the United States gained considerable territory by securing a treaty boundary rather than the natural boundary of the Missouri River watershed. The line of 49° was extended westward to the Pacific Ocean under the Treaty of 1846 with Britain (see p. 371). © 2016 Cengage Learning

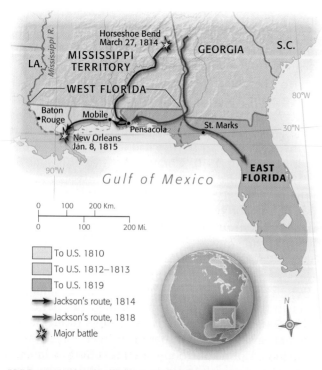

MAP 12.5 The Southeast, 1810–1819 © 2016 Cengage Learning

undefended swamplands. On the pretext that hostile Seminole Indians and fugitive slaves were using Florida as a refuge, Jackson secured a commission to enter Spanish territory, punish the Indians, and recapture the runaways. But he was to respect all posts under the Spanish flag.

Early in 1818 Jackson swept across the Florida border with all the fury of an avenging angel. He hanged two Indian chiefs without ceremony and, after hasty military trials, executed two British subjects for assisting the Indians. He also seized the two most important Spanish posts in the area, St. Marks and then Pensacola, where he deposed the Spanish governor, who was lucky enough to escape Jackson's jerking noose.

Jackson had clearly exceeded his instructions from Washington. Alarmed, President Monroe consulted his cabinet. Its members were for disavowing or disciplining the overzealous Jackson—all except the lone wolf John Quincy Adams, who refused to howl with the pack. An ardent patriot and nationalist, the flinty New Englander took the offensive and demanded huge concessions from Spain.

In the mislabeled **Florida Purchase Treaty** of 1819 (also known as the **Adams-Onís Treaty**), Spain

Stock Montage/Contributor/Getty Images

Andrew Jackson (1767–1845), by Jean François de Vallée, 1815 This portrait of Jackson as a major general in the U.S. Army was painted by a French artist living in New Orleans. It is one of the earliest surviving portraits of Jackson and depicts him at a time when he was known for his stern discipline, iron will ("Old Hickory"), and good luck.

ceded Florida, as well as shadowy Spanish claims to Oregon, in exchange for America's abandonment of equally murky claims to Texas, soon to become part of independent Mexico. The hitherto vague western boundary of Louisiana was made to zigzag northwesterly toward the Rockies to the forty-second parallel and then to turn due west to the Pacific, dividing Oregon from Spanish holdings.

✵ The Menace of Monarchy in America

After the Napoleonic nightmare, the rethroned autocrats of Europe banded together in a kind of monarchical protective association. Determined to restore the good old days, they undertook to stamp out the democratic tendencies that had sprouted from soil they considered richly manured by the ideals of the French Revolution. The world must be made safe *from* democracy.

The crowned despots acted promptly. With complete ruthlessness they smothered the embers of popular rebellions in Italy (1821) and in Spain (1823).

According to the European rumor factory, they were also gazing across the Atlantic. Russia, Austria, Prussia, and France, acting in partnership, would presumably send powerful fleets and armies to the revolted colonies of Spanish America and there restore the autocratic Spanish king to his ancestral domains.

Many Americans were alarmed. Naturally sympathetic to democratic revolutions, they had cheered when the Latin American republics rose from the ruins of monarchy. Americans feared that if the European powers intervened in the New World, the cause of republicanism would suffer irreparable harm. The physical security of the United States—the mother lode of democracy—would be endangered by the proximity of powerful and unfriendly forces.

The southward push of the Russian bear, from the chilly region now known as Alaska, had already publicized the menace of monarchy to North America. In 1821 the tsar of Russia issued a decree extending Russian jurisdiction over one hundred miles of the open sea down to the line of 51°, an area that embraced most of the coast of present-day British Columbia. The energetic Russians had already established trading posts almost as far south as the entrance to San Francisco Bay. (Fort Ross—"Ross" is a corruption of "Russian"—still stands today on the coast of Sonoma County, California.) The fear prevailed in the United States that the Russians were planning to cut the Republic off from California, its prospective window on the Pacific.

Great Britain, still Ruler of the Seas, was now beginning to play a lone-hand role on the complicated international stage. In particular, it recoiled from joining hands with the continental European powers in crushing the newly won liberties of the Spanish Americans. These revolutionaries had thrown open their monopoly-bound ports to outside trade, and British shippers, as well as Americans, had found the profits sweet.

Accordingly, in August 1823 George Canning, the haughty British foreign secretary, approached the American minister in London with a startling proposition. Would the United States combine with Britain in a joint declaration renouncing any interest in acquiring Latin American territory, and specifically warning the European despots to keep their harsh hands off the Latin American republics? The American minister, lacking instructions, referred this fateful scheme to his superiors in Washington.

✵ Monroe and His Doctrine

The tenacious nationalist, Secretary Adams, was hardheaded enough to be wary of Britons bearing gifts. Why should the lordly British, with the mightiest

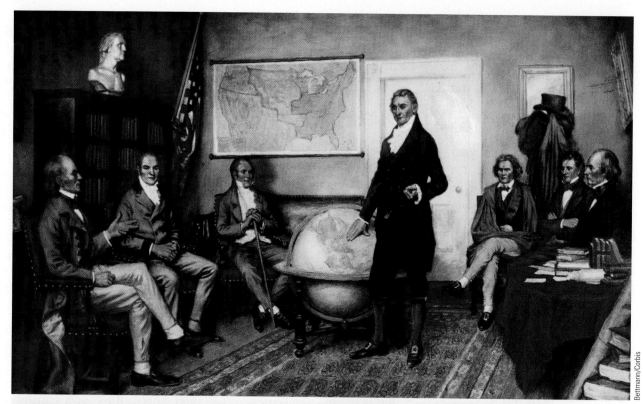

President Monroe Thinking Globally Surrounded by his cabinet, the president is depicted explaining the Monroe Doctrine. Secretary of State John Quincy Adams is the first on the left; Secretary of War John C. Calhoun is the third from the right.

navy afloat, need America as an ally—an America that had neither naval nor military strength? Such a union, argued Adams, was undignified—like a tiny American "cockboat" sailing "in the wake of the British man-of-war."

Adams, ever alert, thought that he detected the joker in the Canning proposal. The British feared that the aggressive Yankees would one day seize Spanish territory in the Americas—perhaps Cuba—which would jeopardize Britain's possessions in the Caribbean. If Canning could seduce the United States into joining with him in support of the territorial integrity of the New World, America's own hands would be morally tied.

A self-denying alliance with Britain would not only hamper American expansion, concluded Adams, but it was also unnecessary. He suspected—correctly—that the European powers had not hatched any definite plans for invading the Americas. In any event the British navy would prevent the approach of hostile fleets because the South American markets had to be kept open at all costs for British merchants. It was presumably safe for Uncle Sam, behind the protective wooden petticoats of the British navy, to blow a defiant, nationalistic blast at all of Europe. The distresses

of the Old World set the stage once again for an American diplomatic coup.

The **Monroe Doctrine** was born late in 1823, when the nationalistic Adams won the nationalistic Monroe over to his way of thinking. The president, in his regular annual message to Congress on December 2, 1823, incorporated a stern warning to the European powers. Its two basic features were (1) noncolonization and (2) nonintervention.

Monroe first directed his verbal volley primarily at the lumbering Russian bear in the Northwest. He proclaimed, in effect, that the era of colonization in the Americas had ended and that henceforth the hunting season was permanently closed. What the great powers had they might keep, but neither they nor any other Old World governments could seize or otherwise acquire more.

At the same time, Monroe trumpeted a warning against foreign intervention. He was clearly concerned with regions to the south, where fears were felt for the fledgling Spanish American republics. Monroe bluntly directed the crowned heads of Europe to keep their hated monarchical systems out of this hemisphere. For its part the United States would not intervene in the war that the Greeks were then fighting against the Turks for their independence.

✦ Monroe's Doctrine Appraised

The ermined monarchs of Europe were angered at Monroe's doctrine. Having resented the incendiary American experiment from the beginning, they were now deeply offended by Monroe's high-flown declaration—all the more so because of the gulf between America's pretentious pronouncements and its puny military strength. But though offended by the upstart Yankees, the European powers found their hands tied, and their frustration increased their annoyance. Even if they had worked out plans for invading the Americas, they would have been helpless before the booming broadsides of the British navy.

Monroe's solemn warning, when issued, made little splash in the newborn republics to the south. Anyone could see that Uncle Sam was only secondarily concerned about his neighbors because he was primarily concerned about defending himself against future invasion. Only a relatively few educated Latin Americans knew of the message, and they generally recognized that the British navy—not the paper pronouncement of James Monroe—stood between them and a hostile Europe.

In truth, Monroe's message did not have much contemporary significance. Americans applauded it and then forgot it. Not until 1845 did President Polk revive it, and not until midcentury did it become an important national dogma.

Even before Monroe's stiff message, the tsar had decided to retreat. This he formally did in the **Russo-American Treaty** of 1824, which fixed his southernmost limits at the line of 54° 40'—the present southern tip of the Alaska panhandle (see Map 12.6).

The Monroe Doctrine might more accurately have been called the Self-Defense Doctrine. President Monroe was concerned basically with the security of his own country—not of Latin America. The United States has never willingly permitted a powerful foreign nation to secure a foothold near its strategic Caribbean vitals. Yet in the absence of the British navy or other allies, the strength of the Monroe Doctrine has never been greater than America's power to eject the trespasser. The doctrine, as often noted, was just as big as the nation's armed forces—and no bigger.

The Monroe Doctrine has had a long career of ups and downs. It was never law—domestic or international. It was not, technically speaking, a pledge or an agreement. It was merely a simple, personalized statement of the policy of President Monroe. What one president says, another may unsay. And Monroe's successors have ignored, revived, distorted, or expanded the original version, chiefly by adding interpretations. Like ivy on a tree, it has grown with America's growth.

Contending Voices
Sizing Up the Monroe Doctrine

Prince Klemens von Metternich (1773–1859), the fabled foreign minister of the Austrian empire from 1809 to 1848, greeted the Monroe Doctrine with scathing contempt in a letter in 1824:

❝The United States of America…have astonished Europe with a new act of revolt.…They have distinctly and clearly announced their intention to set not only power against power, but, to express it more exactly, altar against altar.…If this flood of evil doctrines should extend over the whole of America, what would become of our religious and political institutions, and of the moral force of our governments?❞

A newspaper in the Latin American nation of Colombia, meanwhile, breathed defiance at Europe and lauded Monroe's proclamation:

❝The United States has now begun to play among the civilized nations of the world that powerful and majestic role which befits the oldest and most powerful nation of our hemisphere.…[T]he American continent is now so free and independent that henceforth it cannot be made the theater of colonization by any European power. Indeed the Americans of the North and of the South of this continent shall not again behold in their lands those hordes of foreigners, who, with the cross in one hand and a dagger in the other, would disturb the happiness and the peace which they today enjoy.❞

Why did the European and American perspectives on the Monroe Doctrine diverge so radically?

But the Monroe Doctrine in 1823 was largely an expression of the post-1812 nationalism energizing the United States. Although directed at a specific menace in 1823, and hence a kind of period piece, the doctrine proved to be the most famous of all the long-lived offspring of that nationalism. While giving voice to a spirit of patriotism, it simultaneously deepened the illusion of isolationism. Many Americans falsely concluded, then and later, that the Republic was in fact insulated from European dangers simply because it wanted to be and because, in a nationalistic outburst, Monroe had publicly warned the Old World powers to stay away.

MAP 12.6 The West and Northwest, 1818–1824   The British Hudson's Bay Company moved to secure its claim to the Oregon Country in 1824, when it sent a heavily armed expedition led by Peter Skene Ogden into the Snake River country. In May 1825 Ogden's party descended the Bear River "and found it discharged into a large Lake of 100 miles in length"—one of the first documented sightings by white explorers of the Great Salt Lake. (The mountain man Jim Bridger is usually credited with being the first white man to see the lake.) © 2016 Cengage Learning

Chapter Review

KEY TERMS

War of 1812 (226)

New Orleans, Battle of (228)

Congress of Vienna (229)

Ghent, Treaty of (229)

Hartford Convention (230)

Rush-Bagot agreement (232)

Tariff of 1816 (233)

American System (233)

Era of Good Feelings (234)

panic of 1819 (235)

Land Act of 1820 (236)

Tallmadge amendment (236)

peculiar institution (236)

Missouri Compromise (237)

McCulloch v. *Maryland* (240)

loose construction (240)

Cohens v. *Virginia* (240)

Gibbons v. *Ogden* (240)

Fletcher v. *Peck* (240)

Dartmouth College v. *Woodward* (240)

Anglo-American Convention (241)

Florida Purchase Treaty (Adams-Onís Treaty) (242)

Monroe Doctrine (244)

Russo-American Treaty (245)

PEOPLE TO KNOW

Isaac Brock

Oliver Hazard Perry

Thomas Macdonough

Francis Scott Key

James Monroe

George Canning

CHRONOLOGY

1810   *Fletcher* v. *Peck* ruling asserts right of Supreme Court to invalidate state laws deemed unconstitutional

1811   Venezuela declares independence from Spain

1812   United States declares war on Britain
Madison reelected president

1812–1813   American invasions of Canada fail

1813   Battle of the Thames
Battle of Lake Erie

1814   Battle of Horseshoe Bend
Napoleon exiled to Elba
British burn Washington, D.C.
Battle of Plattsburgh
Treaty of Ghent signed ending War of 1812

1814–1815   Hartford Convention
Congress of Vienna

1815   Battle of New Orleans
Napoleon's army defeated at Waterloo

1816   Second Bank of the United States founded
Protectionist Tariff of 1816
Argentina declares independence from Spain
Monroe elected president

1817   Rush-Bagot agreement limits naval armament on Great Lakes
Madison vetoes internal improvements bill

1818   Jackson invades Florida
Chile, in rebellion since 1810, declares independence from Spain
Anglo-American Convention

1819   Panic of 1819
Spain cedes Florida to United States in Adams-Onís Treaty
McCulloch v. *Maryland*
Dartmouth College v. *Woodward*

1820   Missouri Compromise
Missouri and Maine admitted to Union
Land Act of 1820
Monroe reelected

1821   *Cohens* v. *Virginia*
Austria intervenes to crush popular uprising in Italy

1823   France intervenes to suppresses liberal government in Spain
Secretary Adams proposes Monroe Doctrine

1824   Russo-American Treaty
Gibbons v. *Ogden*

1825   Erie Canal completed

TO LEARN MORE

Jeremy Black, *The War of 1812 in the Age of Napoleon* (2009)

George Dangerfield, *The Awakening of American Nationalism, 1815–1828* (1965)

R. David Edmunds, *Tecumseh and the Quest for Indian Leadership* (1984)

David Heidler, *Old Hickory's War: Andrew Jackson and the Quest for Empire* (2003)

James E. Lewis, *The American Union and the Problem of Neighborhood* (1998)

Arand Otto Mayr and Robert C. Post, eds., *Yankee Enterprise: The Rise of the American System of Manufactures* (1981)

Drew R. McCoy, *The Last of the Fathers: James Madison and the Republican Legacy* (1989)

Dexter Perkins, *A History of the Monroe Doctrine* (1955)

Jack N. Rakove, *James Madison and the Creation of the American Republic* (1990)

Robert Remini, *Henry Clay: Statesman for the Union* (1991)

A complete, annotated bibliography for this chapter—along with brief descriptions of the People to Know—may be found on the *American Pageant* website. The key terms are defined in the glossary at the end of the text.

Chapter 13

The Rise of a Mass Democracy

1824–1840

In the full enjoyment of the gifts of Heaven and the fruits of superior industry, economy, and virtue, every man is equally entitled to protection by law; but when the laws undertake to add to those natural and just advantages artificial distinctions…and exclusive privileges…the humble members of society—the farmers, mechanics, and laborers…have a right to complain of the injustice of their government.

ANDREW JACKSON, 1832

The so-called Era of Good Feelings was never entirely tranquil, but even the illusion of national consensus was shattered by the panic of 1819 and the Missouri Compromise of 1820. Economic distress and the slavery issue raised the political stakes in the 1820s and 1830s. Vigorous political conflict, once feared, came to be celebrated as necessary for the health of democracy. New political parties emerged. New styles of campaigning took hold. A new chapter opened in the history of American—and world—politics, as many European societies began haltingly to expand their electorates and broaden democratic practices. The American political landscape of 1824 was similar, in its broad outlines, to that of 1796. By 1840 it would be almost unrecognizable.

The deference, apathy, and virtually nonexistent party organizations of the Era of Good Feelings yielded to the boisterous democracy, frenzied vitality, and strong political parties of the Jacksonian era. The old suspicion of political parties as illegitimate disrupters of society's natural harmony gave way to an acceptance, even a celebration, of the sometimes wild contentiousness of political life.

In 1828 an energetic new party, the Democrats, captured the White House. By the 1830s the Democrats faced an equally vigorous opposition party, the Whigs. This two-party system institutionalized divisions that had vexed the Revolutionary generation and came to constitute an important part of the nation's checks and balances on political power.

New forms of politicking emerged in this era, as candidates used banners, badges, parades, barbecues, free drinks, and baby kissing to "get out the vote." Voter turnout rose dramatically. Only about one-quarter of eligible voters cast a ballot in the presidential election of 1824, but that proportion doubled in 1828, and in the election of 1840 it reached 78 percent. Everywhere people flexed their political muscles.

⭑ The "Corrupt Bargain" of 1824

The last of the old-style elections was marked by the controversial **corrupt bargain** of 1824. The woods were full of presidential timber as James Monroe, last of the Virginia dynasty, completed his second term. Four candidates towered above the others: John Quincy Adams of Massachusetts, highly intelligent, experienced, and aloof; Henry Clay of Kentucky, the gamy and gallant "Harry of the West"; William H. Crawford of Georgia, an able though ailing giant of a man; and Andrew Jackson of Tennessee, the gaunt and gutsy hero of New Orleans.

All four rivals professed to be "Republicans." Well-organized parties had not yet emerged; their identities were so fuzzy, in fact, that South Carolina's John C. Calhoun appeared as the vice-presidential candidate on both the Adams and Jackson tickets.

The results of the noisy campaign were interesting but confusing. Jackson, the war hero, clearly had the strongest personal appeal, especially in the West, where his campaign against the forces of corruption and privilege in government resonated deeply. He polled almost as many popular votes as his next two

Gift of Mrs. Samuel T. Carson photograph © 1991 The Detroit Institute of Arts (detail). Bridgeman Art Library Ltd.

First State Election in Detroit, Michigan, by Thomas Mickell Burnham This painting shows the "new politics" of the Jacksonian era. Politicians now had to take their message to the common man.

rivals combined, but he failed to win a majority of the electoral vote (see Table 13.1). In such a deadlock, the House of Representatives, as directed by the Twelfth Amendment (see the Appendix), must choose among the top three candidates. Clay was thus eliminated, yet as Speaker of the House, he presided over the very chamber that had to pick the winner.

The influential Clay was in a position to throw the election to the candidate of his choice. He reached his decision by process of elimination. Crawford, recently felled by a paralytic stroke, was out of the picture. Clay hated the "military chieftain" Jackson, his archrival for the allegiance of the West. Jackson, in turn, bitterly resented Clay's public denunciation of his Florida foray in 1818. The only candidate left was the puritanical Adams, with whom Clay—a free-living gambler and duelist—had never established cordial

personal relations. But the two men had much in common politically: both were fervid nationalists and advocates of the American System. Shortly before the final balloting in the House, Clay met privately with Adams and assured him of his support.

Decision day came early in 1825. The House of Representatives met amid tense excitement, with sick members being carried in on stretchers. On the first ballot, thanks largely to Clay's behind-the-scenes influence, Adams was elected president. A few days later, the victor announced that Henry Clay would be the new secretary of state.

The office of secretary of state was the prize plum then, even more so than today. Three of the four preceding secretaries had reached the presidency, and the high cabinet office was regarded as an almost certain pathway to the White House. According to Jackson's supporters, Adams had bribed Clay with the position, making himself, the people's second choice, the victor over Jackson, the people's first choice.

Masses of angry Jacksonians, most of them common folk, raised a roar of protest against this "corrupt bargain." The clamor continued for nearly four years. Jackson condemned Clay as the "Judas of the West," and John Randolph of Virginia publicly assailed

TABLE 13.1 Election of 1824			
Candidates	Electoral Vote	Popular Vote	Popular Percentage
Jackson	99	153,544	42.16%
Adams	84	108,740	31.89
Crawford	41	46,618	12.95
Clay	37	47,136	12.99

the alliance between "the Puritan [Adams] and the black-leg [Clay]," who, he added, "shines and stinks like rotten mackerel by moonlight." Clay, outraged, challenged Randolph to a duel, though poor marksmanship and shaky nerves rendered the outcome bloodless.

No positive evidence has yet been unearthed to prove that Adams and Clay entered into a formal bargain. Clay was a natural choice for secretary of state, and Adams was both scrupulously honest and not given to patronage. Even if a bargain had been struck, it was not necessarily corrupt. Deals of this nature have long been the stock-in-trade of politicians. But the outcry over Adams's election showed that change was in the wind. What had once been common practice was now condemned as furtive, elitist, and subversive of democracy. The next president would not be chosen behind closed doors.

✯ A Yankee Misfit in the White House

John Quincy Adams was a chip off the old family glacier. Short, thickset, and billiard-bald, he was even more frigidly austere than his presidential father, John Adams. Shunning people, he often went for early-morning swims, sometimes stark naked, in the then-pure Potomac River. Essentially a closeted thinker rather than a politician, he was irritable, sarcastic, and tactless. Yet few individuals have ever come to the presidency with a more brilliant record in statecraft, especially in foreign affairs. He ranks as one of the most successful secretaries of state, yet one of the least successful presidents.

A man of scrupulous honor, Adams entered upon his four-year "sentence" in the White House smarting under charges of "bargain," "corruption," and "usurpation." Fewer than one-third of the voters had voted for him. As the first "minority president," he would have found it difficult to win popular support even under the most favorable conditions. He did not possess many of the usual arts of the politician and scorned those who did. He had achieved high office by commanding respect rather than by courting popularity. In an earlier era, an aloof John Adams had won the votes of propertied men by sheer ability. But with the dawning age of backslapping and baby-kissing democracy, his cold-fish son could hardly hope for success at the polls.

While Adams's enemies accused him of striking a corrupt bargain, his political allies wished that he would strike a few more. Whether through high-mindedness or political ineptitude, Adams resolutely declined to oust efficient officeholders in order to create vacancies for his supporters. During his entire administration, he removed only twelve public servants from the federal payroll. Such stubbornness caused countless Adams followers to throw up their hands in despair. If the president would not reward party workers with political plums, why should they labor to keep him in office?

President John Quincy Adams (1767–1848), Daguerreotype by Phillip Haas, 1843 Adams wrote in his diary in June 1819, nearly six years before becoming president, "I am a man of reserved, cold, austere, and forbidding manners: my political adversaries say, a gloomy misanthropist, and my personal enemies an unsocial savage."

Adams's nationalistic views gave him further woes. Much of the nation was turning away from post-Ghent nationalism and toward states' rights and sectionalism. But Adams swam against the tide. Confirmed nationalist that he was, Adams, in his first annual message, urged upon Congress the construction of roads and canals. He renewed George Washington's proposal for a national university and went so far as to advocate federal support for an astronomical observatory.

The public reaction to these proposals was prompt and unfavorable. To many workaday Americans grubbing out stumps, astronomical observatories seemed like a scandalous waste of public funds. The South in particular bristled. If the federal government should take on such heavy financial burdens, it would have to continue the hated tariff duties. Worse, if it could meddle in local concerns like education and roads, it might even try to lay its hand on the "peculiar institution" of black slavery.

Adams's land policy likewise antagonized the westerners. They clamored for wide-open expansion and resented the president's well-meaning attempts to curb feverish speculation in the public domain. The fate of the Cherokee Indians, threatened with eviction from their holdings in Georgia, brought additional bitterness. White Georgians wanted the Cherokees out. The ruggedly honest Adams attempted to deal fairly with the Indians. The Georgia governor, by threatening to resort to arms, successfully resisted the efforts of the Washington government to interpose federal authority on behalf of the Cherokees. Another fateful chapter was thus written in the nullification of the national will—and another nail was driven in Adams's political coffin.

✪ Going "Whole Hog" for Jackson in 1828

Andrew Jackson's next presidential campaign started early—on February 9, 1825, the day of John Quincy Adams's controversial election by the House—and it continued noisily for nearly four years.

Even before the election of 1828, the temporarily united Republicans of the Era of Good Feelings had split into two camps. One was the National Republicans, with Adams as their standard-bearer. The other was the Democratic-Republicans, with the fiery Jackson heading their ticket. Rallying cries of the Jackson zealots were "Bargain and Corruption," "Huzza for Jackson," and "All Hail Old Hickory." Jacksonites planted hickory poles for their hickory-tough hero; Adamsites adopted the oak as the symbol of their oakenly independent candidate.

Jackson's followers presented their hero as a rough-hewn frontiersman and a stalwart champion of the common man. They denounced Adams as a corrupt aristocrat and argued that the will of the people had been thwarted in 1825 by the backstairs "bargain" of Adams and Clay. The only way to right the wrong was to seat Jackson, who would then bring about "reform" by sweeping out the "dishonest" Adams gang.

Much of this talk was political hyperbole. Jackson was no frontier farmer but a wealthy planter. He had been born in a log cabin but now lived in a luxurious manor off the labor of his many enslaved workers. And Adams, though perhaps an aristocrat, was far from corrupt. If anything, his uncompromising morals were too elevated for the job.

Mudslinging reached new lows in 1828, and the electorate developed a taste for bare-knuckle politics. Adams would not stoop to gutter tactics, but many of his backers were less squeamish. They described Jackson's mother as a prostitute and his wife as an adulteress; they printed black-bordered handbills shaped like coffins, recounting his numerous duels and brawls and trumpeting his hanging of six mutinous militiamen.

Jackson men also hit below the belt. President Adams had purchased, with his own money and for his own use, a billiard table and a set of chessmen. In the mouths of rabid Jacksonites, these items became "gaming tables" and "gambling furniture" for the

Rachel Jackson   A devoted wife who did not live to become First Lady, Rachel died a month after the election of 1828. Andrew Jackson was convinced that his enemies' vicious accusations that she was a bigamist and an adulteress had killed her. The more complicated truth was that Andrew Jackson had married Rachel Robards confident that her divorce had been granted. Two years later, when they discovered to their dismay that it had not been, they made haste to correct the marital miscue. Louisa C. Strobel/The Granger Collection

"presidential palace." Criticism was also directed at the large sums Adams had received over the years in federal salaries, well earned though they had been. He was even accused of having procured a servant girl for the lust of the Russian tsar—in short, of having served as a pimp.

On voting day the electorate split on largely sectional lines. Jackson's strongest support came from the West and South (see Map 13.1). The middle states and the Old Northwest were divided, while Adams won the backing of his own New England and the propertied "better elements" of the Northeast. But when the popular vote was converted to electoral votes, General Jackson's triumph could not be denied. Old Hickory had trounced Adams by an electoral count of 178 to 83. Although a considerable part of Jackson's support was lined up by machine politicians in eastern cities, particularly in New York and Pennsylvania, the political center of gravity clearly had shifted away from the conservative eastern seaboard toward the emerging states across the mountains.

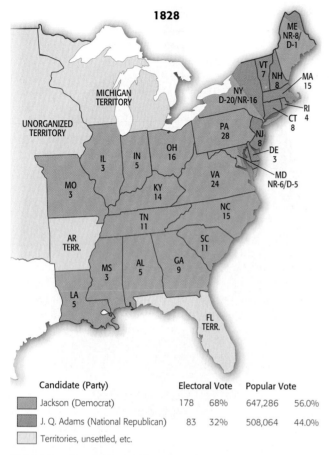

1828

Candidate (Party)	Electoral Vote		Popular Vote	
Jackson (Democrat)	178	68%	647,286	56.0%
J. Q. Adams (National Republican)	83	32%	508,064	44.0%
Territories, unsettled, etc.				

MAP 13.1 Presidential Election of 1828 (with electoral vote by state) Jackson swept the South and West, whereas Adams retained the old Federalist stronghold of the Northeast. Yet Jackson's inroads in the Northeast were decisive. He won twenty of New York's electoral votes and all twenty-eight of Pennsylvania's. If those votes had gone the other way, Adams would have been victorious—by a margin of one vote. © 2016 Cengage Learning

★ "Old Hickory" as President

The new president cut a striking figure—tall, lean, with bushy iron-gray hair brushed high above a prominent forehead, craggy eyebrows, and blue eyes. His irritability and emaciated condition resulted in part from long-term bouts with dysentery, malaria, tuberculosis, and lead poisoning from two bullets that he

One anti-Jackson newspaper declared,

❝General Jackson's mother was a Common Prostitute, brought to this country by the British soldiers! She afterwards married a MULATTO man with whom she had several children, of which number GENERAL JACKSON is one.❞

Contending Voices
Taking the Measure of Andrew Jackson

Andrew Jackson was a military hero to some and an impetuous ruffian to others. A Maryland supporter endorsed Jackson for president in the campaign of 1824 as follows:

❝[As] chief judge of the supreme court of Tennessee, [Jackson] acted until his services in the field were demanded by his country; he then laid down his law books, the sweets of domestic life, and seized his sword to revenge his country's wrongs. The savages were murdering by hundreds, men, women, and children, of our frontier; the tomahawk was reeking with the blood of innocence. It was then, my countrymen, that JACKSON led the van; it was then this noble soldier made his pillow of snow, and had for his roof the canopy of heaven. Yea, countrymen, I might extend my hand-bill to a volume, and I could not then give you a correct idea of the magnanimous and generous soul, of this unparalleled hero.❞

In the same year Thomas Jefferson (1743–1826) wrote of Jackson:

❝When I was President of the Senate he was a Senator; and he could never speak on account of the rashness of his feelings. I have seen him attempt it repeatedly, and as often choke with rage. His passions are no doubt cooler now…but he is a dangerous man.❞

> Do these two observations agree on any aspects of Jackson's character, or do they seem to be describing two different people? Why might Jefferson, himself a revolutionary, regard Jackson as "dangerous"?

carried in his body from near-fatal duels. His autobiography was written in his lined face.

Jackson's upbringing had its shortcomings. Born in the Carolinas and early orphaned, "Mischievous Andy" grew up without parental restraints. As a youth he displayed much more interest in brawling and cockfighting than in his scanty opportunities for reading and spelling. Although he eventually learned to express himself in writing with vigor and clarity, his grammar was always rough-hewn and his spelling original, like that of many contemporaries. He sometimes misspelled a word two different ways in the same letter.

The youthful Carolinian shrewdly moved "up West" to Tennessee, where fighting was prized above writing. There—through native intelligence, force of personality, and powers of leadership—he became a

English novelist Charles Dickens (1812–1870) traveled to the United States just a few years after Alexis de Tocqueville (see "Thinking Globally: Alexis de Tocqueville on Democracy in America and Europe," pp. 254–255). He had his own views on the implications of America's vaunted "equality":

❝The people are all alike too. There is no diversity of character. They travel about on the same errands, say and do the same things in exactly the same manner, and follow in the same dull cheerless round. All down the long table there is scarcely a man who is in anything different from his neighbor.**❞**

judge and a member of Congress. Afflicted with a violent temper, he early became involved in a number of duels, stabbings, and bloody frays. His passions were so profound that on occasion he would choke into silence when he tried to speak.

The first president from the West, the first nominated at a formal party convention (in 1832), and only the second without a college education (Washington was the first), Jackson was unique. His university was adversity. He had risen from the masses, but he was not one of them, except insofar as he shared many of their prejudices. Essentially a frontier aristocrat, he owned many slaves, cultivated broad acres, and lived in one of the finest mansions in America—the Hermitage, near Nashville, Tennessee. More westerner than easterner, more country gentleman than common clay, more courtly than crude, he was hard to fit into a neat category.

Jackson's inauguration seemed to symbolize the ascendancy of the masses. "Hickoryites" poured into Washington from far away, sleeping on hotel floors and in hallways. They were curious to see their hero take office and perhaps hoped to pick up a well-paying office for themselves. Nobodies mingled with notables as the White House, for the first time, was thrown open to the multitude. A milling crowd of rubbernecking clerks and shopkeepers, hobnailed artisans, and grimy laborers surged in, allegedly wrecking the china and furniture and threatening the "people's champion" with cracked ribs. Jackson was hastily spirited through a side door, and the White House miraculously emptied itself when the word was passed that huge bowls of well-spiked punch had been placed on the lawns. Such was "the inaugural brawl."

To conservatives this orgy seemed like the end of the world. "King Mob" reigned triumphant as Jacksonian vulgarity replaced Jeffersonian simplicity. Fainthearted traditionalists shuddered, drew their blinds, and recalled with trepidation the opening scenes of the French Revolution.

✶ The Spoils System

Once in power, the Democrats, famously suspicious of the federal government, demonstrated that they were not above striking some bargains of their own. Under Jackson the **spoils system**—that is, rewarding political supporters with public office—was introduced into the federal government on a large scale. The basic idea was as old as politics. Its name came later from Senator William Marcy's classic remark in 1832, "To the victor belong the spoils of the enemy." The system had already secured a firm hold in New York and Pennsylvania, where well-greased machines ladled out the "gravy" of office.

Jackson defended the spoils system on democratic grounds. "Every man is as good as his neighbor," he declared—perhaps "equally better." As this was believed to be so, and as the routine of office was thought to be simple enough for any upstanding American to learn quickly, why encourage the development of an aristocratic, bureaucratic, officeholding class? Better to bring in new blood, he argued; each generation deserved its turn at the public trough.

Washington was due, it is true, for a housecleaning. No party overturn had occurred since the defeat of the Federalists in 1800, and even that had not produced wholesale evictions. A few officeholders, their commissions signed by President Washington, were lingering on into their eighties, drawing breath and salary but doing little else. But the spoils system was less about finding new blood than about rewarding old cronies. "Throw their rascals out and put our rascals in," the Democrats were essentially saying. The questions asked of each appointee were not "What can he do for the country?" but "What has he done for the party?" or "Is he loyal to Jackson?"

Scandal inevitably accompanied the new system. Men who had openly bought their posts by campaign contributions were appointed to high office. Illiterates, incompetents, and plain crooks were given positions of public trust; men on the make lusted for the spoils—rather than the toils—of office. Samuel Swartwout, despite ample warnings of his untrustworthiness, was awarded the lucrative post of collector of the customs of the port of New York. Nearly nine years later, he "Swartwouted out" for England, leaving his accounts more than a million dollars short—the first person to steal a million from the Washington government.

But despite its undeniable abuse, the spoils system was an important element of the emerging two-party order, cementing as it did loyalty to party over competing claims based on economic class or geographic region. The promise of patronage provided a compelling reason for Americans to pick a party and stick with it through thick and thin.

Alexis de Tocqueville on Democracy in America and Europe

On May 11, 1831, a twenty-six-year-old Frenchman, Alexis de Tocqueville, stepped ashore in New York City and began his fateful acquaintance with Andrew Jackson's America. For nine months he visited the cities of the Atlantic seaboard from Boston to Washington, trekked west to Detroit, and floated down the Ohio and Mississippi Rivers to New Orleans, keenly observing the American scene. Four years later he published the first volume of his monumental work *Democracy in America*. It remains to this day probably the most insightful analysis of American society ever written and provides an indispensable starting point for understanding both the nature of modern democracy and the American national character.

Tocqueville was born in the French Revolutionary era, and he witnessed the so-called July Revolution in France in 1830, which widened the French electorate. He was following closely the agitation in Britain for a broader, more democratic franchise, which culminated in the landmark Reform Bill of 1832. He also knew of the several independent democratic republics that had blossomed in Latin America as the disruptions of the Napoleonic Wars weakened Spain's imperial grip: Venezuela proclaimed its independence in 1811, Argentina in 1816, Chile in 1818, Mexico and Peru in 1821. (Brazil declared its independence from Portugal in 1822, but remained a monarchy until becoming a republic in 1889.) Those events convinced him that democracy was the irresistible wave of the future, but he was far less certain about what that democratic future might mean for human happiness, political stability, and social justice. Thus he studied America to understand Europe's—indeed the world's—fate. "In America I saw more than America," he wrote. "I sought there the image of democracy itself…in order to learn what we have to fear or to hope from its progress."

He announced his central insight in his book's first sentence: "Among the novel objects that attracted my attention during my stay in the United States, nothing struck me more forcibly than the general equality of condition among the people." (He acknowledged the gross inequality of slavery, but he considered slavery to be something that was "peculiar to America, not to democracy.") The "primary fact" of equality, he argued, exercised a "prodigious influence on the whole course of society."

It is easy to understand why the scale and pervasiveness of American equality made such an impression on Tocqueville. Mass democratic participation was already a well-established fact when he arrived. Almost 1.2 million voters—nearly 50 percent of the adult white male population—had cast their ballots in the election that brought Jackson to the White House in 1828. In contrast, France's July Revolution had enfranchised fewer than 200,000 propertied males, less than 1 percent of the total population, in 1830. And Britain's Reform Bill of 1832 would extend voting rights only to some 800,000 male property holders—in a country with 50 percent more people than the United States.

Tocqueville repeatedly remarked on the seething, restless energy that American equality unleashed, and he speculated on two possible futures for the United States. They might be called, respectively, the *centripetal* and *centrifugal* scenarios.

In the first scenario, Tocqueville thought that the doctrine of equality might breed a suffocating conformity that would eventually invoke the power of the state to enforce a stern and repressive consensus—the kind of "tyranny of the majority" that had worried Founders like James Madison. Tocqueville thought he saw signs that such a future was already emerging. "I know of no country in which there is so little independence of mind and real freedom of discussion as in America," he wrote.

In the second scenario, equality might foster radical *individualism*, a word that Tocqueville coined to capture the unique psychology he encountered everywhere in America. "As social conditions become more equal," he wrote, people "acquire the habit of always considering themselves as standing alone, and they are apt to imagine that their whole destiny is in their own hands." In this case, gnawing individual loneliness and even social anarchy might define America's future. "Democracy makes every man forget his ancestors," Tocqueville wrote. "It throws him back forever upon himself alone and threatens in the end to confine him entirely within the solitude of his own heart."

Tocqueville noted several factors that mitigated both of those

Alexis de Tocqueville (1805–1859) The Granger Collection, NYC

Election Day in Philadelphia, by John Lewis Krimmel, 1815 The German immigrant Krimmel recorded as early as 1815 the growing popular interest in elections that would culminate in Jacksonian democracy a decade later. Although politics was serious business, it also provided the occasion for much socializing and merriment. Even disfranchised free blacks, women, and children turned out for the festivities on election day.

grim prospects and held American democracy in a healthy balance: the absence of hostile countries on its borders; a vigorously free press; robust voluntary associations (especially churches and political parties); and, crucially, "habits of the heart," which sustained a sense of civic belonging and responsibility. But Tocqueville raised troubling questions about whether those factors would prove durable. If not, what would the ultimate fate of democracy be?

Ironically, today the United States has markedly *lower* rates of political participation than many other countries, especially those in Europe (see Table 13.2). Can it be that America—the pioneering mass democracy that served as Tocqueville's laboratory and his window on the future—has proved to be less fertile soil for the development of democracy than the Old World societies with which he compared it in the 1830s?

TABLE 13.2 Voter Turnout by Country, 1840–2008

	1840		1900		1960	2008
	Percentage of Voting-Age Population*	Percentage of Eligible Voters†	Percentage of Voting-Age Population	Percentage of Eligible Voters	Percentage of Voting-Age Population	Percentage of Voting-Age Population‡
United States	30 (1841)	79 (1841)	34	73	63	58 (2008)
United Kingdom	4 (1842)	58 (1842)	14 (1902)	49 (1902)	77 (1958)	58 (2005)
France	1	79	33 (1898)	76 (1898)	68 (1961)	77 (2007)
Germany	—	—	26	68	87	72 (2005)
Japan	—	—	—	—	71 (1958)	67 (2005)
Mexico	—	—	—	—	52	64 (2006)

*Voting-age population includes individuals of any race and both genders. For France and the United Kingdom, individuals over the age of twenty are included in population estimates. For the United States, the voting-age population is an approximation of the total population over age twenty-one.

†Virtually all blacks and all women were ineligible to vote in the United States. Landholding requirements severely limited eligibility in the United Kingdom and France.

‡The voting age was reduced to eighteen in the United States, France, the United Kingdom, and Germany in the second half of the twentieth century. The voting age in Mexico was eighteen for both the 1958 and 2000 elections. The voting age in Japan is twenty.

(Sources: *Historical Statistics of the United States*, vol. 5; *State, Economy and Society in Western Europe, 1815–1975*; *International Historical Statistics, 1750–2005: Europe*; and *International Institute for Democracy and Electoral Assistance*.)

✸ The Tricky "Tariff of Abominations"

The touchy tariff issue had been one of John Quincy Adams's biggest headaches. Now Andrew Jackson felt his predecessor's pain. Tariffs protected American industry against competition from European manufactured goods, but they also drove up prices for all Americans and invited retaliatory tariffs on American agricultural exports abroad. The middle states had long been supporters of protectionist tariffs. In the 1820s influential New Englanders like Daniel Webster gave up their traditional defense of free trade to support higher tariffs, too. The wool and textile industries were booming, and forward-thinking Yankees came to believe that their future prosperity would flow from the factory rather than from the sea.

In 1824 Congress had increased the general tariff significantly, but wool manufacturers bleated for still-higher barriers. Ardent Jacksonites now played a cynical political game. They promoted a high-tariff bill, expecting to be defeated, which would give a black eye to President Adams. To their surprise, the tariff passed in 1828, and Andrew Jackson inherited the political hot potato.

Southerners, as heavy consumers of manufactured goods with little manufacturing industry of their own, were hostile to tariffs. They were particularly shocked by what they regarded as the outrageous rates of the Tariff of 1828. Hotheads branded it the "Black Tariff" or the **Tariff of Abominations**. Several southern states adopted formal protests. In South Carolina flags were lowered to half-mast. "Let the *New* England beware how she imitates the *Old*," cried one eloquent South Carolinian.

Why did the South react so angrily against the tariff? Southerners believed, not illogically, that the "Yankee tariff" discriminated against them. The bustling Northeast was experiencing a boom in manufacturing, the developing West was prospering from rising property values and a multiplying population, and the energetic Southwest was expanding into virgin cotton lands. But the Old South was falling on hard times, and the tariff provided a convenient and plausible scapegoat. Southerners sold their cotton and other farm produce in a world market completely unprotected by tariffs but were forced to buy their manufactured goods in an American market heavily protected by tariffs. Protectionism protected Yankee and middle-state manufacturers. The farmers and planters of the Old South felt they were stuck with the bill.

But much deeper issues underlay the southern outcry—in particular, a growing anxiety about possible federal interference with the institution of slavery. The congressional debate on the Missouri

South Carolina Belle Sewing Palmetto Cockade The "Tariff of Abominations" of 1828 drove many people in South Carolina—the "Palmetto State"—to flirt with secession. Anti-tariff protesters wore palmetto blossoms, real or sewn from fabric, to symbolize their defiance of the federal law. The blue cockade indicated support for the ordinance of nullification.

The Granger Collection, NYC; inset: Collection of McKissick Museum, University of South Carolina

John C. Calhoun (1782–1850), leader of South Carolina's offensive to nullify the Tariff of 1832, saw nullification as a way of preserving the Union while preventing secession of the southern states. In his mind he was still a Unionist, even if also a southern sectionalist:

❝I never use the word 'nation' in speaking of the United States. I always use the word 'union' or 'confederacy.' We are not a nation, but a union, a confederacy of equal and sovereign states.❞

During the crisis of 1832, some of his South Carolina compatriots had different ideas. Medals were struck off in honor of Calhoun, bearing the words, "First President of the Southern Confederacy."

unconstitutional. Going a stride beyond the Virginia and Kentucky resolutions of 1798, it bluntly and explicitly proposed that the states should nullify the tariff—that is, they should declare it null and void within their borders.

✴ "Nullies" in South Carolina

The stage was set for a showdown. Through Jackson's first term, the nullifiers—"nullies," they were called—tried strenuously to muster the necessary two-thirds vote for nullification in the South Carolina legislature. But they were blocked by a determined minority of Unionists, scorned as "submission men." Back in Washington, Congress tipped the balance by passing the new Tariff of 1832. Though it pared away the worst "abominations" of 1828, it was still frankly protective and fell far short of meeting southern demands. Worse yet, to many southerners it had a disquieting air of permanence. The **Nullification Crisis** deepened.

South Carolina was now nerved for drastic action. Nullifiers and Unionists clashed head-on in the state election of 1832. "Nullies," defiantly wearing palmetto ribbons on their hats to mark their loyalty to the "Palmetto State," emerged with more than a two-thirds majority. The state legislature then called for a special convention. Several weeks later the delegates, meeting in Columbia, solemnly declared the existing tariff to be null and void within South Carolina. As a further act of defiance, the convention threatened to take South Carolina out of the Union if Washington attempted to collect the customs duties by force.

Such tactics might have intimidated John Quincy Adams, but Andrew Jackson was the wrong president to stare down. The cantankerous general was not a diehard supporter of the tariff, but he would not permit defiance or disunion. His military instincts rasped, Jackson privately threatened to invade the state and have the nullifiers hanged. In public he was only slightly less pugnacious. He dispatched naval and military reinforcements to the Palmetto State, while quietly preparing a sizable army. He also issued a ringing proclamation against nullification, to which the governor of South Carolina, former senator Robert Y. Hayne,

King, Charles Bird (1785–1862) (attr.) John Caldwell Calhoun (1782–1850), Statesman. ca. 1818–25. Oil on canvas. 76.2 x 63.5 cm./National Portrait Gallery, Smithsonian Institution/Art Resource, NY

John C. Calhoun (1782–1850), by John Trumbull, 1827 Calhoun was a South Carolinian, educated at Yale. Beginning as a strong nationalist and Unionist, he reversed himself and became the ablest of the sectionalists and disunionists in defense of the South and slavery. As a foremost nullifier, he died trying to reconcile strong states' rights with a strong Union. In his last years, he advocated a Siamese-twin "dual presidency," probably unworkable, with one president for the North and one for the South. His former plantation home is now the site of Clemson University.

Compromise had kindled those anxieties, and they were further fanned by an aborted slave rebellion in Charleston in 1822, led by a free black named Denmark Vesey. The South Carolinians, still closely tied to the British West Indies, also knew full well that their slave-owning West Indian cousins were feeling the mounting pressure of British abolitionism on the London government. Abolitionism in America might similarly use the power of the government in Washington to suppress slavery in the South. If so, now was the time, and the tariff was the issue, to take a strong stand on principle against all federal encroachments on states' rights.

South Carolinians took the lead in protesting against the "Tariff of Abominations." Their legislature went so far as to publish in 1828, though without formal endorsement, a pamphlet known as *The South Carolina Exposition*. It had been secretly written by John C. Calhoun, one of the few topflight political theorists ever produced by America. (As vice president, he was forced to conceal his authorship.) *The Exposition* denounced the recent tariff as unjust and

At a Jefferson Day dinner on April 13, 1830, in the midst of the nullification controversy, President Andrew Jackson (1767–1845) offered a toast:

❝Our federal Union: It must be preserved.❞

John C. Calhoun rose to his feet to make a countertoast:

❝To the Union, next to our liberty, most dear.❞

responded with a counterproclamation. The lines were drawn. If civil war was to be avoided, one side would have to surrender, or both would have to compromise.

Conciliatory Henry Clay of Kentucky, now in the Senate, stepped forward. An unforgiving foe of Jackson, he had no desire to see his old enemy win new laurels by crushing the Carolinians and returning with the scalp of Calhoun dangling from his belt. Although himself a supporter of tariffs, the gallant Kentuckian therefore threw his influence behind a compromise bill that would gradually reduce the Tariff of 1832 by about 10 percent over a period of eight years. By 1842 the rates would be back at the mildly protective level of 1816.

The **compromise Tariff of 1833** finally squeezed through Congress. Debate was bitter, with most of the opposition naturally coming from protectionist New England and the middle states. Calhoun and the South favored the compromise, so it was evident that Jackson would not have to use firearms and rope. But at the same time, and partly as a face-saving device, Congress passed the **Force Bill**, known among Carolinians as the "Bloody Bill." It authorized the president to use the army and navy, if necessary, to collect federal tariff duties.

South Carolinians welcomed this opportunity to extricate themselves from a dangerously tight corner without loss of face. To the consternation of the Calhounites, no other southern states had sprung to their support, though Georgia and Virginia toyed with the idea. Moreover, an appreciable Unionist minority within South Carolina was gathering guns, organizing militias, and nailing Stars and Stripes to flagpoles. Faced with civil war within and invasion from without, the Columbia convention met again and repealed the ordinance of nullification. As a final but futile gesture of fist-shaking, it nullified the unnecessary Force Bill and adjourned.

Neither Jackson nor the "nullies" won a clear-cut victory in 1833. Clay was the true hero of the hour, hailed in Charleston and Boston alike for saving the country. Armed conflict had been avoided, but the fundamental issues had not been resolved. When next the "nullies" and the Union clashed, compromise would prove more elusive.

✦ The Trail of Tears

Jackson's Democrats were committed to western expansion, but such expansion necessarily meant confrontation with the current inhabitants of the land. More than 125,000 Native Americans lived in the forests and prairies east of the Mississippi in the 1820s. Federal policy toward them varied. Beginning in the 1790s, the

Washington government ostensibly recognized the tribes as separate nations and agreed to acquire land from them only through formal treaties. The Indians were shrewd and stubborn negotiators, but this availed them little when Americans routinely violated their own covenants, erasing and redrawing treaty line after treaty line on their maps as white settlement pushed west.

Many white Americans felt respect and admiration for the Indians and believed that they could be assimilated into white society. Much energy therefore was devoted to "civilizing" and Christianizing the Indians. The Society for Propagating the Gospel Among Indians was founded in 1787, and many denominations sent missionaries into Indian villages. In 1793 Congress

Jackson the "Great Father" An anonymous cartoonist satirizes Jackson's alleged compassion for the Indians, but in fact his feelings toward Native Americans were complicated. He made ruthless war on the Creeks as a soldier, but he also adopted a Creek Indian son (who died of tuberculosis at the age of sixteen). At least in part, his motives for pursuing Indian removal stemmed from his concern that if the Indians were not removed from contact with the whites, they would face certain annihilation.

The "Trail of Tears" In the fall and winter of 1838–1839, the U.S. Army forcibly removed about fifteen thousand Cherokees, some of them in manacles, from their ancestral homelands in the southeastern United States and marched them to Indian Territory (present-day Oklahoma). Freezing weather and inadequate food supplies led to unspeakable suffering. The escorting troops refused to slow the forced march so that the ill could recover, and some four thousand Cherokees died on the 116-day journey.

appropriated $20,000 for the promotion of literacy and agricultural and vocational instruction among the Indians.

Although many tribes violently resisted white encroachment, others followed the path of accommodation. The Cherokees of Georgia made especially remarkable efforts to learn the ways of the whites. They gradually abandoned their seminomadic life and adopted a system of settled agriculture and a notion of private property. Missionaries opened schools among the Cherokees, and the Indian Sequoyah devised a Cherokee alphabet. In 1808 the Cherokee National Council legislated a written legal code, and in 1827 it adopted a written constitution that provided for executive, legislative, and judicial branches of government. Some Cherokees became prosperous cotton planters and even turned to slaveholding. Nearly thirteen hundred enslaved blacks toiled for their Native American masters in the Cherokee nation in the 1820s. For these efforts the Cherokees—along with the Creeks, Choctaws, Chickasaws, and Seminoles—were numbered by whites among the "Five Civilized Tribes."

All this embrace of "civilization" apparently was not good enough for whites. In 1828 the Georgia legislature declared the Cherokee tribal council illegal and asserted its own jurisdiction over Indian affairs and Indian lands. The Cherokees appealed this move to the Supreme Court, which thrice upheld the rights of the Indians. But President Jackson, who clearly wanted to open Indian lands to white settlement, refused to recognize the Court's decisions. In a callous jibe at the Indians' defender, Jackson allegedly snapped, "John Marshall has made his decision; now let him enforce it."*

Feeling some obligation to rescue "this much injured race," Jackson proposed a bodily removal of the remaining eastern tribes—chiefly Cherokees, Creeks, Choctaws, Chickasaws, and Seminoles—beyond the Mississippi. Emigration was supposed to be voluntary because it would be "cruel and unjust to compel the aborigines to abandon the graves of their fathers." Jackson evidently consoled himself with the belief that the Indians could preserve their native cultures in the wide-open West.

Jackson's policy led to the forced uprooting of more than 100,000 Indians. In 1830 Congress passed the **Indian Removal Act**, providing for the transplanting

---

*One hundred sixty years later, in 1992, the state government of Georgia formally pardoned the two white missionaries, Samuel Austin Worcester and Elihu Butler, who figured prominently in the decision Jackson condemned. They had been convicted of living on Cherokee lands without a license from the state government of Georgia. They had served sixteen months at hard labor on a chain gang and later had accompanied the Cherokees on the "Trail of Tears" to Oklahoma.

One survivor of the Indians' forced march in 1838–1839 on the "Trail of Tears" to Indian Territory, farther west, remembered,

"One each day, and all are gone. Looks like maybe all dead before we get to new Indian country, but always we keep marching on. Women cry and make sad wails. Children cry, and many men cry, and all look sad when friends die, but they say nothing and just put heads down and keep on toward west.... She [his mother] speak no more; we bury her and go on."

of all Indian tribes then resident east of the Mississippi (see Map 13.2). Ironically, the heaviest blows fell on the Five Civilized Tribes. In the ensuing decade, countless Indians died on forced marches—notably the Cherokees along the notorious **Trail of Tears**—to the newly established Indian Territory, where they

were to be "permanently" free of white encroachments. The Bureau of Indian Affairs was established in 1836 to administer relations with America's original inhabitants. But as the land-hungry "palefaces" pushed west faster than anticipated, the government's guarantees went up in smoke. The "permanent" frontier lasted about fifteen years.

Suspicious of white intentions from the start, Sauk and Fox braves from Illinois and Wisconsin, ably led by Black Hawk, resisted eviction. They were bloodily crushed in the **Black Hawk War** of 1832 by regular troops, including Lieutenant Jefferson Davis of Mississippi, and by volunteers, including Captain Abraham Lincoln of Illinois.

In Florida the Seminole Indians, joined by runaway black slaves, retreated to the swampy Everglades. For seven years (1835–1842), they waged a bitter guerrilla war that took the lives of some fifteen hundred soldiers. The spirit of the Seminoles was broken in 1837, when the American field commander treacherously seized their leader, Osceola, under a flag of truce. The war dragged on for five more years, but the Seminoles

MAP 13.2 Indian Removals, 1830–1846 © 2016 Cengage Learning

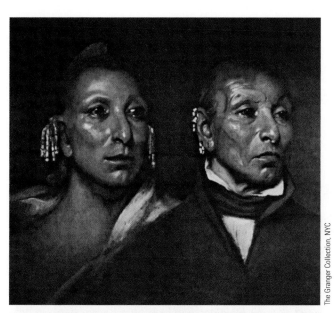

Black Hawk and His Son Whirling Thunder, by John Wesley Jarvis, 1833 Chief Black Hawk and his son are depicted here in captivity. After their surrender in the Black Hawk War of 1832, they were put on public display throughout the United States.

were doomed. Some fled deeper into the Everglades, where their descendants now live, but about four-fifths of them were moved to present-day Oklahoma, where several thousand of the tribe survive.

✷ The Bank War

President Jackson did not hate all banks and all businesses, but he distrusted monopolistic banking and over-big businesses, as did his followers. A man of virulent dislikes, he came to share the prejudices of his own West against the "moneyed monster" known as the Bank of the United States.

What made the bank a monster in Jackson's eyes? The national government minted gold and silver coins in the mid-nineteenth century but did not issue paper money. Paper notes were printed by private banks. Their value fluctuated with the health of the bank and the amount of money printed, giving private bankers considerable power over the nation's economy.

No bank in America had more power than the Bank of the United States. In many ways the bank acted like a branch of government. It was the principal depository for the funds of the Washington government and controlled much of the nation's gold and silver. Its notes, unlike those of many smaller banks, were stable in value. A source of credit and stability, the bank was an important and useful part of the nation's expanding economy.

But the Bank of the United States was a private institution, accountable not to the people, but to its elite circle of moneyed investors. Its president, the brilliant but arrogant Nicholas Biddle, held an immense—and to many unconstitutional—amount of power over the nation's financial affairs. Enemies of the bank dubbed him "Czar Nicolas I" and called the bank a "hydra of corruption," a serpent that grew new heads whenever old ones were cut off.

To some the bank's very existence seemed to sin against the egalitarian credo of American democracy. The conviction formed the deepest source of Jackson's opposition. The bank also won no friends in the West by foreclosing on many western farms and draining "tribute" into eastern coffers. Profit, not public service, was its first priority.

The **Bank War** erupted in 1832, when Daniel Webster and Henry Clay presented Congress with a bill to renew the Bank of the United States' charter. The charter was not set to expire until 1836, but Clay pushed for renewal four years early to make it an election issue in 1832. As Jackson's leading rival for the presidency, Clay, with fateful blindness, looked upon the bank issue as a surefire winner.

Clay's scheme was to ram a recharter bill through Congress and then send it on to the White House. If Jackson signed it, he would alienate his worshipful western followers. If he vetoed it, as seemed certain, he would presumably lose the presidency in the forthcoming election by alienating the wealthy and influential groups in the East. Clay seems not to have fully realized that the "best people" were now only a minority and that they generally feared Jackson anyhow.

The recharter bill slid through Congress on greased skids, as planned, but was killed by a scorching veto from Jackson. The "Old Hero" declared the monopolistic bank to be unconstitutional. Of course, the Supreme Court had earlier declared it constitutional in the case of *McCulloch* v. *Maryland* (1819), but Jackson acted as though he regarded the executive branch as superior to the judicial branch. The old general growled privately, "The Bank ... is trying to kill me, but I will kill it."

Jackson's veto message reverberated with constitutional consequences. It not only squashed the bank bill but vastly amplified the power of the presidency. All previous vetoes had rested almost exclusively on questions of constitutionality. But though Jackson invoked the Constitution in his bank-veto message, he essentially argued that he was vetoing the bill because he personally found it harmful to the nation. In effect, he was claiming for the president alone a power equivalent to two-thirds of the votes in Congress. If the legislative and executive branches were partners in government, he implied, the president was unmistakably the senior partner.

In Mother Bank's Sickroom Pro-bank men Henry Clay, Daniel Webster, and John C. Calhoun consult on the grave illness that is causing Mother Bank to cough up her deposits. While Nicholas Biddle, president of the Bank of the United States, ministers to the patient, U.S. president Andrew Jackson looks on with pleasure.

Henry Clay's political instincts continued to fail him. Delighted with the financial fallacies of Jackson's message but blind to its political appeal, he arranged to have thousands of copies printed as a campaign document. The president's sweeping accusations may indeed have seemed demagogic to the moneyed interests of the East, but they made perfect sense to the common people. The bank issue was now thrown into the noisy arena of the presidential contest of 1832.

Banker Nicholas Biddle (1786–1844) wrote to Henry Clay (August 1, 1832) expressing his satisfaction:

❝ I have always deplored making the Bank a party question, but since the President will have it so, he must pay the penalty of his own rashness. As to the veto message, I am delighted with it. It has all the fury of a chained panther biting the bars of his cage. It is really a manifesto of anarchy . . . and my hope is that it will contribute to relieve the country of the domination of these miserable [Jackson] people. **❞**

✴ "Old Hickory" Wallops Clay in 1832

Clay and Jackson were the chief gladiators in the looming electoral combat. The grizzled old general, who had earlier favored one term for a president and rotation in office, was easily persuaded by his cronies not to rotate himself out of office. Presidential power is a heady brew and can be habit-forming.

The ensuing campaign was raucous. The "Old Hero's" adherents again raised the hickory pole and bellowed, "Jackson Forever: Go the Whole Hog." Admirers of Clay shouted, "Freedom and Clay," while his detractors harped on his dueling, gambling, cockfighting, and fast living.

Novel features made the campaign of 1832 especially memorable. For the first time, a third party entered the field—the newborn **Anti-Masonic party**, which opposed the influence and fearsome secrecy of the Masonic order. Energized by the mysterious disappearance and probable murder in 1826 of a New Yorker who was threatening to expose the secret rituals of the Masons, the Anti-Masonic party quickly became a potent political force in New York and spread its influence throughout the middle Atlantic and New England states. The Anti-Masons appealed to long-standing American suspicions of secret societies, which they condemned as citadels of privilege and monopoly—a note that harmonized with the democratic chorus of the Jacksonians. But since Jackson himself was a Mason and publicly gloried in his membership, the Anti-Masonic party was also an anti-Jackson party. The Anti-Masons also attracted support from many evangelical Protestant groups seeking to use political power to effect moral and religious reforms, such as prohibiting mail delivery on Sunday and otherwise keeping the Sabbath holy. This moral busybodiness was anathema to the Jacksonians, who were generally opposed to all government meddling in social and economic life.

A further novelty of the presidential contest in 1832 was the calling of national nominating conventions (three of them) to name candidates. The Anti-Masons and a group of National Republicans added still another innovation when they adopted formal platforms, publicizing their positions on the issues.

Henry Clay and his overconfident National Republicans enjoyed impressive advantages. Ample funds flowed into their campaign chest, including $50,000 in "life insurance" from the Bank of the United States. Most of the newspaper editors, some of them "bought" with Biddle's bank loans, dipped their pens in acid when they wrote of Jackson.

Yet Jackson, idol of the masses, easily defeated the big-money Kentuckian. A Jacksonian wave again swept over the West and South, surged into Pennsylvania and New York, and even washed into rock-ribbed New England. The popular vote stood at 687,502 to 530,189 for Jackson; the electoral count was a lopsided 219 to 49.

✦ Burying Biddle's Bank

Its charter denied, the Bank of the United States was due to expire in 1836. But Jackson was not one to let the financial octopus die in peace. He was convinced that he now had a mandate from the voters for its extermination, and he feared that the slippery Biddle might try to manipulate the bank (as he did) so as to force its recharter. Jackson therefore decided in 1833 to bury the bank for good by removing federal deposits from its vaults. He proposed depositing no more funds with Biddle and gradually shrinking existing deposits by using them to defray the day-to-day expenses of the government. By slowly siphoning off the government's funds, he would bleed the bank dry and ensure its demise.

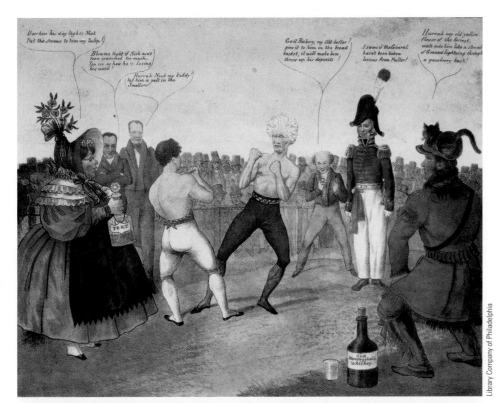

Fistfight Between Old Hickory and Bully Nick, 1834 An aged President Andrew Jackson faces off against the bank's director, aristocratic Nicholas Biddle. Comically presented as sparring pugilists undressed in the style of the popular sport, the two are assisted by their seconds, Daniel Webster and Henry Clay for Biddle, Vice President Martin Van Buren for Jackson.

Removing the deposits involved nasty complications. Even the president's closest advisers opposed this seemingly unnecessary, possibly unconstitutional, and certainly vindictive policy. Jackson, his dander up, was forced to reshuffle his cabinet twice before he could find a secretary of the Treasury who would bend to his iron will. A desperate Biddle called in his bank's loans, evidently hoping to illustrate the bank's importance by producing a minor financial crisis. A number of wobblier banks were driven to the wall by "Biddle's Panic," but Jackson's resolution was firm. If anything, the vengeful conduct of the dying "monster" seemed to justify the earlier accusations of its adversaries.

But the death of the Bank of the United States left a financial vacuum in the American economy and kicked off a lurching cycle of booms and busts. Surplus federal funds were placed in several dozen state institutions—the so-called **pet banks**, chosen for their pro-Jackson sympathies. Without a sober central bank in control, the pet banks and smaller "wildcat" banks—fly-by-night operations that often consisted of little more than a few chairs and a suitcase full of printed notes—flooded the country with paper money.

Jackson tried to rein in the runaway economy in 1836, the year Biddle's bank breathed its last. "Wildcat" currency had become so unreliable, especially in the West, that Jackson authorized the Treasury to issue a **Specie Circular**—a decree that required all public lands to be purchased with "hard," or metallic, money. This drastic step slammed the brakes on the speculative boom, a neck-snapping change of direction that contributed to a financial panic and crash in 1837.

But by then Jackson had retired to his Nashville home, hailed as the hero of his age. His successor would have to deal with the damage.

✵ The Birth of the Whigs

New political parties were gelling as the 1830s lengthened. As early as 1828, the Democratic-Republicans of Jackson had unashamedly adopted the once-tainted name "Democrats." Jackson's opponents, fuming at his ironfisted exercise of presidential power, condemned him as "King Andrew I" and began to coalesce as the Whigs—a name deliberately chosen to recollect eighteenth-century British and Revolutionary American opposition to the monarchy.

The Whig party contained so many diverse elements that it was mocked at first as "an organized incompatibility." Hatred of Jackson and his "executive usurpation" was its only apparent cement in its formative days. The Whigs first emerged as an identifiable group in the Senate, where Clay, Webster, and Calhoun joined forces in 1834 to pass a motion censuring

Jackson for his single-handed removal of federal deposits from the Bank of the United States. Thereafter, the Whigs rapidly evolved into a potent national political force by attracting other groups alienated by Jackson: supporters of Clay's American System, southern states' righters offended by Jackson's stand on nullification, the larger northern industrialists and merchants, and eventually many of the evangelical Protestants associated with the Anti-Masonic party.

Whigs thought of themselves as conservatives, yet they were progressive in their support of active government programs and reforms. Instead of boundless territorial acquisition, they called for internal improvements like canals, railroads, and telegraph lines, and they supported institutions like prisons, asylums, and public schools. The Whigs welcomed the market economy, drawing support from manufacturers in the North, planters in the South, and merchants and bankers in all sections. But they were not simply a party of wealthy fat cats, however dearly the Democrats wanted to paint them as such. By absorbing the Anti-Masonic party, the Whigs blunted much of the Democratic appeal to the common man. The egalitarian anti-Masons portrayed Jackson, and particularly his New York successor Martin Van Buren, as imperious aristocrats. This turned Jacksonian rhetoric on its head: now the Whigs claimed to be the defenders of the common man and declared the Democrats the party of cronyism and corruption.

✵ The Election of 1836

The smooth-tongued and keen-witted vice president, Martin Van Buren of New York, was Jackson's choice for "appointment" as his successor in 1836. The hollow-cheeked Jackson, now nearing seventy, was too old and ailing to consider a third term. But he was not loath to try to serve a third term through Van Buren, something of a "yes man." Leaving nothing to chance, Jackson carefully rigged the nominating convention and rammed his favorite down the throats of the delegates. Van Buren was supported by the Jacksonites without wild enthusiasm, even though he had promised "to tread generally" in the military-booted footsteps of his predecessor.

As the election neared, the still-ramshackle organization of the Whigs showed in their inability to nominate a single presidential candidate. Their long-shot strategy was instead to run several prominent "favorite sons," each with a different regional appeal, and hope to scatter the vote so that no candidate would win a majority. The deadlock would then have to be broken by the House of Representatives, where the Whigs might have a chance. With Henry Clay rudely elbowed aside, the leading Whig "favorite son" was heavy-jawed General William Henry Harrison of Ohio, hero of the

Satiric Bank Note, 1837

Political humor can take more forms than the commonly seen caustic cartoon. Occasionally historians stumble upon other examples, such as this fake bank note. A jibe at Andrew Jackson's money policies, it appeared in New York in 1837 after Jackson's insistence on shutting down the Bank of the United States resulted in the suspension of specie payments. The clever creator of this satiric bank note for six cents left little doubt about the worthlessness of the note or Jackson's responsibility for it. The six cents payable by the "Humbug Glory Bank"—whose symbols were a donkey and a "Hickory Leaf" (for Old Hickory)—were redeemable "in mint drops or Glory at cost." The bank's cashier was "Cunning Reuben," possibly an anti-Semitic allusion to usurious Jewish bankers. Can you identify other ways in which this document takes aim at Jackson's banking policies? What symbols did the note's creator assume the public would comprehend?

SIX CENTS in mint drops or Glory at cost.

"I leave this great people prosperous and happy."—Manager's last kick.

Roman Firmness

6 CENTS

"Better Currency"

Hichory Leaf.

We promise to pay to Tumble Humbug Benton, Seven Months after date at the

HUMBUG GLORY BANK

SIX CENTS *in mint drops or Glory at cost.*

Cunning Reuben Cash'r   Honest Amos Pres't

" In seven months from this time bank rags shall be abolished.—Globe of 1834.

Entered according to Act of Congress, Aug 21st 1837. dy H.L. Winslow an Clerk's Office of Southern District. New-York.

Collection of the New-York Historical Society

Battle of Tippecanoe (see p. 222). The fine-spun schemes of the Whigs availed nothing, however. Van Buren, the dapper "Little Magician," squirmed into office by the close popular vote of 765,483 to 739,795, but by the comfortable margin of 170 to 124 votes (for all the Whigs combined) in the Electoral College.

★ Big Woes for the "Little Magician"

Martin Van Buren, eighth president, was the first to be born under the American flag. Short and slender, bland and bald, the adroit little New Yorker has been described as "a first-class second-rate man." An accomplished strategist and spoilsman—"the wizard of Albany"—he was also a statesman of wide experience in both legislative and administrative life. In intelligence, education, and training, he was above the average of the presidents since Jefferson. The myth of his mediocrity sprouted mostly from a series of misfortunes over which he had no control.

From the outset the new president labored under severe handicaps. As a machine-made candidate, he incurred the resentment of many Democrats—those who objected to having a "bastard politician" smuggled into office beneath the tails of the old general's military coat. Jackson, the master showman, had been a dynamic type of executive whose administration had resounded with furious quarrels and cracked heads. Mild-mannered Martin Van Buren seemed to rattle about in the military boots of his testy predecessor. The people felt let down. Inheriting Andrew Jackson's mantle without his popularity, Van Buren also inherited the ex-president's numerous and vengeful enemies.

Van Buren's four years overflowed with toil and trouble. A pair of short-lived rebellions in Canada in 1837, mostly over political reform but aggravated by unregulated immigration from the United States, stirred up ugly incidents along the northern frontier and threatened to trigger war with Britain. The president's attempt to play a neutral game led to the wail "Woe to Martin Van Buren!" The antislavery agitators in the North were also in full cry. Among other grievances, they were condemning the prospective annexation of Texas (see "Makers of America: Mexican or Texican?" pp. 270–271).

Worst of all, Jackson bequeathed to Van Buren the makings of a searing depression. Much of Van Buren's energy had to be devoted to the purely negative task of battling the panic, and there were not enough rabbits in the "Little Magician's" tall silk hat. Hard times ordinarily blight the reputation of a president, and Van Buren was no exception.

✦ Depression Doldrums and the Independent Treasury

The **panic of 1837** was a symptom of the financial sickness of the times. Its basic cause was rampant speculation prompted by a mania of get-rich-quickism. Gamblers in western lands were doing a "land-office business" on borrowed capital, much of it in the shaky currency of "wildcat banks." The speculative craze spread to canals, roads, railroads, and slaves.

But speculation alone did not cause the crash. Jacksonian finance, including the Bank War and the Specie Circular, gave an additional jolt to an already

The Long Bill Americans who bought on credit, confident that they could make their payments later, were caught off guard by the panic of 1837. Customers like the one shown here found themselves confronted with a "long bill" that they could not pay, particularly when the banks holding their savings collapsed.

Cincinnati Art Museum, Ohio, USA/Gift of Mrs T. E. Houston/The Bridgeman Art Library

teetering structure. Failures of wheat crops, ravaged by the Hessian fly, deepened the distress. Grain prices were forced so high that mobs in New York City, three weeks before Van Buren took the oath, stormed warehouses and broke open flour barrels. The panic really began before Jackson left office, but its full fury burst about Van Buren's bewildered head.

Financial stringency abroad likewise endangered America's economic house of cards. Late in 1836 the failure of two prominent British banks created tremors, and these in turn caused British investors to call in foreign loans. The resulting pinch in the United States, combined with other setbacks, heralded the beginning of the panic. Europe's economic distresses have often become America's distresses, for every major American financial panic has been affected by conditions overseas.

Hardship was acute and widespread. American banks collapsed by the hundreds, including some "pet banks," which carried down with them several million in government funds. Commodity prices drooped, sales of public lands fell off, and customs revenues dried to a rivulet. Factories closed their doors, and unemployed workers milled in the streets.

The Whigs came forward with proposals for active government remedies for the economy's ills. They called for the expansion of bank credit, higher tariffs, and subsidies for internal improvements. But Van Buren, shackled by the Jacksonian philosophy of keeping the government's paws off the economy, spurned all such ideas.

The beleaguered Van Buren tried to apply vintage Jacksonian medicine to the ailing economy through his controversial "Divorce Bill." Convinced that some of the financial fever was fed by the injection of federal funds into private banks, he championed the principle of "divorcing" the government from banking altogether. By establishing a so-called independent

Philip Hone (1780–1851), a New York businessman, described in his diary (May 10, 1837) a phase of the financial crisis:

❝The savings-bank also sustained a most grievous run yesterday. They paid 375 depositors $81,000. The press was awful; the hour for closing the bank is six o'clock, but they did not get through the paying of those who were in at that time till nine o'clock. I was there with the other trustees and witnessed the madness of the people—women nearly pressed to death, and the stoutest men could scarcely sustain themselves; but they held on as with a death's grip upon the evidences of their claims, and, exhausted as they were with the pressure, they had strength to cry 'Pay! Pay!'❞

treasury, the government could lock its surplus money in vaults in several of the larger cities. Government funds would thus be safe, but they would also be denied to the banking system as reserves, thereby shriveling available credit resources.

Van Buren's "divorce" scheme was never highly popular. His fellow Democrats, many of whom longed for the risky but lush days of the "pet banks," supported it only lukewarmly. The Whigs condemned it, primarily because it squelched their hopes for a revived Bank of the United States. After a prolonged struggle, the Independent Treasury Bill passed Congress in 1840. Repealed the next year by the victorious Whigs, the scheme was reenacted by the triumphant Democrats in 1846 and then continued until the Republicans instituted a network of national banks during the Civil War.

✦ Gone to Texas

Americans, greedy for land, continued to covet the vast expanse of Texas, which the United States had abandoned to Spain when acquiring Florida in 1819. The Spanish authorities wanted to populate this virtually unpeopled area, but before they could carry through their contemplated plans, the Mexicans won their independence, in 1821. A new regime in Mexico City thereupon concluded arrangements in 1823 for granting a huge tract of land to Stephen Austin, with the understanding that he would bring into Texas three hundred American families. Immigrants were to be of the established Roman Catholic faith and upon settlement were to become properly Mexicanized.

These two stipulations were largely ignored. Hardy Texas pioneers remained Americans at heart, resenting the trammels imposed by a "foreign" government. They were especially annoyed by the presence of Mexican soldiers, many of whom were ragged ex-convicts.

Energetic and prolific, Texan Americans numbered about thirty thousand by 1835 (see "Makers of

America: Mexican or Texican?" pp. 270–271). Most of them were law-abiding, God-fearing people, but some of them had left the "States" only one or two jumps ahead of the sheriff. "G.T.T." (Gone to Texas) became current descriptive slang. Among the adventurers were Davy Crockett, the famous rifleman, and Jim Bowie, the presumed inventor of the murderous knife that bears his name. Bowie's blade was widely known in the Southwest as the "genuine Arkansas toothpick." A distinguished latecomer and leader was an ex-governor of Tennessee, Sam Houston. His life had been temporarily shattered in 1829 when his bride of a few weeks left him, and he took up transient residence with the Arkansas Indians, who dubbed him "Big Drunk." He subsequently took the pledge of temperance.

The pioneer individualists who came to Texas were not easy to push around. Friction rapidly increased between Mexicans and Texans over issues such as slavery, immigration, and local rights. Slavery was a particularly touchy topic. Mexico emancipated its slaves in 1830 and prohibited the further importation of slaves into Texas, as well as further colonization by troublesome Americans. The Texans refused to honor these decrees. They kept their slaves in bondage, and new American settlers kept bringing more slaves into Texas. When Stephen Austin went to Mexico City in

Samuel ("Sam") Houston (1793–1863) After a promising career in Tennessee as a soldier, lawyer, congressman, and governor, Houston became the chief leader and hero of the Texas rebels. Elected to the U.S. Senate and the governorship of Texas, he was forced into retirement when his love for the Union caused him to spurn the Confederacy in the Civil War.

George Eastman House/Getty Images

"Come and Take It" This mosaic, done in 1959 by Bert Rees of Austin, Texas, shows one of the defenders' cannon, as well as their legendary battle flag of defiance.

1833 to negotiate these differences with the Mexican government, the dictator Santa Anna clapped him in jail for eight months. The explosion finally came in 1835, when Santa Anna wiped out all local rights and started to raise an army to suppress the upstart Texans.

✦ The Lone Star Rebellion

Early in 1836 the Texans declared their independence, unfurled their Lone Star flag, and named Sam Houston commander in chief. Santa Anna, at the head of about six thousand men, swept ferociously into Texas.

Trapping a band of nearly two hundred pugnacious Texans at the **Alamo** in San Antonio, he wiped them out to a man after a thirteen-day siege. The Texans' commander, Colonel W. B. Travis, had declared, "I shall never surrender nor retreat. … Victory or Death." A short time later, a band of about four hundred surrounded and defeated American volunteers, having thrown down their arms at **Goliad**, were butchered as "pirates." All these operations further delayed the Mexican advance and galvanized American opposition.

Slain heroes like Jim Bowie and Davy Crockett, well-known in life, became legendary in death. Texan war cries—"Remember the Alamo!" "Remember Goliad!"

The Battle of the Alamo, 1836 Long celebrated in song and story, the battle was a military defeat but a spiritual victory for the Texas rebels, whose annihilation to a man inspired others and led eventually to independence from Mexico.

and "Death to Santa Anna!"—swept up into the United States. Scores of vengeful Americans seized their rifles and rushed to the aid of relatives, friends, and compatriots.

General Sam Houston's small army retreated to the east, luring Santa Anna to **San Jacinto**, near the site of the city that now bears Houston's name (see Map 13.3). The Mexicans numbered about thirteen hundred men, the Texans about nine hundred. Suddenly, on April 21, 1836, Houston turned. Taking full advantage of the Mexican siesta, the Texans wiped out the pursuing force and captured Santa Anna, who was found cowering in the tall grass near the battlefield. Confronted with thirsty bowie knives, the quaking

dictator was speedily induced to sign two treaties. By their terms he agreed to withdraw Mexican troops and to recognize the Rio Grande as the extreme southwestern boundary of Texas. When released, he repudiated the agreement as illegal because it had been extorted under duress.

These events put the U.S. government in a sticky situation. The Texans, though courageous, could hardly have won their independence without the help in men and supplies from their American cousins. The Washington government, as the Mexicans bitterly complained, had a solemn obligation under international law to enforce its leaky neutrality statutes. But American public opinion, overwhelmingly favorable to the Texans, openly nullified the existing legislation. The federal authorities were powerless to act, and on the day before he left office in 1837, President Jackson even extended the right hand of recognition to the Lone Star Republic, led by his old comrade-in-arms against the Indians, Sam Houston.

Many Texans wanted not just recognition of their independence but outright union with the United States. What nation in its right mind, they reasoned, would refuse so lavish a dowry? The radiant Texas bride, officially petitioning for annexation in 1837, presented herself for marriage. But the expectant groom, Uncle Sam, was jerked back by the black hand of the slavery issue. Antislavery crusaders in the North were opposing annexation with increasing vehemence. They contended that the whole scheme was merely a conspiracy cooked up by the southern "slavocracy" to bring new slave pens into the Union.

At first glance a "slavery plot" charge seemed plausible. Most of the early settlers in Texas, as well as American volunteers during the revolution, had come from the states of the South and Southwest. But scholars have concluded that no proslavery plot existed. Most of the immigrants came from the South and Southwest simply because these states were closer. The explanation was proximity rather than conspiracy. Yet the fact remained that many Texans were slaveholders, and admitting Texas to the Union inescapably meant enlarging American slavery.

✴ Log Cabins and Hard Cider of 1840

Martin Van Buren was renominated by the Democrats in 1840, albeit without terrific enthusiasm. The party had no acceptable alternative to what the Whigs called "Martin Van Ruin."

The Whigs, hungering for the spoils of office, scented victory in the breeze. Pangs of the panic were still being felt, and voters blamed their woes on the party in power. Learning from their mistake in 1836, the Whigs united behind one candidate, Ohio's

MAP 13.3 The Texas Revolution, 1836 General Houston's strategy was to retreat and use defense in depth. His line of supply from the United States was shortened as Santa Anna's lengthened. The Mexicans were forced to bring up supplies by land because the Texas navy controlled the sea. This force consisted of only four small ships, but it was big enough to do the job. © 2016 Cengage Learning

oses Austin, born a Connecticut Yankee in 1761, was determined to be Spanish—if that's what it took to acquire cheap land and freedom from pesky laws. In 1798 he tramped into untracked Missouri, still part of Spanish Louisiana, and pledged his allegiance to the king of Spain. He was not pleased when the Louisiana Purchase of 1803 restored him to American citizenship. In 1820, with his old Spanish passport in his saddlebag, he rode into Spanish Texas and asked for permission to establish a colony of three hundred families.

Austin's request posed a dilemma for the Texas governor. The Spanish authorities had repeatedly stamped out the bands of American horse thieves and squatters who periodically splashed across the Red and Sabine Rivers from the United States into Spanish territory. Yet the Spanish had lured only

Lorenzo de Zavala (1788–1836)   Born in Mexico, Zavala was among the signers of the Texas declaration of independence in 1836, and served briefly as vice president of the Texas republic. The State Preservation Board, Austin, Texas.

some three thousand of their own settlers into Texas during their three centuries of rule. If the land were ever to be wrestled from the Indians and "civilized," maybe Austin's plan could do it. Hoping that this band of the "right sort" of Americans might prevent the further encroachment of the buckskinned border ruffians, the governor reluctantly agreed to Austin's proposal.

Upon Moses Austin's death in 1821, the task of realizing his dream fell to his twenty-seven-year-old son, Stephen. "I bid an everlasting farewell to my native country," Stephen Austin said, and he crossed into Texas on July 15, 1821, "determined to fulfill rigidly all the duties and obligations of a Mexican citizen." (Mexico declared its independence from Spain early in 1821 and finalized its agreement with Austin in 1823.) Soon he learned fluent Spanish and was signing his name as "Don Estévan F. Austin." In his new colony between the Brazos and Colorado Rivers, he allowed "no drunkard, no gambler, no profane swearer, no idler"—and sternly enforced these rules. Not only did he banish several families as "undesirables," but he ordered the public flogging of unwanted interlopers.

Austin fell just three families short of recruiting the three hundred households that his father had contracted to bring to Texas. The original settlers were still dubbed the "Old Three Hundred," the Texas equivalent of New England's Mayflower Pilgrims or the "First Families of Virginia." Mostly Scots-Irish southerners from the trans-Appalachian frontier, the Old Three Hundred were cultured folk by frontier standards; all but four of them were literate. Other settlers followed, from Europe as well as America. Within ten years the "Anglos" (many of them French and German) outnumbered the Mexican residents, or *tejanos*, ten to one and soon evolved a distinctive "Texican" culture. The wide-ranging horse patrols organized to attack Indian camps became the Texas Rangers; Samuel Maverick, whose unbranded calves roamed the limitless prairies, left his surname as a label for rebellious loners who refused to run with the herd; and Jared Groce, an Alabama planter whose caravan of fifty covered wagons and one hundred slaves arrived in 1822, etched the original image of the larger-than-life, big-time Texas operator.

West Side Main Plaza, San Antonio, Texas, by William G. M. Samuel, 1849 (detail)   Even after annexation, Texas retained a strong Spanish Mexican flavor, as the architecture and activities here illustrate.

The original Anglo-Texans brought with them the old Scots-Irish frontiersmen's hostility to authority. They ignored Mexican laws and officials, including restrictions against owning or importing slaves. When the Mexican government tried to impose its will on the Anglo-Texans in the 1830s, they took up their guns. Like the American revolutionaries of the 1770s, who at first demanded only the rights of Englishmen, the Texans began by asking simply for Mexican recognition of their rights as guaranteed by the Mexican constitution of 1824. But bloodshed at the Alamo in 1836, like that at Lexington and Concord in 1775, transformed protest into rebellion.

Texas lay—and still lies—along the frontier where Hispanic and Anglo-American cultures met, mingled, and clashed. In part the Texas Revolution was a contest between those two cultures. But it was also a contest about philosophies of government, pitting liberal frontier ideals of freedom against the conservative concept of centralized control. Stephen Austin sincerely tried to "Mexicanize" himself and his followers—until the Mexican government grew too arbitrary and authoritarian. And not all the Texas revolutionaries were "Anglos." Many *tejanos* fought for Texas independence—seven perished defending the Alamo. Among the fifty-nine signers of the Texas declaration of independence were several Hispanics, including the *tejanos* José Antonio Navarro and Francisco Ruiz. Lorenzo de Zavala, an ardent Mexican liberal who had long resisted the centralizing tendencies of Mexico's dominant political party, was designated vice president of the Texas republic's interim government in 1836. Like the Austins, these *tejanos* and Mexicans had sought in Texas an escape from overbearing governmental authority. Their role in the revolution underscores the fact that the uprising was a struggle between defenders of local rights and the agents of central authority as much as it was a fight between Anglo and Mexican cultures.

© Collection of the New-York Historical Society, USA/The Bridgeman Art Library

Harrison and Tyler Campaign Kerchief, 1840 As the two-party system came into its own by 1840, presidential elections became more public contests. Lively campaigns used banners, posters, flags, and other paraphernalia like this kerchief to whip up voters' support. Log Cabin Whigs took particular interest in attracting female supporters. They gathered up women at campaign stops, supplied them with Harrison kerchiefs for waving at key moments, and included them conspicuously in events. Although women could not vote, they had moral influence on their menfolk that the Whigs hoped to tap.

William Henry Harrison. He was not their ablest statesman—that would have been Daniel Webster or Henry Clay—but he was believed to be their ablest vote-getter.

The aging hero, nearly sixty-eight when the campaign ended, was known for his successes against Indians and the British at the Battles of Tippecanoe (1811) and the Thames (1813). Harrison's views on current issues were only vaguely known. "Old Tippecanoe" was nominated primarily because he was issueless and enemyless—a tested recipe for electoral success that still appeals today. John Tyler of Virginia, an afterthought, was selected as his vice-presidential running mate.

The Whigs, eager to avoid offense, published no official platform, hoping to sweep their hero into office with a frothy huzza-for-Harrison campaign reminiscent of Jackson's triumph in 1828. A dull-witted Democratic editor played directly into Whig hands. Stupidly insulting the West, he lampooned Harrison as an impoverished old farmer who should be content

with a pension, a log cabin, and a barrel of hard cider—the poor westerner's champagne. Whigs gleefully adopted honest hard cider and the sturdy log cabin as symbols of their campaign. Harrisonites portrayed their hero as the poor "Farmer of North Bend," who had been called from his cabin and his plow to drive corrupt Jackson spoilsmen from the "presidential palace." They denounced Van Buren as a supercilious aristocrat, a simpering dandy who wore corsets and ate French food from golden plates. As a jeering Whig campaign song proclaimed,

> *Old Tip, he wears a homespun shirt, He has no ruffled shirt, wirt, wirt.*
> *But Matt, he has the golden plate, and he's a little squirt, wirt, wirt.*

The Whig campaign was a masterpiece of inane hoopla. Log cabins were dished up in every conceivable form. Bawling Whigs, stimulated by fortified cider, rolled huge inflated balls from village to village and state to state—balls that represented the snowballing majority for "Tippecanoe, and Tyler too." In truth, Harrison was not lowborn, but from one of the FFVs ("First Families of Virginia"). He was not poverty-stricken. He did not live in a one-room log cabin, but rather in a sixteen-room mansion on a three-thousand-acre farm. He did not swill down gallons of hard cider (he evidently preferred whiskey). And he did not plow his fields with his own "huge paws." But such details had not mattered when General Jackson rode to victory, and they did not matter now.

The Democrats who hurrahed Jackson into the White House in 1828 now discovered to their chagrin that whooping it up for a backwoods westerner was a game two could play. Harrison won by the surprisingly close margin of 1,274,624 to 1,127,781 popular votes, but by an overwhelming electoral margin of 234 to 60. With hardly a real issue debated, though with hard times blighting the incumbent's fortunes, Van Buren was washed out of Washington on a wave of apple juice. The hard-ciderites had apparently received a mandate to tear down the White House and erect a log cabin.

Although campaigners in 1840 did their best to bury substantive issues beneath the ballyhoo, voters actually faced a stark choice between two economic visions of how to cope with the nation's first major depression. Whigs sought to expand and stimulate the economy, while Democrats favored retrenchment and an end to high-flying banks and aggressive corporations.

Collection of Janice L. and David J. Frent

Martin Van Buren Gags on Hard Cider This 1840 "pull-card" shows Van Buren on the left as an aristocratic fop sipping champagne. When the right-hand card was pulled out, Van Buren's face soured as he discovered that his "champagne" was actually hard cider. The cartoonist clearly sympathized with Van Buren's opponent in the 1840 presidential election, William Henry Harrison, who waged the famous "log cabin and hard cider" campaign.

✦ Politics for the People

The election of 1840 conclusively demonstrated two major changes in American politics since the Era of Good Feelings. The first was the triumph of a populist democratic style. Democracy had been something of a taint in the days of the lordly Federalists. Martha Washington, the first First Lady, was shocked after a presidential reception to find a greasy smear on the wallpaper—left there, she was sure, by an uninvited "filthy democrat."

But by the 1840s, aristocracy was the taint, and democracy was respectable. Politicians were now forced to curry favor with the voting masses. Lucky indeed was the aspiring office seeker who could boast of birth in a log cabin. In 1840 Daniel Webster publicly apologized for not being able to claim so humble a birthplace, though he quickly added that his brothers could. Hopelessly handicapped was the candidate who appeared to be too clean, too well dressed, too grammatical, too highbrowishly intellectual. In truth, most high political offices continued to be filled by "leading citizens." But now these wealthy and prominent men had to forsake all social pretensions and cultivate the common touch if they hoped to win elections.

Snobbish bigwigs, unhappy over the change, sneered at "coonskin congressmen" and at the newly enfranchised "bipeds of the forest." To them the tyranny of "King Numbers" was no less offensive than that of King George. But these critics protested in vain. The common man was at last moving to the center of the national political stage: the sturdy American who donned coarse trousers rather than buff breeches, who sported a coonskin cap rather than a silk top hat, and who wore no man's collar, often not even one of his own. Instead of the old divine right of kings, America was now bowing to the divine right of the people.

✦ The Two-Party System

The second dramatic change resulting from the 1840 election was the formation of a vigorous and durable two-party system. The Jeffersonians of an earlier day had been so successful in absorbing the programs of their Federalist opponents that a full-blown two-party system had never truly emerged in the subsequent Era of Good Feelings. The idea had prevailed that parties of any sort smacked of conspiracy and "faction" and were injurious to the health of the body politic in a virtuous republic. By 1840 political parties had fully

The County Election, **by George Caleb Bingham, 1851–1852**   The artist here gently satirizes the drinking and wheeling and dealing that sometimes marred the electoral process in the boisterous age of Jacksonian politics.

come of age, a lasting legacy of Andrew Jackson's and Martin Van Buren's tenaciousness.

Both national parties, the Democrats and the Whigs, grew out of the rich soil of Jeffersonian republicanism, and each laid claim to different aspects of the republican inheritance. Jacksonian Democrats glorified the liberty of the individual and were fiercely on guard against the inroads of "privilege" into government. Whigs trumpeted the natural harmony of society and the value of community, and were willing to use government to realize their objectives. Whigs also berated those leaders—and they considered Jackson to be one—whose appeals to self-interest fostered conflict among individuals, classes, or sections.

Democrats clung to states' rights and federal restraint in social and economic affairs as their basic doctrines. Whigs tended to favor a renewed national bank, protective tariffs, internal improvements, public schools, and, increasingly, moral reforms such as the prohibition of liquor and eventually the abolition of slavery.

The two parties were thus separated by real differences of philosophy and policy. But they also had much in common. Both were mass-based, "catchall" parties that tried deliberately to mobilize as many voters as possible for their cause. Although it is true that Democrats tended to be more humble folk and Whigs more prosperous, both parties nevertheless commanded the loyalties of all kinds of Americans, from all social classes and in all sections. The social diversity of the two parties had important implications. It fostered horse-trading compromises *within* each party that prevented either from assuming extreme or radical positions. By the same token, the geographical diversity of the two parties retarded the emergence of purely sectional political parties—temporarily suppressing, through compromise, the ultimately uncompromisable issue of slavery. When the two-party system began to creak in the 1850s, the Union was mortally imperiled.

President Andrew Jackson advised a supporter in 1835 on how to tell the difference between Democrats and "Whigs, nullies, and blue-light federalists." In doing so, he neatly summarized the Jacksonian philosophy:

❝The people ought to inquire [of political candidates]—are you opposed to a national bank; are you in favor of a strict construction of the Federal and State Constitutions; are you in favor of rotation in office; do you subscribe to the republican rule that the people are the sovereign power, the officers their agents, and that upon all national or general subjects, as well as local, they have a right to instruct their agents and representatives, and they are bound to obey or resign; in short, are they true Republicans agreeable to the true Jeffersonian creed?**❞**

Varying Viewpoints
What Was Jacksonian Democracy?

Aristocratic, eastern-born historians of the nineteenth century damned Jackson as a backwoods barbarian. They criticized Jacksonianism as democracy run riot—an irresponsible, ill-bred outburst that overturned the electoral system and wrecked the national financial structure.

In the late nineteenth and early twentieth centuries, however, another generation of historians came to the fore, many of whom had grown up in the Midwest and rejected the elitist views of their predecessors. Frederick Jackson Turner and his disciples saw the western frontier as the fount of democratic virtue, and they hailed Jackson as a true hero sprung from the forests of the West to protect the will of the people against the moneyed interests, akin to the progressive reformers of their own day. In his famous 1893 essay, "The Significance of the Frontier in American History," Turner argued that the United States owed the survival of its democratic tradition to the rise of the West, not to its roots in the more conservative, aristocratic East.

When Arthur M. Schlesinger, Jr., published *The Age of Jackson* in 1945, however, the debate on Jacksonianism shifted dramatically. Although he shared the Turnerians' admiration for Jackson the democrat, Schlesinger cast the Jacksonian era not as a sectional conflict, but as a class conflict between poor farmers, laborers, and noncapitalists on the one hand, and the business community—epitomized by the Second Bank of the United States—on the other. In Schlesinger's eyes the Jacksonians justifiably attacked the bank as an institution dangerously independent of democratic oversight. The political mobilization of the urban working classes in support of Jackson particularly attracted Schlesinger's interest.

Soon after Schlesinger's book appeared, the discussion again shifted ground and entirely new interpretations of Jacksonianism emerged. Richard Hofstadter argued in *The American Political Tradition and the Men Who Made It* (1948) that Jacksonian democracy was not a rejection of capitalism, as Schlesinger insisted, but rather the effort of aspiring entrepreneurs to secure laissez-faire policies that would serve their own interests against their entrenched, and monopolistic, eastern competitors. In *The Jacksonian Persuasion* (1957), Marvin Meyers portrayed the Jacksonians as conservative capitalists, torn between fierce commercial ambitions and a desire to cling to the virtues of the agrarian past. In an effort to resolve this contradiction, he argued, they lashed out at scapegoats like the national bank, blaming it for the very changes their own economic energies had unleashed. Lee Benson contended in *The Concept of Jacksonian Democracy* (1961) that the political conflicts of the Jacksonian era did not correspond so much to class divisions as to different ethnic and religious splits within American society. Using new quantitative methods of analysis, Benson found no consistent demarcations—in class, occupation, or region—between the Jacksonians and their rivals. Local and cultural issues such as temperance and religion were far more influential in shaping political life than the national financial questions analyzed by previous historians.

In the 1980s Sean Wilentz and other scholars began to resurrect some of Schlesinger's argument about the importance of class to Jacksonianism. In *Chants Democratic* (1984), Wilentz maintained that Jacksonian politics could not be properly understood without reference to the changing national economy. Artisans watched in horror as new manufacturing techniques put many of them out of business and replaced their craftsmanship with the unskilled hands of wage laborers. To these anxious small producers, America's infatuation with impersonal institutions and large-scale employers threatened the very existence of a republic founded on the principle that its citizens were virtuously self-sufficient. Thus Jackson's attack on the Bank of the United States symbolized the antagonism these individuals felt toward the emergent capitalist economy and earned him their strong allegiance.

The scholarly cycle came full circle with the publication of Charles Sellers's *The Market Revolution: Jacksonian America, 1815–1846* (1991). In many ways this ambitious synthesis offered an updated version of Schlesinger's argument about class conflict. American democracy and free-market capitalism, according to Sellers, were not twins, born from the common parentage of freedom and opportunity, reared in the wide-open young Republic, and mutually supporting each other ever since. Rather, Sellers suggested, they were really adversaries, with Jacksonians inventing mass democracy in order to hold capitalist expansion in check. Like Schlesinger's thesis, Sellers's interpretation provoked a storm of controversy. To supporters, the concept of the "market revolution" (see p. 304) provided a useful organizing tool for seeing social, cultural, political, and economic transformations as interdependent. To critics, Sellers's book suffered from a hopelessly romantic view of preindustrial society and a pronounced ideological bias. In an era of tightly contested elections, they argued, no party could expect to prevail by appealing exclusively to rich or poor along class lines.

Published a decade and a half later, *What Hath God Wrought: The Transformation of America, 1815–1848* (2007), Daniel Walker Howe's equally sweeping synthesis of the period, took a different view of the relationship between commercialization and democracy. Howe argued that mass political participation did not emerge as an antidote to the crushing yoke of industrialization; rather, it evolved out of the same forces that drove market expansion—the "twin revolutions" in transportation and communications. Advances in printing and the proliferation of newspapers were prerequisites for mass political parties, which depended on the largely partisan press to publicize their platforms and rally support. The turnpikes, canals, and railroads that delivered local goods to increasingly distant markets also carried ministers to far-off parishes, setting off a religious revival that helped transform the political landscape. New churches, representing a multiplicity of faiths, created venues for debates on issues ranging from abolition to women's rights, issues that were intentionally kept out of the halls of Congress. Howe argued that Jackson's supporters did not object to new commercial opportunities. At the same time that Jackson worked to dismantle the Bank of the United States, he also funded transportation projects in the territories to promote westward expansion and built harbors along the eastern seaboard to fuel international trade. According to Howe, Jacksonians welcomed commerce, but they disagreed with Whigs over the *direction* of development, favoring a more agrarian, atomized economy.

Chapter Review

KEY TERMS

corrupt bargain (248)
spoils system (253)
Tariff of Abominations (256)
Nullification Crisis (257)
compromise Tariff of 1833 (258)
Force Bill (258)
Indian Removal Act (259)
Trail of Tears (260)

Black Hawk War (260)
Bank War (261)
Anti-Masonic party (262)
pet banks (264)
Specie Circular (264)
panic of 1837 (266)
Alamo (268)
Goliad (268)
San Jacinto, Battle of (269)

PEOPLE TO KNOW

John Quincy Adams
Andrew Jackson
Denmark Vesey
John C. Calhoun
Black Hawk
Nicholas Biddle
Daniel Webster
Henry Clay

Martin Van Buren
Stephen Austin
Sam Houston
Santa Anna
William Henry Harrison

CHRONOLOGY

1822	Vesey slave conspiracy in Charleston, South Carolina
1823	Mexico opens Texas to American settlers
1824	Lack of electoral majority for presidency throws election into House of Representatives
1825	House elects John Quincy Adams president
1828	Tariff of 1828 ("Tariff of Abominations") Jackson elected president *The South Carolina Exposition* published
1830	Indian Removal Act July Revolution in France
1831–1832	Alexis de Tocqueville tours United States
1832	"Bank War"—Jackson vetoes bill to recharter Bank of the United States Reform Bill in Britain expands electorate Tariff of 1832 Black Hawk War Jackson defeats Clay for presidency
1832–1833	South Carolina nullification crisis
1833	Compromise Tariff of 1833 Jackson removes federal deposits from Bank of the United States
1836	Bank of the United States expires Specie Circular issued Bureau of Indian Affairs established Battle of the Alamo Battle of San Jacinto Texas wins independence from Mexico Van Buren elected president
1837	Seminole Indians defeated and eventually removed from Florida United States recognizes Texas republic but refuses annexation Panic of 1837
1838–1839	Cherokee Indians removed on "Trail of Tears"
1840	Independent treasury established Harrison defeats Van Buren for presidency

TO LEARN MORE

Glenn C. Altschuler and Stuart M. Blumin, *Rude Republic: Americans and Their Politics in the Nineteenth Century* (2001)

Andrew Burstein, *The Passions of Andrew Jackson* (2003)

Daniel Feller, *The Jacksonian Promise, 1815–1840* (1995)

Michael D. Green, *The Politics of Indian Removal* (1982)

Daniel Walker Howe, *What Hath God Wrought: The Transformation of America, 1815–1848* (2007)

Louis P. Masur, *1831: Year of Eclipse* (2001)

David Andrew Nichols, *Red Gentlemen and White Savages: Indians, Federalists, and the Search for Order on the American Frontier* (2008)

Lynn Hudson Parsons, *The Birth of Modern Politics: Andrew Jackson, John Quincy Adams, and the Election of 1828* (2009)

Merrill D. Peterson, *The Great Triumvirate: Webster, Clay, and Calhoun* (1987)

Alexis de Tocqueville, *Democracy in America* (1835, 1840)

Sean Wilentz, *The Rise of American Democracy* (2005)

A complete, annotated bibliography for this chapter—along with brief descriptions of the People to Know—may be found on the *American Pageant* website. The key terms are defined in the glossary at the end of the text.

Chapter 14

Forging the National Economy

1790–1860

The progress of invention is really a threat [to monarchy].
Whenever I see a railroad I look for a republic.

RALPH WALDO EMERSON, 1866

The new nation bounded into the nineteenth century in a burst of movement. New England Yankees, Pennsylvania farmers, southern yeomen, cotton lords and their enslaved workers, all pushed west in search of land and opportunity, soon to be joined by vast numbers of immigrants from Europe, who also made their way to the country's fast-growing cities. And not only people were in motion. Newly invented machinery boomed the cultivation of crops and the manufacture of goods, while workers, free and enslaved alike, labored ever longer, harder, and faster. Better roads, faster steamboats, farther-reaching canals, and ribboning railroad lines all moved people, foodstuffs, raw materials, and manufactured goods from coast to coast, from Gulf to Great Lakes, and from American shores to the wider world. The prodigious momentum of burgeoning American capitalism gave rise to an economy that was remarkably dynamic, market driven, continentally scaled, and internationally consequential.

✯ The Westward Movement

The rise of Andrew Jackson, the first president from beyond the Appalachian Mountains, exemplified the relentless westward march of the American people. The West, with its raw frontier, began to acquire its mythical status as the most American part of America. As Ralph Waldo Emerson wrote in 1844, "Europe stretches to the Alleghenies; America lies beyond."

The Republic was young, and so were the people—as late as 1850, half of Americans were under the age of thirty. They were also restless and energetic, seemingly always on the move, and always westward. One "tall tale" of the frontier described chickens that voluntarily crossed their legs every spring, waiting to be tied for the annual move west. By 1840 the "demographic center" of the American population map had crossed the Alleghenies (see Map 14.1). By the eve of the Civil War, it had marched across the Ohio River.

Legend portrays an army of muscular axmen triumphantly carving civilization out of the western woods. But in reality life was downright grim for most pioneer families. Poorly fed, ill-clad, housed in hastily erected shanties (Abraham Lincoln's family lived for a year in a three-sided lean-to made of brush and sticks), they were perpetual victims of disease, depression, and premature death. Above all, unbearable loneliness haunted them, especially the women, who were often cut off from human contact, even their neighbors, for days or even weeks, while confined to the cramped orbit of a dark cabin in a secluded clearing. Breakdowns and even madness were all too frequently the "opportunities" that the frontier offered to pioneer women.

Frontier life could be tough and crude for men as well. No-holds-barred wrestling, which permitted such niceties as the biting off of noses and the gouging out of eyes, was a popular entertainment. Pioneering Americans, marooned by geography, were often ill-informed, superstitious, provincial, and fiercely individualistic. Ralph Waldo Emerson's popular lecture-essay **"Self-Reliance"** struck a deeply responsive chord. Popular literature of the period abounded with portraits of unique, isolated figures like James Fenimore Cooper's heroic Natty Bumppo and Herman

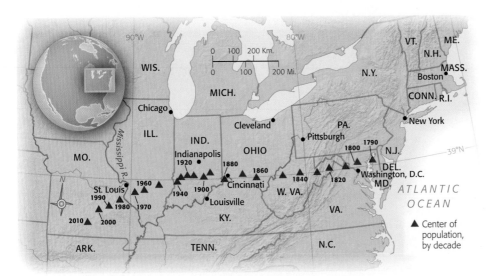

MAP 14.1 Westward Movement of Center of Population, 1790–2010 The triangles indicate the points at which a map of the United States weighted for the population of the country in a given year would balance. Note the remarkable equilibrium of the north-south pull from 1790 to about 1940, and the strong spurt west and south thereafter. The 1980 census revealed that the nation's center of population had at last moved west of the Mississippi River. The map also shows the slowing of the westward movement between 1890 and 1940—the period of heaviest immigration from Europe, which ended up mainly in East Coast cities. © 2016 Cengage Learning

Melville's restless Captain Ahab—just as Jacksonian politics aimed to emancipate the lone-wolf, enterprising businessperson. Yet even in this heyday of "rugged individualism," there were important exceptions. Pioneering men, facing tasks clearly beyond their own individual resources, relied upon the labor of their womenfolk, children, and neighbors—and, in the booming cotton South, their slaves—for logrolling and barn raising. Community was crucial to survival, as were governments, local as well as federal, for help in building internal improvements like canals and roads.

Shaping the Western Landscape

The westward movement also molded the physical environment. Pioneers in a hurry often exhausted the land in the tobacco regions and then pushed on, leaving behind barren and rain-gutted fields. In the Kentucky bottomlands, cane as high as fifteen feet posed a seemingly insurmountable barrier to the plow. But settlers soon discovered that when the cane was burned off, European bluegrass thrived in the charred canefields. "Kentucky bluegrass," as it was somewhat inaccurately called, made ideal pasture for livestock—and lured thousands more American homesteaders into Kentucky.

The American West felt the pressure of civilization in additional ways. By the 1820s American fur-trappers were setting their traplines all over the vast Rocky Mountain region. The fur-trapping empire was based on the **rendezvous** (French for "meeting") system. Each summer, traders ventured from St. Louis to a verdant Rocky Mountain valley, made camp, and waited for the trappers and Indians to arrive with beaver pelts to swap for manufactured goods from the East. This trade thrived for some two decades; by the time beaver hats had gone out of fashion, the hapless beaver had all but disappeared from the region. Trade in buffalo robes also flourished, leading eventually to the virtually total annihilation of the massive bison herds that once blanketed the western prairies. Still farther west, on the California coast, other traders bought up prodigious quantities of sea-otter pelts, driving the once-bountiful otters to the point of near-extinction. Some historians have called this aggressive and often heedless exploitation of the West's natural bounty **ecological imperialism**.

Yet Americans in this period also revered nature and admired its beauty. Indeed the spirit of nationalism fed a growing belief in the uniqueness of the American wilderness. Searching for the United States' distinctive characteristics in this nation-conscious age, many observers found the wild, unspoiled character of the land, especially in the West, to be among the young nation's defining attributes. Other countries might have impressive mountains or sparkling rivers, but none had the pristine, natural beauty of

Major Dougherty's Indian Agency on the Missouri River, by Karl Bodmer, 1833 The Swiss-born and Paris-trained artist Karl Bodmer painted this scene while accompanying German Prince Maximilian on his expedition across the American West. From St. Louis, the party traveled up the Missouri River by steamboat under the protection of John Jacob Astor's Fur Company. Bodmer painted scenes along the way, especially of Indians and their surroundings. Trading posts like this one both promoted commerce with the Indians and served settlers heading west.

America, unspoiled by human hands and reminiscent of a time before the dawn of civilization. This attitude toward wilderness became in time a kind of national mystique, inspiring literature and painting, and eventually kindling a powerful conservation movement.

George Catlin, a painter and student of Native American life, was among the first Americans to advocate the preservation of nature as a deliberate national policy. In 1832 he observed Sioux Indians in South Dakota recklessly slaughtering buffalo in order to trade the animals' tongues for the white man's whiskey. Appalled at this spectacle and fearing for the preservation of Indians and buffalo alike, Catlin proposed the creation of a national park. His idea later bore fruit with the creation of a national park system—the world's first—beginning with Yellowstone Park in 1872.

✳ The March of the Millions

As the American people moved west, they also multiplied at an amazing rate. By midcentury the population was still doubling approximately every twenty-five years, as in fertile colonial days (see Figure 14.1).

By 1860 the original thirteen states had more than doubled in number: thirty-three stars graced the American flag. The United States was the fourth most populous nation in the western world, exceeded only by three European countries—Russia, France, and Austria.

Urban growth continued explosively. In 1790 there had been only two American cities that could boast populations of twenty thousand or more souls: Philadelphia and New York. By 1860 there were forty-three, and about three hundred other places claimed over five thousand inhabitants apiece. New York was the metropolis; New Orleans, the "Queen of the South"; and Chicago, the swaggering lord of the Midwest, destined to be "hog butcher for the world."

Such overrapid urbanization unfortunately brought undesirable by-products. It intensified the problems of smelly slums, feeble street lighting, inadequate policing, impure water, foul sewage, ravenous rats, and improper garbage disposal. Hogs poked their scavenging snouts about many city streets as late as the 1840s. Boston in 1823 pioneered a sewer system, and New York in 1842 abandoned wells and cisterns for a piped-in water supply. The city thus unknowingly eliminated the breeding places of many disease-carrying mosquitoes.

A continuing high birthrate accounted for most of the increase in population, but by the 1840s the tides of immigration were adding hundreds of thousands more. Before this decade immigrants had been flowing in at a rate of sixty thousand a year, but suddenly the influx

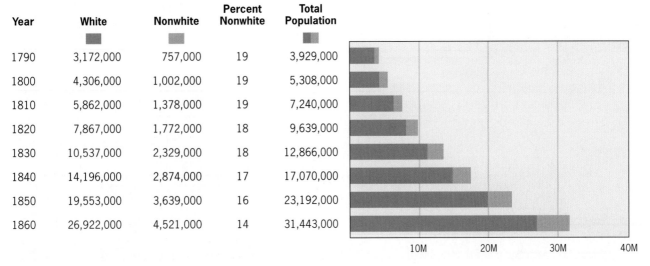

Year	White	Nonwhite	Percent Nonwhite	Total Population
1790	3,172,000	757,000	19	3,929,000
1800	4,306,000	1,002,000	19	5,308,000
1810	5,862,000	1,378,000	19	7,240,000
1820	7,867,000	1,772,000	18	9,639,000
1830	10,537,000	2,329,000	18	12,866,000
1840	14,196,000	2,874,000	17	17,070,000
1850	19,553,000	3,639,000	16	23,192,000
1860	26,922,000	4,521,000	14	31,443,000

FIGURE 14.1 Population Increase, Including Slaves and Indians, 1790–1860 Increasing European immigration and the closing of the slave trade gradually "whitened" the population beginning in 1820. This trend continued into the early twentieth century. © 2016 Cengage Learning

tripled in the 1840s and then quadrupled in the 1850s. During these two feverish decades, over a million and a half Irish, and nearly as many Germans, swarmed down the gangplanks (see Table 14.1). Why did they come?

The immigrants came partly because Europe seemed to be running out of room. The population of the Old World more than doubled in the nineteenth century, and Europe began to generate a seething pool of apparently "surplus" people. They were displaced and footloose in their homelands before they felt the tug of the American magnet. Indeed at least as many people moved about *within* Europe as crossed the Atlantic. America benefited from these people-churning changes but did not set them all in motion. Nor was the United States the sole beneficiary of the process: of the nearly 60 million people who

abandoned Europe in the century after 1840, about 25 million went somewhere other than the United States.

Yet America still beckoned most strongly to the struggling masses of Europe, and the majority of migrants headed for the "land of freedom and opportunity." There was freedom from aristocratic caste and state church; there was abundant opportunity to secure broad acres and better one's condition. Much-read letters sent home by immigrants—"America

TABLE 14.1 Irish and German Immigration by Decade, 1830–1900		
Years	Irish	Germans
1831–1840	207,381	152,454
1841–1850	780,719	434,626
1851–1860	914,119	951,667
1861–1870	435,778	787,468
1871–1880	436,871	718,182
1881–1890	655,482	1,452,970
1891–1900	388,416	505,152
TOTAL	3,818,766	5,000,519

A German immigrant living in Cincinnati wrote to his relatives in Germany in 1847,

❝A lot of people come over here who were well off in Germany but were enticed to leave their fatherland by boastful and imprudent letters from their friends or children and thought they could become rich in America. This deceives a lot of people, since what can they do here? If they stay in the city they can only earn their bread at hard and unaccustomed labor. If they want to live in the country and don't have enough money to buy a piece of land that is cleared and has a house then they have to settle in the wild bush and have to work very hard to clear the trees out of the way so they can sow and plant. But people who are healthy, strong, and hard-working do pretty well.❞

Mouth of the Platte River, 900 Miles Above St. Louis, by George Catlin, 1832 Catlin's West unfolded as a vast panorama of flat, open space peopled only by the Indians shown in the foreground. Catlin believed that capturing the unending prairie on canvas required a new aesthetic, the sublime horizontal, and an acceptance of a landscape bereft of man-built features, without "anything rising above the horizon, which was a perfect straight line around us, like that of the blue and boundless ocean."

letters"—often described in glowing terms the richer life: low taxes, no compulsory military service, and "three meat meals a day." The introduction of trans-oceanic steamships also meant that the immigrants could come speedily and cheaply. The journey to the United States now took ten or twelve days, instead of ten or twelve weeks on a sailing vessel, and was much less expensive than a voyage to more distant immigrant destinations such as Australia, Argentina, or South Africa. The United States also received a far more diverse array of immigrants than did other countries. Argentina, for example, had a higher proportion of immigrants relative to its population than did the United States, but they came mostly from Spain and Italy. In contrast, the United States beckoned to immigrants from dozens of different nations.

✷ The Emerald Isle Moves West

Ireland, already groaning under the heavy hand of British overlords, was prostrated in the mid-1840s. A terrible rot attacked the potato crop, on which the people had become dangerously dependent, and about one-fourth of them were swept away by disease and hunger. Starved bodies were found dead by the roadsides with grass in their mouths. All told, about 2 million perished.

Tens of thousands of destitute souls, fleeing the Land of Famine for the Land of Plenty, flocked to America in the "Black Forties." Ireland's great export has been population, and the Irish take their place beside the Jews and the Africans as a dispersed people (see "Makers of America: The Irish," pp. 284–285).

These uprooted newcomers—too poor to move west and buy the necessary land, livestock, and equipment—swarmed into the larger seaboard cities. Noteworthy were Boston and particularly New York, which rapidly became the largest Irish city in the world. Before many decades had passed, more people of Hibernian blood lived in America than on the "ould sod" of Erin's Isle.

The luckless Irish immigrants received no red-carpet treatment. Forced to live in squalor, they were rudely crammed into the already vile slums. They were scorned by the older American stock, especially "proper" Protestant Bostonians, who regarded the scruffy Catholic arrivals as a social menace. Barely literate "Biddies" (Bridgets) took jobs as kitchen maids. Broad-shouldered "Paddies" (Patricks) were pushed into pick-and-shovel drudgery on canals and railroads, where thousands left their bones as victims of disease and accidental explosions. It was said that an Irishman lay buried under every railroad tie. As wage-depressing competitors for jobs, the Irish were hated by native workers. "No Irish Need Apply" was a sign commonly posted at factory gates and was often abbreviated to

NINA. The Irish, for similar reasons, fiercely resented the blacks, with whom they shared society's basement. Race riots between black and Irish dockworkers flared up in several port cities, and the Irish were generally cool to the abolitionist cause.

The friendless "famine Irish" were forced to fend for themselves. The **Ancient Order of Hibernians**, a semisecret society founded in Ireland to fight rapacious landlords, served in America as a benevolent society, aiding the downtrodden. It also helped to spawn the **Molly Maguires**, a shadowy Irish miners' union that rocked the Pennsylvania coal districts in the 1860s and 1870s.

The Irish tended to remain in low-skill occupations but gradually improved their lot, usually by acquiring modest amounts of property. The education of children was cut short as families struggled to save money to purchase a home. But for humble Irish peasants, cruelly cast out of their homeland, property ownership counted as a grand "success."

Politics quickly attracted these gregarious Gaelic newcomers. They soon began to gain control of powerful city machines, notably New York's **Tammany Hall**, and reaped the patronage rewards. Before long, beguilingly brogued Irishmen dominated police departments in many big cities, where they now drove the "Paddy wagons" that had once carted their brawling forebearers to jail.

American politicians made haste to cultivate the Irish vote, especially in the politically potent state of New York. Irish hatred of the British lost nothing in the transatlantic transplanting. As the Irish Americans increased in number—nearly 2 million arrived between 1830 and 1860—officials in Washington glimpsed political gold in those emerald green hills. Politicians often

Margaret McCarthy, a recent arrival to America, captured much of the complexity of the immigrant experience in a letter she wrote from New York to her family in Ireland in 1850:

❝This is a good place and a good country, but there is one thing that's ruining this place. The emigrants have not money enough to take them to the interior of the country, which obliges them to remain here in New York and the like places, which causes the less demand for labor and also the great reduction in wages. For this reason I would advise no one to come to America that would not have some money after landing here that would enable them to go west in case they would get no work to do here.**❞**

An early-nineteenth-century French traveler recorded his impressions of America and Ireland:

❝I have seen the Indian in his forests and the Negro in his chains, and thought, as I contemplated their pitiable condition, that I saw the very extreme of human wretchedness; but I did not then know the condition of unfortunate Ireland.**❞**

found it politically profitable to fire verbal volleys at London—a process vulgarly known as "twisting the British lion's tail."

✦ The German Forty-Eighters

The influx of refugees from Germany between 1830 and 1860 was hardly less spectacular than that from Ireland. During these troubled years, over a million and a half Germans stepped onto American soil (see "Makers of America: The Germans," pp. 288–289).

The bulk of them were uprooted farmers, displaced by crop failures and other hardships. But a strong sprinkling were liberal political refugees. Saddened by the collapse of the democratic revolutions of 1848, they had decided to leave the autocratic fatherland and flee to America—the brightest hope of democracy.

Germany's loss was America's gain. Zealous German liberals like the lanky and public-spirited Carl Schurz, a relentless foe of slavery and public corruption, contributed richly to the elevation of American political life.

Unlike the Irish, many of the Germanic newcomers possessed a modest amount of material goods. Most of them pushed out to the lush lands of the Middle West, notably Wisconsin, where they settled and established model farms. Like the Irish, they formed an influential body of voters whom American politicians shamelessly wooed. But the Germans were less potent politically because their strength was more widely scattered.

The hand of Germans in shaping American life was widely felt in still other ways. The Conestoga wagon, the Kentucky rifle, and the Christmas tree were all German contributions to American culture. Germans had fled from the militarism and wars of Europe and consequently came to be a bulwark of isolationist sentiment in the upper Mississippi Valley. Better educated on the whole than the stump-grubbing Americans, they warmly supported public schools, including their *Kindergarten* (children's garden). They likewise did much to stimulate art and music. As outspoken champions of freedom, they became relentless enemies of slavery during the fevered years before the Civil War.

For a generation, from 1793 to 1815, war raged across Europe. Ruinous as it was on the Continent, the fighting brought unprecedented prosperity to the long-suffering landsmen of Ireland, groaning since the twelfth century under the yoke of English rule. For as Europe's fields lay fallow, irrigated only by the blood of its farmers, Ireland fed the hungry armies that ravened for food as well as territory. Irish farmers planted every available acre, interspersing the lowly potato amongst their fields of grain. With prices for food products ever mounting, tenant farmers reaped a temporary respite from their perpetual struggle to remain on the land. Most landlords were satisfied by the prosperity and so relaxed their pressure on tenants; others, stymied by the absence of British police forces that had been stripped of manpower to fight in Europe, had little means to enforce eviction notices.

But the peace that brought solace to battle-scarred Europe changed all this. After 1815 war-inflated wheat prices plummeted by half. Hard-pressed landlords resolved to leave vast fields unplanted. Assisted now by a strengthened British constabulary, they vowed to sweep the pesky peasants from the retired acreage. Many of those forced to leave sought work in England; some went to America. Then in 1845 a blight that ravaged the potato crop sounded the final knell for the Irish peasantry. The resultant famine spread desolation throughout the island. In five years more than a million people died. Another million sailed for America.

Of the emigrants, most were young and literate in English, the majority under thirty-five years old. Families typically pooled money to send strong young sons to the New World, where they would earn wages to pay the fares for those who waited at home. These "famine Irish" mostly remained in the port cities of the Northeast, abandoning the farmer's life for the dingy congestion of the urban metropolis.

The disembarking Irish were poorly prepared for urban life. They found progress up the economic ladder painfully slow. Their work as domestic servants or construction laborers was dull and arduous, and mortality rates were astoundingly high. Escape from the potato famine hardly guaranteed a long life to an Irish American; a gray-bearded Irishman was a rare sight in nineteenth-century America. Most of the new arrivals toiled as day laborers. A fortunate few owned boardinghouses or saloons, where their dispirited countrymen sought solace in the bottle. For Irish-born women, opportunities were still scarcer; they worked mainly as domestic servants.

But it was their Roman Catholicism, more even than their penury or their perceived fondness for alcohol, that earned the Irish the distrust and resentment of their native-born, Protestant American neighbors. The core of community and identity for Irish immigrants was their parish church. Worries about safeguarding their children's faith inspired the construction of parish schools, financed by the pennies of struggling, working-class Irish parents.

Outward Bound, the Quay at Dublin, 1854   Thousands fled famine in Ireland by coming to America in the 1840s and 1850s.

St. Patrick's Day Parade in America, Union Square, ca. 1870 This painting shows a St. Patrick's Day parade in New York City. The religious festival was celebrated with greater fanfare in America than in Ireland itself, as Irish immigrants used it to boost their ethnic solidarity and assert their distinctive identity in their adopted country.

If Ireland's green fields scarcely equipped her sons and daughters for the scrap and scramble of economic life in America's cities, life in the Old Country nevertheless had instilled in them an aptitude for politics. Irish Catholic resistance against centuries of English Anglican domination had instructed many Old Country Irish in the ways of mass politics. That political experience readied them for the boss system of the political "machines" in America's northeastern cities. The boss's local representatives met each newcomer soon after he landed in America. Asking only for votes, the machine supplied coal in wintertime, food, and help with the law. Irish voters soon became a bulwark of the Democratic party, reliably supporting the party of Jefferson and Jackson in cities like New York and Boston. As Irish Americans like New York's "Honest John" Kelly themselves became bosses, white-collar jobs in government service opened up to the Irish. They became building inspectors, aldermen, and even policemen—an astonishing irony for a people driven from their homeland by the nightsticks and bayonets of the British police.

Yet the Germans—often dubbed "damned Dutchmen"—were occasionally regarded with suspicion by their old-stock American neighbors. Seeking to preserve their language and culture, they sometimes settled in compact "colonies" and kept aloof from the surrounding community. Accustomed to the "Continental Sunday" and uncurbed by Puritan tradition, they made merry on the Sabbath and drank huge quantities of an amber beverage called *bier* (beer), which dates its real popularity in America to their coming. Their Old World drinking habits, like those of the Irish, spurred advocates of temperance in the use of alcohol to redouble their reform efforts.

✴ Flare-ups of Antiforeignism

The invasion by this so-called immigrant "rabble" in the 1840s and 1850s inflamed the prejudices of American "nativists." They feared that these foreign hordes would outbreed, outvote, and overwhelm the old "native" stock. Not only did the newcomers take jobs from "native" Americans, but the bulk of the displaced Irish were Roman Catholics, as were a substantial minority of the Germans. The Church of Rome was still widely regarded by many old-line Americans as a "foreign" church; convents were commonly referred to as "popish brothels."

Roman Catholics were now on the move. Seeking to protect their children from Protestant indoctrination in the public schools, they began in the 1840s to construct an entirely separate Catholic educational system—an enormously expensive undertaking for a poor immigrant community, but one that revealed the strength of its religious commitment. They had formed a negligible minority during colonial days, and their numbers had increased gradually. But with the enormous influx of the Irish and Germans in the 1840s and 1850s, the Catholics became a powerful religious group. In 1840 they had ranked fifth, behind the Baptists, Methodists, Presbyterians, and Congregationalists. By 1850, with some 1.8 million communicants, they had bounded into first place—a position they have never lost.

Older-stock Americans were alarmed by these mounting figures. They professed to believe that in due time the "alien riffraff" would "establish" the Catholic Church at the expense of Protestantism and would introduce "popish idols." The noisier American "nativists" rallied for political action. In 1849 they formed the Order of the Star-Spangled Banner, which soon developed into the formidable American party, more commonly known as the **Know-Nothing party**, a name derived from its secretiveness. "Nativists" agitated for rigid restrictions on immigration and naturalization and for laws authorizing the deportation of alien paupers. They also promoted a lurid literature of

Crooked Voting A bitter "nativist" cartoon charging Irish and German immigrants with "stealing" elections.

exposure, much of it pure fiction. The authors, sometimes posing as escaped nuns, described the shocking sins they imagined the cloisters concealed, including the secret burial of babies. One of these sensational books—Maria Monk's ***Awful Disclosures*** (1836)—sold over 300,000 copies.

Even uglier was occasional mass violence. As early as 1834, a Catholic convent near Boston was burned by a howling mob, and in ensuing years a few scattered attacks fell upon Catholic schools and churches. The most frightful flare-up occurred during 1844 in Philadelphia, where the Irish Catholics fought back against the threats of the "nativists." The City of Brotherly Love did not quiet down until two Catholic churches had been burned and some thirteen citizens had been killed and fifty wounded in several days of fighting. These outbursts of intolerance, though infrequent and generally localized in the larger cities, remain an unfortunate blot on the record of America's treatment of minority groups.

Immigrants were undeniably making America a more pluralistic society—one of the most ethnically and racially varied in the history of the world—and perhaps it was small wonder that cultural clashes would occur. Why, in fact, were such episodes not even more frequent and more violent? Part of the answer lies in the robustness of the American economy. The vigorous growth of the economy in these years both attracted immigrants in the first place and ensured that, once arrived, they could claim their share of American wealth without jeopardizing the wealth of others. Their hands and brains, in fact, helped fuel economic expansion. Immigrants and the American economy, in short, needed one another. Without the newcomers, a preponderantly agricultural United States might well have been condemned to watch in envy as the **Industrial Revolution** swept through nineteenth-century Europe.

Creeping Mechanization

A group of gifted British inventors, beginning about 1750, perfected a series of machines for the mass production of textiles. This harnessing of steam multiplied the power of human muscles some ten-thousandfold and ushered in the modern factory system—and with it, the so-called Industrial Revolution. It was accompanied by a no-less-spectacular transformation in agricultural production and in the methods of transportation and communication.

The factory system gradually spread from Britain—"the world's workshop"—to other lands. It took a generation or so to reach western Europe, and then the United States. Why was the youthful American Republic, eventually to become an industrial giant, so slow to embrace the machine?

For one thing, land was cheap in America. Land-starved descendants of land-starved peasants were not going to coop themselves up in smelly factories when they might till their own acres in God's fresh air and sunlight. Labor was therefore generally scarce, and enough nimble hands to operate the machines were hard to find—until immigrants began to pour ashore in the 1840s. Money for capital investment, moreover, was not plentiful in pioneering America, whose Industrial Revolution, like that of many a developing country in later centuries, awaited an influx of foreign capital—which in turn awaited assurance of secure property rights, sufficient infrastructure, an adequate work force, and political stability. Without

such capital, raw materials lay undeveloped, undiscovered, or unsuspected. The Republic was one day to become the world's leading coal producer, but much of the coal burned in colonial times was imported all the way from Britain.

The young country also had difficulty producing goods of high enough quality and cheap enough cost to compete with mass-produced European products. Long-established British factories in particular provided cutthroat competition. Their superiority was attested by the fact that a few unscrupulous Yankee manufacturers, out to make a dishonest dollar, stamped their own products with fake English trademarks.

The British also enjoyed a monopoly of the textile machinery, whose secrets they were anxious to hide from foreign competitors. Parliament enacted laws, in harmony with the mercantile system, forbidding the export of the machines or the emigration of mechanics able to reproduce them.

Although a number of small manufacturing enterprises existed in the early Republic, the future industrial colossus was still snoring. Not until well past the middle of the nineteenth century did the value of the output of the factories exceed that of the farms.

Whitney Ends the Fiber Famine

Samuel Slater has been acclaimed the "Father of the Factory System" in America, and seldom can the paternity of a movement more properly be ascribed to one person. A skilled British mechanic of twenty-one, he was attracted by bounties being offered to British workers familiar with the textile machines. After memorizing the plans for the machinery, he escaped in disguise to America, where he won the backing of Moses Brown, a Quaker capitalist in Rhode Island. Laboriously reconstructing the essential apparatus with the aid of a blacksmith and a carpenter, he put into operation in 1791 the first efficient American machinery for spinning cotton thread.

The ravenous mechanism was now ready, but where was the cotton fiber? Handpicking one pound of lint from three pounds of seed was a full day's work for one slave, and this process was so expensive that American-made cotton cloth was relatively rare.

Another mechanical genius, Massachusetts-born Eli Whitney, now made his mark. After graduating from Yale, he journeyed to Georgia to serve as a private tutor while preparing for the law. There he was told that the poverty of the South would be relieved if someone could only invent a workable device for separating the seed from the short-staple cotton fiber. Within ten days, in 1793, he built a crude machine called the **cotton gin** (short for engine) that was fifty times more effective than the handpicking process.

Between 1820 and 1920, a sea of Germans lapped at America's shores and seeped into its very heartland. Their numbers surpassed those of any other immigrant group, even the prolific and often-detested Irish. Yet this Germanic flood, unlike its Gaelic equivalent, stirred little panic in the hearts of native-born Americans because the Germans largely stayed to themselves, far from the madding crowds and nativist fears of northeastern cities. They prospered with astonishing ease, building towns in Wisconsin, agricultural colonies in Texas, and religious communities in Pennsylvania. They added a decidedly Germanic flavor to the heady brew of reform and community building that so animated antebellum America.

These "Germans" actually hailed from many different Old World lands, because there was no unified nation of Germany until 1871, when the ruthless and crafty Prussian Otto von Bismarck assembled the German state out of a mosaic of independent principalities, kingdoms, and duchies. Until that time, "Germans" came to America as Prussians, Bavarians, Hessians, Rhinelanders, Pomeranians, and Westphalians. They arrived at different times and for many different reasons. Some, particularly the so-called Forty-Eighters—the refugees from the abortive democratic revolutions of 1848—hungered for the democracy they had failed to win in Germany. Others, particularly Jews, Pietists, and Anabaptist groups like the Amish and the Mennonites, coveted religious freedom. And they came not only to America. Like the Italians later, many Germans sought a new life in Brazil, Argentina, and Chile. But the largest number ventured into the United States.

Typical German immigrants arrived with fatter purses than their Irish counterparts. Small landowners or independent artisans in their native countries, they did not have to settle for bottom-rung industrial employment in the grimy factories of the Northeast and instead could afford to push on to the open spaces of the American West.

In Wisconsin these immigrants found a home away from home, a place with a climate, soil, and geography much like central Europe's. Milwaukee, a crude frontier town before the Germans' arrival, became the "German Athens." It boasted a German theater, German beer gardens, a German volunteer fire company, and a German-English academy. In distant Texas, German settlements like New Braunfels and Fredericksburg flourished. When the famous landscape architect and writer Frederick Law Olmsted stumbled upon these prairie outposts of Teutonic culture in 1857, he was shocked to be "welcomed by a figure in a blue flannel shirt and pendant beard, quoting Tacitus." These German colonies in the frontier Southwest mixed high European elegance with Texas ruggedness. Olmsted described a visit to a German household where the settlers drank "coffee in tin cups upon Dresden saucers" and sat upon "barrels for seats, to hear a Beethoven symphony on the grand piano."

"Little Germany" Cincinnati's "Over-the-Rhine" district in 1887.

These Germanic colonizers of America's heartland also formed religious communities, none more distinctive or durable than the Amish settlements of Pennsylvania, Indiana, and Ohio. The Amish took their name from their founder and leader, the Swiss Anabaptist Jacob Amman. Like other Anabaptist groups, they shunned extravagance and reserved baptism for adults, repudiating the tradition of infant baptism practiced by most Europeans. For this they were persecuted, even imprisoned, in Europe. Seeking escape from their oppression, some five hundred Amish ventured to Pennsylvania in the 1700s, followed by three thousand in the years from 1815 to 1865.

In America they formed enduring religious communities—isolated enclaves where they could shield themselves from the corruption and the conveniences of the modern world. To this day the German-speaking Amish still travel in horse-drawn carriages and farm without heavy machinery. No electric lights brighten the darkness that nightly envelops their tidy farmhouses; no ringing telephones punctuate the reverent tranquility of their mealtime prayer; no ornaments relieve the austere simplicity of their black garments. The Amish remain a stalwart, traditional community in a rootless, turbulent society, a living testament to the religious ferment and social experiments of the antebellum era.

Marriage Plate, Bucks County, Pennsylvania, ca. 1806 The Germans who settled the "Pennsylvania Dutch" communities in the eighteenth century preserved ancient traditions of handicraft and art, as exemplified by this whimsical "marriage plate" made by a sixteen-year-old potter named John Leidy. The inscription reads, "Rather would I single live than the wife the breeches [trousers] give."

1895-78 John Leidy I, Dish, 1797, Philadelphia Museum of Art: Gift of A.C. Harrison, 1895

Jean-Louis Atlan/Sygma/Corbis

Amish Country, Near Lancaster, Pennsylvania For more than two centuries, the Amish people have preserved their traditional way of life.

Francis Cabot Lowell's Mill, Waltham, Massachusetts, 1826, and Cotton Industry; Carding, Drawing, and Roving; Engraving, 1835   Built in 1814, Lowell's mill (left) was a marvel of manufacturing efficiency. It combined all phases of production, including spinning and weaving, under one roof. The mill's labor force (right) was composed primarily of young women from the local farming communities.

Few machines have ever wrought so wondrous a change. The gin affected not only the history of America but that of the world. Almost overnight the raising of cotton became highly profitable, and the South was tied hand and foot to the throne of King Cotton. Human bondage had been dying out, but the insatiable demand for cotton reriveted the chains on the limbs of the downtrodden southern blacks.

South and North both prospered. Slave-driving planters cleared more acres for cotton, pushing the Cotton Kingdom westward off the depleted tidewater plains, over the Piedmont, and onto the black loam bottomlands of Alabama and Mississippi. Humming gins poured out avalanches of snowy fiber for the spindles of the Yankee machines, though for decades to come the mills of Britain bought the lion's share of southern cotton. The American phase of the Industrial Revolution, which first blossomed in cotton textiles, was well on its way.

Factories at first flourished most actively in New England, though they branched out into the more populous areas of New York, New Jersey, and Pennsylvania. The South, increasingly wedded to the production of cotton, could boast of comparatively little manufacturing. Its capital was bound up in slaves; its local consumers for the most part were desperately poor.

New England was singularly favored as an industrial center for several reasons. Its narrow belt of stony soil made farming difficult and hence made manufacturing attractive. A relatively dense population provided labor and accessible markets, shipping brought in capital, and snug seaports made easy the import of raw materials and the export of the finished products.

Finally, the rapid rivers—notably the Merrimack in Massachusetts—provided abundant water power to turn the cogs of the machines. By 1860 more than 400 million pounds of southern cotton poured annually into the gaping maws of over a thousand mills, mostly in New England.

Marvels in Manufacturing

America's factories spread slowly until about 1807, when there began the fateful sequence of the embargo, nonintercourse, and the War of 1812. Stern necessity dictated the manufacture of substitutes for normal imports, while the stoppage of European commerce was temporarily ruinous to Yankee shipping. Both capital and labor were driven from the waves onto the factory floor, as New England, in the striking phrase of John Randolph, exchanged the trident for the distaff. Generous bounties were offered by local authorities for homegrown goods, "Buy American" and "Wear American" became popular slogans, and patriotism prompted the wearing of baggy homespun garments. President Madison donned some at his inauguration, where he was said to have been a walking argument for the better processing of native wool.

But the manufacturing boomlet broke abruptly with the peace of Ghent in 1815. British competitors unloaded their dammed-up surpluses at ruinously low prices, and American newspapers were so full of British advertisements for goods on credit that little space was left for news. In one Rhode Island district, all 150 mills were forced to close their doors, except the original Slater plant. Responding to pained outcries, Congress provided some relief when it passed the mildly protective Tariff of 1816—among the earliest political contests to control the shape of the economy.

As the factory system flourished, it embraced numerous other industries in addition to textiles. Prominent among them was the manufacturing of firearms, and here the wizardly Eli Whitney again appeared with an extraordinary contribution. Frustrated in his earlier efforts to monopolize the cotton gin, he turned to the mass production of muskets for the U.S. Army. Up to this time, each part of a firearm had been hand-tooled, and if the trigger of one broke, the trigger of another might or might not fit. About 1798 Whitney seized upon the idea of having machines make each part, so that all the triggers, for example, would be as much alike as the successive imprints of a copperplate engraving. Journeying to Washington, he reportedly dismantled ten of his new muskets in the presence of skeptical officials, scrambled the parts together, and then quickly reassembled ten different muskets.

The principle of interchangeable parts was widely adopted by 1850. It gave rise to a host of other innovations, including Samuel Colt's fabled revolver, and it ultimately became the basis of modern mass-production, assembly-line methods that set the northern states on the path to thoroughgoing industrialization. Ironically, the same Yankee Eli Whitney, by perfecting the cotton gin, had also given slavery a renewed lease on life, making the Civil War more likely. Yet by nourishing the North's industrial revolution, Whitney conferred upon the Union a massive advantage when that showdown finally came.

The sewing machine, invented by Elias Howe in 1846 and perfected by Isaac Singer, gave another strong boost to northern industrialization. The sewing machine became the foundation of the ready-made clothing industry, which took root about the time of the Civil War. It drove many a seamstress from the shelter of the private home to the factory, where, like a human robot, she tended the clattering mechanisms.

Each momentous new invention seemed to stimulate still more imaginative inventions. For the decade ending in 1800, only 306 patents were registered in Washington; but the decade ending in 1860 saw the amazing total of 28,000. Yet in 1838 the clerk of the **Patent Office** resigned in despair, complaining that all worthwhile inventions had been discovered.

Technical advances spurred equally important changes in the form and legal status of business

The Growth in Cotton Production and Consumption Whitney's gin (left) made possible the mass cultivation of upland, or short-stable, cotton, which was unprofitable to raise when its seeds had to be laboriously removed by hand. As cotton production pushed farther south and west, taking slavery with it, it provisioned a growing northern textile industry. Calico, or patterned cotton cloth, was hand-produced by wood-block printing with colored dyes, as shown here at right. The availability of plentiful, cheap cloth vastly expanded women's wardrobes.

Said Abraham Lincoln (1809–1865) in a lecture in 1859,

❝The patent system secured to the inventor for a limited time exclusive use of his invention, and thereby added the fuel of interest to the fire of genius in the discovery and production of new and useful things.**❞**

Ten years earlier Lincoln had received patent no. 6469 for a scheme to buoy steamboats over shoals. It was never practically applied, but he remains the only president ever to have secured a patent.

organizations. The principle of **limited liability** aided the concentration of capital by permitting the individual investor, in cases of legal claims or bankruptcy, to risk no more than his own share of the corporation's stock. Fifteen Boston families formed one of the earliest investment capital companies, the Boston Associates. They eventually dominated the textile, railroad, insurance, and banking business of Massachusetts. Laws of "free incorporation," first passed in New York in 1848, meant that businessmen could create corporations without applying for individual charters from the legislature.

Samuel F. B. Morse's telegraph was among the inventions that tightened the sinews of an increasingly complex business world. A distinguished but poverty-stricken portrait painter, Morse finally secured from Congress, to the accompaniment of the usual jeers, an appropriation of $30,000 to support his experiment with "talking wires." In 1844 Morse strung a wire forty miles from Washington to Baltimore and tapped out the historic message, "What hath God wrought?" The invention brought fame and fortune to Morse, as he put distantly separated people in almost instant communication with one another. By the eve of the Civil War, a web of singing wires spanned nearly the entire continent, revolutionizing news gathering, diplomacy, and finance.

Thus, by the time of the fabled London World's Fair in 1851, known as the Great Exhibition, American products were prominent among the world's commercial wonders. Fairgoers crowded into the dazzling Crystal Palace to see McCormick's reaper, Morse's telegraph, Colt's firearms, and Charles Goodyear's vulcanized rubber goods.

✷ Workers and "Wage Slaves"

One ugly outgrowth of the factory system was an increasingly acute labor problem. Hitherto manufacturing had been done in the home, or in the small shop, where the master craftsman and his apprentice, rubbing elbows at the same bench, could maintain an intimate and friendly relationship. The Industrial Revolution submerged this personal association in the impersonal ownership of stuffy factories in "spindle cities." Around these, like tumors, the slumlike hovels of the "wage slaves" tended to cluster.

Clearly the early factory system did not shower its benefits evenly on all. While many owners grew plump, working people often wasted away at their workbenches. Hours were long, wages were low, and meals were skimpy and hastily gulped. Workers were forced to toil in unsanitary buildings that were poorly ventilated, lighted, and heated. They were forbidden by law to form labor unions to raise wages, for such cooperative activity was regarded as a criminal conspiracy. Not surprisingly, only twenty-four recorded strikes occurred before 1835.

Especially vulnerable to exploitation were child workers. In 1820 a significant portion of the nation's industrial toilers were children under ten years of age. Victims of factory labor, many children were mentally blighted, emotionally starved, physically stunted, and even brutally whipped in special "whipping rooms." In Samuel Slater's mill of 1791, the first machine tenders were seven boys and two girls, all under twelve years of age.

By contrast, the lot of most adult wage workers improved markedly in the 1820s and 1830s. In the full flush of Jacksonian democracy, many of the states granted the laboring man the vote. Brandishing the ballot, he first strove to lighten his burden through workingmen's parties. Eventually many workers gave their loyalty to the Democratic party of Andrew Jackson, whose attack on the Bank of the United States and against all forms of "privilege" reflected their anxieties about the emerging capitalist economy. In addition to such goals as the ten-hour day, higher wages, and tolerable working conditions, they demanded public education for their children and an end to the inhuman practice of imprisonment for debt.

One observer in 1836 published a newspaper account of conditions in some of the New England factories:

❝The operatives work thirteen hours a day in the summer time, and from daylight to dark in the winter. At half past four in the morning the factory bell rings, and at five the girls must be in the mills.... So fatigued...are numbers of girls that they go to bed soon after receiving their evening meal, and endeavor by a comparatively long sleep to resuscitate their weakened frames for the toil of the coming day.**❞**

Courtesy of the Connecticut State Library

The Granger Collection, NYC

Coexistence of the Craftsman's Shop and the Factory, 1860 These two images recorded workers laboring in very different kinds of work places in the same year. The painting, "The Wheelwright's Shop," by Edwin Tryon Billings (right), captures the survival of a small-scale, intimate shop producing hand-made wheels for carts and carriages. The daguerreotype (left) shows an operator working the Lock Frame Jigging Machine in Samuel Colt's state-of-the-art Hartford, Connecticut, gun factory. As different as they were, both jobs required skill and focus.

Employers, abhorring the rise of the "rabble" in politics, fought the ten-hour day to the last ditch. They argued that reduced hours would lessen production, increase costs, and demoralize the workers. Laborers would have so much leisure time that the Devil would lead them into mischief. A red-letter gain was at length registered for labor in 1840, when President Van Buren established the ten-hour day for federal employees on public works. In ensuing years a number of states gradually fell into line by reducing the hours of working people.

Day laborers at last learned that their strongest weapon was to lay down their tools, even at the risk of prosecution under the law. Dozens of strikes erupted in the 1830s and 1840s, most of them for higher wages, some for the ten-hour day, and a few for such unusual goals as the right to smoke on the job. The workers usually lost more strikes than they won, for the employer could resort to such tactics as the importing of strikebreakers—often derisively called "scabs" or "rats," and often fresh off the boat from the Old World. Labor long raised its voice against the unrestricted inpouring of wage-depressing and union-busting immigrant workers.

Labor's early and painful efforts at organization had netted some 300,000 trade unionists by 1830. But such encouraging gains were dashed on the rocks of hard times following the severe depression of 1837. As unemployment spread, union membership shriveled. Yet toilers won a promising legal victory in 1842. The supreme court of Massachusetts ruled in the case of **Commonwealth v. Hunt** that labor unions were not illegal conspiracies, provided that their methods were "honorable and peaceful." This enlightened decision did not legalize the strike overnight throughout the country, but it was a significant signpost of the times. Trade unions still had a rocky row to hoe, stretching ahead for about a century, before they could meet management on relatively even terms.

Violence broke out along the New York waterfront in 1836 when laborers striking for higher wages attacked "scabs." Philip Hone's (1780–1851) diary records,

❝ The Mayor, who acts with vigour and firmness, ordered out the troops, who are now on duty with loaded arms.... These measures have restored order for the present, but I fear the elements of disorder are at work; the bands of Irish and other foreigners, instigated by the mischievous councils of the trades-union and other combinations of discontented men, are acquiring strength and importance which will ere long be difficult to quell. **❞**

The Invention of the Sewing Machine

Historians of technology examine not only the documentary evidence of plans and patents left behind by inventors, but surviving machines themselves. In 1845 Elias Howe, a twenty-six-year-old apprentice to a Boston watchmaker, invented a sewing machine that could make 250 stitches a minute, five times what the swiftest hand-sewer could do. A year later Howe received a patent for his invention, but because the hand-cranked machine could only stitch straight seams for a short distance before requiring resetting,

it had limited commercial appeal. Howe took his sewing machine abroad, where he worked with British manufacturers to improve it, and then returned to America and combined his patent with those of other inventors, including Isaac M. Singer. Hundreds of thousands of sewing machines were produced beginning in the 1850s for the commercial manufacture of clothing, books, shoes, and many other products and also for home use. The sewing machine became the first widely advertised consumer product. Due

to its high cost, the Singer company introduced an installment buying plan, which helped place sewing machines in most middle-class households. Why was the sewing machine able to find eager customers in commercial workshops and home sewing rooms alike? How might the sewing machine have changed other aspects of American life, such as work patterns, clothing styles, and retail selling? What other advances in technology might have been necessary for the invention of the sewing machine?

National Museum of American History, Smithsonian Institution, Behring Center

✸ Women and the Economy

Women were also sucked into the clanging mechanism of factory production. Farm women and girls had an important place in the preindustrial economy, spinning yarn, weaving cloth, and making candles,

soap, butter, and cheese. New factories such as the textile mills of New England undermined these activities, cranking out manufactured goods much faster than they could be made by hand at home. Yet these same factories offered employment to the very young women whose work they were displacing. Factory jobs

STRIVE TO EXCEL.

W. S. & C. H. THOMSON'S SKIRT MANUFACTORY.

The Sewing Floor of Thompson's Skirt Factory, 1859 The burgeoning textile industry provided employment for thousands of women in antebellum America—and also produced the clothes that women wore. This view of a New York City shop in 1859 illustrates the transition from hand-sewing (on the right) to machine-stitching (on the left). It also vividly illustrates the contrast between the kinds of "sewing circles" in which women had traditionally sought companionship to the impersonal mass-production line of the modern manufacturing plant. Note especially the stark exhortation on the wall: "Strive to Excel."

promised greater economic independence for women, as well as the means to buy the manufactured products of the new market economy.

"**Factory girls**" typically toiled six days a week, earning a pittance for dreary, limb-numbing, earsplitting stints of twelve or thirteen hours—"from dark to dark." The Boston Associates, nonetheless, proudly pointed to their textile mill at Lowell, Massachusetts, as a showplace factory. The workers were virtually all New England farm girls, carefully supervised on and off the job by watchful matrons. Escorted regularly to church from their company boardinghouses and forbidden to form unions, they had few opportunities to share dissatisfactions over their grueling working conditions.

But factory jobs of any kind were still unusual for women. Opportunities for women to be economically self-supporting were scarce and consisted mainly of nursing, domestic service, and especially teaching. The dedicated Catharine Beecher, unmarried daughter of a famous preacher and sister of Harriet Beecher Stowe, tirelessly urged women to enter the teaching profession. She eventually succeeded beyond her dreams, as men left teaching for other lines of work and schoolteaching became a thoroughly "feminized" occupation. Other work "opportunities" for women beckoned

in household service. Perhaps one white family in ten employed servants at midcentury, most of whom were poor white, immigrant, or black women. About 10 percent of white women were working for pay outside their own homes in 1850, and estimates are that about 20 percent of all women had been employed at some time prior to marriage.

The vast majority of working women were single. Upon marriage they left their paying jobs and took up their new work (without wages) as wives and mothers. In the home they were enshrined in a **cult of domesticity**, a widespread cultural creed that glorified the customary functions of the homemaker. From their pedestal, married women commanded immense moral power, and they increasingly made decisions that altered the character of the family itself.

Women's changing roles and the spreading Industrial Revolution brought some important changes in the life of the nineteenth-century home—the traditional "women's sphere." Love, not parental "arrangement," more and more frequently determined the choice of a spouse—yet parents often retained the power of veto. Families thus became more closely knit and affectionate, providing the emotional refuge that made the threatening impersonality of big-city industrialism tolerable to many people.

A woman worker in the Lowell mills wrote a friend in 1844,

"You wish to know minutely of our hours of labor. We go in [to the mill] at five o'clock; at seven we come out to breakfast; at half-past seven we return to our work, and stay until half-past twelve. At one, or quarter-past one four months in the year, we return to our work, and stay until seven at night. Then the evening is all our own, which is more than some laboring girls can say, who think nothing is more tedious than a factory life."

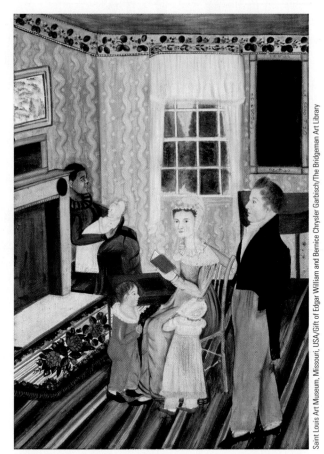

York, Pennsylvania, Family with Negro Servant, ca. 1828 This portrait of a Pennsylvania family presents a somewhat idealized picture of the home as the woman's sphere. The wife and mother sits at the center of activity; while she reads to the children, the husband and father stands by somewhat superfluously. A black servant cares for an infant in the corner, suggesting the prosperous status of this household.

Most striking, families grew smaller. The average household had nearly six members at the end of the eighteenth century but fewer than five members a century later. The "fertility rate," or number of births among women ages fourteen to forty-five, dropped sharply among white women in the years after the Revolution and, in the course of the nineteenth century as a whole, fell by half. Birth control was still a taboo topic for polite conversation, and contraceptive technology was primitive, but clearly some form of family limitation was being practiced quietly and effectively in countless families, rural and urban alike. Women undoubtedly played a large part—perhaps the leading part—in decisions to have fewer children. This newly assertive role for women has been called "domestic feminism" because it signified the growing power and independence of women, even while they remained wrapped in the "cult of domesticity."

Smaller families, in turn, meant child-centered families because where children are fewer, parents can lavish more care on them individually. European visitors to the United States in the nineteenth century often complained about the unruly behavior of American "brats." But though American parents may have increasingly spared the rod, they did not spoil their children. Lessons were enforced by punishments other than the hickory stick. When the daughter of novelist Harriet Beecher Stowe neglected to do her homework, her mother sent her from the dinner table and gave her "only bread and water in her own apartment." What Europeans saw as permissiveness was in reality the consequence of an emerging new idea of child-rearing, in which the child's will was not to be simply broken, but rather shaped.

In the little republic of the family, as in the Republic at large, good citizens were raised not to be meekly obedient to authority, but to be independent individuals who could make their own decisions on the basis of internalized moral standards. Thus the outlines of the "modern" family were clear by mid-century: it was small, affectionate, and child-centered, and it provided a special arena for the talents of women. Feminists of a later day might decry the stifling atmosphere of the nineteenth-century middle-class white home, but to many women of the time, it seemed a big step upward from the conditions of grinding toil—often alongside men in the fields—in which their mothers had lived.

✴ Western Farmers Reap a Revolution in the Fields

As smoke-belching factories altered the eastern skyline, flourishing farms were changing the face of the West. The trans-Allegheny region—especially the Ohio-Indiana-Illinois tier—was fast becoming the nation's breadbasket. Before long it would become a granary to the world.

Pioneer families first hacked a clearing out of the forest and then planted their painfully furrowed fields to corn. The yellow grain was amazingly versatile. It could be fed to hogs ("corn on the hoof") or distilled into liquor ("corn in the bottle"). Both these products could be transported more easily than the bulky grain itself, and they became the early western farmer's staple market items. So many hogs were butchered, traded, or shipped at Cincinnati that the city was known as the "Porkopolis" of the West.

Most western produce was at first floated down the Ohio-Mississippi River system, to feed the lusty appetite of the booming Cotton Kingdom. But western farmers were as hungry for profits as southern slaves and planters were for food. These tillers, spurred on by the easy availability of seemingly boundless acres, sought ways to bring more and more land into cultivation.

Ingenious inventors came to their aid. One of the first obstacles that frustrated the farmers was the thickly matted soil of the West, which snagged and snapped fragile wooden plows. John Deere of Illinois in 1837 finally produced a steel plow that broke the stubborn soil. Sharp and effective, it was also light enough to be pulled by horses, rather than oxen.

In the 1830s Virginia-born Cyrus McCormick contributed the most wondrous contraption of all: a mechanical mower-reaper. The clattering cogs of McCormick's horse-drawn machine were to the western farmers what the cotton gin was to the southern planters. Seated on his red-chariot reaper, a single husbandman could do the work of five men with sickles and scythes.

No other American invention cut so wide a swath as the **McCormick reaper**. It made ambitious capitalists out of humble plowmen, who now scrambled for more acres on which to plant more fields of billowing wheat. Subsistence farming gave way to food production for both domestic and foreign markets, as large-scale ("extensive"), specialized, cash-crop agriculture came to dominate the trans-Allegheny West. With it followed mounting indebtedness, as farmers bought more land and more machinery to work it. Soon hustling farmer-businesspeople were annually harvesting a larger crop than the South—which was becoming self-sufficient in food production—could devour. They began to dream of markets elsewhere—in the mushrooming factory towns of the East or across the far-away Atlantic. But they were still largely landlocked. Commerce moved north and south on the river systems. Before it could begin to move east-west in bulk, a transportation revolution would have to occur.

McCormick's Miraculous Reaper   This illustration shows an early test of Cyrus McCormick's mechanical reaper near his home in Virginia in 1831. The reaper was best suited, however, to the horizonless fields of wheat on the rolling prairies of the Midwest. By the 1850s McCormick's Chicago factory was cranking out more than twenty thousand reapers a year for midwestern farmers.

McCormick Reaper Works, 1850s Contrast this hectic scene of "mass production" with the simple workplace depicted in "The Wheelwright's Shop" on p. 293.

Wisconsin Historical Society

✦ Highways and Steamboats

In 1789, when the Constitution was launched, primitive methods of travel were still in use. Waterborne commerce, whether along the coast or on the rivers, was slow, uncertain, and often dangerous. Stagecoaches and wagons lurched over bone-shaking roads. Passengers would be routed out to lay nearby fence rails across muddy stretches, and occasionally horses would drown in muddy pits while wagons sank slowly out of sight.

Cheap and efficient carriers were imperative if raw materials were to be transported to factories and if finished products were to be delivered to consumers. On December 3, 1803, a firm in Providence, Rhode Island, sent a shipment of yarn to a point sixty miles away, notifying the purchaser that the consignment could be expected to arrive in "the course of the winter."

A promising improvement came in the 1790s, when a private company completed the Lancaster Turnpike in Pennsylvania. It was a broad, hard-surfaced highway that thrust sixty-two miles westward from Philadelphia to Lancaster. As drivers approached the tollgate, they were confronted with a barrier of sharp pikes, which were turned aside when they paid their toll. Hence the term **turnpike**.

The Lancaster Turnpike proved to be a highly successful venture, returning as high as 15 percent annual dividends to its stockholders. It attracted a rich trade to Philadelphia and touched off a turnpike-building boom that lasted about twenty years. It also stimulated western development. The turnpikes

beckoned to the canvas-covered Conestoga wagons, whose creakings heralded a westward advance that would know no real retreat.

Western road building, always expensive, encountered many obstacles. One pesky roadblock was the noisy states' righters, who opposed federal aid to local projects. Eastern states also protested against being bled of their populations by the westward-reaching arteries.

Westerners scored a notable triumph in 1811 when the federal government started construction of the National Road, also known as the Cumberland Road, in honor of its starting point in Cumberland, Maryland. Although construction was interrupted by the War of 1812 and by states' righters' complaints about federal grants for internal improvements, the road reached Vandalia, Illinois, 591 miles to the west, in 1839. Later extensions brought it from Baltimore, on Chesapeake Bay, to the banks of the Mississippi River in St. Louis.

The steamboat craze, which overlapped the turnpike craze, was touched off by an ambitious painter-engineer named Robert Fulton. He installed a powerful steam engine in a vessel that posterity came to know as the *Clermont* but that a dubious public dubbed "Fulton's Folly." On a historic day in 1807, the quaint little ship, belching sparks from its single smokestack, churned steadily from New York City up the Hudson River toward Albany. It made the run of 150 miles in 32 hours.

The success of the steamboat was sensational. People could now in large degree defy wind, wave, tide, and downstream current. Within a few years, Fulton had changed all of America's navigable streams into

Mississippi in Time of Peace, by Mrs. Frances Flora Bond Palmer, 1865 By the mid-nineteenth century, steamboats had made the Mississippi a bustling river highway—as it remains today.

two-way arteries, thereby doubling their carrying capacity. Hitherto keelboats had been pushed up the Mississippi, with quivering poles and raucous profanity, at less than one mile an hour—a process that was prohibitively expensive. Now the steamboats could churn rapidly against the current, ultimately attaining speeds in excess of ten miles an hour. The mighty Mississippi had met its master.

By 1820 there were some sixty steamboats on the Mississippi and its tributaries; by 1860 about one thousand, some of them luxurious river palaces. Keen rivalry among the swift and gaudy steamers led to memorable races. Excited passengers would urge the captain to pile on wood at the risk of bursting the boilers, which all too often exploded, with tragic results for the floating firetraps. When the steamer *Sultana* blew up in April 1865, the explosion killed seventeen hundred passengers, including many Union prisoners of war being repatriated to the North.

Chugging steamboats played a vital role in the opening of the West and South, both of which were richly endowed with navigable rivers. Like bunches of grapes on a vine, population clustered along the banks of the broad-flowing streams. Cotton growers and other farmers made haste to take up and turn over the now-profitable soil. Not only could they float their produce out to market, but hardly less important, they could ship in at low cost their shoes, hardware, and other manufactured necessities.

✳ "Clinton's Big Ditch" in New York

A canal-cutting craze paralleled the boom in turnpikes and steamboats (see Map 14.2). A few canals had been built around falls and elsewhere in colonial days, but ambitious projects lay in the future. Resourceful New Yorkers, cut off from federal aid by states' righters, themselves dug the **Erie Canal**, linking the Great Lakes with the Hudson River. They were blessed with the driving leadership of Governor DeWitt Clinton, whose grandiose project was scoffingly called "Clinton's Big Ditch" or "the Governor's Gutter."

Begun in 1817, the canal eventually ribboned 363 miles. On its completion in 1825, a garlanded canal boat glided from Buffalo, on Lake Erie, to the Hudson River and on to New York harbor. There, with colorful ceremony, Governor Clinton emptied a cask of water from the lake to symbolize "the marriage of the waters."

The water from Clinton's keg baptized the Empire State. Mule-drawn passengers and bulky freight could now be handled with thrift and dispatch, at the dizzy speed of five miles an hour. The cost of shipping a ton of grain from Buffalo to New York City fell from $100 to $5, and the time of transit from about twenty days to six.

Ever-widening economic ripples followed the completion of the Erie Canal. The value of land along the route skyrocketed, and new cities—such as Rochester and Syracuse—blossomed. Industry in the state boomed. The new profitability of farming in the Old

MAP 14.2 Major Rivers, Roads, and Canals, 1825–1860 © 2016 Cengage Learning

Northwest—notably in Ohio, Michigan, Indiana, and Illinois—attracted thousands of European immigrants to the unaxed and untaxed lands now available. Flotillas of steamships soon plied the Great Lakes, connecting with canal barges at Buffalo. Interior waterside villages like Cleveland, Detroit, and Chicago exploded into mighty cities.

Other profound economic and political changes followed the canal's completion. The price of potatoes in New York City was cut in half, and many dispirited New England farmers, no longer able to face the ruinous competition, abandoned their rocky holdings and went elsewhere. Some became mill hands, thus speeding the industrialization of America. Others, finding it easy to go west over the Erie Canal, took up new farmland south of the Great Lakes, where they were joined by thousands of New Yorkers and other northerners. Still others shifted to fruit, vegetable, and dairy farming. The transformations in the Northeast—canal consequences—showed how long-established local market structures could be swamped by the emerging behemoth of a continental economy. And as American products began to flow into international markets, even far-off Europeans began to feel the effects of America's economic vitality. Before long, Italian and Polish peasants, displaced from their marginal farms by the arrival of cheap American grains, would come to America to build new lives.

✦ The Iron Horse

The most significant contribution to the development of such an economy proved to be the railroad. It was fast, reliable, cheaper than canals to construct, and not frozen over in winter. Able to go almost anywhere, even through the Allegheny barrier, it defied terrain and weather. The first railroad appeared in the United States in 1828, and new lines spread with amazing swiftness. Andrew Jackson rode to his first presidential inauguration in 1829 in a horse-drawn carriage. At the end of his second term, eight years later, he departed from Washington in a railway car. By 1860, on the eve of the Civil War, the United States boasted thirty thousand miles of railroad track, three-fourths of it in the rapidly industrializing North (see Map 14.3).

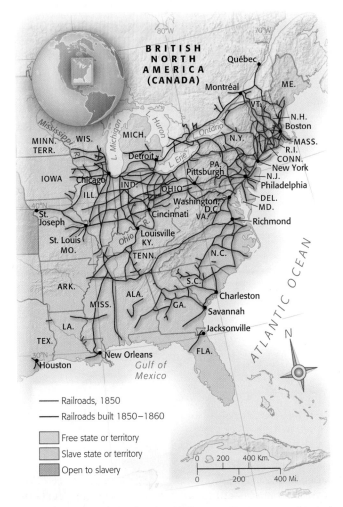

MAP 14.3 The Railroad Revolution Note the explosion of new railroad construction in the 1850s and its heavy concentration in the North. © 2016 Cengage Learning

At first the railroad faced strong opposition from vested interests, especially canal backers. Anxious to protect its investment in the Erie Canal, the New York legislature in 1833 prohibited the railroads from carrying freight—at least temporarily. Early railroads were also considered a dangerous public menace, for flying sparks could set fire to nearby haystacks and houses, and appalling railway accidents could turn the wooden "miniature hells" into flaming funeral pyres for their riders.

Railroad pioneers had to overcome other obstacles as well. Brakes were so feeble that the engineer might miss the station twice, both arriving and backing up. Arrivals and departures were conjectural, and numerous differences in gauge (the distance between the rails) meant frequent changes of trains for passengers. In 1840 there were seven transfers between Philadelphia and Charleston. But gauges gradually became standardized, better brakes did brake, safety devices were adopted, and the Pullman "sleeping palace" was introduced in 1859. America at long last was being bound together with braces of iron, later to be made of steel.

✦ Cables, Clippers, and Pony Riders

Other forms of transportation and communication were binding together the United States and the world. A crucial development came in 1858 when Cyrus Field, called "the greatest wire-puller in history," organized a joint Anglo-American-Canadian venture to stretch a cable under the deep North Atlantic waters from Newfoundland to Ireland. Although this initial cable went dead after three weeks of public rejoicing, a heavier cable laid in 1866 permanently linked the American and European continents.

The United States merchant marine encountered rough sailing during much of the early nineteenth century. American vessels had been repeatedly laid up by the embargo, the War of 1812, and the panics of 1819 and 1837. American naval designers made few contributions to maritime progress. A pioneer American steamer, the *Savannah*, crept across the Atlantic in 1819, but it used sail most of the time and was pursued for a day by a British captain who thought it afire.

In the 1840s and 1850s, a golden age dawned for American shipping. Yankee naval yards, notably Donald McKay's at Boston, began to send down the ways sleek new craft called **clipper ships**. Long, narrow, and majestic, they glided across the sea under towering masts and clouds of canvas. In a fair breeze, they could outrun any steamer.

The stately clippers sacrificed cargo space for speed, and their captains made killings by hauling high-value

Poster-Timetable for Baltimore & Susquehanna Railroad, 1840 Advertising the Baltimore & Susquehanna's train schedule alone was not sufficient to get passengers to their destinations. A typical trip often entailed coordinating legs on other railroad lines, stagecoaches, and canal boats.

New York Clipper Ship, *Challenge*

MAP 14.4 Main Routes West Before the Civil War Mark Twain described his stagecoach trip to California in the 1860s in *Roughing It*: "We began to get into country, now, threaded here and there with little streams. These had high, steep banks on each side, and every time we flew down one bank and scrambled up the other, our party inside got mixed somewhat. First we would all be down in a pile at the forward end of the stage,…and in a second we would shoot to the other end, and stand on our heads. And…as the dust rose from the tumult, we would all sneeze in chorus, and the majority of us would grumble, and probably say some hasty thing, like: 'Take your elbow out of my ribs!—can't you quit crowding?'" © 2016 Cengage Learning

cargoes in record times. They wrested much of the tea-carrying trade between the Far East and Britain from their slower-sailing British competitors, and they sped thousands of impatient adventurers to the goldfields of California and Australia.

But the hour of glory for the clipper was relatively brief. On the eve of the Civil War, the British had clearly won the world race for maritime ascendancy with their iron tramp steamers ("teakettles"). Although slower and less romantic than the clipper, these vessels were steadier, roomier, more reliable, and hence more profitable.

No story of rapid American communication would be complete without including the Far West. By 1858 horse-drawn overland stagecoaches, immortalized by Mark Twain's *Roughing It*, were a familiar sight. Their

dusty tracks stretched from the banks of the muddy Missouri River clear to California (see Map 14.4).

Even more dramatic was the **Pony Express**, established in 1860 to carry mail speedily the two thousand lonely miles from St. Joseph, Missouri, to Sacramento, California. Daring, lightweight riders, leaping onto wiry ponies saddled at stations approximately ten miles apart, could make the trip in an amazing ten days. These unarmed horsemen galloped on, summer or winter, day or night, through dust or snow, past Indians and bandits. The speeding postmen missed only one trip, though the whole enterprise lost money heavily and folded after only eighteen legend-leaving months.

Just as the clippers had succumbed to steam, so were the express riders unhorsed by Samuel Morse's

As late as 1877, stagecoach passengers were advised in print,

❝ Never shoot on the road as the noise might frighten the horses.... Don't point out where murders have been committed, especially if there are women passengers.... Expect annoyances, discomfort, and some hardships. **❞**

clacking keys, which began tapping messages to California in 1861. The swift ships and the fleet ponies ushered out a dying technology of wind and muscle. In the future, machines would be in the saddle.

✦ The Transport Web Binds the Union

More than anything else, the desire of the East to tap the West stimulated the **transportation revolution**. Until about 1830 the produce of the western region drained southward to the cotton belt or to the heaped-up wharves of New Orleans. The steamboat vastly aided the reverse flow of finished goods up the watery western arteries and helped bind West and South together. But the truly revolutionary changes in commerce and communication came in the three decades before the Civil War, as canals and railroad tracks radiated out from the East, across the Alleghenies and into the blossoming heartland. The ditch-diggers and tie-layers were attempting nothing less than a conquest of nature itself. They would offset the "natural" flow of trade on the interior rivers by laying down an impressive grid of "internal improvements."

The builders succeeded beyond their wildest dreams. The Mississippi was increasingly robbed of its traffic, as goods moved eastward on chugging trains, puffing lake boats, and mule-tugged canal barges. Governor Clinton had in effect picked up the mighty Father of Waters and flung it over the Alleghenies, forcing it to empty into the sea at New York City. By the 1840s the city of Buffalo handled more western produce than New Orleans. Between 1836 and 1860, grain shipments through Buffalo increased a staggering sixtyfold. New York City became the seaboard queen of the nation, a gigantic port through which a vast hinterland poured its wealth and to which it daily paid economic tribute.

By the eve of the Civil War, a truly continental economy had emerged. The principle of division of labor, which spelled productivity and profits in the factory, applied on a national scale as well. Each region now specialized in a particular type of economic activity. The South raised cotton for export to New England and Britain; the West grew grain and livestock to feed factory workers in the East and in Europe; the East made machines and textiles for the South and the West.

The economic pattern thus woven had fateful political and military implications. Many southerners regarded the Mississippi as a silver chain that naturally linked together the upper valley states and the Cotton Kingdom. They would become convinced, as secession approached in the 1850s, that some or all of these states would have to secede with them or be strangled. But they would overlook the man-made links that increasingly bound the upper Mississippi Valley to the East in intimate commercial union. Southern rebels would have to fight not only Northern armies but the tight bonds of an interdependent continental economy. Economically, the two northerly sections were conjoined twins.

✦ The Market Revolution

No less revolutionary than the political upheavals of the antebellum era was the **market revolution** that transformed a subsistence economy of scattered farms and tiny workshops into a national network of industry and commerce (see Map 14.5). Greater mechanization and a more robust market-oriented economy raised new legal questions about winners and losers. How tightly should patents protect inventions? Should the government regulate monopolies? Who should own the technologies and networks that made America hum in the 1840s and 1850s?

Under Chief Justice John Marshall, the U.S. Supreme Court vigilantly protected contract rights by requiring state governments to grant irrevocable charters. Monopolies easily developed, as new companies found it difficult to break into markets. After Marshall died in 1835, the climate began to change, and the winds of economic opportunity blew more freely. When the proprietors of Boston's Charles River Bridge (which included Harvard College) sued the owners of the new Warren Bridge for unconstitutionally violating their original contract, the new chief justice, Roger B. Taney, sided with the newcomers and argued that "the rights of the community" outweighed any exclusive corporate rights. Taney's decision opened new entrepreneurial channels and encouraged greater competition. So did the passage of more liberal state incorporation laws beginning in the 1830s, granting investors the benefit of "limited liability" if their companies were sued or went bankrupt.

As more and more Americans—mill workers as well as farmhands, women as well as men—linked their economic fate to the burgeoning market economy, the self-sufficient households of colonial days were transformed. Most families had once raised all their own food, spun their own wool, and bartered with their neighbors for the few necessities they could not make themselves. In growing numbers they now scattered to work for wages in the mills, or they planted just a few crops for sale at market and used the money to buy goods made by strangers in far-off factories. As store-bought fabric, candles, and soap replaced homemade products, a quiet revolution occurred in the household division of labor and status. Traditional women's work was rendered superfluous and devalued. The home itself, once a center of economic production in which all family members cooperated, grew into a place of refuge from the world of work, a refuge that became increasingly the special and separate sphere of women.

Revolutionary advances in manufacturing and transportation brought increased prosperity to all

The famed English writer Charles Dickens (1812–1870) traveled to the United States in 1842 and was sharply critical of certain aspects of the national character:

❝Another prominent feature is the love of 'smart' dealing which gilds over many a swindle and gross breach of trust; many a defalcation [embezzlement], public and private; and enables many a knave to hold his head up with the best, who well deserves a halter.❞

Americans, but they also widened the gulf between the rich and the poor. Millionaires had been rare in the early days of the Republic, but by the eve of the Civil War, several specimens of colossal financial success were strutting across the national stage. Spectacular was the case of fur-trader and real estate speculator

MAP 14.5 Industry and Agriculture, 1860 Still a nation of farmers on the eve of the Civil War, Americans had nevertheless made an impressive start on their own Industrial Revolution, especially in the Northeast. © 2016 Cengage Learning

Chicago, 1857 A modest village of a few hundred souls in the 1830s, Chicago was a teeming metropolis just two decades later—one of the fastest-growing cities in the world. A food and livestock processing center and transportation hub, it served the vast farming area of the western plains, a remarkably productive agricultural region and breadbasket to the world.

John Jacob Astor, who left an estate of $30 million on his death in 1848.

Cities bred the greatest extremes of economic inequality. Unskilled workers, then as always, fared worst. Many of them came to make up a floating mass of "drifters," buffeted from town to town by the shifting prospects for menial jobs. These wandering workers accounted at various times for up to half the population of the brawling industrial centers. Although their numbers were large, they left little behind them but the homely fruits of their transient labor. Largely unstoried and unsung, they are among the forgotten men and women of American history.

Many myths about "social mobility" grew up over the buried memories of these unfortunate day laborers. Mobility did exist in industrializing America—but not in the proportions that legend often portrays. Rags-to-riches success stories were relatively few.

Yet America, with its dynamic society and wide-open spaces, undoubtedly provided more "opportunity" than did the contemporary countries of the Old World—which is why millions of immigrants packed their bags and headed for New World shores. Moreover, a rising tide lifts all boats, and the improvement in overall standards of living was real. Wages for unskilled workers in a labor-hungry America rose about 1 percent a year from 1820 to 1860. This general prosperity helped defuse the potential class conflict that might otherwise have exploded—and that did explode in many European countries.

Chapter Review

KEY TERMS

"Self-Reliance" (278)

rendezvous (279)

ecological imperialism (279)

Ancient Order of Hibernians (283)

Molly Maguires (283)

Tammany Hall (283)

Know-Nothing party (286)

Awful Disclosures (286)

Industrial Revolution (286)

cotton gin (287)

Patent Office (291)

limited liability (292)

Commonwealth v. *Hunt* (293)

factory girls (295)

cult of domesticity (295)

McCormick reaper (297)

turnpike (298)

Erie Canal (299)

clipper ships (301)

Pony Express (303)

transportation revolution (304)

market revolution (304)

PEOPLE TO KNOW

Samuel Slater

Eli Whitney

Elias Howe

Isaac Singer

Samuel F. B. Morse

John Deere

Cyrus McCormick

Robert Fulton

DeWitt Clinton

Cyrus Field

John Jacob Astor

CHRONOLOGY

ca. 1750	Industrial Revolution begins in Britain
1791	Samuel Slater builds first U.S. textile factory
1793	Eli Whitney invents cotton gin
1798	Whitney develops interchangeable parts for muskets
1807	Robert Fulton's first steamboat Embargo spurs American manufacturing
1811	Cumberland Road construction begins
1817	Erie Canal construction begins
1825	Erie Canal completed
1828	First railroad in United States
1830s	Cyrus McCormick invents mechanical mower-reaper
1834	Anti-Catholic riot in Boston
1837	John Deere develops steel plow
1840	President Van Buren establishes ten-hour day for federal employees
1842	Massachusetts declares labor unions legal in *Commonwealth* v. *Hunt*
ca. 1843–1868	Era of clipper ships
1844	Samuel Morse invents telegraph Anti-Catholic riot in Philadelphia
1845–1849	Potato famine in Ireland
1846	Elias Howe invents sewing machine
1848	First general incorporation laws in New York Democratic revolutions collapse in Germany
1849	American, or Know-Nothing, party formed
1851	London World's Fair
1852	Cumberland Road completed
1858	Cyrus Field lays first transatlantic cable
1860	Pony Express established
1861	First transcontinental telegraph
1866	Permanent transatlantic cable established

TO LEARN MORE

John Bodnar, *The Transplanted: A History of Immigrants in Urban America* (1985)

Christopher Clark, *Social Change in America: From the Revolution Through the Civil War* (2006)

Thomas C. Cochran, *Frontiers of Change: Early Industrialism in America* (1981)

Hasia Diner, *Erin's Daughters in America* (1983)

David H. Hounshell, *From the American System to Mass Production, 1800–1932: The Development of Manufacturing Technology in the United States* (1984)

Paul E. Johnson, *Sam Patch, the Famous Jumper* (2003)

Gerard Koeppel, *Bond of Union: Building the Erie Canal and the American Empire* (2009)

Bruce Levine, *The Spirit of 1848: German Immigrants, Labor Conflict, and the Coming of the Civil War* (1992)

David Nye, *Consuming Power: A Social History of American Energies* (1998)

Michael O'Malley, *Keeping Watch: A History of American Time* (1996)

Augustus J. Veenendaal, *American Railroads in the Nineteenth Century* (2003)

A complete, annotated bibliography for this chapter—along with brief descriptions of the People to Know—may be found on the *American Pageant* website. The key terms are defined in the glossary at the end of the text.

Chapter 15

The Ferment of Reform and Culture

1790–1860

*We [Americans] will walk on our own feet; we will work
with our own hands; we will speak our own minds.*

RALPH WALDO EMERSON, "THE AMERICAN SCHOLAR," 1837

A *third revolution accompanied* the reformation of American politics and the transformation of the American economy in the mid-nineteenth century. It consisted of a diffuse yet deeply felt commitment to improve the character of ordinary Americans, to make them more upstanding, God-fearing, and literate. Some high-minded souls were disillusioned by the rough-and-tumble realities of democratic politics. Others, notably women, were excluded from the political game altogether. As the young Republic grew, increasing numbers of Americans poured their considerable energies into an astonishing variety of religious revivals and reform movements.

Reform campaigns of all types flourished in sometimes bewildering abundance. There was not "a reading man" who was without some scheme for a new utopia in his "waistcoat pocket," claimed Ralph Waldo Emerson. Reformers promoted better public schools and rights for women, as well as miracle medicines, polygamy, celibacy, rule by prophets, and guidance by spirits. Societies were formed against alcohol, tobacco, profanity, and the transit of mail on the Sabbath. Eventually overshadowing all other reforms was the great crusade against slavery (see "Early Abolitionism" and "Radical Abolitionism" on pp. 351–353).

Many reformers drew their crusading zeal from religion. Beginning in the late 1790s and boiling over into the early nineteenth century, the Second Great Awakening swept through America's Protestant churches, fundamentally reshaping the nation's religious landscape, and powerfully reaffirming religion's central role in American society, as a generation of believers embarked on their missions to perfect the world.

✴ Reviving Religion

Church attendance was still a regular ritual for about three-fourths of the 23 million Americans in 1850. Alexis de Tocqueville declared that there was "no country in the world where the Christian religion retains a greater influence over the souls of men than in America." Yet the religion of these years was not the old-time religion of colonial days. The austere Calvinist rigor had long been seeping out of the American churches. The rationalist ideas of the French Revolutionary era had done much to soften the older orthodoxy. Thomas Paine's widely circulated book ***The Age of Reason*** (1794) had shockingly declared that all churches were "set up to terrify and enslave mankind, and monopolize power and profit." American anticlericalism was seldom that virulent, but many of the Founding Fathers, including Jefferson and Franklin, embraced the liberal doctrines of **Deism** that Paine promoted. Deists relied on reason rather than revelation, on science rather than the Bible. They rejected the concept of original sin and denied Christ's divinity. Yet Deists believed in a Supreme Being who had created a knowable universe and endowed human beings with a capacity for moral behavior.

The comforting teachings of Deism evolved from a long trend in American religious history. Since Puritan times, American Protestants had grappled mightily with the relationship between free will and human salvation. For the great many affected by Calvinism, the doctrines of predestination and human depravity had always been thorny, even gloomy. More than a century of theological wrangling had moved

Protestants of various stripes toward a view of humanity that stressed the essential goodness of human nature rather than its vileness, that emphasized the possibility of salvation through good works, and that pictured God not as a stern Creator but as a loving Father. During the eighteenth century, such sentiments had flourished most among America's newer denominations—Methodist, Baptist, and Unitarian—but they also made inroads into the older and more rigidly hewn pulpits and pews of the Puritan churches: Presbyterian and Congregationalist.

This ferment propelled a wave of roaring revivals during the early decades of the nineteenth century. Sweeping up even more people than the First Great Awakening, the **Second Great Awakening** was one of the most momentous episodes in the history of American religion. This tidal wave of spiritual fervor left in its wake countless converted souls, many shattered and reorganized churches, and numerous new sects. It also encouraged an effervescent evangelicalism that bubbled up into innumerable areas of American life—including prison reform, the temperance cause, the women's movement, and the crusade to abolish slavery.

The Second Great Awakening was spread to the masses by huge "camp meetings." As many as twenty-five thousand people would gather for an encampment of several days to drink the frothy gospel as served up by an itinerant preacher. Thousands of spiritually starved souls "got religion" at these gatherings. In their ecstasy they engaged in frenzies of rolling, dancing, barking, and jerking. Many of the "saved" soon backslid into their former sinful ways, but the revivals boosted church membership and further buttressed the nation's religious core. Countless Americans heeded God's call. They joined reform-minded benevolent societies and carried their missionary creed to Africa, Asia, Hawaii, and to the Indian tribes of the American West.

Methodists and Baptists reaped the most abundant harvest of souls from the fields fertilized by revivalism. Both sects stressed personal conversion (contrary to predestination), a relatively democratic control of church affairs, and a rousing emotionalism. As a frontier jingle ran,

> The devil hates the Methodists
> Because they sing and shout the best.

Powerful Peter Cartwright (1785–1872) was the best known of the Methodist "circuit riders," or traveling frontier preachers. This ill-educated but sinewy servant of the Lord ranged for a half-century from Tennessee to Illinois, calling upon sinners to repent. With bellowing voice and flailing arms, he converted thousands of souls to the Lord. Not only did he lash the Devil with his tongue, but with his fists he knocked out rowdies who tried to break up his meetings. His Christianity was definitely muscular.

Bell-voiced Charles Grandison Finney was the greatest of the revival preachers. Trained as a lawyer, Finney abandoned the bar to become an evangelist

Religious Camp Meeting, by J. Maze Burbank, 1839 At huge, daylong encampments, repentant sinners dedicated themselves to lives of personal rectitude and social reform. Fire-and-brimstone preachers like the one depicted here inspired convulsions, speaking in tongues, and ecstatic singing and dancing among the converted. Out of this religious upheaval grew many of the movements for social improvement in the pre–Civil War decades, including the abolitionist crusade.

Charles Grandison Finney (1792–1875), 1834 The charismatic Finney appears here at age forty-two, at the height of his career as an evangelist. A mesmerizer of audiences, he was said to have converted over a half million people. In 1834, Finney had just led a series of enormously successful revivals in cities along the Erie Canal. The next year he would establish a theology department at the newly founded Oberlin College in Ohio, where he helped train a generation of ministers and served as president from 1851 to 1866.

Oberlin College Archives, Oberlin, Ohio

In his lecture "Hindrances to Revivals," delivered in the 1830s, Charles Grandison Finney (1792–1875) proposed the excommunication of drinkers and slaveholders:

"Let the churches of all denominations speak out on the subject of temperance, let them close their doors against all who have anything to do with the death-dealing abomination, and the cause of temperance is triumphant. A few years would annihilate the traffic. Just so with slavery.... It is a great national sin. It is a sin of the church. The churches by their silence, and by permitting slaveholders to belong to their communion, have been consenting to it.... The church cannot turn away from this question. It is a question for the church and for the nation to decide, and God will push it to a decision."

and most fervent enthusiasts of religious revivalism. They made up the majority of new church members, and they were most likely to stay within the fold when the tents were packed up and the traveling evangelists left town. Perhaps women's greater ambivalence than men about the changes wrought by the expanding market economy made them such eager converts to piety. It helped as well that evangelicals preached a gospel of female spiritual worth and offered women an active role in bringing their husbands and families back to God. That accomplished, many women turned to saving the rest of society. They formed a host of benevolent and charitable organizations and spearheaded crusades for most, if not all, of the era's ambitious reforms.

Denominational Diversity

Revivals also furthered the fragmentation of religious faiths. Western New York, where many descendants of New England Puritans had settled, was so blistered by sermonizers preaching "hellfire and damnation" that it came to be known as the **Burned-Over District**.

Millerites, or Adventists, who mustered several hundred thousand adherents, rose from the super-heated soil of the Burned-Over District in the 1830s. Named after the eloquent and commanding William Miller, they interpreted the Bible to mean that Christ would return to earth on October 22, 1844. Donning their go-to-meeting clothes, they gathered in prayerful assemblies to greet their Redeemer. The failure of Jesus to descend on schedule dampened but did not destroy the movement.

after a deeply moving conversion experience as a young man. Tall and athletically built, Finney held huge crowds spellbound with the power of his oratory and the pungency of his message. He led massive revivals in Rochester and New York City in 1830 and 1831. Finney preached a version of the old-time religion, but he was also an innovator. He devised the "anxious bench," where repentant sinners could sit in full view of the congregation, and he encouraged women to pray aloud in public. Holding out the promise of a perfect Christian kingdom on earth, Finney denounced both alcohol and slavery. He eventually served as president of Oberlin College in Ohio, which he helped to make a hotbed of revivalist activity and abolitionism.

A key feature of the Second Great Awakening was the feminization of religion, in terms of both church membership and theology. Middle-class women, the wives and daughters of businessmen, were the first

Mormon Trekkers Crossing the Mississippi on the Ice Driven out of Illinois after the murder of founder Joseph Smith in 1844, the Mormons wintered near Council Bluffs, Iowa Territory, before beginning the long overland trek to Utah.

Like the First Great Awakening, the Second Great Awakening tended to widen the lines between classes and regions. The more prosperous and conservative denominations in the East were somewhat less shaken by revivalism, and Episcopalians, Presbyterians, Congregationalists, and Unitarians continued to rise mostly from the wealthier, urbanized, better-educated levels of society. Methodists, Baptists, and the members of the other new sects spawned by the swelling evangelistic fervor tended to come from less prosperous, less "learned" communities in the rural South and West.

Religious diversity further reflected social cleavages when the churches faced up to the slavery issue. By 1844–1845 both the southern Baptists and the southern Methodists had split with their northern brethren over human bondage. The Methodists came to grief over the case of a slaveowning bishop in Georgia, whose second wife added several household slaves to his estate. In 1857 the Presbyterians, North and South, parted company. The secession of the southern churches foreshadowed the secession of the southern states. First the churches split, then the political parties split, and then the Union split.

✴ A Desert Zion in Utah

The smoldering spiritual embers of the Burned-Over District kindled one especially ardent flame in 1830. In that year Joseph Smith—a rugged visionary, proud

of his prowess at wrestling—reported that he had received some golden plates from an angel. When deciphered, they constituted the Book of Mormon, and the Church of Jesus Christ of Latter-Day Saints (the **Mormons**) was launched. It was a native American product, a new religion, destined to spread its influence worldwide.

After establishing a religious oligarchy, Smith ran into serious opposition from his non-Mormon neighbors, first in Ohio and then in Missouri and Illinois. His cooperative sect antagonized rank-and-file Americans, who were individualistic and dedicated to free enterprise. The Mormons aroused further anger by voting as a unit and by openly but understandably drilling their militia for defensive purposes. Accusations of polygamy likewise arose and increased in intensity, for Joseph Smith was reputed to have several wives.

Continuing hostility finally drove the Mormons to desperate measures. In 1844 Joseph Smith and his brother were murdered and mangled by a mob in Carthage, Illinois, and the movement seemed near collapse. The falling torch was seized by a remarkable Mormon Moses named Brigham Young. Stern and austere in contrast to Smith's charm and affability, the barrel-chested Brigham Young had received only eleven days of formal schooling. But he quickly proved to be an aggressive leader, an eloquent preacher, and a gifted administrator. Determined to escape further persecution, Young in 1846–1847

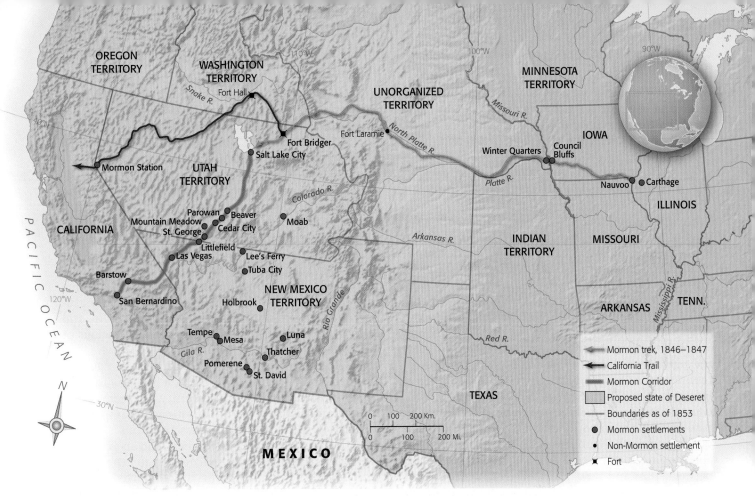

MAP 15.1 The Mormon World After Joseph Smith's murder at Carthage in 1844, the Mormons abandoned their thriving settlement at Nauvoo, Illinois (which had about twenty thousand inhabitants in 1845), and set out for the valley of the Great Salt Lake, then still part of Mexico. When the Treaty of Guadalupe Hidalgo (see "Fighting Mexico for Peace" on p. 375) in 1848 brought the vast Utah Territory into the United States, the Mormons rapidly expanded their desert colony, which they called Deseret, especially along the "Mormon Corridor" that stretched from Salt Lake to southern California. © 2016 Cengage Learning

led his oppressed and despoiled Latter-Day Saints over vast rolling plains to Utah as they sang "Come, Come, Ye Saints."

Overcoming pioneer hardships, the Mormons soon made the desert bloom like a new Eden by means of ingenious and cooperative methods of irrigation. The crops of 1848, threatened by hordes of crickets, were saved when flocks of gulls appeared, as if by a miracle, to gulp down the invaders. (A monument to the seagulls stands in Salt Lake City today.)

Semiarid Utah grew remarkably. By the end of 1848, some five thousand settlers had arrived, and other large bands were to follow them (see Map 15.1). Many dedicated Mormons in the 1850s actually made the thirteen-hundred-mile trek across the plains pulling two-wheeled carts.

Under the rigidly disciplined management of Brigham Young, the community became a prosperous frontier theocracy and a cooperative commonwealth. Young married as many as twenty-seven women—some

of them wives in name only—and begot fifty-six children. The population was further swelled by thousands of immigrants from Europe, where the Mormons had established a flourishing missionary movement.

A crisis developed when the Washington government was unable to control the hierarchy of Brigham Young, who had been made territorial governor in 1850. A federal army marched in 1857 against the Mormons, who harassed its lines of supply and rallied to die in their last dusty ditch. Fortunately the quarrel

Polygamy was an issue of such consequence that it was bracketed with slavery in the Republican national platform of 1856:

❝It is both the right and the imperative duty of Congress to prohibit in the Territories those twin relics of barbarism—Polygamy and Slavery.❞

was finally adjusted without serious bloodshed. The Mormons later ran afoul of the antipolygamy laws passed by Congress in 1862 and 1882, and their unique marital customs delayed statehood for Utah until 1896.

✯ Free Schools for a Free People

Tax-supported primary schools were scarce in the early years of the Republic. They had the odor of pauperism about them because they existed chiefly to educate the children of the poor—the so-called ragged schools. Advocates of "free" public education met stiff opposition. A midwestern legislator cried that he wanted only this simple epitaph when he died: "Here lies an enemy of public education."

Well-to-do, conservative Americans gradually saw the light. If they did not pay to educate "other folkses brats," the "brats" might grow up into a dangerous, ignorant rabble—armed with the vote. Taxation for education was an insurance premium that the wealthy paid for stability and democracy.

Tax-supported public education, though miserably lagging in the slavery-cursed South, triumphed between 1825 and 1850. Hard-toiling laborers wielded increased influence and demanded instruction for their children. Most important was the gaining of manhood suffrage for whites in Jackson's day. A free

vote cried aloud for free education. A civilized nation that was both ignorant and free, declared Thomas Jefferson, "never was and never will be."

The famed little red schoolhouse—with one room, one stove, one teacher, and often eight grades—became the shrine of American democracy. Regrettably, it was an imperfect shrine. Early free schools stayed open only a few months of the year. Schoolteachers, most of them men in this era, were too often ill-trained, ill-tempered, and ill-paid. They frequently put more stress on "lickin'" (with a hickory stick) than on "larnin'." These knights of the blackboard often "boarded around" in the community, and some knew scarcely more than their older pupils. They usually taught only the "three Rs"—"readin', 'ritin', and 'rithmetic." To many rugged Americans, suspicious of "book larnin'," this was enough.

Reform was urgently needed. Into the breach stepped Horace Mann (1796–1859), a brilliant and idealistic graduate of Brown University. As secretary of the Massachusetts Board of Education, he campaigned effectively for more and better schoolhouses, longer school terms, higher pay for teachers, and an expanded curriculum. His influence radiated out to other states, and impressive improvements were chalked up. Yet education remained an expensive luxury for many communities. As late as 1860, the nation counted only about a hundred public secondary schools—and

The Country School, by Winslow Homer, 1871 Stark and simple by latter-day standards, the one-room schoolhouse nevertheless contributed richly to the development of the young Republic.

nearly a million white adult illiterates. Black slaves in the South were legally forbidden to receive instruction in reading or writing, and even free blacks, in the North as well as the South, were usually excluded from the schools.

Educational advances were aided by improved textbooks, notably those of Noah Webster (1758–1843), a Yale-educated Connecticut Yankee who was known as the "Schoolmaster of the Republic." His "reading lessons," used by millions of children in the nineteenth century, were partly designed to promote patriotism. Webster devoted twenty years to his famous dictionary, published in 1828, which helped to standardize the American language.

Equally influential was Ohioan William H. McGuffey (1800–1873), a teacher-preacher of rare power. His grade-school readers, first published in the 1830s, sold 122 million copies in the following decades. *McGuffey's Readers* hammered home lasting lessons in morality, patriotism, and idealism.

✷ Higher Goals for Higher Learning

Higher education was likewise stirring. The religious zeal of the Second Great Awakening led to the planting of many small, denominational, liberal arts colleges, chiefly in the South and West. Too often they were academically anemic, established more to satisfy local pride than genuinely to advance the cause of learning. Like their more venerable, ivy-draped brethren, the new colleges offered a narrow, tradition-bound curriculum of Latin, Greek, mathematics, and moral philosophy. On new and old campuses alike, there was little intellectual vitality and much boredom.

The first state-supported universities sprang up in the South, beginning with North Carolina in 1795.

Federal land grants nourished the growth of state institutions of higher learning. Conspicuous among the early group was the University of Virginia, founded in 1819. It was largely the brainchild of Thomas Jefferson, who designed its beautiful architecture and who at times watched its construction through a telescope from his hilltop home. He dedicated the university to freedom from religious or political shackles, and modern languages and the sciences received unusual emphasis.

Women's higher education was frowned upon in the early decades of the nineteenth century. A woman's place was believed to be in the home, and training in needlecraft seemed more important than training in algebra. In an era when the clinging-vine bride was the ideal, coeducation was regarded as frivolous. Prejudices also prevailed that too much learning injured the feminine brain, undermined health, and rendered a young lady unfit for marriage. The teachers of Susan B. Anthony, the future feminist, refused to instruct her in long division.

Women's schools at the secondary level began to attain some respectability in the 1820s, thanks in part to the dedicated work of Emma Willard (1787–1870). In 1821 she established the Troy (New York) Female Seminary. Oberlin College, in Ohio, jolted traditionalists in 1837 when it opened its doors to women as well as men. (Oberlin had already created shock waves by admitting black students.) In the same year, Mary Lyon established an outstanding women's school, Mount Holyoke Seminary (later College), in South Hadley, Massachusetts. Mossback critics scoffed that "they'll be educatin' cows next."

Adults who craved more learning satisfied their thirst for knowledge at private subscription libraries or, increasingly, at tax-supported libraries. House-to-house peddlers also did a lush business in feeding the public

Oberlin College Archives, Oberlin, Ohio

The Women Graduates of the Oberlin College Class of 1855 Oberlin was the first coeducational institution of higher education in the United States, accepting women in 1837, two years after it had welcomed African Americans. Feminists continued to press for coeducation, and by 1872 ninety-seven American universities accepted women. At some of these institutions, however, such as Radcliffe College of Harvard University and Barnard College of Columbia University, women were educated in associated schools, not alongside male students.

appetite for culture. Traveling lecturers helped to carry learning to the masses through the **lyceum** lecture associations, which numbered about three thousand by 1835. The lyceums provided platforms for speakers in such areas as science, literature, and moral philosophy. Talented talkers like Ralph Waldo Emerson journeyed thousands of miles on the lyceum circuits, casting their pearls of civilization before appreciative audiences.

Magazines flourished in the pre–Civil War years, but most of them withered after a short life. The *North American Review*, founded in 1815, was the long-lived leader of the intellectuals. *Godey's Lady's Book*, founded in 1830, survived until 1898 and attained the enormous circulation (for those days) of 150,000. It was devoured devotedly by millions of women, many of whom read the dog-eared copies of their relatives and friends.

✦ An Age of Reform

As the young Republic grew, reform campaigns of all types flourished in sometimes bewildering abundance as the driving forces of religious revival and the rapid growth of a market economy converged. Some reformers were simply crackbrained cranks. But most were intelligent, inspired idealists, usually

touched by the fire of evangelical religion then licking through the sanctuaries and steeples of American churches. The optimistic promises of the Second Great Awakening inspired countless souls to do battle against earthly evils. These modern idealists dreamed anew the old Puritan vision of a perfected society: free from cruelty, war, intoxicating drink,

In presenting her case to the Massachusetts legislature for more humane treatment for the mentally ill, Dorothea Dix (1802–1887) quoted from the notebook she carried with her as she traveled around the state:

❝ *Lincoln.* A woman in a cage. *Medford.* One idiotic subject chained, and one in a close stall for seventeen years. *Pepperell.* One often doubly chained, hand and foot; another violent; several peaceable now….*Dedham.* The insane disadvantageously placed in the jail. In the almshouse, two females in stalls…; lie in wooden bunks filled with straw; always shut up. One of these subjects is supposed curable. The overseers of the poor have declined giving her a trial at the hospital, as I was informed, on account of expense.**❞**

discrimination, and—ultimately—slavery. Women were particularly prominent in these reform crusades, especially in their own struggle for suffrage. For many middle-class women, the reform campaigns provided a unique opportunity to escape the confines of the home and enter the arena of public affairs.

Imprisonment for debt continued to be a nightmare, though its extent has been exaggerated. As late as 1830, hundreds of penniless people were languishing in filthy holes, sometimes for owing less than one dollar. The poorer working classes were especially hard hit by this merciless practice. But as the embattled laborer won the ballot and asserted himself, state legislatures gradually abolished debtors' prisons.

Reformers likewise tackled noxious criminal codes in the states, in accord with more enlightened European practices. They succeeded in reducing the number of capital offenses and helped eliminate brutal punishments, such as whipping and branding. A refreshing idea was taking hold that prisons should reform as well as punish—hence "reformatories," "houses of correction," and "penitentiaries" (for penance).

Sufferers of so-called insanity were still being treated with incredible cruelty. The medieval concept had been that the mentally deranged were cursed with unclean spirits; the nineteenth-century idea was that they were willfully perverse and depraved—to

be treated only as beasts. Many crazed persons were chained in jails or poor-houses with sane people.

Into this dismal picture stepped a formidable New England teacher-author, Dorothea Dix (1802–1887). A physically frail woman afflicted with persistent lung trouble, she possessed infinite compassion and willpower. She traveled some sixty thousand miles in eight years and assembled her damning reports on insanity and asylums from firsthand observations. Though she never raised her voice, Dix's message was loud and clear. Her classic petition of 1843 to the Massachusetts legislature, describing cells so foul that visitors were driven back by the stench, turned legislative stomachs and hearts. Her persistent prodding resulted in improved conditions and in a gain for the concept that the demented were not willfully perverse but mentally ill.

Agitation for peace also gained momentum in the pre–Civil War years. In 1828 the American Peace Society was formed, with a ringing declaration of war on war. A leading spirit was William Ladd, who orated when his legs were so badly ulcerated that he had to sit on a stool. His ideas were finally to bear some fruit in the international organizations for collective security of the twentieth century. The American peace crusade, linked with a European counterpart, was making promising progress by midcentury, but it was set back by the bloodshed of the Crimean War in Europe and the Civil War in America.

(left) The Stepping Mill, Auburn Prison, New York, 1823; (right) Portrait of Dorothea Dix by Samuel Bell Waugh, 1868 Reformers like Dorothea Dix believed that idleness was a scourge and prescribed rigorous exercise regimens for prisoners. At the experimental prison in Auburn, chained prisoners were obliged to turn this wheel for long periods of time.

✸ Demon Rum—The "Old Deluder"

The ever-present drink problem attracted dedicated reformers. Custom, combined with a hard and monotonous life, led to the excessive drinking of hard liquor, even among women, clergymen, and members of Congress. Weddings and funerals all too often became disgraceful brawls, and occasionally a drunken mourner would fall into the open grave with the corpse. Heavy drinking decreased the efficiency of labor, and poorly safeguarded machinery operated under the influence of alcohol increased the danger of accidents occurring at work. Drunkenness also fouled the sanctity of the family, threatening the spiritual welfare—and physical safety—of women and children.

After earlier and feebler efforts, the **American Temperance Society** was formed in Boston in 1826. Within a few years, about a thousand local groups sprang into existence. They implored drinkers to sign the temperance pledge and organized children's clubs, known as the "Cold Water Army." Temperance crusaders also made effective use of pictures, pamphlets, and lurid lecturers, some of whom were reformed drunkards. A popular temperance song ran,

We've done with our days of carousing,
Our nights, too, of frolicsome glee;
For now with our sober minds choosing,
We've pledged ourselves never to spree.

The most popular anti-alcohol tract of the era was T. S. Arthur's melodramatic novel, *Ten Nights in a Barroom and What I Saw There* (1854). It described in shocking detail how a once-happy village was ruined by Sam Slade's tavern. The book was second only to Stowe's *Uncle Tom's Cabin* as a best seller in the 1850s, and it enjoyed a highly successful run on the stage. Its touching theme song began with the words of a little girl:

Father, dear father, come home with me now,
The clock in the belfry strikes one.

Early foes of Demon Drink adopted two major lines of attack. One was to stiffen the individual's will to resist the wiles of the little brown jug. The moderate reformers thus stressed "temperance" rather than "teetotalism," or the total elimination of intoxicants. But less patient zealots came to believe that temptation should be removed by legislation. Prominent among this group was Neal S. Dow of Maine, a blue-nosed reformer who, as a mayor of Portland and an employer of labor, had often witnessed the debauching effect of alcohol—to say nothing of the cost to his pocketbook of work time lost because of drunken employees.

Dow—the "Father of Prohibition"—sponsored the so-called **Maine Law of 1851**. This drastic new statute, hailed as "the law of Heaven Americanized," prohibited the manufacture and sale of intoxicating liquor. Other states in the North followed Maine's example, and by 1857 about a dozen had passed various

Signing the Pledge, Lithograph, 1846 Temperance reformers decried many evils of alcohol, but they fulminated especially against its corrupting influence on family life. Here a former drinker pledges to abstain hereafter, while his hopeful wife and children look on.

The Granger Collection, NYC

prohibitory laws. But these figures are deceptive, for within a decade some of the statutes were repealed or declared unconstitutional, if not openly flouted.

It was clearly impossible to legislate thirst for alcohol out of existence, especially in localities where public sentiment was hostile. Yet on the eve of the Civil War, the prohibitionists had registered inspiring gains. There was much less drinking among women than earlier in the century and probably much less per capita consumption of hard liquor.

✳ Women in Revolt

When the nineteenth century opened, it was still a man's world, both in America and in Europe. A wife was supposed to immerse herself in her home and subordinate herself to her lord and master (her husband). Like black slaves, she could not vote; like black slaves, she could be legally beaten by her overlord "with a reasonable instrument." When she married, she could not retain title to her property; it passed to her husband.

Yet American women, though legally regarded as perpetual minors, fared better than their European cousins. French visitor Alexis de Tocqueville noted that in his native France, rape was punished only lightly, whereas in America it was one of the few crimes punishable by death.

Despite these relative advantages, women were still "the submerged sex" in America in the early part of the century. But as the decades unfolded, women increasingly surfaced to breathe the air of freedom and self-determination. In contrast to women in colonial times, many women now avoided marriage altogether—about 10 percent of adult women remained "spinsters" at the time of the Civil War.

Gender differences were strongly emphasized in nineteenth-century America—largely because the burgeoning market economy was increasingly separating women and men into sharply distinct economic roles. Women were thought to be physically and emotionally weak, but also artistic and refined. Endowed with finely tuned moral sensibilities, they were the keepers of society's conscience, with special responsibility to teach the young how to be good and productive citizens of the Republic. Men were considered strong but crude, always in danger of slipping into some savage or beastly way of life if not guided by the gentle hands of their loving ladies.

The home was a woman's special sphere, the centerpiece of the "cult of domesticity." Even reformers like Catharine Beecher, who urged her sisters to seek employment as teachers, endlessly celebrated the role of the good homemaker. But some women increasingly felt that the glorified sanctuary of the home was

Stellar Suffragists Elizabeth Cady Stanton (left) and Susan B. Anthony (right) were two of the most persistent battlers for rights. Their National Woman Suffrage Association fought for women's equality in courts and workplaces as well as at the polls. Napoleon Sarony/Bettmann/CORBIS

in fact a gilded cage. They yearned to tear down the bars that separated the private world of women from the public world of men.

Clamorous female reformers—most of them white and well-to-do—began to gather strength as the century neared its halfway point. Most were broad-gauge battlers; while demanding rights for women, they joined in the general reform movement of the age, fighting for temperance and the abolition of slavery. Like men, they had been touched by the evangelical spirit that offered the promise of earthly reward for human endeavor. Neither foul eggs nor foul words, when hurled by disapproving men, could halt women heartened by these doctrines.

The women's rights movement was mothered by some arresting characters. Prominent among them was Lucretia Mott, a sprightly Quaker whose ire had been aroused when she and her fellow female delegates to the London antislavery convention of 1840 were not recognized. Elizabeth Cady Stanton, a mother of seven who had insisted on leaving "obey" out of her marriage ceremony, shocked fellow feminists by going so far as to advocate suffrage for women.

What It Would Be If Some Ladies Had Their Own Way The men in this antifeminist cartoon are sewing, tending the baby, and washing clothes. The scene seemed absurd then, but not a century later.

Quaker-reared Susan B. Anthony, a militant lecturer for women's rights, fearlessly exposed herself to rotten garbage and vulgar epithets. She became such a conspicuous advocate of female rights that progressive women everywhere were called "Suzy Bs."

Other feminists challenged the man's world. Dr. Elizabeth Blackwell, a pioneer in a previously forbidden profession for women, was the first female graduate of a medical college. The talented Grimké sisters, Sarah and Angelina, championed antislavery. Lucy Stone retained her maiden name after marriage—hence the latter-day "Lucy Stoners," who follow her example. Amelia Bloomer revolted against the current "street sweeping" female attire by donning a short skirt with Turkish trousers—"bloomers," they were called—amid much bawdy ridicule about "Bloomerism" and "loose habits." A jeering male rhyme of the times jabbed,

> Gibbey, gibbey gab
> The women had a confab
> And demanded the rights
> To wear the tights
> Gibbey, gibbey gab.

Unflinching feminists met in 1848 in a memorable **Woman's Rights Convention at Seneca Falls**, New York. The defiant Stanton read a "Declaration of Sentiments," which in the spirit of the Declaration of Independence declared that "all men and women are created equal." One resolution formally demanded the ballot for females. Amid scorn and denunciation from press and pulpit, the Seneca Falls meeting launched the modern women's rights movement.

The crusade for women's rights was eclipsed by the campaign against slavery in the decade before the Civil War. Still, any white male, even an idiot, over the age of twenty-one could vote, while no woman could. Yet women were gradually being admitted to colleges, and some states, beginning with Mississippi in 1839, were even permitting wives to own property after marriage.

When early feminist Lucy Stone (1818–1893) married fellow abolitionist Henry B. Blackwell (1825–1909) in West Brookfield, Massachusetts, in 1855, they added the following vow to their nuptial ceremony:

❝While acknowledging our mutual affection by publicly assuming the relation of husband and wife, yet in justice to ourselves and a great principle, we deem it a duty to declare that this act on our part implies no…promise of voluntary obedience to such of the present laws of marriage, as refuse to recognize the wife as an independent, rational being, while they confer upon the husband an injurious and unnatural superiority.❞

Dress as Reform

Among the many social movements that swept nineteenth-century America, dress reform emerged in the 1840s as a critique of materialism and the constraints that fashion imposed on women. Medical professionals, social reformers, and transcendentalist intellectuals all argued that corsets constricting vital organs and voluminous skirts dragging along garbage-strewn streets unfairly restricted women's mobility, prevented women from bearing healthy children, and even induced serious sickness and death. The "Bloomer costume" depicted in this illustration from 1853 included Turkish-style trousers, a

jacket, and a short overskirt that came to the knees. Named after reformer Amelia Bloomer (1818–1894), who publicized the new style in her magazine, *The Lily*, the bloomer dress was first adopted by utopian communities such as the Owenites in New Harmony, Indiana, and the Oneidans in New York. Radical social critic Henry David Thoreau also advocated rational dress as a way of rejecting the artificial desires created by industrialization. But while applauded by reformers, new-style dress was viciously ridiculed by mainstream society, as this print demonstrates. Critics claimed that women blurred

gender distinctions by adopting "male" attire, endangering the family and even American civilization. After only a decade, practitioners gave up wearing bloomers in public, adopting plain and simplified clothing instead. But Owenites, some Mormons, women's rights advocates, farmers, and travelers on the overland trail continued to wear bloomers in private. How did dress reform intersect with other religious and social movements of the era? Why did bloomers upset so many antebellum Americans? Have there been other historical eras when new styles of dress came to symbolize broader social change?

BLOOMER COSTUMES OR WOMAN'S EMANCIPATION.

Harry T. Peters 'America on Stone' Collection, National Museum of American History, Smithsonian Institution.

✹ Wilderness Utopias

Bolstered by the utopian spirit of the age, various reformers, ranging from the high-minded to the "lunatic fringe," set up more than forty communities of a cooperative, communistic, or "communitarian" nature. Seeking human betterment, a wealthy and idealistic

Scottish textile manufacturer, Robert Owen, founded in 1825 a communal society of about a thousand people at **New Harmony**, Indiana. Little harmony prevailed in the colony, which, in addition to hard-working visionaries, attracted a sprinkling of radicals, work-shy theorists, and outright scoundrels. The colony sank in a morass of contradiction and confusion.

Contending Voices
The Role of Women

The emerging movement for women's social and political rights was often dismissed with sarcasm and contempt. With the title "Women out of their Latitude," a writer in an Albany, New York, newspaper in 1848 mocked the Seneca Falls Convention:

❝We are sorry to see that the women, in several parts of this State, are holding what they call 'Woman's Rights Conventions,' and setting forth a formidable list of those Rights, in a parody upon the Declaration of American Independence....The women who attend these meetings, no doubt at the expense of their more appropriate duties...are holding conventions and making an agitatory movement, with the object of revolutionizing public opinion....Now it requires no argument to prove that this is all wrong.**❞**

A reform-minded newspaper replied:

❝This is disposing of the matter very easily. *No argument can be given,* and so he says none is required. Then he presumes to dictate the place of women—the 'latitude,' as his heading has it. He talks of the awful change in society—the breaking away from the custom of *six thousand years ago,* as if women, or any institution among men remained now as they were in the darkness of ignorance and vice when women did the chief physical labor of the world.**❞**

Why did feelings run so high on this issue?

Brook Farm in Massachusetts, comprising two hundred acres of grudging soil, was started in 1841 with the brotherly and sisterly cooperation of about twenty intellectuals committed to the philosophy of transcendentalism (see p. 329). They prospered reasonably well until 1846, when they lost by fire a large new communal building shortly before its completion. The whole venture in "plain living and high thinking" then collapsed in debt. The Brook Farm experiment inspired Nathaniel Hawthorne's classic novel *The Blithedale Romance* (1852).

A more radical experiment was the **Oneida Community**, founded in New York in 1848. It practiced free love ("complex marriage"), birth control (through "male continence," or *coitus reservatus*), and the eugenic selection of parents to produce superior offspring. This curious enterprise flourished for more than thirty years, largely because its artisans made superior steel traps and Oneida Community (silver) Plate (see "Makers of America: The Oneida Community," pp. 324–325).

Various communistic experiments, mostly small in scale, have been attempted since the founding of Jamestown in 1607. But in competition with democratic free enterprise and free land, virtually all of them sooner or later failed or changed their methods. Among the longest-lived sects were the **Shakers**, founded in England in 1747 and brought to America in 1774 by Mother Ann Lee. She moved her tiny band of followers to upstate New York—the first of a score or so of American Shaker communities. The Shakers attained a membership of about six thousand in 1840, but since their monastic customs prohibited both marriage and sexual relations, they were virtually extinct by 1940.

✦ The Dawn of Scientific Achievement

Early Americans, confronted with pioneering problems, were more interested in practical gadgets than in pure science. Jefferson, for example, was a gifted amateur inventor who won a gold medal for a new type of plow. Noteworthy also were the writings of the mathematician Nathaniel Bowditch (1733–1838) on practical navigation and of the oceanographer Matthew F. Maury (1806–1873) on ocean winds and currents. These writers promoted safety, speed, and economy. But as far as basic science was concerned, Americans were best known for borrowing and adapting the findings of Europeans.

Yet the Republic was not without scientific talent. The most influential American scientist of the first half of the nineteenth century was Professor Benjamin Silliman (1779–1864), a pioneer chemist and geologist who taught and wrote brilliantly at Yale College for more than fifty years. Professor Louis Agassiz (1807–1873), a distinguished French Swiss immigrant, served for a quarter of a century at Harvard College. A path-breaking student of biology who sometimes carried snakes in his pockets, he insisted on original research and deplored the reigning overemphasis on memory work. Professor Asa Gray (1810–1888) of Harvard College, the Columbus of American botany, published over 350 books, monographs, and papers. His textbooks set new standards for clarity and interest.

Lovers of American bird lore owed much to the French-descended naturalist John J. Audubon (1785–1851), who painted wildfowl in their natural habitat. His magnificently illustrated *Birds of America* attained considerable popularity. The Audubon Society for the protection of birds was named after him, although as a young man he shot much feathered game for sport.

Medicine in America, despite a steady growth of medical schools, was still primitive by modern

Fotosearch/Stringer/Archive Photos/Getty Images

Harvesting, by Olof Krans, ca. 1896 The Shakers' emphasis on communal work and separation of the sexes was captured in this painting of the Bishop Hill Colony in Illinois. Krans, born in Sweden, arrived at Bishop Hill with his family in 1850 when he was twelve. Trained as a housepainter, he turned later in life to recording on canvas the simplicity of daily life that he remembered from his youth.

Victoria and Albert Museum, London, Great Britain/Art Resource, NY

National Portrait Gallery, Smithsonian Institution /Art Resource, NY

(left) Passenger Pigeons, by John Audubon; (right) John J. Audubon (1785–1851) An astute naturalist and a gifted artist, Audubon drew the birds of America in loving detail. Ironically, he had to go to Britain in the 1820s to find a publisher for his pioneering depictions of the unique beauty of American wildlife. Born in Haiti and educated in France, he achieved fame as America's greatest ornithologist. The passenger pigeons shown here once numbered in the billions in North America but were extinct by 1900, thanks to aggressive hunting and trapping. This was perhaps the greatest mass slaughter of wildlife in history.

John Humphrey Noyes (1811–1886), the founder of the Oneida Community, repudiated the old Puritan doctrines that God was vengeful and that sinful mankind was doomed to dwell in a vale of tears. Noyes believed in a benign deity, in the sweetness of human nature, and in the possibility of a perfect Christian community on earth. "The more we get acquainted with God," he declared, "the more we shall find it our special duty to be happy."

That sunny thought was shared by many early nineteenth-century American utopians (a word derived from Greek that slyly combines the meanings of "a good place" and "no such place"). But Noyes added some wrinkles of his own. The key to happiness, he taught, was the suppression of selfishness. True Christians should possess no private property—nor should they indulge in exclusive emotional relationships, which bred jealousy, quarreling, and covetousness. Material things and sexual partners alike, Noyes preached, should be shared. Marriage should not be monogamous. Instead all members of the community should be free to love one another in "complex marriage." Noyes called his system "Bible Communism."

Tall and slender, with piercing blue eyes and reddish hair, the charismatic Noyes began voicing these ideas in his hometown of Putney, Vermont, in the 1830s. He soon attracted a group of followers who called themselves the Putney Association, a kind of extended family whose members farmed five hundred acres by day and sang and prayed together in the evenings. They sustained their spiritual intensity by submitting to "Mutual Criticism," in which the person being criticized would sit in silence while other members frankly discussed his or her faults and merits. "I was, metaphorically, stood upon my head and allowed to drain till all the self-righteousness had dripped out of me," one man wrote of his experience with Mutual Criticism.

The Putney Association also indulged in sexual practices that outraged the surrounding community's sense of moral propriety. Indicted for adultery in 1847, Noyes led his followers to Oneida, in the supposedly more tolerant region of New York's Burned-Over District, the following year. Several affiliated communities were also established, the most important of which was at Wallingford, Connecticut.

The Oneidans struggled in New York until they were joined in the 1850s by Sewell Newhouse, a clever inventor of steel animal traps. The manufacture of Newhouse's traps, and other products such as sewing silk and various types of bags, put the Oneida Community on a sound financial footing. By the 1860s Oneida was a flourishing commonwealth of some three hundred people. Men and women shared equally in all the community's tasks, from field to factory to kitchen. The members lived under one roof in Mansion House, a sprawling building that boasted central heating, a well-stocked library, and a common dining hall, as well as the "Big Hall," where members gathered nightly for prayer and entertainment. Children at the age of three were removed from direct parental care and raised communally in the Children's House until the age of thirteen or fourteen, when they took up jobs in the community's industries. They imbibed their religious doctrines with their school lessons:

> *I-spirit*
> *With me never shall stay,*
> *We-spirit*
> *Makes us happy and gay.*

Oneida's apparent success fed the utopian dreams of others, and for a time it became a great tourist attraction. Visitors from as far away as Europe came to picnic on the shady lawns, speculating on the sexual secrets that Mansion House guarded, while their hosts fed them strawberries and cream and entertained them with music.

But eventually the same problems that had driven Noyes and his band from Vermont began to shadow their lives at Oneida. Their New York neighbors grew

The Founding Father   John Humphrey Noyes (1811–1886)

Mansion House A sprawling, resplendent building, it formed the center of the Oneida Community's life and was a stunning specimen of mid-nineteenth-century architectural and engineering achievement.

increasingly horrified at the Oneidans' licentious sexual practices, including the selective breeding program by which the community matched mates and gave permission—or orders—to procreate, without regard to the niceties of matrimony. "It was somewhat startling to me," one straight-laced visitor commented, "to hear *Miss* _____ speak about her baby."

Yielding to their neighbors' criticisms, the Oneidans gave up complex marriage in 1879. Soon other "communistic" practices withered away as well. The communal dining hall became a restaurant, where meals were bought with money, something many Oneidans had never used before. In 1880 the Oneidans abandoned communism altogether and became a joint-stock company specializing in the manufacture of silver tableware. Led by Noyes's son Pierrepont, Oneida Community, Ltd., grew into the world's leading manufacturer of stainless steel knives, forks, and spoons, until foreign competition forced it into bankruptcy in 2006. As for Mansion House, it still stands in central New York, but it now serves as a museum and private residence. Ironically, what grew from Noyes's religious vision was not utopia but a mighty capitalist corporation that finally succumbed to the "creative destruction" that is capitalism's essence.

A Bag Bee on the Lawn of Mansion House The fledgling community supported itself in part by manufacturing bags. Men and women shared equally in the bag-making process.

An outbreak of cholera occurred in New York City in 1832, and a wealthy businessman, Philip Hone (1780–1851), wrote in his diary for the Fourth of July,

❝ The alarm about the cholera has prevented all the usual jollification under the public authority.... The Board of Health reports today twenty new cases and eleven deaths since noon yesterday. The disease is here in all its violence and will increase. God grant that its ravages may be confined, and its visit short. **❞**

standards. Bleeding remained a common cure and a curse as well. Smallpox plagues were still dreaded, and the yellow fever epidemic of 1793 in Philadelphia took several thousand lives. "Bring out your dead!" was the daily cry of the corpse-wagon drivers.

People everywhere complained of ill health— malaria, the "rheumatics," the "miseries," and the chills. Illness often resulted from improper diet, hurried eating, perspiring and cooling off too rapidly, and ignorance of germs and sanitation. "We was sick every fall, regular," wrote the mother of future president James Garfield. Life expectancy was still dismayingly short—about forty years for a white person born in 1850, and less for blacks. The suffering from decayed or ulcerated teeth was enormous; tooth extraction was often practiced by the muscular village blacksmith.

Self-prescribed patent medicines were common (one dose for people, two for horses) and included Robertson's Infallible Worm Destroying Lozenges. Fad diets proved popular, including the whole-wheat bread and crackers regimen of Sylvester Graham. Among home remedies was the rubbing of tumors with dead toads. The use of medicine by regular doctors was often harmful, and Dr. Oliver Wendell Holmes declared in 1860 that if the medicines, as then employed, were thrown into the sea, humans would be better off and the fish worse off.

Victims of surgical operations were ordinarily tied down, often after a stiff drink of whiskey. The surgeon then sawed or cut with breakneck speed, undeterred by the piercing shrieks of the patient. A priceless boon for medical progress came in the early 1840s, when several American doctors and dentists, working independently, successfully employed laughing gas and ether as anesthetics.

✹ Artistic Achievements

As early as the 1770s, Revolutionary Americans anticipated that a great cultural flourishing would accompany America's political awakening. Optimistic commentators spoke of the "rising glory" of America,

sharing the British philosopher George Berkeley's prediction in 1752 that "westward the course of empire takes its way...time's noblest offspring is its last." But while American political thought sparkled with originality, the nation's earliest cultural forays proved less than spectacular. Flush with political independence, Americans strained to achieve cultural autonomy and create a national art worthy of their aspirations.

Architecturally, America chose to imitate Old World styles rather than create indigenous ones. Early national builders articulated a plain **Federal Style** of architecture that borrowed from classical Greek and Roman examples and emphasized symmetry, balance, and restraint. Public buildings incorporated a neoclassical vocabulary of columns, domes, and pediments to suggest venerable ancient models for America's novel republican experiment. Charles Bulfinch's design of the Massachusetts State House (1798) and Benjamin Latrobe's early-nineteenth-century additions to the U.S. Capitol and President's House (now White House) showcased this neoclassical obsession.

A remarkable **Greek Revival** came between 1820 and 1850, partly stimulated by the heroic efforts of the Greeks in the 1820s to wrest independence from the "terrible Turk." Popularized in pattern books for carpenters, plain and porticoed Greek Revival houses proliferated across America, especially in New York's Burned-Over District and the Old Northwest. About midcentury, strong interest developed in a revival of medieval Gothic forms, with their emphasis on pointed arches, sloped roofs, and large, stained-glass windows.

Talented Thomas Jefferson, architect of revolution, was one of the ablest American architects of his generation. Inspired by the sixteenth-century Venetian architect Andrea Palladio, Jefferson's Virginia hilltop home, Monticello, arose as perhaps the most stately mansion in the nation and an iconic example of the Palladian style. Jefferson also modeled Richmond's new state capitol on an ancient Roman temple, the Maison Carrée, which he had visited while minister to France. The quadrangle of the University of Virginia at Charlottesville, another of Jefferson's creations, remains one of the finest examples of neoclassical architecture in America.

Early American painting also struggled to find a distinctive national style. Imitative portraiture and history painting predominated in the late eighteenth century, as American artists attempted to cover their provincial culture with a civilizing veneer. Painting suffered from the dollar-grabbing of a raw civilization; from the hustle, bustle, and absence of leisure; from the lack of a wealthy class to sit for portraits— and then pay for them. Some of the earliest painters, including Benjamin West, were enticed to go to England, where they found both training and patrons. America exported artists and imported art.

The Library of Virginia

Virginia State Capitol, 1785–1788 With the coming of the American Revolution, Virginia Governor Thomas Jefferson urged that the state capital move from Williamsburg to Richmond. There he designed a new, neoclassical capitol building inspired by the Maison Carrée, an exceedingly well-preserved Roman temple in Nîmes, France. The Virginia State Capitol became the Capitol of the Confederacy during the Civil War.

Painting, like the theater, also suffered from the Puritan prejudice that art was a sinful waste of time—and often obscene. John Adams boasted that "he would not give a sixpence for a bust of Phidias or a painting by Raphael." When Edward Everett, the eminent Boston scholar and orator, placed a statue of Apollo in his home, he had its naked limbs draped.

Competent painters nevertheless emerged. Gilbert Stuart (1755–1828), a restless Rhode Islander and one of the most gifted of the early group, wielded his brush in Britain in competition with the best artists. Returning to America in 1793, he produced several portraits of Washington, all of them somewhat idealized and dehumanized. (One of them appears on the familiar one-dollar bill.) Truth to tell, by the time he posed for Stuart, the famous general had lost his natural teeth and some of the original shape of his face. Charles Willson Peale (1741–1827), a Marylander, painted some sixty portraits of Washington, who patiently sat for about fourteen of them. John Trumbull (1756–1843), who had fought in the Revolutionary War, recaptured its heroic scenes and spirit on scores of striking canvases.

After the War of 1812, American painters turned increasingly from human portraits and history paintings to pastoral mirrorings of local landscapes. In America's vast wilderness the new nation's painters finally found their distinctive muse. The **Hudson River school** of the 1820s and 1830s excelled in this type of romantic art. Its leading lights, British-born Thomas Cole and New Jerseyan Asher Durand,

celebrated the raw sublimity and grand divinity of nature. Cole's canvases, including *The Oxbow* (1836), portrayed the ecological threat of human encroachment on once-pristine environments. His masterpiece five-part series *The Course of Empire* (1833–1836) depicted the cyclical rise and fall of human civilization—a powerful analogy for nineteenth-century Americans anxious about industrialization and expansion. Around midcentury a group of "luminist" painters, including German-born Albert Bierstadt, dramatically and sometimes fancifully rendered majestic natural landscapes in the same romantic tradition.

At the same time, new technologies reframed the artistic landscape. Portrait painters gradually encountered some unwelcome competition from the invention of a crude photograph known as the daguerreotype, perfected about 1839 by a Frenchman, Louis Daguerre. Cheap and easily reproducible lithographs, most notably from the New York City firm of Currier and Ives, offered picturesque scenes and city views to millions of consumers.

Music was slowly shaking off the restraints of colonial days, when the prim Puritans had frowned upon nonreligious singing. Rhythmic and nostalgic "darky" tunes, popularized by whites, were becoming immense hits by midcentury. Special favorites were the uniquely American **minstrel shows**, featuring white actors with blackened faces playing stock plantation characters. (For the survival of blackface performance into the twentieth century, see "Examining the Evidence: *The Jazz Singer,* 1927," p. 709.) "Dixie," later adopted by

The Oxbow, by Thomas Cole, 1836 This rendering of the oxbow of the Connecticut River near Northampton, Massachusetts, after a thunderstorm is considered one of Cole's (1801–1848) masterpieces. A leader of the so-called Hudson River school, Cole wandered on foot over the mountains and rivers of New York State and New England, making pencil studies from which he painted in his studio during the winter. He and other members of this group transformed their realistic sketches into lyrical, romantic celebrations of the beauty of the American wilderness.

the Confederates as their battle hymn, was written in 1859, ironically in New York City by an Ohioan. The most famous southern songs, also ironically, came from a white Pennsylvanian, Stephen C. Foster (1826–1864). His one excursion into the South occurred in 1852, after he had published "Camptown Races" (1850), "Old Folks at Home" (1851), and "Oh! Susanna" (1848), the anthem of California gold-rushers. Foster made a valuable contribution to American folk music by capturing the plaintive spirit of the slaves. An odd and pathetic figure, he finally lost both his art and his popularity and died in a charity ward after drowning his sorrows in drink. Lacking adequate copyright protections, songwriters in this era earned pennies, not profits.

✴ The Blossoming of a National Literature

"In the four quarters of the globe," sneered a British critic of 1820, "who reads an American book, or goes to an American play, or looks at an American picture or statue?" Like their sisterly artistic pursuits, early American literary efforts also fell short of initial expectations. Despite an unusually literate population,

post-Revolutionary America imported or plagiarized much of its "polite" reading matter from Britain.

Busy conquering a continent, Americans poured most of their creative efforts into practical outlets. Praiseworthy were political essays, like *The Federalist* (1787–1788) of Hamilton, Jay, and Madison; pamphlets, like Tom Paine's *Common Sense* (1776); and political orations, like the masterpieces of Daniel Webster. In the category of nonreligious books published before 1820, Benjamin Franklin's *Autobiography* (1818) is one of the few that achieved genuine distinction. His narrative is a classic in its simplicity, clarity, and inspirational quality. Even so, it records only a fragment of "Old Ben's" long, fruitful, and amorous life.

After 1820 a confident cohort of young American authors finally began to answer the call for an authentic national literature. Their rise corresponded with the wave of nationalism following the War of 1812 and the arrival of **romanticism** on American shores. Conceived as a reaction against the hyper-rational Enlightenment, romanticism originated in the revolutionary salons of continental Europe and England. In direct contrast to neoclassicism, romanticism emphasized imagination over reason, nature over civilization, intuition over calculation, and the self over society. Emotion, expression, and experimentation were core values. Upsetting the restrained, clocklike universe of the eighteenth-century *philosophes*, nineteenth-century romantics elevated primal nature in all its sublime and picturesque glory. They celebrated human potential and prized the heroic genius of the individual artist. Infused with romantic energy, American literature flowered in the mid-nineteenth century as never before.

Washington Irving (1783–1859), born in New York City, was the first American to win international recognition as a literary figure. Steeped in the traditions of New Netherland, he published in 1809 his amusing *Knickerbocker's History of New York*, with its "local color" caricatures of the Dutch. When the family business failed, Irving was forced to turn to the goose-feather pen. In 1819–1820 he published *The Sketch Book*, which brought him immediate fame at home and abroad. Combining a pleasing style with delicate charm and quiet humor, he used English as well as American themes and included such immortal Gothic tales as "Rip Van Winkle" and "The Legend of Sleepy Hollow." Europe was amazed to find at last an American with a feather in his hand, not in his hair. Later turning to Spanish locales and biography, Irving did much to interpret America to Europe and Europe to America. He was, said the Englishman William Thackeray, "the first ambassador whom the New World of letters sent to the Old."

James Fenimore Cooper (1789–1851) followed on Irving's coattails and gained world fame making New World themes respectable. Expelled from Yale, he eventually married into a wealthy family and settled down on the New York frontier. Reading one day to his wife from an insipid English novel, Cooper remarked in disgust that he could write a better book himself. His wife challenged him to do so—and he did.

After an initial failure, Cooper launched an illustrious career in 1821 with his second novel, *The Spy*—an absorbing tale of the American Revolution. His stories of the sea were meritorious and popular, but his fame rests most enduringly on his five *Leatherstocking Tales*, featuring a dead-eye rifleman named Natty Bumppo, a solitary and self-reliant hero who mingles easily with nature's "noble savages" in stirring adventures like *The Last of the Mohicans* (1826). Cooper's novels sold well to Europeans, some of whom came to think of all American people as born with tomahawk in hand. Actually Cooper's deepest theme was an exploration of the viability and destiny of America's republican experiment; he contrasted the undefiled purity of "natural men," children of the untrammeled wilderness, with the artificiality and corruption of modern civilization. Cooper's emblematic tales of the vanishing frontier offered literary analogues of the Hudson River school's visual landscapes.

Along with Irving and Cooper, the third member of New York's trailblazing Knickerbocker Group was the belated Puritan William Cullen Bryant (1794–1878), transplanted from Massachusetts. At age sixteen he wrote the meditative and melancholy "Thanatopsis" (published in 1817), which was one of the first high-quality poems produced in the United States. Critics could hardly believe that it had been written on "this side of the water." Although Bryant continued with poetry, he made his living by editing the influential *New York Evening Post*. For over fifty years, he set a model for journalism that was dignified, liberal, and conscientious.

✴ Trumpeters of Transcendentalism

A golden age in American literature dawned in the second quarter of the nineteenth century, when an amazing outburst shook New England. One of the mainsprings of this literary flowering was **transcendentalism**, especially around Boston, which preened itself as "the Athens of America."

The transcendentalist movement of the 1830s resulted in part from a liberalizing of the straight-jacket Puritan theology. It also owed much to foreign influences, including the German romantic philosophers and the religions of Asia. The transcendentalists rejected the prevailing empiricist theory, derived from John Locke, that all knowledge comes to the mind through the senses. Truth, rather, "transcends" the senses: it cannot be found by observation alone. Every person possesses an inner light that can illuminate the highest truth and put him or her in direct touch with God, or the "Oversoul."

These mystical doctrines of transcendentalism defied precise definition, but they underlay concrete beliefs. Foremost was a stiff-backed individualism in

Washington Irving's (1783–1859) popular folktale "Rip Van Winkle" (1819) offered a shrewd allegory for the dramatic changes sweeping the early Republic. In this short story, the fictional Rip sleeps through the American Revolution. Upon awakening after twenty years, he finds his fellow village people

❝haranguing vehemently about rights of citizens—election—members of congress—liberty—Bunker's hill—heroes of seventy-six—and other words, that were a perfect Babylonish jargon to the bewildered Van Winkle.**❞**

Portrait of Washington Irving and His Literary Friends at Sunnyside, 1864   This apocryphal gathering of America's founding generation of writers, many of them now sadly unread, was imagined to take place in the library of Washington Irving's Hudson River home. Surrounding Irving, seated in the armchair at center, are fourteen accomplished creators of history, philosophy, fiction, and poetry: (seated, left to right) William Gilmore Simms, Fitz-Greene Halleck, William Hickling Prescott, Irving, Ralph Waldo Emerson, James Fennimore Cooper, George Bancroft; (standing, left to right) Henry Theodore Tuckerman, Oliver Wendell Holmes, Nathaniel Hawthorne, Henry Wadsworth Longfellow, Nathaniel Parker Willis, James Kirke Paulding, William Cullen Bryant, John Pendleton Kennedy. The portrait itself represented a collaborative effort of artists. Felix Octavius Carr Darley did the original drawing, with the help of photographs taken by Matthew Brady. Christian Schussele made a four-by-six-foot oil painting of the scene, and Thomas Oldham Barlow rendered it as a steel-plate engraving for distribution to a wide public.

matters religious as well as social. Closely associated was a commitment to self-reliance, self-culture, and self-discipline. These traits naturally bred hostility to authority and to formal institutions of any kind, as well as to all conventional wisdom. Finally came a romantic exaltation of the dignity of the individual, whether black or white—the mainspring of a whole array of humanitarian reforms.

Best known of the transcendentalists was Boston-born Ralph Waldo Emerson (1803–1882). Tall, slender, and intensely blue-eyed, he mirrored serenity in his noble features. Trained as a Unitarian minister, he early forsook his pulpit and ultimately reached a wider audience by pen and platform. He was a never-failing favorite as a lyceum lecturer and for twenty years took a western tour every winter. Perhaps his most thrilling public effort was a Phi Beta Kappa address, **"The American Scholar,"** delivered at Harvard College

in 1837. This brilliant appeal was an intellectual declaration of independence, for it urged American writers to throw off European traditions and delve into the riches of their own backyards.

Hailed as both a poet and a philosopher, Emerson was not of the highest rank as either. He was more influential as a practical philosopher and public intellectual. Through his fresh and vibrant essays he enriched countless thousands of humdrum lives. Catching the individualistic mood of the Republic, he stressed self-reliance, self-improvement, self-confidence, optimism, and freedom, though he also criticized American triumphalism of the Jacksonian brand. By the 1850s he was an outspoken critic of slavery, and he ardently supported the Union cause in the Civil War.

Henry David Thoreau (1817–1862) was Emerson's close associate—a poet, a mystic, a transcendentalist,

In 1849 Henry David Thoreau (1817–1862) published "Resistance to Civil Government" (later renamed "On the Duty of Civil Disobedience"), asserting,

❝All men recognize the right of revolution; the right to refuse allegiance to and to resist the government, when its tyranny or its inefficiency are great and unendurable. But almost all say that such is not the case now.... I say, when a sixth of the population of a nation which has undertaken to be the refuge of liberty are slaves, and a whole country is unjustly overrun and conquered by a foreign army, and subjected to military law, I think that it is not too soon for honest men to rebel and revolutionize. What makes this duty more urgent is the fact, that the country so overrun is not our own, but ours is the invading army.❞

In 1958 civil rights leader Martin Luther King, Jr. (1929–1968) connected his theory of nonviolent resistance to Henry David Thoreau's pedigree:

❝At this point [in the planning of the 1955 Montgomery, Alabama, bus boycott] I began to think about Thoreau's *Essay on Civil Disobedience*. I remembered how, as a college student, I had been moved when I first read this work. I became convinced that what we were preparing to do in Montgomery was related to what Thoreau had expressed. We were simply saying to the white community, 'We can no longer lend our cooperation to an evil system.'❞

and a nonconformist. Condemning a government that supported slavery, he refused to pay his Massachusetts poll tax and was jailed for a night.* A gifted prose writer, he is well known for *Walden: Or Life in the Woods* (1854). The book is a record of Thoreau's two years of simple existence in a hut that he built on the edge of Walden Pond, near Concord, Massachusetts. *Walden* epitomized the romantic quest for isolation from society's corruptions. A stiff-necked individualist, Thoreau believed that he should reduce his bodily wants so as to gain time to pursue truth through study and meditation. Thoreau's *Walden* and his essay "On the Duty of Civil Disobedience" (1849) exercised a strong influence in furthering idealistic thought, both in America and abroad. His writings later encouraged Mahatma Gandhi to resist British rule in India and, still later, inspired the development of American civil rights leader Martin Luther King, Jr.'s thinking about nonviolence.

Precocious Margaret Fuller (1810–1850) befriended Emerson around the time of his Phi Beta Kappa address in 1837 and soon joined the Boston circle of transcendentalists. She edited the movement's journal, *The Dial*, for two years after its founding in 1840. In the same year, she launched her series of "Conversations," or paid seminars designed to promote scholarly dialogue among local elite women (and some invited men). Known for her sparkling conversational wit, Fuller also wrote prolifically. In 1845, she published *Woman in the Nineteenth Century*, a powerful critique of gender roles and an iconic statement of the budding feminist movement. After an influential stint as literary editor of Horace Greeley's *New York*

Tribune, Fuller sailed for Europe and eventually took part in the struggle to bring unity and republican government to Italy. She died tragically in a shipwreck off New York's Fire Island while returning to the United States in 1850.

Bold, brassy, and swaggering was the open-collared figure of Brooklyn's Walt Whitman (1819–1892). In his famous collection of poems *Leaves of Grass* (1855), he gave free rein to his gushing genius with what he called a "barbaric yawp." His landmark "Song of Myself," with its unabashed first-person speaker, celebrated the romantic artist-hero in free verse. Highly emotional and unconventional, Whitman dispensed with titles, stanzas, rhymes, and at times even regular meter. He located divinity in commonplace natural objects (e.g., leaves of grass) as well as the human body. Whitman even handled sex with shocking frankness, although he laundered his verses in later editions, and his book was banned in Boston.

Whitman's *Leaves of Grass* was at first a financial failure. The only three enthusiastic reviews that it received were written by the author himself—anonymously. But in time the once-withered *Leaves of Grass*, revived and honored, won for Whitman an enormous following in both America and Europe and gained him the informal title "Poet Laureate of Democracy." Singing with transcendental abandon of his love for the masses, he caught the exuberant enthusiasm of an expanding America that had turned its back on the Old World:

> *All the Past we leave behind;*
> *We debouch upon a newer, mightier world, varied world;*
> *Fresh and strong the world we seize—world of labor*
> *   and the march—*
> *Pioneers! O Pioneers!*

Here at last was the native art for which critics had been crying.

---

*The story (probably apocryphal) is that Emerson visited Thoreau at the jail and asked, "Why are you here?" The reply came, "Why are you *not* here?"

✴ Glowing Literary Lights

Certain other literary giants were not actively associated with the transcendentalist movement, though not completely immune to its influences. Professor Henry Wadsworth Longfellow (1807–1882), who for many years taught modern languages at Harvard College, was one of the most popular poets ever produced in America. Handsome and urbane, he lived a generally serene life, except for the tragic deaths of two wives, the second of whom perished before his eyes when her dress caught fire. Writing for the genteel classes, he was adopted by the less cultured masses. His wide knowledge of European literature supplied him with many themes, but some of his most admired narrative poems—*Evangeline* (1847), *The Song of Hiawatha* (1855), and *The Courtship of Miles Standish* (1858)—were based on American traditions. Immensely popular in Europe, Longfellow was the first American ever to be enshrined in the Poets' Corner of Westminster Abbey.

A fighting Quaker with piercing dark eyes, John Greenleaf Whittier (1807–1892) was the uncrowned poet laureate of the antislavery crusade. Less talented as a writer than Longfellow, he was vastly more important in influencing social action. His abolitionist poems cried aloud against inhumanity, injustice, and intolerance, against

> *The outworn rite, the old abuse,*
> *The pious fraud transparent grown*

Undeterred by insults and the stoning of mobs, Whittier helped arouse a callous America on the slavery issue. He also left behind a legacy of "local color" sketches and verse dedicated to his native New England.

Many-sided professor James Russell Lowell (1819–1891), who succeeded Professor Longfellow at Harvard, ranks as one of America's better poets. He was also a distinguished essayist, literary critic, and diplomat, as well as editor of Boston's *Atlantic Monthly* and *North American Review*—a diffusion of talents that hampered his poetical output. Lowell is remembered as a political satirist in his *Biglow Papers*, especially those of 1846–1848 opposing the Mexican War. Written partly as poetry in the Yankee dialect, the *Papers* condemned in blistering terms the alleged slavery-expansion designs of the Polk administration.

Two women writers whose work remains enormously popular today also sprouted from this New

Louisa May Alcott (1832–1888)   This color lithograph printed by Louis Prang in 1888 made Alcott's image accessible to her many loyal readers. In search of independence for herself and financial security for her family, Alcott worked as a seamstress, governess, teacher, and housemaid until her writing finally brought her success. Her much-loved, largely autobiographical novel *Little Women* has remained in print continuously from 1868 until our own day.

England literary soil. Louisa May Alcott (1832–1888) grew up in Concord, Massachusetts, in the bosom of transcendentalism, alongside neighbors Emerson, Thoreau, and Fuller. Her philosopher father Bronson Alcott occupied himself more with ideas than with earning a living, leaving his daughter to write *Little Women* (1868) and other books to support her mother and sisters. Not far away in Amherst, Massachusetts, poet Emily Dickinson (1830–1886) lived as a recluse but created her own original world through precious gems of poetry. Her seclusion was but an extreme example of the romantic artist's desire for social remove. In deceptively spare language and simple rhyme schemes, Dickinson explored universal themes of nature, love, death, and immortality. Although she hesitated during her lifetime to publish more than a dozen of her poems, when she died, nearly two thousand of them were found among her papers and eventually made their way into print.

The most noteworthy literary figure produced by the South before the Civil War was novelist William Gilmore Simms (1806–1870). Quantitatively, at least, he was great: eighty-two books flowed from his ever-moist pen, winning for him the title "the Cooper of the South." His favorite themes, captured in titles like *The Yemasee* (1835) and *The Cassique of Kiawah* (1859), dealt with the southern frontier in colonial days and with the South during the Revolutionary War. Enormously popular in his own day, Simms ardently promoted southern literature and won the esteem of many northern writers, including Irving, Bryant, and Herman Melville, among others. Yet his national and international reputation suffered after the Civil War, no doubt due to his overt proslavery and secessionist sentiments.

✦ Literary Individualists and Dissenters

Not all writers in these years believed so keenly in human goodness and social progress. A clique of contrary-minded authors plumbed the darker realms of human experience, exploring pain, fear, and grief, along with the supernatural and the subconscious. Edgar Allan Poe (1809–1849), who spent much of his youth in Virginia, was an eccentric genius. Orphaned at an early age, cursed with ill health, and married to a child-wife of thirteen who fell fatally ill of tuberculosis, he suffered hunger, cold, poverty, and debt. Failing at suicide, he took refuge in the bottle and dissipated his talent early. Poe was a gifted lyric poet, as the mesmerizing rhythms of "The Raven" (1845) attest. A master stylist, he also excelled in the short story, especially of the Gothic horror type, in which he shared his alcoholic nightmares with fascinated readers. If he did not invent the modern detective story, he at least set new high standards in tales like "The Murders in the Rue Morgue" (1841).

Poe was fascinated by the ghostly and ghastly, as in "The Fall of the House of Usher" (1839) and other stories. Obsessed with romantic antiheroes on the verge of mental disintegration, he reflected a morbid sensibility distinctly at odds with the usually optimistic tone of American culture. Partly for this reason, Poe has perhaps been even more prized by Europeans than by Americans. His brilliant career was cut short when he was found drunk in a Baltimore gutter and shortly thereafter died.

Two other writers reflected the continuing Calvinist obsession with original sin and with the never-ending struggle between good and evil. In somber Salem, Massachusetts, writer Nathaniel Hawthorne (1804–1864) grew up in an atmosphere heavy with the memories of his Puritan forebears and the tragedy of his father's premature death on an ocean voyage. His masterpiece was *The Scarlet Letter* (1850), which describes the Puritan practice of forcing an adulteress to wear a scarlet "A" on her clothing. The tragic tale chronicles the psychological effects of sin on the guilty heroine Hester Prynne, a classic romantic outcast, and her secret lover Arthur Dimmesdale, the father of her baby and a minister of the gospel in Puritan Boston. In *The Marble Faun* (1860), Hawthorne dealt with a group of young American artists who witness a mysterious murder in Rome. The book explores the concepts of the omnipresence of evil and the dead hand of the past weighing upon the present.

Herman Melville (1819–1891), an orphaned and ill-educated New Yorker, went to sea as a youth and served eighteen adventuresome months on a whaler. "A whale ship was my Yale College and my Harvard," he wrote. Jumping ship in the South Seas, he lived among cannibals, from whom he providently escaped uneaten. His exotic tales of the South Seas were immediately popular, but his masterpiece, *Moby Dick* (1851), was not. This epic novel is a complex allegory of good and evil, told by its narrator Ishmael in terms of the conflict between a whaling captain, Ahab, and a giant white whale, Moby Dick. The monomaniacal Captain Ahab, having lost a leg to the marine monster, lives only for revenge. His deterministic pursuit finally ends when Moby Dick rams and sinks Ahab's ship, leaving only one survivor. The whale's exact identity and Ahab's motives remain obscure. In the end the untamed sea, like the terrifyingly impersonal and unknowable universe of Melville's imagination, simply rolls on.

Moby Dick was widely ignored at the time of its publication; people were accustomed to more straightforward and upbeat prose. A disheartened Melville continued to write unprofitably for some years, part of the time eking out a living as a customs inspector

Capturing a Sperm Whale, painted by William Page from a sketch by C. B. Hulsart, 1835   This painting and Melville's *Moby Dick* vividly portray the hazards of whaling. Despite the dangers, it proved to be an important industry from colonial times to the end of the nineteenth century.

in New York City, and then died in relative obscurity. Ironically, his brooding masterpiece about the mysterious white whale had to wait until the more jaded twentieth century for readers and for proper recognition.

✦ Portrayers of the Past

A distinguished group of American historians was emerging at the same time that other writers were winning distinction. Energetic George Bancroft (1800–1891), who as secretary of the navy helped found the Naval Academy at Annapolis in 1845, has deservedly received the title "Father of American History." He published a spirited, superpatriotic history of the United States to 1789 in six (originally ten) volumes (1834–1876), a work that grew out of his vast researches in dusty archives in Europe and America.

Two other historians are read with greater pleasure and profit today. William H. Prescott (1796–1859), who accidentally lost the sight of an eye while

in college, conserved his remaining weak vision and published classic accounts of the conquest of Mexico (1843) and Peru (1847). Francis Parkman (1823–1893), whose eyes were so defective that he wrote in darkness with the aid of a guiding machine, penned a brilliant series of volumes beginning in 1851. In epic style he chronicled the struggle between France and Britain in colonial times for the mastery of North America.

Early American historians of prominence were almost without exception New Englanders, largely because the Boston area provided well-stocked libraries and a stimulating literary tradition. These writers numbered abolitionists among their relatives and friends and hence were disposed to view unsympathetically the slavery-cursed South. This "made in New England" interpretation dominated the writing of American history until the close of the nineteenth century, when pressure for national reconciliation overcame regional bias. "The history of the United States has been written by Boston," one pro-southern historian bitterly complained, "and largely written wrong."

[*Varying Viewpoints*]
Reform: Who? What? How? and Why?

Early chronicles of the antebellum period universally lauded the era's reformers, portraying them as idealistic, altruistic crusaders intent on improving American society.

After World War II, however, some historians began to detect selfish and even conservative motives underlying the apparent benevolence of the reformers. This view described the advocates of reform as anxious, upper-class men and women threatened by the ferment of life in antebellum America. The pursuit of reforms like temperance, asylums, prisons, and mandatory public education represented a means of asserting "social control." In this vein, one historian described a reform movement as "the anguished protest of an aggrieved class against a world they never made." In Michael Katz's treatment of early educational reform, proponents were community leaders who sought a school system that would ease the traumas of America's industrialization by inculcating business-oriented values and discipline in the working classes.

The wave of reform activity in the 1960s prompted a reevaluation of the reputations of the antebellum reformers. These more recent interpretations found much to admire in the authentic religious commitments of reformers and especially in the participation of women, who sought various social improvements as an extension of their function as protectors of the home and family.

The scholarly treatment of abolitionism is a telling example of how reformers and their campaigns have risen and fallen in the estimation of historians. To northern historians writing in the late nineteenth century, abolitionists were courageous men and women so devoted to uprooting the evil of slavery that they were willing to dedicate their lives to a cause that often ostracized them from their communities. By the mid-twentieth century, an interpretation more favorable to the South prevailed, one that blamed the fanaticism of the abolitionists for the Civil War. But as the racial climate in the United States began to change during the 1960s, historians such as Benjamin Quarles and James Brewer Stewart once again showed sympathy for the abolitionist struggle, and by the end of the twentieth century abolitionist men and women, white as well as black, were revered as ideologically committed individuals dedicated not just to freeing the enslaved but to saving the moral soul of America.

Scholars animated by the modern feminist movement have inspired a reconsideration of women's reform activity. It had long been known, of course, that women were active participants in charitable organizations. But not until Nancy Cott, Kathryn Sklar, Mary Ryan, and other historians began to look more closely at what Cott has called "the bonds of womanhood" did the links between women's domestic lives and their public benevolent behavior fully emerge. Carroll Smith-Rosenberg showed in her study of the New York Female Moral Reform Society, for example, that members who set out at first to convert prostitutes to evangelical Protestantism and to close down the city's many brothels soon developed an ideology of female autonomy that rejected male dominance. When men behaved in immoral or illegal ways, women reformers claimed that they had the right—even the duty—to leave the confines of their homes and actively work to purify society. More recently, historians Nancy Hewitt and Lori Ginzberg have challenged the assumption that all women reformers embraced a single definition of female identity. Instead they have emphasized the importance of class differences in shaping women's reform work, which led inevitably to tensions within female ranks. Giving more attention to the historical evolution of female reform ideology, Ginzberg has also detected a shift from an early focus on moral uplift to a more class-based appeal for social control.

Historians of the suffrage movement have emphasized another kind of exclusivity among women reformers—the boundaries of race. Ellen DuBois has shown that after a brief alliance with the abolitionist movement, many female suffrage reformers abandoned the cause of black liberation in an effort to achieve their own goal with less controversy. Whatever historians may conclude about the liberating or leashing character of early reform, it is clear by now that they have to contend with the ways in which class, gender, and race divided reformers, making the plural—*reform movements*—the more accurate depiction of the impulse to "improve" that pervaded American society in the early nineteenth century.

Most recently, historians of all kinds of reform have highlighted the transatlantic dimensions of these movements. American reformers corresponded with and adopted ideas from their European counterparts, participating in waves of reform that extended well beyond the shores of the United States.

Chapter Review

KEY TERMS

The Age of Reason (309)
Deism (309)
Second Great Awakening (310)
Burned-Over District (311)
Mormons (312)
lyceum (316)
American Temperance Society (318)
Maine Law of 1851 (318)
Woman's Rights Convention at Seneca Falls (320)

New Harmony (321)
Brook Farm (322)
Oneida Community (322)
Shakers (322)
Federal Style (326)
Greek Revival (326)
Hudson River school (327)
minstrel shows (327)
romanticism (328)
transcendentalism (329)
"The American Scholar" (330)

PEOPLE TO KNOW

Peter Cartwright
Charles Grandison Finney
Joseph Smith
Brigham Young
Horace Mann
Dorothea Dix
Neal S. Dow
Lucretia Mott
Elizabeth Cady Stanton
Susan B. Anthony
Lucy Stone
Amelia Bloomer
Robert Owen
John J. Audubon

Stephen C. Foster
James Fenimore Cooper
Ralph Waldo Emerson
Henry David Thoreau
Walt Whitman
Henry Wadsworth Longfellow
Louisa May Alcott
Emily Dickinson
Edgar Allan Poe
Nathaniel Hawthorne
Herman Melville
Francis Parkman

CHRONOLOGY

1747	Shaker movement founded in Manchester, England
1770s	First Shaker communities established in New York
1790s	Second Great Awakening begins
1794	Thomas Paine publishes *The Age of Reason*
1795	University of North Carolina founded
1819	Jefferson founds University of Virginia
1819–1820	Irving publishes *The Sketch Book*
1821	Emma Willard establishes Troy (New York) Female Seminary
1825	New Harmony commune established
1826	American Temperance Society founded
Cooper publishes *The Last of the Mohicans*
1828	Noah Webster publishes dictionary
American Peace Society founded
1830	Joseph Smith founds Mormon Church
Godey's Lady's Book first published
1830–1831	Finney conducts revivals in eastern cities
1835	Lyceum movement flourishes

1836	Cole's *The Oxbow* debuts
1837	Oberlin College admits female students
Mary Lyon establishes Mount Holyoke Seminary
Emerson delivers "The American Scholar" address
1840	London antislavery convention refuses to recognize female delegates
1841	Brook Farm commune established
1843	Dorothea Dix petitions Massachusetts legislature on behalf of the insane
1845	Poe publishes "The Raven"
1846–1847	Mormon migration to Utah
1848	Seneca Falls Woman's Rights Convention held
Oneida Community established
Foster's "Oh! Susanna" debuts
1850	Hawthorne publishes *The Scarlet Letter*
1851	Melville publishes *Moby Dick*
Maine passes first law prohibiting liquor
1854	Thoreau publishes *Walden*
1855	Whitman publishes *Leaves of Grass*

TO LEARN MORE

Robert Abzug, *Cosmos Crumbling: American Reform and the Religious Imagination* (1994)

Anne M. Boylan, *The Origins of Women's Activism: New York and Boston, 1797–1840* (2002)

Nathan O. Hatch, *The Democratization of American Christianity* (1989)

Joseph Hawes, *Children in Urban Society* (1971)

Daniel Walker Howe, *What Hath God Wrought: The Transformation of America, 1815–1848* (2007)

Paul Johnson, *A Shopkeeper's Millennium: Society and Revivals in Rochester, New York, 1815–1837* (1978)

Joseph F. Kett, *Rites of Passage: Adolescence in America* (1976)

Spencer Klaw, *Without Sin: The Life and Death of the Oneida Community* (1993)

Sally G. McMillen, *Seneca Falls and the Origins of the Women's Rights Movement* (2008)

Steven Mintz and Susan Kellogg, *Domestic Revolutions: A Social History of American Family Life* (1988)

William Rorabaugh, *The Alcoholic Republic* (1979)

Caroline Winterer, *The Culture of Classicism: Ancient Greece and Rome in American Intellectual Life, 1780–1910* (2002)

A complete, annotated bibliography for this chapter—along with brief descriptions of the People to Know—may be found on the *American Pageant* website. The key terms are defined in the glossary at the end of the text.

Part Three

Testing the New Nation

1820–1877

The Civil War of 1861 to 1865 was the awesome trial by fire of American nationhood and of the American soul. All Americans knew, said Abraham Lincoln, that slavery "was somehow the cause of this war." The war tested, in Lincoln's ringing phrase at Gettysburg, whether any nation "dedicated to the proposition that all men are created equal…can long endure." How did this great and bloody conflict come about? And what were its results?

American slavery was by any measure a "peculiar institution." Slavery was rooted in both racism and economic exploitation and depended for its survival on brutal repression. Yet the American slave population was the only enslaved population in history that grew by means of its own biological reproduction—a fact that suggests to many historians that conditions under slavery in the United States were somehow less punitive than those in other slave societies. Indeed a distinctive and durable African American culture managed to flourish under

slavery, further suggesting that the slave regime provided some "space" for African American cultural development. But however benignly it might be painted, slavery still remained a cancer in the heart of American democracy, a moral outrage that mocked the nation's claim to be a model of social and political enlightenment. As time went on, more and more voices called more and more stridently for its abolition.

The nation lived uneasily with slavery from the outset. Thomas Jefferson was only one among many in the founding generation who felt acutely the conflict between the high principle of equality and the ugly reality of slavery. The federal government in the early Republic took several steps to check the growth of slavery. It banned slavery in the Old Northwest in 1787, prohibited the further importation of slaves after 1808, and declared in the Missouri Compromise of 1820 that the vast western territories secured in the Louisiana Purchase were forever closed to slavery north of the state

Collection of the New-York Historical Society, USA/The Bridgeman Art Library

Returning from the Cotton Fields in South Carolina Enslaved African American planted and picked virtually all the cotton that formed the foundation of the nineteenth-century southern economy. The white South ferociously defended its "peculiar institution" of slavery, which ended at last only in the fires of the Civil War.

The 1st Virginia Regiment These Virginia militiamen were photographed in 1859 while attending the trial of the abolitionist John Brown for treason against the state of Virginia. Two years later their regiment formed part of the Confederate army that struck for southern independence.

of Missouri. Antislavery sentiment even abounded in the South in the immediate post-Revolutionary years. But as time progressed, and especially after Eli Whitney's invention of the cotton gin in the 1790s, the southern planter class became increasingly dependent on slave labor to wring profits from the sprawling plantations that carpeted the South. As cotton cultivation spread westward, the South's stake in slavery grew deeper, and the abolitionist outcry grew louder.

The controversy over slavery significantly intensified following the war with Mexico in the 1840s. "Mexico will poison us," predicted the philosopher Ralph Waldo Emerson, and he proved to be distressingly prophetic. The lands acquired from Mexico—most of the present-day American Southwest, from Texas to California—reopened the question of extending slavery into the western territories. The decade and a half that followed the Mexican War—from 1846 to 1861—witnessed a series of ultimately ineffective efforts to come to grips with that question, including the ill-starred Compromise of 1850, the conflict-breeding Kansas-Nebraska Act of 1854, and the Supreme Court's inflammatory decision in the *Dred Scott* case of 1857.

Ultimately, the slavery question was settled by force of arms, in the Civil War itself.

The Civil War, as Lincoln observed, was assuredly about slavery. But as Lincoln also repeatedly insisted, the war was about the viability of the Union as well and about the strength of democracy itself. Could a democratic government, built on the principle of popular consent, rightfully deny some of its citizens the same right to independence that the American revolutionaries had exercised in seceding from the British Empire in 1776? Southern rebels, calling the conflict "The War for Southern Independence," asked that question forcefully, but ultimately it, too, was answered not in the law courts or in the legislative halls but on the battlefield.

The Civil War unarguably established the supremacy of the Union, and it ended slavery as well. But as the victorious Union set about the task of "reconstruction" after the war's end in 1865, a combination of weak northern will and residual southern power frustrated the goal of making the emancipated blacks full-fledged American citizens. The Civil War in the end brought nothing but freedom—though over time, freedom proved a powerful tool indeed.

Chapter 16

The South and the Slavery Controversy

1793–1860

*Those who deny freedom to others deserve it not for themselves,
and, under a just God, cannot long retain it.*

ABRAHAM LINCOLN, 1859

At the dawn of the Republic, slavery faced an uncertain future. Touched by Revolutionary idealism, some southern leaders, including Thomas Jefferson, were talking openly of freeing their slaves. Others predicted that the iron logic of economics would eventually expose slavery's unprofitability, speeding its demise.

But the introduction of Eli Whitney's cotton gin in 1793 scrambled all those predictions. Whitney's invention made possible the wide-scale cultivation of short-staple cotton. The white fiber rapidly became the dominant southern crop, eclipsing tobacco, rice, and sugar. The explosion of cotton cultivation created an insatiable demand for new fields to plant and new labor to work them. The slave was chained to the gin and the planter to the slave. As the nineteenth century opened, the reinvigoration of southern slavery carried fateful implications for blacks and whites alike—and threatened the survival of the nation itself.

✷ "Cotton Is King!"

As time passed, the Cotton Kingdom developed into a huge agricultural factory, pouring out avalanches of the fluffy fiber. Quick profits drew planters to the loamy bottomlands of the Gulf states. As long as the soil was still vigorous, the yield was bountiful and the rewards were high. Caught up in an economic spiral, the planters bought more slaves and land to grow more cotton, so as to buy still more slaves and land.

Northern shippers reaped a large part of the profits from the cotton trade. They would load bulging bales of cotton at southern ports, transport them to England, sell their fleecy cargo for pounds sterling, and buy needed manufactured goods for sale in the United States. To a large degree, the prosperity of both North and South—and of England, too—rested on the bent backs of enslaved bondsmen.

So did the young nation's growing wealth. Cotton accounted for half the value of all American exports after 1840, and export earnings provided much of the capital that stoked the Republic's economic growth. The American South produced more than half of the entire world's supply of cotton—a fact that held foreign nations in partial bondage. Britain was then the leading industrial power. Its most important single manufacture in the 1850s was cotton cloth, from which about one-fifth of its population, directly or indirectly, drew its livelihood. About 75 percent of this precious supply of fiber came from the white-carpeted acres of the South.

Southern leaders were fully aware that Britain was tied to them by cotton threads, and this dependence gave them a heady sense of power. In their eyes "Cotton was King," the gin was his throne, and the black bondsmen were his vassals. If war should ever break out between North and South, northern warships would presumably cut off the outflow of cotton. Fiber-famished British factories would then close their gates, starving mobs would force the London government to break the blockade, and the South would triumph. Cotton appeared to be a powerful monarch indeed.

✦ The Planter "Aristocracy"

Before the Civil War, the South was in some respects not so much a democracy as an oligarchy—or a government by the few, in this case heavily influenced by a planter aristocracy. In 1850 only 1,733 families owned more than one hundred slaves each, and this select group provided the cream of the political and social leadership of the section and nation. Here was the mint-julep South of the tall-columned and white-painted plantation mansion—the "big house," where dwelt the "cottonocracy."

The planter aristocrats, with their blooded horses and Chippendale chairs, enjoyed a lion's share of southern wealth. They could educate their children in the finest schools, often in the North or abroad. Their money provided the leisure for study, reflection, and statecraft, as was notably true of men like John C. Calhoun (a Yale graduate) and Jefferson Davis (a West Point graduate). They felt a keen sense of obligation to serve the public. It was no accident that Virginia and the other southern states produced a higher proportion of front-rank statesmen before 1860 than the "dollar-grubbing" North.

But even in its best light, dominance by a favored aristocracy was basically undemocratic. It widened the gap between rich and poor. It hampered tax-supported public education because the rich planters could and did send their children to private institutions.

A favorite author of elite southerners was Sir Walter Scott, whose manors and castles, graced by brave Ivanhoes and fair Rowenas, helped them idealize a feudal society, even when many of their economic activities were undeniably capitalistic. Southern aristocrats, who sometimes staged jousting tournaments, strove to perpetuate a type of medievalism that had died out in Europe—or was rapidly dying out.* Mark Twain later accused Sir Walter Scott of having had a hand in starting the Civil War. The British novelist, Twain said, aroused the southerners to fight for a decaying social structure—"a sham civilization."

The plantation system also shaped the lives of southern women. The mistress of a great plantation commanded a sizable household staff of mostly female slaves. She gave daily orders to cooks, maids, seamstresses, laundresses, and body servants. Relationships between mistresses and slaves ranged from affectionate to atrocious. Some mistresses showed tender regard for their bondswomen, and some enslaved women took pride in their status as "members" of the household. But slavery strained even the bonds

---

*Oddly enough, by legislative enactment, jousting became the official state sport of Maryland in 1962.

Interior of the Cotton Bureau in New Orleans, by Edgar Degas, 1873 Although this painting dates from 1873, French impressionist painter Edgar Degas (1834–1917) captured the insouciant self-confidence of cotton traders in the pre–Civil War era. As cotton cultivation spread into the new states of the trans-Appalachian Southwest, the entire Cotton Kingdom paid tribute to New Orleans, Queen City of the South, and the port through which millions of cotton bales flowed out to British textile mills.

Erich Lessing/Art Resource, NY

Harvesting Cotton   This Currier & Ives print shows slaves of both sexes harvesting cotton, which was then "ginned," baled, carted to the riverbank, and taken by paddle wheeler downriver to New Orleans for shipment to New England or overseas.

of womanhood. Virtually no slaveholding women believed in abolition, and relatively few protested when the husbands and children of their slaves were sold. One plantation mistress harbored a special affection for her slave Annica but noted in her diary that "I whipt Annica" for insolence.

✦ Slaves of the Slave System

Unhappily, the moonlight-and-magnolia tradition concealed much that was worrisome, distasteful, and sordid. Plantation agriculture was wasteful, largely because King Cotton and his money-hungry subjects despoiled the good earth. Quick profits led to excessive cultivation, or "land butchery," which in turn caused a heavy leakage of population to the West and Northwest.

The economic structure of the South became increasingly monopolistic. As the land wore thin, many small farmers sold their holdings to more prosperous neighbors and went north or west. The big got bigger and the small smaller. When the Civil War finally erupted, a large percentage of southern farms had passed from the hands of the families that had originally cleared them.

Another cancer in the bosom of the South was the financial instability of the plantation system. The temptation to overspeculate in land and slaves caused many planters, including Andrew Jackson in his later years, to plunge in beyond their depth. Although the enslaved blacks might in extreme cases be fed for as little as ten cents a day, there were other expenses. The slaves represented a heavy investment of capital, perhaps $1,200 each in the case of prime field hands, and they might deliberately injure themselves or run away. An entire slave quarter might be wiped out by disease or even by lightning, as happened in one instance to twenty ill-fated blacks.

Dominance by King Cotton likewise led to a dangerous dependence on a one-crop economy, whose price level was at the mercy of world conditions. The whole system discouraged a healthy diversification of agriculture and particularly of manufacturing.

Southern planters resented watching the North grow fat at their expense. They were pained by the heavy outward flow of commissions and interest to northern middlemen, bankers, agents, and shippers. Staunch sons and daughters of the South, especially by the 1850s, deplored the fact that when born, they were wrapped in Yankee-made swaddling clothes and that they spent the rest of their lives in servitude to Yankee manufacturing. When they died, they were laid in coffins held together with Yankee nails and were buried in graves dug with Yankee shovels. The South furnished the corpse and the hole in the ground.

The Cotton Kingdom also repelled large-scale European immigration, which added so richly to the manpower and wealth of the North. In 1860 only 4.4 percent of the southern population was foreign-born, as compared with 18.7 percent for the North.

Thomas Jefferson (1743–1826) wrote in 1786,

❝What a stupendous, what an incomprehensible machine is man! Who can endure toil, famine, stripes, imprisonment & death itself in vindication of his own liberty, and the next moment…inflict on his fellow men a bondage, one hour of which is fraught with more misery than ages of that which he rose in rebellion to oppose.❞

Unlike George Washington, Jefferson freed only a couple of his slaves in his will; the rest were sold to pay off his large debts.

German and Irish immigration to the South was generally discouraged by the competition of slave labor, by the high cost of fertile land, and by European ignorance of cotton growing. The diverting of non-British immigration to the North caused the white South to become the most Anglo-Saxon section of the nation.

✴ The White Majority

Only a handful of southern whites lived in Grecian-pillared mansions. Below those 1,733 families in 1850 who owned a hundred or more slaves were the less wealthy slaveowners (see Figure 16.1). They totaled in 1850 some 345,000 families, representing about 1,725,000 white persons. Over two-thirds of these families—255,268 in all—owned fewer than ten slaves each. All told, only about one-fourth of white southerners owned slaves or belonged to a slaveowning family.

The smaller slaveowners did not own a majority of the slaves, but they made up a majority of the masters. These lesser masters were typically small farmers. With the striking exception that their households contained a slave or two, or perhaps an entire slave family, the style of their lives probably resembled that of small farmers in the North more than it did that of the southern planter aristocracy. They lived in modest farmhouses and sweated beside their bondsmen in the cotton fields, laboring callus for callus just as hard as their slaves.

Beneath the slaveowners on the population pyramid was the great body of whites who owned no slaves at all. By 1860 their numbers had swelled to 6,120,825—three-quarters of all southern whites. Shouldered off the richest bottomlands by the mighty planters, they scratched a simple living from the thinner soils of the backcountry and the mountain valleys (see Maps 16.1 and 16.2). To them the riches of the Cotton Kingdom were a distant dream, and they often sneered at the lordly pretensions of the cotton "snobocracy." These red-necked farmers participated in the market economy scarcely at all. As subsistence farmers, they raised corn and hogs, not cotton, and often lived isolated lives, punctuated periodically by extended socializing and sermonizing at religious camp meetings.

Some of the least prosperous nonslaveholding whites were scorned even by slaves as "poor white trash." Known also as "hillbillies," "crackers," or "clay eaters," they were often described as listless, shiftless, and misshapen. Later investigations have revealed that many of them were not simply lazy but sick, suffering from malnutrition and parasites, especially hookworm.

All these whites without slaves had no direct economic stake in the preservation of slavery, yet they were among the stoutest defenders of the slave system. Why? The answer is not far to seek.

The carrot on the stick ever dangling before their eyes was the hope of buying a slave or two and of parlaying their paltry holdings into riches—all in accord with the "American dream" of upward social mobility. They also took fierce pride in their presumed racial superiority, which would be watered down if the enslaved blacks were freed. Many of the poorer whites were hardly better off economically than the slaves; some, indeed, were not so well-off. But even the most wretched whites could take perverse comfort from the

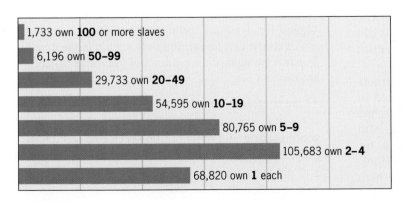

FIGURE 16.1 Slaveowning Families, 1850 More than half of all slaveholding families owned fewer than four slaves. In contrast, 2 percent of slaveowners owned more than fifty slaves each. A tiny slaveholding elite held a majority of slave property in the South. The great majority of white southerners owned no slaves at all. © 2016 Cengage Learning

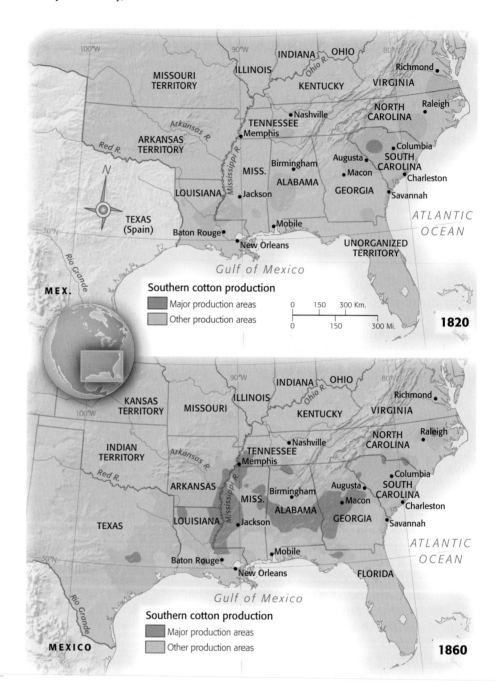

MAP 16.1 Southern Cotton Production and Distribution of Slaves, 1820 and 1860

© 2016 Cengage Learning

knowledge that they outranked someone in status: the still more wretched African American slave. Thus did the logic of economics join with the illogic of racism in buttressing the slave system.

In a special category among white southerners were the mountain whites, more or less marooned in the valleys of the Appalachian range that stretched from western Virginia to northern Georgia and Alabama. Civilization had largely passed them by, and they still lived under spartan frontier conditions. They were a kind of living ancestry, for some of them retained Elizabethan speech forms and habits that had long since died out in Britain.

"Arthur Lee, Freeman," petitioned the General Assembly of Virginia in 1835 for permission to remain in the state despite a law against the residency of free blacks. After asserting his upstanding moral character, he implored,

❝ He therefore most respectfully and earnestly prays that you will pass a law permitting him on the score of long and meritorious service to remain in the State, together with his wife and four children, and not force him in his old age to seek a livelihood in a new Country. **❞**

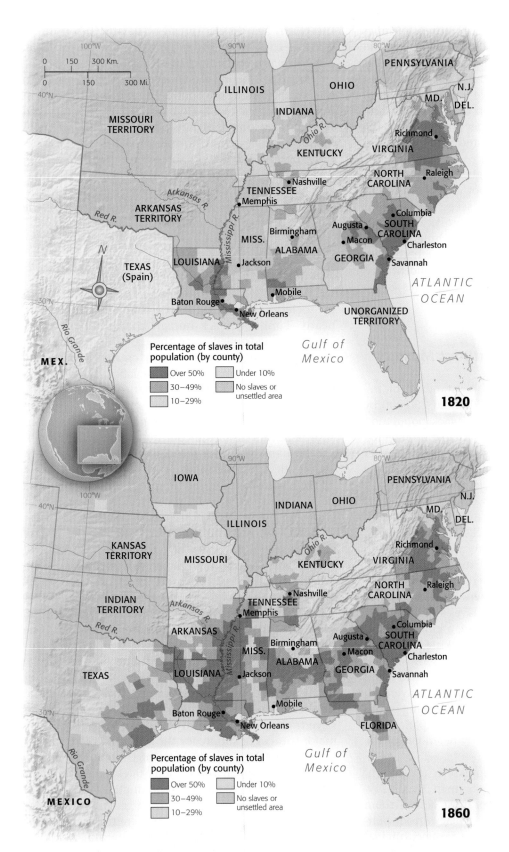

MAP 16.2 Southern Cotton Production and Distribution of Slaves, 1820 and 1860
The philosopher Ralph Waldo Emerson, a New Englander, declared in 1856, "I do not
see how a barbarous community and a civilized community can constitute a state.
I think we must get rid of slavery or we must get rid of freedom." © 2016 Cengage Learning

As independent small farmers, hundreds of miles distant from the heart of the Cotton Kingdom and rarely if ever in sight of a slave, these mountain whites had little in common with the whites of the flatlands. Many of them, including future president Andrew Johnson of Tennessee, hated both the haughty planters and their gangs of blacks. They looked upon the impending strife between North and South as "a rich man's war but a poor man's fight."

When the war came, the tough-fibered mountain whites constituted a vitally important peninsula of Unionism jutting down into the secessionist Southern sea. They ultimately played a significant role in crippling the Confederacy. Their attachment to the Union party of Abraham Lincoln was such that for generations after the Civil War, the only concentrated Republican strength in the solid South was to be found in the southern highlands.

✦ Free Blacks: Slaves Without Masters

Precarious in the extreme was the standing of the South's free blacks, who numbered about 250,000 by 1860. In the upper South, the free black population traced its origins to a wavelet of emancipation inspired by the idealism of Revolutionary days. In the deeper South, many free blacks were mulattoes, usually the emancipated children of a white planter and his black mistress. Throughout the South were some free blacks who had purchased their freedom with earnings from labor after hours. Many free blacks owned property, especially in New Orleans, where a sizable mulatto community prospered. Some, such as William T. Johnson, the "barber of Natchez," even owned slaves. He was the master of fifteen bondsmen; his diary records that in June 1848 he flogged two slaves and a mule.

The free blacks in the South were a kind of "third race." They were prohibited from working in certain occupations and forbidden from testifying against whites in court. They were always vulnerable to being hijacked back into slavery by unscrupulous slave traders. As free men and women, they were walking examples of what might be achieved by emancipation and hence were resented and detested by defenders of the slave system.

Free blacks were also unpopular in the North, where about another 250,000 of them lived. Several states forbade their entrance, most denied them the right to vote, and some barred blacks from public schools. In 1835 New Hampshire farmers hitched their oxen to a small schoolhouse that had dared to enroll fourteen black children and dragged it into a swamp. Northern blacks were especially hated by the pick-and-shovel Irish immigrants, with whom they competed for menial jobs. Much of the agitation in the North against the spread of slavery into the new territories in the 1840s and 1850s grew out of racial prejudice, not humanitarian idealism.

Antiblack feeling was in fact frequently stronger in the North than in the South. The gifted and eloquent former slave Frederick Douglass, an abolitionist and self-educated orator of rare power, was several times mobbed and beaten by northern rowdies. It was sometimes observed that white southerners, who were often suckled and reared by black nurses, liked the black as an individual but despised the race. The white northerner, on the other hand, often professed to like the race but disliked individual blacks.

✦ Plantation Slavery

In society's basement in the South of 1860 were nearly 4 million black human chattels. Their numbers had quadrupled since the dawn of the century, as the booming cotton economy created a seemingly unquenchable demand for slave labor. Legal importation of African slaves into America ended in 1808, when Congress outlawed slave imports. Britain had abolished the slave trade (but not slavery itself) in 1807, a milestone in the continuing struggle to establish human rights as a principle of international law. In the decades thereafter, the Royal Navy's **West Africa Squadron** seized hundreds of slave ships and freed thousands of grateful captives. Yet despite that effort, as many as 3 million enslaved Africans were shipped to Brazil and the West Indies in the several decades after 1807. In the United States, the price of "black ivory" was so high in the years before the Civil War that uncounted thousands of blacks were smuggled into the South, despite the death penalty for slavers. Although several slave traders were captured, southern juries repeatedly acquitted them. Only one slave trader, N. P. Gordon, was ever executed, and this took place in New York in 1862, the second year of the Civil War.

Ironically, the suppression of the international slave trade fostered the growth of a vigorous *internal* slave trade, as upper South states like Virginia became major sources of supply for the booming cotton economy of the Deep South. Most of the increase in the slave population in the United States came not from imports, but from natural reproduction—a fact that owed something to the accident of geography that the slave South lay outside the area where tropical diseases took such a grisly human toll. The natural reproduction of enslaved African Americans also distinguished North American slavery from slavery in more southerly New World societies and implied much about the tenor of the slave regime and the conditions of family life under slavery in the United States.

SOLOMON IN HIS PLANTATION SUIT.

Solomon Nor Theep

A Market in People (left) Held captive in a net, a slave sits on the Congo shore, waiting to be sold and shipped. (right) Once in the United States, slaves continued to be treated like commodities. Even free blacks in the northern states were at risk of being enslaved. Solomon Northrup (1808–1863?), shown on the right, was a musician living in upstate New York in 1841, when he was kidnapped by slave traders, shipped to New Orleans, and sold at auction. He spent twelve years enslaved on a Louisiana plantation. Regaining his freedom at last, he wrote a sensational account of his experience, "Twelve Years a Slave," published in 1853. More than 150 years later the book became the basis for a major Hollywood film.

Above all, the planters regarded their slaves as investments into which they had sunk nearly $2 billion of their capital by 1860. Slaves were the primary form of wealth in the South, and as such they were cared for as any asset is cared for by a prudent capitalist. Accordingly, they were sometimes, though by no means always, spared dangerous work, like putting a roof on a house. If a neck was going to be broken, the master preferred it to be that of a wage-earning Irish laborer rather than that of a prime field hand, worth $1,800 by 1860 (a price that had quintupled since 1800). Tunnel blasting and swamp draining were often consigned to itinerant gangs of expendable Irishmen because those perilous tasks were "death on niggers and mules."

Slavery was profitable for the great planters, though it hobbled the economic development of the region as a whole. The profits from the cotton boom sucked ever more slaves from the upper to the lower South, so that by 1860 the Deep South states of South Carolina, Florida, Mississippi, Alabama, and Louisiana each had a majority or near-majority of blacks and accounted for about half of all slaves in the South.

Breeding slaves in the way that cattle are bred was not openly encouraged. But thousands of blacks from the soil-exhausted slave states of the Old South, especially tobacco-depleted Virginia, were "sold down the river" to toil as field-gang laborers on the cotton frontier of the lower Mississippi Valley. Women who bore thirteen or fourteen babies were prized as "rattlin' good breeders," and some of these fecund females were promised their freedom when they had produced ten. White masters all too frequently would force their attentions on female slaves, fathering a sizable mulatto population, most of which remained enchained.

Slave auctions were brutal sights. The open selling of human flesh under the hammer, sometimes alongside cattle and horses, was among the most revolting aspects of slavery. On the auction block, families were

In 1852 Maria Perkins, a woman enslaved in Virginia, wrote plaintively to her husband about the disruption that the commercial traffic in slaves was visiting upon their family:

❝ I write you a letter to let you know of my distress my master has sold albert to a trader on Monday court day and myself and other child is for sale also and I want you to let hear from you very soon before next cort if you can I dont know when I dont want you to wait till Christmas I want you to tell Dr Hamelton and your master if either will buy me they can attend to it know and then I can go after-wards I dont want a trader to get me they asked me if I had got any person to buy me and I told them no they took me to the court houste too they never put me up a man buy the name of brady bought albert and is gone I dont know whare they say he lives in Scottesville my things is in several places some is in staunton and if I should be sold I dont know what will become of them I dont expect to meet with the luck to get that way till I am quite heart sick nothing more I am and ever will be your kind wife Maria Perkins. **❞**

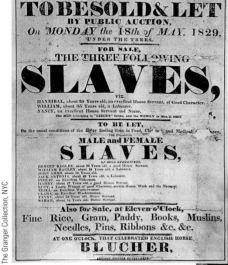

A Slave Auction   Abraham Lincoln said in 1865, "Whenever I hear anyone arguing for slavery, I feel a strong impulse to see it tried on him personally."

separated with distressing frequency, usually for economic reasons such as bankruptcy or the division of "property" among heirs. The sundering of families in this fashion was perhaps slavery's greatest psychological horror. Abolitionists decried the practice, and Harriet Beecher Stowe seized on the emotional power of this theme by putting it at the heart of the plot of her acclaimed 1852 novel, *Uncle Tom's Cabin.*

✦ Life Under the Lash

White southerners often romanticized about the happy life of their singing, dancing, banjo-strumming, joyful "darkies." But how did the slaves actually live? There is no simple answer to this question. Conditions varied greatly from region to region, from large plantation to small farm, and from master to master. Everywhere, of course, slavery meant hard work, ignorance, and oppression. The slaves—both men and women—usually toiled from dawn to dusk in the fields under the watchful eyes and ready whip-hand of a white overseer or black "driver." They had no civil or political rights, other than minimal protection from arbitrary murder or unusually cruel punishment. Some states offered further protections, such as banning the sale of a child under the age of ten away from his or her mother. But all such laws were difficult to enforce, since slaves were forbidden to testify in court or even to have their marriages legally recognized.

Floggings were common, for the whip was the substitute for the wage-incentive system and the most visible symbol of the planter's mastery. Strong-willed slaves were sometimes sent to **breakers**, whose technique consisted mostly in lavish laying on of the lash. As an abolitionist song of the 1850s lamented,

> *To-night the bond man, Lord*
> *Is bleeding in his chains;*
> *And loud the falling lash is heard*
> *On Carolina's plains!*

But savage beatings made sullen laborers, and lash marks hurt resale values. There are, to be sure, sadistic monsters in any population, and the planter class contained its share. But the typical planter had too much of his own prosperity riding on the backs of his slaves to beat them bloody on a regular basis.

By 1860 most slaves were concentrated in the **black belt** of the Deep South that stretched from South Carolina and Georgia into the new southwest states of Alabama, Mississippi, and Louisiana. This was the region of the southern frontier into which the explosively growing CottonKingdom had burst in a few short decades. As on all frontiers, life was often rough and raw, and in general the lot of the slave was harder here than in the more settled areas of the Old South.

A majority of blacks lived on larger plantations that harbored communities of twenty or more slaves. In some counties of the Deep South, especially along the lower Mississippi River, blacks accounted for more than 75 percent of the population. There the family life of slaves tended to be relatively stable, and a distinctive African American slave culture developed. Forced separations of spouses, parents, and children were evidently more common on smaller plantations and in the upper South. Slave marriage vows sometimes proclaimed, "Until death or *distance* do you part."

With impressive resilience, blacks managed to sustain family life in slavery, and most slaves were raised in stable two-parent households. Continuity of family identity across generations was evidenced in the widespread practice of naming children for grandparents or

The Cruelty of Slavery   Slaveowners used devices like this collar with bells to discipline and patrol their slaves. This female slave shown toiling in New Orleans has such a collar riveted around her neck, designed to prevent her from hiding from her master or escaping. Image and inset: The Historic New Orleans Collection, 1937.2.3

adopting the surname not of a current master but of a forebear's master. African Americans also displayed their African cultural roots when they avoided marriage between first cousins, in contrast to the frequent intermarriage of close relatives among the ingrown planter aristocracy.

African roots were also visible in the slaves' religious practices. Though heavily Christianized by the itinerant evangelists of the Second Great Awakening, blacks in slavery molded their own distinctive religious forms from a mixture of Christian and African elements. They emphasized those aspects of the Christian heritage that seemed most pertinent to their own situation—especially the captivity of the Israelites in Egypt. One of their most haunting spirituals implored,

Tell old Pharaoh
"Let my people go."

And another lamented,

Nobody knows de trouble I've had
Nobody knows but Jesus

African practices also persisted in the **responsorial** style of preaching, in which the congregation frequently

Slave Nurse and Young White Master Southern whites would not allow slaves to own property or exercise civil rights, but, paradoxically, they often entrusted them with the raising of their own precious children. Many a slave "mammy" served as a surrogate mother for the offspring of the planter class.

punctuated the minister's remarks with assents and amens—an adaptation of the give-and-take between caller and dancers in the African ringshout dance.

✦ The Burdens of Bondage

Slavery was intolerably degrading to the victims. They were deprived of the dignity and sense of responsibility that come from independence and the right to make choices. They were denied an education, because reading brought ideas, and ideas brought discontent. Many states passed laws forbidding their instruction, and perhaps nine-tenths of adult slaves at the beginning of the Civil War were totally illiterate. For all slaves—indeed for virtually all blacks, slave or free—the "American dream" of bettering one's lot through study and hard work was a cruel and empty mockery.

Not surprisingly, victims of the "peculiar institution" devised countless ways to throw sand in its gears. When workers are not voluntarily hired and adequately compensated, they can hardly be expected to work with alacrity. Accordingly, slaves often slowed the pace of their labor to the barest minimum that would spare them the lash, thus fostering the myth of black "laziness" in the minds of whites. They filched food from the "big house" and pilfered other goods that had been produced or purchased by their labor. They sabotaged expensive equipment, stopping the work routine altogether until repairs were accomplished. Occasionally they even poisoned their masters' food.

The slaves also universally pined for freedom. Many took to their heels as runaways, frequently in search of a separated family member. A black girl, asked if her mother was dead, replied, "Yessir, master, she is dead, but she's free." Others rebelled, though never successfully. In 1800 an armed insurrection led by a slave named Gabriel in Richmond, Virginia, was foiled by informers, and its leaders were hanged. Denmark Vesey, a free black, led another ill-fated rebellion in Charleston, South Carolina, in 1822. Also betrayed by informers, Vesey and more than thirty followers were publicly strung from the gallows. In 1831 the semiliterate Nat Turner, a visionary black preacher, led an uprising that slaughtered about sixty Virginians, mostly women and children. Reprisals were swift and bloody, and **Nat Turner's rebellion** was soon extinguished.

An especially dramatic episode involved the enslaved Africans who rebelled aboard the Spanish slave ship ***Amistad*** in 1839. They seized command of the vessel off the coast of Cuba and attempted to sail back to Africa but were driven ashore on Long Island. After two years of imprisonment and several trials, former president John Quincy Adams finally secured their

Arise! Arise! and weep no more dry up your tears, we shall part no more, Come rose we go to Tennessee, that happy Shore to old virginia never — never — return. —

Slaves Being Marched from Staunton, Virginia, to Tennessee, by Lewis Miller, 1853 In this folk painting of slaves in transit from the upper South to the new cotton lands of the lower South, couples travel together and children accompany parents. In reality the forced movement of slaves often involved the painful separation of family members.

freedom in a brilliant, moving argument before the U.S. Supreme Court in 1841, and the Africans returned to the British colony of Sierra Leone, in West Africa.

The dark taint of slavery also left its mark on whites. It fostered the brutality of the whip, the bloodhound, and the branding iron. White southerners increasingly lived in a state of imagined siege, surrounded by potentially rebellious blacks inflamed by abolitionist propaganda from the North. Their fears bolstered an intoxicating theory of biological racial superiority and turned the South into a reactionary backwater in an era of progress—one of the last bastions of slavery in the Western world. The defenders of slavery were forced to degrade themselves, along with their victims. As Booker T. Washington, a distinguished black leader and former slave, later observed, whites could not hold blacks in a ditch without getting down there with them.

✴ Early Abolitionism

The inhumanity of the "peculiar institution" gradually caused antislavery societies to sprout forth. Abolitionist sentiment first stirred at the time of the Revolution, especially among Quakers (see Map 16.3). Because of the widespread loathing of blacks, some of the earliest abolitionist efforts focused on transporting blacks bodily back to Africa. The **American Colonization Society** was founded for this purpose in 1817, and in 1822 the Republic of **Liberia**, on the fever-stricken West African coast, was established for former slaves. Its capital, Monrovia, was named after President Monroe. Some fifteen thousand freed blacks were transported there over the

Contending Voices
Perspectives on Race and Slavery

American slavery was inextricably bound up with American attitudes about race. William A. Smith (1802–1870), a southern clergyman college president, defended slavery on explicitly racial grounds in 1856:

❝ [Africans] are a distinct race of people, separated by strongly marked lines of moral and physical condition from those amongst whom they reside. This difference is so strongly marked that there can be no spontaneous amalgamation by intermarriage, and consequently no reciprocity of social rights and privileges between the races.... They must therefore continue to exist as a separate race. ❞

At its founding meeting in 1833, the American Anti-Slavery Society declared

❝ that all persons of color who possess the qualifications which are demanded of others ought to be admitted forthwith to the enjoyment of the same privileges, and the exercise of the same prerogatives, as others; and that the paths of preferment, of wealth, and of intelligence should be opened as widely to them as to persons of a white complexion. ❞

> What common ground, if any, lay between those two positions?

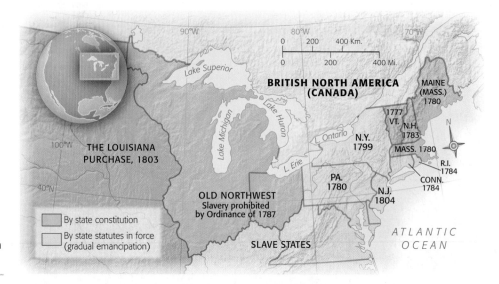

MAP 16.3 Early Emancipation in the North © 2016 Cengage Learning

next four decades. But most blacks had no wish to be transplanted into a strange civilization after having become partially Americanized. By 1860 virtually all southern slaves were no longer Africans, but native-born African Americans, with their own distinctive history and culture. Yet the colonization idea appealed to some antislaveryites, including Abraham Lincoln, until the time of the Civil War.

In the 1830s the abolitionist movement took on new energy and momentum, mounting to the proportions of a crusade. American abolitionists took heart in 1833 when their British counterparts, inspired by the redoubtable William Wilberforce,

Tag Identifying Slaves and Free Blacks in Charleston
All slaves in Charleston, South Carolina, were reminded of their status as property by the tags they were forced to wear, marked with their skills—such as porter or mechanic or carpenter—and the year the tag was issued. After 1848 even free blacks had to wear tags, ensuring that no African American could be anonymous in the city. The badge above was issued to a freed slave in Charleston, South Carolina, sometime after 1848. American Numismatic Society

a member of Parliament and an evangelical Christian reformer whose family had been touched by the preaching of George Whitefield (see Chapter 5), unchained the slaves in the West Indies (see "Thinking Globally: The Struggle to Abolish Slavery," pp. 356–357). (Wilberforce University in Ohio, an African American college that later sent many missionaries to Africa, is named for him.)

As with Wilberforce, the religious spirit of the Second Great Awakening now inflamed the hearts of many American abolitionists against the sin of slavery. Prominent among them was lanky, tousle-haired Theodore Dwight Weld, who had been evangelized by Charles Grandison Finney in New York's Burned-Over District in the 1820s. Self-educated and simple in manner and speech, Weld appealed with special power and directness to his rural audiences of untutored farmers.

Spiritually inspired by Finney, Weld was materially aided by two wealthy and devout New York merchants, the brothers Arthur and Lewis Tappan. In 1832 they paid his way to Lane Theological Seminary in Cincinnati, Ohio, which was presided over by the formidable Lyman Beecher, father of a remarkable brood, including novelist Harriet Beecher Stowe, reformer Catharine Beecher, and preacher-abolitionist Henry Ward Beecher. Expelled along with several other students in 1834 for organizing an eighteen-day debate on slavery, Weld and his fellow "Lane Rebels"—full of the energy and idealism of youth—fanned out across the Old Northwest preaching the antislavery gospel. Humorless and deadly earnest, Weld also assembled a potent propaganda pamphlet, *American Slavery as It Is* (1839). Its compelling arguments made it among the most effective abolitionist tracts and greatly influenced Harriet Beecher Stowe's *Uncle Tom's Cabin.*

ANTI-SLAVERY EVENTS

DURING THE YEAR ENDING 5TH MARCH

1863.

AM I NOT A MAN AND A BROTHER

AM I NOT A WOMAN AND A SISTER

" Can we behold, unheeding,
Life's holiest feelings crush'd ;—
While *Woman's* heart is bleeding,
Shall *Woman's* voice be hush'd ?"

Boston Athenaeum

"Am I Not a Man and a Brother? Am I Not a Woman and a Sister?" A popular appeal.

✷ Radical Abolitionism

On New Year's Day, 1831, a shattering abolitionist blast came from the bugle of William Lloyd Garrison, a mild-looking reformer of twenty-six. The emotionally high-strung son of a drunken father and a spiritual child of the Second Great Awakening, Garrison published in Boston the first issue of his militantly antislavery newspaper, ***The Liberator***. With this mighty paper broadside, Garrison triggered a thirty-year war of words and in a sense fired one of the opening barrages of the Civil War.

Stern and uncompromising, Garrison nailed his colors to the masthead of his weekly. He proclaimed in strident tones that under no circumstances would he tolerate the poisonous weed of slavery but would stamp it out at once, root and branch:

> *I will be as harsh as truth and as uncompromising as justice....I am in earnest—I will not equivocate—I will not excuse—I will not retreat a single inch—and I WILL BE HEARD!*

Other dedicated abolitionists rallied to Garrison's standard, and in 1833 they founded the **American Anti-Slavery Society**. Prominent among them was Wendell Phillips, a Boston patrician known as "abolition's golden trumpet." A man of strict principle, he would eat no cane sugar and wear no cotton cloth, since both were produced by southern slaves.

Black abolitionists distinguished themselves as living monuments to the cause of African American freedom. Their ranks included David Walker, whose incendiary ***Appeal to the Colored Citizens of the World*** (1829) advocated a bloody end to white supremacy. Also noteworthy were Sojourner Truth, a freed black woman in New York who fought tirelessly for black emancipation and women's rights, and Martin Delany, one of the few black leaders to take seriously the notion of the mass recolonization of Africa. In 1859 he visited West Africa's Niger Valley seeking a suitable site for relocation.

The greatest of the black abolitionists was Frederick Douglass. Escaping from bondage in 1838 at the age of twenty-one, he was "discovered" by the abolitionists in 1841 when he gave a stunning impromptu speech at an antislavery meeting in Massachusetts. Thereafter he lectured widely for the cause, despite frequent beatings and threats against his life. In 1845 he published his classic autobiography, ***Narrative of the Life of Frederick Douglass***. It depicted his remarkable origins as the son of a black slave woman and a white father, his struggle to learn to read and write, and his eventual escape to the North.

Douglass was as flexibly practical as Garrison was stubbornly principled. Garrison often appeared to be more interested in his own righteousness than in the substance of the slavery evil itself. He repeatedly demanded that the "virtuous" North secede from the "wicked" South. Yet he did not explain how the creation of an independent slave republic would bring an end to the "damning crime" of slavery. Renouncing politics, on the Fourth of July, 1854, he publicly burned a copy of the Constitution as "a covenant with death and an agreement with hell" (a phrase he borrowed from a Shaker condemnation of marriage). Critics, including some of his former supporters, charged that Garrison was cruelly probing the moral wound in America's underbelly but offering no acceptable balm to ease the pain.

Douglass, on the other hand, along with other abolitionists, increasingly looked to politics to end the

Frederick Douglass (1817?–1895), the remarkable ex-slave, told of Mr. Covey, a white owner who bought a single female slave "as a breeder." She gave birth to twins at the end of the year:

❝ At this addition to the human stock Covey and his wife were ecstatic with joy. No one dreamed of reproaching the woman or finding fault with the hired man, Bill Smith, the father of the children, for Mr. Covey himself had locked the two up together every night, thus inviting the result. **❞**

Bellegrove Plantation, Donaldsville, Louisiana, Built 1857

The sugar-growing Bellegrove Plantation—on the banks of the Mississippi River ninety-five miles north of New Orleans—was laid out on a grander scale than many southern plantations. In this rendering from an advertisement for Bellegrove's sale in 1867, the planter John Orr's home was identified as a "mansion," and quarters for his field hands proved extensive: twenty double cabins built for slaves (now for "Negroes") and a dormitory, described in the ad but not pictured here, housing 150 laborers. Because of the unhealthy work involved in cultivating sugar cane, such as the constant digging of drainage canals to keep the cane from rotting in standing water, many planters hired immigrant (usually Irish) labor to keep their valuable slaves out of physical danger. The presence of a hospital between the slave cabins and the mansion indicates the very real threat to health. The layout of Bellegrove reflects the organization of production as well as the social relations on a sugar plantation. The storehouse where preserved sugar awaited shipping stood closest to the Mississippi River, the principal transportation route, whereas the sugar house, the most important building on the plantation, with its mill, boilers, and cooking vats for converting syrup into sugar, dominated the canefields. Although the "big house" and slave quarters stood in close proximity, hedges surrounding the planter's home shut out views of both sugar production and labor. Within the slave quarters, the overseer's larger house signified his superior status, while the arrangement of cabins ensured his supervision of domestic as well as work life. What else does the physical layout of the plantation reveal about settlement patterns, sugar cultivation, and social relationships along the Mississippi?

The Historic New Orleans Collection, 1970.13.2 i-iv.

blight of slavery. These political abolitionists backed the Liberty party in 1840, the Free Soil party in 1848, and eventually the Republican party in the 1850s. In the end, most abolitionists, including even the pacifistic Garrison himself, followed the logic of their beliefs and supported a frightfully costly fratricidal war as the price of emancipation.

High-minded and courageous, the abolitionists were men and women of goodwill and various colors who faced the cruel choice that people of good conscience in many ages have had thrust upon them: when is evil so enormous that it must be denounced, even at the risk of precipitating bloodshed and butchery?

Sojourner Truth Also known simply as "Isabella," she held audiences spellbound with her deep, resonant voice and the religious passion with which she condemned the sin of slavery. This photo was taken about 1870.

Frederick Douglass (1817?–1895) Born a slave in Maryland, Douglass escaped to the North and became the most prominent of the black abolitionists. Gifted as an orator, writer, and editor, he continued to battle for the civil rights of his people after emancipation. Near the end of a distinguished career, he served as U.S. minister to Haiti. Photo by Fotosearch/Getty Images

✹ The South Lashes Back

Antislavery sentiment was not unknown in the South, and in the 1820s antislavery societies were more numerous south of the **Mason-Dixon line*** than north of it. But after about 1830, the voice of white southern abolitionism was silenced. In a last gasp of southern questioning of slavery, the Virginia legislature debated and eventually defeated various emancipation proposals in 1831–1832. That debate marked a turning point. Thereafter all the slave states tightened their slave codes and moved to prohibit emancipation of any kind, voluntary or compensated. Nat Turner's rebellion in 1831 sent a wave of hysteria sweeping over the snowy cotton fields, and planters in growing numbers, recollecting the massive slave revolt that had erupted in Haiti in the 1790s, slept with pistols by their pillows. Although Garrison had no demonstrable connection with the Turner conspiracy, his *Liberator* appeared at about the same time, and he was bitterly condemned as a terrorist and an

*Originally the southern boundary of colonial Pennsylvania.

inciter of murder. The state of Georgia offered $5,000 for his arrest and conviction.

The nullification crisis of 1832 further implanted haunting fears in white southern minds, conjuring up nightmares of black incendiaries and abolitionist

After hearing Frederick Douglass speak in Bristol, England, in 1846, Mary A. Estlin wrote to an American abolitionist,

❝ [T]here is but one opinion of him. Wherever he goes he arouses sympathy in your cause and love for himself. . . . Our expectations were highly roused by his narrative, his printed speeches, and the eulogisms of the friends with whom he has been staying: but he far exceeds the picture we had formed both in outward graces, intellectual power and culture, and eloquence. **❞** *

*From Clare Taylor, ed., *British and American Abolitionists: An Episode in Transatlantic Understanding* (Edinburgh University Press, 1974), p. 282.

The Struggle to Abolish Slavery

hen slaves in the French Caribbean colony of Saint-Domingue, inspired by the Revolutionary fervor that had seized mainland France, rose up and demanded "liberty, equality, and fraternity" for themselves, they became, in 1794, the first enslaved people in the New World to win their freedom. They went on to proclaim their independence from France in 1804 by creating the Republic of Haiti. Meanwhile, in 1802, Napoleon had reinstated slavery in what remained of his Caribbean empire. It would take another revolution in France, in 1848, to secure permanent emancipation throughout the French Caribbean.

Table 16.1 documents the long, 250-year struggle to abolish slavery throughout the world. Agitators outraged by the scourge of human bondage and committed to ending it, known as abolitionists, shared antislavery sentiments and strategies across national boundaries. From the late seventeenth through the mid-nineteenth century, British and American abolitionists wove dense networks of mutual support. They shared writings, lecturers, and funding and jointly sponsored conferences such as the World's Anti-Slavery Convention of 1840 in London, which became famous for inspiring the American women's rights movement when it refused to seat female delegates.

But the political fortunes of abolitionist movements, and hence the timing of the longed-for day of freedom, varied sharply from nation to nation. In France emancipation was twice tied to revolutions. In Great Britain massive citizens' petition campaigns, orchestrated by venerable lifelong abolitionist leaders such as William Wilberforce, brought enormous popular pressure to bear on the government. Parliament eventually responded by outlawing the slave trade in 1807 and then, three days before Wilberforce died in 1833, prohibiting slavery itself throughout most of the British Empire.

The antislavery impulse in the United States sprung from a variety of sources. Some abolitionists opposed the brutality of the trade in human beings because they idealistically believed that the end of slavery was tied directly to humanity's progress. Others wished for the economic and labor systems in the South to more closely resemble northern models of free labor. Ideas about what might come after abolition were similarly diverse; while some hoped that former slaves might continue to work in their communities, others supported colonization, the repatriation of freemen to countries in Africa.

The Granger Collection, NYC

World's Anti-Slavery Convention, London, 1840 The convention assembled antislavery advocates from around the world, but it refused to seat female delegates. Women were allowed to observe, but not to take part in, the official proceedings. The frustrations of the unseated American representatives led to the historic Woman's Rights Convention at Seneca Falls, New York, in 1848 (see p. 320).

In the United States as in Britain, abolitionism became a robust social movement, propelled not least by women and free blacks. The issue had first become highly politicized in the 1770s, though during the Constitutional Convention delegates had chosen not to ban slavery in the new United States. By the 1830s, debates had heated up again as abolitionists objected to the expansion of slavery into the growing western territories of the country. But the roots of the "peculiar institution" in the United States ran wide and deep. Even though the American slave trade was ended in 1808, a widespread internal trade continued, and it took the Union's victory in a bloody Civil War in 1865 to eradicate slavery once and for all. Elsewhere in the Americas, enslaved peoples secured their freedom gradually and, in stark contrast to the United States, peacefully. Emancipation typically became possible only after the achievement of independence from Spain, where abolitionism never gained much traction. Cuba, still a Spanish colony into the 1890s, was among the last places in the New World to set its slaves free.

TABLE 16.1 Comparative Abolition of Slavery

Country	Date Abolished	Notes
Mexico	1829	The slave trade was prohibited in 1824, but slavery itself was not abolished until 1829, eight years after Mexico gained independence from Spain.
Great Britain	1833	The slave trade was ended in 1807, but slavery was not abolished until 1833. The abolition of slavery did not apply to British India, where slavery persisted until 1860.*
France	1848	Slavery was first abolished in 1794 but was reestablished by Napoleon Bonaparte in 1802. In 1848 the Second Republic replaced the July Monarchy and abolished slavery in all French colonies.
Bolivia	1851	All slaves born since independence (1825) were freed in 1831, but slavery was not abolished entirely until 1851.
Ecuador	1852	At the time of independence in 1821, all children born to slaves after that date were declared free, but slavery persisted until 1852.
Peru	1854	At the time of independence in 1821, all children born to slaves after that date were declared free, but slavery was not abolished entirely until 1854.
Argentina	1854	Emancipation, first begun in 1813, was completed in 1854.
Venezuela	1854	Gradual emancipation began when independence was fully secured in 1821, but slavery was not completely abolished until 1854.
Russia	1861	Peter the Great first abolished slavery in 1723 by converting household slaves into serfs. Tsar Alexander II freed Russia's 22 million serfs in 1861.
Netherlands	1863	Slavery was abolished in all Dutch colonies.
United States	1865	The slave trade was ended in 1808, but slavery was not abolished entirely until after the Civil War, with the ratification of the Thirteenth Amendment. Slavery was abolished earlier in the North, in the decades after the Revolution, often through gradual emancipation.
Paraguay	1869	Gradual emancipation began in 1842, but slavery was not abolished until 1869.
Cuba	1886	Gradual emancipation began in 1870; the Spanish government freed the remaining slaves in 1886.
Brazil	1888	The slave trade was abolished in 1851. A gradual emancipation law was first passed in 1871, but slavery was not abolished entirely until 1888.
Korea	1894	State-owned slaves were emancipated in 1801. Although slavery was formally abolished in 1894, it persisted in some regions until the 1930s.
China	1949	The emperor abolished slavery toward the end of the Xing dynasty, in 1910, but it persisted until the communist government proclaimed abolition in 1949.
Saudi Arabia	1962	Slavery was abolished under pressure from the United Nations and moderate Arab states.
Yemen	1962	Leaders of the newly proclaimed Yemen Arab Republic abolished slavery after overthrowing the imamate in 1962.

*The British East India Company had sovereignty over India until 1858, when the British government took over—and abolished slavery shortly thereafter.

Sources: Martin A. Klein, *Historical Dictionary of Slavery and Abolition* (2002); Robert Fogel, *Without Consent of Contract* (1994); Herbert Klein, *African Slavery in Latin America and the Caribbean* (1986); Edward Alpers, Gwyn Campbell, and Michael Salman, eds., *Slavery and Resistance in Africa and Asia* (2005); Jerome Alan Cohen, R. Randle Edwards, and Fu-mei Chang Chen, *Essays on China's Legal Tradition* (1980).

devils. Jailings, whippings, and lynchings now greeted rational efforts to discuss the slavery problem in the South.

Proslavery whites responded by launching a massive defense of slavery as a positive good. In doing so, they forgot their own section's previous doubts about the morality of the "peculiar institution." Slavery, they claimed, was supported by the authority of the Bible and the wisdom of Aristotle. It was good for the Africans, who were lifted from the barbarism of the jungle and clothed with the blessings of Christian civilization. Slavemasters strongly encouraged religion in the slave quarters. A catechism for blacks contained such passages as

Q. Who gave you a master and a mistress?
A. God gave them to me.
Q. Who says that you must obey them?
A. God says that I must.

White apologists also claimed that master-slave relationships really resembled those of a family. On many plantations, especially those of the Old South of Virginia and Maryland, this argument had a certain plausibility. A slave's tombstone bore this touching inscription:

JOHN:
A faithful servant:
and true friend:

Kindly, and considerate:
Loyal, and affectionate:
The family he served
Honours him in death:
But, in life they gave him love:
For he was one of them

Southern whites were quick to contrast the "happy" lot of their "servants" with that of the overworked northern wage slaves, including sweated women and stunted children. The blacks mostly toiled in the fresh air and sunlight, not in dark and stuffy factories. They did not have to worry about slack times or unemployment, as did the "hired hands" of the North. Provided with a jail-like form of Social Security, they were cared for in sickness and old age, unlike northern workers, who were set adrift when they had outlived their usefulness.

These curious proslavery arguments only widened the chasm between a backward-looking South and a forward-looking North—and indeed much of the rest of the Western world. The southerners reacted defensively to the pressure of their own fears and bristled before the merciless nagging of the northern abolitionists. Increasingly the white South turned in upon itself and grew hotly intolerant of any embarrassing questions about the status of slavery.

In Defense of Slavery This pair of illustrations contrasts the supposedly benevolent slave regime of the South with the harshness of working life in England, where starvation wages and unemployment blighted workers' lives. Apologists for slavery frequently invoked this comparison between allegedly paternalistic slavemasters and the uncaring capitalists who captained the Industrial Revolution.

Regrettably, also, the controversy over free people endangered free speech in the entire country. Piles of petitions poured in upon Congress from the antislavery reformers, and in 1836 sensitive southerners drove through the House the so-called **Gag Resolution**. It required all such antislavery appeals to be tabled without debate. This attack on the right of petition aroused the sleeping lion in the aged ex-president, Representative John Quincy Adams, and he waged a successful eight-year fight for its repeal.

Southern whites likewise resented the flooding of their mails with incendiary abolitionist literature. Even if blacks could not read, they could interpret the inflammatory drawings, such as those that showed masters knocking out slaves' teeth with clubs. In 1835 a mob in Charleston, South Carolina, looted the post office and burned a pile of abolitionist propaganda. Capitulating to southern pressures, the Washington government in 1835 ordered southern postmasters to destroy abolitionist material and called on southern state officials to arrest federal postmasters who did not comply. Such was "freedom of the press" as guaranteed by the Constitution.

★ The Abolitionist Impact in the North

Abolitionists—especially the extreme Garrisonians—were for a long time unpopular in many parts of the North. Northerners had been brought up to revere the Constitution and to regard the clauses on slavery as a lasting bargain. The ideal of Union, hammered home by the thundering eloquence of Daniel Webster and others, had taken deep root, and Garrison's wild talk of secession grated harshly on northern ears.

The North also had a heavy economic stake in Dixieland. By the late 1850s, southern planters owed northern bankers and other creditors about $300 million, and much of this immense sum would be lost—as, in fact, it later was—should the Union dissolve. New England textile mills were fed with cotton raised by the slaves, and a disrupted labor system might cut off this vital supply and bring unemployment. The Union during these critical years was partly bound together with cotton threads, tied by lords of the loom in collaboration with the so-called lords of the lash. It was not surprising that strong hostility developed in the North against the boat-rocking tactics of the radical antislaveryites.

Repeated tongue-lashings by the extreme abolitionists provoked many mob outbursts in the North, some led by respectable gentlemen. A gang of young toughs broke into Lewis Tappan's New York house in 1834 and demolished its interior while a crowd in the street cheered. In 1835 Garrison, with a rope tied around him, was dragged through the streets of Boston by the so-called Broadcloth Mob but escaped almost miraculously. Reverend Elijah P. Lovejoy of Alton, Illinois, not content to assail slavery, impugned the chastity of Catholic women. His printing press was destroyed four times, and in 1837 he was killed in a ferocious gun battle with an anti-abolitionist mob and became "the martyr abolitionist." So unpopular were the antislavery zealots that ambitious politicians, like Lincoln, usually avoided the taint of Garrisonian abolition like the plague.

Yet by the 1850s the abolitionist outcry had made a deep dent in the northern mind. Many citizens had come to see the South as the land of the unfree and the home of a hateful institution. Few northerners were prepared to abolish slavery outright, but a growing number, including Lincoln, opposed extending it to the western territories. People of this stamp, commonly called "free-soilers," swelled their ranks as the Civil War approached.

[*Varying Viewpoints*]
What Was the True Nature of Slavery?

By the early twentieth century, the predictable accounts of slavery written by partisans of the North or South had receded in favor of a romantic vision of the Old South conveyed through popular literature, myth, and, increasingly, scholarship. That vision was persuasively validated by the publication of Ulrich Bonnell Phillips's landmark study, *American Negro Slavery* (1918). Phillips made three key arguments. First, he claimed that slavery was a dying economic institution, unprofitable to the slaveowner and an obstacle to the economic development of the South as a whole. Second, he contended that slavery was a rather benign institution and that the planters, contrary to abolitionist charges of ruthless exploitation, treated their chattels with kindly paternalism. Third, he reflected the dominant racial attitudes of his time in his belief that blacks were inferior and submissive by nature and did not abhor the institution that enslaved them.

For nearly a century, historians have debated these assertions, sometimes heatedly. More sophisticated economic analysis has refuted Phillips's claim that slavery would have withered away without a war. Economic historians have demonstrated that slavery was a viable, profitable, expanding economic system and that slaves constituted a worthwhile investment for their owners. The price of a prime field hand rose dramatically, even in the 1850s.

No such definitive conclusion has yet been reached in the disputes over slave treatment. Frank Tannenbaum's classic comparative study, *Slave and Citizen* (1947), argued that slavery was more humane in Latin America than in the United States, leaving a legacy of less sharply defined racial castes there. Beginning in the late 1950s, historians came increasingly to emphasize the harshness of the U.S. slave system. One study, Stanley Elkins's *Slavery* (1959), went so far as to compare the "peculiar institution" to the Nazi concentration camps of World War II. Both were "total institutions," Elkins contended, which "infantilized" their victims.

Still later, scholars such as Eugene Genovese moved beyond debating whether slavery was kind or cruel. Without diminishing the deprivations and pains of slavery, Genovese conceded that slavery embraced a strange form of paternalism, a system that reflected not the benevolence of southern slaveholders, but their need to control and coax work out of their reluctant and often recalcitrant "investments." Furthermore, within this paternalistic system, black slaves were able to make reciprocal demands of their white owners and to protect a "cultural space" of their own in which family and religion particularly could flourish. The crowning paradox of slaveholder paternalism was that in treating their property more humanely, slaveowners implicitly recognized the humanity of their slaves and thereby subverted the racist underpinnings upon which their slave society existed.

The revised conceptions of the master-slave relationship also spilled over into the debate about slave personality. Elkins accepted Phillips's portrait of the slave as a childlike "Sambo" but saw it as a consequence of slavery rather than a congenital attribute of African Americans. Kenneth Stampp, rejecting the Sambo stereotype, stressed the frequency and variety of slave resistance, both mild and militant. A third view, imaginatively documented in the work of Lawrence Levine, argued that the Sambo character was an act, an image that slaves used to confound their masters without incurring punishment. Levine's *Black*

Culture and Black Consciousness (1977) shares with books by John Blassingame and Herbert Gutman an emphasis on the tenacity with which slaves maintained their own culture and kin relations, despite the hardships of bondage. Most recently, historians have attempted to avoid the polarity of repression versus autonomy. They assert the debasing oppression of slavery, while also acknowledging slaves' ability to resist the dehumanizing effects of enslavement. For example, Walter Johnson's *Soul by Soul* (1999) details the horrors of the slave market but explains the multitude of ways that enslaved people could influence their own sale and position. The challenge before historians today is to capture the vibrancy of slave culture and its legacy for African American society after emancipation, without diminishing the brutality of life under the southern slave regime.

A new sensitivity to gender, spurred by the growing field of women's history, has also expanded the horizons of slavery studies. Historians such as Elizabeth Fox-Genovese, Jacqueline Jones, and Jennifer Morgan have focused on the ways in which slavery differed for men and women, both slaves and slaveholders. Enslaved black women, for example, had the unique task of negotiating an identity out of their multiple responsibilities as plantation laborers, caretakers of white women and children, and anchors of their families. They were also, in a crude but quite real sense, engines for generating capital, as their offspring became slaveholder assets. By tracing the interconnectedness of race and gender in the American South, these historians have also shown how slavery shaped conceptions of masculinity and femininity within southern society, further distinguishing its culture from that of the North.

Scholarship on slavery continues to grow. Work by Philip D. Morgan and Ira Berlin has drawn attention to how both the institution of slavery and the experience of the enslaved changed over time. They have contended that slavery was far from monolithic. Rather, it adapted to particular geographic and environmental factors, which influenced the diet and work routines of slaves and shaped the degree of autonomy in family life and culture that slaves were able to carve out. Slavery also changed from one generation to the next. As southern slaveholders responded to new social and economic conditions, they gradually altered the legal status of slaves, making slavery a hereditary condition, outlawing manumission in many places, rendering freedom for the enslaved increasingly difficult to attain, and placing onerous restrictions on the work opportunities and mobility of free African Americans. One of the most recent and overarching syntheses of Atlantic slavery, David Brion Davis's *Inhuman Bondage* (2008), stresses the dehumanization inherent to slavery, especially in harsh New World systems.

Chapter Review

KEY TERMS

West Africa Squadron (346)
breakers (349)
black belt (349)
responsorial (350)
Nat Turner's rebellion (350)
Amistad (350)
American Colonization Society (351)
Liberia (351)

The Liberator (353)
American Anti-Slavery Society (353)
Appeal to the Colored Citizens of the World (353)
Narrative of the Life of Frederick Douglass (353)
Mason-Dixon line (355)
Gag Resolution (359)

PEOPLE TO KNOW

William T. Johnson
Nat Turner
William Wilberforce
Theodore Dwight Weld
William Lloyd Garrison
David Walker
Sojourner Truth
Martin Delany
Frederick Douglass

CHRONOLOGY

1793	Whitney's cotton gin transforms southern economy
1800	Gabriel slave rebellion in Virginia
1807	Britain abolishes slave trade
1808	Congress outlaws slave trade / Royal Navy forms West Africa Squadron
1817	American Colonization Society formed
1820	Missouri Compromise
1822	Vesey slave rebellion in Charleston, South Carolina / Republic of Liberia established in Africa
1829	Walker publishes *Appeal to the Colored Citizens of the World*
1831	Nat Turner slave rebellion in Virginia / Garrison begins publishing *The Liberator*
1831–1832	Virginia legislature debates slavery and emancipation
1833	British abolish slavery in West Indies / American Anti-Slavery Society founded
1834	Abolitionist students expelled from Lane Theological Seminary
1835	U.S. Post Office orders destruction of abolitionist mail / "Broadcloth Mob" attacks Garrison
1836	House of Representatives passes "Gag Resolution"
1837	Mob kills abolitionist Lovejoy in Alton, Illinois
1839	Weld publishes *American Slavery as It Is* / Slave revolt aboard *Amistad*
1845	Douglass publishes *Narrative of the Life of Frederick Douglass*
1848	Free Soil party organized

TO LEARN MORE

Erskine Clarke, *Dwelling Place: A Plantation Epic* (2005)

Frederick Douglass, *Narrative of the Life of Frederick Douglass* (1845)

John Hope Franklin, *From Slavery to Freedom* (8th ed., 2000)

John Craig Hammond, *Slavery, Freedom, and Expansion in the Early American West* (2007)

Anya Jabour, *Scarlett's Sisters: Young Women in the Old South* (2007)

Julie Roy Jeffrey, *The Great Silent Army of Abolitionism: Ordinary Women in the Antislavery Movement* (1998)

Walter Johnson, *Soul by Soul: Life Inside the Antebellum Slave Market* (2001)

Stephanie McCurry, *Masters of Small Worlds: Yeoman Households, Gender Relations, and the Political Culture of the Antebellum South* (1995)

Melton Alonza McLaurin, *Celia, a Slave* (1991)

Joshua Rothman, *Notorious in the Neighborhood: Sex and Families Across the Color Line in Virginia, 1787–1861* (2003)

James B. Stewart, *Holy Warriors* (1976)

Gavin Wright, *Slavery and American Economic Development* (2006)

A complete, annotated bibliography for this chapter—along with brief descriptions of the People to Know—may be found on the *American Pageant* website. The key terms are defined in the glossary at the end of the text.

Chapter 17

Manifest Destiny and Its Legacy

1841–1848

Our manifest destiny [is] to overspread the continent allotted by Providence for the free development of our yearly multiplying millions.

JOHN L. O'SULLIVAN, 1845*

Territorial expansion dominated American diplomacy and politics in the 1840s. Settlers swarming into the still-disputed Oregon Country aggravated relations with Britain, which had staked its own claims in the Pacific Northwest. The clamor to annex Texas to the Union provoked bitter tension with Mexico, which continued to regard Texas as a Mexican province in revolt. And when Americans began casting covetous eyes on Mexico's northernmost province, the great prize of California, open warfare erupted between the United States and its southern neighbor. Victory over Mexico added vast new domains to the United States, but it also raised thorny questions about the status of slavery in the newly acquired territories—questions that would be answered in blood in the Civil War of the 1860s.

⭐ The Accession of "Tyler Too"

A horde of hard-ciderites descended upon Washington early in 1841, clamoring for the spoils of office. Newly elected President Harrison, bewildered by the uproar, was almost hounded to death by Whig spoilsmen.

The real leaders of the Whig party regarded "Old Tippecanoe" as little more than an impressive figurehead. Daniel Webster, as secretary of state, and Henry Clay, the uncrowned king of the Whigs and their ablest spokesman in the Senate, would grasp the helm. The aging general was finally forced to rebuke the overzealous

Clay and pointedly remind him that he, William Henry Harrison, was president of the United States.

Unluckily for Clay and Webster, their schemes soon hit a fatal snag. Before the new term had fairly started, Harrison contracted pneumonia. Wearied by official functions and plagued by office seekers, the enfeebled old warrior died after only four weeks in the White House—by far the shortest administration in American history, following by far the longest inaugural address.

The "Tyler too" part of the Whig ticket, hitherto only a rhyme, now claimed the spotlight. What manner of man did the nation now find in the presidential chair? Six feet tall, slender, blue-eyed, and fair-haired, with classical features and a high forehead, John Tyler was a Virginia gentleman of the old school—gracious and kindly, yet stubbornly attached to principle. He had earlier resigned from the Senate, quite unnecessarily, rather than accept distasteful instructions from the Virginia legislature. Still a lone wolf, he had forsaken the Jacksonian Democratic fold for that of the Whigs, largely because he could not stomach the dictatorial tactics of Jackson.

Tyler's enemies accused him of being a Democrat in Whig clothing, but this charge was only partially true. The Whig party, like the Democratic party, was something of a catchall, and the accidental president belonged to the minority wing, which embraced a number of Jeffersonian states' righters. Tyler had in fact been put on the ticket partly to attract the vote of this fringe group, many of whom were influential southern gentry.

Yet Tyler, high-minded as he was, should never have consented to run on the ticket. Although the dominant Clay-Webster group had published no platform,

*Earliest known use of the term *Manifest Destiny*, sometimes called "Manifest Desire."

every alert politician knew what the unpublished platform contained. And on virtually every major issue, the obstinate Virginian was at odds with the majority of his adoptive Whig party, which was pro-bank, pro–protective tariff, and pro–internal improvements. "Tyler too" rhymed with "Tippecanoe," but there the harmony ended. As events turned out, President Harrison, the Whig, served for only 4 weeks, whereas Tyler, the ex-Democrat who was still largely a Democrat at heart, served for 204 weeks.

★ John Tyler: A President Without a Party

After their hard-won, hard-cider victory, the Whigs brought their not-so-secret platform out of Clay's waistcoat pocket. To the surprise of no one, it outlined a strongly nationalistic program.

Financial reform came first. The Whig Congress hastened to pass a law ending the independent treasury system, and President Tyler, disarmingly agreeable, signed it. Clay next drove through Congress a bill for a "Fiscal Bank," which would establish a new Bank of the United States.

Tyler's hostility to a centralized bank was notorious, and Clay—the "Great Compromiser"—would have done well to conciliate him. But the Kentuckian, robbed repeatedly of the presidency by lesser men, was in an imperious mood and riding for a fall. When the bank bill reached the presidential desk, Tyler flatly vetoed it on both practical and constitutional grounds. A drunken mob gathered late at night near the White House and shouted insultingly, "Huzza for Clay!" "A Bank! A Bank!" "Down with the Veto!"

The stunned Whig leaders tried once again. Striving to pacify Tyler's objections to a "Fiscal Bank," they passed another bill providing for a "Fiscal Corporation." But the president, still unbending, vetoed the offensive substitute. The Democrats were jubilant: they had been saved from another financial "monster" only by the pneumonia that had felled Harrison.

Whig extremists, seething with indignation, condemned Tyler as "His Accidency" and as an "Executive Ass." Widely burned in effigy, he received numerous letters threatening him with death. A wave of influenza then sweeping the country was called the "Tyler grippe." To the delight of Democrats, the stiff-necked Virginian was formally expelled from his party by a caucus of Whig congressmen, and a serious attempt to impeach him was broached in the House of Representatives. His entire cabinet resigned in a body, except Secretary of State Webster, who was then in the midst of delicate negotiations with England.

The proposed Whig tariff also felt the prick of the president's well-inked pen. Tyler appreciated the necessity of bringing additional revenue to the Treasury. But old Democrat that he was, he looked with a frosty eye on the major tariff scheme of the Whigs because it provided, among other features, for a distribution among the states of revenue from the sale of public lands in the West. Tyler could see no point in squandering federal money when the federal Treasury was not overflowing, and he again wielded an emphatic veto.

Chastened Clayites redrafted their tariff bill. They chopped out the offensive dollar-distribution scheme and pushed down the rates to about the moderately protective level of 1832, roughly 32 percent on dutiable goods. Tyler had no fondness for a protective tariff, but realizing the need for additional revenue, he reluctantly signed the **Tariff of 1842**. In subsequent months the pressure for higher customs duties slackened as the country gradually edged its way out of the depression. The Whig slogan, "Harrison, Two Dollars a Day and Roast Beef," was reduced by unhappy Democrats to "Ten Cents a Day and Bean Soup."

★ A War of Words with Britain

Hatred of Britain during the nineteenth century came to a head periodically and had to be lanced by treaty settlement or by war. The poison had festered ominously by 1842.

Anti-British passions were composed of many ingredients. At bottom lay the bitter, red-coated memories of the two Anglo-American wars. In addition, the genteel pro-British Federalists had died out, eventually yielding to the boisterous Jacksonian Democrats. British travelers, sniffing with aristocratic noses at the crude scene, wrote acidly of American tobacco spitting, slave auctioneering, lynching, eye gouging, and other unsavory features of the rustic Republic. Travel books penned by these critics, whose views were avidly read on both sides of the Atlantic, stirred up angry outbursts in America.

But the literary fireworks did not end there. British magazines added fuel to the flames when, enlarging on the travel books, they launched sneering attacks on Yankee shortcomings. American journals struck back with "you're another" arguments, thus touching

Frances Trollope (1780–1863), an English writer disillusioned by the failure of a utopian community she had joined in Tennessee, wrote scathingly of the Americans in 1832,

❝Other nations have been called thin-skinned, but the citizens of the Union have, apparently, no skins at all; they wince if a breeze blows over them unless it be tempered with adulation.❞

The Land of Liberty, 1847 This British cartoon reflected the contemptuous view of American culture, politics, and diplomacy that was common in early nineteenth-century Britain.

The Granger Collection, NYC

off the "Third War with England." Fortunately, this British-American war was fought with paper broadsides, and only ink was spilled. British authors, including Charles Dickens, entered the fray with gall-dipped pens, for they were being denied rich royalties by the absence of an American copyright law.*

Sprawling America, with expensive canals to dig and railroads to build, was a borrowing nation in the nineteenth century. Imperial Britain, with its overflowing coffers, was a lending nation. The well-heeled creditor is never popular with the down-at-the-heels debtor, and the phrase "bloated British bond-holder" rolled bitterly from many an American tongue. When the panic of 1837 broke and several states defaulted on their bonds or repudiated them openly, honest Englishmen assailed Yankee trickery. One of them offered a new stanza for an old song:

> *Yankee Doodle borrows cash,*
> *Yankee Doodle spends it,*
> *And then he snaps his fingers at*
> *The jolly flat [simpleton] who lends it.*

---

*Not until 1891 did Congress extend copyright privileges to foreign authors.

Troubles of a more dangerous sort came closer to home in 1837 when a short-lived insurrection erupted in Canada. It was supported by such a small minority of Canadians that it never had a real chance of success. Yet hundreds of hot-blooded Americans, hoping to strike a blow for freedom against the hereditary enemy, furnished military supplies or volunteered for armed service. The Washington regime tried arduously, though futilely, to uphold its weak neutrality regulations. But again, as in the case of Texas, it simply could not enforce unpopular laws in the face of popular opposition.

A provocative incident on the Canadian frontier brought passions to a boil in 1837. An American steamer, the **Caroline**, was carrying supplies to the insurgents across the swift Niagara River. It was finally attacked on the New York shore by a determined British force, which set the vessel on fire. Lurid American illustrators showed the flaming ship, laden with shrieking souls, plummeting over Niagara Falls. The craft in fact sank short of the plunge, and only one American was killed.

This unlawful invasion of American soil—a counterviolation of neutrality—had alarming aftermaths. Washington officials lodged vigorous but ineffective protests. Three years later, in 1840, the incident was dramatically revived in the state of New York. A Canadian named McLeod, after allegedly boasting in a tavern of his part in the *Caroline* raid, was arrested and indicted for murder. The London Foreign Office, which regarded the *Caroline* raiders as members of a sanctioned armed force and not as criminals, made clear that his execution would mean war. Fortunately, McLeod was freed after establishing an alibi. It must have been airtight, for it was good enough to convince a New York jury. The tension forthwith eased, but it snapped taut again in 1841, when British officials in the Bahamas offered asylum to 130 Virginia slaves who had rebelled and captured the American ship **Creole**. Britain had abolished slavery within its empire in 1833, raising southern fears that its Caribbean possessions would become Canada-like havens for escaped slaves.

✦ Manipulating the Maine Maps

An explosive controversy of the early 1840s involved the Maine boundary dispute. The St. Lawrence River is icebound several months of the year, as the British, remembering the War of 1812, well knew. They were determined, as a defensive precaution against the Yankees, to build a road westward from the seaport of Halifax to Québec. But the proposed route ran through disputed territory—claimed also by Maine under the misleading peace treaty of 1783. Tough-knuckled lumberjacks from both Maine and Canada entered the disputed no-man's-land of the tall-timbered Aroostook River valley. Ugly fights flared up, and both sides summoned the local militia. The small-scale lumber-jack clash, which was dubbed the **Aroostook War**, threatened to widen into a full-dress shooting war.

As the crisis deepened in 1842, the London Foreign Office took an unusual step. It sent to Washington a nonprofessional diplomat, the conciliatory financier Lord Ashburton, who had married a wealthy American woman. He speedily established cordial relations with Secretary Webster, who had recently been lionized during a visit to Britain.

The two statesmen, their nerves frayed by pro-tracted negotiations in the heat of a Washington summer, finally agreed to compromise on the Maine boundary (see Map 17.1). On the basis of a rough, split-the-difference arrangement, the Americans were to retain some 7,000 square miles of the 12,000 square miles of wilderness in dispute. The British got less land but won the desired Halifax-Québec route. During the negotiations the *Caroline* affair, malingering since 1837, was patched up by an exchange of diplomatic notes.

An overlooked bonus sneaked by in the small print of the same treaty: the British, in adjusting the U.S.-Canadian boundary farther west, surrendered 6,500 square miles. The area was later found to contain the priceless Mesabi iron ore of Minnesota.

✯ The Lone Star of Texas Shines Alone

During the uncertain eight years since 1836, Texas had led a precarious existence. Mexico, refusing to rec-ognize Texas's independence, regarded the Lone Star

MAP 17.1 Maine Boundary Settlement, 1842 © 2016 Cengage Learning

Republic as a province in revolt, to be reconquered in the future. Mexican officials loudly threatened war if the American eagle should ever gather the fledgling republic under its protective wings.

The Texans were forced to maintain a costly military establishment. Vastly outnumbered by their Mexican foe, they could not tell when he would strike again. Mexico actually did make two halfhearted raids that, though ineffectual, foreshadowed more fearsome efforts. Confronted with such perils, Texas was driven to open negotiations with Britain and France, in the hope of securing the defensive shield of a protectorate. In 1839 and 1840, the Texans concluded treaties with France, Holland, and Belgium.

Britain was intensely interested in an independent Texas. Such a republic would check the southward surge of the American colossus, whose bulging biceps posed a constant threat to nearby British possessions in the New World. A puppet Texas, dancing to strings pulled by Britain, could be turned upon the Yankees. Subsequent clashes would create a smokescreen diver-sion, behind which foreign powers could move into the Americas and challenge the insolent Monroe Doctrine. French schemers were likewise attracted by the hoary game of divide and conquer. These actions would result, they hoped, in the fragmentation and militarization of America.

Dangers threatened from other foreign quarters. British abolitionists were busily intriguing for a foot-hold in Texas. If successful in freeing the few blacks there, they presumably would inflame the nearby slaves of the South. In addition, British merchants regarded Texas as a potentially important free-trade area—an offset to the tariff-walled United States. British manufacturers likewise perceived that those vast Texas plains constituted one of the great cotton-producing areas of the future. An independent Texas would relieve British looms of their chronic depen-dence on American fiber—a supply that might be cut off in time of crisis by embargo or war.

✯ The Belated Texas Nuptials

Partly because of the fears aroused by British schemers, Texas became a leading issue in the presidential cam-paign of 1844. The foes of expansion assailed annexation, while southern hotheads cried, "Texas or Disunion." The pro-expansion Democrats under James K. Polk finally triumphed over the Whigs under Henry Clay, the hardy perennial candidate. Lame duck president Tyler there-upon interpreted the narrow Democratic victory, with dubious accuracy, as a "mandate" to acquire Texas.

Eager to crown his troubled administration with this splendid prize, Tyler deserves much of the credit

St. Louis in 1846, by Henry Lewis   Thousands of pioneers like these pulling away from St. Louis said farewell to civilization as they left the Mississippi River and headed across the untracked plains to Oregon in the 1840s.

for shepherding Texas into the fold. Many antislavery Whigs feared that Texas in the Union would be red meat to nourish the lusty "slave power." Aware of their opposition, Tyler despaired of securing the needed two-thirds vote for a treaty in the Senate. He therefore arranged for annexation by a joint resolution. This solution required only a simple majority in both houses of Congress. After a spirited debate, the resolution passed early in 1845, and Texas was formally invited to become the twenty-eighth star on the American flag.

Thomas J. Green (1801–1863), who served as a brigadier general in the Texas Revolution, published a pamphlet in 1845 to make the case for American support of an independent Texas:

❝Both the government of the United States and Texas are founded upon the same political code. They have the same common origin—the same language, laws, and religion—the same pursuits and interests; and though they may remain independent of each other as to government, they are identified in weal and wo'—they will flourish side by side and the blight which affects the one will surely reach the other.❞

Mexico angrily charged that the Americans had despoiled it of Texas. There was truth to this claim, especially in 1836 when the Texans first seceded, but considerably less so in 1845, when the area was no longer Mexico's to be despoiled of. By then, the situation had become even more complex. More than a decade of widespread Comanche raids had further demonstrated the weakness of Mexican influence in the region. As the years stretched out, realistic observers could see that Mexico would not be able to reconquer its lost province. The most astute observers could further see that victory in war against Mexico would not resolve all tensions. A powerful and integrated network of Comanche tribes still had to be reckoned with. By 1845 the Lone Star Republic had become a danger spot, inviting foreign intrigue that menaced the American people. The continued existence of Texas as an independent nation threatened to involve the United States in a series of ruinous wars, both in America and in Europe. Americans were in a "lick all creation" mood when they sang "Uncle Sam's Song to Miss Texas":

If Mexy back'd by secret foes,
*   Still talks of getting you, gal;*
Why we can lick 'em all you know
*   And then annex 'em too, gal.*

What other power would have spurned the imperial domain of Texas? The bride was so near, so rich, so fair, so willing. Whatever the peculiar circumstances of the Texas Revolution, the United States can hardly be accused of unseemly haste in achieving annexation. Nine long years were surely a decent wait between the beginning of the courtship and the consummation of the marriage.

★ Oregon Fever Populates Oregon

The so-called Oregon Country was an enormous wilderness. It sprawled magnificently west of the Rockies to the Pacific Ocean, and north of California to the line of 54° 40′—the present southern tip of the Alaska panhandle. All or substantial parts of this immense area were claimed at one time or another by four nations: Spain, Russia, Britain, and the United States.

Two claimants dropped out of the scramble. Spain, though the first to raise its banner in Oregon, bartered away its claims to the United States in the so-called Florida Treaty of 1819. Russia retreated to the line of 54° 40′ by the treaties of 1824 and 1825 with America and Britain. These two remaining rivals now had the field to themselves.

British claims to Oregon were strong—at least to that portion north of the Columbia River. They were based squarely on prior discovery and exploration, on treaty rights, and on actual occupation. The most important colonizing agency was the far-flung Hudson's Bay Company, which was trading profitably with the Indians of the Pacific Northwest for furs.

Americans, for their part, could also point pridefully to exploration and occupation. Captain Robert

In winning Oregon, the Americans had great faith in their procreative powers. Boasted one congressman in 1846,

"Our people are spreading out with the aid of the American multiplication table. Go to the West and see a young man with his mate of eighteen; after the lapse of thirty years, visit him again, and instead of two, you will find twenty-two. That is what I call the American multiplication table."

Gray in 1792 had stumbled upon the majestic Columbia River, which he named after his ship; and the famed Lewis and Clark expedition of 1804–1806 had ranged overland through the Oregon Country to the Pacific. This shaky American toehold was ultimately strengthened by the presence of missionaries and other settlers, a sprinkling of whom reached the grassy Willamette River valley, south of the Columbia, in the 1830s. These men and women of God, in saving the soul of the Indian, were instrumental in saving the soil of Oregon for the United States. They stimulated interest in a faraway domain that countless Americans had earlier assumed would not be settled for centuries.

Scattered American and British pioneers in Oregon continued to live peacefully side by side. At the time of negotiating the Anglo-American Convention of 1818 (see p. 241), the United States had sought to divide the vast domain at the forty-ninth parallel. But

Pundt and Koenig's General Store, Omaha City, Nebraska, 1858 Settlers bound for Colorado and California stopped here for provisions before venturing farther west across the open plains. Huntington Library/SuperStock

the British, who regarded the Columbia River as the St. Lawrence of the West, were unwilling to yield this vital artery. A scheme for peaceful "joint occupation" was thereupon adopted, pending future settlement.

The handful of Americans in the Willamette Valley was suddenly multiplied in the early 1840s, when "Oregon fever" seized hundreds of restless pioneers. In increasing numbers, their creaking covered wagons jolted over the two-thousand-mile Oregon Trail as the human rivulet widened into a stream.* By 1846 about five thousand Americans had settled south of the Columbia River, some of them tough "border ruffians," expert with bowie knife and "revolving pistol."

The British, in the face of this rising torrent of humanity, could muster only seven hundred or so subjects north of the Columbia. Losing out lopsidedly in the population race, they were beginning to see the wisdom of arriving at a peaceful settlement before being engulfed by their neighbors.

A curious fact is that only a relatively small segment of the Oregon Country was in actual controversy by 1845. The area in dispute consisted of the rough quadrangle between the Columbia River on the south and east, the forty-ninth parallel on the north, and the Pacific Ocean on the west. Britain had repeatedly offered the line of the Columbia; America had repeatedly offered the forty-ninth parallel. The whole fateful issue was now tossed into the presidential election of 1844, where it was largely overshadowed by the question of annexing Texas.

✳ A Mandate (?) for Manifest Destiny

The two major parties nominated their presidential standard-bearers in May 1844. Ambitious but often frustrated Henry Clay, easily the most popular man in the country, was enthusiastically chosen by the Whigs at Baltimore. The Democrats, meeting there later, seemed hopelessly deadlocked. Van Buren's opposition to annexing Texas ensured his defeat, given domination of the party by southern expansionists. Finally party delegates trotted out and nominated James K. Polk of Tennessee, America's first "dark-horse" or "surprise" presidential candidate.

Polk may have been a dark horse, but he was hardly an unknown or decrepit nag. Speaker of the House of Representatives for four years and governor of Tennessee for two terms, he was a determined, industrious, ruthless, and intelligent public servant.

Manifest Destiny: A Caricature The spirit of Manifest Destiny swept the nation in the 1840s and threatened to sweep it to extremes. This cartoon from 1848 lampoons proslavery Democratic presidential candidate Lewis Cass as a veritable war machine, bent on the conquest of territory ranging from New Mexico to Cuba and even Peru.

Sponsored by Andrew Jackson, his friend and neighbor, he was rather implausibly touted by Democrats as yet another "Young Hickory." Whigs attempted to jeer him into oblivion with the taunt "Who is James K. Polk?" They soon found out.

The campaign of 1844 was in part an expression of the mighty emotional upsurge known as **Manifest Destiny**. Countless citizens in the 1840s and 1850s, feeling a sense of mission, believed that Almighty God had "manifestly" destined the American people for a hemispheric career. They would irresistibly spread their uplifting and ennobling democratic institutions over at least the entire continent, and possibly over South America as well. Land greed and ideals—"empire" and "liberty"—were thus conveniently conjoined.

Expansionist Democrats were strongly swayed by the intoxicating spell of Manifest Destiny. They came out flat-footedly in their platform for the "Reannexation of Texas"[†] and the "Reoccupation of Oregon," all the way to 54° 40'. Outbellowing the Whig logcabinites in the game of slogans, they shouted "All of Oregon or None." (The slogan **"Fifty-four forty or fight"** was not coined until two years later, in 1846.) They also condemned Clay as a "corrupt bargainer," a dissolute character, and a slaveowner. (Their own candidate, Polk, also owned slaves—a classic case of the pot calling the kettle black.)

---

*The average rate of progress in covered wagons was one to two miles an hour. This amounted to about one hundred miles a week, or about five months for the entire journey. Thousands of humans, in addition to horses and oxen, died en route. One estimate is seventeen deaths a mile for men, women, and children.

---

†The United States had given up its claims to Texas in the so-called Florida Purchase Treaty (Adams-Onís Treaty) with Spain in 1819 (see p. 242).

Smithsonian American Art Museum, Washington, DC/Art Resource, NY

Westward the Course of Empire Takes Its Way   This romantic tribute to the spirit of Manifest Destiny was commissioned by Congress in 1860 and may still be seen in the Capitol.

The Whigs, as noisemakers, took no backseat. They countered with such slogans as "Hooray for Clay" and "Polk, Slavery, and Texas, or Clay, Union, and Liberty." They also spread the lie that a gang of Tennessee slaves had been seen on their way to a southern market branded with the initials J. K. P. (James K. Polk).

On the crucial issue of Texas, the acrobatic Clay tried to ride two horses at once. The "Great Compromiser" appears to have compromised away the presidency when he wrote a series of confusing letters. They seemed to say that while he personally favored annexing slaveholding Texas (an appeal to the South), he also favored postponement (an appeal to the North). He might have lost more ground if he had not "straddled," but he certainly alienated the more ardent antislaveryites.

In the stretch drive, "Dark Horse" Polk nipped Henry Clay at the wire, 170 to 105 votes in the Electoral College and 1,338,464 to 1,300,097 in the popular column. Clay would have won if he had not lost New York State by a scant 5,000 votes. There the tiny antislavery **Liberty party** absorbed nearly 16,000 votes, many of which would otherwise have gone to the unlucky Kentuckian. Ironically, the anti-Texas Liberty party, by spoiling Clay's chances and helping to ensure the election of pro-Texas Polk, hastened the annexation of Texas.

Land-hungry Democrats, flushed with victory, proclaimed that they had received a mandate from the voters to take Texas. But a presidential election is seldom, if ever, a clear-cut mandate on anything. The only way to secure a true reflection of the voters' will is to hold a special election on a given issue. The picture that emerged in 1844 was one not of mandate but of muddle. What else could there have been when the results were so close, the personalities so colorful, and the issues so numerous—including Oregon, Texas, the tariff, slavery, the bank, and internal improvements? Yet this unclear "mandate" was interpreted by President Tyler as a crystal-clear charge to annex Texas—and he signed the joint resolution three days before leaving the White House.

✴ Polk the Purposeful

"Young Hickory" Polk, unlike "Old Hickory" Jackson, was not an impressive figure. Of middle height (five feet eight inches), lean, white-haired (worn long), gray-eyed, and stern-faced, he took life seriously and drove himself mercilessly into a premature grave. His burdens were increased by an unwillingness to delegate authority. Methodical and hard-working but not brilliant, he was shrewd, narrow-minded, conscientious, and persistent. "What he went for he fetched," wrote a contemporary.

TABLE 17.1 House Vote on Tariff of 1846		
Region	For	Against
New England	9	19
Middle states	18	44
West and Northwest	29	10
South and Southwest	58	20
Total	114	93

Purposeful in the highest degree, he developed a positive four-point program and with remarkable success achieved it completely in less than four years.

One of Polk's goals was a lowered tariff. His secretary of the Treasury, wispy Robert J. Walker, devised a tariff-for-revenue bill that reduced the average rates of the Tariff of 1842 from about 32 percent to 25 percent. With the strong support of low-tariff southerners, the **Walker Tariff** bill made its way through Congress, though not without loud complaints from the Clayites, especially in New England and the middle states, who cried that American manufacturing would be ruined (see Table 17.1). But these prophets of doom missed the mark. The Walker Tariff of 1846 proved to be an excellent revenue producer, largely because it was followed by boom times and heavy imports.

A second objective of Polk was the restoration of the independent treasury, unceremoniously dropped by the Whigs in 1841. Pro-bank Whigs in Congress raised a storm of opposition, but victory at last rewarded the president's efforts in 1846.

The third and fourth points on Polk's "must list" were the acquisition of California and the settlement of the Oregon dispute (see Map 17.2).

"Reoccupation" of the "whole" of Oregon had been promised by northern Democrats in the campaign of 1844. But southern Democrats, once they had annexed Texas, rapidly cooled off. Polk, himself a southerner, had no intention of insisting on the 54° 40' pledge of his own platform. But feeling bound by the three offers of his predecessors to London, he again proposed the compromise line of 49°. The British minister in Washington, on his own initiative, brusquely spurned this olive branch.

The next move on the Oregon chessboard was up to Britain. Fortunately for peace, the ministry began to experience a change of heart. British anti-expansionists ("Little Englanders") were now persuaded that the Columbia River was not after all the St. Lawrence of the West and that the turbulent American hordes might one day seize the Oregon Country. Why fight a hazardous war over this wilderness on behalf of an unpopular monopoly, the Hudson's Bay Company, which had already "furred out" much of the area anyhow?

Early in 1846 the British, hat in hand, came around and themselves proposed the line of 49°. President Polk, irked by the previous rebuff, threw the decision squarely into the lap of the Senate. The senators speedily accepted the offer and approved the subsequent treaty, despite a few diehard shouts of "Fifty-four forty forever!" and "Every foot or not an inch!" The fact that the United States was then a month deep in a war with Mexico doubtless influenced the Senate's final vote.

Satisfaction with the Oregon settlement among Americans was not unanimous. The northwestern states, hotbed of Manifest Destiny and "fifty-four fortyism," joined the antislavery forces in condemning what they regarded as a base betrayal by the South. Why *all* of Texas but not *all* of Oregon? Because, retorted the expansionist Senator Benton of Missouri, "Great Britain is powerful and Mexico is weak."

So Polk, despite all the campaign bluster, got neither "fifty-four forty" nor a fight. But he did get something that in the long run was better: a reasonable compromise without a rifle being raised.

✦ Misunderstandings with Mexico

Faraway California was another worry of Polk's. He and other disciples of Manifest Destiny had long coveted its verdant valleys, and especially the

MAP 17.2 The Oregon Controversy, 1846 © 2016 Cengage Learning

Fort Vancouver, Oregon Country, ca. 1846 Fort Vancouver, on the Columbia River near its confluence with the Willamette River, was the economic hub of the Oregon Country during the early years of settlement. Founded as a Hudson's Bay Company fur-trading outpost, the fort was handed over to the Americans when Britain ceded the Oregon Country to the United States in 1846.

spacious bay of San Francisco. This splendid harbor was widely regarded as America's future gateway to the Pacific Ocean.

The population of California in 1845 was curiously mixed. It consisted of perhaps thirteen thousand sun-blessed Spanish Mexicans and as many as seventy-five thousand dispirited Indians. There were fewer than a thousand "foreigners," mostly Americans, some of whom had "left their consciences" behind them as they rounded Cape Horn. Given time, these transplanted Yankees might yet bring California into the Union by "playing the Texas game."

Polk was eager to buy California from Mexico, but relations with Mexico City were dangerously embittered. Among other friction points, the United States had claims against the Mexicans for some $3 million in damages to American citizens and their property. The revolution-riddled regime in Mexico had formally agreed to assume most of this debt but had been forced to default on its payments.

A more serious bone of contention was Texas. The Mexican government, after threatening war if the United States should acquire the Lone Star Republic, had recalled its minister from Washington following annexation. Diplomatic relations were completely severed.

Deadlock with Mexico over Texas was further tightened by a question of boundaries. During the long era of Spanish Mexican occupation, the southwestern boundary of Texas had been the Nueces River. But the expansive Texans, on rather far-fetched grounds, were claiming the more southerly Rio Grande instead. Polk, for his part, felt a strong moral obligation to defend Texas in its claim, once it was annexed.

The Mexicans were far less concerned about this boundary quibble than was the United States. In their eyes all of Texas was still theirs, although temporarily in revolt, and a dispute over the two rivers seemed pointless. Yet Polk was careful to keep American troops out of virtually all of the explosive no-man's-land between the Nueces and the Rio Grande, as long as there was any real prospect of peaceful adjustment.

The golden prize of California continued to cause Polk much anxiety. Disquieting rumors (now known to have been ill-founded) were circulating that Britain was about to buy or seize California—a grab that Americans could not tolerate under the Monroe Doctrine. In a last desperate throw of the dice, Polk dispatched John Slidell to Mexico City as minister late in 1845. The new envoy, among other alternatives, was instructed to offer a maximum of $25 million for California and territory to the east. But the proud Mexican people would not even permit Slidell to present his "insulting" proposition.

✵ American Blood on American (?) Soil

A frustrated Polk was now prepared to force a showdown. On January 13, 1846, he ordered four thousand men, under General Zachary Taylor, to march from the Nueces River to the Rio Grande, provocatively near Mexican forces. Polk's presidential diary reveals that he expected at any moment to hear of a clash. When none occurred after an anxious wait, he informed his cabinet on May 9, 1846, that he proposed to ask Congress to declare war on the basis of (1) unpaid claims and (2) Slidell's rejection. These, at best, were rather flimsy pretexts. Two cabinet members spoke up and said that they would feel better satisfied if Mexican troops should fire first.

That very evening, as fate would have it, news of bloodshed arrived. On April 25, 1846, Mexican troops had crossed the Rio Grande and attacked General Taylor's command, with a loss of sixteen Americans killed or wounded.

Polk, further aroused, sent a vigorous war message to Congress. He declared that despite "all our efforts" to avoid a clash, hostilities had been forced upon the country by the shedding of "American blood upon the American soil." A patriotic Congress overwhelmingly voted for war, and enthusiastic volunteers cried, "Ho for the Halls of the Montezumas!" and "Mexico or Death!" Inflamed by the war fever, even antislavery Whig bastions melted and joined with the rest of the nation, though they later condemned "Jimmy Polk's war." As James Russell Lowell of Massachusetts lamented,

Massachusetts, God forgive her,
She's akneelin' with the rest.

In his message to Congress, Polk was making history—not writing it. Like many presidents with ambitious foreign-policy goals, he felt justified in bending the truth if that was what it took to bend a reluctant public toward war. If he had been a historian, Polk would have explained that American blood had been shed on soil that the Mexicans had good reason to regard as their own. A gangling, rough-featured Whig congressman from Illinois, one Abraham Lincoln, introduced certain resolutions that requested information as to the precise "spot" on American soil where American blood had been shed. He pushed his **spot resolutions** with such persistence that he came to be known as the "spotty Lincoln," who could die of "spotted fever." The more extreme antislavery agitators of the North, many of them Whigs, branded the president a liar— "Polk the Mendacious."

Did Polk provoke war? California was an imperative point in his program, and Mexico would not sell it at any price. The only way to get it was to use force or wait for an internal American revolt. Yet delay seemed

dangerous, for the claws of the British lion might snatch the ripening California fruit from the talons of the American eagle. Grievances against Mexico were annoying yet tolerable; in later years America endured even worse ones. But in 1846 patience had ceased to be a virtue, as far as Polk was concerned. Bent on grasping California by fair means or foul, he pushed the quarrel to a bloody showdown.

Both sides, in fact, were spoiling for a fight. Feisty Americans, especially southwestern expansionists, were eager to teach the Mexicans a lesson. The Mexicans, in turn, were burning to humiliate the "Bullies of the North." Possessing a considerable standing army, heavily overstaffed with generals, they boasted of invading the United States, freeing the black slaves, and lassoing whole regiments of Americans. They were hoping that the quarrel with Britain over Oregon would blossom into a full-dress war, as it came near doing, and further pin down the hated *yanquis*. A conquest of Mexico's vast and arid expanses seemed fantastic, especially in view of the bungling American invasion of Canada in 1812.

Both sides were fired by moral indignation. The Mexican people could fight with the flaming sword of righteousness, for had not the "insolent" Yankee picked a fight by polluting their soil? Many earnest Americans, on the other hand, sincerely believed that Mexico was the aggressor.

✵ The Mastering of Mexico

Polk wanted California—not war. But when war came, he hoped to fight it on a limited scale and then pull out when he had captured the prize. The dethroned Mexican dictator Santa Anna, then exiled with his teenage bride in Cuba, let it be known that if the American blockading squadron would permit him to slip into Mexico, he would sell out his country. Incredibly, Polk agreed to this discreditable intrigue. But the double-crossing Santa Anna, once he returned to Mexico, proceeded to rally his countrymen to a desperate defense of their soil.

American operations in the Southwest and in California were completely successful (see Map 17.3). In 1846 General Stephen W. Kearny led a detachment of seventeen hundred troops over the famous Santa Fe Trail from Fort Leavenworth to Santa Fe. This sun-baked outpost, with its drowsy plazas, was easily captured. But before Kearny could reach California, the fertile province was won. When war broke out, Captain John C. Frémont, the dashing explorer, just "happened" to be there with several dozen well-armed men. In helping to overthrow Mexican rule in 1846, he collaborated with American naval officers and with the local Americans, who had hoisted the banner of the short-lived **California Bear Flag Republic**.

General Zachary Taylor meanwhile had been spearheading the main thrust. Known as "Old Rough and Ready" because of his iron constitution and incredibly unsoldierly appearance—he sometimes wore a Mexican straw hat—he fought his way across the Rio Grande into Mexico. After several gratifying victories, he reached **Buena Vista**. There, on February 22–23, 1847, his weakened force of five thousand men was attacked by some twenty thousand march-weary troops under Santa Anna. The Mexicans were finally repulsed with extreme difficulty, and overnight Zachary Taylor became the "Hero of Buena Vista." One Kentuckian was heard to say that "Old Zack" would be elected president in 1848 by "spontaneous combustion."

Sound American strategy now called for a crushing blow at the enemy's vitals—Mexico City. General Taylor, though a good leader of modest-sized forces, could not win decisively in the semideserts of northern Mexico. The command of the main expedition, which pushed inland from the coastal city of Veracruz early in 1847, was entrusted to General Winfield Scott. A handsome giant of a man, Scott had emerged as a hero from the War of 1812 and had later earned the nickname "Old Fuss and Feathers" because of his resplendent uniforms and strict discipline. He was severely handicapped in the Mexican campaign by inadequate numbers of troops, by expiring enlistments, by a more numerous enemy, by mountainous terrain, by disease, and by political backbiting at home. Yet he succeeded in battling his way up to Mexico City by September 1847 in one of the most brilliant campaigns in American military annals. He proved to be the most distinguished general produced by his country between the Revolution and the Civil War.

MAP 17.3 Major Campaigns of the Mexican War © 2016 Cengage Learning

✪ Fighting Mexico for Peace

Polk was anxious to end the shooting as soon as he could secure his territorial goals. Accordingly, he sent along with Scott's invading army the chief clerk of the State Department, Nicholas P. Trist, who among other weaknesses was afflicted with an overfluid pen. Trist and Scott arranged for an armistice with Santa Anna, at a cost of $10,000. The wily dictator pocketed the bribe and then used the time to bolster his defenses.

Negotiating a treaty with a sword in one hand and a pen in the other was ticklish business. Polk, disgusted with his blundering envoy, abruptly recalled Trist. The wordy diplomat then dashed off a sixty-five-page letter explaining why he was not coming home. The president was furious. But Trist, grasping a fleeting opportunity to negotiate, signed the **Treaty of Guadalupe Hidalgo** on February 2, 1848, and forwarded it to Washington.

The terms of the treaty were breathtaking. They confirmed the American title to Texas and yielded the enormous area stretching westward to Oregon and the ocean and embracing coveted California. This total expanse, including Texas, was about one-half of Mexico. The United States agreed to pay $15 million for the land and to assume the claims of its citizens against Mexico in the amount of $3,250,000 (see "Makers of America: The Californios," pp. 378–379).

Polk submitted the treaty to the Senate. Although Trist had proved highly annoying, he had generally followed his original instructions. And speed was imperative. The antislavery Whigs in Congress—dubbed "Mexican Whigs" or "**Conscience Whigs**"—were denouncing this "damnable war" with increasing heat. Having secured control of the House in 1847, they were even threatening to vote down supplies for the armies in the field. If they had done so, Scott probably would have been forced to retreat, and the fruits of victory might have been tossed away.

Another peril impended. A swelling group of expansionists, intoxicated by Manifest Destiny, was clamoring for all of Mexico. If America had seized it, the nation would have been saddled with an expensive and vexatious policing problem. Farseeing southerners like Calhoun, alarmed by the mounting anger of antislavery agitators, realized that the South would do well not to be too greedy. The treaty was finally approved by the Senate, 38 to 14. Oddly enough, it was condemned both by those opponents who wanted all of Mexico and by opponents who wanted none of it.

Victors rarely pay an indemnity, especially after a costly conflict has been "forced" on them. Yet Polk, who had planned to offer $25 million before fighting the war, arranged to pay $18,250,000 after winning it. Cynics have charged that the Americans were pricked by guilty consciences; apologists have pointed proudly to the "Anglo-Saxon spirit of fair play." A decisive factor was the need for haste, while there was still a responsible Mexican government to carry out the treaty and before political foes in the United States, notably the antislavery zealots, sabotaged Polk's expansionist program.

Contending Voices
Warring over the Mexican War

The war against Mexico was both warmly applauded and hotly condemned. The prowar New York Evening Post *trumpeted in 1848:*

❝ Now we ask, whether any man can coolly contemplate the idea of recalling our troops from the [Mexican] territory we at present occupy...and...resign this beautiful country to the custody of the ignorant cowards and profligate ruffians who have ruled it for the last twenty-five years? Why, humanity cries out against it. Civilization and Christianity protest against this reflux of the tide of barbarism and anarchy.❞

The eminent Kentuckian and founder of the Whig party, Henry Clay (1777–1852), though a "war hawk" in the War of 1812, strongly opposed the expansionism of the 1840s, which contributed to his defeat by Democrat James K. Polk in the presidential election of 1844. His son Henry died fighting in the battle of Buena Vista in February 1847. Nine months later, Clay made a passionate antiwar speech in Lexington, Kentucky. In the audience was newly elected Illinois congressman Abraham Lincoln, who later called the Mexican War "unnecessary." Clay said:

❝ Of all the dangers and misfortunes which could befall this nation, I should regard that of its becoming a warlike and conquering power, the most direful and fatal....This is no war of defense, but one unnecessary and of offensive aggression. It is Mexico that is defending her fire-sides, her castles and her altars, not we.❞

Was the war against Mexico wise or unwise, just or unjust?

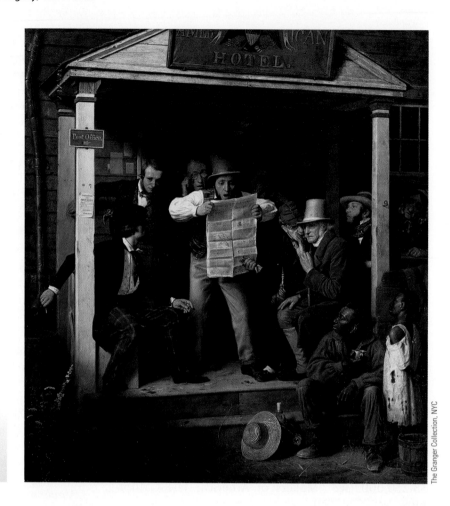

War News from Mexico, by Richard Caton Woodville The newfangled telegraph kept the nation closely informed of events in far-off Mexico.

✸ Profit and Loss in Mexico

As wars go, the Mexican War was a small one. It cost some thirteen thousand American lives, most of them taken by disease. But the fruits of the fighting were enormous.

America's total expanse, already vast, was increased by about one-third (counting Texas)—an addition even greater than that of the Louisiana Purchase. A sharp stimulus was given to the spirit of Manifest Destiny, for as the proverb has it, the appetite comes with eating.

The Mexican War proved to be the blood-spattered schoolroom of the Civil War. The campaigns provided priceless field experience for most of the officers destined to become leading generals in the forthcoming conflict, including Captain Robert E. Lee and Lieutenant Ulysses S. Grant. The Military Academy at West Point, founded in 1802, fully justified its existence through the well-trained officers. Useful also was the navy, which did valuable work in throwing a crippling blockade around Mexican ports. A new academy at Annapolis had just been established by Navy Secretary and historian George Bancroft in 1845. The Marine Corps, in existence since 1798, won new laurels and to this day sings in its stirring hymn about the "Halls of Montezuma."

The army waged war without defeat and without a major blunder, despite formidable obstacles and a half-dozen or so achingly long marches. Chagrined British critics, as well as other foreign skeptics, reluctantly revised upward their estimate of Yankee military prowess. Opposing armies, moreover, emerged with increased respect for each other. The Mexicans, though poorly led, fought heroically. At Chapultepec, near Mexico City, the teenage lads of the military academy there (*los niños*) perished to a boy.

Long-memoried Mexicans have never forgotten that their northern enemy tore away about half of their country. The argument that they were lucky not to lose all of it, and that they had been paid something for their land, has scarcely lessened their bitterness. The war also marked an ugly turning point in relations between the United States and Latin America as a whole. Hitherto, Uncle Sam had been regarded with some complacency, even friendliness. Henceforth, he was increasingly feared as the "Colossus of the North." Suspicious neighbors to the south condemned him as a greedy and untrustworthy bully, who might next despoil them of their soil.

Most ominous of all, the war rearoused the snarling dog of the slavery issue, and the beast did not stop yelping until drowned in the blood of the Civil War. Abolitionists assailed the Mexican conflict as one provoked by the southern "slavocracy" for its own evil purposes. As James Russell Lowell had Hosea Biglow drawl in his Yankee dialect,

> *They jest want this Californy*
> *So's to lug new slave-states in*
> *To abuse ye, an' to scorn ye,*
> *An' to plunder ye like sin.*

In line with Lowell's charge, the bulk of the American volunteers were admittedly from the South and Southwest. But, as in the case of the Texas Revolution, the basic explanation was proximity rather than conspiracy.

Quarreling over slavery extension also erupted on the floors of Congress. In 1846, shortly after the shooting started, Polk had requested an appropriation of $2 million with which to buy a peace. Representative David Wilmot of Pennsylvania, fearful of the southern "slavocracy," introduced a fateful amendment. It stipulated that slavery should never exist in any of the territory to be wrested from Mexico.

The fiercely contested Wilmot amendment twice passed the House, but not the Senate. Southern members, unwilling to be robbed of prospective slave states, fought the restriction tooth and nail. Antislavery men, in Congress and out, battled no less bitterly for the exclusion of slaves. The **Wilmot Proviso** never became federal law, but it was eventually endorsed by the legislatures of all but one of the free states, and it came to symbolize the burning issue of slavery in the territories. It was this issue of slavery's extension into the newly acquired lands in the West, more than any other, that drove the broadest and hottest wedge between North and South.

Seen in historical perspective, the opening shots of the Mexican War were the opening shots of the Civil War. President Polk left the nation the splendid physical heritage of California and the Southwest but also the ugly moral heritage of a toxic slavery dispute. "Mexico will poison us," said the philosopher Ralph Waldo Emerson. Even the great champion of the South, John C. Calhoun, had prophetically warned that "Mexico is to us the forbidden fruit...the penalty of eating it would be to subject our institutions to political death." Mexicans could later take some satisfaction in knowing that the territory wrenched from them by sword and musket proved to be a venomous apple of discord that could well be called Santa Anna's revenge.

Storming the Fortress of Chapultepec, Mexico, 1847 The American success at Chapultepec contributed heavily to the final victory over Mexico. One American commander lined up several Irish American deserters on a gallows facing the castle and melodramatically dropped the trapdoors beneath them just as the United States flag was raised over the captured battlement. According to legend, the flag was raised by First Lieutenant George Pickett, later immortalized as the leader of "Pickett's charge" in the Civil War Battle of Gettysburg, 1863.

West Point Museum Collection, United States Military Academy

In 1848 the United States, swollen with the spoils of war, reckoned the costs and benefits of the conflict with Mexico. Thousands of Americans had fallen in battle, and millions of dollars had been invested in a war machine. For this expenditure of blood and money, the nation was repaid with ample land—and with people, the former citizens of Mexico who now became, whether willingly or not, Americans. The largest single addition to American territory in history, the Mexican Cession stretched the United States from sea to shining sea. It secured Texas, brought in vast tracts of the desert Southwest, and included the great prize—the fruited valleys and port cities of California. There, at the conclusion of the Mexican War, dwelled some thirteen thousand Californios—descendants of the Spanish and Mexican conquerors who had once ruled California.

The Spanish had first arrived in California in 1769, extending their New World empire and outracing Russian traders to bountiful San Francisco Bay.

Father Junipero Serra, an enterprising Franciscan friar, soon established twenty-one missions along the coast (see Map 17.4). Indians in the iron grip of the missions were encouraged to adopt Christianity and were often forced to toil endlessly as farmers and herders, in the process suffering disease and degradation. These frequently maltreated mission Indians occupied the lowest rungs on the ladder of Spanish colonial society.

Upon the loftiest rungs perched the Californios. Pioneers from the Mexican heartland of New Spain, they had trailed Serra to California, claiming land and civil offices in their new home. Yet even the proud Californios had deferred to the all-powerful Franciscan missionaries until Mexico threw off the Spanish colonial yoke in 1821, whereupon the infant Mexican government turned an anxious eye toward its frontier outpost.

Mexico now emptied its jails to send settlers to the sparsely populated north, built and garrisoned fortresses, and, most important, transferred authority

Dance of Native Californians at San Francisco de Assis Mission, 1816, by Ludwig Choris   In the sixty years that they operated, the twenty-one California missions employed 142 priests and baptized 87,787 Indians. Missions became a combination of churches, towns, schools, farms, factories, and prisons.

Gianni Dagli Orti/The Art Archive at Art Resource, NY

The Landowner and His Foreman, by Julio Michard, 1839 This California ranchero's way of life was soon to be extinguished when California became part of the United States in 1848 and thousands of American gold-seekers rushed into the state the following year.

San Francisco Solano
1823

San Rafael
1817
San Francisco de Asís
San Francisco 1776

San José
1797

Santa Clara
1777

Santa Cruz
1791

San Juan Bautista
1797

Monterey

San Carlos
Borromeo   Soledad
1770   1791

San Antonio
de Padua
1771

PACIFIC
OCEAN

San Miguel
1797

San Luis Obispo
1772

La Purísima   Santa Ynez
Concepción   1804
1787

Santa Barbara   San Buenaventura
1786   1782

San Fernando Rey
1797

San Gabriel
1771

San Juan Capistrano
1776

San Luis Rey
1798

San Diego de Alcalá
1769

SIERRA NEVADA

Mission

Presidio (Fort)

El Camino Réal
(Royal Road)

0   30   60 Km.

0   30   60 Mi.

122°W

120°W

38°N

36°N

34°N

N

MAP 17.4 Spanish Missions and Presidios © 2016 Cengage Learning

from the missions to secular (that is, governmental) authorities. This "secularization" program attacked and eroded the immense power of the missions and of their Franciscan masters—with their bawling herds of cattle, debased Indian workers, millions of acres of land, and lucrative foreign trade. The frocked friars had commanded their fiefdoms so self-confidently that earlier reform efforts had dared to go no further than levying a paltry tax on the missions and politely requesting that the missionaries limit their floggings of Indians to fifteen lashes per week. But during the 1830s, the power of the missions weakened, and much of their land and their assets was confiscated by the Californios. Vast *ranchos* (ranches) formed, and from those citadels the Californios ruled in their turn until the Mexican War.

The Californios' glory faded in the wake of the American victory, even though in some isolated places they clung to their political offices for a decade or two. Overwhelmed by the inrush of Anglo gold-diggers—some eighty-seven thousand after the discovery at Sutter's Mill in 1848—and undone by the waning of the pastoral economy, the Californios saw their recently acquired lands and their recently established political power slip through their fingers. When the Civil War broke out in 1861, so harshly did the word *Yankee* ring in their ears that many Californios supported the South.

By 1870 the Californios' brief ascendancy had utterly vanished—a short and sad tale of riches to rags in the face of the Anglo onslaught. Half a century later, beginning in 1910, hundreds of thousands of young Mexicans would flock into California and the Southwest. They would enter a region liberally endowed with Spanish architecture and artifacts, bearing the names of Spanish missions and Californio *ranchos*. But they would find it a land dominated by Anglos, a place far different from that which their Californio ancestors had settled so hopefully in earlier days.

379

Chapter Review

KEY TERMS

Tariff of 1842 (364)
Caroline (365)
Creole (365)
Aroostook War (366)
Manifest Destiny (369)
"Fifty-four forty or fight" (369)
Liberty party (370)
Walker Tariff (371)

spot resolutions (373)
California Bear Flag Republic (374)
Buena Vista, Battle of (374)
Guadalupe Hidalgo, Treaty of (375)
Conscience Whigs (375)
Wilmot Proviso (377)

PEOPLE TO KNOW

John Tyler
James K. Polk
Stephen W. Kearny
John C. Frémont

Winfield Scott
Nicholas P. Trist
David Wilmot

CHRONOLOGY

1837	Canadian rebellion and *Caroline* incident
1839	"Aroostook War" breaks out over Maine boundary
1840	Antislavery Liberty party organized
1841	Harrison dies after four weeks in office Tyler assumes presidency
1842	Webster-Ashburton treaty
1844	Polk defeats Clay in "Manifest Destiny" election
1845	United States annexes Texas
1846	Walker Tariff; Independent treasury restored; United States settles Oregon dispute with Britain; United States and Mexico clash over Texas boundary; Kearny takes Santa Fe; Frémont conquers California; Wilmot Proviso passes House of Representatives
1846–1848	Mexican War
1847	Battle of Buena Vista; Scott takes Mexico City
1848	Treaty of Guadalupe Hidalgo

TO LEARN MORE

William Cronon, *Nature's Metropolis: Chicago and the Great West* (1992)
Iris Engstrand et al., *Culture y Cultura: Consequences of the U.S.-Mexican War, 1846–1848* (1998)
John Mack Faragher, *Sugar Creek: Life on the Illinois Prairie* (1986)
Sam W. Haynes and Christopher Morris, eds., *Manifest Destiny and Empire: American Antebellum Expansionism* (1997)
Robert W. Johannsen, *To the Halls of the Montezumas: The Mexican War in the American Imagination* (1985)
Theodore J. Karamanski, *Fur Trade and Exploration: Opening the Far Northwest, 1821–1852* (1983)
James McCaffrey, *Army of Manifest Destiny: The American Soldier in the Mexican War* (1992)
Dale Morgan, ed., *Overland in 1846: Diaries and Letters of the California-Oregon Trail* (1963)
Martha Sandweiss, *Print and Legend: Photography and the American West* (2002)
Michael L. Tate, *Indians and Emigrants: Encounters on the Overland Trails* (2006)
Richard Bruce Winders, *Crisis in the Southwest: The United States, Mexico, and the Struggle over Texas* (2002)

A complete, annotated bibliography for this chapter—along with brief descriptions of the People to Know—may be found on the *American Pageant* website. The key terms are defined in the glossary at the end of the text.

Chapter 18

Renewing the Sectional Struggle

1848–1854

*Secession! Peaceable secession! Sir, your eyes and
mine are never destined to see that miracle.*

DANIEL WEBSTER, SEVENTH OF MARCH SPEECH, 1850

The year 1848, highlighted by a rash of revolutions in Europe, was filled with unrest in America. The Treaty of Guadalupe Hidalgo had officially ended the war with Mexico, but it had initiated a new and perilous round of political warfare in the United States. The vanquished Mexicans had been forced to relinquish an enormous tract of real estate, including Texas, California, and all the area between. The acquisition of this huge domain raised anew the burning issue of extending slavery into the territories. Northern antislaveryites had rallied behind the Wilmot Proviso, which flatly prohibited slavery in any territory acquired in the Mexican War. Southern senators had blocked the passage of the proviso, but the issue would not die. Ominously, debate over slavery in the area of the Mexican Cession threatened to disrupt the ranks of both Whigs and Democrats and split national politics along North-South sectional lines.

✵ The Popular Sovereignty Panacea

Each of the two great political parties was a vital bond of national unity, for each enjoyed powerful support in both North and South. If they should be replaced by two purely sectional groupings, the Union would be in peril. To politicians, the wisest strategy seemed to be to sit on the lid of the slavery issue and ignore the boiling beneath. Even so, the cover bobbed up and down ominously in response to the agitation of zealous northern abolitionists and impassioned southern "fire-eaters."

Anxious Democrats were forced to seek a new standard-bearer in 1848. President Polk, broken in health by overwork and chronic diarrhea, had pledged himself to a single term. The Democratic National Convention at Baltimore turned to an aging leader, General Lewis Cass, a veteran of the War of 1812. Although a senator and diplomat of wide experience and considerable ability, he was sour-visaged and somewhat pompous. His enemies dubbed him General "Gass" and quickly noted that *Cass* rhymed with *jackass*. The Democratic platform, in line with the lid-sitting strategy, was silent on the burning issue of slavery in the territories.

But Cass himself had not been silent. His views on the extension of slavery were well known because he was the reputed father of **popular sovereignty**. This was the doctrine that stated that the sovereign people of a territory, under the general principles of the Constitution, should themselves determine the status of slavery.

Popular sovereignty had a persuasive appeal. The public liked it because it accorded with the democratic tradition of self-determination. Politicians liked it because it seemed a comfortable compromise between the free-soilers' bid for a ban on slavery in the territories and southern demands that Congress protect slavery in the territories. Popular sovereignty tossed the slavery problem into the laps of the people in the various territories. Advocates of the principle thus hoped to dissolve the most stubborn national issue of the day into a series of local issues. Yet popular sovereignty had one fatal defect: it might serve to spread the blight of slavery.

✯ Political Triumphs for General Taylor

The Whigs, meeting in Philadelphia, cashed in on the "Taylor fever." They nominated frank and honest Zachary Taylor, the "Hero of Buena Vista," who had never held civil office or even voted for president. Henry Clay, the living embodiment of Whiggism, should logically have been nominated. But Clay had made too many speeches—and too many enemies.

As usual, the Whigs pussyfooted in their platform. Eager to win at any cost, they dodged all troublesome issues and merely extolled the homespun virtues of their candidate. The self-reliant old frontier fighter had not committed himself on the issue of slavery extension. But as a wealthy resident of Louisiana, living on a sugar plantation, he owned scores of slaves.

Ardent antislavery men in the North, distrusting both Cass and Taylor, organized the **Free Soil party**. Aroused by the conspiracy of silence in the Democratic and Whig platforms, the Free-Soilers made no bones about their own stand. They came out four-square for the Wilmot Proviso and against slavery in the territories. Going beyond other antislavery groups, they broadened their appeal by advocating federal aid for internal improvements and by urging free government homesteads for settlers.

The new party assembled a strange assortment of new fellows in the same political bed. It attracted industrialists miffed at Polk's reduction of protective tariffs. It appealed to Democrats resentful of Polk's settling for part of Oregon while insisting on all of Texas—a disparity that suggested a menacing southern dominance in the Democratic party. It harbored many northerners whose hatred was directed not so much at slavery as at blacks and who gagged at the prospect of sharing the newly acquired western territories with African Americans. It also contained a large element of "Conscience Whigs," heavily influenced by the abolitionist crusade, who condemned slavery on moral grounds. The Free-Soilers trotted out wizened former president Van Buren and marched into the fray, shouting, "Free soil, free speech, free labor, and free men." These freedoms provided the bedrock on which the Free-Soilers built their party. They condemned slavery not so much for enslaving blacks but for destroying the chances of free white workers to rise up from wage-earning dependence to the esteemed status of self-employment. They argued that only with free soil in the West could a traditional American commitment to upward mobility continue to flourish. If forced to compete with slave labor, more costly wage labor would inevitably wither away, and with it the chance for the American worker to own property. As the first widely inclusive party organized around the issue of slavery and confined to a single section, the Free Soil party foreshadowed the emergence of the Republican party six years later.

General Zachary Taylor (1784–1850) This Democratic campaign cartoon of 1848 charges that Taylor's reputation rested on Mexican skulls.

Library of Congress Prints and Photographs Division [LC-USZC2-3760]

With the slavery issue officially shoved under the rug by the two major parties, the politicians on both sides opened fire on personalities. The amateurish Taylor had to be carefully watched, lest his indiscreet pen puncture the reputation won by his sword. His admirers puffed him up as a gallant knight and a Napoleon, and sloganized his remark, allegedly uttered during the Battle of Buena Vista, "General Taylor never surrenders." Taylor's wartime popularity pulled him through. He harvested 1,360,967 popular and 163 electoral votes, as compared with Cass's 1,222,342 popular and 127 electoral votes. Free-Soiler Van Buren, although winning no state, polled 291,263 ballots and apparently diverted enough Democratic strength from Cass in the crucial state of New York to throw the election to Taylor.

✯ "Californy Gold"

Tobacco-chewing President Taylor—with his stumpy legs, rough features, heavy jaw, black hair, ruddy complexion, and squinty gray eyes—was a military square peg in a political round hole. He would have been spared much turmoil if he could have continued to sit on the slavery lid. But the discovery of gold on the American River near Sutter's Mill, California, early in 1848, blew the cover off (see Map 18.1).

A horde of adventurers poured into the valleys of California. Singing "O Susannah!" and shouting "Gold! Gold! Gold!" they began tearing frantically at the yellow-graveled streams and hills. A fortunate few of the bearded miners "struck it rich" at the "diggings." But the luckless many, who netted blisters instead of nuggets, probably would have been money well ahead if they had stayed at home unaffected by "gold fever," which was often followed by more deadly fevers. The most reliable profits were made by those who mined the miners, notably by charging outrageous rates for laundry and other personal services. Some soiled clothing was even sent as far away as the Hawaiian Islands for washing. Many of the "forty-niners" who flopped in California kept chasing their dream of gold in even more distant places, notably Australia in 1851.

The **California gold rush** attracted tens of thousands of people to the future Golden State almost overnight, completely overwhelming the one-horse territorial government. A distressingly high proportion of the newcomers were lawless men, accompanied or followed by virtueless women. A contemporary song ran,

> *Oh what was your name in the States?*
> *Was it Thompson or Johnson or Bates?*
> *Did you murder your wife,*
> *And fly for your life?*
> *Say, what was your name in the States?*

An outburst of crime inevitably resulted from the presence of so many miscreants and outcasts. Robbery, claim jumping, and murder were commonplace, and such violence was only partly discouraged by rough vigilante justice. In San Francisco, from 1848 to 1856, there were scores of lawless killings but only three semilegal hangings.

A married woman wrote from the California goldfields to her sister in New England in 1853,

"i tell you the woman are in great demand in this country no matter whether they are married or not you need not think strange if you see me coming home with some good looking man some of these times with a pocket full of rocks.... it is all the go here for Ladys to leave there Husbands two out of three do it there is a first rate Chance for a single woman she can have her choice of thousands i wish mother was here she could marry a rich man and not have to lift her hand to do her work.**"**

MAP 18.1 California Gold Rush Country Miners from all over the world swarmed over the rivers that drained the western slope of California's Sierra Nevada. Their nationalities and religions, their languages, and their ways of life are recorded in the colorful place names they left behind. © 2016 Cengage Learning

A majority of Californians, as decent and law-abiding citizens needing protection, grappled earnestly with the problem of erecting an adequate state government. Privately encouraged by President Taylor, they drafted a constitution in 1849 that excluded slavery and then boldly applied to Congress for admission. California would thus bypass the usual territorial stage, thwarting southern congressmen seeking to block free soil. Southern politicians, alarmed by the Californians' "impertinent" stroke for freedom, arose in violent opposition. Would California prove to be the golden straw that broke the back of the Union?

The idea that many ne'er-do-wells went west is found in the Journals (January 1849) of Ralph Waldo Emerson (1803–1882):

"If a man is going to California, he announces it with some hesitation; because it is a confession that he has failed at home.**"**

Placer Miners in California Cheap but effective, placer mining consisted of literally "washing" the gold out of surface deposits. No deep excavation was required. This crew of male and female miners in California in 1852 was using a "long tom" sluice that washed relatively large quantities of ore.

✴ Sectional Balance and the Underground Railroad

The South of 1850 was relatively well-off. It then enjoyed, as it had from the beginning, more than its share of the nation's leadership. It had seated in the White House the war hero Zachary Taylor, a Virginia-born, slaveowning planter from Louisiana. It boasted a majority in the cabinet and on the Supreme Court. If outnumbered in the House, the South had equality in the Senate, where it could at least neutralize northern maneuvers. Its cotton fields were expanding, and cotton prices were profitably high. Few sane people, North or South, believed that slavery was seriously threatened where it already existed below the Mason-Dixon line. The fifteen slave states could easily veto any proposed constitutional amendment.

Yet the South was deeply worried, as it had been for several decades, by the ever-tipping political balance. There were then fifteen slave states and fifteen free states. The admission of California

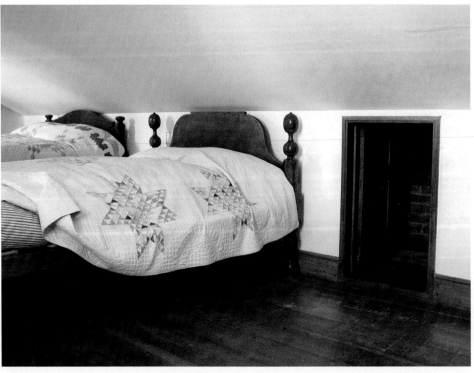

A Stop on the Underground Railroad Escaping slaves could be hidden in this small upstairs room of Levi and Catharine Coffin's House in Newport, Indiana. The beds were moved in front of the door to hide its existence. The Coffins were Quakers from North Carolina who, during twenty years in Newport, helped more than 2,000 fleeing slaves safely reach Canada—and freedom.

Harriet Tubman (on left) with Some of the Slaves She Helped to Free John Brown called her "General Tubman" for her effective work in helping slaves escape to Canada on the Underground Railroad. During the Civil War, she served as a Union spy behind Confederate lines. Herself illiterate, she worked after the war to bring education to the freed slaves in North Carolina.

would destroy the delicate equilibrium in the Senate, perhaps forever. Potential slave territory under the American flag was running short, if it had not in fact disappeared. Agitation had already developed in the territories of New Mexico and Utah for admission as nonslave states. The fate of California might well establish a precedent for the rest of the Mexican Cession territory—an area purchased largely with southern blood.

Texas nursed an additional grievance of its own. It claimed a huge area east of the Rio Grande and north to the forty-second parallel, embracing in part about half the territory of present-day New Mexico (see Map 18.2). The federal government was proposing to detach this prize, while hot-blooded Texans were threatening to descend upon Santa Fe and seize what they regarded as rightfully theirs. The explosive quarrel foreshadowed shooting.

Many southerners were also angered by the nagging agitation in the North for the abolition of slavery in the District of Columbia. They looked with alarm on the prospect of a ten-mile-square oasis of free soil thrust between slaveholding Maryland and slaveholding Virginia.

Even more disagreeable to the South was the loss of runaway slaves, many of whom were assisted north by the **Underground Railroad**. This virtual freedom train consisted of an informal chain of "stations" (antislavery homes) through which scores of "passengers" (runaway slaves) were spirited by "conductors" (usually white and black abolitionists) from the slave states to the free-soil sanctuary of Canada.

The most amazing of these "conductors" was an illiterate runaway slave from Maryland, fearless Harriet Tubman. During nineteen forays into the South, she rescued more than three hundred slaves, including her aged parents, and deservedly earned the title "Moses." Lively imaginations later exaggerated the reach of the

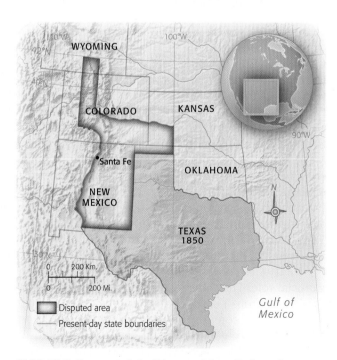

MAP 18.2 Texas and the Disputed Area Before the Compromise of 1850 © 2016 Cengage Learning

Underground Railroad and its "stationmasters," but its importance was undisputed.

By 1850 southerners were demanding a new and more stringent fugitive-slave law. The old one, passed by Congress in 1793, had proved inadequate to cope with runaways, especially since unfriendly state authorities failed to provide needed cooperation. Unlike cattle thieves, the abolitionists who ran the Underground Railroad did not gain personally from their lawlessness. But to the slaveowners, the loss was infuriating, whatever the motives. The moral judgments of the abolitionists seemed, in some ways, more galling than outright theft. They reflected not only a holier-than-thou attitude but a refusal to obey the laws solemnly passed by Congress.

Estimates indicate that the South in 1850 was losing perhaps 1,000 runaways a year out of its total of some 4 million slaves. In fact, more blacks probably gained their freedom by self-purchase or voluntary emancipation than ever escaped. But the principle weighed heavily with the slavemasters. They rested their argument on the Constitution, which they claimed (not entirely implausibly) protected slavery, and on the laws of Congress, which explicitly provided for slave-catching. "Although the loss of property is felt," said a southern senator, "the loss of honor is felt still more."

✦ Twilight of the Senatorial Giants

Southern fears were such that Congress was confronted with catastrophe in 1850. Free-soil California was banging on the door for admission. "Fire-eaters" in the South were voicing ominous threats of secession. In October 1849 southerners had announced their intention to convene the following year in Nashville, Tennessee, to consider withdrawing from the Union. The failure of Congress to act could easily mean the failure of the United States as a country. The crisis brought into the congressional forum the most distinguished assemblage of statesmen since the Constitutional Convention of 1787—the Old Guard of the dying generation and the young gladiators of the new. That "immortal trio"—Clay, Calhoun, and Webster—appeared together for the last time on the public stage.

Henry Clay, now seventy-three years of age, played a crucial role. The "Great Compromiser" had come to the Senate from Kentucky to reprise the role he had played twice before, in the Missouri and nullification crises. The once-glamorous statesman—though disillusioned, enfeebled, and racked by a cruel cough—was still eloquent, conciliatory, and captivating. He proposed and skillfully defended a series of compromises. He was ably seconded by thirty-seven-year-old Senator Stephen A. Douglas of Illinois, the "Little Giant" (five feet four inches), whose role was less spectacular but even more important. Clay urged with all his persuasiveness that the North and South both make concessions and that the North partially yield by enacting a more feasible fugitive-slave law.

Senator John C. Calhoun, the "Great Nullifier," then sixty-eight and dying of tuberculosis, championed the South in his last formal speech. Too weak to deliver it himself, he sat bundled up in the Senate chamber, his eyes glowing within a stern face, while a younger colleague read his fateful words. "I have, Senators, believed from the first that the agitation on the subject of slavery would, if not prevented by some timely and effective measure, end in disunion." Although approving the purpose of Clay's proposed concessions, Calhoun rejected them as not providing adequate safeguards for southern rights. His impassioned plea was to leave slavery alone, return runaway slaves, give the South its rights as a minority, and restore the political balance. He had in view, as was later revealed, an utterly unworkable scheme of electing two presidents, one from the North and one from the South, each wielding a veto.

Calhoun died in 1850, before the debate was over, murmuring the sad words, "The South! The South! God knows what will become of her!" Appreciative fellow citizens in Charleston erected to his memory an imposing monument, which bore the inscription "Truth, Justice, and the Constitution." Calhoun had labored to preserve the Union and had taken his stand on the Constitution, but his proposals in their behalf almost undid both.

Daniel Webster next took the Senate spotlight to uphold Clay's compromise measures in his last great speech, a three-hour effort. Now sixty-eight years old and suffering from a liver complaint aggravated by high living, he had lost some of the fire in his magnificent voice. Speaking deliberately and before overflowing galleries, he urged all reasonable concessions to the South, including a new fugitive-slave law with teeth.

As for slavery in the territories, asked Webster, why legislate on the subject? To do so was an act of sacrilege, for Almighty God had already passed the Wilmot Proviso. The good Lord had decreed—through climate, topography, and geography—that a plantation economy, and hence a slave economy, could not profitably exist in the Mexican Cession territory.* Webster sanely concluded that compromise, concession, and sweet reasonableness would provide the only solutions. "Let us not be pygmies," he pleaded, "in a case that calls for men."

If measured by its immediate effects, Webster's famed **Seventh of March speech** of 1850 was his finest. It helped turn the tide in the North toward compromise. The clamor for printed copies became

---

*Webster was wrong here; within one hundred years, California had become one of the great cotton-producing states of the Union.

Ralph Waldo Emerson, the philosopher and moderate abolitionist, was outraged by Webster's support of concessions to the South in the Fugitive Slave Act. In February 1851 he wrote in his journal,

" I opened a paper to-day in which he [Webster] pounds on the old strings [of liberty] in a letter to the Washington Birthday feasters at New York. 'Liberty! liberty!' Pho! Let Mr. Webster, for decency's sake, shut his lips once and forever on this word. The word *liberty* in the mouth of Mr. Webster sounds like the word *love* in the mouth of a courtesan. **"**

so great that Webster mailed out more than 100,000, remarking that 200,000 would not satisfy the demand. His tremendous effort visibly strengthened Union sentiment. It was especially pleasing to the banking and commercial centers of the North, which stood to lose millions of dollars by secession. One prominent Washington banker canceled two notes of Webster's totaling $5,000 and sent him a personal check for $1,000 and a message of congratulations.

But the Free-Soilers and abolitionists, who had assumed Webster was one of them, upbraided him as a traitor, worthy of bracketing with Benedict Arnold. The poet John Greenleaf Whittier lamented,

So fallen! so lost! the light withdrawn
Which once he wore!
The glory from his gray hairs gone
For evermore!

These reproaches were most unfair. Webster had long regarded slavery as evil but disunion as worse.

Deadlock and Danger on Capitol Hill

The stormy congressional debate of 1850 was not finished, for the Young Guard from the North were yet to have their say. This was the group of newer leaders who, unlike the aging Old Guard, had not grown up with the Union. They were more interested in purging and purifying it than in patching and preserving it.

William H. Seward, the wiry and husky-throated freshman senator from New York, was the able spokesman for many of the younger northern radicals. A strong anti-slaveryite, he came out unequivocally against concession. He seemed not to realize that compromise had brought the Union together and that when the sections could no longer compromise, they would have to part company.

Seward argued earnestly that Christian legislators must obey God's moral law as well as man's mundane law. He therefore appealed, with reference to excluding slavery in the territories, to an even "higher law" than the Constitution. This alarming phrase, wrenched from its context, may have cost him the presidential nomination and the presidency in 1860.

As the great debate in Congress ran its heated course, deadlock seemed certain. Blunt old President Taylor, who had allegedly fallen under the influence of men like "Higher Law" Seward, seemed bent on vetoing any compromise passed by Congress. His military ire was aroused by the threats of Texas to seize Santa Fe. He appeared to be doggedly determined to "Jacksonize" the dissenters, if need be, by leading an army against the Texans in person and hanging all "damned traitors." If troops had begun to march, the South probably would have rallied to the defense of Texas, and the Civil War might have erupted in 1850.

Breaking the Congressional Logjam

At the height of the controversy in 1850, President Taylor unknowingly helped the cause of concession by dying suddenly, probably of an acute intestinal disorder. Portly, round-faced Vice President Millard Fillmore, a colorless and conciliatory New York lawyer-politician, took over the reins. As presiding officer of the Senate, he had been impressed with the arguments for conciliation, and he gladly signed the series of compromise measures that passed Congress after seven long months of stormy debate. The balancing of interests in the **Compromise of 1850** was delicate in the extreme (see Table 18.1).

TABLE 18.1 Compromise of 1850	
Concessions to the North	Concessions to the South
California admitted as a free state	The remainder of the Mexican Cession area to be formed into the territories of New Mexico and Utah, without restriction on slavery, hence open to popular sovereignty
Territory disputed by Texas and New Mexico to be surrendered to New Mexico	Texas to receive $10 million from the federal government as compensation
Abolition of the slave trade (but not slavery) in the District of Columbia	A more stringent fugitive-slave law going beyond that of 1793

The struggle to get these measures accepted by the country was hardly less heated than in Congress. In the northern states, "Union savers" like Senators Clay, Webster, and Douglas orated on behalf of the compromise. The ailing Clay himself delivered more than seventy speeches, as a powerful sentiment for acceptance gradually crystallized in the North. It was strengthened by a growing spirit of goodwill, which sprang partly from a feeling of relief and partly from an upsurge of prosperity enriched by California gold.

But the "fire-eaters" of the South were still violently opposed to concessions. One extreme South Carolina newspaper avowed that it loathed the Union and hated the North as much as it did Hell itself. A movement in the South to boycott northern goods gained some headway, but in the end the southern Unionists, assisted by the warm glow of prosperity, prevailed.

In June 1850 the assemblage of southern extremists met in Nashville, ironically near the burial place of Andrew Jackson. The delegates not only took a strong position in favor of slavery but condemned the compromise measures then being hammered out in Congress. Meeting again in November after the bills had passed, the convention proved to be a dud. By that time southern opinion had reluctantly accepted the verdict of Congress.

Like the calm after a storm, a second Era of Good Feelings dawned. Disquieting talk of secession subsided. Peace-loving people, both North and South, were determined that the compromises should be a "finality" and that the explosive issue of slavery should be buried. But this placid period proved all too brief.

✴ Balancing the Compromise Scales

Who got the better deal in the Compromise of 1850? The answer is clearly the North (see Map 18.3). California, as a free state, tipped the Senate balance permanently against the South. The territories of New Mexico and Utah were open to slavery on the basis of popular sovereignty. But the iron law of nature—the "highest law" of all—had loaded the dice in favor of free soil. Southerners urgently needed more slave territory to restore the "sacred balance." If they could not carve new states out of the recent conquests from Mexico, where else might they get them? The Caribbean was one answer.

Even the apparent gains of the South rang hollow. Disgruntled Texas was to be paid $10 million toward discharging its indebtedness, but in the long run this was a modest sum. The immense area in dispute had been torn from the side of slaveholding Texas and was almost certain to be free. The South had halted the drive toward abolition in the District of Columbia, at least temporarily, by permitting the outlawing of the

Henry Clay Proposing the Compromise of 1850 This engraving captures one of the most dramatic moments in the history of the United States Senate. Vice President Millard Fillmore presides, while on the floor sit several of the "Senatorial Giants" of the era, including Daniel Webster, Stephen A. Douglas, and John C. Calhoun.

slave *trade* in the federal district. But even this move was an entering wedge toward complete emancipation in the nation's capital.

Most alarming of all, the drastic new **Fugitive Slave Law** of 1850—"the Bloodhound Bill"—stirred up a storm of opposition in the North. The fleeing slaves could not testify in their own behalf, and they were denied a jury trial. These harsh practices, some citizens feared, threatened to create dangerous precedents for white Americans. The federal commissioner who handled the case of a fugitive would receive five dollars if the runaway were freed and ten dollars if not—an arrangement that strongly resembled a bribe. Freedom-loving northerners who aided the slave to escape were liable to heavy fines and jail sentences. They might even be ordered to join the slave-catchers, and this possibility rubbed salt into old sores.

So abhorrent was this "Man-Stealing Law" that it touched off an explosive chain reaction in the North. Many shocked moderates, hitherto passive, were driven into the swelling ranks of the antislaveryites. When a runaway slave from Virginia was captured in Boston in 1854, he had to be removed from the city under heavy federal guard through streets lined with sullen Yankees and shadowed by black-draped buildings festooned with flags flying upside down. One prominent Bostonian who witnessed this grim spectacle wrote that "we went to bed one night old-fashioned, conservative, Compromise Union Whigs and waked up stark mad Abolitionists."

The Underground Railroad stepped up its timetable, and infuriated northern mobs rescued slaves from their pursuers. Massachusetts, in a move toward nullification suggestive of South Carolina in 1832, made it a penal offense for any state official to enforce the new federal statute. Other states passed "personal liberty laws," which denied local jails to federal officials and otherwise hampered enforcement. The abolitionists rent the heavens with their protests against the man-stealing statute. A meeting presided over by William Lloyd Garrison in 1851 declared, "We execrate it, we spit upon it, we trample it under our feet."

Beyond question, the Fugitive Slave Law was an appalling blunder on the part of the South. No single irritant of the 1850s was more persistently galling to both sides, and none did more to awaken in the North a spirit of antagonism against the South. The southerners in turn were embittered because the northerners would not in good faith execute the law—the one real and immediate southern "gain" from the

MAP 18.3 Slavery After the Compromise of 1850 Regarding the Fugitive Slave Law provisions of the Compromise of 1850, Ralph Waldo Emerson declared in May 1851 at Concord, Massachusetts, "The act of Congress…is a law which every one of you will break on the earliest occasion—a law which no man can obey, or abet the obeying, without loss of self-respect and forfeiture of the name of gentleman." Privately he wrote in his journal, "This filthy enactment was made in the nineteenth century, by people who could read and write. I will not obey it, by God." © 2016 Cengage Learning

Protesting the Fugitive Slave Law, 1850 The cartoonist makes bitter sport of the hated law and heaps scorn on Daniel Webster, on his hands and knees at the right, who voted for the law as part of the Compromise of 1850. The outspoken abolitionist William Lloyd Garrison is depicted much more favorably on the left.

Great Compromise. Slave-catchers, with some success, redoubled their efforts.

Should the shooting showdown have come in 1850? From the standpoint of the secessionists, yes; from the standpoint of the Unionists, no. Time was fighting for the North. With every passing decade, this huge section was forging further ahead in population and wealth—in crops, factories, foundries, ships, and railroads.

Delay also added immensely to the moral strength of the North—to its will to fight for the Union. In 1850 countless thousands of northern moderates were unwilling to pin the South to the rest of the nation with bayonets. But the inflammatory events of the 1850s did much to bolster the Yankee will to resist secession, whatever the cost. This one feverish decade gave the North time to accumulate the material and moral strength that provided the margin of victory. Thus the Compromise of 1850, from one point of view, won the Civil War for the Union (see Map 18.4).

✦ Defeat and Doom for the Whigs

Meeting in Baltimore, the Democratic nominating convention of 1852 startled the nation. Hopelessly deadlocked, it finally stampeded to the second "dark-horse" candidate in American history, an unrenowned lawyer-politician, Franklin Pierce, from the hills of New Hampshire. The Whigs tried to jeer him back into obscurity with the cry "Who is Frank Pierce?" Democrats replied, "The Young Hickory of the Granite Hills."

Pierce was a weak and indecisive figure. Youngish, handsome, militarily erect, smiling, and convivial, he had served without real distinction in the Mexican War. As a result of a painful groin injury that caused him to fall off

Contending Voices
The Compromise of 1850

Two senatorial giants hotly debated the nature—and future—of the Union as they tried to hammer out the Compromise of 1850:

John C. Calhoun (1782–1850), South Carolina:

❝If you, who represent the stronger portion, cannot agree to settle…[then] let the states we both represent agree to separate and part in peace. If you are unwilling we should part in peace, tell us so; and we shall know what to do, when you reduce the question to submission or resistance.❞

Daniel Webster (1782–1852) of Massachusetts replied:

❝There can be no such thing as a peaceable secession. Peaceable secession is an utter impossibility.…I see that disruption must produce such a war as I will not describe.❞

Who proved the more accurate prophet?

a horse, he was known as the "Fainting General," though scandalmongers pointed to a fondness for alcohol. But he was enemyless because he had been inconspicuous, and as a prosouthern northerner, he was acceptable to the slavery wing of the Democratic party. His platform revived the Democrats' commitment to territorial expansion as pursued by President Polk and emphatically endorsed the Compromise of 1850, Fugitive Slave Law and all.

The Whigs, also convening in Baltimore, missed a splendid opportunity to capitalize on their record in statecraft. Able to boast of a praiseworthy achievement in the Compromise of 1850, they might logically have nominated President Fillmore or Senator Webster, both of whom were associated with it. But having won in the past only with military heroes, they turned to another, "Old Fuss and Feathers" Winfield Scott, perhaps the ablest American general of his generation. Although he was a huge and impressive figure, his manner bordered on haughtiness. His personality not only repelled the masses but eclipsed his genuinely statesmanlike achievements. The Whig platform praised the Compromise of 1850 as a lasting arrangement, though less enthusiastically than the Democrats.

With slavery and sectionalism to some extent soft-pedaled, the campaign again degenerated into a dull and childish attack on personalities. Democrats ridiculed Scott's pomposity; Whigs charged that Pierce was the hero of "many a well-fought *bottle*." Democrats cried exultantly, "We Polked 'em in '44; we'll Pierce 'em in '52."

Luckily for the Democrats, the Whig party was hopelessly split. Antislavery Whigs of the North swallowed Scott as their nominee but deplored his platform, which endorsed the hated Fugitive Slave Law. The current phrase ran, "We accept the candidate but spit on the platform." Southern Whigs, who doubted Scott's loyalty to the Compromise of 1850 and especially the Fugitive Slave Law, accepted the platform but spat on the candidate. More than five thousand Georgia Whigs—"finality men"—voted in vain for Webster, although he had died nearly two weeks before the election.

General Scott, victorious on the battlefield, met defeat at the ballot box. His friends remarked whimsically that he was not used to "running." Actually, he was stabbed in the back by his fellow Whigs, notably in the South. In addition, Free Soil party candidate

MAP 18.4 The Legal Status of Slavery, from the Revolution to the Civil War © 2016 Cengage Learning

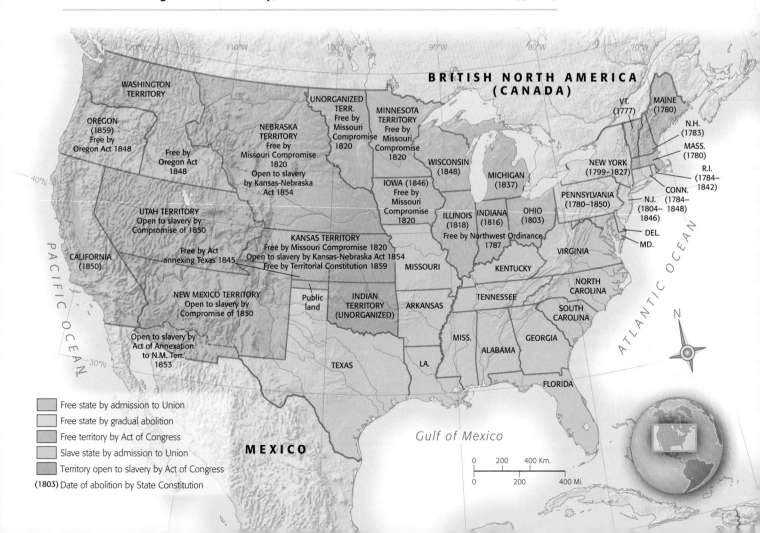

John P. Hale, senator from New Hampshire, siphoned off northern Whig votes that might have gone to Scott. Hale walked away with a respectable 5 percent of the popular vote. The pliant Pierce won in a landslide, 254 electoral votes to 42, although the popular count was closer, 1,601,117 to 1,385,453.

The election of 1852 was fraught with frightening significance, though it may have seemed tame at the time. It marked the effective end of the disorganized Whig party and, within a few years, its complete death. The Whigs' demise augured the eclipse of *national* parties and the worrisome rise of purely *sectional* political alignments. The Whigs were governed at times by the crassest opportunism, and they won only two presidential elections (1840, 1848) in their colorful career, both with war heroes. They finally choked to death trying to swallow the distasteful Fugitive Slave Law. But their great contribution—and a noteworthy one indeed—was to help uphold the ideal of the Union through their electoral strength in the South and through the eloquence of leaders like Henry Clay and Daniel Webster. Both of these statesmen, by unhappy coincidence, died during the 1852 campaign. But the good they had done lived after them and contributed powerfully to the eventual preservation of a *united* United States.

✴ Expansionist Stirrings South of the Border

The intoxicating victory in the Mexican War, coupled with the discovery of gold in California just nine days before the war's end, reinvigorated the spirit of Manifest Destiny. The rush to the Sierra Nevada goldfields

aroused particular concerns about the fate of Central America. Since the days of Balboa, this narrow neck of land had stimulated dreams of a continuous Atlantic-to-Pacific transportation route that would effectively sever the two American continents (see Map 18.5). Whoever controlled that route would hold imperial sway over all maritime nations, especially the United States.

Increasing British encroachment into the area—including the British seizure of the port of San Juan del Norte (renamed Greytown) on Nicaragua's "Mosquito Coast"—drove the governments of both the United States and New Granada (later Colombia) to conclude an important treaty in 1848. It guaranteed the American right of transit across the isthmus in return for Washington's pledge to maintain the "perfect neutrality" of the route so that the "free transit of traffic might not be interrupted." The agreement later provided a fig leaf of legal cover for Theodore Roosevelt's assertion of American control of the Panama Canal Zone in 1903. It also led to the construction of the first "transcontinental" railroad. Completed in 1855 at a cost of thousands of lives lost to pestilence and accident, it ran forty-eight miles from coast to coast through the green hell of the Panamanian jungle. A full-blown confrontation with Britain was avoided by the **Clayton-Bulwer Treaty** in 1850, which stipulated that neither America nor Britain would fortify or seek exclusive control over any future isthmian waterway (later rescinded by the Hay-Pauncefote Treaty of 1901; see p. 627).

Southern "slavocrats" cast especially covetous eyes southward in the 1850s. They lusted for new slave territory after the Compromise of 1850 seemingly closed most of the Mexican Cession to the "peculiar institution." In 1856 a Texan proposed a toast that was

MAP 18.5 Central America, ca. 1850, Showing British Possessions and Proposed Canal Routes Until President Theodore Roosevelt swung into action with his big stick in 1903, a Nicaraguan canal, closer to the United States, was generally judged more desirable than a canal across Panama. © 2016 Cengage Learning

drunk with gusto: "To the Southern republic bounded on the north by the Mason and Dixon line and on the South by the Isthmus of Tehuantepec [southern Mexico], including Cuba and all other lands on our Southern shore." Nicaragua beckoned beguilingly. A brazen American adventurer, William Walker, tried repeatedly to grab control of this Central American country. (He had earlier tried and failed to seize Baja California from Mexico and turn it into a slave state.) Backed by an armed force recruited largely in the South, he installed himself as president in July 1856 and promptly legalized slavery. One southern newspaper proclaimed to the planter aristocracy that Walker—the "gray-eyed man of destiny"—"now offers Nicaragua to you and your slaves, at a time when you have not a friend on the face of the earth." But a coalition of Central American nations formed an alliance to overthrow him. President Pierce withdrew diplomatic recognition, and the gray-eyed man's destiny was to crumple before a Honduran firing squad in 1860.

Sugar-rich Cuba, lying just off the nation's southern doorstep, was also an enticing prospect for annexation. This remnant of Spain's once-mighty New World empire already held a large population of enslaved blacks, and it might be carved into several states, restoring the political balance in the Senate. President Polk had considered offering Spain $100 million for Cuba, but the proud Spaniards replied that they would sooner see the island sunk into the sea than in the hands of the hated Yankees.

Rebuffed as buyers, some southern adventurers now undertook to shake the tree of Manifest Destiny. During 1850–1851 two "filibustering" (from the Spanish *filibustero*, meaning "freebooter" or "pirate") expeditions, each numbering several hundred armed men, descended upon Cuba. Both feeble efforts were repelled, and the last one ended in tragedy when the leader and fifty followers—some of them from the "best families" of the South—were summarily shot or strangled. So outraged were the southerners that an angry mob sacked Spain's consulate in New Orleans.

Spanish officials in Cuba rashly forced a showdown in 1854, when they seized the American steamer

Black Warrior on a technicality. Now was the time for President Pierce, dominated as he was by the South, to provoke a war with Spain and seize Cuba. The major powers of Europe—England, France, and Russia—were about to become bogged down in the Crimean War and hence were unable to aid Spain.

An incredible cloak-and-dagger episode followed. The secretary of state instructed the American ministers in Spain, England, and France to prepare confidential recommendations for the acquisition of Cuba. Meeting initially at Ostend, Belgium, the three envoys drew up a top-secret dispatch, soon known as the **Ostend Manifesto**. This startling document urged that the administration offer $120 million for Cuba. If Spain refused, and if its continued ownership endangered American interests, the United States would "be justified in wresting" the island from the Spanish.

The secret Ostend Manifesto quickly leaked out. Northern free-soilers, already angered by the Fugitive Slave Law and other gains for slavery, rose up in wrath against the "manifesto of brigands." The shackled black hands of Harriet Beecher Stowe's Uncle Tom, whose plight had already stung the conscience of the North, now held the South back. The red-faced Pierce administration hurriedly dropped its reckless schemes for Cuba. The slavery issue thus checked territorial expansion in the 1850s.

✴ The Allure of Asia

The acquisition of California and Oregon had made the United States a Pacific power—or would-be power. How could Americans now tap more deeply the supposedly rich markets of Asia? Rivalry with the British lion once again played a role. Britain had recently humbled China in the **Opium War**, fought to secure the right of British traders to peddle opium in the Celestial Kingdom. At the war's conclusion in 1842, Britain gained free access to five so-called treaty ports, as well as outright control of the island of Hong Kong (where it remained for another century and a half). Prodded by Boston merchants fearful of seeing Britain horn in on their lucrative trade with China, President Tyler thereupon dispatched Caleb Cushing, a dashing Massachusetts lawyer-scholar, to secure comparable concessions for the United States. Cushing's four warships arrived at Macao, in southern China, in early 1844, bearing gifts that included a weathervane and a pair of six-shooters.

Impressed by Cushing's charm and largesse—and also eager for a counterweight to the meddlesome British—silk-gowned Chinese diplomats signed the **Treaty of Wanghia**, the first formal diplomatic agreement between the United States and China, on July 3, 1844. Cushing was interested in commerce, not

The first platform of the newly born (antislavery) Republican party in 1856 lashed out at the Ostend Manifesto, with its transparent suggestion that Cuba be seized. The plank read,

❝Resolved, That the highwayman's plea, that 'might makes right,' embodied in the Ostend Circular, was in every respect unworthy of American diplomacy, and would bring shame and dishonor upon any Government or people that gave it their sanction.**❞**

Commodore Perry's Gift of a Railway to the Japanese in 1853 (woodblock print), Hiroshige, Ando or Utagawa (1797–1858)/Private Collection/The Bridgeman Art Library

Commodore Matthew Perry in Japan, 1853 Among Perry's gifts to the Japanese was a miniature railway, complete with engine, cars, and track, which made a vivid impression on the Japanese artist who created this work.

colonies, and he secured some vital rights and privileges from the Chinese. "Most favored nation" status afforded the United States any and all trading terms accorded to other powers. "Extraterritoriality" provided for trying Americans accused of crimes in China before American officials, not in Chinese courts. (Cushing was prompted to seek this particular immunity by the memory of a seaman on a U.S. vessel who had been strangled to death by Chinese authorities for what was apparently the accidental drowning of a Chinese woman.) American trade with China flourished thanks to Cushing's treaty, though it never reached the proportions his backers had dreamed of. More immediately important was the opportunity it opened for American missionaries, thousands of whom soon flooded prayerfully through the treaty ports to convert the "heathen Chinese." Fatefully, America had now aligned itself with the Western powers that chronically menaced China's cultural integrity. All of them would one day reap a bitter harvest of resentment.

Success in China soon inspired a still more consequential mission to pry open the bamboo gates of Japan. After some disagreeable experiences with the European world, Japan, at about the same time Jamestown was settled, withdrew into an almost airtight cocoon of isolationism and remained there for more than two centuries. The long-ruling warrior dynasty known as the Tokugawa Shogunate was so protective of Japan's insularity that it prohibited shipwrecked foreign sailors from leaving and refused to readmit Japanese sailors who had been washed up on foreign shores. Meanwhile, industrial and democratic revolutions were convulsing the Western world, while Japan

remained placidly secluded. By 1853 Japan was ready to emerge from its self-imposed quarantine.

In 1852 President Millard Fillmore dispatched to Japan a fleet of warships commanded by Commodore Matthew C. Perry. The brother of the hero of the Battle of Lake Erie in 1813, Perry prepared diligently for his mission, voraciously reading about Japan, querying whalers about Pacific Ocean currents, and collecting specimens of American technology with which to impress the Japanese. His four awesome, smoke-belching "black ships" steamed into Edo (later Tokyo) Bay on July 8, 1853, inciting near-panic among the shocked Japanese. After tense negotiations, during which Perry threatened to blast his way ashore if necessary, Perry stepped onto the beach, preceded by two conspicuously tall African American flag bearers. From elaborately carved gold-trimmed boxes, Perry produced silk-bound letters requesting free trade and friendly relations. He handed them to the wary Japanese delegation and then tactfully withdrew, promising to return the following year to receive the Japanese reply.

True to his word, Perry returned in February 1854 with an even larger force of seven men-of-war. Once again he combined bluster and grace, plying the Japanese with gifts, including a miniature steam locomotive and 350 feet of track. With this display of pomp and bravado, he persuaded the Japanese to sign the landmark **Treaty of Kanagawa** on March 31, 1854. It provided for proper treatment of shipwrecked sailors, American coaling rights in Japan, and the establishment of consular relations. Perry had inserted only a commercial toe in the door, but he had cracked Japan's two-century shell of isolation wideopen. Within little more than a decade, the "Meiji Restoration" would end the era of the Shogunate and propel the Land of the Rising Sun headlong into the modern world—and an eventual epochal military clash with the United States.

✦ Pacific Railroad Promoters and the Gadsden Purchase

Acute transportation problems were another legacy of the Mexican War. The newly acquired prizes of California and Oregon might just as well have been islands some eight thousand miles west of the nation's capital. The sea routes to and from the Isthmus of Panama, to say nothing of those around South America, were too long. Covered-wagon travel past bleaching animal bones was possible, but slow and dangerous. A popular song recalled,

> They swam the wide rivers and crossed the tall peaks,
> And camped on the prairie for weeks upon weeks.
> Starvation and cholera and hard work and slaughter,
> They reached California spite of hell and high water.

Feasible land transportation was imperative—or the newly won possessions on the Pacific Coast might break away. Camels were even proposed as the answer. Several score of these temperamental beasts—"ships of the desert"—were imported from the Near East, but mule-driving Americans did not adjust to them. A transcontinental railroad was clearly the only real solution to the problem.

Railroad promoters, both North and South, had projected many drawing-board routes to the Pacific Coast. But the estimated cost in all cases was so great that for many years there could obviously be only one line. Should its terminus be in the North or in the South? The favored section would reap rich rewards in wealth, population, and influence. The South, losing the economic race with the North, was eager to extend a railroad through adjacent southwestern territory all the way to California.

Another chunk of Mexico now seemed desirable because the campaigns of the recent war had shown that the best railway route ran slightly south of the Mexican border. Secretary of War Jefferson Davis, a Mississippian, arranged to have James Gadsden, a prominent South Carolina railroad man, appointed minister to Mexico. Finding Santa Anna in power for the sixth and last time, and as usual in need of money, Gadsden made gratifying headway. He negotiated a treaty in 1853, which ceded to the United States the **Gadsden Purchase** for $10 million (see Map 18.6). The transaction aroused much criticism among northerners, who objected to paying a huge sum for a cactus-strewn desert nearly the size of Gadsden's South Carolina. Undeterred, the Senate approved the pact, in the process shortsightedly eliminating a window on the Sea of Cortez.

No doubt the Gadsden Purchase enabled the South to claim the coveted railroad with even greater insistence. A southern track would be easier to build because the mountains were less high and because the route, unlike the proposed northern lines, would not pass through unorganized territory. Texas was already a state at this point, and New Mexico (with the Gadsden Purchase added) was a formally organized territory, with federal troops available to provide protection against marauding tribes of Indians. Any northern or central railroad line would have to be thrust through the unorganized territory of Nebraska, where the buffalo and Indians roamed.

Northern railroad boosters quickly replied that if organized territory were the test, then Nebraska should be organized. Such a move was not premature because thousands of land-hungry pioneers were already poised on the Nebraska border. But all schemes proposed in Congress for organizing the territory were greeted with apathy or hostility by many southerners. Why should the South help create new free-soil states and thus cut its own throat by facilitating a northern railroad?

MAP 18.6 The Gadsden Purchase, 1853 © 2016 Cengage Learning

✦ Douglas's Kansas-Nebraska Scheme

At this point in 1854, Senator Stephen A. Douglas of Illinois delivered a counterstroke to offset the Gadsden thrust for southern expansion westward. A squat, bull-necked, and heavy-chested figure, the "Little Giant" radiated the energy and breezy optimism of the self-made man. An ardent booster for the West, he longed to break the North-South deadlock over westward expansion and stretch a line of settlements across the continent. He had also invested heavily in Chicago real estate and in railway stock and was eager to have the Windy City become the eastern terminus of the proposed Pacific railroad. He would thus endear himself to the voters of Illinois, benefit his section, and enrich his own purse.

A veritable "steam engine in breeches," Douglas threw himself behind a legislative scheme that would enlist the support of a reluctant South. The proposed Territory of Nebraska would be sliced into two territories, Kansas and Nebraska (see Map 18.7). Their status regarding slavery would be settled by popular sovereignty—a democratic concept to which Douglas and his western constituents were deeply attached. Kansas, which lay due west of slaveholding Missouri, would presumably choose to become a slave state. But Nebraska, lying west of free-soil Iowa, would presumably become a free state.

Douglas's Kansas-Nebraska scheme flatly contradicted the Missouri Compromise of 1820, which had forbidden slavery in the proposed Nebraska Territory north of the sacred 36° 30' line. The only way to open the region to popular sovereignty was to repeal the ancient compact outright. This bold step Douglas was now prepared to take, even at the risk of shattering the uneasy truce patched together by the Compromise of 1850.

Many southerners, who had not conceived of Kansas as slave soil, rose to the bait. Here was a chance to gain one more slave state. The pliable President Pierce, under the thumb of southern advisers, threw his full weight behind the Kansas-Nebraska Bill.

But the Missouri Compromise, then thirty-four years old, could not be brushed aside lightly. Whatever Congress passes it can repeal, but by this time the North had come to regard the sectional pact as almost as sacred as the Constitution itself. Free-soil members of Congress struck back with a vengeance. They met their match in the violently gesticulating Douglas, who was the ablest rough-and-tumble debater of his generation. Employing twisted logic and oratorical fireworks, he rammed the bill through Congress with strong support from many southerners. So heated were political passions that bloodshed was barely averted. Some members carried a concealed revolver or a bowie knife—or both.

Douglas's motives in prodding anew the snarling dog of slavery have long puzzled historians. His personal interests have already been mentioned. In addition, his foes accused him of angling for the presidency in 1856. Yet his admirers have argued plausibly in his defense that if he had not championed the ill-omened bill, someone else would have.

The truth seems to be that Douglas acted somewhat impulsively and recklessly. His heart did not bleed over the issue of slavery, and he declared repeatedly that he did not care whether it was voted up or down in the territories. What he failed to perceive was that hundreds of thousands of his fellow citizens in

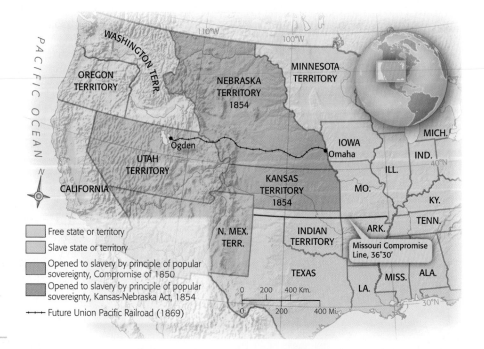

MAP 18.7 Kansas and Nebraska, 1854 The future Union Pacific Railroad (completed in 1869) is shown. Note the Missouri Compromise line of 36° 30' (1820). © 2016 Cengage Learning

Free state or territory

Slave state or territory

Opened to slavery by principle of popular sovereignty, Compromise of 1850

Opened to slavery by principle of popular sovereignty, Kansas-Nebraska Act, 1854

⟶ Future Union Pacific Railroad (1869)

The Kansas-Nebraska Act • 397

Douglas Hatches a Slavery Problem   Note the already hatched Missouri Compromise, Squatter Sovereignty, and Filibuster (in Cuba), and the about-to-hatch Free Kansas and Dred Scott decision. So bitter was the outcry against Douglas at the time of the Kansas-Nebraska controversy that he claimed with exaggeration that he could have traveled from Boston to Chicago at night by the light from his burning effigies.

the North *did* feel deeply on this moral issue. They regarded the repeal of the Missouri Compromise as an intolerable breach of faith, and they would henceforth resist to the last trench all future southern demands for slave territory. As Abraham Lincoln said, the North wanted to give to pioneers in the West "a clean bed, with no snakes in it."

Genuine leaders, like skillful chess players, must foresee the possible effects of their moves. Douglas predicted a "hell of a storm," but he grossly underestimated its proportions. His critics in the North, branding him a "Judas" and a "traitor," greeted his name with frenzied boos, hisses, and "three groans for Doug." But he still enjoyed a high degree of popularity among his following in the Democratic party, especially in Illinois, a stronghold of popular sovereignty.

✦ Congress Legislates a Civil War

The **Kansas-Nebraska Act**—a curtain-raiser to a terrible drama—was one of the most momentous measures ever to pass Congress. By one way of reckoning, it greased the slippery slope to Civil War.

Antislavery northerners were angered by what they condemned as an act of bad faith by the "Nebrascals" and their "Nebrascality." All future compromise with the South would be immeasurably more difficult, and without compromise there was bound to be conflict.

Henceforth the Fugitive Slave Law of 1850, previously enforced in the North only halfheartedly, was a dead letter. The Kansas-Nebraska Act wrecked two compromises: that of 1820, which it repealed specifically, and that of 1850, which northern opinion repealed indirectly. Emerson wrote, "The Fugitive [Slave] Law did much to unglue the eyes of men, and now the Nebraska Bill leaves us staring." Northern abolitionists and southern "fire-eaters" alike saw less and less they could live with. The growing legion of antislaveryites gained numerous recruits, who resented the grasping move by the "slavocracy" for Kansas. The southerners, in turn, became inflamed when the free-soilers tried to control Kansas, contrary to the presumed "deal."

The proud Democrats—a party now over half a century old—were shattered by the Kansas-Nebraska Act. They did elect a president in 1856, but he was the last one they were to boost into the White House for twenty-eight long years.

Undoubtedly the most durable offspring of the Kansas-Nebraska blunder was the new Republican party. It sprang up spontaneously in the Middle West, notably in Wisconsin and Michigan, as a mighty moral protest against the gains of slavery. Gathering together dissatisfied elements, it soon included disgruntled Whigs (among them Abraham Lincoln), Democrats, Free-Soilers, Know-Nothings, and other foes of the Kansas-Nebraska Act. The hodgepodge party spread eastward with the swiftness of a prairie fire and with the zeal of a religious crusade. Unheard-of and unheralded at the beginning of 1854, when the nativist Know-Nothings instead seemed to be the rising party of the North, it elected a Republican Speaker of the House of Representatives within two years. Never really a third-party movement, its wide wingspan gave it flight overnight as the second major political party—and a purely sectional one at that.

At long last the dreaded sectional rift had appeared. The new Republican party would not be allowed south of the Mason-Dixon line. Countless southerners subscribed wholeheartedly to the sentiment that it was "a nigger stealing, stinking, putrid, abolition party." The Union was in dire peril.

Massachusetts senator Charles Sumner (1811–1874) described the Kansas-Nebraska Bill as "at once the worst and the best Bill on which Congress ever acted." It was the worst because it represented a victory for the slave power in the short run. But it was the best, he said prophetically, because it

❝annuls all past compromises with slavery, and makes all future compromises impossible. Thus it puts freedom and slavery face to face, and bids them grapple. Who can doubt the result?❞

Chapter Review

KEY TERMS

popular sovereignty (381)
Free Soil party (382)
California gold rush (383)
Underground Railroad (385)
Seventh of March speech (386)
Compromise of 1850 (387)
Fugitive Slave Law (389)
Clayton-Bulwer Treaty (392)
Ostend Manifesto (393)
Opium War (393)
Wanghia, Treaty of (393)
Kanagawa, Treaty of (394)
Gadsden Purchase (395)
Kansas-Nebraska Act (397)

PEOPLE TO KNOW

Lewis Cass
Zachary Taylor
Harriet Tubman
Millard Fillmore
Franklin Pierce
William Walker
Caleb Cushing
Matthew C. Perry

CHRONOLOGY

1844 Caleb Cushing signs Treaty of Wanghia with China

1848 British seize port of San Juan del Norte in Nicaragua
Treaty of Guadalupe Hidalgo ends Mexican War
Taylor defeats Cass and Van Buren for presidency

1849 California gold rush

1850 Fillmore assumes presidency after Taylor's death
Compromise of 1850, including Fugitive Slave Law
Clayton-Bulwer Treaty with Britain

1851 Australian gold rush

1852 Pierce defeats Scott for presidency

1853 Gadsden Purchase from Mexico

1854 Commodore Perry opens Japan
Ostend Manifesto proposes seizure of Cuba
Kansas-Nebraska Act repeals Missouri Compromise of 1820
Republican party organized

1856 William Walker becomes president of Nicaragua and legalizes slavery

1868 Meiji Restoration in Japan

TO LEARN MORE

William J. Cooper, *Liberty and Slavery: Southern Politics to 1860* (1983)

David H. Donald, Jean H. Baker, and Michael F. Holt, *The Civil War and Reconstruction* (rev. ed., 2001)

Kenneth S. Greenberg, *Masters and Statesmen: The Political Culture of American Slavery* (1985)

Keith P. Griffler, *Frontline of Freedom: African Americans and the Forging of the Underground Railroad in the Ohio Valley* (2004)

Bruce Levine, *Half Slave and Half Free: The Roots of the Civil War* (1992)

James M. McPherson, *Battle Cry of Freedom: The Civil War Era* (1988)

David M. Potter, *The Impending Crisis, 1848–1861* (1976)

Richard H. Sewell, *A House Divided: Sectionalism and Civil War, 1848–1860* (1988)

Robert Trennert, *Alternative to Extinction: Federal Indian Policy and the Beginnings of the Reservation System, 1846–1851* (1975)

A complete, annotated bibliography for this chapter—along with brief descriptions of the People to Know—may be found on the *American Pageant* website. The key terms are defined in the glossary at the end of the text.

Chapter 19

Drifting Toward Disunion

1854–1861

A house divided against itself cannot stand. I believe this government cannot endure permanently half slave and half free.

ABRAHAM LINCOLN, 1858

The slavery question continued to churn the cauldron of controversy throughout the 1850s. As moral temperatures rose, prospects for a peaceful political solution to the slavery issue simply evaporated. Kansas Territory erupted in violence between proslavery and antislavery factions in 1855. Two years later the Supreme Court's incendiary *Dred Scott* decision extended formal protection to slavery in all the territories of the West. Attitudes on both sides progressively hardened. When in 1860 the newly formed Republican party nominated for president Abraham Lincoln, an outspoken opponent of the further expansion of slavery, the stage was set for all-out civil war.

★ Stowe and Helper: Literary Incendiaries

Sectional tensions were further strained in 1852, and later, by an inky phenomenon. Harriet Beecher Stowe, a wisp of a woman and the mother of a half-dozen children, published her heartrending novel **Uncle Tom's Cabin**. Dismayed by the passage of the Fugitive Slave Law, she was determined to awaken the North to the wickedness of slavery by laying bare its terrible inhumanity, especially the cruel splitting of families. Her wildly popular book relied on powerful imagery and touching pathos. "God wrote it," she explained in later years—a reminder that the deeper sources of her antislavery sentiments lay in the evangelical religious crusades of the Second Great Awakening.

The success of the novel at home and abroad was sensational. Several hundred thousand copies were published in the first year, and the totals soon ran into the millions as the tale was translated into more than a score of languages. It was also put on the stage in "Tom shows" for lengthy runs. No other novel in American history—perhaps in all history—can be compared with it as a political force. To millions of people, it made slavery appear almost as evil as it really was.

When Mrs. Stowe was introduced to President Lincoln in 1862, he reportedly remarked with twinkling eyes, "So you're the little woman who wrote the book that made this great war." The truth is that *Uncle Tom's Cabin* did help start the Civil War—and win it. The South condemned that "vile wretch in petticoats" when it learned that hundreds of thousands of fellow Americans were reading and believing her "unfair" indictment. Mrs. Stowe had never witnessed slavery first hand in the Deep South, but she had seen it briefly during a visit to Kentucky, and she had lived for many years in Ohio, a center of Underground Railroad activity.

Uncle Tom, endearing and enduring, left a profound impression on the North. Uncounted thousands of readers swore that henceforth they would have nothing to do with the enforcement of the Fugitive Slave Law. The tale was devoured by millions of impressionable youths in the 1850s—some of whom later became the Boys in Blue who volunteered to fight the Civil War through to its grim finale. The memory of a beaten and dying Uncle Tom helped sustain them in their determination to wipe out the plague of slavery.

Harriet Beecher Stowe (1811–1896), 1853 This oil portrait of Stowe was painted a year after she published *Uncle Tom's Cabin*. Her pen helped to change the course of history. National Portrait Gallery, Smithsonian Institution/Art Resource, NY

135,000 SETS, 270,000 VOLUMES SOLD.

UNCLE TOM'S CABIN

FOR SALE HERE.

AN EDITION FOR THE MILLION, COMPLETE IN 1 Vol., PRICE 37 1-2 CENTS.
"   "   IN GERMAN, IN 1 Vol., PRICE 50 CENTS.
"   "   IN 2 Vols,. CLOTH, 6 PLATES, PRICE $1.50.
SUPERB ILLUSTRATED EDITION, IN 1 Vol., WITH 153 ENGRAVINGS,
PRICES FROM $2.50 TO $5.00.

The Greatest Book of the Age.

The Granger Collection, New York

"The Book That Made This Great War" Lincoln's celebrated remark to author Harriet Beecher Stowe reflected the enormous emotional impact of her impassioned novel.

The novel was immensely popular abroad, especially in Britain and France. Countless readers wept over the kindly Tom and the angelic Eva, while deploring the brutal Simon Legree. When the guns in America finally began to boom, the common people of England sensed that the triumph of the North would spell the end of the slave system. The governments in London and Paris seriously considered intervening on behalf of the South, but they were sobered by the realization that many of their own people, aroused by the "Tommania," might not support them.

Another trouble-brewing book appeared in 1857, five years after the debut of Uncle Tom. Titled ***The Impending Crisis of the South***, it was written by Hinton R. Helper, a nonaristocratic white from North Carolina. Hating both slavery and blacks, he attempted to prove by an array of statistics that indirectly the nonslaveholding whites were the ones who suffered most from the millstone of slavery. Unable to secure a publisher in the South, he finally managed to find one in the North.

Helper's influence was negligible among the poorer whites to whom he addressed his message. Yet the South's planter elite certainly took note of Helper's audacity, which fueled their fears that the nonslaveholding majority might abandon them. *The Impending Crisis of the South,* with its "dirty allusions," was banned in the South and fed to the flames at book-burning parties. In the North untold thousands of copies, many in

In the closing scenes of Harriet Beecher Stowe's novel, Uncle Tom's brutal master, Simon Legree, orders the $1,200 slave savagely beaten (to death) by two fellow slaves. Through tears and blood, Tom exclaims,

❝'No !no! no! my soul an't yours, Mas'r! You haven't bought it,—ye can't buy it! It's been bought and paid for, by one that is able to keep it,—no matter, no matter, you can't harm me!' 'I can't,' said Legree, with a sneer; 'we'll see,—we'll see! Here, Sambo, Quimbo, give this dog such a breakin' in as he won't get over, this month!'**❞**

Harriet Beecher Stowe, *Uncle Tom's Cabin*

As works of fiction, novels pose tricky problems to historians, whose principal objective is to get the factual record straight. Works of the imagination are notoriously unreliable as descriptions of reality, and only rarely is it known with any degree of certainty what a reader might have felt when confronting a particular fictional passage or theme. Yet a novel like Harriet Beecher Stowe's *Uncle Tom's Cabin* had such an unarguably large impact on the American (and worldwide) debate over slavery that historians have inevitably looked to it for evidence of the mid-nineteenth-century ideas and attitudes to which Stowe appealed. The passage quoted here is especially rich in such evidence—and even offers an explanation for the logic of the novel's title. Stowe cleverly aimed to mobilize not simply her readers' sense of injustice but also their emotions on behalf of the antislavery cause. Why is the *cabin* described here so central to Stowe's novel?

What sentimental values does the cabin represent? What is the nature of the threat to those values? What does it say about nineteenth-century American culture that Stowe's appeal to sentiment succeeded so much more dramatically in exciting anti-slavery passions than did the factual and moral arguments of many other (mostly male) abolitionists?

THE February morning looked gray and drizzling through the window of Uncle Tom's cabin. It looked on downcast faces, the images of mournful hearts. The little table stood out before the fire, covered with an ironing-cloth; a coarse but clean shirt or two, fresh from the iron, hung on the back of a chair by the fire, and Aunt Chloe had another spread out before her on the table. Carefully she rubbed and ironed every fold and every hem, with the most scrupulous exactness, every now and then raising her hand to her face to wipe off the tears that were coursing down her cheeks.

Tom sat by, with his Testament open on his knee, and his head leaning upon his hand; — but neither spoke. It was yet early, and the children lay all asleep together in their little rude trundle-bed.

Tom, who had, to the full, the gentle, domestic heart, which, woe for them! has been a peculiar characteristic of his unhappy race, got up and walked silently to look at his children.

"It's the last time," he said.

University of Virginia Library

condensed form, were distributed as campaign literature by the Republicans. Southerners were further embittered when they learned that their northern brethren were spreading these wicked "lies." Thus did southerners, reacting much as they did to *Uncle Tom's Cabin*, become increasingly unwilling to sleep under the same federal roof with their hostile Yankee bedfellows.

✴ The North-South Contest for Kansas

The rolling plains of Kansas had meanwhile been providing an example of the worst possible workings of popular sovereignty, although admittedly under abnormal conditions.

Newcomers who ventured into Kansas were a motley lot. Most of the northerners were just ordinary westward-moving pioneers in search of richer lands beyond the sunset. But a small part of the inflow was financed by groups of northern abolitionists or free-soilers. The most famous of these antislavery organizations was the **New England Emigrant Aid Company**, which sent about two thousand people to the troubled area to forestall the South—and also to make a profit. Shouting "Ho for Kansas," many of them carried the deadly new breech-loading Sharps rifles, nicknamed "Beecher's Bibles" after the Reverend Henry Ward Beecher (Harriet Beecher Stowe's brother), who had helped raise money for their purchase. Many of the

Kansas-bound pioneers sang John Greenleaf Whittier's marching song (1854):

> We cross the prairie as of old
> The pilgrims crossed the sea,
> To make the West, as they the East,
> The homestead of the free!

Southern spokesmen, now more than ordinarily touchy, raised furious cries of betrayal. They had supported the Kansas-Nebraska scheme of Senator Douglas with the unspoken understanding that Kansas would become slave and Nebraska free. The northern "Nebrascals," allegedly by foul means, were now apparently out to "abolitionize" *both* Kansas and Nebraska.

A few southern hotheads, quick to respond in kind, attempted to "assist" small groups of well-armed slaveowners to Kansas. Some carried banners proclaiming,

> Let Yankees tremble, abolitionists fall,
> Our motto is, "Give Southern Rights to All."

But planting blacks on Kansas soil was a losing game. Slaves were valuable and volatile property, and foolish indeed were owners who would take them where bullets were flying and where the soil might be voted free under popular sovereignty. The census of 1860 found only 2 slaves among 107,000 souls in all Kansas Territory and only 15 in Nebraska. There was much truth in the charge that the whole quarrel over slavery in the territories revolved around "an imaginary Negro in an impossible place."

Crisis conditions in Kansas rapidly worsened (see Map 19.1). When the day came in 1855 to elect members of the first territorial legislature, proslavery "border ruffians" poured in from Missouri to vote early and often. The slavery supporters triumphed and then set up their own puppet government at Shawnee Mission. The free-soilers, unable to stomach this fraudulent conspiracy, established an extralegal regime of their own in Topeka. The confused Kansans thus had their choice between two governments—one based on fraud, the other on illegality.

Tension mounted as settlers also feuded over conflicting land claims. The breaking point came in 1856 when a gang of proslavery raiders, alleging provocation, shot up and burned part of the free-soil town of Lawrence. This outrage was but the prelude to a bloodier tragedy.

✦ Kansas in Convulsion

The fanatical figure of John Brown now stalked upon the Kansas battlefield. Spare, gray-bearded, and iron-willed, he was obsessively dedicated to the abolitionist cause. The power of his glittering gray eyes was such, so he claimed, that his stare could force a dog or cat to slink out of a room. Becoming involved in dubious dealings, including horse stealing, he moved to Kansas from Ohio with part of his large family. Brooding over the recent attack on Lawrence, "Old Brown" of Osawatomie led a band of his followers to Pottawatomie Creek in May 1856. There they literally hacked to pieces five surprised men, presumed to be proslaveryites. This terrorist butchery besmirched the free-soil cause and brought vicious retaliation from the proslavery forces.

Civil war in Kansas thus erupted in 1856 and continued intermittently until it merged with the large-scale Civil War of 1861–1865. Altogether, the Kansas conflict destroyed millions of dollars' worth of property, paralyzed agriculture in certain areas, and cost scores of lives.

MAP 19.1 Bleeding Kansas, 1854–1860 "Enter every election district in Kansas … and vote at the point of a bowie knife or revolver," one proslavery agitator exhorted a Missouri crowd. Proslavery Missouri senator David Atchison declared that "there are 1,100 men coming over from Platte County to vote, and if that ain't enough we can send 5,000—enough to kill every Goddamned abolitionist in the Territory." © 2016 Cengage Learning

National Portrait Gallery, Smithsonian Institution/Art Resource, NY

John Brown (1800–1859) This daguerreotype of the militant abolitionist Brown tells a tale of two men, the sitter and the photographer. It was taken in 1847 when Brown was running a wool-brokerage house in Springfield, Massachusetts, and working closely with other New England abolitionists, including Frederick Douglass. Brown made his way to the Hartford studio of free black photographer Augustus Washington, who was the son of an Asian woman and a former black slave and well known in abolitionist circles. Six years later, Washington would close his successful studio and take his family to Liberia, convinced that American blacks would do better in their own country in Africa than as free men in the United States (see "Early Abolitionism" and "Radical Abolitionism" in Chapter 16, pp. 351–353).

Yet by 1857 Kansas had enough people, chiefly free-soilers, to apply for statehood on a popular-sovereignty basis. The proslavery forces, then in the saddle, devised a tricky document known as the **Lecompton Constitution**. The people were not allowed to vote for or against the constitution as a whole, but for the constitution either "with slavery" or "with no slavery." If they voted against slavery, one of the remaining provisions of the constitution would protect the owners of slaves already in Kansas. So whatever the outcome, there would still be black bondage in Kansas. Many free-soilers, infuriated by this ploy,

boycotted the polls. Left to themselves, the proslavery-ites approved the constitution with slavery late in 1857.

The scene next shifted to Washington. President Pierce had been succeeded by the no-less-pliable James Buchanan, who was also strongly under southern influence. Blind to sharp divisions within his own Democratic party, Buchanan threw the weight of his administration behind the notorious Lecompton Constitution. But Senator Douglas, who had championed true popular sovereignty, would have none of this semipopular fraudulency. Deliberately tossing away his strong support in the South for the presidency, he fought courageously for fair play and democratic principles. The outcome was a compromise that, in effect, submitted the entire Lecompton Constitution to a popular vote. The free-soil voters thereupon thronged to the polls and snowed it under. Kansas remained a territory until 1861, when the southern secessionists left Congress.

President Buchanan, by antagonizing the numerous Douglas Democrats in the North, hopelessly divided the once-powerful Democratic party. Until then, it had been the only remaining *national* party, for the Whigs were dead and the Republicans were sectional. With the disruption of the Democrats came the snapping of one of the last important strands in the rope that was barely binding the Union together.

✷ "Bully" Brooks and His Bludgeon

Bleeding Kansas also spattered blood on the floor of the Senate in 1856. Senator Charles Sumner of Massachusetts, a tall and imposing figure, was a leading abolitionist—one of the few prominent in political life. Highly educated but cold, humorless, intolerant, and egotistical, he had made himself one of the most disliked men in the Senate. Brooding over the turbulent miscarriage of popular sovereignty, he delivered a blistering speech titled "The Crime Against Kansas." Sparing few epithets, he condemned the proslavery men as "hirelings picked from the drunken spew and vomit of an uneasy civilization." He also referred insultingly to South Carolina and to its white-haired senator Andrew Butler, one of the best-liked members of the Senate.

Hot-tempered Congressman Preston S. Brooks of South Carolina now took vengeance into his own hands. Ordinarily gracious and gallant, he resented the insults to his state and to its senator, a distant cousin. His code of honor called for a duel, but in the South one fought only with one's social equals. And had not the coarse language of the Yankee, who probably would reject a challenge, dropped him to a lower order? To Brooks, the only alternative was to chastise the senator as one would beat an unruly dog. On May 22, 1856, he approached Sumner, then sitting at his

Senate desk, and pounded the orator with an eleven-ounce cane until it broke. The victim fell bleeding and unconscious to the floor, while several nearby senators refrained from interfering.

Sumner had been provocatively insulting, but this counteroutrage put Brooks in the wrong. The House of Representatives could not muster enough votes to expel the South Carolinian, but he resigned and was triumphantly reelected. Southern admirers deluged Brooks with canes, some of them gold-headed, to replace the one that had been broken. The injuries to Sumner's head and nervous system were serious. He was forced to leave his seat for three and a half years and go to Europe for treatment that was both painful and costly. Meanwhile, Massachusetts defiantly reelected him, leaving his seat eloquently empty. Bleeding Sumner was thus joined with bleeding Kansas as a political issue.

The free-soil North was mightily aroused against the "uncouth" and "cowardly" "Bully" Brooks. Copies of Sumner's abusive speech, otherwise doomed to obscurity, were sold by the tens of thousands. Every blow that struck the senator doubtless made thousands of Republican votes. The South, although not unanimous in approving Brooks, was angered not only because Sumner had made such an intemperate speech but because it had been so extravagantly applauded in the North.

The Sumner-Brooks clash and the ensuing reactions revealed how dangerously inflamed passions were becoming, North and South. It was ominous that the cultured Sumner should have used the language of a barroom bully and that the gentlemanly Brooks should have employed the tactics and tools of a thug.

Regarding the Brooks assault on Sumner, the Illinois State Journal, *one of the more moderate antislavery journals, declared,*

❝Brooks and his Southern allies have deliberately adopted the monstrous creed that any man who dares to utter sentiments which they deem wrong or unjust, shall be brutally assailed.❞

One of the milder southern responses came from the Petersburg (Virginia) Intelligencer:

❝Although Mr. Brooks ought to have selected some other spot for the altercation than the Senate chamber, if he had broken every bone in Sumner's carcass it would have been a just retribution upon this slanderer of the South and her individual citizens.❞

Emotion was displacing thought. The blows rained on Sumner's head were, broadly speaking, among the first blows of the Civil War.

✦ "Old Buck" Versus "The Pathfinder"

With bullets whining in Kansas, the Democrats met in Cincinnati to nominate their presidential standard-bearer of 1856. They shied away from both the weak-kneed President Pierce and the dynamic Douglas.

Preston Brooks Caning Charles Sumner, 1856 Cartoonist John Magee of Philadelphia depicted Brooks's beating of Sumner in the Senate as a display of southern ruthlessness in defending slavery, ironically captioned "southern chivalry."

SOUTHERN CHIVALRY — ARGUMENT versus CLUB'S.

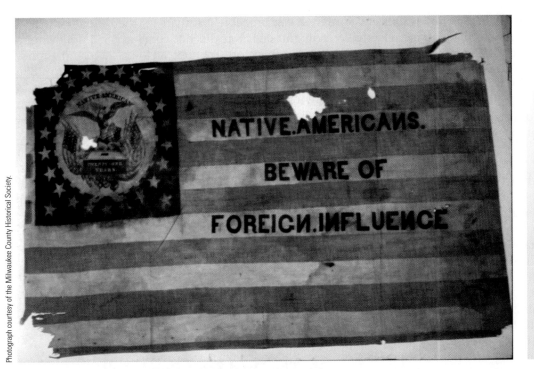

Photograph courtesy of the Milwaukee County Historical Society.

NATIVE.AMERICANS.
BEWARE OF
FOREIGN.INFLUENCE

Know-Nothing Banner, 1856 The Know-Nothing party feared that slavery and other sectional issues were blinding Americans to the real danger in their midst—uncontrolled immigration and foreign influence. The party ran ex-President Millard Fillmore for president in 1856, using banners like this one to alert voters to the threat presented by recent Irish and German immigrants, many of them Catholic.

Each was too indelibly tainted by the Kansas-Nebraska Act. The delegates finally chose James Buchanan (pronounced by many Buck-anan), who was muscular, white-haired, and tall (six feet), with a short neck and a protruding chin. Because of an eye defect, he carried his head cocked to one side. A well-to-do Pennsylvania lawyer, he had been serving as minister to London during the recent Kansas-Nebraska uproar. He was therefore "Kansas-less" and, hence, relatively enemyless. But in a crisis that called for giants, "Old Buck" Buchanan was mediocre, irresolute, and confused.

Delegates of the fast-growing Republican party met in Philadelphia with bubbling enthusiasm. "Higher Law" Seward was their most conspicuous leader, and he probably would have arranged to win the nomination had he been confident that this was a "Republican year." The final choice was Captain John C. Frémont, the so-called Pathfinder of the West—a dashing but erratic explorer-soldier-surveyor who was supposed to find the path to the White House. The black-bearded and flashy young adventurer was virtually without political experience, but like Buchanan he was not tarred with the Kansas brush. The Republican platform came out vigorously against the extension of slavery into the territories, while the Democrats declared no less emphatically for popular sovereignty.

An ugly dose of antiforeignism was injected into the campaign, even though slavery extension loomed largest. The recent influx of immigrants from Ireland and Germany had alarmed "nativists," as many old-stock Protestants were called. They organized the American party, also known as the Know-Nothing

party because of its secretiveness, and in 1856 nominated the lackluster ex-president Millard Fillmore. Antiforeign and anti-Catholic, these superpatriots adopted the slogan "Americans Must Rule America." Remnants of the dying Whig party likewise endorsed Fillmore, and they and the Know-Nothings threatened to cut into Republican strength.

Republicans fell in behind Frémont with the zeal of crusaders. Shouting "We Follow the Pathfinder" and "We Are Buck Hunting," they organized glee clubs, which sang (to the tune of "The Marseillaise"),

Arise, arise ye brave!
And let our war-cry be,
Free speech, free press, free soil, free men,
Fré-mont and victory!

"And free love," sneered the Buchanan supporters ("Buchaneers").

Mudslinging bespattered both candidates. "Old Fogy" Buchanan was assailed because he was a bachelor: the fiancée of his youth had died after a lovers'

Spiritual overtones developed in the Frémont campaign, especially over slavery. The Independent, a prominent religious journal, saw in Frémont's nomination "the good hand of God." As election day neared, it declared,

❝Fellow-Christians! Remember it is for Christ, for the nation, and for the world that you vote at this election! Vote as you pray! Pray as you vote!**❞**

quarrel. Frémont was reviled because of his illegitimate birth, for his young mother had left her elderly husband, a Virginia planter, to run away with a French adventurer. In due season she gave birth to John in Savannah, Georgia—further to shame the South. More harmful to Frémont was the allegation, which alienated many bigoted Know-Nothings and other "nativists," that he was a Roman Catholic.

★ The Electoral Fruits of 1856

A bland Buchanan, although polling less than a majority of the popular vote, won handily (see Map 19.2). His tally in the Electoral College was 174 to 114 for Frémont, with Fillmore garnering 8. The popular vote was 1,832,955 for Buchanan to 1,339,932 for Frémont, and 871,731 for Fillmore.

Why did the rousing Republicans go down to defeat? Frémont lost much ground because of grave doubts as to his honesty, capacity, and sound judgment. Perhaps more damaging were the violent threats of the southern "fire-eaters" that the election of a sectional "Black Republican" would be a declaration of war on them, forcing them to secede. Many northerners, anxious to save both the Union and their profitable business connections with the South, were thus intimidated into voting for Buchanan. Innate conservatism triumphed, assisted by so-called southern bullyism.

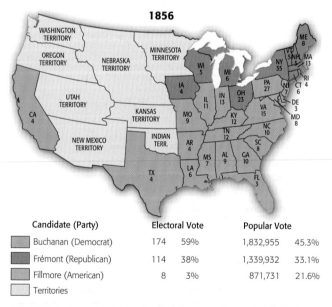

1856

Candidate (Party)	Electoral Vote		Popular Vote	
Buchanan (Democrat)	174	59%	1,832,955	45.3%
Frémont (Republican)	114	38%	1,339,932	33.1%
Fillmore (American)	8	3%	871,731	21.6%
Territories				

MAP 19.2 Presidential Election of 1856 (electoral vote by state)   The fateful split of 1860 was foreshadowed. The regional polarization in 1856, shown here, was to be even sharper four years later, as illustrated by Maps 19.3 and 19.4 later in this chapter. © 2016 Cengage Learning

It was probably fortunate for the Union that secession and civil war did not come in 1856, following a Republican victory. Frémont, an ill-balanced and second-rate figure, was no Abraham Lincoln. And in 1856 the North was more willing to let the South depart in peace than it would be in 1860. Dramatic events from 1856 to 1860 were to arouse hundreds of thousands of still-apathetic northerners to a fighting pitch.

Yet the Republicans in 1856 could rightfully claim a "victorious defeat." The new party—a mere two-year-old toddler—had made an astonishing showing against the well-oiled Democratic machine. Whittier exulted:

> Then sound again the bugles,
>   Call the muster-roll anew;
> If months have well-nigh won the field,
>   What may not four years do?

The election of 1856 cast a long shadow forward, and politicians, North and South, peered anxiously toward 1860.

★ The Dred Scott Bombshell

The **Dred Scott v. Stanford** decision, handed down by the Supreme Court on March 6, 1857, abruptly ended the two-day presidential honeymoon of the unlucky bachelor, James Buchanan. This pronouncement was one of the opening paper-gun blasts of the Civil War.

Basically, the case was simple. Dred Scott, a black slave, had lived with his master for five years in Illinois and Wisconsin Territory. Backed by interested abolitionists, he sued for freedom on the basis of his long residence on free soil.

The Supreme Court proceeded to twist a simple legal case into a complex political issue. It ruled, not surprisingly, that Dred Scott was a black slave and not a citizen, and hence could not sue in federal courts.* The tribunal could then have thrown out the case on these technical grounds alone. But a majority decided to go further, under the leadership of emaciated Chief Justice Roger B. Taney from the slave state of Maryland. A sweeping judgment on the larger issue of slavery in the territories seemed desirable, particularly to forestall arguments by two free-soil justices who were preparing dissenting opinions. The prosouthern majority evidently hoped in this way to lay the odious question to rest.

Taney's thunderclap rocked the free-soilers back on their heels. A majority of the Court decreed that because a slave was private property, he or she could be taken into *any* territory and legally held there in slavery. The reasoning was that the Fifth Amendment

---

*This part of the ruling, denying blacks their citizenship, seriously menaced the precarious position of the South's quarter-million free blacks.

Dred Scott with His Wife and Daughters, 1857 This slave's long legal battle for his freedom, culminating in the Supreme Court's *Dred Scott* decision in 1857, helped to ignite the Civil War. Widespread publicity about the fate of Scott and his family strengthened antislavery sentiment in the North. Articles like this one in *Frank Leslie's Illustrated Newspaper* appealed to the same sentimental regard for the idealized family that Harriet Beecher Stowe so artfully mobilized in *Uncle Tom's Cabin* (see "Examining the Evidence: Harriet Beecher Stowe, *Uncle Tom's Cabin*," p. 401).

The decision of Chief Justice Roger B. Taney (1777–1864) in the case of Dred Scott referred to the status of slaves when the Constitution was adopted:

❝They had for more than a century before been regarded as beings of an inferior order; and altogether unfit to associate with the white race, either in social or political relations; and so far inferior that they had no rights which the white man was bound to respect.... This opinion was at that time fixed and universal in the civilized portion of the white race.**❞**

Taney's statement accurately described historical attitudes, but it deeply offended antislaveryites when applied to conditions in 1857.

Foes of slavery extension, especially the Republicans, were infuriated by the Dred Scott setback. Their chief rallying cry had been the banishing of bondage from the territories. They now insisted that the ruling of the Court was merely an opinion, not a decision, and no more binding than the views of a "southern debating society." Republican defiance of the exalted tribunal was intensified by an awareness that a majority of its members were southerners and by the conviction that it had debased itself—"sullied the ermine"—by wallowing in the gutter of politics.

Southerners in turn were inflamed by all this defiance. They began to wonder anew how much longer they could remain joined to a section that refused to honor the Supreme Court, to say nothing of the constitutional compact that had established it.

✴ The Financial Crash of 1857

Bitterness caused by the *Dred Scott* decision was deepened by hard times, which dampened a period of feverish prosperity. Then the **panic of 1857** burst about Buchanan's harassed head. The storm was not so bad economically as the panic of 1837, but psychologically it was probably the worst of the nineteenth century.

What caused the crash? Inpouring California gold played its part by helping to inflate the currency. The demands of the Crimean War in Russia (1853–1856) had overstimulated the growing of grain, while frenzied speculation in land and railroads had further ripped the economic fabric. When the collapse came, over five thousand businesses failed within a year. Unemployment, accompanied by hunger meetings in urban areas, was widespread. "Bread or Death" stated one desperate slogan.

clearly forbade Congress to deprive people of their property without due process of law. The Court, to be consistent, went further. The Missouri Compromise, banning slavery north of 36° 30′, had been repealed three years earlier by the Kansas-Nebraska Act. But its spirit was still venerated in the North. Now the Court ruled that the Compromise of 1820 had been unconstitutional all along: Congress had no power to ban slavery from the territories, regardless even of what the territorial legislatures themselves might want.

Southerners were delighted with this unexpected victory. Champions of popular sovereignty were aghast, including Senator Douglas and a host of northern Democrats. Another lethal wedge was thus driven between the northern and southern wings of the once-united Democratic party.

Picture Research Consultants & Archives

Panic on Wall Street, 1857 The panic of 1857 further burdened President Buchanan, already reeling from the armed clashes in Kansas and the controversy over the *Dred Scott* decision.

The North, including its grain growers, was hardest hit. The South, enjoying favorable cotton prices abroad, rode out the storm with flying colors. Panic conditions seemed further proof that cotton was king and that its economic kingdom was stronger than that of the North. This fatal delusion helped drive the overconfident southerners closer to a shooting showdown.

Financial distress in the North, especially in agriculture, gave a new vigor to the demand for free farms of 160 acres from the public domain. For several decades interested groups had been urging the federal government to abandon its ancient policy of selling the land for revenue. Instead, the argument ran, acreage should be given outright to the sturdy pioneers as a reward for risking health and life to develop it.

A scheme to make outright gifts of homesteads encountered two-pronged opposition. Eastern industrialists had long been unfriendly to free land; some of them feared that their underpaid workers would be drained off to the West. The South was even more bitterly opposed, partly because gang-labor slavery could not flourish on a mere 160 acres. Free farms would merely fill up the territories more rapidly with freesoilers and further tip the political balance against the South. In 1860, after years of debate, Congress finally passed a homestead act—one that made public lands available at a nominal sum of twenty-five cents an acre. But the homestead act was stabbed to death by the veto pen of President Buchanan, near whose elbow sat leading southern sympathizers.

The panic of 1857 also created a clamor for higher tariff rates. Several months before the crash, Congress, embarrassed by a large Treasury surplus, had enacted the **Tariff of 1857**. The new law, responding to pressures from the South, reduced duties to about 20 percent on dutiable goods—the lowest point since the War of 1812. Hardly had the revised rates been placed on the books when financial misery descended like a black pall. Northern manufacturers, many of them Republicans, noisily blamed their misfortunes on the low tariff. As the surplus melted away in the Treasury, industrialists in the North pointed to the need for higher duties. But what really concerned them was their desire for increased protection. Thus the panic of 1857 gave the Republicans two surefire economic issues for the election of 1860: protection for the unprotected and farms for the farmless.

✦ An Illinois Rail-Splitter Emerges

The Illinois senatorial election of 1858 now claimed the national spotlight. Senator Stephen A. Douglas's term was about to expire, and the Republicans decided to run against him a rustic Springfield lawyer, one Abraham Lincoln. The Republican candidate—6 feet 4 inches in height and 180 pounds in weight—presented an awkward but arresting figure. Lincoln's legs, arms, and neck were abnormally long; his head was crowned by coarse, black, and unruly hair; and his face was sad, sunken, and weather-beaten.

Lincoln was no silver-spoon child of the elite. Born in 1809 in a Kentucky log cabin to impoverished parents, he attended a frontier school for not more than a year; being an avid reader, he was mainly self-educated.

In 1832, when Abraham Lincoln (1809–1865) became a candidate for the Illinois legislature, he delivered a speech at a political gathering:

❝I presume you all know who I am. I am humble Abraham Lincoln. I have been solicited by many friends to become a candidate for the Legislature. My [Whiggish] politics are short and sweet, like the old woman's dance. I am in favor of a national bank. I am in favor of the internal-improvement system, and a high protective tariff. These are my sentiments and political principles. If elected, I shall be thankful; if not, it will be all the same.**❞**

He was elected two years later.

All his life he said, "git," "thar," and "heered." Although narrow-chested and somewhat stoop-shouldered, he shone in his frontier community as a wrestler and weight lifter, and spent some time, among other pioneering pursuits, as a splitter of logs for fence rails. A superb teller of earthy and amusing stories, he would oddly enough plunge into protracted periods of melancholy.

Lincoln's private and professional lives were not especially noteworthy. He married "above himself" socially, into the influential Todd family of Kentucky, and the temperamental outbursts of his high-strung wife, known by her enemies as the "she wolf," helped to school him in patience and forbearance. After reading a little law, he gradually emerged as one of the dozen or so better-known trial lawyers in Illinois, although still accustomed to carrying important papers in his stovepipe hat. He was widely referred to as "Honest Abe," partly because he would refuse cases that he had to suspend his conscience to defend.

The rise of Lincoln as a political figure was less than rocketlike. After making his mark in the Illinois legislature as a Whig politician of the logrolling variety, he served one undistinguished term in Congress, 1847–1849. Until 1854, when he was forty-five years of age, he had done nothing to establish a claim to statesmanship. But the passage of the Kansas-Nebraska Act in that year lighted within him unexpected fires. After mounting the Republican bandwagon, he emerged as one of the foremost politicians and orators of the Northwest. At the Philadelphia convention of 1856, where John C. Frémont was nominated, Lincoln actually received 110 votes for the vice-presidential nomination.

✦ The Great Debate: Lincoln Versus Douglas

Lincoln, as Republican nominee for the Senate seat, boldly challenged Douglas to a series of joint debates. This was a rash act because the stumpy senator was probably the nation's most devastating debater. Douglas promptly accepted Lincoln's challenge, and seven meetings—the famed **Lincoln-Douglas debates**—were arranged from August to October 1858.

At first glance the two contestants seemed ill-matched. The well-groomed and polished Douglas, with his bearlike figure and bullhorn voice, presented a striking contrast to the lanky Lincoln, with his baggy clothes and unshined shoes. Moreover, "Old Abe," as he was called in both affection and derision, had a piercing, high-pitched voice and was often ill at ease when he began to speak. But as he threw himself into an argument, he seemed to grow in height, while his glowing eyes lighted up a rugged face. He relied on logic rather than on table thumping.

Abraham Lincoln, a Most Uncommon Common Man This daguerreotype is the earliest-known photograph of Abraham Lincoln, taken at age thirty-seven when he was a frontier lawyer in Springfield and congressman-elect from Illinois.

The most famous debate came at Freeport, Illinois, where Lincoln nearly impaled his opponent on the horns of a dilemma. Suppose, he queried, the people of a territory should vote slavery down. The Supreme Court in the *Dred Scott* decision had decreed that they could not. Who would prevail, the Court or the people?

Legend to the contrary, Douglas and some southerners had already publicly answered the **Freeport question**. The "Little Giant" therefore did not hesitate to meet the issue head-on, honestly and consistently. His reply to Lincoln became known as the **Freeport Doctrine**. No matter how the Supreme Court ruled, Douglas argued, slavery would stay down if the people voted it down. Laws to protect slavery would have to be passed by the territorial legislatures. These would not be forthcoming in the absence of popular approval, and black bondage would soon disappear. Douglas, in truth, had American history on his side. Where public opinion does not support the federal government, as in the case of Jefferson's embargo (see "The Hated Embargo" in Chapter 11, pp. 218–220), the law is almost impossible to enforce.

Lincoln and Douglas Debate, 1858 Thousands attended each of the seven Lincoln-Douglas debates. Douglas is shown here sitting to Lincoln's right in the debate at Charleston, Illinois, in September. On one occasion Lincoln quipped that Douglas's logic would prove that a horse chestnut was a chestnut horse.

The upshot was that Douglas defeated Lincoln for the Senate seat. The "Little Giant's" loyalty to popular sovereignty, which still had a powerful appeal in Illinois, probably was decisive. Senators were then chosen by state legislatures; and in the general election that followed the debates, more pro-Douglas members were elected than pro-Lincoln members. Yet thanks to

Lincoln expressed his views on the relation of the black and white races in 1858, in his first debate with Stephen A. Douglas:

❝I, as well as Judge Douglas, am in favor of the race to which I belong, having the superior position. I have never said anything to the contrary, but I hold that notwithstanding all this, there is no reason in the world why the negro is not entitled to all the natural rights enumerated in the Declaration of Independence, the right to life, liberty, and the pursuit of happiness. I hold that he is as much entitled to those rights as the white man. I agree with Judge Douglas he is not my equal in many respects—certainly not in color, perhaps not in moral or intellectual endowment. But in the right to eat the bread, without leave of anybody else, which his own hand earns, he is my equal and the equal of Judge Douglas, and the equal of every living man.**❞**

inequitable apportionment, the districts carried by Douglas supporters represented a smaller population than those carried by Lincoln supporters. "Honest Abe" thus won a clear moral victory.

Lincoln possibly was playing for larger stakes than just the senatorship. Although defeated, he had shambled into the national limelight in company with the most prominent northern politicians. Newspapers in the East published detailed accounts of the debates, and Lincoln began to emerge as a potential Republican nominee for president. But Douglas, in winning Illinois, hurt his own chances of winning the presidency, while further splitting his splintering party. After his opposition to the Lecompton Constitution for Kansas and his further defiance of the Supreme Court at Freeport, southern Democrats were determined to break up the party (and the Union) rather than accept him. The Lincoln-Douglas debate platform thus proved to be one of the preliminary battlefields of the Civil War.

✦ John Brown: Murderer or Martyr?

The gaunt, grim figure of John Brown of bleeding Kansas infamy now once again took the stage. After studying the tactics of the black rebels Toussaint L'Ouverture (see p. 213) and Nat Turner (see p. 350), he hatched a daring scheme to invade the South secretly with a handful of followers, call upon the slaves to rise, furnish them with arms, and establish a kind of black free state as a sanctuary. Brown secured several thousand dollars for firearms from northern abolitionists and finally arrived in hilly western Virginia with some twenty men, including several blacks. At scenic **Harpers Ferry**, he seized the federal arsenal in October 1859, incidentally killing seven innocent people, including a free black, and injuring ten or so more. But the slaves, largely ignorant of Brown's strike, failed to rise, and the wounded Brown and the remnants of his tiny band were quickly captured by U.S. Marines under the command of Lieutenant Colonel Robert E. Lee. Ironically, within two years Lee would become the preeminent general in the Confederate army.

"Old Brown" was convicted of murder and treason after a hasty but legal trial. His presumed insanity was supported by affidavits from seventeen friends and relatives, who were trying to save his neck. Actually thirteen of his near relations were regarded as insane, including his mother and grandmother. Governor Wise of Virginia would have been wiser, so his critics say, if he had only clapped the culprit into a lunatic asylum.

But Brown—"God's angry man"—was given every opportunity to pose and to enjoy martyrdom. Though perhaps of unsound mind, he was clever enough to see that he was worth much more to the abolitionist cause dangling from a rope than in any other way. His demeanor during the trial was dignified and courageous, his last words ("this *is* a beautiful country") were to become legendary, and he marched up the scaffold steps without flinching. His conduct was so exemplary, his devotion to freedom so inflexible, that he took on an exalted character, however deplorable his previous record may have been. So the hangman's trap was sprung, and Brown plunged not into oblivion but into world fame. A memorable marching song of the impending Civil War ran,

> *John Brown's body lies a-mould'ring in the grave,*
> *His soul is marching on.*

The effects of Harpers Ferry were inflammatory. In the eyes of the South, already embittered, "Osawatomie Brown" was a wholesale murderer and an apostle of treason. Many southerners asked how they could possibly remain in the Union while a "murderous gang of abolitionists" was financing armed bands to "Brown" them. Moderate northerners, including Republican leaders, openly deplored this mad exploit. But the South naturally concluded that the violent abolitionist view was shared by the entire North, dominated by "Brown-loving" Republicans.

Abolitionists and other ardent free-soilers were infuriated by Brown's execution. Many of them were ignorant of his bloody past and his even more bloody purposes, and they were outraged because the Virginians had hanged so earnest a reformer who was working for so righteous a cause. On the day of his execution,

Contending Voices
Judging John Brown

Upon hearing of John Brown's execution, escaped slave and abolitionist Harriet Tubman (ca. 1820–1913) paid him the highest tribute for his self-sacrifice:

❝I've been studying, and studying upon it, and its clar to me, it wasn't John Brown that died on that gallows. When I think how he gave up his life for our people, and how he never flinched, but was so brave to the end; its clar to me it wasn't mortal man, it was God in him.❞

Not all opponents of slavery, however, shared Tubman's reverence for Brown. Republican presidential candidate Abraham Lincoln dismissed Brown as deluded:

❝[The Brown] affair, in its philosophy, corresponds with the many attempts, related in history, at the assassination of kings and emperors. An enthusiast broods over the oppression of a people till he fancies himself commissioned by Heaven to liberate them. He ventures the attempt, which ends in little else than his own execution.❞

Did John Brown help or harm the antislavery cause?

free-soil centers in the North tolled bells, fired guns, lowered flags, and held rallies. Some spoke of "Saint John" Brown, and the serene Ralph Waldo Emerson compared the new martyr-hero with Jesus. The gallows became a cross. E. C. Stedman wrote,

> *And Old Brown,*
> *Osawatomie Brown,*
> *May trouble you more than ever, when you've nailed his*
> *   coffin down!*

The ghost of the martyred Brown would not be laid to rest.

✦ The Disruption of the Democrats

Beyond question the presidential election of 1860 was the most fateful in American history. On it hung the issue of peace or civil war.

Deeply divided, the Democrats met in Charleston, South Carolina, with Douglas the leading candidate of the northern wing of the party. But the southern "fire-eaters" regarded him as a traitor, as a result of his unpopular stand on the Lecompton Constitution and the Freeport Doctrine. After a bitter wrangle over the platform, the delegates from most of the cotton states walked out. When the remainder could not scrape together the necessary two-thirds vote for Douglas, the entire body dissolved. The first tragic secession was the secession of southerners from the Democratic National Convention. Departure became habit-forming.

The Democrats tried again in Baltimore. This time the Douglas Democrats, chiefly from the North, were firmly in the saddle. Many of the cotton-state delegates again took a walk, and the rest of the convention enthusiastically nominated their hero. The platform came out squarely for popular sovereignty and, as a sop to the South, against obstruction of the Fugitive Slave Law by the states.

Last Moments of John Brown, by Thomas Hovenden
Sentenced to be hanged, John Brown wrote to his brother, "I am quite cheerful in view of my approaching end, being fully persuaded that I am worth inconceivably more to hang than for any other purpose....I count it all joy. 'I have fought the good fight,' and have, as I trust, 'finished my course.'" This painting of Brown going to his execution may have been inspired by the journalist Horace Greeley, who was not present but wrote that "a black woman with a little child stood by the door. He stopped for a moment, and stooping, kissed the child." That scene never took place, as Brown was escorted from the jail only by a detachment of soldiers. But this painting has become famous as a kind of allegorical expression of the pathos of Brown's martyrdom for the abolitionist cause.

The Metropolitan Museum of Art/Art Resource, NY

Angered southern Democrats promptly organized a rival convention in Baltimore, in which many of the northern states were unrepresented. They selected as their leader the stern-jawed vice president, John C. Breckinridge, a man of moderate views from the border state of Kentucky. The platform favored the extension of slavery into the territories and the annexation of slave-populated Cuba.

A middle-of-the-road group, fearing for the Union, hastily organized the **Constitutional Union party**, sneered at as the "Do Nothing" or "Old Gentleman's" party. It consisted mainly of former Whigs and Know-Nothings, a veritable "gathering of graybeards." Desperately anxious to elect a compromise candidate, they met in Baltimore and nominated for the presidency John Bell of Tennessee. They went into battle ringing hand bells for Bell and waving handbills for "The Union, the Constitution, and the Enforcement of the Laws."

✦ A Rail-Splitter Splits the Union

Elated Republicans, scenting victory in the breeze as their opponents split hopelessly, gathered in Chicago in a huge, boxlike wooden structure called the Wigwam. William H. Seward was by far the best known of the contenders. But his radical utterances, including his "irrepressible conflict" speech at Rochester in 1858, had ruined his prospects.* His numerous enemies coined the slogan "Success Rather Than Seward." Lincoln, the favorite son of Illinois, was definitely a "Mr. Second Best," but he was a stronger candidate because he had made fewer enemies. Overtaking Seward on the third ballot, he was nominated amid scenes of the wildest excitement.

The Republican platform had a seductive appeal for just about every important nonsouthern group: for the free-soilers, nonextension of slavery; for the northern manufacturers, a protective tariff; for the immigrants, no abridgment of rights; for the Northwest, a Pacific railroad; for the West, internal improvements at federal expense; and for the farmers, free homesteads from the public domain. Alluring slogans included "Vote Yourselves a Farm" and "Land for the Landless."

Southern secessionists promptly served notice that the election of the "baboon" Lincoln—the "abolitionist" rail-splitter—would split the Union. In fact, "Honest Abe," though hating slavery, was no outright abolitionist. As late as February 1865, he was inclined to favor cash compensation to the owners of freed slaves. But for the time being, he saw fit, perhaps

---

*Seward had referred to an "irrepressible conflict" between slavery and freedom, though not necessarily a bloody one.

THE NATIONAL GAME. THREE "OUTS" AND ONE "RUN".
ABRAHAM WINNING THE BALL.

Library of Congress Prints and Photographs Division

Lincoln Hits a Home Run in 1860 Currier & Ives, the producer of popular, inexpensive prints, portrayed Lincoln's victory over (from left to right) John Bell, Stephen Douglas, and John C. Breckinridge as a baseball game. Baseball developed in New York in the 1840s, and by 1860 the National Association of Baseball Players boasted fifty clubs, several playing regular schedules and charging admission. This cartoon is thought to be the first time baseball was used as a metaphor for politics. Note that Lincoln is beardless. By February 1861, when he left Springfield, Illinois, by train for the White House, he was fully bearded, having followed the advice of an eleven-year-old girl from Westfield, New York, who urged him to grow whiskers because "you would look a great deal better for your face is so thin."

mistakenly, to issue no statements to quiet southern fears. He had already put himself on record, and fresh statements might stir up fresh antagonisms.

As the election campaign ground noisily forward, Lincoln enthusiasts staged roaring rallies and parades, complete with pitch-dripping torches and oilskin capes. They extolled "High Old Abe," the "Woodchopper of the West," and the "Little Giant Killer," while groaning dismally for "Poor Little Doug." Enthusiastic "Little Giants" and "Little Dougs" retorted with "We want a statesman, not a rail-splitter, as President." Douglas himself waged a vigorous speaking campaign, even in the South, and threatened to put the noose with his own hands around the neck of the first secessionist.

The returns, breathlessly awaited, proclaimed a sweeping victory for Lincoln (see Table 19.1).

Candidate	Popular Vote	Percentage of Popular Vote	Electoral Vote
Lincoln	1,865,593	39.79%	180 (every vote of the free states except for 3 of New Jersey's 7 votes)
Douglas	1,382,713	29.40	12 (only Missouri and 3 of New Jersey's 7 votes)
Breckinridge	848,356	18.20	72 (all the cotton states)
Bell	592,906	12.61	39 (Virginia, Kentucky, Tennessee)

TABLE 19.1 Election of 1860

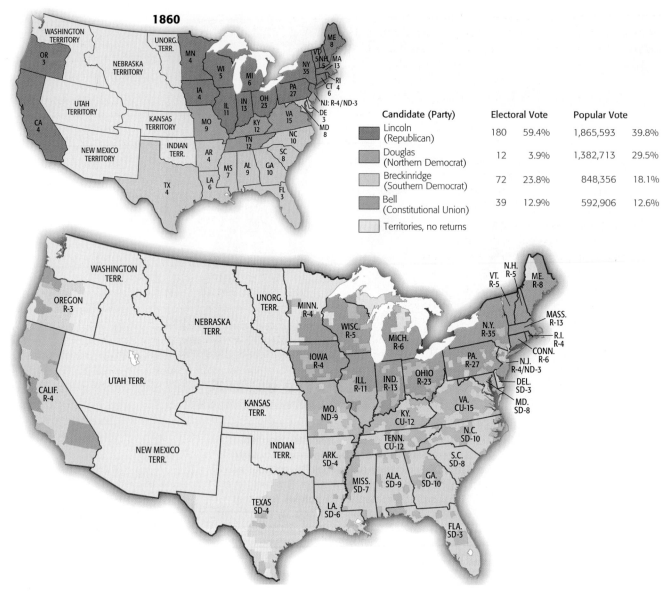

MAP 19.3 Presidential Election of 1860: Electoral Vote by State (top) and Popular Vote by County (bottom)   It is a surprising fact that Lincoln, often rated among the greatest presidents, ranks near the bottom in percentage of popular votes. In all the eleven states that seceded, he received only a scattering of one state's votes—about 1.5 percent in Virginia. The vote by county for Lincoln was virtually all cast in the North. The northern Democrat, Douglas, was also nearly shut out in the South, which divided its votes between Breckinridge and Bell. (Note that only citizens of states could vote; inhabitants of territories could not.) © 2016 Cengage Learning

✦ The Electoral Upheaval of 1860

Awkward "Abe" Lincoln had run a curious race. To a greater degree than any other holder of the nation's highest office (except John Quincy Adams), he was a minority president. Sixty percent of the voters preferred some other candidate. He was also a sectional president, for in ten southern states, where he was not allowed on the ballot, he polled no popular votes. The election of 1860 was virtually two elections: one in the North, the other in the South (see Map 19.3). South Carolinians rejoiced over Lincoln's victory; they now had their excuse to secede. In winning the North, the "rail-splitter" had split off the South.

Douglas, though scraping together only twelve electoral votes, made an impressive showing. Boldly breaking with tradition, he campaigned energetically on his own behalf. (Presidential candidates customarily maintained a dignified silence.) He drew important strength from all sections and ranked a fairly close second in the popular-vote column. In fact, the Douglas Democrats and the Breckinridge Democrats together amassed 365,476 more votes than did Lincoln.

A myth persists that if the Democrats had only united behind Douglas, they would have triumphed. Yet the cold figures tell a different story. Even if the "Little Giant" had received all the electoral votes cast for all three of Lincoln's opponents, the "rail-splitter" would have won, 169 to 134 instead of 180 to 123. Lincoln still would have carried the populous states of the North and the Northwest. On the other hand, if the Democrats had not broken up, they could have entered the campaign with higher enthusiasm and better organization and might have won.

Significantly, the verdict of the ballot box did not indicate a strong sentiment for secession (see Map 19.4). Breckinridge, while favoring the extension of slavery, was no disunionist. Although the candidate of the "fire-eaters," he polled fewer votes in the slave states than the combined strength of his opponents, Douglas and Bell. He even failed to carry his own Kentucky.

Yet the South, despite its electoral defeat, was not all that badly off in terms of political power. It retained a five-to-four majority on the Supreme Court. And although the Republicans had elected Lincoln to the presidency, they controlled neither the Senate nor the House of Representatives. The federal government could not touch slavery in those states where it existed except by a constitutional amendment, and such an amendment could be defeated by one-fourth of the states. The fifteen slave states numbered nearly one-half of the total—a fact not fully appreciated by southern firebrands.

Nonetheless, hot passions, not cool reason, now began to drive events. South Carolina, which had

> *One reason why the Crittenden Compromise failed in December 1860 was the prevalence of an attitude reflected in a private letter of Senator James Henry Hammond (1807–1864) of South Carolina on April 19:*
>
> **❝**I firmly believe that the slave-holding South is now the controlling power of the world—that no other power would face us in hostility. Cotton, rice, tobacco, and naval stores command the world; and we have sense to know it, and are sufficiently Teutonic to carry it out successfully. The North without us would be a motherless calf, bleating about, and die of mange and starvation.**❞**

threatened to go out if the "sectional" Lincoln came in, proved as good as its word. Four days after the election of the "Illinois baboon" by "insulting" majorities, its legislature voted unanimously to call a special convention. Meeting at Charleston in December 1860, the delegates unanimously voted to leave the Union. The fuse had now been lit that would eventually ignite a chain reaction of secession.

✦ The Collapse of Compromise

Impending bloodshed spurred frantic last-ditch attempts at compromise—in the American tradition. The most promising of these efforts was sponsored by Senator John Jordan Crittenden of Kentucky, on whose shoulders had fallen the mantle of a fellow Kentuckian, Henry Clay.

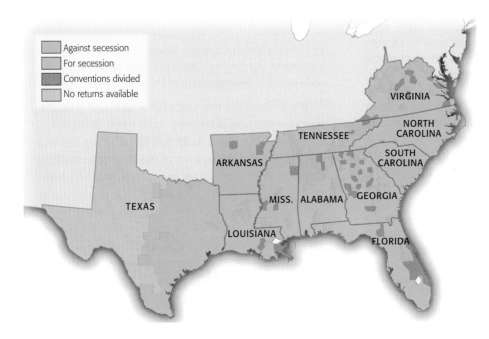

Against secession
For secession
Conventions divided
No returns available

VIRGINIA

TENNESSEE NORTH CAROLINA

SOUTH CAROLINA

ARKANSAS

TEXAS MISS. ALABAMA GEORGIA

LOUISIANA

FLORIDA

MAP 19.4 Southern Opposition to Secession, 1860–1861 (showing vote by county) This county vote shows the opposition of the antiplanter, antislavery mountain whites in the Appalachian region. There was also considerable resistance to secession in Texas, where Governor Sam Houston, who led the Unionists, was deposed by secessionists. © 2016 Cengage Learning

The proposed **Crittenden amendments** to the Constitution, proposed within days of South Carolina's secession vote, were designed to appease the South. Slavery in the territories was to be prohibited north of 36° 30′, but south of that line it was to be given federal protection in all territories existing or "hereafter to be acquired" (such as Cuba). Future states, north or south of 36° 30′, could come into the Union with or without slavery, as they should choose. In short, the slavery supporters were to be guaranteed full rights in the southern territories, as long as they were territories, regardless of the wishes of the majority under popular sovereignty. Federal protection in a territory south of 36° 30′ might conceivably, though improbably, turn the entire area permanently to slavery.

President-elect Lincoln flatly rejected the Crittenden scheme, which offered some slight prospect of success, and all hope of compromise evaporated. For this refusal he must bear a heavy responsibility. Yet he had been elected on a platform that opposed the extension of slavery, and he felt that as a matter of principle, he could not afford to yield, even though gains for slavery in the territories might be only temporary. Larger gains might come later in Cuba and Mexico. Crittenden's proposal, said Lincoln, "would amount to a perpetual covenant of war against every people, tribe, and state owning a foot of land between here and Tierra del Fuego."

✴ The Secessionist Exodus

As the new year dawned and the Crittenden Compromise spiraled toward failure, six other states of the lower South, though somewhat less united, followed the leader over the precipice: Alabama, Mississippi, Florida, Georgia, Louisiana, and Texas. Four more were to join them in the spring, bringing the total to eleven.

With the eyes of destiny upon them, the first seven seceders, formally meeting at Montgomery, Alabama, in February 1861, created a government known as the **Confederate States of America**. As their president they chose Jefferson Davis, a dignified and austere recent member of the U.S. Senate from Mississippi. He was a West Pointer and a former cabinet member with wide military and administrative experience; but he suffered from chronic ill health, as well as from a frustrated ambition to be a Napoleonic strategist.

The crisis, already critical enough, was deepened by the "lame duck"* interlude. Lincoln, although elected president in November 1860, could not take

*The "lame duck" period was shortened to ten weeks in 1933 by the Twentieth Amendment (see the Appendix).

Jefferson Davis (1808–1889), President of the Confederacy   Faced with grave difficulties, he was probably as able a man for the position as the Confederacy could have chosen. Ironically, Davis and Lincoln had both sprung from the same Kentucky soil. The Davis family had moved south from Kentucky, the Lincoln family north.

Chicago History Museum

office until four months later, on March 4, 1861. During this period of protracted uncertainty, when he was still a private citizen in Illinois, the secessionist movement gathered further momentum.

The state of South Carolina, leader of the secessionist movement, justified its retreat from the Union in its declaration of independence of December 1860:

❝We affirm that the ends for which this [Federal] government was instituted have been defeated, and the government itself has been made destructive of them by the action of the non-slaveholding states.... For twenty five years this agitation has been steadily increasing, until it has now secured to its aid the power of the common government. Observing the forms of the constitution, a sectional party has found within that article establishing the executive department the means of subverting the constitution itself.**❞**

Three days after Lincoln's election, Horace Greeley's influential New York Tribune *(November 9, 1860) declared,*

❝ If the cotton States shall decide that they can do better out of the Union than in it, we insist on letting them go in peace. The right to secede may be a revolutionary one, but it exists nevertheless.... Whenever a considerable section of our Union shall deliberately resolve to go out, we shall resist all coercive measures designed to keep it in. We hope never to live in a republic, whereof one section is pinned to the residue by bayonets. ❞

After the secession movement got well under way, Greeley's Tribune *changed its tune.*

President Buchanan, the aging incumbent, has been blamed for not holding the seceders in the Union by sheer force—for wringing his hands instead of secessionist necks. Never a vigorous man and habitually conservative, he was now nearly seventy, and although devoted to the Union, he was surrounded by prosouthern advisers. As an able lawyer wedded to the Constitution, he did not believe that the southern states could legally secede. Yet he could find no authority in the Constitution for stopping them with guns. And even if he had used force on South Carolina in December 1860, the fighting almost certainly would

have erupted three months sooner than it did and under less favorable circumstances for the Union. The North would have appeared as the heavy-handed aggressor. And the crucial Border States, so vital to the Union, probably would have been driven into the arms of their "wayward sisters."

"Oh for one hour of Jackson!" cried the advocates of strong-arm tactics. But "Old Buck" Buchanan was not "Old Hickory," and he was faced with a far more complex and serious problem. One important reason why he did not resort to force was that the tiny standing army of some fifteen thousand men, then widely scattered, was urgently needed to suppress the Indians in the West. Public opinion in the North, at that time, was far from willing to unsheathe the sword. Fighting would merely shatter all prospects of adjustment, and until the guns began to boom, there was still a flickering hope of reconciliation rather than a contested divorce. The weakness lay not so much in Buchanan as in the Constitution and in the Union itself. Ironically, when Lincoln became president in March, he essentially continued Buchanan's wait-and-see policy.

✴ Farewell to Union

Secessionists who parted company with their sister states left for a number of avowed reasons, mostly relating in some way to slavery. They were alarmed by the inexorable tipping of the political balance against them—"the despotic majority of numbers."

The Eagle's Nest, 1861 The American eagle jealously guards her nest of states and bids defiance to the rebels.

James Russell Lowell (1819–1891), the northern poet and essayist, wrote in the Atlantic Monthly *shortly after the secessionist movement began,*

❝The fault of the free States in the eyes of the South is not one that can be atoned for by any yielding of special points here and there. Their offense is that they are free, and that their habits and prepossessions are those of freedom. Their crime is the census of 1860. Their increase in numbers, wealth, and power is a standing aggression. It would not be enough to please the Southern States that we should stop asking them to abolish slavery: what they demand of us is nothing less than that we should abolish the spirit of the age. Our very thoughts are a menace.❞

Regarding the Civil War, the London Times *(November 7, 1861) editorialized,*

❝The contest is really for empire on the side of the North, and for independence on that of the South, and in this respect we recognize an exact analogy between the North and the Government of George III, and the South and the Thirteen Revolted Provinces.❞

The "crime" of the North, observed James Russell Lowell, was the census returns. Southerners were also dismayed by the triumph of the new sectional Republican party, which seemed to threaten their rights as a slaveholding minority. They were weary of free-soil criticism, abolitionist nagging, and northern interference, ranging from the Underground Railroad to John Brown's raid. "All we ask is to be let alone," declared Confederate president Jefferson Davis in an early message to his congress.

Many southerners supported secession because they felt sure that their departure would be unopposed, despite "Yankee yawp" to the contrary. They were confident that the clodhopping and codfishing Yankee would not or could not fight. They believed that northern manufacturers and bankers, so heavily dependent on southern cotton and markets, would not dare to cut their own economic throats with their own unionist swords. But should war come, the immense debt owed to northern creditors by the South—happy thought—could be promptly repudiated, as it later was.

Southern leaders regarded secession as a golden opportunity to cast aside their generations of "vassalage" to the North. An independent Dixieland could develop its own banking and shipping and trade directly with Europe. The low Tariff of 1857 had passed largely with southern votes. But who could tell when the "greedy" northern Republicans would win control of Congress and drive through their own oppressive protective tariff? For decades this fundamental friction had pitted the North, with its growing development of a manufacturing economy, against the South, with an economy hugely dependent on agricultural exports, especially cotton.

Worldwide impulses of nationalism—then stirring in Italy, Germany, Poland, and elsewhere—were fermenting in the South. This huge area, with its distinctive culture, was not so much a section as a subnation. It could not view with complacency the possibility of being lorded over, then or later, by what it regarded as a hostile nation of northerners.

The principles of self-determination—of the Declaration of Independence—seemed to many southerners to apply perfectly to them. Few, if any, of the seceders felt that they were doing anything wrong or immoral. The thirteen original states had voluntarily entered the Union, and now seven—ultimately eleven—southern states were voluntarily withdrawing from it.

Historical parallels ran even deeper. In 1776 thirteen American colonies, led by the rebel George Washington, had seceded from the British Empire by throwing off the yoke of King George III. In 1860–1861, eleven American states, led by the rebel Jefferson Davis, were seceding from the Union by throwing off the yoke of "King" Abraham Lincoln. With that burden gone, the South was confident that it could work out its own peculiar destiny more quietly, happily, and prosperously.

The Civil War: Repressible or Irrepressible?

Few topics have generated as much controversy among American historians as the causes of the Civil War. Looming over the entire debate is the stark fact that the United States was the only slaveowning society that had to fight a war to rid itself of slavery. The very names employed to describe the conflict—notably "Civil War" or "War Between the States" or even "War for Southern Independence"—reveal much about the various authors' points of view. Interpretations of the great conflict have naturally differed according to section and have been charged with both emotional and moral fervor. Yet despite long and keen interest in the origins of the conflict, the causes of the Civil War remain as passionately debated today as they were a century ago.

The so-called Nationalist School of the late nineteenth century claimed that slavery caused the Civil War. Defending the necessity and inevitability of the war, these northern-oriented historians credited the conflict with ending slavery and preserving the Union. But in the early twentieth century, progressive historians, led by Charles and Mary Beard, presented a more skeptical interpretation. The Beards argued that the war was not fought over slavery per se, but rather was a deeply rooted economic struggle between an industrial North and an agricultural South. Anointing the Civil War the "Second American Revolution," the Beards claimed that the war precipitated vast changes in American class relations and shifted the political balance of power by magnifying the influence of business magnates and industrialists while destroying the plantation aristocracy of the South.

Shaken by the disappointing results of World War I, a new wave of historians argued that the Civil War, too, had actually been a big mistake. Rejecting the nationalist interpretation that the clash was inevitable, James G. Randall and Avery Craven asserted that the war had been a "repressible conflict." Neither slavery nor the economic differences between North and South were sufficient causes for war. Instead Craven and others attributed the bloody confrontation to the breakdown of political institutions, the passion of overzealous reformers, and the ineptitude of a blundering generation of political leaders.

Following the Second World War, however, a neonationalist view regained authority, echoing earlier views in depicting the Civil War as an unavoidable conflict between two societies, one slave and one free. For Allan Nevins and David M. Potter, irreconcilable differences in morality, politics, culture, social values, and economies increasingly eroded the ties between the sections and inexorably set the United States on the road to Civil War.

Eric Foner and Eugene Genovese emphasized each section's nearly paranoid fear that the survival of its distinctive way of life was threatened by the expansion of the other section. In *Free Soil, Free Labor, Free Men* (1970), Foner emphasized that most northerners detested slavery not because it enslaved blacks, but because its existence—and particularly its rapid extension—threatened the position of free white laborers. This "free labor ideology" increasingly became the foundation stone upon which the North claimed its superiority over the South. Eugene Genovese has argued that the South felt similarly endangered. Convinced that the southern labor system was more humane than the northern factory system, southerners saw northern designs to destroy their way of life lurking at every turn—and every territorial battle. The focus on the irreconcilable interests of the free and slave sections as the central cause of the war has been carried into more recent scholarship by historians such as John Ashworth and David L. Lightner.

Some historians have placed party politics at the center of their explanations for the war. For them, no event was more consequential than the breakdown of the Jacksonian party system. When the slavery issue tore apart both the Democratic and the Whig parties, the last ligaments binding the nation together were snapped, and the war inevitably came.

Historians of the "Ethnocultural School," especially Michael Holt, have acknowledged the significance of the collapse of the established parties but have offered a different analysis of how that breakdown led to war. They have noted that the two great national parties before the 1850s focused attention on issues such as the tariff, banking, and internal improvements, thereby muting sectional differences over slavery. According to this argument, the erosion of the traditional party system was due not to growing differences over slavery, but to a temporary *consensus* between the two parties in the 1850s on almost all national issues *other than* slavery. In this peculiar political atmosphere, the slavery issue rose to the fore, encouraging the emergence of Republicans in the North and secessionists in the South. In the absence of regular, national, two-party conflict over economic issues, purely regional parties (like the Republicans) coalesced. They identified their opponents not simply as competitors for power but as threats to their way of life, even to the life of the Republic itself.

Chapter Review

KEY TERMS

Uncle Tom's Cabin (399)

The Impending Crisis of the South (400)

New England Emigrant Aid Company (401)

Lecompton Constitution (403)

Bleeding Kansas (403)

Dred Scott v. Stanford (406)

panic of 1857 (407)

Tariff of 1857 (408)

Lincoln-Douglas debates (409)

Freeport question (409)

Freeport Doctrine (409)

Harpers Ferry (411)

Constitutional Union party (412)

Crittenden amendments (416)

Confederate States of America (416)

PEOPLE TO KNOW

Harriet Beecher Stowe

Henry Ward Beecher

James Buchanan

Charles Sumner

Preston S. Brooks

Dred Scott

Roger B. Taney

Stephen A. Douglas

Abraham Lincoln

John Brown

John C. Breckinridge

John Jordan Crittenden

CHRONOLOGY

1852	Harriet Beecher Stowe publishes *Uncle Tom's Cabin*
1853–1856	Crimean War in Russia
1854	Kansas-Nebraska Act Republican party forms
1856	Buchanan defeats Frémont and Fillmore for presidency Sumner beaten by Brooks in Senate chamber Brown's Pottawatomie Massacre
1856–1861	Civil war in "bleeding Kansas"
1857	*Dred Scott* decision Lecompton Constitution rejected
1857	Panic of 1857 Tariff of 1857 Hinton R. Helper publishes *The Impending Crisis of the South*
1858	Lincoln-Douglas debates
1859	Brown raids Harpers Ferry
1860	Lincoln wins four-way race for presidency South Carolina secedes from Union Crittenden Compromise fails
1861	Seven seceding states form Confederate States of America

TO LEARN MORE

Frederick J. Blue, *Charles Sumner and the Conscience of the North* (1994)

Nicole Etcheson, *Bleeding Kansas: Contested Liberty in the Civil War Era* (2004)

Paul Finkelman, ed., *And His Soul Goes Marching On: Responses to John Brown and the Harpers Ferry Raid* (1995)

Eric Foner, *Free Soil, Free Labor, Free Men: The Ideology of the Republican Party Before the Civil War* (1995)

Joan Hedrick, *Harriet Beecher Stowe: A Life* (1994)

Ward M. McAfee, ed., *The Slaveholding Republic* (2001)

Stephen B. Oates, *To Purge This Land with Blood* (1970)

Kenneth M. Stampp, *America in 1857: A Nation on the Brink* (1990)

Harriet Beecher Stowe, *Uncle Tom's Cabin* (1852)

A complete, annotated bibliography for this chapter—along with brief descriptions of the People to Know—may be found on the *American Pageant* website. The key terms are defined in the glossary at the end of the text.

Chapter 20

Girding for War: The North and the South

1861–1865

I consider the central idea pervading this struggle is the necessity that is upon us, of proving that popular government is not an absurdity. We must settle this question now, whether in a free government the minority have the right to break up the government whenever they choose. If we fail it will go far to prove the incapability of the people to govern themselves.

ABRAHAM LINCOLN, MAY 7, 1861

*A*braham Lincoln solemnly took the presidential oath of office on March 4, 1861, after having slipped into Washington at night, partially disguised to thwart assassins. He thus became president not of the *United* States of America, but of the *dis-United* States of America. Seven had already departed; eight more teetered on the edge. The girders of the unfinished Capitol dome loomed nakedly in the background, as if to symbolize the imperfect state of the Union. Before the nation was restored—and the slaves freed at last—the American people would endure four years of anguish and bloodshed, and Lincoln would face tortuous trials of leadership such as have been visited upon few presidents.

✸ The Menace of Secession

Lincoln's inaugural address was firm yet conciliatory: there would be no conflict unless the South provoked it. Secession, the president declared, was wholly impractical because "physically speaking, we cannot separate."

Here Lincoln put his finger on a profound geographical truth. The North and South were conjoined twins, bound inseparably together. If they had been divided by the Pyrenees or the Danube River, a sectional divorce might have been more feasible. But the Appalachian Mountains and the mighty Mississippi River both ran the wrong way.

Uncontested secession would create new controversies. What share of the national debt should the South be forced to take with it? What portion of the jointly held federal territories, if any, should the Confederate states be allotted—areas so largely won with Southern blood? How would the fugitive-slave issue be resolved? The Underground Railroad would certainly redouble its activity, and it would have to transport its passengers only across the Ohio River, not all the way to Canada. Was it conceivable that all such problems could have been solved without ugly armed clashes?

Secretary of State William H. Seward (1801–1872) entertained the dangerous idea that if the North picked a fight with one or more European nations, the South would once more rally around the flag. On April Fools' Day, 1861, he submitted to Lincoln a memorandum:

❝I would demand explanations from Spain and France, categorically, at once. I would seek explanations from Great Britain and Russia.... And, if satisfactory explanations are not received from Spain and France...would convene Congress and declare war against them.**❞**

Lincoln quietly but firmly quashed Seward's scheme.

Bombardment of Fort Sumter, South Carolina, April 1861 At 4:30 the morning of April 12, a Confederate battery at Fort Johnson opened fire on the Union Forces at Fort Sumter in Charleston Harbor. Residents of Charleston cheered from their rooftops as the beleaguered garrison briefly returned fire, surrendered, and then fled.

A *united United* States had hitherto been the paramount republic in the Western Hemisphere. If this powerful democracy should break into two hostile parts, the European nations would be delighted. They could gleefully transplant to America their ancient concept of the balance of power. Playing the no-less-ancient game of divide and conquer, they could incite one snarling fragment of the *dis-United* States against the other. The colonies of the European powers in the New World, notably those of Britain, would thus be made safer against the rapacious Yankees. And European imperialists, with no unified republic to stand across their path, could more easily defy the Monroe Doctrine and seize territory in the Americas.

✦ South Carolina Assails Fort Sumter

The issue of the divided Union came to a head over the matter of federal forts in the South. As the seceding states left, they seized the United States' arsenals, mints, and other public property within their borders. When Lincoln took office, only two significant forts in the South still flew the Stars and Stripes. The more important of the pair was square-walled **Fort Sumter**, in Charleston harbor, with fewer than a hundred men.

Ominously, the choices presented to Lincoln by Fort Sumter were all bad. This stronghold had provisions that would last only a few weeks—until the middle of April 1861. If no supplies were forthcoming, its commander would have to surrender without firing a shot. Lincoln, quite understandably, did not feel that

such a weak-kneed course squared with his obligation to protect federal property. But if he sent reinforcements, the South Carolinians would undoubtedly fight back; they could not tolerate a federal fort blocking the mouth of their most important Atlantic seaport.

After agonizing indecision, Lincoln adopted a middle-of-the-road solution. He notified the South Carolinians that an expedition would be sent to *provision* the garrison, though not to *reinforce* it. He promised "no effort to throw in men, arms, and ammunition." But to Southern eyes "provision" still spelled "reinforcement."

A Union naval force was next started on its way to Fort Sumter—a move that the South regarded as an act of aggression. On April 12, 1861, the cannon of the Carolinians opened fire on the fort, while crowds in Charleston applauded and waved handkerchiefs. After a thirty-four-hour bombardment, which took no lives, the dazed garrison surrendered.

The shelling of the fort electrified the North, which at once responded with cries of "Remember Fort Sumter" and "Save the Union." Hitherto countless Northerners had been saying that if the Southern states wanted to go, they should not be pinned to the rest of the nation with bayonets. "Wayward sisters, depart in peace" was a common sentiment, expressed even by the commander of the army, war hero General Winfield Scott, now so feeble at seventy-five that he had to be boosted onto his horse.

But the assault on Fort Sumter provoked the North to a fighting pitch: the fort was lost, but the Union was saved. Lincoln had turned a tactical defeat into a calculated victory. Southerners had wantonly fired upon the glorious Stars and Stripes, and honor demanded an armed response. Lincoln promptly (April 15) issued a call to the states for seventy-five thousand militiamen, and volunteers sprang to the colors in such enthusiastic numbers that many were turned away—a mistake that was not often repeated. On April 19 and 27, the president proclaimed a leaky blockade of Southern seaports.

The call for troops, in turn, aroused the South much as the attack on Fort Sumter had aroused the North. Lincoln was now waging war—from the Southern view an aggressive war—on the Confederacy. Virginia, Arkansas, and Tennessee, all of which had earlier voted down secession, reluctantly joined their embattled sister states, as did North Carolina (see Map 20.1). Thus the seven states became eleven as the "submissionists" and "Union shriekers" were overcome. Richmond, Virginia, replaced Montgomery, Alabama, as the Confederate capital—too near Washington for strategic comfort on either side.

✯ Brothers' Blood and Border Blood

The only slave states left were the crucial **Border States**. This group consisted of Missouri, Kentucky, Maryland, and Delaware. If the North had fired the first shot, some or all of these doubtful states probably would have seceded, and the South might well have succeeded. The border group actually contained a white population more than half that of the entire

Confederacy. Maryland, Kentucky, and Missouri would almost double the manufacturing capacity of the South and increase by nearly half its supply of horses and mules. The strategic prize of the Ohio River flowed along the northern border of Kentucky and **West Virginia**—the "mountain white" area that somewhat illegally tore itself from the side of Virginia to become a free state in mid-1861. Two of the Ohio River's navigable tributaries, the Cumberland and Tennessee Rivers, penetrated deep into the heart of Dixie, where much of the Confederacy's grain, gunpowder, and iron was produced. Small wonder that Lincoln reportedly said he *hoped* to have God on his side, but he *had* to have Kentucky.

In dealing with the Border States, President Lincoln did not rely solely on moral suasion but successfully used methods of dubious legality. In Maryland he declared martial law where needed and sent in troops, because this state threatened to cut off Washington from the North. Lincoln also deployed Union soldiers in western Virginia and notably in Missouri, where they fought beside Unionists in a local civil war within the larger Civil War.

Any official statement of the North's war aims was profoundly influenced by the teetering Border States. At the very outset, Lincoln was obliged to declare publicly that he was not fighting to free the blacks. An antislavery declaration would no doubt have driven the Border States into the welcoming arms of the South. An antislavery war was also extremely

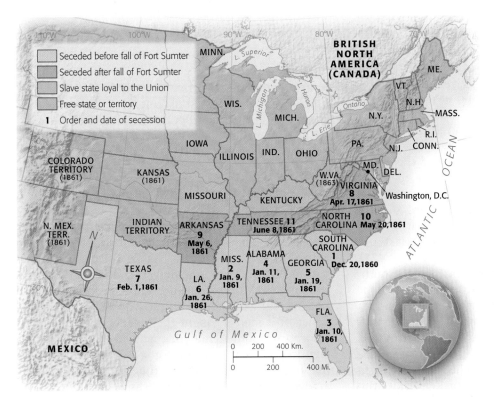

MAP 20.1 Seceding States (with dates and order of secession) Note the long interval—nearly six months—between the secession of South Carolina, the first state to go, and that of Tennessee, the last state to leave the Union. These six months were a time of terrible trial for moderate Southerners. When a Georgia statesman pleaded for restraint and negotiations with Washington, he was rebuffed with the cry, "Throw the bloody spear into this den of incendiaries!" © 2016 Cengage Learning

Abraham Lincoln (1809–1865), Kentucky-born like Jefferson Davis, was aware of Kentucky's crucial importance. In September 1861 he remarked,

❝ I think to lose Kentucky is nearly the same as to lose the whole game. Kentucky gone, we cannot hold Missouri, nor, I think, Maryland. These all against us, and the job on our hands is too large for us. We would as well consent to separation at once, including the surrender of this capital [Washington]. ❞

unpopular in the so-called Butternut region of southern Ohio, Indiana, and Illinois. That area had been settled largely by Southerners who had carried their racial prejudices with them when they had crossed the Ohio River (see "Makers of America: Settlers of the Old Northwest," pp. 238–239). It was to be a hotbed of pro-Southern sentiment throughout the war. Sensitive to this delicate political calculus, Lincoln insisted repeatedly—even though undercutting his moral high ground—that his paramount purpose was to save the Union at all costs. Thus the war began not as one between slave soil and free soil, but one for the Union—with slaveholders on both sides and many proslavery sympathizers in the North.

Slavery also colored the character of the war in the West. In Indian Territory (present-day Oklahoma), most of the Five Civilized Tribes—the Cherokees, Creeks, Choctaws, Chickasaws, and Seminoles—sided with the Confederacy. Some of these Indians, notably the Cherokees, owned slaves and thus felt themselves to be making common cause with the slaveowning South. To secure their loyalty, the Confederate government agreed to take over federal payments to the tribes and invited the Native Americans to send delegates to the Confederate congress. In return the tribes supplied troops to the Confederate army. Meanwhile, a rival faction of Cherokees and most of the Plains Indians sided with the Union, only to be rewarded after the war with a relentless military campaign to herd them onto reservations or into oblivion.

Unhappily, the conflict between "Billy Yank" and "Johnny Reb" was a brothers' war (see "Makers of America: Billy Yank and Johnny Reb," pp. 426–427). There were many Northern volunteers from the Southern states and many Southern volunteers from the Northern states. The "mountain whites" of the South sent north some 50,000 men, and the loyal slave states contributed some 300,000 soldiers to the Union. In many a family of the Border States, one brother rode north to fight with the Blue, another south to fight with the Gray. Senator Crittenden of Kentucky, who

Contending Voices
War Aims: Emancipation or Union?

On August 19, 1862, Horace Greeley (1811–1872), a passionate abolitionist and editor of the New York Tribune, *published an open letter to President Lincoln expressing disappointment that the president had not embraced full and unqualified emancipation.*

❝ Had you, Sir, in your Inaugural Address . . . proclaimed that Rebellion would strike the shackles from the slaves of every traitor, the wealthy and the cautious would have been supplied with a powerful inducement to remain loyal. As it was, every coward in the South soon became a traitor from fear; for Loyalty was perilous, while Treason seemed comparatively safe . . . The Rebels from the first have been eager to confiscate, imprison, scourge and kill: we have fought wolves with the devices of sheep. ❞

Lincoln replied on August 22, even as he was about to announce the Emancipation Proclamation:

❝ If I could save the Union without freeing any slave, I would do it; and if I could save it by freeing all the slaves, I would do it; and if I could do it by freeing some and leaving others alone, I would also do that. ❞

> Why did Lincoln not champion emancipation earlier in the war?

had fathered the abortive Crittenden Compromise, also had fathered two sons: one became a general in the Union army, the other a general in the Confederate army. Lincoln's own Kentucky-born wife had four brothers who fought for the Confederacy.

✴ The Balance of Forces

When war broke out, the South seemed to have great advantages. The Confederacy could fight defensively behind interior lines. The North had to invade the vast territory of the Confederacy, conquer it, and drag it bodily back into the Union. In fact, the South did not have to win the war in order to win its independence. If it merely fought the invaders to a draw and stood firm, Confederate independence would be won. Fighting on their own soil for self-determination and preservation of their way of life, Southerners at first enjoyed an advantage in morale as well.

Library of Congress Prints and Photographs Division [LC-DIG-cwpb-00156]

Friendly Enemies The man on the right is George Armstrong Custer. The youngest general in the Union army, this brilliant young officer survived the Civil War only to lose his life and that of every soldier under his command to Sioux warriors at the Battle of the Little Bighorn in 1876—"Custer's Last Stand." The man on the left is Lt. James B. Washington, a Confederate prisoner. He and Custer had been classmates at West Point.

Militarily, the South from the opening volleys of the war had the most talented officers. Most conspicuous among a dozen or so first-rate commanders was gray-haired General Robert E. Lee, whose knightly bearing and chivalric sense of honor embodied the Southern ideal. Lincoln had unofficially offered him command of the Northern armies, but when Virginia

seceded, Lee felt honor-bound to go with his native state. Lee's chief lieutenant for much of the war was black-bearded Thomas J. ("Stonewall") Jackson, a gifted tactical theorist and a master of speed and deception.

Besides their brilliant leaders, ordinary Southerners were also bred to fight. Accustomed to managing horses and bearing arms from boyhood, they made excellent cavalrymen and foot soldiers. Their high-pitched "rebel yell" ("yeeeahhh") was designed to strike terror into the hearts of fuzz-chinned Yankee recruits. "There is nothing like it on this side of the infernal region," one Northern soldier declared. "The peculiar corkscrew sensation that it sends down your backbone can never be told. You have to feel it."

As one immense farm, the South seemed to be handicapped by the scarcity of factories. Yet by seizing federal weapons, running Union blockades, and developing their own ironworks, Southerners managed to obtain sufficient weaponry. "Yankee ingenuity" was not confined to Yankees.

Nevertheless, as the war dragged on, grave shortages of shoes, uniforms, and blankets disabled the South. Even with immense stores of food on Southern farms, civilians and soldiers often went hungry because of supply problems. "Forward, men! They have cheese in their haversacks," cried one Southern officer as he attacked the Yankees. Much of the hunger was caused by a breakdown of the South's rickety transportation system, especially where the railroad tracks were cut or destroyed by the Yankee invaders.

The economy was the greatest Southern weakness; it was the North's greatest strength. The North was not only a huge farm but a sprawling factory as well (see Table 20.1). Yankees boasted about three-fourths of the nation's wealth, including three-fourths of the thirty thousand miles of railroads.

The North also controlled the sea. With its vastly superior navy, it established a blockade that, though a sieve at first, soon choked off Southern supplies and eventually shattered Southern morale. Its sea power also

TABLE 20.1 Manufacturing by Sections, 1860					
Section	Number of Establishments	Capital Invested	Average Number of Laborers	Annual Value of Products	Percentage of Total Value
New England	20,671	$ 257,477,783	391,836	$ 468,599,287	24.8%
Middle states	53,387	435,061,964	546,243	802,338,392	42.5
Western states	36,785	194,212,543	209,909	384,606,530	20.4
Southern states	20,631	95,975,185	110,721	155,531,281	8.3
Pacific states	8,777	23,380,334	50,204	71,229,989	3.8
Territories	282	3,747,906	2,333	3,556,197	0.2
TOTAL	140,533	$1,009,855,715	1,311,246	$1,885,861,676	

The Prussian general Helmuth von Moltke (1800–1891) allegedly remarked that the American Civil War was merely a contest waged by "armed mobs." Whether he meant it or not, the Prussian's famous insult actually contains an important insight. Unlike the professional standing armies of nineteenth-century Europe, the Civil War armies were over-whelmingly amateur and volunteer. Taken from all walks of life, citizen-soldiers gave the Civil War drama its uniquely plebeian cast.

With 2 million men in Union blue and 1 million men in Confederate gray, Civil War soldiers repre-sented a vast cross section of American society. (At nearly 10 percent of the 1860 population, the same rate of mobilization would amount to more than 27 million troops today.) Most soldiers had been farm-ers or farm laborers. Poor unskilled workers, despite vehement antidraft rhetoric to the contrary, were actu-ally underrepresented. Most troops were native-born,

but immigrants did serve in rough proportion to their presence in the general population. Black fighting men accounted for about 10 percent of Union enlist-ments by war's end (see "Blacks Battle Bondage," pp. 446–447). Perhaps one-third of the soldiers were married. Nearly 40 percent were under twenty-two years of age at the time of enlistment.

Inheritors of the values of Jacksonian mass democracy and Victorian sentiments, Civil War citizen-soldiers brought strong ideological commitments to the struggle. Neither army regulars nor reluctant conscripts, these men fought in the name of country, duty, honor, manhood, and righteousness. Though enemies, Union and Confederate soldiers shared a common commitment to the patriotic "spirit of '76" and the cause of liberty, independence, and republi-can government. A man's moral obligation to defend his country and preserve his personal reputation pro-vided added motivation. Many interpreted the war as a religious crusade. In short, convictions, not coercion, created Civil War armies.

Despite their similarities, "Billy Yank" (the ordinary Union soldier) and "Johnny Reb" (the typical Confederate) were not necessarily cut from the same cloth. Both armies reflected the societies from which they came. Billy Yank tended to be more literate, intellectual, practi-cal, and efficient, while Johnny Reb was often more jocular, emotional, religious, and per-sonally concerned about the war. Defense of home and hearth meant more to Confederate troops, for the simple reason that most of the fighting occurred on Southern soil. Above all else, the men in gray maintained a distinctive rural individualism and homegrown disrespect for authority. Their counterparts in blue, often familiar with the strict regimen of Northern cit-ies and factories, adapted more quickly to army discipline.

One aspect of soldiering Johnny Reb and Billy Yank shared was the dull routine of camp life. For all its promises of adventure, the life of a Civil War soldier could be downright boring and unpleasant. Men spent fifty days in camp for every one in battle. Reveille, roll call, and drill were daily chores. A soldier's first con-cern was usually his stomach, even when pork ("sowbelly"), beef ("salt horse"), coffee, and bread (or its unwelcome substitute, "hardtack")

A Union Private

Library of Congress Prints and Photographs Division [LC-DIG-ppmsca-37010] were in abundance. Food shortages plagued both armies, especially the Confederates as the war progressed. Uniforms deteriorated from "finery" to "tatters," as did moral standards. Gambling, drinking, stealing, swearing, and Sabbath-breaking proliferated; even widespread religious revivals could not keep up.

The gravest hardship of all, however, was disease. Germs—especially camp and campaign maladies like dysentery, diarrhea, typhoid, and malaria—took twice as many lives as bullets. By modern standards the mortality rates of wounded soldiers were appallingly high. (World War II marked the first time in American warfare that more soldiers died from combat wounds than from sickness and disease.) Without proper medical understanding of sterilization or sanitation, the risk of sepsis (bacterial infection) accompanied every wound. Head, chest, and stomach wounds were usually considered fatal; arm and leg injuries often resulted in amputation. Only the presence of nurses made life in field hospitals tolerable. Overcoming the vocal hostility of male army doctors and the filth, stench, and agony of these hospitals, some twenty thousand women volunteered as nurses during the war. Working with the maimed and the dying was never pleasant, but female nurses earned the respect of countless wounded soldiers for their dedicated service.

Yet for all its brutality, not even the field hospital could match the traumatic experience of combat. Tension mounted in the final moments before battle, as officers strove to maintain close-order ranks in the face of harrowing enemy gunfire. Artillery shells blanketed the battlefield with a smoky haze. Bullets zinged through the air like a driving rain. Once soldiers joined the action, a rush of adrenaline could transform frightened civilians into frenzied and ferocious fighters. First-timers likened the experience to "seeing the elephant" (an antebellum expression of awe). One sight of mangled limbs or one whiff of decaying flesh was often enough to push men over the edge. "Even when I sleep," a Massachusetts soldier moaned, "I hear the whistling of the shells and the shouts and groans, and to sum it up in two [*sic*] words it is *horrible*." Given the extraordinary stress of battle, many men avoided combat as much as they could.

Shell-shocked and weary, most soldiers returned home from the war utterly transformed. For nearly

Library of Congress

A Confederate Soldier

a decade and a half, silence reigned, as veterans and civilians entered into a tacit agreement to put the ordeal behind them. By 1880 interest revived in the war, and a new battle over its proper meaning commenced. Ignoring the conflict's original significance as a moral victory for slave emancipation, many Americans embraced a new reconciliationist and white supremacist script. In the interest of sectional harmony and national prosperity, Northerners abandoned earlier commitments to black rights. A reunion of sections spelled a division of races. Casting aside their original ideological convictions, many Americans came to regard the conflict as a tragic brothers' war meaningful only for its show of martial valor. Principles that had compelled 3 million men to enlist and caused 620,000 to die were largely forgotten. Instead a sentimental, sanitized, and whitened version of the Civil War became commonplace by the late nineteenth century. Von Moltke's "armed mobs" came to be remembered as the noblest of knights.

National Archives and Records Administration

The Technology of War One of the new machines of destruction that made the Civil War the first mechanized war, this eight-and-a-half-ton federal mortar sat on a railroad flatcar in Petersburg, Virginia, ready to hurl two-hundred-pound missiles as far as two and a half miles. This powerful artillery piece rode on the tracks of a captured Southern railroad—itself another artifact of modern technology that figured heavily in the war. Of the 31,256 miles of railroad track in the United States in 1861, less than 30 percent, or 9,283 miles, were in the Confederate states, soon reduced by Union capture and destruction to 6,000 miles. The Confederate government's failure to understand the military importance of railroads contributed substantially to its defeat.

enabled the North to exchange huge quantities of grain for munitions and supplies from Europe, thus adding the output from the factories of Europe to its own.

The Union also enjoyed a much larger reserve of manpower. The loyal states had a population of some 22 million; the seceding states had 9 million people, including about 3.5 million slaves. Adding to the

North's overwhelming supply of soldiery were ever-more immigrants from Europe, who continued to pour into the North even during the war (see Table 20.2). Over 800,000 newcomers arrived between 1861 and 1865, most of them British, Irish, and German. Large numbers of them were induced to enlist in the Union army. Altogether about one-fifth of the Union forces were foreign-born, and in some units military commands were given in four different languages.

Whether immigrant or native, ordinary Northern boys were much less prepared than their Southern counterparts for military life. Yet the Northern "clodhoppers" and "shop-keepers" eventually adjusted themselves to soldiering and became known for their discipline and determination.

The North was much less fortunate in its higher commanders. Lincoln was forced to use a costly trial-and-error method to sort out effective leaders from the many incompetent political officers, until he finally uncovered a

TABLE 20.2 Immigration to United States, 1860–1866

Year	Total	Britain	Ireland	Germany	All Others
1860	153,640	29,737	48,637	54,491	20,775
1861	91,918	19,675	23,797	31,661	16,785
1862	91,985	24,639	23,351	27,529	16,466
1863	176,282	66,882	55,916	33,162	20,322
1864	193,418	53,428	63,523	57,276	19,191
1865*	248,120	82,465	29,772	83,424	52,459
1866	318,568	94,924	36,690	115,892	71,062

*Only the first three months of 1865 were war months.

general, Ulysses Simpson Grant, who was determined to slog his way to victory at whatever cost in life and limb.

In the long run, as the Northern strengths were brought to bear, they outweighed those of the South. But when the war began, the chances for Southern independence were unusually favorable—certainly better than the prospects for success of the thirteen colonies in 1776. The turn of a few events could easily have produced a different outcome.

The might-have-beens are fascinating. *If* the Border States had seceded, *if* the uncertain states of the upper Mississippi Valley had turned against the Union, *if* a wave of Northern defeatism had demanded an armistice, and *if* Britain and/or France had broken the Union's naval blockade of Southern ports, the South might well have won. All of these possibilities almost became realities, but none of them actually occurred, and lacking their impetus, the South could not hope to win.

✦ Dethroning King Cotton

Successful revolutions, including the American Revolution of 1776, have generally succeeded because of foreign intervention. The South counted on it, did not get it, and lost. Of all the Confederacy's potential assets, none counted more weightily than the prospect of foreign intervention. Europe's ruling classes were openly sympathetic to the Confederate cause. They had long abhorred the incendiary example of the American democratic experiment, and they cherished a kind of fellow-feeling for the South's semifeudal, aristocratic social order.

In contrast, the masses of workingpeople in Britain, and to some extent in France, were pulling and praying for the North. Many of them had read *Uncle Tom's Cabin*, and they sensed that the war—though at the outset officially fought only over the question of union—might extinguish slavery if the North emerged victorious. The common folk of Britain could not yet cast the ballot, but they could cast the brick. Their certain hostility to any official intervention on behalf of the South evidently had a sobering effect on the British government. Thus the dead hands of Uncle Tom helped Uncle Sam by restraining the British and French ironclads from piercing the Union blockade. Yet the fact remained that British textile mills depended on the American South for 75 percent of their cotton supplies. Wouldn't silent looms force London to speak? Humanitarian sympathies aside, Southerners counted on hard economic need to bring Britain to their aid. Why did King Cotton fail them?

He failed in part because he had been so lavishly productive in the immediate prewar years of 1857–1860. Enormous exports of cotton in those years had piled up surpluses in British warehouses. When the shooting started in 1861, British manufacturers had on hand a hefty oversupply of fiber. The real pinch

Recruiting Immigrants for the Union Army This poster in several languages appeals to immigrants to enlist. Immigrant manpower provided the Union with both industrial and military muscle.

did not come until about a year and a half later, when thousands of hungry operatives were thrown out of work. But by this time Lincoln had announced his slave-emancipation policy, and the "wage slaves" of Britain were not going to demand a war to defend the slaveowners of the South.

The American minister to Britain wrote,

❝The great body of the aristocracy and the commercial classes are anxious to see the United States go to pieces [but] the middle and lower class sympathise with us [because they] see in the convulsion in America an era in the history of the world, out of which must come in the end a general recognition of the right of mankind to the produce of their labor and the pursuit of happiness.❞

The direst effects of the "cotton famine" in Britain were relieved in several ways. Hunger among unemployed workers was partially eased when certain kindhearted Americans sent over several cargoes of foodstuffs. As Union armies penetrated the South, they captured or bought considerable supplies of cotton and shipped them to Britain; the Confederates also ran a limited quantity through the blockade. In addition, the cotton growers of Egypt and India, responding to high prices, increased their output and captured a share of the world cotton market that they held on to well after the war's conclusion. Finally, booming war industries in England, which supplied both the North and the South, relieved unemployment.

King Wheat and King Corn—the monarchs of Northern agriculture—proved to be more potent potentates than King Cotton. During these war years, the North, blessed with ideal weather, produced bountiful crops of grain and harvested them with McCormick's mechanical reaper. In the same period, the British suffered a series of bad harvests. They were forced to import huge quantities of grain from America, which happened to have the cheapest and

As the Civil War neared the end of its third year, the London Times *(January 7, 1864) could boast,*

❝We are as busy, as rich, and as fortunate in our trade as if the American war had never broken out, and our trade with the States had never been disturbed. Cotton was no King, notwithstanding the prerogatives which had been loudly claimed for him.**❞**

most abundant supply. If the British had broken the blockade to gain cotton, they would have provoked the North to war and would have lost this precious granary. Unemployment for some seemed better than hunger for all. Hence one Yankee journal could exult,

Wave the stars and stripes high o'er us,
Let every freeman sing . . .
Old King Cotton's dead and buried;
*   brave young Corn is King.*

✦ The Decisiveness of Diplomacy

America's diplomatic front has seldom been so critical as during the Civil War. The South never wholly abandoned its dream of foreign intervention, and Europe's rulers schemed to take advantage of America's distress.

The first major crisis with Britain came over the **Trent affair**, late in 1861. A Union warship cruising on the high seas north of Cuba stopped a British mail steamer, the *Trent*, and forcibly removed two Confederate diplomats bound for Europe.

Britons were outraged: upstart Yankees could not so boldly offend the Mistress of the Seas. War preparations buzzed, and red-coated troops embarked for Canada, with bands blaring "I Wish I Was in Dixie." The London Foreign Office prepared an ultimatum demanding surrender of the prisoners and an apology. But luckily, slow communications gave passions on both sides a chance to cool. Lincoln came to see the *Trent* prisoners as "white elephants" and reluctantly released them. "One war at a time," he reportedly said.

Another major crisis in Anglo-American relations arose over the unneutral building in Britain of Confederate commerce-raiders, notably the **Alabama**. These vessels were not warships within the meaning of loopholed British law because they left their shipyards unarmed and picked up their guns elsewhere. The *Alabama* escaped in 1862 to the Portuguese Azores, and there took on weapons and a crew from two British ships that followed it. Although flying the Confederate flag and officered by Confederates, it was manned by Britons and never entered a Confederate port. Britain was thus the chief naval base of the Confederacy.

THE PENDING CONFLICT.

Library of Congress Prints and Photographs Division [LC-US262-42025]

The Pending Conflict, 1863 Great Britain and France look on while the Americans struggle. Despite repeated pleas from Confederate diplomats for recognition and aid, both France and Britain refrained from intervening in the American conflict—not least because of the Union's demonstrated strength on the battlefield and its economic importance to European importers.

The *Alabama* lighted the skies from Europe to the Far East with the burning hulks of Yankee merchantmen. All told, this "British pirate" captured over sixty vessels. Competing British shippers were delighted, while an angered North had to divert naval strength from its blockade for wild-goose chases. The barnacled *Alabama* finally accepted a challenge from a stronger Union cruiser off the coast of France in 1864 and was quickly destroyed.

The *Alabama* was beneath the waves, but the issue of British-built Confederate raiders stayed afloat. Under prodding by the American minister, Charles Francis Adams, the British gradually perceived that allowing such ships to be built was a dangerous precedent that might someday be used against them. In 1863 London openly violated its own leaky laws and seized another raider being built for the South. But despite greater official efforts by Britain to remain truly neutral, Confederate commerce-destroyers, chiefly British-built, captured more than 250 Yankee ships, severely crippling the American merchant marine, which never fully recovered. Glowering Northerners looked farther north and talked openly of securing revenge by grabbing Canada when the war was over.

✴ Foreign Flare-ups

A final Anglo-American crisis was touched off in 1863 by the **Laird rams**—two Confederate warships being constructed in the shipyard of John Laird and Sons in Great Britain. Designed to destroy the wooden ships of the Union navy with their iron rams and large-caliber guns, they were far more dangerous than the swift but lightly armed *Alabama*. If delivered to the South, they probably would have sunk the blockading squadrons and then brought Northern cities under their fire. In retaliation the North doubtless would have invaded Canada, and a full-dress war with Britain would have erupted. But Minister Adams took a hard line, warning that "this is war" if the rams were released. At the last minute, the London government relented and bought the two ships for the Royal Navy. Everyone seemed satisfied—except the disappointed Confederates. Britain also eventually repented its sorry role in the *Alabama* business. It agreed in 1871 to submit the *Alabama* dispute to arbitration, and in 1872 paid American claimants $15.5 million for damages caused by wartime commerce-raiders.

American rancor was also directed at Canada, where despite the vigilance of British authorities, Southern agents plotted to burn Northern cities. One Confederate raid into Vermont left three banks plundered and one American citizen dead. Hatred of England burned especially fiercely among Irish Americans, and they unleashed their fury on Canada. They raised several tiny "armies" of a few hundred green-shirted men and launched invasions of Canada, notably in 1866 and 1870. The Canadians condemned the Washington government for permitting such violations of neutrality, but the administration was hampered by the presence of so many Irish American voters.

As fate would have it, two great nations emerged from the fiery furnace of the American Civil War. One was a reunited United States, and the other was a united Canada. The British Parliament established the **Dominion of Canada** in 1867. It was partly designed to bolster the Canadians, both politically and spiritually, against the possible vengeance of the United States.

Emperor Napoleon III of France, taking advantage of America's preoccupation with its own internal problems, dispatched a French army to occupy Mexico City in 1863. The following year he installed on the ruins of the crushed republic his puppet, Austrian archduke Maximilian, as emperor of Mexico. Both sending the army and enthroning Maximilian were flagrant violations of the Monroe Doctrine. Napoleon was gambling that the Union would collapse and thus America would be too weak to enforce its "hands-off" policy in the Western Hemisphere.

The North, as long as it was convulsed by war, pursued a walk-on-eggs policy toward France. The Washington government gave aid to the resistance movement headed by Mexico's beloved national hero (and the first full-blooded Indian president of Mexico) Benito Juárez. But when the shooting stopped in 1865, Secretary of State Seward, speaking with the authority of nearly a million war-tempered bayonets, prepared to march south. Napoleon realized that his costly gamble was doomed. He reluctantly took "French leave" of his ill-starred puppet in 1867, and Maximilian soon crumpled ingloriously before a Mexican firing squad.

✴ President Davis Versus President Lincoln

The Confederate government, like King Cotton, harbored fatal weaknesses. Its constitution, borrowing liberally from that of the Union, contained one deadly defect. Created by secession, it could not logically deny future secession to its constituent states. President Davis, while making his bow to states' rights, had in view a well-knit central government. But determined states' rights supporters fought him bitterly to the end. The Richmond regime encountered difficulty even in persuading certain state troops to serve outside their own borders. The governor of Georgia, a belligerent states' righter, at times seemed ready to secede from the secession and fight both sides. States' rights were no less damaging to the Confederacy than Yankee firepower.

Sharp-featured Jefferson Davis—tense, humorless, legalistic, and stubborn—was repeatedly in hot water. Although an eloquent orator and an able administrator, he at no time enjoyed real personal popularity and was often at loggerheads with his congress. At times there was serious talk of impeachment. Unlike Lincoln, Davis was somewhat imperious and inclined to defy rather than lead public opinion. Suffering acutely from neuralgia and other nervous disorders (including a tic), he overworked himself with the details of both civil government and military operations. No one could doubt his courage, sincerity, integrity, and devotion to the South, but the task proved beyond his powers. It was probably beyond the powers of any mere mortal.

Lincoln also had his troubles, but on the whole they were less prostrating. The North enjoyed the prestige of a long-established government, financially stable and fully recognized both at home and abroad. Lincoln, the inexperienced prairie politician, proved superior to the more experienced but less flexible Davis. Able to relax with droll stories at critical times,

Lincoln at Antietam (also known as Sharpsburg), October 1862 Deeply committed to his responsibilities as commander in chief, President Lincoln visited Union forces on the battlefield several times during the war. With him here at Antietam are the detective Allan Pinkerton (on the left), who provided intelligence to the Union army, and General John McClernand, who often accompanied the president on his travels.

Library of Congress Prints and Photographs Division [LC-B8171-7929]

"Old Abe" grew as the war dragged on. Tactful, quiet, patient, yet firm, he developed a genius for interpreting and leading a fickle public opinion. Holding aloft the banner of Union with inspiring utterances, he demonstrated charitableness toward the South and forbearance toward backbiting colleagues. "Did [Secretary of War Edwin] Stanton say I was a damned fool?" he reportedly replied to a tale-bearer. "Then I dare say I must be one, for Stanton is generally right and he always says what he means."

✦ Limitations on Wartime Liberties

"Honest Abe" Lincoln, when inaugurated, laid his hand on the Bible and swore a solemn oath to uphold the Constitution. Then, feeling driven by necessity, he proceeded to tear a few holes in that hallowed document. He understandably concluded that if he did not do so, and patch the parchment later, there might not be a Constitution of a *united United* States to mend. The "rail-splitter" was no hairsplitter.

But such infractions were not, in general, sweeping. Congress, as is often true in times of crisis, generally accepted or confirmed the president's questionable acts. Lincoln, though accused of being a "Simple Susan Tyrant," did not believe that his ironhanded authority would continue once the Union was preserved. As he pointedly remarked in 1863, a man suffering from "temporary illness" would not persist in feeding on bitter medicines for "the remainder of his healthful life."

Congress was not in session when war erupted, so Lincoln gathered the reins into his own hands. Brushing aside legal objections, he boldly proclaimed a blockade. (His action was later upheld by the Supreme Court.) He arbitrarily increased the size of the Federal army—something that only Congress can do under the Constitution (see Art. I, Sec. VIII, para. 12). (Congress later approved.) He directed the secretary of the Treasury to advance $2 million without appropriation or security to three private citizens for military purposes—a grave irregularity contrary to the Constitution (see Art. I, Sec. IX, para. 7). He suspended the precious privilege of the **writ of habeas corpus**, so that anti-Unionists might be summarily arrested. In taking this step, he defied a dubious ruling by the chief justice that the safeguards of habeas corpus could be set aside only by the authorization of Congress (see Art. I, Sec. IX, para. 2).

Lincoln's regime was guilty of many other highhanded acts. For example, it arranged for "supervised" voting in the Border States. There the intimidated citizen, holding a colored ballot indicating his party preference, had to march between two lines of armed troops. The federal officials also ordered the suspension of certain newspapers and the arrest of their editors on grounds of obstructing the war.

Amputation on the Battlefields of Virginia A surgeon wearing a hat and a sword amputates the leg of a wounded soldier, while an anesthetist (facing the camera) holds a sponge dipped in chloroform over the patient's nose. A surgical assistant ties a tourniquet to stem the flow of blood. Other soldiers, dressed in Zouave uniforms modeled on North African designs, which were popular among some Northern and Southern regiments, watch closely, likely aware of the dangers accompanying such crude surgery. An estimated 30 percent of amputees died from postoperative complications, most often infections.

Jefferson Davis was less able than Lincoln to exercise arbitrary power, mainly because of confirmed states' righters who fanned an intense spirit of localism. To the very end of the conflict, the owners of horse-drawn vans in Petersburg, Virginia, prevented the sensible joining of the incoming and outgoing tracks of a militarily vital railroad. The South seemed willing to lose the war before it would surrender local rights—and it did.

✳ Volunteers and Draftees: North and South

Ravenous, the gods of war demanded men—lots of men. Northern armies were at first manned solely by volunteers, with each state assigned a quota based on population. But in 1863, after volunteering had slackened, Congress passed a federal conscription law for the first time on a nationwide scale in the United States. The provisions were grossly unfair to the poor.

Rich boys, including young John D. Rockefeller, could hire substitutes to go in their places or purchase exemption outright by paying $300. "Three-hundred-dollar men" was the scornful epithet applied to these slackers. Draftees who did not have the necessary cash complained that their banditlike government demanded "three hundred dollars or your life."

The draft was especially damned in the Democratic strongholds of the North, notably in New York City. A frightful riot broke out in 1863, touched off largely by underprivileged and antiblack Irish Americans, who shouted, "Down with Lincoln!" and "Down with the draft!" For several days the **New York draft riots** put the city at the mercy of a rampaging, pillaging mob. Scores of lives were lost, and the victims included many lynched blacks. Elsewhere in the North, conscription met with resentment and an occasional minor riot.

More than 90 percent of the Union troops were volunteers because social and patriotic pressures to enlist were strong. As able-bodied men became scarcer, generous bounties for enlistment were offered by federal, state, and local authorities. An enterprising and money-wise volunteer might legitimately pocket more than $1,000.

With money flowing so freely, an unsavory crew of "bounty brokers" and "substitute brokers" sprang up, at home and abroad. They combed the poorhouses of the British Isles and western Europe, and many an Irishman or German was befuddled with whiskey and induced to enlist. A number of the slippery "bounty

The New York City Anti-Draft Rioters, 1863 Mostly Irish American mobs convulsed the city for days and were in the end put down only by a merciless application of Federal firepower.

TABLE 20.3	Number of Men in Uniform at Date Given	
Date	Union	Confederate
July 1861	186,751	112,040
January 1862	575,917	351,418
March 1862	637,126	401,395
January 1863	918,121	446,622
January 1864	860,737	481,180
January 1865	959,460	445,203

boys" deserted, volunteered elsewhere, and netted another handsome haul. The records reveal that one "bounty jumper" repeated his profitable operation thirty-two times. But desertion was by no means confined to "bounty jumpers." The rolls of the Union army recorded about 200,000 deserters of all classes, and the Confederate authorities were plagued with a runaway problem of similar dimensions.

Like the North, the South at first relied mainly on volunteers. But since the Confederacy was much less populous, it scraped the bottom of its manpower barrel much more quickly (see Table 20.3). Quipsters observed that any man who could see lightning and hear thunder was judged fit for service. The Richmond regime, robbing both "cradle and grave" (ages seventeen to fifty), was forced to resort to conscription as early as April 1862, nearly a year earlier than the Union.

Confederate draft regulations also worked serious injustices. As in the North, a rich man could hire a substitute or purchase exemption. Slaveowners or overseers with twenty slaves might also claim exemption. These special privileges, later modified, made for bad feelings among the less prosperous, many of whom complained that this was "a rich man's war but a poor man's fight." Why sacrifice one's life to save an affluent neighbor's slaves? No large-scale draft riots broke out in the South, as in New York City. But the Confederate conscription agents often found it prudent to avoid those areas inhabited by sharpshooting mountain whites, who were branded "Tories," "traitors," and "Yankee-lovers."

✵ The Economic Stresses of War

Blessed with a lion's share of the wealth, the North rode through the financial breakers much more smoothly than the South. Excise taxes on tobacco and alcohol were substantially increased by Congress. An income tax was levied for the first time in the nation's experience, and although the rates were painlessly low by later standards, they netted millions of dollars.

Customs receipts likewise proved to be important revenue-raisers. Early in 1861, after enough antiprotection Southern members had seceded, Congress passed the **Morrill Tariff Act**, superseding the low Tariff of 1857. It increased the existing duties some 5 to 10 percent, boosting them to about the moderate level of the Walker Tariff of 1846. But these modest rates were soon pushed sharply upward by the necessities of war. The increases were designed partly to raise additional revenue and partly to provide more protection for the prosperous manufacturers who were being plucked by the new internal taxes. A protective tariff thus became identified with the Republican party, as American industrialists, mostly Republicans, waxed fat on these welcome benefits.

The Washington Treasury also issued greenbacked paper money, totaling nearly $450 million, at face value. This printing-press currency was inadequately supported by gold, and hence its value was determined by the nation's credit. **Greenbacks** thus fluctuated with the fortunes of Union arms and at one low point were worth only 39 cents on the gold dollar. The holders of the notes, victims of creeping inflation, were indirectly taxed as the value of the currency slowly withered in their hands.

Yet borrowing far outstripped both greenbacks and taxes as a money-raiser. The Federal Treasury netted $2,621,916,786 through the sale of bonds, which bore interest and which were payable at a later date. The modern technique of selling these issues to the people directly through "drives" and payroll deductions had not yet been devised. Accordingly, the Treasury was forced to market its bonds through the private banking house of Jay Cooke and Company, which received a commission of three-eighths of 1 percent on all sales. With both profits and patriotism at stake, the bankers succeeded in making effective appeals to citizen purchasers.

A financial landmark of the war was the **National Banking System**, authorized by Congress in 1863. Launched partly as a stimulant to the sale of government bonds, it was also designed to establish a standard bank-note currency. (The country was then flooded with depreciated "rag money" issued by unreliable bankers.) Banks that joined the National Banking System could buy government bonds and issue sound paper money backed by them. The war-born National Banking Act thus turned out to be the

A contemporary (October 22, 1863) Richmond diary portrays the ruinous effects of inflation:

❝ A poor woman yesterday applied to a merchant in Carey Street to purchase a barrel of flour. The price he demanded was $70. 'My God!' exclaimed she, 'how can I pay such prices? I have seven children; what shall I do?' 'I don't know, madam,' said he coolly, 'unless you eat your children.' **❞**

first significant step taken toward a unified banking network since 1836, when the "monster" Bank of the United States was killed by Andrew Jackson. Spawned by the war, this new system continued to function for fifty years, until replaced by the Federal Reserve System in 1913.

An impoverished South was beset by different financial woes. Customs duties were choked off as the coils of the Union blockade tightened. Large issues of Confederate bonds were sold at home and abroad, amounting to nearly $400 million. The Richmond regime also increased taxes sharply and imposed a 10 percent levy on farm produce. But in general the states' rights Southerners were immovably opposed to heavy direct taxation by the central authority: only about 1 percent of the total income was raised in this way.

As revenue began to dry up, the Confederate government was forced to print blue-backed paper money with complete abandon. "Runaway inflation" occurred as Southern presses continued to grind out the poorly backed treasury notes, totaling in all more than $1 billion. The Confederate paper dollar finally sank to the point where it was worth only 1.6 cents when Lee surrendered. Overall, the war inflicted a 9,000 percent inflation rate on the Confederacy, contrasted with 80 percent for the Union.

✪ The North's Economic Boom

Wartime prosperity in the North was little short of miraculous. The marvel is that a divided nation could fight a costly conflict for four long years and then emerge seemingly more prosperous than ever before.

New factories, sheltered by the friendly umbrella of the new protective tariffs, mushroomed forth. Soaring prices, resulting from inflation, unfortunately pinched the day laborer and the white-collar worker to some extent. But the manufacturers and businesspeople raked in "the fortunes of war."

The Civil War bred a millionaire class for the first time in American history, though a few individuals of extreme wealth could have been found earlier. Many of these newly rich were noisy, gaudy, brassy, and given to extravagant living. Their emergence merely illustrates the truth that some gluttony and greed always mar the devotion and self-sacrifice called forth by war. The story of speculators and peculators

Booth at the Sanitary Fair in Chicago, 1863 The Chicago Sanitary Fair was the first of many such fairs throughout the nation to raise funds for soldier relief efforts. Mainly organized by women, the fair sold captured Confederate flags, battle relics, handicrafts like these potholders (above), and donated items, including President Lincoln's original draft of the Emancipation Proclamation (which garnered $3,000 in auction). When the fair closed, the Chicago headquarters of the U.S. Sanitary Commission had raised $100,000, and its female managers had gained organizational experience that many would put to work in the postwar movement for women's rights. Image and inset: Chicago History Museum was roughly the same in both camps. But graft was more flagrant in the North than in the South, partly because there was more to steal.

Yankee "sharpness" appeared at its worst. Dishonest agents, putting profits above patriotism, palmed off aged and blind horses on government purchasers. Unscrupulous Northern manufacturers supplied shoes with cardboard soles and fast-disintegrating uniforms of reprocessed or "shoddy" wool rather than virgin wool. Hence the reproachful term "shoddy millionaires" was doubly fair. One profiteer reluctantly admitted that his profits were "painfully large."

Newly invented laborsaving machinery enabled the North to expand economically, even though the cream of its manpower was being drained off to the fighting front. The sewing machine wrought wonders in fabricating uniforms and military footwear.

The marriage of military need and innovative machinery largely ended the production of custom-tailored clothing. Graduated standard measurements were introduced, creating "sizes" that were widely used in the civilian garment industry forever after.

Clattering mechanical reapers, which numbered about 250,000 by 1865, proved hardly less potent than thundering guns. They not only released tens of thousands of farm boys for the army but fed them their field rations. They produced vast surpluses of grain that, when sent abroad, helped dethrone King Cotton. They provided profits with which the North was able to buy munitions and supplies from abroad. They contributed to the feverish prosperity of the North—a prosperity that enabled the Union to weather the war with flying colors.

Other industries were humming. The discovery of petroleum gushers in 1859 had led to a rush of "Fifty-Niners" to Pennsylvania. The result was the birth of a new industry, with its "petroleum plutocracy" and "coal oil Johnnies." Pioneers continued to push westward during the war, altogether an estimated 300,000 people. Major magnets were free gold nuggets and free land under the **Homestead Act** of 1862. Strong propellants were the federal draft agents. The only major Northern industry to suffer a crippling setback was the ocean-carrying trade, which fell prey to the *Alabama* and other raiders.

The Civil War was a women's war, too. The protracted conflict opened new opportunities for women. When men departed in uniform, women often took their jobs. In Washington, D.C., five hundred women clerks ("government girls") became government workers, with over one hundred in the Treasury Department alone. The booming military demand for shoes and clothing, combined with technological marvels like the sewing machine, likewise drew countless women into industrial employment. Before the war one industrial worker in four had been female; during the war the ratio rose to one in three.

Other women, on both sides, stepped up to the fighting front—or close behind it. More than four hundred women accompanied husbands and sweethearts into battle by posing as male soldiers. Other women took on dangerous spy missions. One woman was executed for smuggling gold to the Confederacy. Dr. Elizabeth Blackwell, America's first female physician, helped organize the **U.S. Sanitary Commission** to assist the Union armies in the field. The commission trained nurses, collected medical supplies, and equipped hospitals. Commission work helped many women to acquire the organizational skills and the self-confidence that would propel the women's movement forward after the war. Heroically energetic Clara Barton and dedicated Dorothea Dix, superintendent of nurses for the Union army, helped transform nursing from a lowly service into a respected profession—and in the process opened up another major sphere of employment for women in the postwar era. Equally renowned in the South was Sally Tompkins, who ran a Richmond infirmary for wounded Confederate soldiers and was awarded the rank of captain by Confederate president Jefferson Davis. Still other women, North as well as South, organized bazaars and fairs that raised millions of dollars for the relief of widows, orphans, and disabled soldiers.

✴ A Crushed Cotton Kingdom

The South fought to the point of exhaustion. The suffocation caused by the blockade, together with the destruction wrought by invaders, took a terrible toll. Possessing 30 percent of the national wealth in 1860, the South claimed only 12 percent in 1870. Before the war the average per capita income of Southerners (including slaves) was about two-thirds that of Northerners. The Civil War squeezed the average Southern income to two-fifths of the Northern level, where it remained for the rest of the century. The South's bid for independence exacted a cruel and devastating cost.

Transportation collapsed. The South was even driven to the economic cannibalism of pulling up rails from the less-used lines to repair the main ones. Window weights were melted down into bullets; gourds replaced dishes; pins became so scarce that they were loaned with reluctance.

To the brutal end, the South mustered remarkable resourcefulness and spirit. Women buoyed up their menfolk, many of whom had seen enough of war at first hand to be heartily sick of it. A proposal was made by a number of women that they cut off their long hair and sell it abroad. But the project was not adopted, partly because of the blockade. The self-sacrificing women took pride in denying themselves the silks and satins of their Northern sisters. The chorus of a song, "The Southern Girl," touched a cheerful note:

So hurrah! hurrah! For Southern Rights, hurrah!
Hurrah! for the homespun dress the Southern ladies wear.

At war's end the Northern Captains of Industry had conquered the Southern Lords of the Manor. A crippled South left the capitalistic North free to work its own way, with high tariffs and other benefits. The manufacturing moguls of the North, ushering in the full-fledged Industrial Revolution, were headed for increased dominance over American economic and political life. Hitherto the agrarian "slavocracy" of the South had partially checked the ambitions of the rising plutocracy of the North. Now cotton capitalism had lost out to industrial capitalism. The South of 1865 was to be rich in little but amputees, war heroes, ruins, and memories.

Chapter Review

KEY TERMS

Fort Sumter (422)
Border States (423)
West Virginia (423)
Trent affair (430)
Alabama (430)
Laird rams (431)
Dominion of Canada (431)
writ of habeas corpus (432)

New York draft riots (433)
Morrill Tariff Act (434)
greenbacks (434)
National Banking System (434)
Homestead Act (436)
U.S. Sanitary Commission (436)

PEOPLE TO KNOW

Charles Francis Adams
Napoleon III
Maximilian
Jefferson Davis

Elizabeth Blackwell
Clara Barton
Sally Tompkins

CHRONOLOGY

1861	Confederate government formed
	Lincoln takes office (March 4)
	Fort Sumter fired on (April 12)
	Morrill Tariff Act passed
	Four upper South states secede (April–June)
	Trent affair
	Lincoln suspends writ of habeas corpus
1862	Confederacy enacts conscription
	Homestead Act

1862–1864	*Alabama* raids Northern shipping
1863	Union enacts conscription
	New York City draft riots
	National Banking System established
1863–1864	Napoleon III installs Archduke Maximilian as emperor of Mexico
1864	*Alabama* sunk by Union warship

TO LEARN MORE

Daniel Aaron, *The Unwritten War: American Writers and the Civil War* (1973)

David W. Blight, *Race and Reunion: The Civil War in American Memory* (2001)

Richard J. Carwardine, *Lincoln* (2003)

LaWanda Cox, *Lincoln and Black Freedom* (1981)

David H. Donald, *Lincoln* (1995)

——, ed., *Why the North Won the Civil War* (1960)

Drew Gilpin Faust, *The Creation of Confederate Nationalism* (1988)

——, *Mothers of Invention: Women of the Slaveholding South in the American Civil War* (1996)

William Freehling, *The South vs. The South: How Anti-Confederate Southerners Shaped the Course of the Civil War* (2001)

Doris Kearns Goodwin, *Team of Rivals: The Political Genius of Abraham Lincoln* (2005)

Elizabeth D. Leonard, *Yankee Women: Gender Battles in the Civil War* (1994)

Randall M. Miller et al., *Religion and the American Civil War* (1998)

A complete, annotated bibliography for this chapter—along with brief descriptions of the People to Know—may be found on the *American Pageant* website. The key terms are defined in the glossary at the end of the text.

Chapter 21

The Furnace of Civil War

1861–1865

My paramount object in this struggle is to save the Union,
and is not either to save or to destroy slavery.

ABRAHAM LINCOLN, 1862

When President Lincoln issued his call to the states for seventy-five thousand militiamen on April 15, 1861, he envisioned them serving for only ninety days. Reaffirming his limited war aims, he declared that he had "no purpose, directly or indirectly, to interfere with slavery in the States where it exists." With a swift flourish of federal force, he hoped to show the folly of secession and rapidly return the rebellious states to the Union. But the war was to be neither brief nor limited. When the guns fell silent four years later, hundreds of thousands of soldiers on both sides lay dead, slavery was ended forever, and the nation faced the challenge of reintegrating the defeated but still recalcitrant South into the Union.

✴ Bull Run Ends the "Ninety-Day War"

Northern newspapers, at first sharing Lincoln's expectation of a quick victory, raised the cry "On to Richmond!" In this yeasty atmosphere, a Union army of some thirty thousand men drilled near Washington in the summer of 1861. It was ill-prepared for battle, but the press and the public clamored for action. Lincoln eventually concluded that an attack on a smaller Confederate force at **Bull Run (Manassas Junction)**, some thirty miles southwest of Washington, might be worth a try. If successful, it would demonstrate the superiority of Union arms. It might even lead to the capture of the Confederate capital at Richmond, one hundred miles to the south. If Richmond fell, secession would be thoroughly discredited, and the

Union could be restored without damage to the economic and social system of the South.

Raw Yankee recruits swaggered out of Washington toward Bull Run on July 21, 1861, as if they were headed for a sporting event. Congressmen and spectators trailed along with their lunch baskets to witness the fun. At first the battle went well for the Yankees. But Thomas J. ("Stonewall") Jackson's gray-clad warriors stood like a stone wall (here he won his nickname), and Confederate reinforcements arrived unexpectedly. Panic seized the green Union troops, many of whom fled in shameful confusion. The Confederates,

An observer behind the Union lines described the Federal troops' pell-mell retreat from the battlefield at Bull Run:

"We called to them, tried to tell them there was no danger, called them to stop, implored them to stand. We called them cowards, denounced them in the most offensive terms, put out our heavy revolvers, and threatened to shoot them, but all in vain; a cruel, crazy, mad, hopeless panic possessed them, and communicated to everybody about in front and rear. The heat was awful, although now about six; the men were exhausted—their mouths gaped, their lips cracked and blackened with powder of the cartridges they had bitten off in battle, their eyes staring in frenzy; no mortal ever saw such a mass of ghastly wretches.**"**

The Army of the Potomac Marching up Pennsylvania Avenue, Washington, D.C., 1861 In this painting Union troops parade before the Battle of Bull Run. Colorfully uniformed, they are a regiment of Zouaves, who adopted the name and style of military dress from a legendarily dashing French infantry unit recruited from Berber tribesmen in North Africa. But bright uniforms were not enough to win battles, and these troops were soon to be routed by the Confederates.

themselves too exhausted or disorganized to pursue, feasted on captured lunches.

The "military picnic" at Bull Run, though not decisive militarily, bore significant psychological and political consequences, many of them paradoxical. Victory was worse than defeat for the South because it inflated an already dangerous overconfidence. Many of the Southern soldiers promptly deserted, some boastfully to display their trophies, others feeling that the war was now surely over. Southern enlistments fell off sharply, and preparations for a protracted conflict slackened. Defeat was better than victory for the Union because it dispelled all illusions of a one-punch war and caused the Northerners to buckle down to the staggering task at hand. It also set the stage for a war that would be waged not merely for the cause of Union but also, eventually, for the abolitionist ideal of emancipation.

✴ "Tardy George" McClellan and the Peninsula Campaign

Northern hopes brightened later in 1861, when General George B. McClellan was given command of the Army of the Potomac, as the major Union force near Washington was now called. Red-haired and red-mustached, strong and stocky, McClellan was a brilliant, thirty-four-year-old West Pointer. As a serious student of warfare who was dubbed "Young Napoleon,"

he had seen plenty of fighting, first in the Mexican War and then as an observer of the Crimean War in Russia.

Cocky George McClellan embodied a curious mixture of virtues and defects. He was a superb organizer and drillmaster, and he injected splendid morale into the Army of the Potomac. Hating to sacrifice his troops, he was idolized by his men, who affectionately called him "Little Mac." But he was a perfectionist who seems not to have realized that an army is never ready to the last button and that wars cannot be won without running some risks. He consistently but erroneously believed that the enemy outnumbered him, partly because his intelligence reports from the head of Pinkerton's Detective Agency were unreliable. He was overcautious—Lincoln once accused him of having "the slows"—and he addressed the president in an arrogant tone that a less forgiving person would never have tolerated. Privately the general referred to his chief as a "baboon."

As McClellan doggedly continued to drill his army without moving it toward Richmond, the derisive Northern watchword became "All Quiet Along the Potomac." The song of the hour was "Tardy George" (McClellan). After threatening to "borrow" the army if it was not going to be used, Lincoln finally issued firm orders to advance.

A reluctant McClellan at last decided upon a waterborne approach to Richmond, which lies at the western base of a narrow peninsula formed by the James and York Rivers—hence the name given to

Preparing for Battle These troops of the 69th New York State Militia, a largely Irish regiment, were photographed attending Sunday morning Mass in May 1861, just weeks before the Battle of Bull Run. Because the regiment was camped near Washington, D.C., women were able to visit.

this historic encounter: the **Peninsula Campaign** (see Map 21.1). McClellan warily inched toward the Confederate capital in the spring of 1862 with about 100,000 men. After taking a month to capture historic Yorktown, which bristled with imitation wooden cannon, he finally came within sight of the spires of Richmond. At this crucial juncture, Lincoln diverted McClellan's anticipated reinforcements to chase "Stonewall" Jackson, whose lightning feints in the Shenandoah Valley seemed to put Washington, D.C., in jeopardy. Stalled in front of Richmond, McClellan was further frustrated when "Jeb" Stuart's Confederate cavalry rode completely around his army on reconnaissance. Then General Robert E. Lee launched a devastating counterattack—the Seven Days' Battles—June 26–July 2, 1862. The Confederates slowly drove McClellan back to the sea. The Union forces abandoned the Peninsula Campaign as a costly failure, and Lincoln temporarily abandoned McClellan as commander of the Army of the Potomac—though Lee's army had suffered some twenty thousand casualties to McClellan's ten thousand.

Lee had achieved a brilliant, if bloody, triumph. Yet the ironies of his accomplishment are striking. If McClellan had succeeded in taking Richmond and ending the war in mid-1862, the Union would

MAP 21.1 Peninsula Campaign, 1862 © 2016 Cengage Learning

Abraham Lincoln (1809–1865) treated the demands of George McClellan for reinforcements and his excuses for inaction with infinite patience. One exception came when the general complained that his horses were tired. On October 24, 1862, Lincoln wrote,

❝ I have just read your dispatch about sore-tongued and fatigued horses. Will you pardon me for asking what the horses of your army have done since the battle of Antietam that fatigues anything? **❞**

A Confederate soldier assigned to burial detail after the Seven Days' Battles (1862) wrote,

❝ The sights and smells that assailed us were simply indescribable...corpses swollen to twice their original size, some of them actually burst asunder with the pressure of foul gasses....The odors were so nauseating and so deadly that in a short time we all sickened and were lying with our mouths close to the ground, most of us vomiting profusely. **❞**

probably have been restored with minimal disruption to the "peculiar institution." Slavery would have survived, at least for a time. By his successful defense of Richmond and defeat of McClellan, Lee had in effect ensured that the war would endure until slavery was uprooted and the Old South thoroughly destroyed. Lincoln himself, who had earlier professed his unwillingness to tamper with slavery where it already existed, now declared that the rebels "cannot experiment for ten years trying to destroy the government and if they fail still come back into the Union unhurt." He began to draft an emancipation proclamation.

Union strategy now turned toward total war (see Map 21.2). As finally developed, the Northern military plan had six components: first, slowly suffocate the South by blockading its coasts; second, liberate the slaves and hence undermine the very economic foundations of the Old South; third, cut the Confederacy in half by seizing control of the Mississippi River backbone; fourth, chop the Confederacy to pieces by sending troops through Georgia and the Carolinas; fifth, decapitate it by capturing its capital at Richmond; and sixth (this was Ulysses Grant's idea especially), try everywhere to engage the enemy's main strength and to grind it into submission.

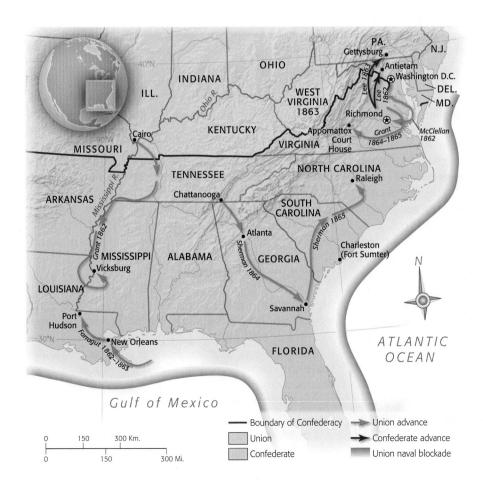

MAP 21.2 Main Thrusts, 1861–1865 Northern strategists at first believed that the rebellion could be snuffed out quickly by a swift, crushing blow. But the stiffness of Southern resistance to the Union's early probes, and the North's inability to strike with sufficient speed and severity, revealed that the conflict would be a war of attrition, long and bloody. © 2016 Cengage Learning

Battle Between the *Monitor* and the *Merrimac*, off Hampton Roads, Virginia, March 8–9, 1862
This was the first naval battle between two, powered ironclad warships. The Confederate *Merrimac* having previously sunk two Union ships in an attempt to break through their blockade, fought the Union *Monitor* in a battle lasting nine hours. Neither vessel seriously damaged the other, but their inconclusive duel changed the nature of naval warfare ever after.

✦ The War at Sea

The blockade started leakily: it was not clamped down all at once but was extended by degrees. A watertight patrol of some thirty-five hundred miles of coast was impossible for the hastily improvised Northern navy, which counted converted yachts and ferryboats in its fleet. But blockading was simplified by concentrating on the principal ports and inlets where dock facilities were available for loading bulky bales of cotton.

How was the blockade regarded by the naval powers of the world? Ordinarily, they probably would have defied it, for it was never completely effective and was especially sievelike at the outset. But Britain, the greatest maritime nation, recognized it as binding and warned its shippers that they ignored it at their peril. Britain plainly did not want to tie its hands in a future war by insisting that Lincoln maintain impossibly high blockading standards.

Blockade-running was risky but profitable, as the growing scarcity of Southern goods drove prices skyward. The most successful blockade runners were swift, gray-painted steamers, scores of which were specially built in Scotland. A leading rendezvous was the West Indies port of Nassau, in the British Bahamas, where at one time thirty-five of the speedy ships rode at anchor. The low-lying craft would take on cargoes of arms brought in by tramp steamers from Britain, leave with fraudulent papers for "Halifax" (Canada), and then return a few days later with a cargo of cotton. The risks were great, but the profits would mount to 700 percent and more for lucky gamblers. Two successful voyages might well pay for capture on a third. The lush days of blockade-running finally passed as Union squadrons gradually pinched off the leading Southern ports, from New Orleans to Charleston.

The Northern navy enforced the blockade with high-handed practices. Yankee captains, for example, would seize British freighters on the high seas, if laden with war supplies for the tiny port of Nassau and other halfway stations. The justification was that obviously these shipments were "ultimately" destined, by devious routes, for the Confederacy.

London, although not happy, acquiesced in this disagreeable doctrine of "ultimate destination" or "continuous voyage." British blockaders might need to take advantage of the same far-fetched interpretation

When news reached Washington that the Merrimack had sunk two wooden Yankee warships with ridiculous ease, President Lincoln, much "excited," summoned his advisers. Secretary of the Navy Gideon Welles (1802–1878) recorded,

"The most frightened man on that gloomy day...was the Secretary of War [Stanton]. He was at times almost frantic.... The *Merrimack*, he said, would destroy every vessel in the service, could lay every city on the coast under contribution, could take Fortress Monroe.... Likely the first movement of the *Merrimack* would be to come up the Potomac and disperse Congress, destroy the Capitol and public buildings.**"**

in a future war—as in fact they did in the world war of 1914–1918.

The most alarming Confederate threat to the blockade came in 1862. Resourceful Southerners raised and reconditioned a former wooden U.S. warship, the **Merrimack**, and plated its sides with old iron railroad rails. Renamed the *Virginia*, this clumsy but powerful monster easily destroyed two wooden ships of the Union navy in the Virginia waters of Chesapeake Bay; it also threatened catastrophe to the entire Yankee blockading fleet. (Actually the homemade ironclad was not a seaworthy craft.)

A tiny Union ironclad, the **Monitor**, built in about one hundred days, arrived on the scene in the nick of time. For four hours, on March 9, 1862, the little "Yankee cheesebox on a raft" fought the wheezy *Merrimack* to a standstill. Britain and France had already built several powerful ironclads, but the first battle-testing of these new craft heralded the doom of wooden warships. A few months after the historic battle, the Confederates destroyed the *Merrimack* to keep it from the grasp of advancing Union troops.

✷ The Pivotal Point: Antietam

Robert E. Lee, having broken the back of McClellan's assault on Richmond, next moved northward. At the **Second Battle of Bull Run** (August 29–30, 1862), he encountered a Federal force under General John Pope. A handsome, dashing, soldierly figure, Pope boasted that in the western theater of war, from which he had recently come, he had seen only the backs of the enemy. Lee quickly gave him a front view, furiously attacking Pope's troops and inflicting a crushing defeat.

Emboldened by this success, Lee daringly thrust into Maryland. He hoped to strike a blow that would

not only encourage foreign intervention but also seduce the still-wavering Border State and its sisters from the Union. The Confederate troops sang lustily:

Thou wilt not cower in the dust,
Maryland! my Maryland!
Thy gleaming sword shall never rust,
Maryland! my Maryland!

But the Marylanders did not respond to the siren song. The presence among the invaders of so many blanketless, hatless, and shoeless soldiers dampened the state's ardor.

Events finally converged toward a critical battle at **Antietam** Creek, Maryland. Lincoln, yielding to popular pressure, hastily restored "Little Mac" to active command of the main Northern army. His soldiers tossed their caps skyward and hugged his horse as they hailed his return. Fortune shone upon McClellan when two Union soldiers found a copy of Lee's battle plans wrapped around a packet of three cigars dropped by a careless Confederate officer. With this crucial piece of intelligence in hand, McClellan succeeded in halting Lee at Antietam on September 17, 1862, in one of the bitterest and bloodiest days of the war.

Antietam was more or less a draw militarily. But Lee, finding his thrust parried, retired across the Potomac. McClellan, from whom much more had been hoped, was removed from his field command for the second and final time. His numerous critics, condemning him for not having boldly pursued the ever-dangerous Lee, finally got his scalp.

The landmark Battle of Antietam was one of the decisive engagements of world history—probably the most decisive of the Civil War. Jefferson Davis was perhaps never again so near victory as on that fateful summer day. The British and French governments were on the verge of diplomatic mediation, a form of interference sure to be angrily resented by the North. An almost certain rebuff by Washington might well have spurred Paris and London into armed collusion with Richmond. But both capitals cooled off when the Union displayed unexpected power at Antietam, and their chill deepened with the passing months.

Bloody Antietam was also the long-awaited "victory" that Lincoln needed for launching his **Emancipation Proclamation**. The abolitionists had long been clamoring for action: Wendell Phillips was denouncing the president as a "first-rate second-rate man." By midsummer of 1862, with the Border States safely in the fold, Lincoln was ready to move. But he believed that to issue such an edict on the heels of a series of military disasters would be folly. It would seem like a confession that the North, unable to conquer the South, was forced to call upon the slaves to

The Killing Fields of Antietam   These Confederate corpses testify to the awful slaughter of the battle. The twelve-hour fight at Antietam Creek ranks as the bloodiest single day of the war, with more than ten thousand Confederate casualties and even more on the Union side. "At last the battle ended," one historian wrote, "smoke heavy in the air, the twilight quivering with the anguished cries of thousands of wounded men."

murder their masters. Lincoln therefore decided to wait for the outcome of Lee's invasion.

Antietam served as the needed emancipation springboard. The halting of Lee's offensive was just enough of a victory to justify Lincoln's issuing, on September 23, 1862, the preliminary Emancipation Proclamation. This hope-giving document announced that on January 1, 1863, the president would issue a final proclamation.

On the scheduled date, he fully redeemed his promise. "If my name ever goes into history," Lincoln declared, "it will be for this act, and my whole soul is in it." With a fateful stroke of the president's pen, the Civil War now became more of a moral crusade as well as what Lincoln called a "remorseless revolutionary struggle." After January 1, 1863, Lincoln said, "the character of the war will be changed. It will be one of subjugation. . . . The [old] South is to be destroyed and replaced by new propositions and ideas."

✦ A Proclamation Without Emancipation

Lincoln's Emancipation Proclamation of 1863 declared "forever free" the slaves in those Confederate areas still in rebellion. Bondsmen in the loyal Border States

were not affected, nor were those in specific conquered areas in the South—all told, about 800,000. The tone of the document was dull and legalistic (one historian has said that it had all the moral grandeur of a bill of lading). But if Lincoln stopped short of a clarion call for a holy war to achieve freedom, he pointedly concluded his historic document by declaring that the proclamation was "an act of justice" and calling for "the considerate judgment of mankind and the gracious favor of Almighty God."

The presidential pen did not formally strike the shackles from a single slave. Where Lincoln could presumably free the slaves—that is, in the loyal Border States—he refused to do so, lest he spur disunion. Where he could not—that is, in the Confederate states—he tried to. In short, where he *could* he would not, and where he *would* he could not. Thus the Emancipation Proclamation was stronger on proclamation than emancipation.

Yet much unofficial do-it-yourself liberation did take place. Thousands of jubilant slaves, learning of the proclamation, flocked to the invading Union armies, stripping already run-down plantations of their work force. In this sense the Emancipation Proclamation was heralded by the drumbeat of running feet. But many fugitives would have come anyhow, as

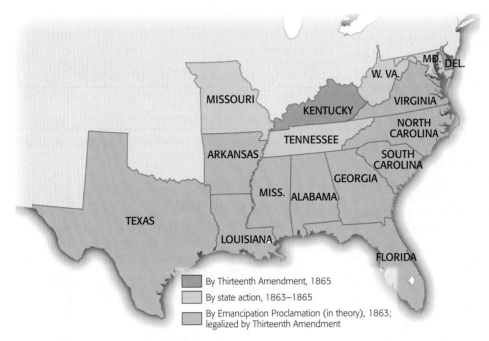

MAP 21.3 Emancipation in the South President Lincoln believed that emancipation of the slaves, accompanied by compensation to their owners, would be fairest to the South. He formally proposed such an amendment to the Constitution in December 1862. What finally emerged was the Thirteenth Amendment of 1865, which freed all slaves *without* compensation. © 2016 Cengage Learning

Map legend:
- By Thirteenth Amendment, 1865
- By state action, 1863–1865
- By Emancipation Proclamation (in theory), 1863; legalized by Thirteenth Amendment

they had from the war's outset. One in seven Southern slaves ran away to Union camps. Their presence in the camps and their perseverance against all odds convinced many Northern soldiers of slavery's evils and helped put emancipation atop Lincoln's agenda. By issuing the proclamation, Lincoln addressed the refugees' plight and strengthened the moral cause of the Union at home and abroad. At the same time, Lincoln's proclamation clearly foreshadowed the ultimate doom of slavery (see Map 21.3). This was legally achieved by action of the individual states and by their ratification of the **Thirteenth Amendment** (see the Appendix) in 1865, eight months after the Civil War had ended. The Emancipation Proclamation also fundamentally changed the nature of the war because it effectively removed any chance of a negotiated settlement. Both sides now knew that the war would be a fight to the finish.

Public reactions to the long-awaited proclamation of 1863 were varied. "God bless Abraham Lincoln," exulted the antislavery editor Horace Greeley in his *New York Tribune*. But many ardent abolitionists complained that Lincoln had not gone far enough. On the other hand, formidable numbers of Northerners, especially in the "Butternut" regions of the Old Northwest and the Border States, felt that he had gone too far. A cynical Democratic rhymester quipped,

> *Honest old Abe, when the war first began,*
> *Denied abolition was part of his plan;*
> *Honest old Abe has since made a decree,*
> *The war must go on till the slaves are all free.*
> *As both can't be honest, will some one tell how,*
> *If honest Abe then, he is honest Abe now?*

Opposition mounted in the North against supporting an "abolition war"; ex-president Pierce and others felt that emancipation should not be "inflicted" on the slaves. Many Boys in Blue, especially from the

---

Contending Voices
The Controversy over Emancipation

Not everyone in the North welcomed Lincoln's Emancipation Proclamation, as this condemnation from the Cincinnati Enquirer *reveals:*

❝The hundreds of thousands, if not millions of slaves [the act] will emancipate will come North and West and will either be competitors with our white mechanics and laborers, degrading them by competition, or they will have to be supported as paupers and criminals at the public expense.❞

Lincoln defended his policies toward blacks in an open letter to Democrats on August 26, 1863:

❝You say you will not fight to free negroes. Some of them seem willing to fight for you; but, no matter. Fight you, then, exclusively to save the Union. I issued the proclamation on purpose to aid you in saving the Union.❞

How were the causes of emancipating the slaves and saving the Union related in Lincoln's mind and strategy?

Border States, had volunteered to fight for the Union, not against slavery. Desertions increased sharply. The crucial congressional elections in the autumn of 1862 went heavily against the administration, particularly in New York, Pennsylvania, and Ohio. Democrats even carried Lincoln's Illinois, although they did not secure control of Congress.

The Emancipation Proclamation caused an outcry to rise from the South that "Lincoln the fiend" was trying to stir up the "hellish passions" of a slave insurrection. Aristocrats of Europe, noting that the proclamation applied only to rebel slaveholders, were inclined to sympathize with Southern protests. But the Old World working classes, especially in Britain, reacted otherwise. They sensed that the proclamation spelled the ultimate doom of slavery, and many laborers were more determined than ever to oppose intervention. Gradually the diplomatic position of the Union improved.

The North now had much the stronger moral cause. In addition to preserving the Union, it had committed itself to freeing the slaves. The moral position of the South was correspondingly diminished.

⭐ Blacks Battle Bondage

As Lincoln moved to emancipate the slaves, he also took steps to enlist blacks in the armed forces. Although some African Americans had served in the Revolution and the War of 1812, the regular army contained no blacks at the war's outset, and the War Department refused to accept those free Northern blacks who tried

In August 1863 Lincoln wrote to Grant that enlisting black soldiers

❝works doubly, weakening the enemy and strengthening us.**❞**

In December 1863 he announced,

❝It is difficult to say they are not as good soldiers as any.**❞**

In August 1864 he said,

❝Abandon all the posts now garrisoned by black men, take 150,000 [black] men from our side and put them in the battlefield or cornfield against us, and we would be compelled to abandon the war in three weeks.**❞**

to volunteer. (The Union navy, however, enrolled many blacks, mainly as cooks, stewards, and firemen.)

But as manpower ran low and emancipation was proclaimed, black enlistees were accepted, sometimes over ferocious protests from Northern as well as Southern whites. By war's end some 180,000 blacks served in the Union army, most of them from the slave states, but many from the free-soil North. Blacks accounted for about 10 percent of the total enlistments in the Union forces on land and sea and included two Massachusetts regiments raised largely through the efforts of the ex-slave Frederick Douglass.

The Fabled 54th Massachusetts Infantry Regiment This bas-relief by famed sculptor Augustus Saint-Gaudens stands today in front of the Massachusetts Statehouse in Boston. It commemorates the all-black volunteer regiment, led by the white Boston patrician Robert Gould Shaw, that suffered heavy casualties during the Union siege of Fort Wagner, South Carolina, in 1863.
AP Images/Nikki Kahn

A Bit of War History: Contraband, Recruit, Veteran, by Thomas Waterman Wood, 1865–1866 This painting dramatically commemorates the contributions and sacrifices of the 180,000 African Americans who served in the Union army during the Civil War.

Black fighting men unquestionably had their hearts in the war against slavery that the Civil War had become after Lincoln proclaimed emancipation. Service also offered them a chance to prove their manhood and to strengthen their claim to full citizenship at war's end. Participating in about five hundred engagements, they received a total of twenty-two Congressional Medals of Honor—the highest military award. Their casualties were extremely heavy; more than thirty-eight thousand died, whether from battle, sickness, or reprisals from vengeful masters. Many, when captured, were put to death as slaves in revolt, for not until 1864 did the South recognize them as prisoners of war. In one notorious case, several black soldiers were massacred after they had formally surrendered at Fort Pillow, Tennessee. Thereafter vengeful black units cried "Remember Fort Pillow" as they swung into battle and vowed to take no prisoners.

For reasons of pride, prejudice, and principle, the Confederacy could not bring itself to enlist slaves until a month before the war ended, and then it was too late. Meanwhile, tens of thousands were forced into labor battalions, the building of fortifications, the supplying of armies, and other war-connected activities. Slaves, moreover, were "the stomach of the Confederacy," for they kept the farms going while the white men fought.

Involuntary labor did not imply slave support for the Confederacy. In many ways the actions of Southern slaves hamstrung the Confederate war effort and subverted the institution of slavery. Fear of slave insurrection necessitated Confederate "home guards," keeping many eligible young white men from the front. Everyday forms of slave resistance, such as slowdowns, strikes, and open defiance, diminished productivity and undermined discipline. When Union troops neared, slave assertiveness increased. As "intelligent contraband," slaves served as Union spies, guides, and scouts or provided shelter to escaped Northern prisoners of war. By war's end nearly half a million slaves took the ultimate risk of revolting "with their feet," abandoning their plantations. Many who remained, especially in the urban South, negotiated new working conditions in factories and on farms. Although they stopped short of violent uprising, slaves contributed powerfully to the collapse of slavery and the disintegration of the antebellum Southern way of life.

An affidavit by a Union sergeant described the fate of one group of black Union troops captured by the Confederates:

❝All the negroes found in blue uniform or with any outward marks of a Union soldier upon him was killed—I saw some taken into the woods and hung—Others I saw stripped of all their clothing and they stood upon the bank of the river with their faces riverwards and then they were shot—Still others were killed by having their brains beaten out by the butt end of the muskets in the hands of the Rebels.❞

MAP 21.4 The Battle of Gettysburg, 1863 With the failure of Pickett's charge, the fate of the Confederacy was sealed—though the Civil War dragged on for almost two more bloody years. © 2016 Cengage Learning

✦ Lee's Last Lunge at Gettysburg

After Antietam, Lincoln replaced McClellan as commander of the Army of the Potomac with General A. E. Burnside, whose ornate side-whiskers came to be known as "burnsides" or "sideburns." Protesting his unfitness for this responsibility, Burnside proved it when he launched a rash frontal attack on Lee's strong position at **Fredericksburg**, Virginia, on December 13, 1862. A chicken could not have lived in the line of fire, remarked one Confederate officer. More than ten thousand Northern soldiers were killed or wounded in "Burnside's Slaughter Pen."

A new slaughter pen was prepared when General Burnside yielded his command to Joseph ("Fighting Joe") Hooker, an aggressive officer but a headstrong subordinate. At Chancellorsville, Virginia, on May 2–4, 1863, Lee daringly divided his numerically inferior force and sent "Stonewall" Jackson to attack the Union flank. The strategy worked. Hooker, temporarily dazed by a near-hit from a cannonball, was badly beaten but

not crushed. This victory was probably Lee's most brilliant, but it was dearly bought. Jackson was mistakenly shot by his own men in the gathering dusk and died a few days later. "I have lost my right arm," lamented Lee. Southern folklore relates how Jackson outflanked the angels while galloping into heaven.

Lee now prepared to follow up his stunning victory by invading the North again, this time through Pennsylvania. A decisive blow would add strength to the noisy peace prodders in the North and would also encourage foreign intervention—still a Southern hope. Three days before the battle was joined, Union general George G. Meade—scholarly, unspectacular, and abrupt—was aroused from his sleep at 2 a.m. with the unwelcome news that he would replace Hooker.

Quite by accident, Meade took his stand atop a low ridge flanking a shallow valley near quiet little **Gettysburg**, Pennsylvania (see Map 21.4). There his 92,000 men in blue locked in furious combat with Lee's 76,000 gray-clad warriors. The battle seesawed across the rolling green slopes for three agonizing days, July 1–3, 1863, and the outcome was in doubt until the very end. The failure of General George Pickett's magnificent but futile charge finally broke the back of the Confederate attack—and broke the heart of the Confederate cause.

Pickett's charge has been called the "high tide of the Confederacy." It defined both the northernmost point reached by any significant Southern force and the last real chance for the Confederates to win the war. As the Battle of Gettysburg raged, a Confederate peace delegation was moving under a flag of truce toward the Union lines near Norfolk, Virginia. Jefferson Davis hoped his negotiators would arrive in Washington from the south just as Lee's triumphant army marched on it from Gettysburg to the north. But the victory at Gettysburg belonged to Lincoln, who refused to allow the Confederate peace mission to pass through Union lines. From now on, the Southern cause was doomed. Yet the men of Dixie fought on for nearly two years longer, through sweat, blood, and weariness of spirit.

Later in that dreary autumn of 1863, with the graves still fresh, Lincoln journeyed to Gettysburg to dedicate the cemetery. He read a two-minute address, following a two-hour speech by the orator of the day, a former president of Harvard. Lincoln's noble remarks were branded by the London *Times* as "ludicrous" and

by Democratic editors as "dishwatery" and "silly." The **Gettysburg Address** attracted relatively little attention at the time, but the president was speaking for the ages.

✵ The War in the West

Events in the western theater of the war at last provided Lincoln with an able general who did not have to be shelved after every reverse. Ulysses S. Grant had been a mediocre student at West Point, distinguishing himself only in horsemanship, although he did fairly well in mathematics. After fighting creditably in the Mexican War, he was stationed at isolated frontier posts, where boredom and loneliness drove him to drink. Resigning from the army to avoid a court-martial for drunkenness, he failed at various business ventures, and when war came, he was working in his father's leather store in Illinois for $50 a month.

Grant did not cut much of a figure. The shy and silent shopkeeper was short, stooped, awkward, stubble-bearded, and sloppy in dress. He managed with some difficulty to secure a colonelcy in the volunteers. From then on, his military experience—combined with his boldness, resourcefulness, and tenacity—catapulted him on a meteoric rise.

Library of Congress Prints and Photographs Division [LC-USZ61-903]

National Archives

General Ulysses S. Grant and General Robert E. Lee Trained at West Point, Grant (left) proved to be a better general than a president. Oddly, he hated the sight of blood and recoiled from rare beef. Lee (right), a gentlemanly general in an ungentlemanly business, remarked when the Union troops were bloodily repulsed at Fredericksburg, "It is well that war is so terrible, or we should get too fond of it."

Abraham Lincoln's Gettysburg Address

Political speeches are unfortunately all too often composed of claptrap, platitudes, and just plain bunk—and they are frequently written by someone other than the person delivering them. But Abraham Lincoln's address at the dedication of the cemetery at the Gettysburg battlefield on November 19, 1863, has long been recognized as a masterpiece of political oratory and as a foundational document of the American political system, as weighty a statement of the national purpose as the Declaration of Independence (which it deliberately echoes in its statement that all men are created equal) or even the Constitution itself. In just 272 simple but eloquent words that Lincoln himself indisputably wrote, he summarized the case for American nationhood. What were his principal arguments? What values did he invoke? What did he think was at stake in the Civil War? (Conspicuously, he made no direct mention of slavery in this address.) Another speech that Lincoln gave in 1861 offers some clues. He said, "I have often inquired of myself what great principle or idea it was that kept this [nation] together. It was not the mere separation of the colonies from the motherland, but that sentiment in the Declaration of Independence which gave liberty not alone to the people of this country, but hope to the world, for all future time."

MAP 21.5 The Mississippi River and Tennessee, 1862–1863 © 2016 Cengage Learning

barrel to each of my other generals." There is no evidence that Grant's drinking habits seriously impaired his military performance.

Other Union thrusts in the West were in the making. In the spring of 1862, a flotilla commanded by David G. Farragut joined with a Northern army to strike the South a blow by seizing New Orleans. With Union gunboats both ascending and descending the Mississippi, the eastern part of the Confederacy was left with a jeopardized back door. Through this narrowing entrance, between **Vicksburg**, Mississippi, and Port Hudson, Louisiana, flowed herds of vitally needed cattle and other provisions from Louisiana and Texas. The fortress of Vicksburg, located on a hairpin turn of the Mississippi, was the South's sentinel protecting the lifeline to the western sources of supply.

General Grant was now given command of the Union forces attacking Vicksburg and in the teeth of grave difficulties displayed rare skill and daring. The siege of Vicksburg was his best-fought campaign of the war. The beleaguered city at length surrendered, on July 4, 1863, with the garrison reduced to eating mules and rats. Five days later came the fall of Port Hudson, the last Southern bastion on the Mississippi. The spinal cord of the Confederacy was now severed, and, in Lincoln's quaint phrase, the Father of Waters at last flowed "unvexed to the sea."

The Union victory at Vicksburg came the day after the Confederate defeat at Gettysburg. The political significance of these back-to-back military successes

Grant's first signal success came in the northern Tennessee theater (see Map 21.5). After heavy fighting, he captured **Fort Henry and Fort Donelson** on the Tennessee and Cumberland Rivers in February 1862. When the Confederate commander at Fort Donelson asked for terms, Grant bluntly demanded "an unconditional and immediate surrender."

Grant's triumph in Tennessee was crucial. It not only riveted Kentucky more securely to the Union but also opened the gateway to the strategically important region of Tennessee, as well as to Georgia and the heart of Dixie. Grant next attempted to exploit his victory by capturing the junction of the main Confederate north-south and east-west railroads in the Mississippi Valley at Corinth, Mississippi. But a Confederate force foiled his plans in a gory battle at **Shiloh**, just over the Tennessee border from Corinth, on April 6–7, 1862. Though Grant successfully counterattacked, the impressive Confederate showing at Shiloh confirmed that there would be no quick end to the war in the West.

Lincoln resisted all demands for the removal of "Unconditional Surrender" Grant, insisting, "I can't spare this man; he fights." When talebearers later told Lincoln that Grant drank too much, the president allegedly replied, "Find me the brand, and I'll send a

In the southern tier of Ohio, Indiana, and Illinois, sympathy for the South combined with hostility to the Northeast to stimulate talk of a "Northwest Confederacy" that would itself secede from the Union and make a separate peace with the Confederacy. These sentiments were fueled by economic grievances stemming from the closure of the Mississippi River to trade, and they gained strength after Lincoln's Emancipation Proclamation. Warned one Ohio congressman in January 1863,

❝If you of the East, who have found this war against the South, and for the negro, gratifying to your hate or profitable to your purse, will continue it...[be prepared for] eternal divorce between the West and the East.**❞**

Another Ohio congressman, giving great urgency to the Union effort to reopen the Mississippi River, declared,

❝The erection of the states watered by the Mississippi and its tributaries into an independent Republic is the talk of every other western man.**❞**

was monumental. Reopening the Mississippi helped to quell the Northern peace agitation in the "Butternut" area of the Ohio River valley. Confederate control of the Mississippi had cut off that region's usual trade routes down the Ohio-Mississippi River system to New Orleans, thus adding economic pain to that border section's already shaky support for the "abolition war." The twin victories also conclusively tipped the diplomatic scales in favor of the North, as Britain stopped delivery of the Laird rams to the Confederates (see "Foreign Flare-ups" in Chapter 20, p. 431) and as France killed a deal for the sale of six naval vessels to the Richmond government. By the end of 1863, all Confederate hopes for foreign help were irretrievably lost.

⭐ Sherman Scorches Georgia

General Grant, the victor of Vicksburg, was now transferred to the east Tennessee theater, where Confederates had driven Union forces from the battlefield at Chickamauga into the city of Chattanooga, to which they then laid siege. Grant won a series of desperate engagements in November 1863 in the vicinity of besieged Chattanooga, including Missionary Ridge and Lookout Mountain (the "Battle Above the Clouds"). Chattanooga was liberated, the state was cleared of Confederates, and the way was thus opened for an invasion of Georgia. Grant was rewarded by being made general in chief.

Georgia's conquest was entrusted to General William Tecumseh Sherman. Red-haired and red-bearded, grim-faced and ruthless, he captured Atlanta in September 1864 and burned the city in November of that year. He then daringly left his supply base, lived off the country for some 250 miles, and weeks later emerged at Savannah on the sea. A rousing Northern song ("Marching Through Georgia") said,

> "Sherman's dashing Yankee boys will never reach the coast!"
> So the saucy rebels said—and 't was a handsome boast.

But Sherman's hated "Blue Bellies," sixty thousand strong, cut a sixty-mile swath of destruction through Georgia. They burned buildings, leaving only the blackened chimneys ("Sherman's Sentinels"). They tore up railroad rails, heated them red-hot, and twisted them into "iron doughnuts" and "Sherman's hairpins." They bayoneted family portraits and ran off with valuable "souvenirs." "War...is all hell," admitted Sherman later, and he proved it by his efforts to "make Georgia howl." One of the major purposes of **Sherman's march** was to destroy supplies destined for the Confederate army and to weaken the morale of the men at the front by waging war on their homes (see Map 21.6).

Sherman was a pioneer practitioner of "total war." His success in "Shermanizing" the South was attested by increasing numbers of Confederate desertions. Although his methods were brutal, he probably shortened the struggle and hence saved lives. But there can

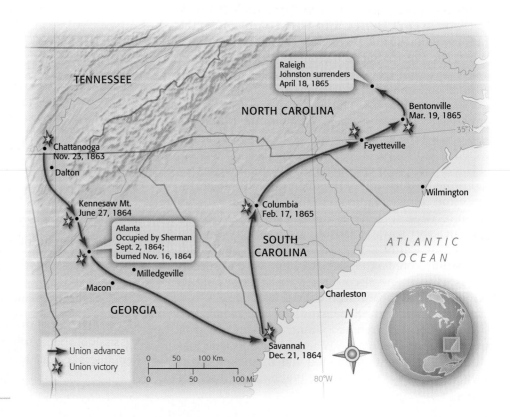

MAP 21.6 Sherman's March, 1864–1865 © 2016 Cengage Learning

A letter picked up on a dead Confederate in North Carolina and addressed to his "deer sister" concluded that

"it was "dam fulishness" trying to "lick shurmin." He had been getting "nuthin but hell & lots uv it" ever since he saw the "dam yanks," and he was "tirdeuv it." He would head for home now, but his old horse was "plaid out." If the "dam yankees" had not got there yet, it would be a "dam wunder." They were thicker than "lise on a hen and a dam site ornerier.**"**

be no doubt that the discipline of his army at times broke down, as roving riffraff (Sherman's "bummers") engaged in an orgy of pillaging. "Sherman the Brute" was universally damned in the South.

After seizing Savannah as a Christmas present for Lincoln, Sherman's army veered north into South Carolina, where the destruction was even more vicious. Many Union soldiers believed that this state, the "hell-hole of secession," had wantonly provoked the war. The capital city, Columbia, burst into flames, in all probability the handiwork of the Yankee invader. Crunching northward, Sherman's conquering army had rolled deep into North Carolina by the time the war ended.

✦ The Politics of War

Presidential elections come by the calendar and not by the crisis. As fate would have it, the election of 1864 fell most inopportunely in the midst of war.

Political infighting in the North added greatly to Lincoln's cup of woe. Factions within his own party, distrusting his ability or doubting his commitment to abolition, sought to tie his hands or even remove him from office. Conspicuous among his critics was a group led by the overambitious secretary of the Treasury, Salmon Chase. Especially burdensome to Lincoln was the creation of the **Congressional Committee on the Conduct of the War**, formed in late 1861. It was dominated by "radical" Republicans who resented the expansion of presidential power in wartime and who pressed Lincoln zealously on emancipation.

Most dangerous of all to the Union cause were the Northern Democrats. Deprived of the talent that had departed with the Southern wing of the party, those Democrats remaining in the North were left with the taint of association with the seceders. Tragedy befell the Democrats—and the Union—when their gifted leader, Stephen A. Douglas, died of typhoid fever seven weeks after the war began. Unshakably devoted to the Union, he probably could have kept much of his following on the path of loyalty.

Lacking a leader, the Democrats divided. A large group of "War Democrats" patriotically supported the Lincoln administration, but tens of thousands of "Peace Democrats" did not. At the extreme were the so-called **Copperheads**, named for the poisonous snake that strikes without a warning rattle. Copperheads openly obstructed the war through attacks against the draft, against Lincoln, and especially, after 1863, against emancipation. They denounced the president as the "Illinois Ape" and condemned the "Nigger War." They commanded considerable political strength in the southern parts of Ohio, Indiana, and Illinois.

Notorious among the Copperheads was a sometime congressman from Ohio, Clement L. Vallandigham. This tempestuous character possessed brilliant oratorical gifts and unusual talents for stirring up trouble. A Southern partisan, he publicly demanded an end to the "wicked and cruel" war. The civil courts in Ohio were open, and he should have been tried in them for sedition. But he was convicted by a military tribunal in 1863 for treasonable utterances and was then sentenced to prison. Lincoln decided that if Vallandigham liked the Confederates so much, he ought to be banished to their lines. This was done.

Vallandigham was not so easily silenced. Working his way to Canada, he ran for the governorship of Ohio on foreign soil and polled a substantial but insufficient vote. He returned to his own state before the war ended, and although he defied "King Lincoln" and spat upon a military decree, he was not further prosecuted. The strange case of Vallandigham inspired Edward Everett Hale to write his moving but fictional story of Philip Nolan, ***The Man Without a Country*** (1863), which was immensely popular in the North and which helped stimulate devotion to the Union. The fictional Nolan was a young army officer found guilty of participation in the Aaron Burr plot of 1806 (see "The Aaron Burr Conspiracies," Chapter 11, pp. 215–216). He had cried out in court, "Damn the United States! I wish I may never hear of the United States again!" For this outburst he was condemned to a life of eternal exile on American warships.

✦ The Election of 1864

As the election of 1864 approached, Lincoln's precarious authority depended on his retaining Republican support while spiking the threat from the Peace Democrats and Copperheads.

Fearing defeat, the Republican party executed a clever maneuver. Joining with the War Democrats, it proclaimed itself to be the **Union party** (see Figure 21.1). Thus the Republican party passed temporarily out of existence.

Lincoln's renomination at first encountered surprisingly strong opposition. Hostile factions whipped up

Sherman's March to the Sea, engraving after E.O.C. Darley, Photo by Ben Lourie. Collection of David M. Sherman, Washington, D.C./Picture Research Consultants & Archive

Sherman's March to the Sea, 1863–1864   Sherman's army inflicted cruel destruction along its route, an early instance of a tactic that came to characterize modern warfare, in which civilians are considered legitimate targets.

considerable agitation to shelve homely "Old Abe" in favor of his handsome nemesis, Secretary of the Treasury Chase. Lincoln was accused of lacking force, of being overready to compromise, of not having won the war, and of having shocked many sensitive souls by his ill-timed and earthy jokes. ("Prince of Jesters," one journal called him.) But the "ditch Lincoln" move collapsed, and he was nominated by the Union party without serious dissent.

Lincoln's running mate was ex-tailor Andrew Johnson, a loyal War Democrat from Tennessee who had been a small slaveowner when the conflict began. He was placed on the Union party ticket to "sew up" the election by attracting War Democrats and the voters in the Border States and, sadly, with no proper regard for the possibility that Lincoln might die in office. Southerners and Copperheads alike condemned both

candidates as birds of a feather: two ignorant, third-rate, boorish, backwoods politicians born in log cabins.

Embattled Democrats—regular and Copperhead—nominated the deposed and overcautious war hero General McClellan. The Copperheads managed to force into the Democratic platform a plank denouncing the prosecution of the war as a failure. But McClellan, who could not otherwise have faced his old comrades-in-arms, repudiated this defeatist declaration.

The campaign was noisy and nasty. The Democrats cried, "Old Abe removed McClellan. We'll now remove Old Abe." They also sang, "Mac Will Win the Union Back." Union party supporters shouted for "Uncle Abe and Andy" and urged, "Vote as you shot." Their most effective slogan, growing out of a remark by Lincoln, was "Don't swap horses in the middle of the river."

NORTHERN DEMOCRATS | REPUBLICANS

COPPERHEADS | PEACE DEMOCRATS | WAR DEMOCRATS

FIGURE 21.1 Union Party, 1864   The blue area represents the Union party. © 2016 Cengage Learning

Women at War Women on both sides of the Civil War organized to protect hearth and home. Though women bearing arms, like this militia, were rare, two uniformed "Ginny Rebs" were found dead at Gettysburg, and it is believed that 400-plus "Bonnie Yanks" fought in men's clothes. (The "physical" was a handshake.)

Lincoln's reelection was at first gravely in doubt. The war was going badly, and Lincoln himself gave way to despondency, fearing that political defeat was imminent. The anti-Lincoln Republicans, taking heart, started a new movement to "dump" Lincoln in favor of someone else.

But the atmosphere of gloom was changed electrically, as balloting day neared, by a succession of Northern victories. Admiral Farragut captured Mobile, Alabama, after defiantly shouting the now-famous order, "Damn the torpedoes! Go ahead." General Sherman seized Atlanta. General ("Little Phil") Sheridan laid waste the verdant Shenandoah Valley of Virginia so thoroughly that in his words "a crow could not fly over it without carrying his rations with him."

The president pulled through, but nothing more than necessary was left to chance. At election time many Northern soldiers were furloughed home to support Lincoln at the polls. One Pennsylvania veteran voted forty-nine times—once for himself and once for each absent member of his company. Other Northern soldiers were permitted to cast their ballots at the front.

THE TRUE ISSUE OR "THATS WHATS THE MATTER".

McClellan as Mediator, 1865 This 1864 poster shows Presidents Lincoln and Davis trying to tear the country in half, while former general George McClellan, the candidate of the Democratic party, attempts to mediate.

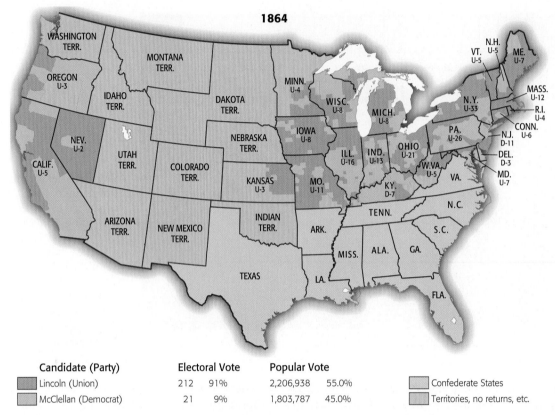

1864

Candidate (Party)	Electoral Vote		Popular Vote	
Lincoln (Union)	212	91%	2,206,938	55.0%
McClellan (Democrat)	21	9%	1,803,787	45.0%

Confederate States

Territories, no returns, etc.

MAP 21.7 Presidential Election of 1864 (showing popular vote by county) Lincoln also carried California, Oregon, and Nevada, but there was a considerable McClellan vote in each. Note McClellan's strength in the Border States and in the southern tier of Ohio, Indiana, and Illinois—the so-called "Butternut" region. © 2016 Cengage Learning

Lincoln, bolstered by the "bayonet vote," vanquished McClellan by 212 electoral votes to 21, losing only Kentucky, Delaware, and New Jersey (see Map 21.7). But "Little Mac" ran a closer race than the electoral count indicates. He netted a healthy 45 percent of the popular vote, 1,803,787 to Lincoln's 2,206,938, piling up much support in the Southerner-infiltrated states of the Old Northwest, in New York, and also in his native state of Pennsylvania.

One of the most crushing losses suffered by the South was the defeat of the Northern Democrats in 1864. The removal of Lincoln was the last ghost of a hope for a Confederate victory, and the Southern soldiers would wishfully shout, "Hurrah for McClellan!" When Lincoln triumphed, desertions from the sinking Southern ship increased sharply.

✦ Grant Outlasts Lee

After Gettysburg, Grant was brought in from the West over Meade, who was blamed for failing to pursue the defeated but always dangerous Lee. Lincoln needed a

general who, employing the superior resources of the North, would have the intestinal stamina to drive ever forward, regardless of casualties. A soldier of bulldog tenacity, Grant was the man for this meat-grinder type of warfare. His overall basic strategy was to assail the enemy's armies simultaneously, so that they could not assist one another and hence could be destroyed piecemeal. His personal motto was "When in doubt, fight." A grimly determined Grant, with more than 100,000 men, struck toward Richmond. He engaged Lee in a series of furious battles in the Wilderness of Virginia, during May and June of 1864, notably in the leaden hurricane of the "Bloody Angle" and "Hell's Half Acre." In this **Wilderness Campaign**, Grant suffered about 50,000 casualties, or nearly as many men as Lee commanded at the start. But Lee lost about as heavily in proportion (see Map 21.8).

In a ghastly gamble, on June 3, 1864, Grant ordered a frontal assault on the impregnable position of Cold Harbor. The Union soldiers advanced to almost certain death with papers pinned on their backs bearing their names and addresses. In a few minutes, about seven thousand men were killed or wounded.

MAP 21.8 Grant's Virginia Campaign, 1864–1865   The Wilderness Campaign pitted soldier against desperate soldier in some of the most brutal and terrifying fighting of the Civil War. "No one could see the fight fifty feet from him," a Union private recalled of his month spent fighting in Virginia. "The lines were very near each other, and from the dense underbrush and the tops of trees came puffs of smoke, the 'ping' of the bullets and the yell of the enemy. It was a blind and bloody hunt to the death, in bewildering thickets, rather than a battle." © 2016 Cengage Learning

Public opinion in the North was appalled by this "blood and guts" type of fighting. Critics cried that "Grant the Butcher" had gone insane. But Grant's reputation was undeserved, while Lee's was overrated. Lee's rate of loss (at one casualty for every five soldiers) was the highest of any general in the war. By contrast, Grant lost one of ten. Grant had intended to fight battles out in the open, a tactic he had perfected in the West. It was Lee, not Grant, who turned the eastern campaign into a war of attrition fought in the trenches. With fewer men, Lee could no longer seize the offensive, as he had at Chancellorsville or Gettysburg. Lee's new defensive posture in turn forced Grant into some brutal arithmetic. Grant could trade two men for one and still beat the enemy to his knees. "I propose to fight it out on this line," he wrote, "if it takes all summer." It did—and it also took all autumn, all winter, and a part of the spring.

In February 1865 the Confederates, tasting the bitter dregs of defeat, tried desperately to negotiate for peace between the "two countries." Lincoln himself met with Confederate representatives aboard a Union ship moored at Hampton Roads, Virginia, to discuss peace terms. But Lincoln could accept nothing short of Union and emancipation, and the Southerners could accept nothing short of independence. So the tribulation wore on—amid smoke and agony—to its terrible climax.

The end came with dramatic suddenness. Rapidly advancing Northern troops captured Richmond and cornered Lee at **Appomattox Courthouse** in Virginia, in April 1865. Grant—stubble-bearded and informally dressed—met with Lee on the ninth, Palm Sunday, and granted generous terms of surrender. Among other concessions, the hungry Confederates were allowed to keep their horses for spring plowing.

Tattered Southern veterans—"Lee's Ragamuffins"—wept as they took leave of their beloved commander. The elated Union soldiers cheered, but they were silenced by Grant's stern admonition, "The war is over; the rebels are our countrymen again."

Lincoln traveled to conquered Richmond and sat in Jefferson Davis's evacuated office just forty hours after the Confederate president had left it. "Thank God I have lived to see this," he said. With a small escort of sailors, he walked the blasted streets of the city. Freed slaves began to recognize him, and crowds

The Burning of Richmond, April 1865 The proud Confederate capital, after holding out against repeated Union assaults, was evacuated and burned in the final days of the war.

gathered to see and touch "Father Abraham." One black man fell to his knees before the Emancipator, who said to him, "Don't kneel to me. This is not right. You must kneel to God only, and thank Him for the liberty you will enjoy hereafter." Sadly, as many freed slaves were to discover, the hereafter of their full liberty was a long time coming.

✯ The Martyrdom of Lincoln

On the night of April 14, 1865 (Good Friday), only five days after Lee's surrender, Ford's Theater in Washington witnessed its most sensational drama. A half-crazed, fanatically pro-Southern actor, John Wilkes Booth, slipped behind Lincoln as he sat in his box and shot him in the head. After lying unconscious all night, the Great Emancipator died the following morning. "Now he belongs to the ages," remarked the once-critical Secretary Stanton—probably the finest words he ever spoke.

Lincoln expired in the arms of victory, at the very pinnacle of his fame. From the standpoint of his reputation, his death could not have been better timed if he

had hired the assassin. A large number of his countrymen had not suspected his greatness, and many others had even doubted his ability. But his dramatic death helped to erase the memory of his shortcomings and caused his nobler qualities to stand out in clearer relief.

The full impact of Lincoln's death was not at once apparent to the South. Hundreds of bedraggled

The New York Herald *editorialized on April 16, 1865, that the South had the most to lose from Lincoln's assassination:*

❝In the death of President Lincoln we feel the pressure of a heavy national calamity; but the great and irrevocable decree of the loyal States that Union must and shall be preserved will lose nothing of its force, but will be immensely if not terribly strengthened. In striking Abraham Lincoln and his kindly disposed Secretary of State the assassins struck at the best friends in the government to the prostrate rebels of the South.❞

ex-Confederate soldiers cheered, as did some Southern civilians and Northern Copperheads, when they learned of the assassination. This reaction was only natural because Lincoln had kept the war grinding on to the bitter end. If he had only been willing to stop the shooting, the South would have won.

As time wore on, increasing numbers of Southerners perceived that Lincoln's death was a calamity for them. Belatedly they recognized that his kindliness and moderation would have been the most effective shields between them and vindictive treatment by the victors. The assassination unfortunately increased the bitterness in the North, partly because of the fantastic rumor that Jefferson Davis had plotted it.

A few historians have argued that Andrew Johnson, now president-by-bullet, was crucified in Lincoln's stead. The implication is that if the "rail-splitter" had lived, he would have suffered Johnson's fate of being impeached by the embittered members of his own party, who demanded harshness, not forbearance, toward the South.

The crucifixion thesis does not stand up under scrutiny. Lincoln no doubt would have clashed with Congress; in fact, he had already found himself in some hot water. The legislative branch normally struggles to win back the power that has been wrested from it by the executive in time of crisis. But the sure-footed and experienced Lincoln could hardly have blundered into the same quicksands that engulfed Johnson. Lincoln was a victorious president, and there is no arguing with victory. In addition to his powers of leadership refined in the war crucible, Lincoln possessed in full measure tact, sweet reasonableness, and an uncommon amount of common sense. Andrew Johnson, hot-tempered and impetuous, lacked all of these priceless qualities.

Ford's Theater, with its tragic murder of Lincoln, set the stage for the wrenching ordeal of Reconstruction.

✸ The Aftermath of the Nightmare

The Civil War took a grisly toll in gore, about as much as all of America's subsequent wars combined. More than 600,000 men died in action or of disease, and in all over a million were killed or seriously wounded. The number of dead, amounting to 2 percent of the entire nation's population, greatly exceeded the number of Americans killed in World War II. The modern equivalent would be a loss of some 6 million American lives. To its lasting

Anne S. K. Brown Military Collection, Brown University Library

President Lincoln's Funeral Procession, New York City, 1865 Lincoln's body traveled by train to lie in state in fourteen cities before arriving at his final resting place of Springfield, Illinois. In New York City, 160,000 mourners accompanied his hearse as the funeral procession slowly made its way down Broadway. Scalpers sold choice window seats for four dollars and up. Blacks were barred from participating, until the mayor changed his mind at the last minute—but only if they marched at the rear.

The Era of Nationalism

The American Civil War was rooted in America's "peculiar institution" of slavery as well as uniquely American controversies about westward expansion. But it was also part of a wider phenomenon that transformed many parts of the world in the mid-nineteenth century: nationalism. To be sure, some ancient societies, such as the Greeks and the Hebrews, had a sense of themselves as distinct peoples who shared a common culture and history. But the creation of robust nation-states with strong central governments ruling over large populations that considered themselves part of an enduring community was of decidedly modern origin. Nationalism was anchored in the French and American Revolutions, with their emphasis on popular sovereignty and on a government that expressed the will of a population that saw itself not just as a random assembly of persons, but as a distinctive and coherent "people," often bonded by religion and language. Nationalism also owed much to modern technologies like the steamship, railroad, and telegraph, which extended both the emotional range of fellow feeling and the geographical reach of centralized authority. The convergence of these several

nineteenth-century developments, intellectual as well as material, made possible the creation of the "virtual communities" called nations.

In the early nineteenth century, only Britain and France could claim to be nation-states in the modern sense. Central Europe remained a patchwork of major and minor principalities. Italy, in the words of the Austrian diplomat Klemens von Metternich, was merely "a geographic expression," as several small duchies and overgrown city-states uneasily coexisted on the Italian peninsula. Canada, a scattering of disconnected provinces, was more a mapmaker's convention than a functioning political entity. Both Spain and Japan looked united on the map, but both notoriously lacked internal cohesion. And in the United States, sectional and state loyalties continued to compete with notions of a *national* identity.

But within just a dozen years, between 1859 and 1871, Prince Otto von Bismarck created modern Germany; Count Camillo di Cavour united Italy ("We have made Italy; now we must make Italians," quipped one Italian wit); a new Meiji emperor

launched Japan on a dramatic program of rapid modernization; the British North America Act of 1867 forged a unified Canada; and the American Civil War, in Abraham Lincoln's words, gave the United States "a new birth of freedom" as a unified country, as well as a significantly invigorated federal government. Before the Civil War, it was said, the United States *were*; after the Civil War, the United States *was*.

These several consolidations created the model for modern states that has prevailed ever since. The rise of nationalism fostered the growth of unprecedentedly powerful governments able to command deep loyalty from millions of people and consequently to marshal enormous economic and military resources—for good or ill. Nationalism was everywhere accompanied by some degree of political democratization and the expansion of public services, as freshly created or reinvigorated central governments sought to secure the loyalty of peoples newly brought under their sway. Bismarck, for example, supported universal suffrage and social insurance

Count Camillo di Cavour (1810–1861)
Hulton-Deutsch Collection/Corbis

Prince Otto von Bismark (1815–1898)
Bettmann/Corbis

Abraham Lincoln (1809–1865) Library of Congress Prints and Photographs Division [LC-USZ62-13016]

for German workers (establishing precedents that would much later be adopted in the United States). The new Italy and Meiji Japan adopted fairly liberal voting laws and programs for universal education. Britain's Reform Bill of 1867 enfranchised 1.5 million adult, male, urban householders, effectively doubling the British electorate.

In the United States, Civil War–era constitutional amendments at least nominally guaranteed the right to vote to adult African American males, while the federal government adopted ambitious plans to facilitate the construction of transcontinental railroads, distribute public lands under the Homestead Act, and support higher education under the Morrill Land-Grant College Act. The Civil War defined a historic pivot in the role of federal power. Of the twelve amendments to the Constitution passed before 1865, eleven were designed to *limit* the authority of the federal government. Of the fifteen amendments passed since the Civil War, nine contain the phrase "Congress shall have the power to *enforce* this article by appropriate legislation."

The words *nation* and *native* derive from the same Latin root, denoting birth or birthplace. Nationalism is at bottom a sentiment of common feeling or shared identity, generally among people born in the same place. It therefore implies boundaries, territorial as well as psychological. It defines who is included as well as who is excluded.

("No nation imagines itself coterminous with mankind," writes one scholar of nationalism.) It can breed exclusionary and nativist pathologies, as well as chauvinism, jingoism, and imperialism. The United States was no exception to these patterns. Nativists mounted increasingly effective anti-immigrant campaigns in the post–Civil War era, beginning with the Chinese Exclusion Act of 1882 and culminating in the highly restrictionist National Origins Act of 1924. As Germany and Italy acquired colonies in Africa and Japan tightened its grip on Taiwan, Korea, and parts of Manchuria, the United States also joined the imperial scramble, annexing the Philippines, Puerto Rico, Guam, and Samoa before the century's end.

Prisoners from the Front, by Winslow Homer, 1866   This celebrated painting reflects the artist's firsthand observations of the war. Homer brilliantly captured the enduring depths of sectional animosity. The Union officer somewhat disdainfully asserts his command of the situation; the beaten and disarmed Confederates exhibit an out-at-the-elbows pride and defiance.

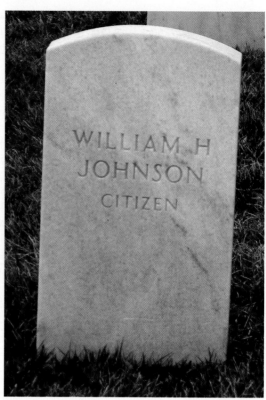

Grave of William H. Johnson, 1864   Johnson was a free black man who worked as Lincoln's personal valet in Springfield and accompanied him to Washington, D.C., when he assumed the presidency. When lighter-skinned mulatto White House staffers rejected him for his dark skin, Lincoln helped Johnson find other employment in the Treasury and Navy Departments, writing "The bearer of this card, William Johnson (colored), came with me from Illinois, and is a worthy man, as I believe. A. Lincoln." In November 1863 Lincoln requested that Johnson accompany him to deliver his famous address at Gettysburg, where they both contracted smallpox. Lincoln recovered in a few days; Johnson, with a more severe case, died in January 1864. Lincoln arranged for him to be buried at Arlington National Cemetery and wrote the one-word epitaph for his tombstone: "Citizen," a succinct and stinging rebuke of the racist reasoning of the *Dred Scott* decision.

hurt, the nation lost the cream of its young manhood and potential leadership. In addition, tens of thousands of babies went unborn because potential fathers were at the front.

Direct monetary costs of the conflict totaled about $15 billion. But this colossal figure does not include continuing expenses, such as pensions and interest on the national debt. The intangible costs—dislocations, disunities, wasted energies, lowered ethics, blasted lives, bitter memories, and burning hates—cannot be calculated.

The greatest constitutional decision of the century, in a sense, was written in blood and handed down at Appomattox Courthouse, near which Lee surrendered. The extreme states' righters were crushed. The national government, tested in the fiery furnace of war, emerged unbroken. Nullification and secession, those twin nightmares of previous decades, were laid to rest.

Beyond doubt the Civil War—the nightmare of the Republic—was the supreme test of American democracy. It finally answered the question, in the words of Lincoln at Gettysburg, whether a nation dedicated to such principles "can long endure." The preservation of democratic ideals, though not an officially announced war aim, was subconsciously one of the major objectives of the North.

Victory for Union arms also provided inspiration to the champions of democracy and liberalism the world over (see "Thinking Globally: The Era of Nationalism," pp. 460–461). The great English **Reform Bill of 1867**, under which Britain became a true political democracy, was passed two years after the Civil War ended. American democracy had proved itself, and its success was an additional argument used by the disfranchised British masses in securing similar blessings for themselves.

The "Lost Cause" of the South was lost, but few Americans today would argue that the result was not for the best. The shameful cancer of slavery was sliced away by the sword, and African Americans were at last in a position to claim their rights to life, liberty, and the pursuit of happiness. The nation was again united politically, though for many generations still divided spiritually by the passions of the war. Grave dangers were averted by a Union victory, including the indefinite prolongation of the "peculiar institution," the unleashing of the slave power on weak Caribbean neighbors, and the transformation of the area from Panama to Hudson Bay into an armed camp, with several heavily armed and hostile states constantly snarling and sniping at one another. America still had a long way to go to make the promises of freedom a reality for all its citizens, black and white. But emancipation laid the necessary groundwork, and a united and democratic United States was free to fulfill its destiny as the dominant republic of the hemisphere—and eventually of the world.

What Were the Consequences of the Civil War?

With the end of the Civil War in 1865, the United States was permanently altered, despite the reunification of the Union and the Confederacy. Slavery was officially banned, secession was a dead issue, and industrial growth surged forward. For the first time, the United States could securely consider itself a singular nation rather than a union of states. Though sectional differences remained, there would be no return to the unstable days of precarious balancing between Northern and Southern interests. With the Union's victory, power rested firmly with the North, and it would orchestrate the future development of the country. According to historian Eric Foner, the war redrew the economic and political map of the country.

The constitutional impact of the terms of the Union victory created some of the most far-reaching transformations. The first twelve amendments to the Constitution, ratified before the war, had all served to limit government power. In contrast, the Thirteenth Amendment, which abolished slavery, and the revolutionary Fourteenth Amendment, which conferred citizenship and guaranteed civil rights to all those born in the United States, marked unprecedented expansions of federal power.

Historian James McPherson has noted still other ways in which the Civil War extended the authority of the central government. It expanded federal powers of taxation. It encouraged the government to develop the National Banking System, print currency, and conscript an army. It made the federal courts more influential. And through the Freedmen's Bureau, which aided former slaves in the South, it instituted the first federal social welfare agency. With each of these actions, the nation moved toward a more powerful federal government, invested with the authority to protect civil rights, aid its citizens, and enforce laws in an aggressive manner that superseded state powers. A recent book by Drew Gilpin Faust, *Republic of Suffering* (2008), goes further, suggesting that Civil War–era experiences with death and tragedy were key to the modernization of America, in terms of both scientific advancement and private belief.

Yet some scholars have disputed whether the Civil War marked an absolute watershed in American history. They correctly note that racial inequality scandalously persisted after the Civil War, despite the abolition of slavery and the supposed protections extended by federal civil rights legislation. Others have argued that the industrial growth of the post–Civil War era had its real roots in the Jacksonian era, and thus cannot be ascribed solely to war. Thomas Cochran has even argued that the Civil War may have retarded overall industrialization rather than advancing it. Regional differences between North and South endured, moreover, even down to the present day.

Even so, the argument that the Civil War launched a modern America remains convincing. The lives of Americans, white and black, North and South, were transformed by the war experience. Industry entered a period of unprecedented growth, having been stoked by the transportation and military needs of the Union army. The emergence of new, national legal and governmental institutions marked the birth of the modern American state. All considered, it is hard to deny that the end of the Civil War brought one chapter of the nation's history to a close, while opening another.

Chapter Review

KEY TERMS

Bull Run (Manassas Junction), Battle of (438)

Peninsula Campaign (440)

Merrimack (443)

Monitor (443)

Bull Run, Second Battle of (443)

Antietam, Battle of (443)

Emancipation Proclamation (443)

Thirteenth Amendment (445)

Fredericksburg, Battle of (448)

Gettysburg, Battle of (448)

Gettysburg Address (449)

Fort Henry and Fort Donelson, Battle of (451)

Shiloh, Battle of (451)

Vicksburg, siege of (451)

Sherman's march (452)

Congressional Committee on the Conduct of the War (453)

Copperheads (453)

The Man Without a Country (453)

Union party (453)

Wilderness Campaign (456)

Appomattox Courthouse (457)

Reform Bill of 1867 (462)

PEOPLE TO KNOW

Thomas J. ("Stonewall")
Jackson

George B. McClellan

Robert E. Lee

John Pope

A. E. Burnside

Joseph ("Fighting Joe")
Hooker

George G. Meade

George Pickett

Ulysses S. Grant

William Tecumseh Sherman

Salmon Chase

Clement L.
Vallandigham

John Wilkes Booth

CHRONOLOGY

1861   First Battle of Bull Run

1862   Grant takes Fort Henry and Fort Donelson
Battle of Shiloh
McClellan's Peninsula Campaign
Seven Days' Battles
Second Battle of Bull Run
Naval battle of *Merrimack* (*Virginia*) and *Monitor*
Battle of Antietam
Preliminary Emancipation Proclamation
Battle of Fredericksburg
Northern army seizes New Orleans

1863   Final Emancipation Proclamation
Battle of Chancellorsville
Battle of Gettysburg
Fall of Vicksburg
Fall of Port Hudson

1864   Sherman's march through Georgia
Grant's Wilderness Campaign
Battle of Cold Harbor
Lincoln defeats McClellan for presidency

1865   Hampton Roads Conference
Lee surrenders to Grant at Appomattox
Lincoln assassinated
Thirteenth Amendment ratified

1867   Reform Bill expands British electorate

TO LEARN MORE

William Blair, *Virginia's Private War: Feeding Body and Soul in the Confederacy, 1861–1865* (1998)

David W. Blight, *Frederick Douglass' Civil War: Keeping Faith in Jubilee* (1989)

Drew Gilpin Faust, *This Republic of Suffering: Death and the American Civil War* (2008)

Joseph Glatthaar, *Forged in Battle: The Civil War Alliance of Black Soldiers and White Officers* (1990)

Allen C. Guelzo, *Lincoln's Emancipation Proclamation: The End of Slavery in America* (2004)

Leon Litwack, *Been in the Storm So Long* (1979)

Robert R. Mackey, *The Uncivil War: Irregular Warfare in the Upper South, 1861–1865* (2004)

Reid Mitchell, *The Vacant Chair: The Northern Soldier Leaves Home* (1993)

Scott Reynolds Nelson and Carol Sheriff, *A People at War: Civilians and Soldiers in America's Civil War, 1854–1877* (2007)

Geoffrey C. Ward, *The Civil War: An Illustrated History* (1990)

Bell I. Wiley, *The Life of Billy Yank* (1952)

———, *The Life of Johnny Reb* (1943)

A complete, annotated bibliography for this chapter—along with brief descriptions of the People to Know—may be found on the *American Pageant* website. The key terms are defined in the glossary at the end of the text.

Chapter 22

The Ordeal of Reconstruction

1865–1877

With malice toward none, with charity for all, with firmness in the right as God gives us to see the right, let us strive on to finish the work we are in, to bind up the nation's wounds, to care for him who shall have borne the battle and for his widow and orphan, to do all which may achieve and cherish a just and lasting peace among ourselves and with all nations.

ABRAHAM LINCOLN, SECOND INAUGURAL, MARCH 4, 1865

The battle was done, the buglers silent. Bone-weary and bloodied, the American people, North and South, now faced the staggering challenges of peace. Four questions loomed large. How would the South, physically devastated by war and socially revolutionized by emancipation, be rebuilt? How would liberated blacks fare as free men and women? How would the Southern states be reintegrated into the Union? And who would direct the process of Reconstruction—the Southern states themselves, the president, or Congress?

★ The Problems of Peace

Other questions also clamored for answers. What should be done with the captured Confederate ringleaders, all of whom were liable to charges of treason? During the war a popular Northern song had been "Hang Jeff Davis to a Sour Apple Tree," and even innocent children had lisped it. Davis was temporarily clapped into irons during the early days of his two-year imprisonment. But he and his fellow "conspirators" were finally released, partly because the odds were that no Virginia jury would convict them. All rebel leaders were finally pardoned by President Johnson as a sort of Christmas present in 1868. But Congress did not remove all remaining civil disabilities until thirty years later and only posthumously restored Davis's citizenship more than a century later.

Dismal indeed was the picture presented by the war-racked South when the rattle of musketry faded.

Not only had an age perished, but a civilization had collapsed, in both its economic and its social structure. The moonlight-and-magnolia Old South, largely imaginary in any case, had forever gone with the wind.

Handsome cities of yesteryear, such as Charleston and Richmond, were rubble-strewn and weed-choked. An Atlantan returned to his once-fair hometown and remarked, "Hell has laid her egg, and right here it hatched."

Economic life had creaked to a halt. Banks and businesses had locked their doors, ruined by runaway inflation. Factories were smokeless, silent, dismantled. The transportation system had broken down completely. Before the war five different railroad lines had converged on Columbia, South Carolina; now the nearest connected track was twenty-nine miles away. Efforts to untwist the rails corkscrewed by Sherman's soldiers proved bumpily unsatisfactory.

Agriculture—the economic lifeblood of the South—was almost hopelessly crippled. Once-white-carpeted cotton fields now yielded a lush harvest of nothing but green weeds. The slave-labor system had collapsed, seed was scarce, and livestock had been driven off by plundering Yankees. Pathetic instances were reported of men hitching themselves to plows, while women and children gripped the handles. Not until 1870 did the seceded states produce as large a cotton crop as that of the fateful year 1860, and much of that yield came from new acreage in the Southwest.

The princely planter aristocrats were humbled by the war—at least temporarily. Reduced to proud poverty, they faced charred and gutted mansions, lost investments, and almost worthless land. Their investments of more than $2 billion in slaves, their primary form of wealth, had evaporated with emancipation.

Beaten but unbent, many high-spirited white Southerners remained dangerously defiant. They cursed the "damnyankees" and spoke of "your government" in Washington instead of "our government." One Southern bishop refused to pray for President Andrew Johnson, though Johnson proved to be in sore need of divine guidance. Conscious of no crime, these former Confederates continued to believe that their view of secession was correct and that the "lost cause" was still a just war. One popular anti-Union song ran,

I'm glad I fought agin her, I only wish we'd won,
And I ain't axed any pardon for anything I've done.

Such attitudes boded ill for the prospects of painlessly binding up the Republic's wounds.

✦ Freedmen Define Freedom

Confusion abounded in the still-smoldering South about the precise meaning of "freedom" for blacks. Emancipation took effect haltingly and unevenly in different parts of the conquered Confederacy. As Union armies marched in and out of various localities, many blacks found themselves emancipated and then re-enslaved. A North Carolina slave estimated that he had celebrated freedom about twelve times. Blacks from one Texas county fleeing to the free soil of the liberated county next door were attacked by slave-owners as they swam across the river that marked the county line. The next day trees along the riverbank were bent with swinging corpses—a grisly warning to others dreaming of liberty. Other planters resisted emancipation more legalistically, stubbornly protesting that slavery was lawful until state legislatures or the Supreme Court declared otherwise. For many slaves the shackles of bondage were not struck off in a single mighty blow; long-suffering blacks often had to wrench free of their chains link by link.

The variety of responses to emancipation, by whites as well as blacks, illustrated the sometimes startling complexity of the master-slave relationship. Loyalty to the plantation master prompted some slaves to resist the liberating Union armies, while other slaves' pent-up bitterness burst forth violently on the day of liberation. Many newly emancipated slaves, for example, joined Union troops in pillaging their masters' possessions. In one instance a group of Virginia slaves laid twenty lashes on the back of their former master—a painful dose of his own favorite medicine.

Prodded by the bayonets of Yankee armies of occupation, all masters were eventually forced to recognize their slaves' permanent freedom. The once-commanding planter would assemble his former human chattels in front of the porch of the "big house" and announce their liberty. Though some blacks initially responded to news of their emancipation with suspicion and uncertainty, they soon celebrated their newfound freedom. Many took new names in place of the ones given by their masters and demanded that whites formally address them as "Mr." or "Mrs." Others abandoned the coarse cottons that had been their only clothing as slaves and sought silks, satins, and other finery. Though many whites perceived such behavior as insubordinate,

Charleston, South Carolina, in Ruins, April 1865 Rebel troops evacuating Charleston blew up military supplies to deny them to General William Tecumseh Sherman's forces. The explosions ignited fires that all but destroyed the city.

Library of Congress

they were forced to recognize the realities of emancipation. "Never before had I a word of impudence from any of our black folk," wrote one white Southerner, "but they are not ours any longer."

Tens of thousands of emancipated blacks took to the roads, some to test their freedom, others to search for long-lost spouses, parents, and children. Emancipation thus strengthened the black family, and many newly freed men and women formalized "slave marriages" for personal and pragmatic reasons, including the desire to make their children legal heirs. Other blacks left their former masters to work in towns and cities, where existing black communities provided protection and mutual assistance. Whole communities sometimes moved together in search of opportunity. From 1878 to 1880, some twenty-five thousand blacks from Louisiana, Texas, and Mississippi surged in a mass exodus to Kansas. The westward flood of these "Exodusters" was stemmed only when steamboat captains refused to transport more black migrants across the Mississippi River.

Houston H. Holloway, age twenty at the time of his emancipation, recalled his feelings upon hearing of his freedom:

❝ I felt like a bird out of a cage. Amen. Amen. Amen. I could hardly ask to feel any better than I did that day….The week passed off in a blaze of glory.**❞**

The reunion of long-lost relatives also inspired joy; one Union officer wrote home,

❝ Men are taking their wives and children, families which had been for a long time broken up are united and oh! such happiness. I am glad I am here.**❞**

The church became the focus of black community life in the years following emancipation. As slaves, blacks had worshiped alongside whites, but now they formed their own churches pastored by

The Tuskegee University Archives, Tuskegee University

Educating Young Freedmen and Freedwomen, 1870s Freed slaves in the South regarded schooling as the key to improving their children's lives and the fulfillment of a long-sought right that had been denied blacks in slavery. These well-dressed schoolchildren are lined up outside their rural, one-room schoolhouse alongside their teachers, both black and white.

Examining the Evidence

Letter from a Freedman to His Old Master, 1865

What was it like to experience the transition from slavery to freedom? Four million Southern blacks faced this exhilarating and formidable prospect with the end of the war. For historians, recovering the African American perspective on emancipation is challenging. Unlike their white masters, freed blacks left few written records. But one former slave captured in a letter to his "Old Master" (whose surname he bore) the heroic determination of many blacks to build new independent and dignified lives for themselves and their families.

During the war Jourdon Anderson escaped slavery in Tennessee with his wife and two daughters. After relocating to the relative safety of Ohio, he received a communication from his former owner asking him to return. In his bold reply, reportedly "dictated by the old servant" himself, Anderson expressed his family's new expectations for life as free people and an uneasiness about his former master's intentions. He made reference to his "comfortable home," his daughters' schooling, the church that he and his wife were free to attend regularly, and the peace of mind that came with knowing that "my girls [would not be] brought to shame by the violence and wickedness of their young masters." To test the white man's sincerity, Anderson and his wife asked for the astronomical figure of $11,680 in back wages from decades as slaves. He closed by reiterating that "the great desire of my life is to give my children an education and have them form virtuous habits." This rare letter demonstrates that many black correspondents may have been illiterate, but they were hardly inarticulate. And they asserted themselves as parents, workers, and citizens not only from the distance of a former free state like Ohio but also deep within the former slave states of the South. Was the tone of Anderson's letter (and postscript) serious or tongue-in-cheek? What did "freedom" mean for Anderson and other blacks in the months following emancipation? How did the eventual accomplishments of Reconstruction correspond with the initial expectations of people like Anderson and his former owner?

Letter from a Freedman to his Old Master.

The following is a genuine document. It was *dictated* by the old servant, and contains his ideas and forms of expression. [Cincinnati Commercial.

DAYTON, Ohio, August 7, 1865.

To my Old Master, Col. P. H. ANDERSON, Big Spring, Tennessee.

SIR: I got your letter and was glad to find that you had not forgotten Jordan, and that you wanted me to come back and live with you again, promising to do better for me than anybody else can. I have often felt uneasy about you. I thought the Yankees would have hung you long before this for harboring Rebs they found at your house. I suppose they never heard about your going to Col. Martin's to kill the Union soldier that was left by his company in their stable. Although you shot at me twice before I left you, I did not want to hear of your being hurt, and am glad you are still living. It would do me good to go back to the dear old home again and see Miss Mary and Miss Martha and Allen, Esther, Green and Lee. Give my love to them all, and tell them I hope we will meet in the better world, if not in this. I would have gone back to see you all when I was working in the Nashville Hospital, but one of the neighbors told me Henry intended to shoot me if he ever got a chance.

I want to know particularly what the good chance is you propose to give me. I am doing tolerably well here; I get $25 a month, with victuals and clothing; have a comfortable home for Mandy (the folks here call her Mrs. Anderson), and the children, Milly Jane and Grundy, go to school and are learning well; the teacher says Grundy has a head for a preacher. They go to Sunday-School, and Mandy and me attend church regularly. We are kindly treated; sometimes we over-

As to my freedom, which you say I can have, there is nothing to be gained on that score, as I got my free-papers in 1864 from the Provost-Marshal-General of the Department at Nashville. Mandy says she would be afraid to go back without some proof that you are sincerely disposed to treat us justly and kindly—and we have concluded to test your sincerity by asking you to send us our wages for the time we served you. This will make us forget and forgive old sores, and rely on your justice and friendship in the future. I served you faithfully for thirty-two years, and Mandy twenty years, at $25 a month for me, and $2 a week for Mandy. Our earnings would amount to $11,680. Add to this the interest for the time our wages has been kept back and deduct what you paid for our clothing and three doctor's visits to me, and pulling a tooth for Mandy, and the balance will show what we are in justice entitled to. Please send the money by Adams Express, in care of V. Winters, esq., Dayton, Ohio. If you fail to pay us for faithful labors in the past we can have little faith in your promises in the future.

P. S.—Say howdy to George Carter, and thank him for taking the pistol from you when you were shooting at me.

New-York Tribune Tuesday, August 22, 1865

468

their own ministers. Black churches grew robustly. The 150,000-member black Baptist Church of 1850 reached 500,000 by 1870, while the African Methodist Episcopal Church quadrupled in size from 100,000 to 400,000 in the first decade after emancipation. These churches formed the bedrock of black community life, and they soon gave rise to other benevolent, fraternal, and mutual aid societies. All these organizations helped blacks protect their newly won freedom.

Emancipation also meant education for many blacks. Learning to read and write had been a privilege generally denied to them under slavery. Freedmen wasted no time establishing societies for self-improvement, which undertook to raise funds to purchase land, build schoolhouses, and hire teachers. One member of a North Carolina education society asserted that "a schoolhouse would be the first proof of their *independence.*" Southern blacks soon found, however, that the demand outstripped the supply of qualified black teachers. They accepted the aid of Northern white women sent by the American Missionary Association, who volunteered their services as teachers. They also turned to the federal government for help. The freed blacks were going to need all the friends—and power—they could muster in Washington.

✵ The Freedmen's Bureau

Abolitionists had long preached that slavery was a degrading institution. Now the emancipators were faced with the brutal reality that the freedmen were overwhelmingly unskilled, unlettered, without property or money, and with scant knowledge of how to survive as free people. To cope with this problem throughout the conquered South, Congress created the **Freedmen's Bureau** on March 3, 1865.

On paper at least, the bureau was intended to be a kind of primitive welfare agency. It was to provide food, clothing, medical care, and education both to freedmen and to white refugees. Heading the bureau was a warmly sympathetic friend of blacks, Union general Oliver O. Howard, who later founded and served as president of Howard University in Washington, D.C.

Women from the North enthusiastically embraced the opportunity to go south and teach in Freedmen's Bureau schools for emancipated blacks. One volunteer explained her motives:

❝ I thought I must do something, not having money at my command, what could I do but give myself to the work.... I would go to them, and give them my life if necessary. **❞**

The bureau achieved its greatest successes in education. It taught an estimated 200,000 blacks how to read. Many former slaves had a passion for learning, partly because they wanted to close the gap between themselves and whites and partly because they longed to read the Word of God. In one elementary class in North Carolina sat four generations of the same family, ranging from a six-year-old child to a seventy-five-year-old grandmother.

But in other areas, the bureau's accomplishments were meager—or even mischievous. Although the bureau was authorized to settle former slaves on forty-acre tracts confiscated from the Confederates, little land actually made it into blacks' hands. Instead local administrators often collaborated with planters in expelling blacks from towns and cajoling them into signing labor contracts to work for their former masters. Still, the white South resented the bureau as a meddlesome federal interloper that threatened to upset white racial dominance. President Andrew Johnson, who shared the white supremacist views of most white Southerners, repeatedly tried to kill it, and it expired in 1872.

✵ Johnson: The Tailor President

Few presidents have ever been faced with a more perplexing sea of troubles than that confronting Andrew Johnson. What manner of man was this medium-built, dark-eyed, black-haired Tennessean, now chief executive by virtue of the bullet that killed Lincoln?

No citizen, not even Lincoln, has ever reached the White House from humbler beginnings. Born to impoverished parents in North Carolina and orphaned early, Johnson never attended school but was apprenticed to a tailor at age ten. Ambitious to get ahead, he taught himself to read, and later his wife taught him to write and do simple arithmetic. Like many another self-made man, he was inclined to overpraise his maker.

Johnson early became active in politics in Tennessee, where he had moved when seventeen years old. He shone as an impassioned champion of poor whites against the planter aristocrats, although he himself ultimately owned a few slaves. He excelled as a two-fisted stump speaker before angry and heckling crowds, who on occasion greeted his political oratory with cocked pistols, not just cocked ears. Elected to Congress, he attracted much favorable attention in the North (but not the South) when he refused to secede with his own state. After Tennessee was partially "redeemed" by Union armies, he was appointed war governor and served courageously in an atmosphere of danger.

Political exigency next thrust Johnson into the vice presidency. Lincoln's Union party in 1864 needed to attract support from the War Democrats and

Crushed by the Constitution President Andrew Johnson revered the U.S. Constitution but eventually felt its awesome weight in his impeachment trial.

other pro-Southern elements, and Johnson, a Democrat, seemed to be the ideal man. Unfortunately, he appeared at the vice-presidential inaugural ceremonies the following March in a scandalous condition. He had recently been afflicted with typhoid fever, and although not known as a heavy drinker, he was urged by his friends to take a stiff bracer of whiskey. This he did—with unfortunate results.

"Old Andy" Johnson was no doubt a man of parts—unpolished parts. He was intelligent, able, forceful, and gifted with homespun honesty. Steadfastly devoted to duty and to the people, he was a dogmatic champion of states' rights and the Constitution. He would often present a copy of the document to visitors, and he was buried with one as a pillow.

Yet the man who had raised himself from the tailor's bench to the president's chair was a misfit. A Southerner who did not understand the North, a Tennessean who had earned the distrust of the South, a Democrat who had never been accepted by the Republicans, a president who had never been elected to the office, he was not at home in a Republican White House. Hotheaded, contentious, and stubborn, he was the wrong man in the wrong place at the wrong time. A Reconstruction policy devised by angels might well have failed in his tactless hands.

★ Presidential Reconstruction

Even before the shooting war had ended, the political war over Reconstruction had begun. Abraham Lincoln believed that the Southern states had never legally withdrawn from the Union. Their formal restoration to the Union would therefore be relatively simple. Accordingly, Lincoln in 1863 proclaimed his **"10 percent" Reconstruction plan**. It decreed that a state could be reintegrated into the Union when the equivalent of at least 10 percent of its total voters in the presidential election of 1860 had taken an oath of allegiance to the United States and pledged to abide by emancipation. The next step would be formal erection of a state government. Lincoln would then recognize the purified regime.

Lincoln's proclamation provoked a sharp reaction in Congress, where Republicans feared the restoration of the planter aristocracy to power and the possible re-enslavement of blacks. Republicans therefore rammed through Congress in 1864 the **Wade-Davis Bill**. The bill required that 50 percent of a state's voters take the oath of allegiance and demanded stronger safeguards for emancipation than Lincoln's as the price of readmission to the Union. Lincoln "pocket-vetoed" this bill by refusing to sign it after Congress had adjourned. Republicans were outraged. They refused to seat delegates from Louisiana after that state had reorganized its government in accordance with Lincoln's 10 percent plan in 1864.

The controversy surrounding the Wade-Davis Bill had revealed deep differences between the president and Congress. Unlike Lincoln, many in Congress insisted that the seceders had indeed left the Union—had "committed suicide" as republican states—and had therefore forfeited all their rights. They could be readmitted only as "conquered provinces" on such conditions as Congress should decree.

This episode further revealed differences among Republicans. Two factions were emerging. The majority

TABLE 22.1	Principal Reconstruction Proposals and Plans
Year	**Proposal or Plan**
1864–1865	Lincoln's 10 percent proposal
1865–1866	Johnson's version of Lincoln's proposal
1866–1867	Congressional plan: 10 percent plan with Fourteenth Amendment
1867–1877	Congressional plan of military Reconstruction: Fourteenth Amendment plus black suffrage, later established nationwide by Fifteenth Amendment

moderate group tended to agree with Lincoln that the seceded states should be restored to the Union as simply and swiftly as reasonable—though on Congress's terms, not the president's. The minority radical group believed that the South should atone more painfully for its sins. Before the South should be restored, the radicals wanted its social structure uprooted, the haughty planters punished, and the newly emancipated blacks protected by federal power.

Some of the radicals were secretly pleased when the assassin's bullet felled Lincoln, for the martyred president had shown tenderness toward the South. Spiteful "Andy" Johnson, who shared their hatred for the planter aristocrats, would presumably also share their desire to reconstruct the South with a rod of iron.

Johnson soon disillusioned them. He agreed with Lincoln that the seceded states had never legally been outside the Union. Thus he quickly recognized several of Lincoln's 10 percent governments, and on May 29, 1865, he issued his own Reconstruction proclamation (see Table 22.1). It disfranchised certain leading Confederates, including those with taxable property worth more than $20,000, though they might petition him for personal pardons. It called for special state conventions, which were required to repeal the ordinances of secession, repudiate all Confederate debts, and ratify the slave-freeing Thirteenth Amendment. States that

complied with these conditions, Johnson declared, would be swiftly readmitted to the Union.

Johnson, savoring his dominance over the high-toned aristocrats who now begged his favor, granted pardons in abundance. Bolstered by the political resurrection of the planter elite, the recently rebellious states moved rapidly in the second half of 1865 to organize governments. But as the pattern of the new governments became clear, Republicans of all stripes grew furious.

✵ The Baleful Black Codes

Among the first acts of the new Southern regimes sanctioned by Johnson was the passage of the iron-toothed **Black Codes**. These laws were designed to regulate the affairs of the emancipated blacks, much as the slave statutes had done in pre–Civil War days. Mississippi passed the first such law in November 1865, and other Southern states soon followed suit. The Black Codes varied in severity from state to state (Mississippi's was the harshest and Georgia's the most lenient), but they had much in common. The Black Codes aimed, first of all, to ensure a stable and subservient labor force. The crushed Cotton Kingdom could not rise from its weeds until the fields were once again put under hoe and plow—and many whites wanted to make sure that they retained the tight control they had exercised over black field hands and plow drivers in the days of slavery.

Dire penalties were therefore imposed by the codes on blacks who "jumped" their labor contracts, which usually committed them to work for the same employer for one year, and generally at pittance wages. Violators could be made to forfeit back wages or could be forcibly dragged back to work by a paid "Negro-catcher." In Mississippi the captured freedmen could be fined and then hired out to pay their fines—an arrangement that closely resembled slavery itself.

The codes also sought to restore as nearly as possible the pre-emancipation system of race relations. Freedom was legally recognized, as were some other privileges, such as the right to marry. But all the codes forbade a black to serve on a jury; some even barred

Before President Andrew Johnson (1808–1875) softened his Southern policy, his views were radical. Speaking on April 21, 1865, he declared,

❝It is not promulgating anything that I have not heretofore said to say that traitors must be made odious, that treason must be made odious, that traitors must be punished and impoverished. They must not only be punished, but their social power must be destroyed. If not, they will still maintain an ascendancy, and may again become numerous and powerful; for, in the words of a former Senator of the United States, 'When traitors become numerous enough, treason becomes respectable.'❞

blacks from renting or leasing land. A black could be punished for "idleness" by being sentenced to work on a chain gang. Nowhere were blacks allowed to vote.

These oppressive laws mocked the ideal of freedom so recently purchased by buckets of blood. The Black Codes imposed terrible burdens on the unfettered blacks, struggling against mistreatment and poverty to make their way as free people. The worst features of the Black Codes would eventually be repealed, but their revocation could not by itself lift the liberated blacks into economic independence. Lacking capital, and with little to offer but their labor, thousands of impoverished former slaves slipped into the status of sharecropper farmers, as did many landless whites. Luckless sharecroppers gradually sank into a morass of virtual peonage and remained there for generations. Formerly slaves to masters, countless blacks as well as poorer whites in effect became slaves to the soil and to their creditors. Yet the dethroned planter aristocracy resented even this pitiful concession to freedom. Sharecropping was the "wrong policy," said one planter. "It makes the laborer too independent; he becomes a partner, and has a right to be consulted."

The Black Codes made an ugly impression in the North. If the former slaves were being re-enslaved, people asked one another, had not the Boys in Blue spilled their blood in vain? Had the North really won the war?

✦ Congressional Reconstruction

These questions grew more insistent when the congressional delegations from the newly reconstituted Southern states presented themselves in the Capitol in December 1865. To the shock and disgust of the Republicans, many former Confederate leaders were on hand to claim their seats.

The appearance of these ex-rebels was a natural but costly blunder. Voters of the South, seeking able representatives, had turned instinctively to their experienced statesmen. But most of the Southern leaders were tainted by active association with the "lost cause." Among them were four former Confederate generals, five colonels, and various members of the Richmond cabinet and Congress. Worst of all, there was the shrimpy but brainy Alexander Stephens, ex–vice president of the Confederacy, still under indictment for treason.

The presence of these "whitewashed rebels" infuriated the Republicans in Congress. The war had been fought to restore the Union, but not on these kinds

Sharecroppers Picking Cotton Although many freed slaves found themselves picking cotton on their former masters' plantations, they took comfort that they were at least paid wages and could work as a family unit. In time, however, they became ensnared in the web of debt that their planter bosses spun to keep a free labor force tightly bound to them.

National Archives

of terms. The Republicans were in no hurry to embrace their former enemies—virtually all of them Democrats—in the chambers of the Capitol. While the South had been "out" from 1861 to 1865, the Republicans in Congress had enjoyed a relatively free hand. They had passed much legislation that favored the North, such as the Morrill Tariff, the **Pacific Railroad Act**, and the Homestead Act. Now many Republicans balked at giving up this political advantage. On the first day of the congressional session, December 4, 1865, they banged shut the door in the face of the newly elected Southern delegations.

Looking to the future, the Republicans were alarmed to realize that a restored South would be stronger than ever in national politics. Before the war a black slave had counted as three-fifths of a person in apportioning congressional representation. Now the slave was five-fifths of a person. Eleven Southern states had seceded and been subdued by force of arms. But now, owing to full counting of free blacks, the rebel states were entitled to twelve more votes in Congress, and twelve more presidential electoral votes, than they had previously enjoyed. Again, angry voices in the North raised the cry, Who won the war?

Republicans had good reason to fear that ultimately they might be elbowed aside. Southerners might join hands with Democrats in the North and win control of Congress or maybe even the White House. If this happened, they could perpetuate the Black Codes, virtually re-enslaving blacks. They could dismantle the economic program of the Republican party by lowering tariffs, rerouting the transcontinental railroad, repealing the free-farm Homestead Act, and possibly even repudiating the national debt. President Johnson thus deeply disturbed the congressional Republicans when he announced on December 6, 1865, that the recently rebellious states had satisfied his conditions and that in his view the Union was now restored.

✴ Johnson Clashes with Congress

A clash between president and Congress was now inevitable. It exploded into the open in February 1866, when the president vetoed a bill (later repassed) extending the life of the controversial Freedmen's Bureau.

Aroused, the Republicans swiftly struck back. In March 1866 they passed the **Civil Rights Bill**, which conferred on blacks the privilege of American citizenship and struck at the Black Codes. President Johnson resolutely vetoed this forward-looking measure on constitutional grounds, but in April congressmen steamrollered it over his veto—something they repeatedly did henceforth. The hapless president, dubbed "Sir Veto" and "Andy Veto," had his presidential

Contending Voices
Radical Republicans and Southern Democrats

Representative Thaddeus Stevens (1792–1868), a leading radical Republican, argued in September 1865 for a sweeping plan of compulsory land redistribution and political reform to smash the Southern plantation system:

❝The whole fabric of southern society *must* be changed, and never can it be done if this opportunity is lost....If the South is ever to be made a safe republic let her lands be cultivated by the toil of the owners or the free labor of intelligent citizens.❞

Two months later, the new governor of South Carolina, James Lawrence Orr (1822–1873), voiced elite Southerners' insistence that emancipated slaves must be kept tied to the South's prewar economic system, even if now by contract rather than bondage:

❝[Emancipated slaves] must be restrained from theft, idleness, vagrancy and crime, and taught the absolute necessity of strictly complying with their contracts for labor....The labor of every negro in the State is needed, if not to till the soil, in some other useful employment—for the culture of cotton and rice; and, in menial occupations, it is very doubtful whether any laborers in this country or in Europe can supply his place.❞

Why were these competing visions of the political future of the post–Civil War South so linked to labor and land policies?

wings clipped, as Congress increasingly assumed the dominant role in running the government. One critic called Johnson "the dead dog of the White House."

Republicans now feared that the Southerners might one day win control of Congress and repeal the hated civil rights law. So the lawmakers undertook to rivet the principles of the Civil Rights Bill into the Constitution as the **Fourteenth Amendment**. The proposed amendment, approved by Congress and sent to the states in June 1866 and ratified in 1868, was among the most sweeping amendments ever passed and proved to be a major pillar of constitutional law ever after. It (1) conferred civil rights, including citizenship but excluding a specific guarantee of the franchise, on the freedmen; (2) reduced proportionately

An Inflexible President, 1866 This Republican cartoon shows Johnson knocking blacks out of the Freedmen's Bureau by his veto.

Picture Research Consultants & Archives

the representation of a state in Congress and in the Electoral College if it denied blacks the ballot, thereby abolishing the original Constitution's notorious "3/5ths" clause but stopping short of a constitutional guarantee of the right to vote; (3) disqualified from federal and state office former Confederates who as federal officeholders had once sworn "to support the Constitution of the United States"; and (4) guaranteed the federal debt, while repudiating all Confederate debts. (See the text of the Fourteenth Amendment in the Appendix.)

The radical faction was disappointed that the Fourteenth Amendment did not grant the right to vote, but all Republicans were agreed that no state should be welcomed back into the Union fold without first ratifying the Fourteenth Amendment. Yet President Johnson advised the Southern states to reject it, and all of the "sinful eleven," except Tennessee, defiantly spurned the amendment. Their spirit was reflected in a Southern song:

And I don't want no pardon for what I was or am,
I won't be reconstructed and I don't give a damn.

✷ Swinging 'Round the Circle with Johnson

As 1866 lengthened, the battle grew between the Congress and the president. The root of the controversy was Johnson's "10 percent" governments that had passed the most stringent Black Codes. Congress had tried to temper the worst features of the codes by extending the life of the embattled Freedmen's Bureau and passing the Civil Rights Bill. Both measures Johnson had vetoed. Now the issue was Southern acceptance of the principles enshrined in the Fourteenth Amendment. The Republicans would settle for nothing less. Indeed, they soon insisted on even more.

The crucial congressional elections of 1866—more crucial than some presidential elections—were fast approaching. Johnson was naturally eager to escape from the clutch of Congress by securing a majority favorable to his soft-on-the-South policy. Invited to dedicate a Chicago monument to Stephen A. Douglas, he undertook to speak at various cities en route in support of his views.

Johnson's famous "swing 'round the circle," beginning in the late summer of 1866, was a seriocomedy of errors. The president delivered a series of "give 'em hell" speeches, in which he accused the radicals in Congress of having planned large-scale antiblack riots and murder in the South. As he spoke, hecklers hurled insults at him. Reverting to his stump-speaking days in Tennessee, he shouted back angry retorts, amid cries of "You be damned" and "Don't get mad, Andy." The dignity of his high office sank to a new low, as the old charges of drunkenness were revived.

As a vote-getter, Johnson was highly successful—for the opposition. His inept speechmaking heightened the cry "Stand by Congress" against the "Tailor of the Potomac." When the ballots were counted, the Republicans had rolled up more than a two-thirds majority in both houses of Congress.

✷ Republican Principles and Programs

The Republicans now had a veto-proof Congress and virtually unlimited control of Reconstruction policy. But moderates and radicals still disagreed over the best course to pursue in the South.

The radicals in the Senate were led by the courtly and principled idealist Charles Sumner, long since

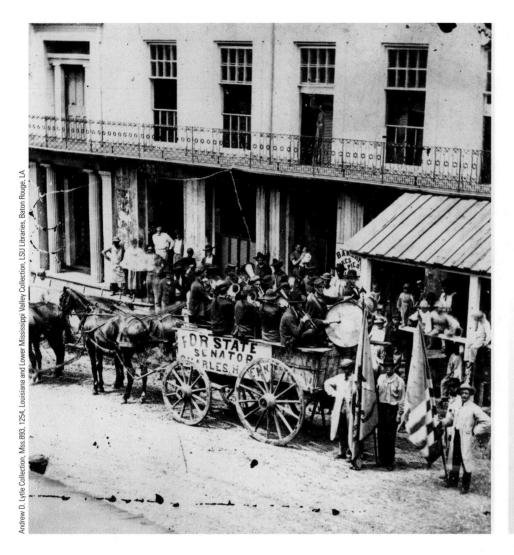

Andrew D. Lytle Collection, Mss. 893, 1264, Louisiana and Lower Mississippi Valley Collection, LSU Libraries, Baton Rouge, LA

Republicans Campaigning in Baton Rouge, Louisiana, 1868 The soldiers' caps and regimental flags demonstrate the continuing federal military presence in the Reconstruction South. Radical Republican congressman Thaddeus Stevens said that Reconstruction must "revolutionize Southern institutions, habits, and manners.... The foundation of their institutions … must be broken up and relaid, or all our blood and treasure have been spent in vain."

recovered from his prewar caning on the Senate floor, who tirelessly labored not only for black freedom but for racial equality. In the House the most powerful radical was Thaddeus Stevens, crusty and vindictive congressman from Pennsylvania. Seventy-four years old in 1866, he was a curious figure, with a protruding lower lip, a heavy black wig covering his bald head, and a deformed foot. An unswerving friend of blacks, he had defended runaway slaves in court without fee and, before dying, insisted on burial in a black cemetery. His affectionate devotion to blacks was matched by his vitriolic hatred of rebellious white Southerners. A masterly parliamentarian with a razor-sharp mind and withering wit, Stevens was a leading figure on the Joint (House-Senate) Committee on Reconstruction.

Still opposed to rapid restoration of the Southern states, the radicals wanted to keep them out as long as possible and apply federal power to bring about a drastic social and economic transformation in the South. But moderate Republicans, invoking the principles of states' rights and self-government, recoiled from the full implications of the radical program. They preferred

policies that restrained the states from abridging citizens' rights, rather than policies that directly involved the federal government in individual lives. The actual policies adopted by Congress showed the influence of both these schools of thought, though the moderates, as the majority faction, had the upper hand. And one thing both groups had come to agree on by 1867 was the necessity to enfranchise black voters, even if it took federal troops to do it.

Reconstruction by the Sword

Against a backdrop of vicious and bloody race riots that had erupted in several Southern cities, Congress passed the **Reconstruction Act** on March 2, 1867 (see Map 22.1). Supplemented by later measures, this drastic legislation divided the South into five military districts, each commanded by a Union general and policed by blue-clad soldiers, about twenty thousand all told. The act also temporarily disfranchised tens of thousands of former Confederates.

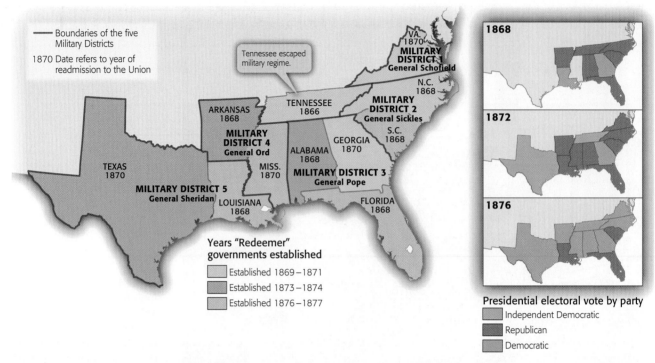

MAP 22.1 Military Reconstruction, 1867 (five districts and commanding generals)   For many white Southerners, military Reconstruction amounted to turning the knife in the wound of defeat. An often-repeated story of later years had a Southerner remark, "I was sixteen years old before I discovered that damnyankee was two words." © 2016 Cengage Learning

Congress additionally laid down stringent conditions for the readmission of the seceded states. The wayward states were required to ratify the Fourteenth Amendment, giving the former slaves their rights as citizens. The bitterest pill of all to white Southerners was the stipulation that they guarantee in their state constitutions full suffrage for their former adult male slaves. Yet the act, reflecting moderate sentiment, stopped short of giving the freedmen land or education at federal expense. The overriding purpose of the moderates was to create an electorate in Southern states that would vote those states back into the Union on acceptable terms and thus free the federal government from direct responsibility for the protection of black rights. As later events would demonstrate, this approach proved woefully inadequate to the cause of justice for blacks.

The radical Republicans were still worried. The danger loomed that once the unrepentant states were readmitted, they would amend their constitutions so as to withdraw the ballot from blacks. The only iron-clad safeguard was to incorporate black suffrage in the federal Constitution. A pattern was emerging: just as the Fourteenth Amendment had constitutionalized the principles of the Civil Rights Bill, now Congress sought to provide constitutional protection for the

suffrage provisions in the Reconstruction Act. This goal was finally achieved by the **Fifteenth Amendment**, passed by Congress in 1869 and ratified by the required number of states in 1870 (see the Appendix).

Military Reconstruction of the South not only usurped certain functions of the president as commander in chief but set up a martial regime of dubious legality. The Supreme Court had already ruled, in the case *Ex parte Milligan* (1866), that military tribunals could not try civilians, even during wartime, in areas where the civil courts were open. Peacetime military rule seemed starkly contrary to the spirit of the Constitution. But the circumstances were extraordinary in the Republic's history, and for the time being the Supreme Court avoided offending the Republican Congress.

Prodded into line by federal bayonets, the Southern states got on with the task of constitution making. By 1870 all of them had reorganized their governments and had been accorded full rights (see Table 22.2). The hated "bluebellies" remained until the new Republican regimes—usually called "radical" regimes—appeared to be firmly entrenched. Yet when the federal troops finally left a state, its government swiftly passed back into the hands of white **Redeemers**, or "Home Rule" regimes, which were inevitably Democratic. Finally, in

TABLE 22.2 Southern Reconstruction by State			
State	Readmitted to Representation in Congress	Home Rule (Democratic or "Redeemer" Regime) Reestablished	Comments
Tennessee	July 24, 1866		Ratified Fourteenth Amendment in 1866 and hence avoided military Reconstruction*
Arkansas	June 22, 1868	1874	
North Carolina	June 25, 1868	1870	
Alabama	June 25, 1868	1874	
Florida	June 25, 1868	1877	Federal troops restationed in 1877, as result of Hayes-Tilden electoral bargain
Louisiana	June 25, 1868	1877	Same as Florida
South Carolina	June 25, 1868	1877	Same as Florida
Virginia	January 26, 1870	1869	
Mississippi	February 23, 1870	1876	
Texas	March 30, 1870	1874	
Georgia	[June 25, 1868] July 15, 1870	1872	Readmitted June 25, 1868, but returned to military control after expulsion of blacks from legislature

*For many years Tennessee was the only state of the secession to observe Lincoln's birthday as a legal holiday. Many states in the South still observe the birthdays of Jefferson Davis and Robert E. Lee.

1877, the last federal muskets were removed from state politics, and the "solid" Democratic South congealed.

✳ No Women Voters

The passage of the three Reconstruction-era Amendments—the Thirteenth, Fourteenth, and Fifteenth—delighted former abolitionists but deeply disappointed advocates of women's rights. Women had played a prominent part in the prewar abolitionist movement and had often pointed out that both women

At a constitutional convention in Alabama, freed people affirmed their rights in the following declaration:

❝We claim exactly the same rights, privileges and immunities as are enjoyed by white men—we ask nothing more and will be content with nothing less.... The law no longer knows white nor black, but simply men, and consequently we are entitled to ride in public conveyances, hold office, sit on juries and do everything else which we have in the past been prevented from doing solely on the ground of color.❞

and blacks lacked basic civil rights, especially the crucial right to vote. The struggle for black freedom and the crusade for women's rights, therefore, were one and the same in the eyes of many women. Yet during the war, feminist leaders such as Elizabeth Cady Stanton and Susan B. Anthony had temporarily suspended their own demands and worked wholeheartedly for the cause of black emancipation. The **Woman's Loyal League** had gathered nearly 400,000 signatures on petitions asking Congress to pass a constitutional amendment prohibiting slavery.

Now, with the war ended and the Thirteenth Amendment passed, feminist leaders believed that their time had come. They reeled with shock, however, when the wording of the Fourteenth Amendment, which defined equal national citizenship, for the first time inserted the word *male* into the Constitution in referring to a citizen's right to vote. Both Stanton and Anthony campaigned actively against the Fourteenth Amendment despite the pleas of Frederick Douglass, who had long supported woman suffrage but believed that this was "the Negro's hour." When the Fifteenth Amendment proposed to prohibit denial of the vote on the basis of "race, color, or previous condition of servitude," Stanton and Anthony wanted the word *sex* added to the list. They lost this battle, too. Fifty years would pass before the Constitution granted women the right to vote.

The prominent suffragist and abolitionist Susan B. Anthony (1820–1906) was outraged over the proposed exclusion of women from the Fourteenth Amendment. In a conversation with her former male allies Wendell Phillips and Theodore Tilton, she reportedly held out her arm and declared,

❝ Look at this, all of you. And hear me swear that I will cut off this right arm of mine before I will ever work for or demand the ballot for the negro and not the woman. **❞**

✦ The Realities of Radical Reconstruction in the South

Blacks now had freedom, of a sort. Their friends in Congress had only haltingly and somewhat belatedly secured the franchise for them. Both Presidents Lincoln and Johnson had proposed to give the ballot gradually to selected blacks who qualified for it through education, property ownership, or military service. Moderate Republicans and even many radicals at first hesitated to bestow suffrage on the freedmen. The Fourteenth Amendment, in many ways the heart of the Republican program for Reconstruction, had fallen short of guaranteeing the right to vote. (It envisioned for blacks the same status as that of women—citizenship without voting rights.) But by 1867 hesitation had given way to a hard determination to enfranchise the former slaves wholesale and immediately, while thousands of white Southerners were being denied the vote. By glaring contrast, most of the Northern states, before ratification of the Fifteenth Amendment in 1870, withheld the ballot from their tiny black minorities. White Southerners naturally concluded that the Republicans were hypocritical in insisting that blacks in the South be allowed to vote.

Having gained their right to suffrage, Southern black men seized the initiative and began to organize politically. Their primary vehicle became the **Union League**, originally a pro-Union organization based in the North. Assisted by Northern blacks, freedmen turned the league into a network of political clubs that educated members in their civic duties and campaigned for Republican candidates. The league's mission soon expanded to include building black churches and schools, representing black grievances before local employers and government, and recruiting militias to protect black communities from white retaliation.

Though African American women did not obtain the right to vote, they too assumed new political roles. Black women faithfully attended the parades and rallies common in black communities during the early years of Reconstruction and helped assemble mass meetings in the newly constructed black churches. They even showed up at the constitutional conventions held throughout the South in 1867, monitoring the proceedings and participating in informal votes outside the convention halls.

Freedmen Voting, Richmond, Virginia, 1871 The exercise of democratic rights by former slaves constituted a political and social revolution in the South and was bitterly resented by whites.

But black men elected as delegates to the state constitutional conventions held the greater political authority. They formed the backbone of the black political community. At the conventions, they sat down with whites to hammer out new state constitutions, which most importantly provided for universal male suffrage. Though the subsequent elections produced no black governors or majorities in state senates, black political participation expanded exponentially during Reconstruction. Between 1868 and 1876, fourteen black congressmen and two black senators, Hiram Revels and Blanche K. Bruce, both of Mississippi, served in Washington, D.C. Blacks also served in state governments as lieutenant governors and representatives, and in local governments as mayors, magistrates, sheriffs, and justices of the peace.

The sight of former slaves holding office deeply offended their onetime masters, who lashed out with particular fury at the freedmen's white allies, labeling them **scalawags** and **carpetbaggers**. The so-called scalawags were Southerners, often former Unionists and Whigs. The former Confederates accused them, often with wild exaggeration, of plundering the treasuries of the Southern states through their political influence in the radical governments. The carpetbaggers, on the other hand, were supposedly sleazy Northerners who had packed all their worldly goods into a carpetbag suitcase at war's end and had come south to seek personal power and profit. In fact, most were former Union soldiers and Northern businessmen and professionals who wanted to play a role in modernizing the "New South."

How well or badly did the radical regimes rule? The radical legislatures passed much desirable legislation and introduced many sorely needed reforms. For the first time in Southern history, steps were taken toward establishing adequate public schools. Tax systems were streamlined; public works were launched; and property rights were guaranteed to women. Many welcome reforms were retained by the all-white "Redeemer" governments that later returned to power.

Despite these achievements, graft ran rampant in many "radical" governments. This was especially true in South Carolina and Louisiana, where conscienceless promoters and other pocket-padders used politically inexperienced blacks as pawns. The worst "black-and-white" legislatures purchased, as "legislative supplies," such "stationery" as hams, perfumes, suspenders, bonnets, corsets, champagne, and a coffin. One "thrifty" carpetbag governor in a single year "saved" $100,000 from a salary of $8,000. Yet this sort of corruption was by no means confined to the South in these postwar years. The crimes of the Reconstruction governments were no more outrageous than the scams and felonies being perpetrated in the North at the same time, especially in Boss Tweed's New York.

Congressman John R. Lynch of Mississippi After John Lynch was freed by the Union army, he got an education at a freedmen's school in Natchez, Mississippi. At age twenty-four, he became speaker of the Mississippi House. In 1872, Lynch joined six other African Americans in Congress, where he made his greatest mark in the long debate over the Civil Rights Act of 1875, barring discrimination in public accommodations. Lynch drew on his own humiliating experiences as a black man in the South to argue for a law prohibiting discrimination on public transportation like trains and at places like inns, restaurants, and theaters. The law passed but was not enforced. It was ruled unconstitutional in 1883.

The Ku Klux Klan

Deeply embittered, some Southern whites resorted to savage measures against "radical" rule. Many whites resented the success and ability of black legislators as much as they resented alleged "corruption." A number of secret organizations mushroomed forth, the most notorious of which was the "Invisible Empire of the South," or **Ku Klux Klan**, founded in Tennessee in 1866. Besheeted nightriders, their horses' hooves muffled, would approach the cabin of an "upstart" black and hammer on the door. In ghoulish tones one thirsty horseman would demand a bucket of water. Then, under pretense of drinking, he would pour it

Dallas Historical Society, Texas, USA /The Bridgeman Art Library

Klansmen in Costume Members of the Ku Klux Klan like these two garbed men utilized terrorist violence on behalf of a political agenda: the disenfranchisement of African Americans and their Republican allies and the reinstatement of white supremacist rule by "Redeemer" governments.

The following excerpt is part of a heartrending appeal to Congress in 1871 by a group of Kentucky blacks:

❝We believe you are not familiar with the description of the Ku Klux Klans riding nightly over the country, going from county to county, and in the county towns, spreading terror wherever they go by robbing, whipping, ravishing, and killing our people without provocation, compelling colored people to break the ice and bathe in the chilly waters of the Kentucky River.

"The [state] legislature has adjourned. They refused to enact any laws to suppress Ku-Klux disorder. We regard them [the Ku-Kluxers] as now being licensed to continue their dark and bloody deeds under cover of the dark night. They refuse to allow us to testify in the state courts where a white man is concerned. We find their deeds are perpetrated only upon colored men and white Republicans. We also find that for our services to the government and our race we have become the special object of hatred and persecution at the hands of the Democratic Party. Our people are driven from their homes in great numbers, having no redress only [except] the United States court, which is in many cases unable to reach them.❞

into a rubber attachment concealed beneath his mask and gown, smack his lips, and declare that this was the first water he had tasted since he was killed at the Battle of Shiloh. If fright did not produce the desired effect, force was employed.

Such tomfoolery and terror proved partially effective. Many ex-bondsmen and white "carpetbaggers," quick to take a hint, shunned the polls. Those stubborn souls who persisted in their "upstart" ways were flogged, mutilated, or even murdered. In one Louisiana parish in 1868, whites in two days killed or wounded two hundred victims; a pile of twenty-five bodies was found half-buried in the woods. By such atrocious practices were blacks "kept in their place"—that is, down. The Klan became a refuge for numerous bandits and cutthroats. Any scoundrel could don a sheet.

Congress, outraged by this night-riding lawlessness, passed the harsh **Force Acts** of 1870 and 1871.

Federal troops were able to stamp out much of the "lash law," but by this time the Invisible Empire had already done its work of intimidation. Many of the outlawed groups continued their tactics in the guise of "dancing clubs," "missionary societies," and "rifle clubs."

White resistance undermined attempts to empower blacks politically. The white South, for many decades, openly flouted the Fourteenth and Fifteenth Amendments. Wholesale disfranchisement of blacks, starting conspicuously about 1890, was achieved by intimidation, fraud, and trickery. Among various underhanded schemes were literacy tests, unfairly administered by whites to the advantage of illiterate

A black leader protested to whites in 1868,

❝It is extraordinary that a race such as yours, professing gallantry, chivalry, education, and superiority, living in a land where ringing chimes call child and sire to the Gospel of God—that with all these advantages on your side, you can make war upon the poor defenseless black man.❞

Hulton Archive/Getty Images

Impeachment Drama The impeachment proceedings against President Andrew Johnson, among the most severe constitutional crises in the Republic's history, were high political theater, and tickets were in sharp demand.

whites. In the eyes of white Southerners, the goal of white supremacy fully justified these dishonorable devices.

✴ Johnson Walks the Impeachment Plank

Radicals meanwhile had been sharpening their hatchets for President Johnson. Annoyed by the obstruction of the "drunken tailor" in the White House, they falsely accused him of maintaining there a harem of "dissolute women." Not content with curbing his authority, they decided to remove him altogether by constitutional processes.*

As an initial step, Congress in 1867 passed the **Tenure of Office Act**—as usual, over Johnson's veto. Contrary to precedent, the new law required the president to secure the consent of the Senate before he could remove his appointees once they had been approved by that body. One purpose was to freeze into the cabinet the secretary of war, Edwin M. Stanton, a holdover from the Lincoln administration. Although outwardly loyal to Johnson, he was secretly serving as a spy and informer for the radicals.

Johnson provided the radicals with a pretext to begin impeachment proceedings when he abruptly dismissed Stanton early in 1868. The House of Representatives immediately voted 126 to 47 to impeach Johnson for "high crimes and misdemeanors," as required by the Constitution, charging him with various violations of the Tenure of Office Act. Two additional articles related to Johnson's verbal assaults on the Congress, involving "disgrace, ridicule, hatred, contempt, and reproach."

✴ A Not-Guilty Verdict for Johnson

With evident zeal the radical-led Senate now sat as a court to try Johnson on the dubious impeachment charges. The House conducted the prosecution. The trial aroused intense public interest and, with one thousand tickets printed, proved to be the biggest show of 1868. Johnson kept his dignity and sobriety and maintained a discreet silence. His battery of attorneys argued that the president, convinced that the Tenure of Office Act was unconstitutional, had fired Stanton merely to put a test case before the Supreme Court. (That slow-moving tribunal finally ruled indirectly in Johnson's favor fifty-eight years later.) House prosecutors, including oily-tongued Benjamin F. Butler and embittered Thaddeus Stevens, had a harder time building a compelling case for impeachment.

On May 16, 1868, the day for the first voting in the Senate, the tension was electric, and heavy breathing could be heard in the galleries. By a margin of only one vote, the radicals failed to muster the two-thirds majority for Johnson's removal. Seven resistant Republican senators, mainly moderates, voted "not guilty."

Several factors shaped the outcome. Fears of creating a destabilizing precedent played a role, as did principled opposition to abusing the constitutional mechanism of checks and balances. Political considerations also figured conspicuously. As the vice presidency remained vacant under Johnson, his successor would have been radical Republican Benjamin Wade, the president pro tempore of the Senate. Wade was disliked by many members of the business community for his high-tariff, soft-money, pro-labor views and was distrusted by moderate Republicans. Meanwhile, Johnson indicated through his attorney that he would stop obstructing Republican policies in return for remaining in office.

*For impeachment, see Art. I, Sec. II, para.5; Art.I, Sec. III, paras.6, 7; Art. II, Sec. IV, in the Appendix.

Diehard radicals were infuriated by their failure to muster a two-thirds majority for Johnson's removal. "The Country is going to the Devil!" cried the crippled Stevens as he was carried from the hall. But the nation, though violently aroused, accepted the verdict with a good temper that did credit to its political maturity. In a less stable republic, an armed uprising might have erupted against the president.

The nation thus narrowly avoided a dangerous precedent that would have gravely weakened one of the three branches of the federal government. Johnson was clearly guilty of bad speeches, bad judgment, and bad temper, but not of "high crimes and misdemeanors." From the standpoint of the radicals, his greatest crime had been to stand inflexibly in their path.

✴ The Purchase of Alaska

Johnson's administration, though enfeebled at home, achieved its most enduring success in the field of foreign relations.

The Russians by 1867 were in a mood to sell the vast and chilly expanse of land now known as Alaska. They had already overextended themselves in North America, and they saw that in the likely event of another war with Britain, they probably would lose their defenseless northern province to the sea-dominant British. Alaska, moreover, had been ruthlessly "furred out" and was a growing economic liability. The Russians were therefore quite eager to unload their "frozen asset" on the Americans, and they put out seductive feelers in Washington. They preferred the United States to any other purchaser, primarily because they wanted to strengthen the American Republic as a barrier against their ancient enemy, Britain.

In 1867 Secretary of State William Seward, an ardent expansionist, signed a treaty with Russia that transferred Alaska to the United States for the bargain price of $7.2 million (see Map 22.2). But Seward's enthusiasm for these frigid wastes was not shared by his ignorant or uninformed countrymen, who jeered at **Seward's Folly,** "Seward's Icebox," "Frigidia," and "Walrussia."

Then why did Congress and the American public sanction the purchase? For one thing Russia, alone among the powers, had been conspicuously friendly to the North during the recent Civil War. Americans did not feel that they could offend their great and good friend, the tsar, by hurling his walrus-covered icebergs back into his face. Besides, the territory was rumored to be teeming with furs, fish, and gold, and it might yet "pan out" profitably—as it later did with natural resources, including oil and gas. So Congress and the country accepted "Seward's Polar Bear Garden," somewhat derisively but nevertheless hopefully.

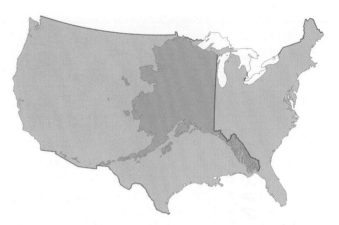

MAP 22.2 Alaska and the Lower Forty-Eight States (a size comparison) © 2016 Cengage Learning

✴ The Heritage of Reconstruction

Many white Southerners regarded Reconstruction as a more grievous wound than the war itself. It left a festering scar that would take generations to heal. They resented the upending of their social and racial system, the political empowerment of blacks, and the insult of federal intervention in their local affairs. Yet few rebellions have ended with the victors sitting down to a love feast with the vanquished. Given the explosiveness of the issues that had caused the war,

The remarkable ex-slave Frederick Douglass (1817?–1895) wrote in 1882,

"Though slavery was abolished, the wrongs of my people were not ended. Though they were not slaves, they were not yet quite free. No man can be truly free whose liberty is dependent upon the thought, feeling, and action of others, and who has himself no means in his own hands for guarding, protecting, defending, and maintaining that liberty. Yet the Negro after his emancipation was precisely in this state of destitution.... He was free from the individual master, but the slave of society. He had neither money, property, nor friends. He was free from the old plantation, but he had nothing but the dusty road under his feet. He was free from the old quarter that once gave him shelter, but a slave to the rains of summer and the frosts of winter. He was, in a word, literally turned loose, naked, hungry, and destitute, to the open sky."

and the bitterness of the fighting, the wonder is that Reconstruction was not far harsher than it was. The fact is that Lincoln, Johnson, and most Republicans had no clear picture at war's end of what federal policy toward the South should be. Policymakers groped for the right policies, influenced as much by Southern responses to defeat and emancipation as by any plans of their own to impose a specific program on the South.

The Republicans acted from a mixture of idealism and political expediency. They wanted both to protect the freed slaves and to promote the fortunes of the Republican party. In the end their efforts backfired badly. Reconstruction conferred only fleeting benefits on blacks and virtually extinguished the Republican party in the South for nearly one hundred years.

Moderate Republicans never fully appreciated the extensive effort necessary to make the freed slaves completely independent citizens, nor the lengths to which Southern whites would go to preserve their system of racial dominance. Had Thaddeus Stevens's radical program of drastic economic reforms and heftier protection of political rights been enacted, things might well have been different. But deep-seated racism, ingrained American resistance to tampering with property rights, and rigid loyalty to the principle of local self-government, combined with spreading indifference in the North to the plight of blacks, formed too formidable an obstacle. Despite good intentions by Republicans, the Old South was in many ways more resurrected than reconstructed, which spelled continuing woe for generations of Southern blacks.

Is This a Republican Form of Government? by Thomas Nast, Harper's Weekly, 1876 The nation's most prominent political cartoonist expressed his despair at the tragic way that Reconstruction had ended—with few real gains for the former slaves.

Harper's Weekly, September 2, 1876//Picture Research Consultants & Archives

[*Varying Viewpoints*]
How Radical Was Reconstruction?

Few topics have triggered as much intellectual warfare as the "dark and bloody ground" of Reconstruction. The period provoked questions—sectional, racial, and constitutional—about which people felt deeply and remain deeply divided even today. Scholarly argument goes back conspicuously to a Columbia University historian, William A. Dunning, whose students in the early 1900s published a series of histories of the Reconstruction South. Dunning and his disciples were influenced by the turn-of-the-century spirit of sectional conciliation as well as by current theories about black racial inferiority. Sympathizing with the white South, they wrote about the Reconstruction period as a kind of national disgrace, foisted upon a prostrate region by vindictive and self-seeking radical Republican politicians. If the South had wronged the North by seceding, the North had wronged the South by reconstructing.

A second cycle of scholarship in the 1920s was impelled by a widespread suspicion that the Civil War itself had been a tragic and unnecessary blunder. Attention now shifted to Northern politicians. Scholars like Howard Beale further questioned the motives of the radical Republicans. To Beale and others, the radicals had masked a ruthless desire to exploit Southern labor and resources behind a false front of "concern" for the freed slaves. Moreover, Northern advocacy of black voting rights was merely a calculated attempt to ensure a Republican political presence in the defeated South. The unfortunate Andrew Johnson, in this view, had valiantly tried to uphold constitutional principles in the face of this cynical Northern onslaught.

Although ignored by his contemporaries, scholar, black nationalist, and founder of the National Association for the Advancement of Colored People W. E. B. Du Bois wrote a sympathetic history of Reconstruction in 1935 that became the basis for historians' interpretations ever since. Following World War II, Kenneth Stampp and others, influenced by the modern civil rights movement, built on Du Bois's argument and claimed that Reconstruction had been a noble though ultimately failed attempt to extend American principles of equity and justice. The radical Republicans and the carpetbaggers were now heroes, whereas Andrew Johnson was castigated for his obstinate racism. By the early 1970s, this view had become orthodoxy, and it generally holds sway today. Yet some scholars, such as Michael Benedict and Leon Litwack, disillusioned with the inability to achieve full racial justice in the 1960s and 1970s, began once more to scrutinize the motives of Northern politicians immediately after the Civil War. They claimed to discover that Reconstruction had never been very radical and that the Freedmen's Bureau and other agencies had merely allowed white planters to maintain their dominance over local politics as well as over the local economy.

More recently, Eric Foner has powerfully reasserted the argument that Reconstruction was a truly radical and noble attempt to establish an interracial democracy. Drawing upon the work of Du Bois, Foner has emphasized the comparative approach to American Reconstruction. Clearly, Foner has admitted, Reconstruction did not create full equality, but it did allow blacks to form political organizations and churches, to vote, and to establish some measure of economic independence. In South Africa, the Caribbean, and other areas once marked by slavery, these opportunities were much harder to come by. Many of the benefits of Reconstruction were erased by whites in the South during the Gilded Age, but in the twentieth century, the constitutional principles and organizations developed during Reconstruction provided the focus and foundation for the post–World War II civil rights movement—which some have called the second Reconstruction. Steven Hahn's *A Nation Under Our Feet: Black Political Struggles in the Rural South from Slavery to the Great Migration* (2003) is the latest contribution to the literature on Reconstruction. Hahn emphasizes the assertiveness and ingenuity of African Americans in creating new political opportunities for themselves after emancipation.

Chapter Review

KEY TERMS

Freedmen's Bureau (469)

"10 percent" Reconstruction plan (470)

Wade-Davis Bill (470)

Black Codes (471)

Pacific Railroad Act (473)

Civil Rights Bill (473)

Fourteenth Amendment (473)

Reconstruction Act (475)

Fifteenth Amendment (476)

Ex parte Milligan (476)

Redeemers (476)

Woman's Loyal League (477)

Union League (478)

scalawags (479)

carpetbaggers (479)

Ku Klux Klan (479)

Force Acts (480)

Tenure of Office Act (481)

Seward's Folly (482)

PEOPLE TO KNOW

Oliver O. Howard

Andrew Johnson

Thaddeus Stevens

Hiram Revels

Edwin M. Stanton

Benjamin Wade

William Seward

CHRONOLOGY

1863	Lincoln announces "10 percent" Reconstruction plan
1864	Lincoln vetoes Wade-Davis Bill
1865	Lincoln assassinated Johnson issues Reconstruction proclamation Congress refuses to seat Southern congressmen Freedmen's Bureau established Southern states pass Black Codes
1866	Congress passes Civil Rights Bill over Johnson's veto Congress passes Fourteenth Amendment Johnson-backed candidates lose congressional election *Ex parte Milligan* case Ku Klux Klan founded
1867	Reconstruction Act Tenure of Office Act United States purchases Alaska from Russia
1868	Johnson impeached and acquitted Johnson pardons Confederate leaders
1870	Fifteenth Amendment ratified
1870–1871	Force Acts
1872	Freedmen's Bureau ended
1877	Reconstruction ends

TO LEARN MORE

Richard N. Current, *Those Terrible Carpetbaggers* (1988)

Eric Foner, *Forever Free: The Story of Emancipation and Reconstruction* (2005)

_____, *Reconstruction: America's Unfinished Revolution, 1863–1877* (1988)

Steven Hahn, *A Nation Under Our Feet: Black Political Struggles in the Rural South from Slavery to the Great Migration* (2003)

James M. McPherson, *Ordeal by Fire: The Civil War and Reconstruction* (1981)

Peggy Pascoe, *What Comes Naturally: Miscegenation Law and the Making of Race in America* (2009)

Michael Perman, *Emancipation and Reconstruction* (rev. ed., 2003)

Lawrence Powell, *New Masters: Northern Planters During the Civil War and Reconstruction* (1980)

Julie Saville, *The Work of Reconstruction: From Slave to Wage Laborer in South Carolina, 1860–1870* (1994)

David O. Stewart, *Impeached: The Trial of President Andrew Johnson and the Fight for Lincoln's Legacy* (2009)

Booker T. Washington, *Up from Slavery* (1901)

Heather Andrea Williams, *Self-Taught: African American Education in Slavery and Freedom* (2005)

A complete, annotated bibliography for this chapter—along with brief descriptions of the People to Know—may be found on the *American Pageant* website. The key terms are defined in the glossary at the end of the text.

DOCUMENTS

Declaration of Independence

In Congress, July 4, 1776

The Unanimous Declaration of the Thirteen United States of America

[Bracketed material in color has been inserted by the authors. For adoption background see pp. 140–141.]

When, in the course of human events, it becomes necessary for one people to dissolve the political bonds which have connected them with another, and to assume, among the powers of the earth, the separate and equal station to which the laws of nature and of nature's God entitle them, a decent respect to the opinions of mankind requires that they should declare the causes which impel them to the separation.

We hold these truths to be self-evident: That all men are created equal; that they are endowed by their Creator with certain unalienable rights; that among these are life, liberty, and the pursuit of happiness; that, to secure these rights, governments are instituted among men, deriving their just powers from the consent of the governed; that whenever any form of government becomes destructive of these ends, it is the right of the people to alter or to abolish it, and to institute new government, laying its foundation on such principles, and organizing its powers in such form, as to them shall seem most likely to effect their safety and happiness. Prudence, indeed, will dictate that governments long established should not be changed for light and transient causes; and accordingly all experience hath shown that mankind are more disposed to suffer, while evils are sufferable, than to right themselves by abolishing the forms to which they are accustomed. But when a long train of abuses and usurpations, pursuing invariably the same object, evinces a design to reduce them under absolute despotism, it is their right, it is their duty, to throw off such government, and to provide new guards for their future security. Such has been the patient sufferance of these colonies; and such is now the necessity which constrains them to alter their former systems of government. The history of the present King of Great Britain is a history of repeated injuries and usurpations, all having in direct object the establishment of an absolute tyranny over these states. To prove this, let facts be submitted to a candid world.

He has refused his assent to laws, the most wholesome and necessary for the public good. [See royal veto, p. 119.]

He has forbidden his governors to pass laws of immediate and pressing importance, unless suspended in their operation till his assent should be obtained; and, when so suspended, he has utterly neglected to attend to them.

He has refused to pass other laws for the accommodation of large districts of people [by establishing new countries], unless those people would relinquish the right of representation in the legislature, a right inestimable to them, and formidable to tyrants only.

He has called together legislative bodies at places unusual, uncomfortable, and distant from the depository of their public records, for the sole purpose of fatiguing them into compliance with his measures [e.g., removal of Massachusetts Assembly to Salem, 1774].

He has dissolved representative houses repeatedly, for opposing, with manly firmness, his invasions on the rights of the people [e.g., Virginia Assembly, 1765].

He has refused for a long time, after such dissolutions, to cause others to be elected; whereby the legislative powers, incapable of annihilation, have returned to the people at large for their exercise; the state remaining, in the mean time, exposed to all the dangers of invasions from without and convulsions within.

He has endeavored to prevent the population [populating] of these states; for that purpose obstructing the laws for naturalization of foreigners; refusing to pass others to encourage their migration hither, and raising the conditions of new appropriations of lands [e.g., Proclamation of 1763, p. 113].

He has obstructed the administration of justice, by refusing his assent to laws for establishing judiciary powers.

He has made judges dependent on his will alone, for the tenure of their offices, and the amount and payment of their salaries. [See Townshend Acts, p. 122.]

He has erected a multitude of new offices, and sent hither swarms of officers to harass our people and eat out their substance. [See enforcement of Navigation Laws, pp. 119, 124.]

He has kept among us, in times of peace, standing armies, without the consent of our legislatures. [See pp. 119, 123.]

He has affected to render the military independent of, and superior to, the civil power.

He has combined with others to subject us to a jurisdiction foreign to our constitution, and unacknowledged by our laws, giving his assent to their acts of pretended legislation:

For quartering large bodies of armed troops among us [see Boston Massacre, p. 123];

For protecting them, by a mock trial, from punishment for any murders which they should commit on the inhabitants of these states [see 1774 "Intolerable Acts," p. 126];

For cutting off our trade with all parts of the world [see Boston Port Act, p. 126];

For imposing taxes on us without our consent [see Stamp Act, pp. 119–120];

For depriving us, in many cases, of the benefits of trial by jury;

For transporting us beyond seas, to be tried for pretended offenses;

For abolishing the free system of English laws in a neighboring province [Quebec], establishing therein an arbitrary government, and enlarging its boundaries, so as to render it at once an example and fit instrument for introducing the same absolute rule into these colonies [Quebec Act, p. 126];

For taking away our charters, abolishing our most valuable laws, and altering fundamentally the forms of our governments [e.g., in Massachusetts, p. 126];

For suspending our own legislatures, and declaring themselves invested with power to legislate for us in all cases whatsoever. [See Stamp Act repeal, pp. 120–121.]

He has abdicated government here, by declaring us out of his protection and waging war against us. [See George III's proclamation of colonies in rebellion, p. 136.]

He has plundered our seas, ravaged our coasts, burned our towns, and destroyed the lives of our people [e.g., the burning of Falmouth (Portland), p. 136].

He is at this time transporting large armies of foreign mercenaries [Hessians, p. 136] to complete the works of death, desolation, and tyranny already begun with circumstances of cruelty and perfidy scarcely paralleled in the most barbarous ages, and totally unworthy the head of a civilized nation.

He has constrained our fellow-citizens, taken captive on the high seas [by impressment], to bear arms against their country, to become the executioners of their friends and brethren, or to fall themselves by their hands.

He has excited domestic insurrection among us [i.e., among slaves], and has endeavored to bring on the inhabitants of our frontiers the merciless Indian savages, whose known rule of warfare is an undistinguished destruction of all ages, sexes, and conditions.

In every stage of these oppressions we have petitioned for redress in the most humble terms; our repeated petitions have been answered only by repeated injury [e.g., p. 136]. A prince, whose character is thus marked by every act which may define a tyrant, is unfit to be the ruler of a free people.

Nor have we been wanting in our attentions to our British brethren. We have warned them, from time to time, of attempts by their legislature to extend an unwarrantable jurisdiction over us. We have reminded them of the circumstances of our emigration and settlement here. We have appealed to their native justice and magnanimity; and we have conjured them, by the ties of our common kindred, to disavow these usurpations, which would inevitably interrupt our connections and correspondence. They, too, have been deaf to the voice of justice and of consanguinity [blood relationship]. We must, therefore, acquiesce in the necessity which denounces [announces] our separation, and hold them, as we hold the rest of mankind, enemies in war, in peace friends.

We, therefore, the representatives of the United States of America, in General Congress assembled, appealing to the Supreme Judge of the world for the rectitude of our intentions, do, in the name and by the authority of the good people of these colonies, solemnly publish and declare, That these United Colonies are, and of right ought to be, FREE AND INDEPENDENT STATES; that they are absolved from all allegiance to the British crown, and that all political connection between them and the state of Great Britain is, and ought to be, totally dissolved; and that, as free and independent states, they have full power to levy war, conclude peace, contract alliances, establish commerce, and do all other acts and things which independent states may of right do. And for the support of this declaration, with a firm reliance on the protection of Divine Providence, we mutually pledge to each other our lives, our fortunes, and our sacred honor.

[Signed by]

JOHN HANCOCK [President]
[and fifty-five others]

Constitution of the United States of America

[Boldface headings and bracketed explanatory matter and marginal comments (both in color) have been inserted for the reader's convenience. Passages that are no longer operative are printed in italic type.]

Article I. **PREAMBLE**

Section I. We the people of the United States, in order to form a more perfect union, establish justice, insure domestic tranquility, provide for the common defense, promote the general welfare, and secure the blessings of liberty to ourselves and our posterity, do ordain and establish this Constitution for the United States of America.

Section II. *Legislative Department*

Congress

Legislative power vested in a two-house Congress. All legislative powers herein granted shall be vested in a Congress of the United States, which shall consist of a Senate and a House of Representatives.

House of Representatives

1. The people elect representatives biennially. The House of Representatives shall be composed of members chosen every second year by the people of the several States, and the electors [voters] in each State shall have the qualifications requisite for electors of the most numerous branch of the State Legislature.

2. Who may be representatives. No person shall be a Representative who shall not have attained the age of twenty-five years, and been seven years a citizen of the United States, and who shall not, when elected, be an inhabitant of that State in which he shall be chosen.

See 1787 compromises, pp. 170–172.

3. Representation in the House based on population; census. Representatives and direct taxes[1] shall be apportioned among the several States which may be included within this Union, according to their respective numbers, *which shall be determined by adding to the whole number of free persons, including those bound to service for a term of years* [apprentices and indentured servants], *and excluding Indians not taxed, three-fifths of all other persons* [slaves].[2] The actual enumeration [census] shall be made within three years after the first meeting of the Congress of the United States, and within every subsequent term of ten years, in such manner as they shall by law direct. The number of Representatives shall not exceed one for every thirty thousand, but each State shall have at least one Representative; *and until such enumeration shall be made, the State of New Hampshire shall be entitled to choose three, Massachusetts eight, Rhode Island and Providence Plantations one, Connecticut five, New York six, New Jersey four, Pennsylvania eight, Delaware one, Maryland six, Virginia ten, North Carolina five, South Carolina five, and Georgia three.*

See 1787 compromises, pp. 170–172.

---

[1]Modified in 1913 by the Sixteenth Amendment re income taxes (see p. 665).

[2]The word *slave* appears nowhere in the original, unamended Constitution. The three-fifths rule ceased to be in force when the Thirteenth Amendment was adopted in 1865 (see p. 66 and amendments below).

4. Vacancies in the House are filled by election. When vacancies happen in the representation from any State, the Executive authority [governor] therefore shall issue writs of election [call a special election] to fill such vacancies.

5. The House selects its Speaker; has sole power to vote impeachment charges (i.e., indictments). The House of Representatives shall choose their Speaker and other officers; and shall have the sole power of impeachment.

See Chase and Johnson trials, pp. 211, 481; Nixon trial preliminaries, pp. 911–914; and discussion of Clinton's impeachment, pp. 972–973.

Section III.   Senate

1. Senators represent the states. The Senate of the United States shall be composed of two Senators from each State, *chosen by the legislature thereof,*[1] for six Years; and each Senator shall have one vote.

2. One-third of senators chosen every two years; vacancies. *Immediately after they shall be assembled in consequence of the first election, they shall be divided as equally as may be into three classes. The seats of the Senators of the first class shall be vacated at the expiration of the second year, of the second class at the expiration of the fourth year, and of the third class at the expiration of the sixth year,* so that one-third may be chosen every second year; *and if vacancies happen by resignation or otherwise, during the recess of the legislature of any State, the Executive* [governor] *thereof may make temporary appointments until the next meeting of the legislature, which shall then fill such vacancies.*[2]

3. Who may be senators. No person shall be a Senator who shall not have attained to the age of thirty years, and been nine years a citizen of the United States, and who shall not, when elected, be an inhabitant of that State for which he shall be chosen.

4. The vice president presides over the Senate. The Vice President of the United States shall be President of the Senate, but shall have no vote, unless they be equally divided [tied].

5. The Senate chooses its other officers. The Senate shall choose their other officers, and also a President *pro tempore*, in the absence of the Vice President, or when he shall exercise the office of the President of the United States.

See Chase and Johnson trials, pp. 211, 481; and discussion of Clinton's impeachment, pp. 972–973.

6. The Senate has sole power to try impeachments. The Senate shall have the sole power to try all impeachments. When sitting for that purpose, they shall be on oath or affirmation. When the President of the United States is tried, the Chief Justice shall preside[3]: and no person shall be convicted without the concurrence of two-thirds of the members present.

7. Penalties for impeachment conviction. Judgment in cases of impeachment shall not extend further than to removal from office, and disqualification to hold and enjoy any office of honor, trust or profit under the United States: but the party convicted shall nevertheless be liable and subject to indictment, trial, judgment and punishment, according to law.

Section IV.   Election and Meetings of Congress

1. Regulation of elections. The times, places and manner of holding elections for Senators and Representatives shall be prescribed in each State by the legislature thereof; but the Congress may at any time by law make or alter such regulations, except as to the places of choosing Senators.

2. Congress must meet once a year. The Congress shall assemble at least once in every year, and such meeting *shall be on the first Monday in December, unless they shall by law appoint a different day.*[4]

---

[1]Repealed in favor of popular election in 1913 by the Seventeenth Amendment.
[2]Changed in 1913 by the Seventeenth Amendment.
[3]The vice president, as next in line, would be an interested party.
[4]Changed in 1933 to January 3 by the Twentieth Amendment (see p. 770 and below).

Section V. Organization and Rules of the Houses

1. Each house may reject members; quorums. Each house shall be the judge of the elections, returns and qualifications of its own members, and a majority of each shall constitute a quorum to do business; but a smaller number may adjourn from day to day, and may be authorized to compel the attendance of absent members, in such manner, and under such penalties, as each house may provide.

See "Bully" Brooks case, pp. 403–404.

2. Each house makes its own rules. Each house may determine the rules of its proceedings, punish its members for disorderly behavior, and with the concurrence of two-thirds, expel a member.

3. Each house must keep and publish a record of its proceedings. Each house shall keep a journal of its proceedings, and from time to time publish the same, excepting such parts as may in their judgment require secrecy; and the yeas and nays of the members of either house on any question shall, at the desire of one-fifth of those present, be entered on the journal.

4. Both houses must agree on adjournment. Neither house, during the session of Congress, shall, without the consent of the other, adjourn for more than three days, nor to any other place than that in which the two houses shall be sitting.

Section VI. Privileges of and Prohibitions upon Congressmen

1. Congressional salaries; immunities. The Senators and Representatives shall receive a compensation for their services, to be ascertained by law and paid out of the treasury of the United States. They shall in all cases except treason, felony and breach of the peace, be privileged from arrest during their attendance at the session of their respective houses, and in going to and returning from the same; and for any speech or debate in either house, they shall not be questioned in any other place [i.e., they shall be immune from libel suits].

2. A congressman may not hold any other federal civil office. No Senator or Representative shall, during the time for which he was elected, be appointed to any civil office under the authority of the United States, which shall have been created, or the emoluments whereof shall have been increased, during such time; and no person holding any office under the United States shall be a member of either house during his continuance in office.

Section VII. Method of Making Laws

See 1787 compromises, p. 171.

1. Money bills must originate in the House. All bills for raising revenue shall originate in the House of Representatives; but the Senate may propose or concur with amendments as on other bills.

Nixon, more than any predecessors, "impounded" billions of dollars voted by Congress for specific purposes because he disapproved of them. The courts generally failed to sustain him, and his impeachment foes regarded wholesale impoundment as a violation of his oath to "faithfully execute" the laws.

2. The president's veto power; Congress may override. Every bill which shall have passed the House of Representatives and the Senate, shall, before it become a law, be presented to the President of the United States; if he approve he shall sign it, but if not he shall return it with his objections to that house in which it shall have originated, who shall enter the objections at large on their journal, and proceed to reconsider it. If after such reconsideration two-thirds of that house shall agree to pass the bill, it shall be sent, together with the objections, to the other house, by which it shall likewise be reconsidered, and, if approved by two-thirds of that house, it shall become a law. But in all such cases the votes of both houses shall be determined by yeas and nays, and the names of the persons voting for and against the bill shall be entered on the journal of each house respectively. If any bill shall not be returned by the President within ten days (Sundays excepted) after it shall have been presented to him, the same shall be a law, in like manner as if he had signed it, unless the Congress by their adjournment prevent its return, in which case it shall not be a law [this is the so-called pocket veto].

3. All measures requiring the agreement of both houses go to president for approval. Every order, resolution, or vote to which the concurrence of the Senate and House of Representatives may be necessary (except on a question of adjournment) shall be presented to the President of the United States; and before the same shall take effect, shall be approved by him, or being disapproved by him, shall be repassed by two-thirds of the Senate and House of Representatives, according to the rules and limitations prescribed in the case of a bill.

Section VIII.   **Powers Granted to Congress**

Congress has certain enumerated powers:

1. It may lay and collect taxes. The Congress shall have power to lay and collect taxes, duties, imposts, and excises, to pay the debts and provide for the common defense and general welfare of the United States; but all duties, imposts and excises shall be uniform throughout the United States;

2. It may borrow money. To borrow money on the credit of the United States;

3. It may regulate foreign and interstate trade. To regulate commerce with foreign nations, and among the several States, and with the Indian tribes;

For 1798 naturalization, see p. 198.

4. It may pass naturalization and bankruptcy laws. To establish an uniform rule of naturalization, and uniform laws on the subject of bankruptcies throughout the United States;

5. It may coin money. To coin money, regulate the value thereof, and of foreign coin, and fix the standard of weights and measures;

6. It may punish counterfeiters. To provide for the punishment of counterfeiting the securities and current coin of the United States;

7. It may establish a postal service. To establish post offices and post roads;

8. It may issue patents and copyrights. To promote the progress of science and useful arts by securing for limited times to authors and inventors the exclusive right to their respective writings and discoveries;

9. It may establish inferior courts. To constitute tribunals inferior to the Supreme Court;

See Judiciary Act of 1789, p. 184.

10. It may punish crimes committed on the high seas. To define and punish piracies and felonies committed on the high seas [i.e., outside the three-mile limit] and offenses against the law of nations [international law];

11. It may declare war; authorize privateers. To declare war,[1] grant letters of marque and reprisal,[2] and make rules concerning captures on land and water;

12. It may maintain an army. To raise and support armies, but no appropriation of money to that use shall be for a longer term than two years;[3]

13. It may maintain a navy. To provide and maintain a navy;

14. It may regulate the army and navy. To make rules for the government and regulation of the land and naval forces;

15. It may call out the state militia. To provide for calling forth the militia to execute the laws of the Union, suppress insurrections, and repel invasions;

See Whiskey Rebellion, pp. 187–188.

16. It shares with the states control of militia. To provide for organizing, arming, and disciplining the militia, and for governing such part of them as may be employed in the service of the United States, reserving to the States respectively the appointment of the officers, and the authority of training the militia according to the discipline prescribed by Congress;

17. It makes laws for the District of Columbia and other federal areas. To exercise exclusive legislation in all cases whatsoever, over such district (not exceeding ten miles square) as may, by cession of particular States, and the acceptance of

---

[1]Note that presidents, though they can provoke war (see the case of Polk, pp. 369–370) or wage it after it is declared, cannot declare it.

[2]Papers issued private citizens in wartime authorizing them to capture enemy ships.

[3]A reflection of fear of standing armies earlier expressed in the Declaration of Independence.

Congress, become the seat of government of the United States,[1] and to exercise like authority over all places purchased by the consent of the legislature of the State, in which the same shall be, for the erection of forts, magazines, arsenals, dock-yards, and other needful buildings;—and

Congress has certain implied powers:

This is the famous "elastic clause"; see p. 187.

18. It may make laws necessary for carrying out the enumerated powers. To make all laws which shall be necessary and proper for carrying into execution the foregoing powers, and all other powers vested by this Constitution in the government of the United States, or in any departure or officer thereof.

Section IX.   Powers Denied to the Federal Government

See 1787 slave compromise, p. 172.

1. Congressional control of slave trade postponed until 1808. *The migration or importation of such persons as any of the States now existing shall think proper to admit shall not be prohibited by the Congress prior to the year 1808; but a tax or duty may be imposed on such importation, not exceeding $10 for each person.*

See Lincoln's unlawful suspension, p. 432.

2. The writ of habeas corpus[2] may be suspended only in cases of rebellion or invasion. The privilege of the writ of habeas corpus shall not be suspended, unless when in cases of rebellion or invasion the public safety may require it.

3. Attainders[3] and ex post facto laws[4] forbidden. No bill of attainder or ex post facto law shall be passed.

4. Direct taxes must be apportioned according to population. No capitation [head or poll tax] or other direct, tax shall be laid, unless in proportion to the census or enumeration herein before directed to be taken.[5]

5. Export taxes forbidden. No tax or duty shall be laid on articles exported from any State.

6. Congress must not discriminate among states in regulating commerce. No preference shall be given by any regulation of commerce or revenue to the ports of one State over those of another; nor shall vessels bound to, or from, one State, be obliged to enter, clear, or pay duties in another.

See Lincoln's unlawful infraction, p. 432.

7. Public money may not be spent without congressional appropriation; accounting. No money shall be drawn from the treasury, but in consequence of appropriations made by law; and a regular statement and account of the receipts and expenditures of all public money shall be published from time to time.

8. Titles of nobility prohibited; foreign gifts. No title of nobility shall be granted by the United States; and no person holding office of profit or trust under them, shall, without the consent of Congress, accept of any present, emolument, office, or title, of any kind whatever, from any king, prince, or foreign state.

Section X.   Powers Denied to the States

Absolute prohibitions on the states:

On contracts, see Fletcher v. Peck, *p. 240.*

1. The states are forbidden to do certain things. No State shall enter into any treaty, alliance, or confederation; grant letters of marque and reprisal [i.e., authorize

---

[1]The District of Columbia, ten miles square, was established in 1791 with a cession from Virginia (see p. 183).

[2]A writ of habeas corpus is a document that enables a person under arrest to obtain an immediate examination in court to ascertain whether he or she is being legally held.

[3]A bill of attainder is a special legislative act condemning and punishing an individual without a judicial trial.

[4]An ex post facto law is one that fixes punishments for acts committed before the law was passed.

[5]Modified in 1913 by the Sixteenth Amendment (see p. 742 and amendments below).

privateers]; coin money; emit bills of credit [issue paper money]; make anything but gold and silver coin a [legal] tender in payment of debts; pass any bill of attainder,[1] ex post facto,[1] or law impairing the obligation of contracts, or grant any title of nobility.

Conditional prohibitions on the states:

Cf. Confederation chaos, pp. 164–165.

2. The states may not levy duties without the consent of Congress. No State shall, without the consent of Congress, lay any imposts or duties on imports or exports, except what may be absolutely necessary for executing its inspection laws: and the net produce of all duties and imposts, laid by any State on imports or exports, shall be for the use of the treasury of the United States; and all such laws shall be subject to the revision and control of the Congress.

3. Certain other federal powers are forbidden the states except with the consent of Congress. No State shall, without the consent of Congress, lay any duty of tonnage [i.e., duty on ship tonnage], keep [nonmilitia] troops or ships of war in time of peace, enter into any agreement or compact with another State, or with a foreign power, or engage in war, unless actually invaded, or in such imminent danger as will not admit of delay.

Article II.   *Executive Department*

Section I.   **President and Vice President**

1. The president is the chief executive; term of office. The executive power shall be vested in a President of the United States of America. He shall hold his office during the term of four years,[2] and, together with the Vice President, chosen for the same term, be elected as follows:

See 1787 compromise, p. 171.

See 1876 Oregon case, p. 494.

2. The president is chosen by electors. Each State shall appoint, in such manner as the legislature thereof may direct, a number of electors, equal to the whole number of Senators and Representatives to which the State may be entitled in the Congress; but no Senator or Representative, or person holding an office of trust or profit under the United States, shall be appointed an elector.

A majority of the electoral votes needed to elect a president. *The electors shall meet in their respective States, and vote by ballot for two persons, of whom one at least shall not be an inhabitant of the same State with themselves. And they shall make a list of all the persons voted for, and of the number of votes for each; which list they shall sign and certify, and transmit sealed to the seat of government of the United States, directed to the President of the Senate. The President of the Senate shall, in the presence of the Senate and House of Representatives, open all the certificates, and the votes shall be counted. The person having the greatest number of votes shall be the President, if such number be a majority of the whole number of electors appointed; and if there be more than*

See Burr-Jefferson disputed election of 1800, pp. 205–206.

one who have such majority, and have an equal number of votes, then the House of Representatives shall immediately choose by ballot one of them for President; and if no person have a majority, then from the five highest on the list the said house shall in like manner choose the President. But in choosing the President the votes shall be taken by States, the representation from each State having one vote; a quorum for this purpose shall consist of a member or members from two-thirds of the States, and a majority of all the States shall be necessary to a choice. In every case, after the choice of the President, the person having the greatest number of votes of the electors shall be the Vice President. But if there should

See Jefferson as vice president in 1796, p. 196.

remain two or more who have equal votes, the Senate shall choose from them by ballot the Vice President.[3]

---

[1]For definitions see footnotes 3 and 4 on preceding page.
[2]No reference to reelection; for anti–third term Twenty-second Amendment, see below.
[3]Repealed in 1804 by the Twelfth Amendment (for text see below).

3. Congress decides time of meeting of Electoral College. The Congress may determine the time of choosing the electors and the day on which they shall give their votes; which day shall be the same throughout the United States.

To provide for foreign-born people, like Alexander Hamilton, born in the British West Indies.

4. Who may be president. No person except a natural-born citizen, *or a citizen of the United States at the time of the adoption of this Constitution*, shall be eligible to the office of President; neither shall any person be eligible to that office who shall not have attained to the age of thirty-five years, and been fourteen years a resident within the United States [i.e., a legal resident].

Modified by Twentieth and Twenty-fifth Amendments below.

5. Replacements for president. In case of the removal of the President from office or of his death, resignation, or inability to discharge the powers and duties of said office, the same shall devolve on the Vice President, and the Congress may by law provide for the case of removal, death, resignation, or inability, both of the President and Vice President, declaring what officer shall then act as President, and such officer shall act accordingly, until the disability be removed, or a President shall be elected.

6. The president's salary. The President shall, at stated times, receive for his services a compensation, which shall neither be increased or diminished during the period for which he shall have been elected, and he shall not receive within that period any other emolument from the United States, or any of them.

7. The president's oath of office. Before he enter on the execution of his office, he shall take the following oath or affirmation:—"I do solemnly swear (or affirm) that I will faithfully execute the office of the President of the United States, and will to the best of my ability preserve, protect and defend the Constitution of the United States."

Section II.   Powers of the President

See cabinet evolution, p. 183.

1. The president has important military and civil powers. The President shall be commander in chief of the army and navy of the United States, and of the militia of the several States, when called into the actual service of the United States; he may require the opinion, in writing, of the principal officer in each of the executive departments, upon any subject relating to the duties of their respective offices, and he shall have power to grant reprieves and pardons for offenses against the United States, except in cases of impeachment.[1]

For president's removal power, see p. 481.

2. The president may negotiate treaties and nominate federal officials. He shall have power, by and with the advice and consent of the Senate, to make treaties, provided two-thirds of the Senators present concur; and he shall nominate, and by and with the advice and consent of the Senate, shall appoint ambassadors, other public ministers and consuls, judges of the Supreme Court, and all other officers of the United States, whose appointments are not herein otherwise provided for, and which shall be established by law: but the Congress may by law vest the appointment of such inferior officers, as they think proper, in the President alone, in the courts of law, or in the heads of departments.

3. The president may fill vacancies during Senate recess. The President shall have power to fill up all vacancies that may happen during the recess of the Senate, by granting commissions which shall expire at the end of their next session.

Section III.   Other Powers and Duties of the President

For president's personal appearances, see p. 664.

Messages; extra sessions; receiving ambassadors; execution of the laws. He shall from time to time give to the Congress information of the state of the Union, and recommend to their consideration such measures as he shall judge necessary and expedient; he may, on extraordinary occasions, convene both houses, or either of

---

[1]To prevent the president's pardoning himself or his close associates, as was feared in the case of Richard Nixon. See p. 928.

them, and in case of disagreement between them, with respect to the time of adjournment, he may adjourn them to such time as he shall think proper; he shall receive ambassadors and other public ministers; he shall take care that the laws be faithfully executed, and shall commission all the officers of the United States.

Section IV. Impeachment

See discussion of Presidents Johnson, p. 481; Nixon, pp. 911–914; and Clinton, pp. 972–973.

Civil officers may be removed by impeachment. The President, Vice President and all civil officers[1] of the United States shall be removed from office on impeachment for, and on conviction of, treason, bribery, and other high crimes and misdemeanors.

Article III. *Judicial Department*

Section I. The Federal Courts

See Judiciary Act of 1789, p. 184.

The judicial power belongs to the federal courts. The judicial power of the United States shall be vested in one Supreme Court, and in such inferior courts as the Congress may from time to time ordain and establish. The judges, both of the Supreme and inferior courts, shall hold their offices during good behavior, and shall, at stated times, receive for their services a compensation which shall not be diminished[2] during their continuance in office.

Section II. Jurisdiction of Federal Courts

1. Kinds of cases that may be heard. The judicial power shall extend to all cases, in law and equity, arising under this Constitution, the laws of the United States, and treaties made, or which shall be made, under their authority;—to all cases affecting ambassadors, other public ministers and consuls;—to all cases of admiralty and maritime jurisdiction;—to controversies to which the United States shall be a party;—to controversies between two or more States;—*between a State and citizens of another State*[3];—between citizens of different States;—between citizens of the same State claiming lands under grants of different States, and between a State, or the citizens thereof, and foreign states, citizens or subjects.

2. Jurisdiction of the Supreme Court. In all cases affecting ambassadors, other public ministers and consuls, and those in which a State shall be a party, the Supreme Court shall have original jurisdiction.[4] In all the other cases before mentioned, the Supreme Court shall have appellate jurisdiction,[5] both as to law and fact, with such exceptions, and under such regulations, as the Congress shall make.

3. Trial for federal crime is by jury. The trial of all crimes, except in cases of impeachment, shall be by jury; and such trial shall be held in the State where the said crimes shall have been committed; but when not committed within any State, the trial shall be at such place or places as the Congress may by law have directed.

---

[1] i.e., all federal executive and judicial officers, but not members of Congress or military personnel.

[2] In 1978, in a case involving federal judges, the Supreme Court ruled that diminution of salaries by inflation was irrelevant.

[3] The Eleventh Amendment (see below) restricts this to suits by a state against citizens of another state.

[4] i.e., such cases must originate in the Supreme Court.

[5] i.e., it hears other cases only when they are appealed to it from a lower federal court or a state court.

Section III. Treason

See Burr trial, p. 216.

1. Treason defined. Treason against the United States shall consist only in levying war against them, or in adhering to their enemies, giving them aid and comfort. No person shall be convicted of treason unless on the testimony of two witnesses to the same overt act, or on confession in open court.

2. Congress fixes punishment for treason. The Congress shall have power to declare the punishment of treason, but no attainder of treason shall work corruption of blood, or forfeiture except during the life of the person attained.[1]

Article IV. *Relations of the States to One Another*

Section I. Credit to Acts, Records, and Court Proceedings

Each state must respect the public acts of the others. Full faith and credit shall be given in each State to the public acts, records, and judicial proceedings of every other State.[2] And the Congress may by general laws prescribe the manner in which such acts, records, and proceedings shall be proved [attested], and the effect thereof.

Section II. Duties of States to States

1. Citizenship in one state is valid in all. The citizens of each State shall be entitled to all privileges and immunities of citizens in the several States.

This stipulation is sometimes openly flouted. In 1978 Governor Jerry Brown of California, acting on humanitarian grounds, refused to surrender to South Dakota an American Indian, Dennis Banks, who was charged with murder in an armed uprising.

Basis of fugitive-slave laws; see pp. 389.

2. Fugitives from justice must be surrendered by the state to which they have fled. A person charged in any State with treason, felony, or other crime, who shall flee from justice, and be found in another State, shall on demand of the executive authority [governor] of the State from which he fled, be delivered up, to be removed to the State having jurisdiction of the crime.

3. Slaves and apprentices must be returned. *No person held to service or labor in one State, under the laws thereof, escaping into another, shall, in consequence of any law or regulation therein, be discharged from such service or labor, but shall be delivered up on claim of the party to whom such service or labor may be due.*[3]

Section III. New States and Territories

e.g., Maine (1820); see p. 236.

1. Congress may admit new states. New States may be admitted by the Congress into this Union; but no new State shall be formed or erected within the jurisdiction of any other State; nor any State be formed by the junction of two or more States, or parts of States, without the consent of the legislatures of the States concerned as well as of the Congress.[4]

2. Congress regulates federal territory and property. The Congress shall have power to dispose of and make all needful rules and regulations respecting the territory or other property belonging to the United States; and nothing in this Constitution shall be so construed as to prejudice any claims of the United States, or of any particular State.

Section IV. Protection to the States

See Cleveland and the Pullman strike, p. 598.

United States guarantees to states representative government and protection against invasion and rebellion. The United States shall guarantee

---

[1] i.e., punishment only for the offender; none for his or her heirs.

[2] e.g., a marriage in one is valid in all.

[3] Invalidated in 1865 by the Thirteenth Amendment (for text see below).

[4] Loyal West Virginia was formed by Lincoln in 1862 from seceded Virginia. This act was of dubious constitutionality and was justified in part by the wartime powers of the president. See pp. 420–421.

to every State in this Union a republican form of government, and shall protect each of them against invasion; and on application of the legislature, or of the executive [governor] (when the legislature cannot be convened), against domestic violence.

Article V. *The Process of Amendment*

The Constitution may be amended in four ways. The Congress, whenever two-thirds of both houses shall deem it necessary, shall propose amendments to this Constitution, or, on the application of the legislature of two-thirds of the several States, shall call a convention for proposing amendments, which, in either case, shall be valid to all intents and purposes, as part of this Constitution, when ratified by the legislatures of three-fourths of the several States, or by conventions in three-fourths thereof, as the one or the other mode of ratification may be proposed by the Congress; provided *that no amendments which may be made prior to the year one thousand eight hundred and eight shall in any manner affect the first and fourth clauses in the ninth section of the first article;*[1] and that no State, without its consent, shall be deprived of its equal suffrage in the Senate.

Article VI. *General Provisions*

This pledge honored by Hamilton, pp. 184–185.

1. The debts of the Confederation are taken over. All debts contracted and engagements entered into, before the adoption of this Constitution, shall be as valid against the United States under this Constitution, as under the Confederation.

2. The Constitution, federal laws, and treaties are the supreme law of the land. This Constitution, and the laws of the United States which shall be made in pursuance thereof; and all treaties made, or which shall be made, under the authority of the United States, shall be the supreme law of the land; and the judges in every State shall be bound thereby, anything in the Constitution or laws of any State to the contrary notwithstanding.

3. Federal and state officers bound by oath to support the Constitution. The Senators and Representatives before mentioned, and the members of the several State legislatures, and all executive and judicial officers, both of the United States and of the several States, shall be bound by oath or affirmation to support this Constitution; but no religious test shall ever be required as a qualification to any office or public trust under the United States.

Article VII. *Ratification of the Constitution*

See 1787 irregularity, pp. 172–173.

The Constitution effective when ratified by conventions in nine states. The ratification of the conventions of nine States shall be sufficient for the establishment of this Constitution between the States so ratifying the same.

Done in Convention by the unanimous consent of the States present, the seventeenth day of September in the year of our Lord one thousand seven hundred and eighty-seven and of the Independence of the United States of America the twelfth. In witness whereof we have hereunto subscribed our names.

[Signed by]

G° WASHINGTON

Presidt and Deputy from Virginia

[and thirty-eight others]

---

[1]This clause, regarding slave trade and direct taxes, became inoperative in 1808.

AMENDMENTS TO THE CONSTITUTION

Amendment I. *Religious and Political Freedom*

For background of Bill of Rights, see p. 184.

Congress must not interfere with freedom of religion, speech or press, assembly, and petition. Congress shall make no law respecting an establishment of religion,[1] or prohibiting the free exercise thereof; or abridging the freedom of speech, or of the press; or the right of the people peaceably to assemble, and to petition the government for a redress of grievances.

Amendment II. *Right to Bear Arms*

The people may bear arms. A well-regulated militia being necessary to the security of a free State, the right of the people to keep and bear arms [i.e., for military purposes] shall not be infringed.[2]

Amendment III. *Quartering of Troops*

See Declaration of Independence and British quartering above.

Soldiers may not be arbitrarily quartered on the people. No soldier shall, in time of peace, be quartered in any house without the consent of the owner, nor in time of war, but in a manner to be prescribed by law.

Amendment IV. *Searches and Seizures*

A reflection of colonial grievances against the crown.

Unreasonable searches are forbidden. The right of the people to be secure in their persons, houses, papers, and effects, against unreasonable searches and seizures, shall not be violated, and no [search] warrants shall issue but upon probable cause, supported by oath or affirmation, and particularly describing the place to be searched, and the persons or things to be seized.

Amendment V. *Right to Life, Liberty, and Property*

When witnesses refuse to answer questions in court, they routinely "take the Fifth Amendment."

The individual is guaranteed certain rights when on trial and the right to life, liberty, and property. No person shall be held to answer for a capital, or otherwise infamous crime, unless on a presentment [formal charge] or indictment of a grand jury, except in cases arising in the naval forces, or in the militia, when in actual service in time of war or public danger; nor shall any person be subject for the same offense to be twice put in jeopardy of life or limb; nor shall be compelled in any criminal case to be a witness against himself, nor be deprived of life, liberty, or property, without due process of law; nor shall private property be taken for public use [i.e., by eminent domain] without just compensation.

Amendment VI. *Protection in Criminal Trials*

See Declaration of Independence above.

An accused person has important rights. In all criminal prosecutions, the accused shall enjoy the right to a speedy and public trial, by an impartial jury of the State and district wherein the crime shall have been committed, which district shall

---

[1] In 1787 "an establishment of religion" referred to an "established church," or one supported by all taxpayers, whether members or not. But the courts have often acted under this article to keep religion, including prayers, out of the public schools.

[2] The courts long held that the right to bear arms was a limited right linked to the maintenance of militias. But in the case of *District of Columbia v. Heller* in 2008, the Supreme Court defined the right to bear arms as an individual right, not contingent on "participation in some corporate body." Yet the Court still left the door open to some kinds of gun-control legislation.

have been previously ascertained by law, and to be informed of the nature and cause of the accusation; to be confronted with the witnesses against him; to have compulsory process [subpoena] for obtaining witnesses in his favor, and to have the assistance of counsel for his defense.

Amendment VII.   *Suits at Common Law*

The rules of common law are recognized. In suits at common law, where the value in controversy shall exceed twenty dollars, the right of trial by jury shall be preserved, and no fact tried by a jury shall be otherwise re-examined in any court of the United States, than according to the rules of the common law.

Amendment VIII.   *Bail and Punishments*

Excessive fines and unusual punishments are forbidden. Excessive bail shall not be required, nor excessive fines imposed, nor cruel and unusual punishment inflicted.

Amendment IX.   *Concerning Rights Not Enumerated*

The Ninth and Tenth Amendments were bulwarks of southern states' rights before the Civil War.

The people retain rights not here enumerated. The enumeration in the Constitution, of certain rights, shall not be construed to deny or disparage others retained by the people.

Amendment X.   *Powers Reserved to the States and to the People*

A concession to states' rights, p. 185.

Powers not delegated to the federal government are reserved to the states and the people. The powers not delegated to the United States by the Constitution, nor prohibited by it to the States, are reserved to the States respectively, or to the people.

Amendment XI.   *Suits Against a State*

The federal courts have no authority in suits by citizens against a state. The judicial power of the United States shall not be construed to extend to any suit in law or equity, commenced or prosecuted against one of the United States by citizens of another State, or by citizens or subjects of any foreign state. [Adopted 1798.]

Amendment XII.   *Election of President and Vice President*

Forestalls repetition of 1800 electoral dispute, pp. 205–206.

See 1876 disputed election. pp. 493–494.

See 1824 election, pp. 248–250.

1. Changes in manner of electing president and vice president; procedure when no presidential candidate receives electoral majority. The electors shall meet in their respective States, and vote by ballot for President and Vice President, one of whom, at least, shall not be an inhabitant of the same state with themselves; they shall name in their ballots the person voted for as President, and in distinct ballots the person voted for as Vice President, and they shall make distinct lists of all persons voted for as President, and of all persons voted for as Vice President, and of the number of votes for each, which lists they shall sign and certify, and transmit sealed to the seat of government of the United States, directed to the President of the Senate;—the President of the Senate shall, in the presence of the Senate and House of Representatives, open all the certificates and the votes shall be counted;—the person having the greatest number of votes for President shall be the President, if such number be a majority of the whole number of electors appointed; and if no person have such majority, then from the persons having the highest numbers not exceeding three on the list of those voted for as President, the House of

Representatives shall choose immediately, by ballot, the President. But in choosing the President, the votes shall be taken by States, the representation from each State having one vote; a quorum for this purpose shall consist of a member or members from two-thirds of the States, and a majority of all the States shall be necessary to a choice. And if the House of Representatives shall not choose a President whenever the right of choice shall devolve upon them, before *the fourth day of March*[1] next following, then the Vice President shall act as President, as in the case of the death or other constitutional disability of the President.

2. Procedure when no vice presidential candidate receives electoral majority. The person having the greatest number of votes as Vice President, shall be the Vice President, if such number be a majority of the whole number of electors appointed; and if no person have a majority, then from the two highest numbers on the list the Senate shall choose the Vice President; a quorum for the purpose shall consist of two-thirds of the whole number of Senators, and a majority of the whole number shall be necessary to a choice. But no person constitutionally ineligible to the office of President shall be eligible to that of Vice President of the United States. [Adopted 1804.]

Amendment XIII.   *Slavery Prohibited*

For background, see pp. 444–445.

Slavery forbidden. 1. Neither slavery[2] nor involuntary servitude, except as a punishment for crime whereof the party shall have been duly convicted, shall exist within the United States, or any place subject to their jurisdiction.

2. Congress shall have power to enforce this article by appropriate legislation. [Adopted 1865.]

Amendment XIV.   *Civil Rights for Ex-slaves,[3] etc.*

For background, see pp. 473–474.

For corporations as "persons," see p. 525.

Abolishes three-fifths rule for slaves, Art. I., Sec. II, para. 3.

1. Ex-slaves made citizens; U.S. citizenship primary. All persons born or naturalized in the United States, and subject to the jurisdiction thereof, are citizens of the United States and of the State wherein they reside. No State shall make or enforce any law which shall abridge the privileges or immunities of citizens of the United States; nor shall any State deprive any person of life, liberty, or property, without due process of law; nor deny to any person within its jurisdiction the equal protection of the laws.

2. When a state denies citizens the vote, its representation shall be reduced. Representatives shall be apportioned among the several States according to their respective numbers, counting the whole number of persons in each State, excluding Indians not taxed. But when the right to vote at any election for the choice of Electors for President and Vice President of the United States, Representatives in Congress, the executive and judicial officers of a State, or the members of the legislature thereof, is denied to any of the male inhabitants of such State, being twenty-one years of age and citizens of the United States, or in any way abridged, except for participation in rebellion, or other crime, the basis of representation therein shall be reduced in the proportion which the number of such make citizens shall bear to the whole number of male citizens twenty-one years of age in such State.[4]

Leading ex-Confederates denied office. See p. 474.

3. Certain persons who have been in rebellion are ineligible for federal and state office. No person shall be a Senator or Representative in Congress, or Elector of President and Vice President, or hold any office, civil or military, under the

---

[1]Changed to January 20 by the Twentieth Amendment (for text see below).

[2]The only explicit mention of slavery in the Constitution.

[3]Occasionally an offender is prosecuted under the Thirteenth Amendment for keeping an employee or other person under conditions approximating slavery.

[4]The provisions concerning "male" inhabitants were modified by the Nineteenth Amendment, which enfranchised women. The legal voting age was changed from twenty-one to eighteen by the Twenty-sixth Amendment.

United States, or under any State, who, having previously taken an oath, as a member of Congress, or as an officer of the United States, or as a member of any State legislature, or as an executive or judicial officer of any State, to support the Constitution of the United States, shall have engaged in insurrection or rebellion against the same, or given aid or comfort to the enemies thereof. But Congress may, by a vote of two-thirds of each house, remove such disability.

The ex-Confederates were thus forced to repudiate their debts and pay pensions to their own veterans, plus taxes for the pensions of Union veterans, their conquerors.

4. Debts incurred in aid of rebellion are void. The validity of the public debt of the United States, authorizing by law, including debts incurred for payment of pensions and bounties for services in suppressing insurrection or rebellion, shall not be questioned. But neither the United States nor any State shall assume or pay any debt or obligation incurred in aid of insurrection or rebellion against the United States, or any claim for the loss or emancipation of any slave; but all such debts, obligations, and claims shall be held illegal and void.

5. Enforcement. The Congress shall have power to enforce, by appropriate legislation, the provisions of this article. [Adopted 1868.]

Amendment XV. *Suffrage for Blacks*

For background, see p. 476.

Black males are made voters. 1. The right of the citizens of the United States to vote shall not be denied or abridged by the United States or by any State on account of race, color, or previous condition of servitude.

2. The Congress shall have power to enforce this article by appropriate legislation. [Adopted 1870.]

Amendment XVI. *Income Taxes*

For background, see p. 664.

Congress has power to lay and collect income taxes. The Congress shall have power to lay and collect taxes on incomes, from whatever source derived, without apportionment among the several States, and without regard to any census or enumeration. [Adopted 1913.]

Amendment XVII. *Direct Election of Senators*

Senators shall be elected by popular vote. 1. The Senate of the United States shall be composed of two Senators from each State, elected by the people thereof, for six years; and each Senator shall have one vote. The electors in each State shall have the qualifications requisite for electors of [voters for] the most numerous branch of the State legislatures.

2. When vacancies happen in the representation of any State in the Senate, the executive authority of such State shall issue writs of election to fill such vacancies: Provided, that the Legislature of any State may empower the executive thereof to make temporary appointments until the people fill the vacancies by election as the Legislature may direct.

3. This amendment shall not be so construed as to affect the election or term of any Senator chosen before it becomes valid as part of the Constitution. [Adopted 1913.]

Amendment XVIII. *National Prohibition*

For background, see pp. 696–697.

The sale or manufacture of intoxicating liquors is forbidden. 1. *After one year from the ratification of this article the manufacture, sale, or transportation of intoxicating liquors within, the importation thereof into, or the exportation thereof from the United States and all territory subject to the jurisdiction thereof, for beverage purposes, is hereby prohibited.*

2. *The Congress and the several States shall have concurrent power to enforce this article by appropriate legislation.*

3. *This article shall be inoperative unless it shall have been ratified as an amendment to the Constitution by the legislatures of the several States, as provided by the Constitution, within seven years from the date of the submission thereof to the States by the Congress.* [Adopted 1919; repealed 1933 by Twenty-first Amendment.]

Amendment XIX.   *Woman Suffrage*

For background, see pp. 679–680.

Women guaranteed the right to vote. 1. The right of citizens of the United States to vote shall not be denied or abridged by the United States or by any State on account of sex.

2. Congress shall have power to enforce this article by appropriate legislation. [Adopted 1920.]

Amendment XX.   *Presidential and Congressional Terms*

Shortens lame duck periods by modifying Art. I, Sec. IV, para. 2.

1. Presidential, vice presidential, and congressional terms of office begin in January. The terms of the President and Vice President shall end at noon on the 20th day of January, and the terms of Senators and Representatives at noon on the 3d day of January, of the years in which such terms would have ended if this article had not been ratified; and the terms of their successors shall then begin.

2. New meeting date for Congress. The Congress shall assemble at least once in every year, and such meeting shall begin at noon on the 3d day of January, unless they shall by law appoint a different day.

3. Emergency presidential and vice presidential succession. If, at the time fixed for the beginning of the term of the President, the President-elect shall have died, the Vice President–elect shall become President. If a President shall not have been chosen before the time fixed for the beginning of his term, or if the President-elect shall have failed to qualify, then the Vice President–elect shall act as President until a President shall have qualified; and the Congress may by law provide for the case wherein neither a President-elect nor a Vice President–elect shall have qualified, declaring who shall then act as President, or the manner in which one who is to act shall be selected, and such persons shall act accordingly until a President or Vice President shall have qualified.

4. The Congress may by law provide for the case of the death of any of the persons from whom the House of Representatives may choose a President whenever the right of choice shall have devolved upon them, and for the case of the death of any of the persons from whom the Senate may choose a Vice President whenever the right of choice shall have devolved upon them.

5. Sections 1 and 2 shall take effect on the 15th day of October following the ratification of this article.

6. This article shall be inoperative unless it shall have been ratified as an amendment to the Constitution by the Legislatures of three-fourths of the several States within seven years from the date of its submission. [Adopted 1933.]

Amendment XXI.   *Prohibition Repealed*

For background, see p. 753.

1. Eighteenth Amendment repealed. The eighteenth article of amendment to the Constitution of the United States is hereby repealed.

2. Local laws honored. The transportation or importation into any State, Territory, or Possession of the United States for delivery or use therein of intoxicating liquors, in violation of the laws thereof, is hereby prohibited.

3. This article shall be inoperative unless it shall have been ratified as an amendment to the Constitution by conventions in the several States, as provided in the Constitution, within seven years from the date of the submission thereof to the States by the Congress. [Adopted 1933.]

Amendment XXII. Anti–Third Term Amendment

Sometimes referred to as the anti–Franklin Roosevelt amendment.

1. Presidential term is limited. No person shall be elected to the office of President more than twice, and no person who has held the office of President, or acted as President, for more than two years of a term to which some other person was elected President shall be elected to the office of President more than once. But this article shall not apply to any person holding the office of President when this article was proposed by the Congress [i.e., Truman], and shall not prevent any person who may be holding the office of President, during the term within which this article becomes operative [i.e., Truman] from holding the office of President or acting as President during the remainder of such term.

2. This article shall be inoperative unless it shall have been ratified as an amendment to the Constitution by the legislatures of three-fourths of the several States within seven years from the date of its submission to the States by the Congress. [Adopted 1951.]

Amendment XXIII. District of Columbia Vote

Designed to give the District of Columbia three electoral votes and to quiet the century-old cry of "No taxation without representation." Yet the District of Columbia still has only one nonvoting member of Congress.

1. Presidential electors for the District of Columbia. The District, constituting the seat of government of the United States, shall appoint in such manner as the Congress shall direct:

A number of electors of President and Vice President equal to the whole number of Senators and Representatives in Congress to which the District would be entitled if it were a State, but in no event more than the least populous State; they shall be in addition to those appointed by the States, but they shall be considered for the purposes of the election of President and Vice President, to be electors appointed by a State; and they shall meet in the District and perform such duties as provided by the twelfth article of amendment.

2. Enforcement. The Congress shall have the power to enforce this article by appropriate legislation. [Adopted 1961.]

Amendment XXIV. Poll Tax

Designed to end discrimination against poor people, including southern blacks who were often denied the vote through inability to pay poll taxes. See p. 888.

1. Payment of poll tax or other taxes not to be prerequisite for voting in federal elections. The right of citizens of the United States to vote in any primary or other election for President or Vice President, for electors for President or Vice President, or for Senator or Representative in Congress, shall not be denied or abridged by the United States or any State by reason of failure to pay any poll tax or other tax.

2. Enforcement. The Congress shall have the power to enforce this article by appropriate legislation. [Adopted 1964.]

Amendment XXV. Presidential Succession and Disability

1. Vice president to become president. In case of the removal of the President from office or of his death or resignation, the Vice President shall become President.[1]

Gerald Ford was the first "appointed president." See p. 911.

2. Successor to vice president provided. Whenever there is a vacancy in the office of the Vice President, the President shall nominate a Vice President who shall take office upon confirmation by a majority vote of both Houses of Congress.

---

[1]The original Constitution (Art. II, Sec. I, para. 5) was vague on this point, stipulating that "the powers and duties" of the president, but not necessarily the title, should "devolve" on the vice president. President Tyler, the first "accidental president," assumed not only the powers and duties but the title as well.

3. Vice president to serve for disabled president. Whenever the President transmits to the President pro tempore of the Senate and the Speaker of the House of Representatives his written declaration that he is unable to discharge the powers and duties of his office, and until he transmits to them a written declaration to the contrary, such powers and duties shall be discharged by the Vice President as Acting President.

4. Procedure for disqualifying or requalifying president. Whenever the Vice President and a majority of either the principal officers of the executive departments or of such other body as Congress may by law provide, transmit to the President pro tempore of the Senate and the Speaker of the House of Representatives their written declaration that the President is unable to discharge the powers and duties of his office, the Vice President shall immediately assume the powers and duties of the office as Acting President.

Thereafter, when the President transmits to the President pro tempore of the Senate and the Speaker of the House of Representatives his written declaration that no inability exists, he shall resume the powers and duties of his office unless the Vice President and a majority of either the principal officers of the executive department[s] or of such other body as Congress may by law provide, transmit within four days to the President pro tempore of the Senate and the Speaker of the House of Representatives their written declaration that the President is unable to discharge the powers and duties of his office. Thereupon Congress shall decide the issue, assembling within forty-eight hours for that purpose if not in session. If the Congress, within twenty-one days after receipt of the latter written declaration, or, if Congress is not in session, within twenty-one days after Congress is required to assemble, determines by two-thirds vote of both Houses that the President is unable to discharge the powers and duties of his office, the Vice President shall continue to discharge the same as Acting President; otherwise, the President shall resume the powers and duties of his office. [Adopted 1967.]

Amendment XXVI. *Lowering Voting Age*

A response to the current revolt of youth. See p. 901.

1. Ballot for eighteen-year-olds. The right of citizens of the United States, who are eighteen years of age or older, to vote shall not be denied or abridged by the United States or any state on account of age.

2. Enforcement. The Congress shall have the power to enforce this article by appropriate legislation. [Adopted 1971.]

Amendment XXVII. *Restricting Congressional Pay Raises*

Reflects anti-incumbent sentiment of early 1990s. First proposed by James Madison in 1789; took 203 years to be ratified.

Congress not allowed to increase its current pay. No law varying the compensation for the services of the Senators and Representatives shall take effect, until an election of Representatives shall have intervened. [Adopted 1992.]

TABLES

Table A.1 Presidential Elections*

Election	Candidates	Parties	Popular Vote	Electoral Vote
1789	GEORGE WASHINGTON	No party designation		69
	JOHN ADAMS			34
	MINOR CANDIDATES			35
1792	GEORGE WASHINGTON	No party designation		132
	JOHN ADAMS			77
	GEORGE CLINTON			50
	MINOR CANDIDATES			5
1796	JOHN ADAMS	Federalist		71
	THOMAS JEFFERSON	Democratic-Republican		68
	THOMAS PINCKNEY	Federalist		59
	AARON BURR	Democratic-Republican		30
	MINOR CANDIDATES			48
1800	THOMAS JEFFERSON	Democratic-Republican		73
	AARON BURR	Democratic-Republican		73
	JOHN ADAMS	Federalist		65
	CHARLES C. PINCKNEY	Federalist		64
	JOHN JAY	Federalist		1
1804	THOMAS JEFFERSON	Democratic-Republican		162
	CHARLES C. PINCKNEY	Federalist		14
1808	JAMES MADISON	Democratic-Republican		122
	CHARLES C. PINCKNEY	Federalist		47
	GEORGE CLINTON	Democratic-Republican		6
1812	JAMES MADISON	Democratic-Republican		128
	DEWITT CLINTON	Federalist		89
1816	JAMES MONROE	Democratic-Republican		183
	RUFUS KING	Federalist		34
1820	JAMES MONROE	Democratic-Republican		231
	JOHN Q. ADAMS	Independent Republican		1
1824	JOHN Q. ADAMS (Min.)†	Democratic-Republican	108,740	84
	ANDREW JACKSON	Democratic-Republican	153,544	99
	WILLIAM H. CRAWFORD	Democratic-Republican	46,618	41
	HENRY CLAY	Democratic-Republican	47,136	37
1828	ANDREW JACKSON	Democratic	647,286	178
	JOHN Q. ADAMS	National Republican	508,064	83
1832	ANDREW JACKSON	Democratic	687,502	219
	HENRY CLAY	National Republican	530,189	49
	WILLIAM WIRT	Anti-Masonic	33,108	7
	JOHN FLOYD	National Republican		11
1836	MARTIN VAN BUREN	Democratic	765,483	170
	WILLIAM H. HARRISON	Whig		73
	HUGH L. WHITE	Whig	739,795	26
	DANIEL WEBSTER	Whig		14
	W. P. MANGUM	Whig		11

* Candidates receiving less than 1 percent of the popular vote are omitted. Before the Twelfth Amendment (1804), the Electoral College voted for two presidential candidates, and the runner-up became vice president. Basic figures are taken primarily from *Historical Statistics of the United States, Colonial Times to 1970* (1975), pp. 1073–1074, and *Statistical Abstract of the United States,* relevant years.
† "Min." indicates minority president—one receiving less than 50 percent of all popular votes.

Presidential Elections (continued)

Election	Candidates	Parties	Popular Vote	Electoral Vote
1840	WILLIAM H. HARRISON	Whig	1,274,624	234
	MARTIN VAN BUREN	Democratic	1,127,781	60
1844	JAMES K. POLK (Min.)†	Democratic	1,338,464	170
	HENRY CLAY	Whig	1,300,097	105
	JAMES G. BIRNEY	Liberty	62,300	0
1848	ZACHARY TAYLOR	Whig	1,360,967	163
	LEWIS CASS	Democratic	1,222,342	127
	MARTIN VAN BUREN	Free Soil	291,263	0
1852	FRANKLIN PIERCE	Democratic	1,601,117	254
	WINFIELD SCOTT	Whig	1,385,453	42
	JOHN P. HALE	Free Soil	155,825	0
1856	JAMES BUCHANAN (Min.)*	Democratic	1,832,955	174
	JOHN C. FRÉMONT	Republican	1,339,932	114
	MILLARD FILLMORE	American	871,731	8
1860	ABRAHAM LINCOLN (Min.)*	Republican	1,865,593	180
	STEPHEN A. DOUGLAS	Democratic	1,382,713	12
	JOHN C. BRECKINRIDGE	Democratic	848,356	72
	JOHN BELL	Constitutional Union	592,906	39
1864	ABRAHAM LINCOLN	Union	2,206,938	212
	GEORGE B. MC CLELLAN	Democratic	1,803,787	21
1868	ULYSSES S. GRANT	Republican	3,013,421	214
	HORATIO SEYMOUR	Democratic	2,706,829	80
1872	ULYSSES S. GRANT	Republican	3,596,745	286
	HORACE GREELEY	Democratic Liberal Republican	2,843,446	66
1876	RUTHERFORD B. HAYES (Min.)*	Republican	4,036,572	185
	SAMUEL J. TILDEN	Democratic	4,284,020	184
1880	JAMES A. GARFIELD (Min.)*	Republican	4,453,295	214
	WINFIELD S. HANCOCK	Democratic	4,414,082	155
	JAMES B. WEAVER	Greenback-Labor	308,578	0
1884	GROVER CLEVELAND (Min.)*	Democratic	4,879,507	219
	JAMES G. BLAINE	Republican	4,850,293	182
	BENJAMIN F. BUTLER	Greenback-Labor	175,370	0
	JOHN P. ST. JOHN	Prohibition	150,369	0
1888	BENJAMIN HARRISON (Min.)*	Republican	5,447,129	233
	GROVER CLEVELAND	Democratic	5,537,857	168
	CLINTON B. FISK	Prohibition	249,506	0
	ANSON J. STREETER	Union Labor	146,935	0
1892	GROVER CLEVELAND (Min.)*	Democratic	5,555,426	277
	BENJAMIN HARRISON	Republican	5,182,690	145
	JAMES B. WEAVER	People's	1,029,846	22
	JOHN BIDWELL	Prohibition	264,133	0
1896	WILLIAM MC KINLEY	Republican	7,102,246	271
	WILLIAM J. BRYAN	Democratic	6,492,559	176
1900	WILLIAM MC KINLEY	Republican	7,218,491	292
	WILLIAM J. BRYAN	Democratic; Populist	6,356,734	155
	JOHN C. WOOLLEY	Prohibition	208,914	0
1904	THEODORE ROOSEVELT	Republican	7,628,461	336
	ALTON B. PARKER	Democratic	5,084,223	140
	EUGENE V. DEBS	Socialist	402,283	0
	SILAS C. SWALLOW	Prohibition	258,536	0

* "Min." indicates minority president—one receiving less than 50 percent of all popular votes.

Presidential Elections (continued)

Election	Candidates	Parties	Popular Vote	Electoral Vote
1908	WILLIAM H. TAFT	Republican	7,675,320	321
	WILLIAM J. BRYAN	Democratic	6,412,294	162
	EUGENE V. DEBS	Socialist	420,793	0
	EUGENE W. CHAFIN	Prohibition	253,840	0
1912	WOODROW WILSON (Min.)*	Democratic	6,296,547	435
	THEODORE ROOSEVELT	Progressive	4,118,571	88
	WILLIAM H. TAFT	Republican	3,486,720	8
	EUGENE V. DEBS	Socialist	900,672	0
	EUGENE W. CHAFIN	Prohibition	206,275	0
1916	WOODROW WILSON (Min.)*	Democratic	9,127,695	277
	CHARLES E. HUGHES	Republican	8,533,507	254
	A. L. BENSON	Socialist	585,113	0
	J. F. HANLY	Prohibition	220,506	0
1920	WARREN G. HARDING	Republican	16,143,407	404
	JAMES M. COX	Democratic	9,130,328	127
	EUGENE V. DEBS	Socialist	919,799	0
	P. P. CHRISTENSEN	Farmer-Labor	265,411	0
1924	CALVIN COOLIDGE	Republican	15,718,211	382
	JOHN W. DAVIS	Democratic	8,385,283	136
	ROBERT M. LA FOLLETTE	Progressive	4,831,289	13
1928	HERBERT C. HOOVER	Republican	21,391,993	444
	ALFRED E. SMITH	Democratic	15,016,169	87
1932	FRANKLIN D. ROOSEVELT	Democratic	22,809,638	472
	HERBERT C. HOOVER	Republican	15,758,901	59
	NORMAN THOMAS	Socialist	881,951	0
1936	FRANKLIN D. ROOSEVELT	Democratic	27,752,869	523
	ALFRED M. LANDON	Republican	16,674,665	8
	WILLIAM LEMKE	Union	882,479	0
1940	FRANKLIN D. ROOSEVELT	Democratic	27,307,819	449
	WENDELL L. WILLKIE	Republican	22,321,018	82
1944	FRANKLIN D. ROOSEVELT	Democratic	25,606,585	432
	THOMAS E. DEWEY	Republican	22,014,745	99
1948	HARRY S TRUMAN (Min.)*	Democratic	24,179,345	303
	THOMAS E. DEWEY	Republican	21,991,291	189
	J. STROM THURMOND	States' Rights Democratic	1,176,125	39
	HENRY A. WALLACE	Progressive	1,157,326	0
1952	DWIGHT D. EISENHOWER	Republican	33,936,234	442
	ADLAI E. STEVENSON	Democratic	27,314,992	89
1956	DWIGHT D. EISENHOWER	Republican	35,590,472	457
	ADLAI E. STEVENSON	Democratic	26,022,752	73
1960	JOHN F. KENNEDY (Min.)*†	Democratic	34,226,731	303
	RICHARD M. NIXON	Republican	34,108,157	219
1964	LYNDON B. JOHNSON	Democratic	43,129,566	486
	BARRY M. GOLDWATER	Republican	27,178,188	52
1968	RICHARD M. NIXON (Min.)*	Republican	31,785,480	301
	HUBERT H. HUMPHREY, JR.	Democratic	31,275,166	191
	GEORGE C. WALLACE	American Independent	9,906,473	46
1972	RICHARD M. NIXON	Republican	47,169,911	520
	GEORGE S. MC GOVERN	Democratic	29,170,383	17

* "Min." indicates minority president—one receiving less than 50 percent of all popular votes.
† Six Democratic electors in Alabama, all eight unpledged Democratic electors in Mississippi, and one Republican elector in Oklahoma voted for Senator Harry F. Byrd.

Presidential Elections (continued)

Election	Candidates	Parties	Popular Vote	Electoral Vote
1976	JIMMY CARTER	Democratic	40,828,657	297
	GERALD R. FORD	Republican	39,145,520	240
1980	RONALD W. REAGAN	Republican	43,899,248	489
	JIMMY CARTER	Democratic	35,481,435	49
	JOHN B. ANDERSON	Independent	5,719,437	0
1984	RONALD W. REAGAN	Republican	52,609,797	525
	WALTER MONDALE	Democratic	36,450,613	13
1988	GEORGE BUSH	Republican	47,946,422	426
	MICHAEL DUKAKIS	Democratic	41,016,429	111
1992	WILLIAM CLINTON (Min.)*	Democratic	44,909,889	370
	GEORGE BUSH	Republican	39,104,545	168
	H. ROSS PEROT	Independent	19,742,267	0
1996	WILLIAM CLINTON (Min.)*	Democratic	47,401,898	379
	ROBERT DOLE	Republican	39,198,482	159
	H. ROSS PEROT	Reform	7,874,283	0
2000	GEORGE W. BUSH (Min.)*	Republican	50,456,002	271
	ALBERT GORE, JR.	Democratic	50,999,897	266
	RALPH NADER	Green	2,783,728	0
2004	GEORGE W. BUSH	Republican	60,693,281	286
	JOHN KERRY	Democratic	57,355,978	252
	RALPH NADER	Green	405,623	0
2008	BARACK OBAMA	Democratic	65,980,131	364
	JOHN MC CAIN	Republican	57,779,170	174
2012	BARACK OBAMA	Democratic	69,915,796	332
	MITT ROMNEY	Republican	60,933,500	206

* "Min." indicates minority president—one receiving less than 50 percent of all popular votes.

Table A.2 Presidents and Vice Presidents

Term	President	Vice President
1789–1793	George Washington	John Adams
1793–1797	George Washington	John Adams
1797–1801	John Adams	Thomas Jefferson
1801–1805	Thomas Jefferson	Aaron Burr
1805–1809	Thomas Jefferson	George Clinton
1809–1813	James Madison	George Clinton (d. 1812)
1813–1817	James Madison	Elbridge Gerry (d. 1814)
1817–1821	James Monroe	Daniel D. Tompkins
1821–1825	James Monroe	Daniel D. Tompkins
1825–1829	John Quincy Adams	John C. Calhoun
1829–1833	Andrew Jackson	John C. Calhoun (resigned 1832)
1833–1837	Andrew Jackson	Martin Van Buren
1837–1841	Martin Van Buren	Richard M. Johnson
1841–1845	William H. Harrison (d. 1841) John Tyler	John Tyler
1845–1849	James K. Polk	George M. Dallas
1849–1853	Zachary Taylor (d. 1850) Millard Fillmore	Millard Fillmore
1853–1857	Franklin Pierce	William R. D. King (d. 1853)

Table A.2 Presidents and Vice Presidents (continued)

Term	President	Vice President
1857–1861	James Buchanan	John C. Breckinridge
1861–1865	Abraham Lincoln	Hannibal Hamlin
1865–1869	Abraham Lincoln (d. 1865) Andrew Johnson	Andrew Johnson
1869–1873	Ulysses S. Grant	Schuyler Colfax
1873–1877	Ulysses S. Grant	Henry Wilson (d. 1875)
1877–1881	Rutherford B. Hayes	William A. Wheeler
1881–1885	James A. Garfield (d. 1881) Chester A. Arthur	Chester A. Arthur
1885–1889	Grover Cleveland	Thomas A. Hendricks (d. 1885)
1889–1893	Benjamin Harrison	Levi P. Morton
1893–1897	Grover Cleveland	Adlai E. Stevenson
1897–1901	William McKinley	Garret A. Hobart (d. 1899)
1901–1905	William McKinley (d. 1901) Theodore Roosevelt	Theodore Roosevelt
1905–1909	Theodore Roosevelt	Charles W. Fairbanks
1909–1913	William H. Taft	James S. Sherman (d. 1912)
1913–1917	Woodrow Wilson	Thomas R. Marshall
1917–1921	Woodrow Wilson	Thomas R. Marshall
1921–1925	Warren G. Harding (d. 1923) Calvin Coolidge	Calvin Coolidge
1925–1929	Calvin Coolidge	Charles G. Dawes
1929–1933	Herbert Hoover	Charles Curtis
1933–1937	Franklin D. Roosevelt	John N. Garner
1937–1941	Franklin D. Roosevelt	John N. Garner
1941–1945	Franklin D. Roosevelt	Henry A. Wallace
1945–1949	Franklin D. Roosevelt (d. 1945) Harry S Truman	Harry S Truman
1949–1953	Harry S Truman	Alben W. Barkley
1953–1957	Dwight D. Eisenhower	Richard M. Nixon
1957–1961	Dwight D. Eisenhower	Richard M. Nixon
1961–1965	John F. Kennedy (d. 1963) Lyndon B. Johnson	Lyndon B. Johnson
1965–1969	Lyndon B. Johnson	Hubert H. Humphrey, Jr.
1969–1974	Richard M. Nixon	Spiro T. Agnew (resigned 1973); Gerald R. Ford
1974–1977	Gerald R. Ford	Nelson A. Rockefeller
1977–1981	Jimmy Carter	Walter F. Mondale
1981–1985	Ronald Reagan	George Bush
1985–1989	Ronald Reagan	George Bush
1989–1993	George Bush	J. Danforth Quayle III
1993–1997	William Clinton	Albert Gore, Jr.
1997–2001	William Clinton	Albert Gore, Jr.
2001–2005	George W. Bush	Richard Cheney
2005–2009	George W. Bush	Richard Cheney
2009–	Barack Obama	Joseph Biden

Table A.3 Admission of States   (See Table 9.3 on p. 193 for order in which the original thirteen entered the Union.)

Order of Admission	State	Date of Admission	Order of Admission	State	Date of Admission
14	Vermont	Mar. 4, 1791	33	Oregon	Feb. 14, 1859
15	Kentucky	June 1, 1792	34	Kansas	Jan. 29, 1861
16	Tennessee	June 1, 1796	35	W. Virginia	June 20, 1863
17	Ohio	Mar. 1, 1803	36	Nevada	Oct. 31, 1864
18	Louisiana	April 30, 1812	37	Nebraska	Mar. 1, 1867
19	Indiana	Dec. 11, 1816	38	Colorado	Aug. 1, 1876
20	Mississippi	Dec. 10, 1817	39	N. Dakota	Nov. 2, 1889
21	Illinois	Dec. 3, 1818	40	S. Dakota	Nov. 2, 1889
22	Alabama	Dec. 14, 1819	41	Montana	Nov. 8, 1889
23	Maine	Mar. 15, 1820	42	Washington	Nov. 11, 1889
24	Missouri	Aug. 10, 1821	43	Idaho	July 3, 1890
25	Arkansas	June 15, 1836	44	Wyoming	July 10, 1890
26	Michigan	Jan. 26, 1837	45	Utah	Jan. 4, 1896
27	Florida	Mar. 3, 1845	46	Oklahoma	Nov. 16, 1907
28	Texas	Dec. 29, 1845	47	New Mexico	Jan. 6, 1912
29	Iowa	Dec. 28, 1846	48	Arizona	Feb. 14, 1912
30	Wisconsin	May 29, 1848	49	Alaska	Jan. 3, 1959
31	California	Sept. 9, 1850	50	Hawaii	Aug. 21, 1959
32	Minnesota	May 11, 1858			

Table A.4 Estimates of Total Costs and Number of Battle Deaths of Major U.S. Wars[1]

War	Total Costs[2] (millions of dollars)	Original Costs (millions of dollars)	Number of Battle Deaths
Iraq War (2003–2011)	N/A	$806,000[3]	3,528[4]
Afghan War (2001–)	N/A	$444,000[5]	1,817[6]
Vietnam Conflict	$352,000	140,600	47,355[7]
Korean Conflict	164,000	54,000	33,629
World War II	664,000	288,000	291,557
World War I	112,000	26,000	53,402
Spanish-American War	6,460	400	385
Civil War { Union only	12,952	3,200	140,414
Civil War { Confederacy (est.)	N.A.	1,000	94,000
Mexican War	147	73	1,733
War of 1812	158	93	2,260
American Revolution	190	100	6,824

[1]Deaths from disease and other causes are not shown. In earlier wars especially, owing to poor medical and sanitary practices, nonbattle deaths substantially exceeded combat casualties.

[2]The difference between total costs and original costs is attributable to continuing postwar payments for items such as veterans' benefits, interest on war debts, and so on.

[3]Through 2011

[4]Through May 9, 2014 for Killed in Action; excludes "non-hostile" deaths for Operation Iraqi Freedom and Operation New Dawn

[5]Through 2011

[6]Through May 9, 2014 for Killed in Action; excludes "non-hostile" deaths for Operation Enduring Freedom

[7]1957–1990

(Sources: *Historical Statistics of the United States, Statistical Abstract of the United States,* relevant years, *The World Almanac and Book of Facts, 1986, Congressional Research Service,* Department of Defense, and Congressional Research Service Reports.)

GLOSSARY OF KEY TERMS

"10 percent" Reconstruction plan (1863): Introduced by President Lincoln, it proposed that a state be readmitted to the Union once 10 percent of its voters had pledged loyalty to the United States and promised to honor emancipation. (470)

Acadians: French residents of Nova Scotia, many of whom were uprooted by the British in 1755 and scattered as far south as Louisiana, where their descendants became known as "Cajuns." (107)

Acoma, Battle of (1599): Fought between Spaniards under Don Juan de Oñate and the Pueblo Indians in present-day New Mexico. Spaniards brutally crushed the Pueblo peoples and established the territory as New Mexico in 1609. (21)

Act of Toleration (1649): Passed in Maryland, it guaranteed toleration to all Christians but decreed the death penalty for those, like Jews and atheists, who denied the divinity of Jesus Christ. Ensured that Maryland would continue to attract a high proportion of Catholic migrants throughout the colonial period. (33)

admiralty courts: Used to try offenders for violating the various Navigation Acts passed by the crown after the French and Indian War. Colonists argued that the courts encroached on their rights as Englishmen because they lacked juries and placed the burden of proof on the accused. (120)

***The Age of Reason* (1794):** Thomas Paine's anticlerical treatise that accused churches of seeking to acquire "power and profit" and to "enslave mankind." (309)

***Alabama* (1862–1864):** British-built and manned Confederate warship that raided Union shipping during the Civil War. One of many built by the British for the Confederacy, despite Union protests. (430)

Alamo: Fortress in Texas where two hundred American volunteers were slain by Santa Anna in 1836. "Remember the Alamo" became a battle cry in support of Texan independence. (268)

Albany Congress (1754): Intercolonial congress summoned by the British government to foster greater colonial unity and assure Iroquois support in the escalating war against the French. (109)

Alien Laws (1798): Acts passed by a Federalist Congress raising the residency requirement for citizenship to fourteen years and granting the president the power to deport dangerous foreigners in times of peace. (198)

American Anti-Slavery Society (1833–1870): Abolitionist society founded by William Lloyd Garrison, who advocated the immediate abolition of slavery. By 1838, the organization had more than 250,000 members across 1,350 chapters. (353)

American Colonization Society: Reflecting the focus of early abolitionists on transporting freed blacks back to Africa, the organization established Liberia, a West African settlement intended as a haven for emancipated slaves. (351)

"The American Scholar" (1837): Ralph Waldo Emerson's address at Harvard College, in which he declared an intellectual independence from Europe, urging American scholars to develop their own traditions. (330)

American System (1820s): Henry Clay's three-pronged system to promote American industry. Clay advocated a strong banking system, a protective tariff, and a federally funded transportation network. (233)

American Temperance Society: Founded in Boston in 1826 as part of a growing effort of nineteenth-century reformers to limit alcohol consumption. (318)

***Amistad* (1839):** Spanish slave ship dramatically seized off the coast of Cuba by the enslaved Africans aboard. The ship was driven ashore in Long Island and the slaves were put on trial. Former president John Quincy Adams argued their case before the Supreme Court, securing their eventual release. (350)

Ancient Order of Hibernians (mid-nineteenth century): Irish semisecret society that served as a benevolent organization for downtrodden Irish immigrants in the United States. (283)

Anglo-American Convention (1818): Signed by Britain and the United States, the pact allowed New England fishermen access to Newfoundland fisheries, established the northern border of Louisiana Territory, and provided for the joint occupation of the Oregon Country for ten years. (241)

Antietam, Battle of (September 1862): Landmark battle in the Civil War that essentially ended in a draw but demonstrated the prowess of the Union army, forestalling foreign intervention and giving Lincoln the "victory" he needed to issue the Emancipation Proclamation. (443)

antifederalists: Opponents of the 1787 Constitution, they cast the document as antidemocratic, objected to the subordination of the states to the central government, and feared encroachment on individuals' liberties in the absence of a bill of rights. (173)

Anti-Masonic party (established ca. 1826): First founded in New York, it gained considerable influence in New England and the mid-Atlantic during the 1832 election, campaigning against the politically influential Masonic order, a secret society. Anti-Masons opposed Andrew Jackson, a Mason, and drew much of their support from evangelical Protestants. (262)

antinomianism: Belief that the elect need not obey the law of either God or man; most notably espoused in the colonies by Anne Hutchinson. (46)

***Appeal to the Colored Citizens of the World* (1829):** Incendiary abolitionist tract advocating the violent overthrow of slavery. Published by David Walker, a southern-born free black. (353)

Appomattox Courthouse: Site where Robert E. Lee surrendered to Ulysses S. Grant in April 1865 after almost a year of brutal fighting throughout Virginia in the "Wilderness Campaign." (457)

Armed Neutrality (1780): Loose alliance of nonbelligerent naval powers, organized by Russia's Catherine the Great, to protect neutral trading rights during the war for American independence. (149)

Arminianism: Belief that salvation is offered to all humans but is conditional on acceptance of God's grace. Different from Calvinism, which emphasizes predestination and unconditional election. (90)

Aroostook War (began 1839): Series of clashes between American and Canadian lumberjacks in the disputed territory of northern Maine, resolved when a permanent boundary was agreed upon in 1842. (366)

Articles of Confederation (1781): First American constitution that established the United States as a loose confederation of states under a weak national Congress, which was not granted the power to regulate commerce or collect taxes. The Articles were replaced by a more efficient Constitution in 1789. (163)

The Association (1774): Nonimportation agreement crafted during the First Continental Congress calling for the complete boycott of British goods. (127)

assumption: Transfer of debt from one party to another. In order to strengthen the union, the federal government assumed states' Revolutionary War debts in 1790, thereby tying the interests of wealthy lenders with those of the national government. (185)

***Awful Disclosures* (1836):** Maria Monk's sensational exposé of alleged horrors in Catholic convents. Its popularity reflected nativist fears of Catholic influence. (286)

Aztecs: Native American empire that controlled present-day Mexico until 1521, when they were conquered by Spanish Hernán Cortés. The Aztecs maintained control over their vast empire through a system of trade and tribute. They came to be known for their advances in mathematics and writing and their use of human sacrifices in religious ceremonies. (6)

Bacon's Rebellion (1676): Uprising of Virginia backcountry farmers and indentured servants led by planter Nathaniel Bacon; initially a response to Governor William Berkeley's refusal to protect backcountry settlers from Indian attacks, the rebellion eventually grew into a broader conflict between impoverished settlers and the planter elite. (64)

Bank of the United States (1791): Chartered by Congress as part of Alexander Hamilton's financial program, the bank printed paper money and served as a depository for Treasury funds. It drew opposition from Jeffersonian Republicans, who argued that the bank was unconstitutional. (187)

Bank War (1832): Battle between President Andrew Jackson and congressional supporters of the Bank of the United States over the bank's renewal. Jackson vetoed the bank bill, arguing that the bank favored moneyed interests at the expense of western farmers. (261)

Barbados slave code (1661): First formal statute governing the treatment of slaves, which provided for harsh punishments against offending slaves but lacked penalties for the mistreatment of slaves by masters. Similar statutes were adopted by southern plantation societies on the North American mainland in the seventeenth and eighteenth centuries. (35)

Bill of Rights (1791): Popular term for the first ten amendments to the U.S. Constitution. The amendments secure key rights for individuals and reserve to the states all powers not explicitly delegated or prohibited by the Constitution. (184)

black belt: Region of the Deep South with the highest concentration of slaves. The "black belt" emerged in the nineteenth century as cotton production became more profitable and slavery expanded south and west. (349)

Black Codes (1865–1866): Laws passed throughout the South to restrict the rights of emancipated blacks, particularly with respect to negotiating labor contracts. Increased Northerners' criticisms of President Andrew Johnson's lenient Reconstruction policies. (471)

Black Hawk War (1832): Series of clashes in Illinois and Wisconsin between American forces and Indian chief Black Hawk of the Sauk and Fox tribes, who unsuccessfully tried to reclaim territory lost under the 1830 Indian Removal Act. (260)

Black Legend: False notion that Spanish conquerors did little but butcher the Indians and steal their gold in the name of Christ. (22)

Bleeding Kansas (1856–1861): Civil war in Kansas over the issue of slavery in the territory, fought intermittently until 1861, when it merged with the wider national Civil War. (403)

blue laws: Also known as sumptuary laws, they are designed to restrict personal behavior in accord with a strict code of morality. Blue laws were passed across the colonies, particularly in Puritan New England and Quaker Pennsylvania. (56)

Border States: Five slave states—Missouri, Kentucky, Maryland, Delaware, and West Virginia—that did not secede during the Civil War. To keep the states in the Union, Abraham Lincoln insisted that the war was not about abolishing slavery but rather protecting the Union. (423)

Boston Massacre (1770): Clash between unruly Bostonian protestors and locally stationed British redcoats, who fired on the jeering crowd, killing or wounding eleven citizens. (123)

Boston Tea Party (1773): Rowdy protest against the British East India Company's newly acquired monopoly on the tea trade. Colonists, disguised as Indians, dumped 342 chests of tea into Boston harbor, prompting harsh sanctions from the British Parliament. (125)

breakers: Slave drivers who employed the lash to brutally "break" the souls of strong-willed slaves. (349)

Brook Farm (1841–1846): Transcendentalist commune founded by a group of intellectuals, who emphasized living plainly while pursuing the life of the mind. The community fell into debt and dissolved when their communal home burned to the ground in 1846. (322)

Buena Vista, Battle of (1847): Key American victory against Mexican forces in the Mexican War. Elevated General Zachary Taylor to national prominence and helped secure his success in the 1848 presidential election. (374)

buffer: In politics, a territory between two antagonistic powers, intended to minimize the possibility of conflict between them. In British North America, Georgia was established as a buffer colony between British and Spanish territory. (37)

Bull Run (Manassas Junction), Battle of (July 1861): First major battle of the Civil War and a victory for the South, it dispelled Northern illusions of swift victory. (438)

Bunker Hill, Battle of (June 1775): Fought on the outskirts of Boston, on Breed's Hill, the battle ended in the colonial militia's retreat, though at a heavy cost to the British. (136)

Burned-Over District: Popular name for western New York, a region particularly swept up in the religious fervor of the Second Great Awakening. (311)

Cahokia (ca. 1100 c.e.): Mississippian settlement near present-day East St. Louis, home to as many as twenty-five thousand Native Americans. (8)

California Bear Flag Republic (1846): Short-lived California republic, established by local American settlers who revolted against Mexico. Once news of the war with Mexico reached the Americans, they abandoned the Republic in favor of joining the United States. (374)

California gold rush (beginning in 1849): Inflow of thousands of miners to northern California after news reports of the discovery of gold at Sutter's Mill in January of 1848 had spread around the world by the end of that year. The onslaught of migrants prompted Californians to organize a government and apply for statehood in 1849. (383)

Calvinism: Dominant theological credo of the New England Puritans based on the teachings of John Calvin. Calvinists believed in predestination—that only "the elect" were destined for salvation. (42)

camp followers: Women and children who followed the Continental Army during the American Revolution, providing vital services such as cooking and sewing in return for rations. (132)

Canadian Shield: First part of the North American landmass to emerge above sea level. (4)

capitalism: Economic system characterized by private property, generally free trade, and open and accessible markets. European colonization of the Americas, and in particular, the discovery of vast bullion deposits, helped bring about Europe's transition to capitalism. (18)

caravel: Small regular vessel with a high deck and three triangular sails. Caravels could sail more closely into the wind, allowing European sailors to explore the western shores of Africa, previously made inaccessible due to prevailing winds on the homeward journey. (12)

***Caroline* (1837):** Diplomatic row between the United States and Britain. Developed after British troops set fire to an American steamer carrying supplies across the Niagara River to Canadian insurgents, during Canada's short-lived insurrection. (365)

carpetbaggers: Pejorative used by Southern whites to describe Northern businessmen and politicians who came to the South after the Civil War to work on Reconstruction projects or invest in Southern infrastructure. (479)

charter: Legal document granted by a government to some group or agency to implement a stated purpose and spelling out the attending rights and obligations. British colonial charters guaranteed inhabitants all the rights of Englishmen, which helped solidify colonists' ties to Britain during the early years of settlement. (28)

***Chesapeake* affair (1807):** Conflict between Britain and the United States that precipitated the 1807 embargo. The conflict developed when a British ship, in search of deserters, fired on the American *Chesapeake* off the coast of Virginia. (218)

civic virtue: Willingness on the part of citizens to sacrifice personal self-interest for the public good. Deemed a necessary component of a successful republic. (179)

civil law: Body of written law enacted through legislative statutes or constitutional provisions. In countries where civil law prevails, judges must apply the statutes precisely as written. (171)

Civil Rights Bill (1866): Passed over Andrew Johnson's veto, the bill aimed to counteract the Black Codes by conferring citizenship on African Americans and making it a crime to deprive blacks of their rights to sue, testify in court, or hold property. (473)

Clayton-Bulwer Treaty (1850): Signed by Great Britain and the United States, it provided that the two nations would jointly protect the neutrality of Central America and that neither power would seek to fortify or exclusively control any future isthmian waterway. Later revoked by the Hay-Pauncefote Treaty of 1901, which gave the United States control of the Panama Canal. (392)

clipper ships (1840s–1850s): Small, swift vessels that gave American shippers an advantage in the carrying trade. Clipper ships were made largely obsolete by the advent of sturdier, roomier iron steamers on the eve of the Civil War. (301)

***Cohens* v. *Virginia* (1821):** Case that reinforced federal supremacy by establishing the right of the Supreme Court to review decisions of state supreme courts in questions involving the powers of the federal government. (240)

Columbian exchange: The transfer of goods, crops, and diseases between New and Old World societies after 1492. (14)

committees of correspondence (1772 and after): Local committees established across Massachusetts, and later in each of the thirteen colonies, to maintain colonial opposition to British policies through the exchange of letters and pamphlets. (124)

common law: Laws that originate from court rulings and customs, as opposed to legislative statutes. The United States Constitution grew out of the Anglo-American common law tradition and thus provided only a general organizational framework for the new federal government. (171)

***Common Sense* (1776):** Thomas Paine's pamphlet urging the colonies to declare independence and establish a republican government. The widely read pamphlet helped convince colonists to support the Revolution. (138)

***Commonwealth* v. *Hunt* (1842):** Massachusetts Supreme Court decision that strengthened the labor movement by upholding the legality of unions. (293)

Compromise of 1850: Admitted California as a free state, opened New Mexico and Utah to popular sovereignty, ended the slave trade (but not slavery itself) in Washington, D.C., and introduced a more stringent fugitive slave law. Widely opposed in both the North and South, it did little to settle the escalating dispute over slavery. (387)

compromise Tariff of 1833: Passed as a measure to resolve the Nullification Crisis, it provided that tariffs be lowered gradually, over a period of ten years, to 1816 levels. (258)

Confederate States of America (1861–1865): Government established after seven southern states seceded from the Union. Later joined by four more states from the upper South. (416)

Congregational Church: Self-governing Puritan congregations without the hierarchical establishment of the Anglican Church. (72)

Congress of Vienna (1814–1815): Convention of major European powers to redraw the boundaries of continental Europe after the defeat of Napoleonic France. (229)

Congressional Committee on the Conduct of the War (1861–1865): Established by Congress during the Civil War to oversee military affairs. Largely under the control of radical Republicans, the committee agitated for a more vigorous war effort and actively pressed Lincoln on the issue of emancipation. (453)

***conquistadores*:** Sixteenth-century Spaniards who fanned out across the Americas, from Colorado to Argentina, eventually conquering the Aztec and Incan empires. (20)

Conscience Whigs (1840s and 1850s): Northern Whigs who opposed slavery on moral grounds. Conscience Whigs sought to prevent the annexation of Texas as a slave state, fearing that the new slave territory would only serve to buttress the southern "slave power." (375)

Constitutional Union party (1860): Formed by moderate Whigs and Know-Nothings in an effort to elect a compromise candidate and avert a sectional crisis. (412)

Convention of 1800: Agreement to formally dissolve the United States' treaty with France, originally signed during the Revolutionary War. The difficulties posed by America's peacetime alliance with France contributed to Americans' long-standing opposition to entangling alliances with foreign powers. (198)

conversion: Intense religious experience that confirmed an individual's place among the "elect," or the "visible saints." Calvinists who experienced conversion were then expected to lead sanctified lives to demonstrate their salvation. (42)

Copperheads: Northern Democrats who obstructed the war effort by attacking Abraham Lincoln, the draft, and, after 1863, emancipation. (453)

Corps of Discovery (1804–1806): Team of adventurers, led by Meriwether Lewis and William Clark, sent by Thomas Jefferson to explore Louisiana Territory and find a water route to the Pacific. Louis and Clark brought back detailed accounts of the West's flora, fauna, and native populations, and their voyage demonstrated the viability of overland travel to the West. (215)

corrupt bargain: Alleged deal between presidential candidates John Quincy Adams and Henry Clay to throw the election, to be decided by the House of Representatives, in Adams's favor. Though never proven, the accusation became the rallying cry for supporters of Andrew Jackson, who had actually garnered a plurality of the popular vote in 1824. (248)

cotton gin (1793): Eli Whitney's invention that sped up the process of harvesting cotton. The gin made cotton cultivation more profitable, revitalizing the southern economy and increasing the importance of slavery in the South. (287)

coureurs de bois: Translated as "runners of the woods," they were French fur-trappers, also known as "voyageurs" (travelers), who established trading posts throughout North America. The fur trade wreaked havoc on the health and folkways of their Native American trading partners. (102)

***Creole* (1841):** American ship captured by a group of rebelling Virginia slaves. The slaves successfully sought asylum in the Bahamas, raising fears among southern planters that the British West Indies would become a safe haven for runaway slaves. (365)

Crittenden amendments (1860): Failed constitutional amendments that would have given federal protection for slavery in all territories south of 36°30' where slavery was supported by popular sovereignty. Proposed in an attempt to appease the South. (416)

cult of domesticity: Pervasive nineteenth-century cultural creed that venerated the domestic role of women. It gave married women greater authority to shape home life but limited opportunities outside the domestic sphere. (295)

***Dartmouth College* v. *Woodward* (1819):** Supreme Court case that sustained Dartmouth University's original charter against changes proposed by the New Hampshire state legislature, thereby protecting corporations from domination by state governments. (240)

Daughters of Liberty: Patriotic groups that played a central role in agitating against the Stamp Act and enforcing nonimportation agreements. (See also Sons of Liberty) (121)

Declaration of Independence (July 4, 1776): Formal pronouncement of independence drafted by Thomas Jefferson and approved by Congress. The Declaration allowed Americans to appeal for foreign aid and served as an inspiration for later revolutionary movements worldwide. (140)

Declaration of the Rights of Man (1789): Declaration of rights adopted during the French Revolution. Modeled after the American Declaration of Independence. (141)

Declaratory Act (1766): Passed alongside the repeal of the Stamp Act, it reaffirmed Parliament's unqualified sovereignty over the North American colonies. (122)

Deism: Eighteenth-century religious doctrine that emphasized reasoned moral behavior and the scientific pursuit of knowledge. Most Deists rejected biblical inerrancy and the divinity of Christ, but they did believe that a Supreme Being created the universe. (309)

disestablish: To separate an official state church from its connection with the government. Following the Revolution, all states disestablished the Anglican Church, though some New England states maintained established Congregational Churches well into the nineteenth century. (178)

Dominion of Canada (established 1867): Unified Canadian government created by Britain to bolster Canadians against potential attacks or overtures from the United States. (431)

Dominion of New England (1686–1689): Administrative union created by royal authority, incorporating all of New England, New York, and East and West Jersey. Placed under the rule of Sir Edmund Andros, who curbed popular assemblies, taxed residents without their consent, and strictly enforced Navigation Laws. Its collapse after the Glorious Revolution in England demonstrated colonial opposition to strict royal control. (50)

Dred Scott v. Stanford (1857): Supreme Court decision that extended federal protection to slavery by ruling that Congress did not have the power to prohibit slavery in any territory. Also declared that slaves, as property, were not citizens of the United States. (406)

ecological imperialism: Historians' term for the spoliation of western natural resources through excessive hunting, logging, mining, and grazing. (279)

Edict of Nantes (1598): Decree issued by the French crown granting limited toleration to French Protestants. Ended religious wars in France and inaugurated a period of French preeminence in Europe and across the Atlantic. Its repeal in 1685 prompted a fresh migration of Protestant Huguenots to North America. (101)

Emancipation Proclamation (1863): Declared all slaves in rebelling states to be free but did not affect slavery in nonrebelling Border States. The proclamation closed the door on possible compromise with the South and encouraged thousands of Southern slaves to flee to Union lines. (443)

Embargo Act (1807): Enacted in response to British and French mistreatment of American merchants, the act banned the export of all goods from the United States to any foreign port. The embargo placed great strains on the American economy, while only marginally affecting its European targets, and was therefore repealed in 1809. (218)

encomienda: Spanish government's policy to "commend," or give, Indians to certain colonists in return for the promise to Christianize them. Part of a broader Spanish effort to subdue Indian tribes in the West Indies and on the North American mainland. (16)

English Civil War (1642–1651): Armed conflict between royalists and parliamentarians, resulting in the victory of pro-Parliament forces and the execution of Charles I. (49)

Era of Good Feelings (1816–1824): Popular name for the period of one-party, Republican, rule during James Monroe's presidency. The term obscures bitter conflicts over internal improvements, slavery, and the national bank. (234)

Erie Canal (completed 1825): New York State canal that linked Lake Erie to the Hudson River. It dramatically lowered shipping costs, fueling an economic boom in upstate New York and increasing the profitability of farming in the Old Northwest. (299)

Ex parte Milligan (1866): Civil War–era case in which the Supreme Court ruled that military tribunals could not be used to try civilians if civil courts were open. (476)

excise tax: Tax on goods produced domestically. Excise taxes, particularly the 1791 tax on whiskey, were a highly controversial component of Alexander Hamilton's financial program. (186)

factory girls: Young women employed in the growing factories of the early nineteenth century, they labored long hours in difficult conditions, living in socially new conditions away from farms and families. (295)

Fallen Timbers, Battle of (1794): Decisive battle between the Miami Confederacy and the U.S. Army. British forces refused to shelter the routed Indians, forcing the latter to attain a peace settlement with the United States. (193)

Farewell Address (1796): George Washington's address at the end of his presidency, warning against "permanent alliances" with other nations. Washington did not oppose all alliances, but believed that the young, fledgling nation should forge alliances only on a temporary basis, in extraordinary circumstances. (195)

Federal Style: Early national style of architecture that borrowed from neoclassical models and emphasized symmetry, balance, and restraint. Famous builders associated with this style included Charles Bulfinch and Benjamin Latrobe. (326)

The Federalist (1788): Collection of essays written by John Jay, James Madison, and Alexander Hamilton and published during the ratification debate in New York to lay out the federalists' arguments in favor of the new Constitution. Since their publication, these influential essays have served as an important source for constitutional interpretation. (176)

federalists: Proponents of the 1787 Constitution, they favored a strong national government, arguing that the checks and balances in the new Constitution would safeguard the people's liberties. (174)

Fifteenth Amendment (ratified 1870): Prohibited states from denying citizens the franchise on account of race. It disappointed feminists, who wanted the amendment to include guarantees for women's suffrage. (476)

"Fifty-four forty or fight" (1846): Slogan adopted by mid-nineteenth-century expansionists who advocated the occupation of Oregon Territory, jointly held by Britain and the United States. Though President Polk had pledged to seize all of Oregon, to 54° 40', he settled on the forty-ninth parallel as a compromise with the British. (369)

First Anglo-Powhatan War (1610–1614): Series of clashes between the Powhatan Confederacy and English settlers in Virginia. English colonists torched and pillaged

Indian villages, applying tactics used in England's campaigns against the Irish. (30)

First Continental Congress (1774): Convention of delegates from twelve of the thirteen colonies that convened in Philadelphia to craft a response to the Intolerable Acts. Delegates established The Association, which called for a complete boycott of British goods. (126)

Fletcher v. Peck (1810): Established firmer protection for private property and asserted the right of the Supreme Court to invalidate state laws in conflict with the federal Constitution. (240)

Florida Purchase Treaty (Adams-Onís Treaty) (1819): Under the agreement, Spain ceded Florida to the United States, and the two nations agreed on the southwestern boundary of the Louisiana Purchase. Spain retained the territory from Texas to California while abandoning its claims to the Oregon country. (242)

Force Acts (1870–1871): Passed by Congress following a wave of Ku Klux Klan violence, the acts banned clan membership, prohibited the use of intimidation to prevent blacks from voting, and gave the U.S. military the authority to enforce the acts. (480)

Force Bill (1833): Passed by Congress alongside the compromise Tariff of 1833, it authorized the president to use the military to collect federal tariff duties. (258)

Fort Henry and Fort Donelson, Battle of (February 1862): Key victory for Union general Ulysses S. Grant, it secured the North's hold on Kentucky and paved the way for Grant's attacks deeper into Tennessee. (451)

Fort Stanwix, Treaty of (1784): Treaty signed by the United States and the pro-British Iroquois granting Ohio Country to the Americans. (152)

Fort Sumter: South Carolina location where Confederate forces fired the first shots of the Civil War in April of 1861, after Union forces attempted to provision the fort. (422)

Fourteenth Amendment (ratified 1868): Constitutional amendment that extended civil rights to freedmen and prohibited states from taking away such rights without due process. (473)

Fredericksburg, Battle of (December 1862): Decisive victory in Virginia for Confederate Robert E. Lee, who successfully repelled a Union attack on his lines. (448)

Free Soil party (1848–1854): Antislavery party in the 1848 and 1852 elections that opposed the extension of slavery into the territories, arguing that the presence of slavery would limit opportunities for free laborers. (382)

Freedmen's Bureau (1865–1872): Created to aid newly emancipated slaves by providing food, clothing, medical care, education, and legal support. Its achievements were uneven and depended largely on the quality of local administrators. (469)

Freeport Doctrine (1858): Declared that since slavery could not exist without laws to protect it, territorial legislatures, not the Supreme Court, would have the final say on the slavery question. First argued by Stephen Douglas in 1858 in response to Abraham Lincoln's "Freeport question." (409)

Freeport question (1858): Raised during one of the Lincoln-Douglas debates by Abraham Lincoln, who asked whether the Court or the people should decide the future of slavery in the territories. (409)

French and Indian War (Seven Years' War) (1756–1763): Nine-year war between the British and the French in North America. It resulted in the expulsion of the French from the North American mainland and helped spark the Seven Years' War in Europe. (107)

Fugitive Slave Law (1850): Passed as part of the Compromise of 1850, it set high penalties for anyone who aided escaped slaves and compelled all law enforcement officers to participate in retrieving runaways. Strengthened the antislavery cause in the North. (389)

Fundamental Orders (1639): Drafted by settlers in the Connecticut River valley, this document was the first "modern constitution" establishing a democratically controlled government. Key features of the document were borrowed for Connecticut's colonial charter and, later, its state constitution. (48)

funding at par: Payment of debts, such as government bonds, at face value. In 1790, Alexander Hamilton proposed that the federal government pay its Revolutionary war debts in full in order to bolster the nation's credit. (185)

Gadsden Purchase (1853): Acquired additional land from Mexico for $10 million to facilitate the construction of a southern transcontinental railroad. (395)

Gag Resolution: Prohibited debate or action on antislavery appeals. Driven through the House by proslavery southerners, the Gag Resolution passed every year for eight years and was eventually overturned with the help of John Quincy Adams. (359)

Gettysburg Address (1863): Abraham Lincoln's oft-quoted speech, delivered at the dedication of the cemetery at Gettysburg battlefield. In the address, Lincoln framed the war as a means to uphold the values of liberty. (449)

Gettysburg, Battle of (July 1863): Civil War battle in Pennsylvania that ended in Union victory, spelling doom for the Confederacy, which never again managed to invade the North. Site of General George Pickett's daring but doomed charge on the Northern lines. (448)

Ghent, Treaty of (1814): Ended the War of 1812 in a virtual draw, restoring prewar borders but failing to address any of the grievances that first brought America into the war. (229)

Gibbons v. Ogden (1824): Suit over whether New York State could grant a monopoly to a ferry operating on interstate waters. The ruling reasserted that Congress had the sole power to regulate interstate commerce. (240)

Glorious (or Bloodless) Revolution (1688–1689): Relatively peaceful overthrow of the unpopular Catholic monarch, James II, who was replaced with Dutch-born William III and Mary II, daughter of James II. William and Mary accepted increased parliamentary oversight and new limits on monarchical authority. (50)

Goliad: Texas outpost where American volunteers, having laid down their arms and surrendered, were massacred by Mexican forces in 1836. The incident, along with the slaughter at the Alamo, fueled American support for Texan independence. (268)

Great Awakening (1730s and 1740s): Religious revival that swept the colonies. Participating ministers, most notably Jonathan Edwards and George Whitefield, placed an emphasis on direct, emotive spirituality. A Second Great Awakening arose in the nineteenth century. (90)

Great Compromise (1787): Popular term for the measure that reconciled the New Jersey and Virginia Plans at the Constitutional Convention, giving states proportional representation in the House and equal representation in the Senate. The compromise broke the stalemate at the convention and paved the way for subsequent compromises over slavery and the Electoral College. (171)

Great English Migration (1630–1642): Migration of seventy thousand refugees from England to the North American colonies, primarily New England and the Caribbean. The twenty thousand migrants who came to Massachusetts largely shared a common sense of purpose—to establish a model Christian settlement in the New World. (44)

Greek Revival: Inspired by the contemporary Greek independence movement, this building style, popular between 1820 and 1850, imitated ancient Greek structural forms in search of a democratic architectural vernacular. (326)

greenbacks: Paper currency issued by the Union Treasury during the Civil War. Inadequately supported by gold, greenbacks fluctuated in value throughout the war, reaching a low of 39 cents on the dollar. (434)

Greenville, Treaty of (1795): Under the terms of the treaty, the Miami Confederacy agreed to cede territory in the Old Northwest to the United States in exchange for cash payment, hunting rights, and formal recognition of their sovereign status. (193)

Guadalupe Hidalgo, Treaty of (1848): Ended the war with Mexico. Mexico agreed to cede territory reaching northwest from Texas to Oregon in exchange for $18.25 million in cash and assumed debts. (375)

Haitian Revolution (1791–1804): War incited by a slave uprising in French-controlled Saint Domingue, resulting in the creation of the first independent black republic in the Americas. (213)

Half-Way Covenant (1662): Agreement allowing unconverted offspring of church members to baptize their children. It signified a waning of religious zeal among second- and third-generation Puritans. (73)

Harpers Ferry: Federal arsenal in Virginia seized by abolitionist John Brown in 1859. Though Brown was later captured and executed, his raid alarmed southerners, who believed that northerners shared in Brown's extremism. (411)

Hartford Convention (1814–1815): Convention of Federalists from five New England states who opposed the War of 1812 and resented the strength of southern and western interests in Congress and in the White House. (230)

headright system: Employed in the tobacco colonies to encourage the importation of indentured servants, the system allowed an individual to acquire fifty acres of land if he paid for a laborer's passage to the colony. (63)

Hessians: German troops hired from their princes by George III to aid in putting down the colonial insurrection. This hardened the resolve of American colonists, who resented the use of paid foreign fighters. (136)

Homestead Act (1862): A federal law that sold settlers 160 acres of land for about $30 if they lived on it for five years and improved it by, for instance, building a house on it. The act helped make land accessible to hundreds of thousands of westward-moving settlers, but many people also found disappointment when their land was infertile or they saw speculators grabbing up the best land. (436)

House of Burgesses: Representative parliamentary assembly created to govern Virginia, establishing a precedent for government in the English colonies. (33)

Hudson River school (mid-nineteenth century): American artistic movement that produced romantic renditions of local landscapes. (327)

Huguenots: French Protestant dissenters, the Huguenots were granted limited toleration under the Edict of Nantes. After King Louis XIV outlawed Protestantism in 1685, many Huguenots fled elsewhere, including to British North America. (101)

***The Impending Crisis of the South* (1857):** Antislavery tract, written by white southerner Hinton R. Helper, arguing that nonslaveholding whites actually suffered most in a slave economy. (400)

impressment: Act of forcibly drafting an individual into military service, employed by the British navy against American seamen in times of war against France, 1793–1815. Impressment was a continual source of conflict between Britain and the United States in the early national period. (217)

Incas: Highly advanced South American civilization that occupied present-day Peru until it was conquered by Spanish forces under Francisco Pizarro in 1532. The Incas developed sophisticated agricultural techniques, such as terrace farming, in order to sustain large, complex societies in the unforgiving Andes Mountains. (6)

indentured servants: Migrants who, in exchange for transatlantic passage, bound themselves to a colonial employer for a term of service, typically between four and seven years. Their migration addressed the chronic labor shortage in the colonies and facilitated settlement. (63)

Indian Removal Act (1830): Ordered the removal of Indian tribes still residing east of the Mississippi to newly established Indian Territory west of Arkansas and Missouri. Tribes resisting eviction were forcibly removed by American forces, often after prolonged legal or military battles. (259)

Industrial Revolution: Shift toward mass production and mechanization that included the creation of the modern factory system. (286)

"Intolerable Acts" (1774): Series of punitive measures passed in retaliation for the Boston Tea Party, closing the Port of Boston, revoking a number of rights in the Massachusetts colonial charter, and expanding the Quartering Act to allow for the lodging of soldiers in private homes. In response, colonists convened the First Continental Congress and called for a complete boycott of British goods. (126)

Iroquois Confederacy (late 1500s): Bound together five tribes—the Mohawks, the Oneidas, the Onondagas, the Cayugas, and the Senecas—in the Mohawk Valley of what is now New York State. (38)

Jamestown (1607): First permanent English settlement in North America founded by the Virginia Company. (28)

Jay's Treaty (1794): Negotiated by Chief Justice John Jay in an effort to avoid war with Britain, the treaty included a British promise to evacuate outposts on U.S. soil and pay damages for seized American vessels, in exchange for which Jay bound the United States to repay pre-Revolutionary war debts and to abide by Britain's restrictive trading policies toward France. (195)

jeremiad: Often-fiery sermons lamenting the waning piety of parishioners first delivered in New England in the mid-seventeenth century; named after the doom-saying Old Testament prophet Jeremiah. (73)

joint-stock company: Short-term partnership between multiple investors to fund a commercial enterprise; such arrangements were used to fund England's early colonial ventures. (27)

Judiciary Act of 1789: Organized the federal legal system, establishing the Supreme Court, federal district and circuit courts, and the office of the attorney general. (184)

Judiciary Act of 1801: Passed by the departing Federalist Congress, it created sixteen new federal judgeships, ensuring a Federalist hold on the judiciary. (210)

Kanagawa, Treaty of (1854): Ended Japan's two-hundred-year period of economic isolation, establishing an American consulate in Japan and securing American coaling rights in Japanese ports. (394)

Kansas-Nebraska Act (1854): Proposed that the issue of slavery be decided by popular sovereignty in the Kansas and Nebraska Territories, thus revoking the 1820 Missouri Compromise. Introduced by Stephen Douglas in an effort to bring Nebraska into the Union and pave the way for a northern transcontinental railroad. (397)

King George's War (1744–1748): North American theater of Europe's War of Austrian Succession that once again pitted British colonists against their French counterparts in the North. The peace settlement did not involve any territorial realignment, leading to conflict between New England settlers and the British government. (105)

King Philip's War (1675–1676): Series of assaults by Metacom, King Philip, on English settlements in New England. The attacks slowed the westward migration of New England settlers for several decades. (49)

King William's War (1689–1697): War fought largely between French trappers, British settlers, and their respective Indian allies. The colonial theater of the larger War of the League of Augsburg in Europe. (103)

Know-Nothing party (1850s): Nativist political party, also known as the American party, that emerged in response to an influx of immigrants, particularly Irish Catholics. (286)

Ku Klux Klan: An extremist, paramilitary, right-wing secret society founded in the mid-nineteenth century and revived during the 1920s. It was antiforeign, antiblack, anti-Jewish, antipacifist, anti-Communist, anti-internationalist, anti-evolutionist, and antibootlegger, but pro–Anglo-Saxon and pro-Protestant. Its members, cloaked in sheets to conceal their identities, terrorized freedmen and sympathetic whites throughout the South after the Civil War. By the 1890s, Klan-style violence and Democratic legislation succeeded in virtually disenfranchising all southern blacks. (479)

Laird rams (1863): Two well-armed ironclad warships constructed for the Confederacy by a British firm. Seeking to avoid war with the United States, the British government purchased the two ships for its Royal Navy instead. (431)

Land Act of 1820: Fueled the settlement of the Northwest and Missouri Territories by lowering the price of public land. Also prohibited the purchase of federal acreage on credit, thereby eliminating one of the causes of the panic of 1819. (236)

Land Ordinance of 1785: Provided for the sale of land in the Old Northwest and earmarked the proceeds toward repaying the national debt. (166)

Lecompton Constitution (1857): Proposed Kansas constitution, whose ratification was unfairly rigged so as to guarantee slavery in the territory. Initially ratified by proslavery forces, it was later voted down when Congress required that the entire constitution be put up for a vote. (403)

Leisler's Rebellion (1689–1691): Armed conflict between aspiring merchants led by Jacob Leisler and the ruling elite of New York. One of many uprisings that erupted across the colonies when wealthy colonists attempted to re-create European social structures in the New World. (76)

Lexington and Concord, Battles of (April 1775): First battles of the Revolutionary War, fought outside of Boston. The colonial militia successfully defended their stores of munitions, forcing the British to retreat to Boston. (127)

***The Liberator* (1831–1865):** Antislavery newspaper published by William Lloyd Garrison, who called for the immediate emancipation of all slaves. (353)

Liberia: West African nation founded in 1822 as a haven for freed blacks, fifteen thousand of whom made their way back across the Atlantic by the 1860s. (351)

Liberty party (1840–1848): Antislavery party that ran candidates in the 1840 and 1844 elections before merging with the Free Soil party. Supporters of the Liberty party sought the eventual abolition of slavery, but in the short term hoped to halt the expansion of slavery into the territories and abolish the domestic slave trade. (370)

limited liability: Legal principle that facilitates capital investment by offering protection for individual investors, who, in cases of legal claims or bankruptcy, cannot be held responsible for more than the value of their individual shares. (292)

Lincoln-Douglas debates (1858): Series of debates between Abraham Lincoln and Stephen Douglas during the U.S. Senate race in Illinois. Douglas won the election, but Lincoln gained national prominence and emerged as the leading candidate for the 1860 Republican nomination. (409)

Long Island, Battle of (August 1776): Battle for the control of New York. British troops overwhelmed the colonial militias and retained control of the city for most of the war. (143)

loose construction: Legal doctrine that the federal government can use powers not specifically granted or prohibited in the Constitution to carry out its constitutionally mandated responsibilities. (240)

Louisiana Purchase (1803): Acquisition of Louisiana Territory from France. The purchase more than doubled the territory of the United States, opening vast tracts for settlement. (214)

Loyalists: American colonists who opposed the Revolution and maintained their loyalty to the king; sometimes referred to as "Tories." (141)

lyceum: (From the Greek name for the ancient Athenian school where Aristotle taught.) Public lecture hall that hosted speakers on topics ranging from science to moral philosophy. Part of a broader flourishing of higher education in the mid-nineteenth century. (316)

Macon's Bill No. 2 (1810): Aimed at resuming peaceful trade with Britain and France, the act stipulated that if either Britain or France repealed its trade restrictions, the United States would reinstate the embargo against the nonrepealing nation. When Napoleon offered to lift his restrictions on British ports, the United States was forced to declare an embargo on Britain, thereby pushing the two nations closer toward war. (220)

Maine Law of 1851: Prohibited the manufacture and sale of alcohol. A dozen other states followed Maine's lead, though most statutes proved ineffective and were repealed within a decade. (318)

***The Man Without a Country* (1863):** Edward Everett Hale's fictional account of a treasonous soldier's journeys in exile. The book was widely read in the North, inspiring greater devotion to the Union. (453)

Manifest Destiny (1840s and 1850s): Belief that the United States was destined by God to spread its "empire of liberty" across North America. Served as a justification for mid-nineteenth-century expansionism. (369)

***Marbury* v. *Madison* (1803):** Supreme Court case that established the principle of "judicial review"—the idea that the Supreme Court had the final authority to determine constitutionality. (211)

market revolution: Eighteenth- and nineteenth-century transformation from a disaggregated, subsistence economy to a national commercial and industrial network. (304)

Mason-Dixon line: Originally drawn by surveyors to resolve the boundaries between Maryland, Delaware, Pennsylvania, and Virginia in the 1760s, it came to symbolize the North-South divide over slavery. (355)

Massachusetts Bay Colony (founded in 1630): Established by non-separating Puritans, it soon grew to be the largest and most influential of the New England colonies. (44)

Mayflower Compact (1620): Agreement to form a majoritarian government in Plymouth, signed aboard the *Mayflower*. Created a foundation for self-government in the colony. (44)

McCormick reaper (1831): Mechanized the harvest of grains, such as wheat, allowing farmers to cultivate larger plots. The introduction of the reaper in the 1830s fueled the establishment of large-scale commercial agriculture in the Midwest. (297)

***McCulloch* v. *Maryland* (1819):** Supreme Court case that strengthened federal authority and upheld the constitutionality of the Bank of the United States by establishing that the State of Maryland did not have power to tax the bank. (240)

mercantilism: Economic theory that closely linked a nation's political and military power to its bullion reserves. Mercantilists generally favored protectionism and colonial acquisition as means to increase exports. (118)

***Merrimack* and *Monitor* (1862):** Confederate and Union ironclads, respectively, whose successes against wooden ships signaled an end to wooden warships. They fought a historic though inconsequential battle in 1862. (443)

mestizos: People of mixed Indian and European heritage, notably in Mexico. (19)

middle passage: Transatlantic voyage slaves endured between Africa and the colonies. Mortality rates were notoriously high. (68)

middlemen: In trading systems, those dealers who operate between the original producers of goods and the retail merchants who sell to consumers. After the eleventh century, European exploration was driven in large part by a desire to acquire alluring Asian goods without paying heavy tolls to Muslim middlemen. (11)

midnight judges (1801): Federal justices appointed by John Adams during the last days of his presidency. Their positions were revoked when the newly elected Republican Congress repealed the Judiciary Act. (210)

minstrel shows: Variety shows performed by white actors in blackface. First popularized in the mid-nineteenth century. (327)

Missouri Compromise (1820): Allowed Missouri to enter as a slave state but preserved the balance between North and South by carving free-soil Maine out of Massachusetts and prohibiting slavery from territories acquired in the Louisiana Purchase, north of the line of 36°30′. (237)

Model Treaty (1776): Sample treaty drafted by the Continental Congress as a guide for American diplomats. Reflected the Americans' desire to foster commercial partnerships rather than political or military entanglements. (148)

Molasses Act (1733): Tax on imported molasses passed by Parliament in an effort to squelch the North American trade with the French West Indies. It proved largely ineffective due to widespread smuggling. (88)

Molly Maguires (1860s–1870s): Secret organization of Irish miners who campaigned, at times violently, against poor working conditions in the Pennsylvania mines. (283)

Monitor: See ***Merrimack***. (443)

Monroe Doctrine (1823): Statement delivered by President James Monroe, warning European powers to refrain from seeking any new territories in the Americas. The United States largely lacked the power to back up the pronouncement, which was actually enforced by the British, who sought unfettered access to Latin American markets. (244)

Mormons: Religious followers of Joseph Smith, who founded a communal, oligarchic religious order in the 1830s, officially known as the Church of Jesus Christ of Latter-Day Saints. Mormons, facing deep hostility from their non-Mormon neighbors, eventually migrated west and established a flourishing settlement in the Utah desert. (312)

Morrill Tariff Act (1861): Increased duties back up to 1846 levels to raise revenue for the Civil War. (434)

nation-states: The term commonly describes those societies in which political legitimacy and authority overlay a large degree of cultural commonality. (8)

Narrative of the Life of Frederick Douglass (1845): Vivid autobiography of the escaped slave and renowned abolitionist Frederick Douglass. (353)

Nat Turner's rebellion (1831): Virginia slave revolt that resulted in the deaths of sixty whites and raised fears among white southerners of further uprisings. (350)

National Banking System (1863): Network of member banks that could issue currency against purchased government bonds. Created during the Civil War to establish a stable national currency and stimulate the sale of war bonds. (434)

Navigation Laws: Series of laws passed, beginning in 1651, to regulate colonial shipping; the acts provided that only English ships would be allowed to trade in English and colonial ports and that all goods destined for the colonies would first pass through England. (50)

Neutrality Proclamation (1793): Issued by George Washington, it proclaimed America's formal neutrality in the escalating conflict between England and France, a statement that enraged pro-French Jeffersonians. (192)

New England Confederation (1643): Weak union of the colonies in Massachusetts and Connecticut led by Puritans for the purposes of defense and organization; an early attempt at self-government during the benign neglect of the English Civil War. (49)

New England Emigrant Aid Company (founded 1854): Organization created to facilitate the migration of free laborers to Kansas in order to prevent the establishment of slavery in the territory. (401)

New Harmony (1825–1827): Communal society of around one thousand members, established in New Harmony, Indiana, by Robert Owen. The community attracted a hodgepodge of individuals, from scholars to crooks, and fell apart due to infighting and confusion after just two years. (321)

New Jersey Plan (1787): "Small-state plan" put forth at the Philadelphia convention, proposing equal representation by state, regardless of population, in a unicameral legislature. Small states feared that the more populous states would dominate the agenda under a proportional system. (170)

new lights: Ministers who took part in the revivalist, emotive religious tradition pioneered by George Whitefield during the Great Awakening. (91)

New Orleans, Battle of (January 1815): Resounding victory of American forces against the British, restoring American confidence and fueling an outpouring of nationalism. Final battle of the War of 1812. (228)

New York draft riots (1863): Uprising, mostly of working-class Irish Americans, in protest of the draft. Rioters were particularly incensed by the ability of the rich to hire substitutes or purchase exemptions. (433)

New York slave revolt (1712): Uprising of approximately two dozen enslaved Africans that resulted in the deaths of nine whites and the brutal execution of twenty-one participating blacks. (81)

***noche triste* (June 30, 1520):** "Sad night," when the Aztecs attacked Hernán Cortés and his forces in the Aztec capital, Tenochtitlán, killing hundreds. Cortés laid siege to the city the following year, precipitating the fall of the Aztec empire and inaugurating three centuries of Spanish rule. (17)

nonimportation agreements (1765 and after): Boycotts against British goods adopted in response to the Stamp Act and, later, the Townshend and Intolerable Acts. The agreements were the most effective form of protest against British policies in the colonies. (121)

Non-Intercourse Act (1809): Passed alongside the repeal of the Embargo Act, it reopened trade with all but the two belligerent nations, Britain and France. The act continued Jefferson's policy of economic coercion, still with little effect. (220)

Northwest Ordinance (1787): Created a policy for administering the Northwest Territories. It included a path to statehood and forbade the expansion of slavery into the territories. (166)

Nullification Crisis (1832–1833): Showdown between President Andrew Jackson and the South Carolina legislature, which declared the 1832 tariff null and void in the state and threatened secession if the federal government tried to collect duties. It was resolved by a compromise negotiated by Henry Clay in 1833. (257)

old lights: Orthodox clergymen who rejected the emotionalism of the Great Awakening in favor of a more rational spirituality. (91)

Old Northwest: Territories acquired by the federal government from the states, encompassing land northwest of the Ohio River, east of the Mississippi River, and south of the Great Lakes. The well-organized management and sale of the land in the territories under the land ordinances of 1785 and 1787 established a precedent for handling future land acquisitions. (165)

Olive Branch Petition (July 1775): Conciliatory measure adopted by the Continental Congress, professing American loyalty and seeking an end to the hostilities. King George rejected the petition and proclaimed the colonies in rebellion. (136)

Oneida Community: One of the more radical utopian communities established in the nineteenth century, it advocated "free love," birth control, and eugenics.

Utopian communities reflected the reformist spirit of the age. (322)

Opium War (1839–1842): War between Britain and China over trading rights, particularly Britain's desire to continue selling opium to Chinese traders. The resulting trade agreement prompted Americans to seek similar concessions from the Chinese. (393)

Orders in Council (1806–1807): Edicts issued by the British crown closing French-owned European ports to foreign shipping. The French responded by ordering the seizure of all vessels entering British ports, thereby cutting off American merchants from trade with both parties. (217)

Ostend Manifesto (1854): Secret Franklin Pierce administration proposal to purchase or, that failing, to wrest militarily Cuba from Spain. Once leaked, it was quickly abandoned due to vehement opposition from the North. (393)

Pacific Railroad Act (1862): Helped fund the construction of the Union Pacific transcontinental railroad with the use of land grants and government bonds. (473)

panic of 1819: Severe financial crisis brought on primarily by the efforts of the Bank of the United States to curb overspeculation on western lands. It disproportionately affected the poorer classes, especially in the West, sowing the seeds of Jacksonian democracy. (235)

panic of 1837: Economic crisis triggered by bank failures, elevated grain prices, and Andrew Jackson's efforts to curb overspeculation on western lands and transportation improvements. In response, President Martin Van Buren proposed the "Divorce Bill," which pulled treasury funds out of the banking system altogether, contracting the credit supply. (266)

panic of 1857: Financial crash brought on by gold-fueled inflation, overspeculation, and excess grain production. Raised calls in the North for higher tariffs and for free homesteads on western public lands. (407)

Paris, Treaty of (1783): Peace treaty signed by Britain and the United States ending the Revolutionary War. The British formally recognized American independence and ceded territory east of the Mississippi while the Americans, in turn, promised to restore Loyalist property and repay debts to British creditors. (155)

Patent Office: Federal government bureau that reviews patent applications. A patent is a legal recognition of a new invention, granting exclusive rights to the inventor for a period of years. (291)

Patriots: colonists who supported the American Revolution; they were also known as "Whigs." (141)

patroonships: Vast tracts of land along the Hudson River in New Netherlands granted to wealthy promoters in exchange for bringing fifty settlers to the property. (53)

Paxton Boys (1764): Armed march on Philadelphia by Scotts-Irish frontiersmen in protest against the Quaker establishment's lenient policies toward Native Americans. (80)

peculiar institution: Widely used term for the institution of American slavery in the South. Its use in the first half of the nineteenth century reflected a growing division between the North, where slavery was gradually abolished, and the South, where slavery became increasingly entrenched. (236)

Peninsula Campaign (1862): Union general George B. McClellan's failed effort to seize Richmond, the Confederate capital. Had McClellan taken Richmond and toppled the Confederacy, slavery would have most likely survived in the South for some time. (440)

Pequot War (1636–1638): Series of clashes between English settlers and Pequot Indians in the Connecticut River valley. Ended in the slaughter of the Pequots by the Puritans and their Narragansett Indian allies. (48)

pet banks: Popular term for pro-Jackson state banks that received the bulk of federal deposits when Andrew Jackson moved to dismantle the Bank of the United States in 1833. (264)

Pinckney's Treaty (1795): Signed with Spain, which, fearing an Anglo-American alliance, granted Americans free navigation of the Mississippi and the disputed territory of Florida. (195)

plantation: Large-scale agricultural enterprise growing commercial crops and usually employing coerced or slave labor. European settlers established plantations in Africa, South America, the Caribbean, and the American South. (13)

Pontiac's uprising (1763): Bloody campaign waged by Ottawa chief Pontiac to drive the British out of Ohio Country. It was brutally crushed by British troops, who resorted to distributing blankets infected with smallpox as a means to put down the rebellion. (113)

Pony Express (1860–1861): Short-lived, speedy mail service between Missouri and California that relied on lightweight riders galloping between closely placed outposts. (303)

Poor Richard's Almanack **(1732–1758):** Widely read annual pamphlet edited by Benjamin Franklin. Best known for its proverbs and aphorisms emphasizing thrift, industry, morality, and common sense. (94)

Popé's Rebellion (1680): Pueblo Indian rebellion that drove Spanish settlers from New Mexico. (21)

popular sovereignty: Notion advanced before the Civil War that the sovereign people of a given territory should decide whether to allow slavery. Seemingly a compromise, it was largely opposed by northern abolitionists, who feared it would promote the spread of slavery to the territories. (381)

predestination: Calvinist doctrine that God has foreordained some people to be saved and some to be damned. Though their fate was irreversible, Calvinists, particularly those who believed they were destined for salvation, sought to lead sanctified lives in order to demonstrate to others that they were in fact members of the "elect." (42)

primogeniture: Legal principle that the oldest son inherits all family property or land. Landowners' younger sons, forced to seek their fortunes elsewhere, pioneered early exploration and settlement of the Americas. (27)

privateers: Privately owned armed ships authorized by Congress to prey on enemy shipping during the Revolutionary War. More numerous than the tiny American navy, privateers inflicted heavy damages on British shippers. (152)

Proclamation of 1763: Decree issued by Parliament in the wake of Pontiac's uprising, prohibiting settlement beyond the Appalachians. Contributed to rising resentment of British rule in the American colonies. (113)

proprietary colonies: Colonies—Maryland, Pennsylvania, and Delaware—under the control of local proprietors, who appointed colonial governors. (95)

Protestant Reformation (sixteenth century): Movement to reform the Catholic Church launched in Germany by Martin Luther. Reformers questioned the authority of the Pope, sought to eliminate the selling of indulgences, and encouraged the translation of the Bible from Latin, which few at the time could read. The Reformation was launched in England in the 1530s when King Henry VIII broke with the Roman Catholic Church. (25)

Puritans: English Protestant reformers who sought to purify the Church of England of Catholic rituals and creeds. Some of the most devout Puritans believed that only "visible saints" should be admitted to church membership. (43)

Quakers: Religious group known for their tolerance, emphasis on peace, and idealistic Indian policy, who settled heavily in Pennsylvania in the seventeenth and eighteenth centuries. (54)

Quartering Act (1765): Required colonies to provide food and quarters for British troops. Many colonists resented the act, which they perceived as an encroachment on their rights. (119)

Quebec Act (1774): Allowed the French residents of Québec to retain their traditional political and religious institutions, and extended the boundaries of the province southward to the Ohio River. Mistakenly perceived by the colonists to be part of Parliament's response to the Boston Tea Party. (126)

Québec, Battle of (1759): Historic British victory over French forces on the outskirts of Québec. The surrender of Québec marked the beginning of the end of French rule in North America. (110)

Queen Anne's War (1702–1713): Second in a series of conflicts between the European powers for control of North America, fought between the English and French colonists in the North, and the English and Spanish in Florida. Under the peace treaty, the French ceded Acadia (Nova Scotia), Newfoundland, and Hudson Bay to Britain. (103)

radical Whigs: Eighteenth-century British political commentators who agitated against political corruption and emphasized the threat to liberty posed by arbitrary power. Their writings shaped American political thought and made colonists especially alert to encroachments on their rights. (117)

Reconstruction Act (1867): Passed by the newly elected Republican Congress, it divided the South into five military districts, disenfranchised former Confederates, and required that Southern states both ratify the Fourteenth Amendment and write state constitutions guaranteeing freedmen the franchise before gaining readmission to the Union. (475)

Redeemers: Southern Democratic politicians who sought to wrest control from Republican regimes in the South after Reconstruction. (476)

Reform Bill of 1867: Granted suffrage to all male British citizens, dramatically expanding the electorate. The success of the American democratic experiment, reinforced by the Union victory in the Civil War, was used as one of the arguments in favor of the bill. (462)

regulars: Trained professional soldiers, as distinct from militia or conscripts. During the French and Indian War, British generals, used to commanding experienced regulars, often showed contempt for ill-trained colonial militiamen. (109)

Regulator movement (1768–1771): Eventually violent uprising of backcountry settlers in North Carolina against unfair taxation and the control of colonial affairs by the seaboard elite. (80)

Reign of Terror (1793–1794): Ten-month period of brutal repression when some forty thousand individuals were executed as enemies of the French Revolution. While many Jeffersonians maintained their faith in the French Republic, Federalists withdrew their already lukewarm support once the Reign of Terror commenced. (192)

rendezvous: The principal marketplace of the Northwest fur trade, which peaked in the 1820s and 1830s. Each summer, traders set up camps in the Rocky Mountains to exchange manufactured goods for beaver pelts. (279)

republican motherhood: Ideal of family organization and female behavior after the American Revolution that stressed the role of women in guiding family members toward republican virtue. (179)

republicanism: Political theory of representative government, based on the principle of popular sovereignty, with a strong emphasis on liberty and civic virtue. Influential in eighteenth-century American political thought, it stood as an alternative to monarchical rule. (117)

responsorial: Call and response style of preaching that melded Christian and African traditions. Practiced by African slaves in the South. (350)

Revolution of 1800: Electoral victory of Democratic Republicans over the Federalists, who lost their congressional majority and the presidency. The peaceful transfer of power between rival parties solidified faith in America's political system. (206)

Roanoke Island (1585): Sir Walter Raleigh's failed colonial settlement off the coast of North Carolina. (26)

romanticism: Early nineteenth-century movement in European and American literature and the arts that, in reaction to the hyper-rational Enlightenment, emphasized imagination over reason, nature over civilization, intuition over calculation, and the self over society. (328)

Royal African Company: English joint-stock company that enjoyed a state-granted monopoly on the colonial slave trade from 1672 until 1698. The supply of slaves to the North American colonies rose sharply once the company lost its monopoly privileges. (68)

royal colonies: Colonies where governors were appointed directly by the king. Though often competent administrators, the governors frequently ran into trouble with colonial legislatures, which resented the imposition of control from across the Atlantic. (95)

Rush-Bagot agreement (1817): Signed by Britain and the United States, it established strict limits on naval armaments in the Great Lakes, a first step in the full demilitarization of the U.S.-Canadian border, completed in the 1870s. (232)

Russo-American Treaty (1824): Fixed the line of 54°40′ as the southernmost boundary of Russian holdings in North America. (245)

Salem witch trials (1692–1693): Series of witchcraft trials launched after a group of adolescent girls in Salem, Massachusetts, claimed to have been bewitched by certain older women of the town. Twenty individuals were put to death before the trials were put to an end by the governor of Massachusetts. (73)

salutary neglect (1688–1763): Unofficial policy of relaxed royal control over colonial trade and only weak enforcement of Navigation Laws. Lasted from the Glorious Revolution to the end of the French and Indian War in 1763. (51)

San Jacinto, Battle of (1836): Resulted in the capture of Mexican dictator Santa Anna, who was forced to withdraw his troops from Texas and recognize the Rio Grande as Texas's southwestern border. (269)

Saratoga, Battle of (October 1777): Decisive colonial victory in upstate New York, which helped secure French support for the Revolutionary cause. (148)

scalawags: Derogatory term for pro-Union Southerners whom Southern Democrats accused of plundering the resources of the South in collusion with Republican governments after the Civil War. (479)

Second Anglo-Powhatan War (1644–1646): Last-ditch effort by the Indians to dislodge Virginia settlements. The resulting peace treaty formally separated white and Indian areas of settlement. (30)

Second Battle of Bull Run (August 1862): Civil War battle that ended in a decisive victory for Confederate general Robert E. Lee, who was emboldened to push further into the North. (443)

Second Continental Congress (1775–1781): Representative body of delegates from all thirteen colonies. Drafted the Declaration of Independence and managed the colonial war effort. (135)

Second Great Awakening (early nineteenth century): Religious revival characterized by emotional mass "camp meetings" and widespread conversion. Brought about a democratization of religion as a multiplicity of denominations vied for members. (310)

Sedition Act (1798): Enacted by the Federalist Congress in an effort to clamp down on Jeffersonian opposition, the law made anyone convicted of defaming government officials or interfering with government policies liable to imprisonment and a heavy fine. The act drew heavy criticism from Republicans, who let the act expire in 1801. (198)

"Self-Reliance" (1841): Ralph Waldo Emerson's popular lecture-essay that reflected the spirit of individualism pervasive in American popular culture during the 1830s and 1840s. (278)

Separatists: Small group of Puritans who sought to break away entirely from the Church of England; after initially settling in Holland, a number of English Separatists made their way to Plymouth Bay, Massachusetts, in 1620. (43)

Seventh of March speech (1850): Daniel Webster's impassioned address urging the North to support the Compromise of 1850. Webster argued that topography and climate would keep slavery from becoming entrenched in Mexican Cession territory and urged northerners to make all reasonable concessions to prevent disunion. (386)

Seward's Folly (1867): Popular term for Secretary of State William Seward's purchase of Alaska from Russia. The derisive term reflected the anti-expansionist sentiments of most Americans immediately after the Civil War. (482)

Shakers (established ca. 1770s): Called "Shakers" for their lively dance worship, they emphasized simple, communal living and were all expected to practice celibacy. First transplanted to America from England by Mother Ann Lee, the Shakers counted six thousand members by 1840, though by the 1940s the movement had largely died out. (322)

Shays's Rebellion (1786): Armed uprising of western Massachusetts debtors seeking lower taxes and an end to property foreclosures. Though quickly put down, the insurrection inspired fears of "mob rule" among leading Revolutionaries. (168)

Sherman's march (1864–1865): Union general William Tecumseh Sherman's destructive march through Georgia. An early instance of "total war," purposely targeting infrastructure and civilian property to diminish morale and undercut the Confederate war effort. (452)

Shiloh, Battle of (April 1862): Bloody Civil War battle on the Tennessee-Mississippi border that left more than twenty-three thousand soldiers dead, wounded, or missing, and ended in a marginal Union victory. (451)

slave codes: Set of laws beginning in 1662 defining racial slavery. They established the hereditary nature of slavery and limited the rights and education of slaves. (69)

Society of the Cincinnati (established 1783): Exclusive, hereditary organization of former officers in the Continental Army. Many resented the pretentiousness of the order, viewing it as a vestige of pre-Revolutionary traditions. (178)

Sons of Liberty: Patriotic groups that played a central role in agitating against the Stamp Act and enforcing nonimportation agreements. (See also **Daughters of Liberty**) (121)

South Carolina slave revolt (Stono River) (1739): Uprising, also known as the Stono Rebellion, of more than fifty South Carolina blacks along the Stono River. They attempted to reach Spanish Florida but were stopped by the South Carolina militia. (81)

Spanish Armada: Spanish fleet defeated in the English Channel in 1588. The defeat of the Armada marked the beginning of the decline of the Spanish Empire. (26)

Specie Circular (1836): U.S. Treasury decree requiring that all public lands be purchased with "hard," or metallic, currency. Issued after small state banks flooded the market with unreliable paper currency, fueling land speculation in the West. (264)

spoils system: Policy of rewarding political supporters with public office, first widely employed at the federal level by Andrew Jackson. The practice was widely abused by unscrupulous office seekers, but it also helped cement party loyalty in the emerging two-party system. (253)

spot resolutions (1846): Measures introduced by Illinois congressman Abraham Lincoln, questioning President James K. Polk's justification for war with Mexico. Lincoln requested that Polk clarify precisely where Mexican forces had attacked American troops. (373)

squatters: Frontier farmers who illegally occupied land owned by others or not yet officially opened for settlement. Many of North Carolina's early settlers were squatters, who contributed to the colony's reputation as being more independent-minded and "democratic" than its neighbors. (36)

Stamp Act Congress (1765): Assembly of delegates from nine colonies who met in New York City to draft a petition for the repeal of the Stamp Act. Helped ease sectional suspicions and promote intercolonial unity. (120)

stamp tax (1765): Widely unpopular tax on an array of paper goods, repealed in 1766 after mass protests erupted across the colonies. Colonists developed the principle of "no taxation without representation" that questioned Parliament's authority over the colonies and laid the foundation for future revolutionary claims. (120)

Sugar Act (1764): Duty on imported sugar from the West Indies. It was the first tax levied on the colonists by the crown and was lowered substantially in response to widespread protests. (119)

Tallmadge amendment (1819): Failed proposal to prohibit the importation of slaves into Missouri Territory and pave the way for gradual emancipation. Southerners vehemently opposed the amendment, which they perceived as a threat to the sectional balance between North and South. (236)

Tammany Hall (established 1789): Powerful New York political machine that primarily drew support from the city's immigrants, who depended on Tammany Hall patronage, particularly social services. (283)

tariff: Tax levied on imports. Traditionally, manufacturers support tariffs as protective and revenue-raising measures, while agricultural interests, dependent on world markets, oppose high tariffs. (186)

Tariff of 1816: First protective tariff in American history, created primarily to shield New England manufacturers from the inflow of British goods after the War of 1812. (233)

Tariff of 1842: Protective measure passed by Congressional Whigs, raising tariffs to pre–compromise tariff of 1833 rates. (364)

Tariff of 1857: Lowered duties on imports in response to a high Treasury surplus and pressure from southern farmers. (408)

Tariff of Abominations (1828): Noteworthy for its unprecedentedly high duties on imports. Southerners vehemently opposed the tariff, arguing that it hurt southern farmers, who did not enjoy the protection of tariffs but were forced to pay higher prices for manufactures. (256)

Tenure of Office Act (1867): Required the president to seek approval from the Senate before removing appointees. When Andrew Johnson removed his secretary of war in violation of the act, he was impeached by the House but remained in office when the Senate fell one vote short of removing him. (481)

Thirteenth Amendment (1865): Constitutional amendment prohibiting all forms of slavery and involuntary servitude. Former Confederate states were required to ratify the amendment prior to gaining reentry into the Union. (445)

three-fifths compromise (1787): Determined that each slave would be counted as three-fifths of a person for the purpose of apportioning taxes and representation. The compromise granted disproportionate political power to southern slave states. (172)

three-sister farming: Agricultural system employed by North American Indians as early as 1000 c.e.; maize, beans, and squash were grown together to maximize yields. (8)

Tippecanoe, Battle of (1811): Resulted in the defeat of Shawnee chief Tenskwatawa, "the Prophet," at the hands of William Henry Harrison in the Indiana wilderness. After the battle, the Prophet's brother, Tecumseh, forged an alliance with the British against the United States. (222)

Tordesillas, Treaty of (1494): Signed by Spain and Portugal, dividing the territories of the New World. Spain received the bulk of territory in the Americas, compensating Portugal with titles to lands in Africa and Asia. (16)

Townshend Acts (1767): External, or indirect, levies on glass, white lead, paper, paint, and tea, the proceeds of which were used to pay colonial governors, who had previously been paid directly by colonial assemblies. Sparked another round of protests in the colonies. (122)

Trail of Tears (1838–1839): Forced march of fifteen thousand Cherokee Indians from their Georgia and Alabama homes to Indian Territory. Some four thousand Cherokees died on the arduous journey. (260)

transcendentalism (mid-nineteenth century): Literary and intellectual movement that emphasized individualism and self-reliance, predicated upon a belief that each person possesses an "inner light" that can point the way to truth and direct contact with God. (329)

transportation revolution: Term referring to a series of nineteenth-century transportation innovations—turnpikes, steamboats, canals, and railroads—that linked local and regional markets, creating a national economy. (304)

***Trent* affair (1861):** Diplomatic row that threatened to bring the British into the Civil War on the side of the Confederacy, after a Union warship stopped a British steamer and arrested two Confederate diplomats on board. (430)

Trenton, Battle of (December 1776): George Washington surprised and captured a garrison of sleeping German Hessians, raising the morale of his crestfallen army and setting the stage for his victory at Princeton a week later. (146)

triangular trade: Exchange of rum, slaves, and molasses between the North American colonies, Africa, and the West Indies. A small but immensely profitable subset of the Atlantic trade. (86)

Tripolitan War (1801–1805): Four-year conflict between the American navy and the North African nation of Tripoli over piracy in the Mediterranean. Jefferson, a staunch noninterventionist, reluctantly deployed American forces, eventually securing a peace treaty with Tripoli. (213)

turnpike: Privately funded, toll-based public road constructed in the early nineteenth century to facilitate commerce. (298)

Tuscarora War (1711–1713): Began with an Indian attack on New Bern, North Carolina. After the Tuscaroras were defeated, remaining Indian survivors migrated northward, eventually joining the Iroquois Confederacy as its sixth nation. (37)

U.S. Sanitary Commission (established 1861): Government agency founded with the help of Elizabeth Blackwell that trained nurses, collected medical supplies, and equipped hospitals in an effort to help the Union army. The commission helped professionalize nursing and gave many women the confidence and organizational skills to propel the women's movement in the postwar years. (436)

***Uncle Tom's Cabin* (1852):** Harriet Beecher Stowe's widely read novel that dramatized the horrors of slavery. It heightened northern support for abolition and escalated the sectional conflict. (399)

Underground Railroad: Informal network of volunteers that helped runaway slaves escape from the South and reach free-soil Canada. Seeking to halt the flow of runaway slaves to the North, southern planters and congressmen pushed for a stronger fugitive slave law. (385)

Union League: Reconstruction-era African American organization that worked to educate Southern blacks about civic life, built black schools and churches, and represented African American interests before government and employers. It also campaigned on behalf of Republican candidates and recruited local militias to protect blacks from white intimidation. (478)

Union party (1864): A coalition party of prowar Democrats and Republicans formed during the 1864 election to defeat antiwar Northern Democrats. (453)

Valley Forge (1777–1778): Encampment where George Washington's poorly equipped army spent a wretched, freezing winter. Hundreds of men died and more than a thousand deserted. The plight of the starving, shivering soldiers reflected the main weakness of the American army—a lack of stable supplies and munitions. (132)

Vicksburg, siege of (1863): Two-and-a-half-month siege of a Confederate fort on the Mississippi River in Tennessee. Vicksburg finally fell to Ulysses S. Grant in July of 1863, giving the Union army control of the Mississippi River and splitting the South in two. (451)

Virginia and Kentucky resolutions (1798–1799): Statements secretly drafted by Jefferson and Madison for the legislatures of Kentucky and Virginia. Argued that states were the final arbiters of whether the federal government overstepped its boundaries and could therefore nullify, or refuse to accept, national legislation they deemed unconstitutional. (200)

Virginia Company: English joint-stock company that received a charter from King James I that allowed it to found the Virginia colony. (28)

Virginia Plan: "Large state" proposal for the new constitution, calling for proportional representation in both houses of a bicameral Congress. The plan favored larger states and thus prompted smaller states to come back with their own plan for apportioning representation. (171)

Virginia Statute for Religious Freedom (1786): Measure enacted by the Virginia legislature prohibiting state support for religious institutions and recognizing freedom of worship. Served as a model for the religion clause of the First Amendment to the Constitution. (178)

voyageurs: See coureurs de bois. (102)

Wade-Davis Bill: Passed by congressional Republicans in response to Abraham Lincoln's "10 percent" Reconstruction plan, it required that 50 percent of a state's voters pledge allegiance to the Union and set stronger safeguards for emancipation. Reflected divisions between Congress and the president, and between radical and moderate Republicans, over the treatment of the defeated South. (470)

Walker Tariff (1846): Revenue-enhancing measure that lowered tariffs from 1842 levels, thereby fueling trade and increasing Treasury receipts. (371)

Wanghia, Treaty of (1844): Signed by the United States and China, it assured the United States the same trading concessions granted to other powers, greatly expanding America's trade with the Chinese. (393)

war hawks (1811–1812): Democratic-Republican congressmen who pressed James Madison to declare war on Britain. Largely drawn from the South and West, the war hawks resented British constraints on American trade and accused the British of supporting Indian attacks against American settlements on the frontier. (221)

War of 1812 (1812–1815): Fought between Britain and the United States largely over the issues of trade and impressment. Though the war ended in a relative draw, it demonstrated America's willingness to defend its interests militarily, earning the young nation newfound respect from European powers. (226)

War of Jenkins's Ear (began in 1739): Small-scale clash between Britain and Spain in the Caribbean and in the buffer colony, Georgia. It merged with the much larger War of Austrian Succession in 1742. (105)

West Africa Squadron (established 1808): British Royal Navy force formed to enforce the abolition of the slave trade in 1807. It intercepted hundreds of slave ships and freed thousands of Africans. (346)

West Virginia (admitted to the Union 1863): Mountainous region that broke away from Virginia in 1861 to form its own state after Virginia seceded from the Union. Most of the residents of West Virginia were independent farmers and miners who did not own slaves and thus opposed the Confederate cause. (423)

Whiskey Rebellion (1794): Popular uprising of whiskey distillers in southwestern Pennsylvania in opposition to an excise tax on whiskey. In a show of strength and resolve by the new central government, Washington put down the rebellion with militia drawn from several states. (187)

Wilderness Campaign (1864–1865): A series of brutal clashes between Ulysses S. Grant's and Robert E. Lee's armies in Virginia, leading up to Grant's capture of Richmond in April of 1865. Having lost Richmond, Lee surrendered to Grant at Appomattox Courthouse. (457)

Wilmot Proviso (1846): Amendment that sought to prohibit slavery from territories acquired from Mexico. Introduced by Pennsylvania congressman David Wilmot, the failed amendment ratcheted up tensions between North and South over the issue of slavery. (377)

Woman's Loyal League (1863–1865): Women's organization formed to help bring about an end to the Civil War and encourage Congress to pass a constitutional amendment prohibiting slavery. (477)

Woman's Rights Convention at Seneca Falls (1848): Gathering of feminist activists in Seneca Falls, New York, where Elizabeth Cady Stanton read her "Declaration of Sentiments," stating that "all men and women are created equal." (320)

writ of habeas corpus: Petition requiring law enforcement officers to present detained individuals before the court to examine the legality of the arrest. Protects individuals from arbitrary state action. Suspended by Lincoln during the Civil War. (432)

XYZ Affair (1797): Diplomatic conflict between France and the United States when American envoys to France were asked to pay a hefty bribe for the privilege of meeting with the French foreign minister. Many in the United States called for war against France, while American sailors and privateers waged an undeclared war against French merchants in the Caribbean. (197)

Yamasee Indians: Defeated by the South Carolinians in the war of 1715–1716. The Yamasee defeat devastated the last of the coastal Indian tribes in the southern colonies. (37)

Yorktown, Battle of (October 1781): George Washington, with the aid of the French army, besieged Cornwallis at Yorktown, while the French naval fleet prevented British reinforcements from coming ashore. Cornwallis surrendered, dealing a heavy blow to the British war effort and paving the way for an eventual peace. (153)

Zenger trial (1734–1735): New York libel case against John Peter Zenger. Established the principle that truthful statements about public officials could not be prosecuted as libel. (95)

INDEX

Tappan, Lewis, 352, 360
Tariff(s), 250; of 1816, 233, 291; of 1832, 257; of 1842, 364, 371; of 1857, 408, 418; of Abominations (1828), 256–257; after American Revolution, 167, 186; colonial, 118; compromise Tariff of 1833, 258; Hamilton and, 186; Morrill (1861), 434, 473; Walker (1846), 371, 434. *See also* Trade
Taverns: colonial, 88–89
Taxation: under Articles of Confederation, 164–165, 174; in Civil War, 434, 435, 463; of colonies, 3, 119–120, 119–123; for education, 314; by England, 51; of farmers, 168; revolts against, 130; in South, 479. *See also* Excise taxes; Income taxes
Taxation through representation, 96
Taylor, Zachary, 383, 384; Compromise of 1850 and, 387; election of 1848 and, 382; in Mexican War, 373, 374
Tea, taxes on, 122–123, 125–126
Teachers: men as, 295, 314; women as, 295, 469
Technology: in Civil War, 428; nationalism and, 460. *See also* Innovations; Inventions
Tecumseh (Shawnee), 221–222, 223, 227 (map)
Tejanos, 270, 271
Telegraph, 159, 292, 301, 303–304
Temperance movement, 159, 286, 310, 318–319
Temperance pledge, 318
10 percent Reconstruction plan, 470, 471, 474
Tenant farming, 284; in England, 27
Ten-hour day, 292, 293
Tennessee, 78, 113, 252, 469; Civil War in, 451, 451 (map); secession by, 423, 423 (map)
Tennessee River region: Civil War and, 423, 451, 451 (map)
Ten Nights in a Barroom and What I Saw There (Arthur), 318
Tenochtitlán, 16, 17, 20, 22
Tenskwatawa ("the Prophet"), 221–222
Tenth Amendment, 184
Tenure of Office Act (1867), 481
Term-limit laws, 195
Terre Haute, naming of, 102
Territories: Northwest Ordinance and, 166; popular sovereignty in, 381, 388, 416; slavery in, 346, 363, 377, 382, 388, 406–407, 416
Terrorism: by Klan, 479–480. *See also* Violence
Texas, 395; annexation of, 269, 363, 366–368, 369, 371, 372, 375; British interests in, 366; France and, 103; German immigrants in, 288; as Lone Star Republic, 269, 270, 366; Mexico and, 267–269, 269 (map), 270–271, 339, 363, 366, 372; New Mexico conflict with, 385, 385 (map), 387, 388; as protectorate, 366; secession of, 416, 423 (map); slavery in, 267–268, 269, 466
Texas Rangers, 270
Texas Revolution (1836), 268–269, 269 (map), 271, 367, 368

Textbooks, 73, 315, 322
Textile industry, 256; British and, 287; southern cotton and, 291, 429, 430; women in, 290, 294–295
Thackeray, William, 329
Thames, Battle of the, 222, 272
"Thanatopsis" (Bryant), 329
Thanksgiving Day, 44
Theater. *See* Drama
Third parties, 189; in 1832, 262–263
Thirteenth Amendment, 445, 463, 471, 477
Thirty Years' War (1618–1648), 53, 130
Thompson's Skirt Factory, 295
Thoreau, Henry David, 321, 330–331
Three Emperors, Battle of, 217
Three-fifths clause, 172, 173, 205, 230–231, 473, 474
Three-sister farming, 8
Ticonderoga, Fort, battle at, 136, 147
Tidewater region, 4
Tierra del Fuego, 25
Tilton, Theodore, 478
Timbuktu, 12
Tippecanoe, Battle of, 222, 265, 272
Tobacco and tobacco industry, 85; blacks and, 81; in Chesapeake region, 32–33, 63–64, 87; Maryland and, 33; soil damage from, 37; Virginia and, 32–33
Tocqueville, Alexis de, 253, 309, 319; on democracy in U.S. and Europe, 254–255
Tokugawa Shogunate, 394
Tompkins, Sally, 436
Topeka, Kansas, free-soilers in, 402
Tordesillas, Treaty of, 16
Tories (American Revolution), 155. *See also* Loyalists
Total war, Civil War as, 441, 452
Town meetings, 51, 72–73, 96–97, 140
Towns. *See* Cities and towns
Townshend, Charles ("Champagne Charley"), 122
Townshend Acts (1767), 122–123
Townshend taxes (1767), 96n
Trade: under Articles of Confederation, 167; British in Spanish America, 104; with China, 163, 393–394; colonial, 51, 87 (map), 112; Embargo Act and, 218, 219, 220; in fish, 85–86; free, 256; fur, 279; global, 14; Hamilton and, 202; in luxury goods, 11; in Napoleonic wars, 217; Native Americans and, 31, 32; New World bullion and, 19; prerevolution, 161; triangular, 86. *See also* Commerce; Economy; Slave trade; Tariff(s)
Trade embargo. *See* Embargo Act (1807)
Trade routes: in 1492, 11 (map)
Trade unions, 293
Trading posts: in Africa, 12; commerce and, 280; for fur trade, 103 (map); Russian in North America, 243
Trafalgar, Battle of, 217
Trail(s): main routes West before Civil War, 303 (map); Oregon, 369
Trail of Tears, 259, 260
Trans-Allegheny area: as nation's breadbasket, 296–297; Spanish

interests in, 154; state land claims and, 163, 164 (map)
Trans-Appalachian area, 155
Transatlantic telegraph, 301
Transatlantic view of history, 156, 335
Transcendentalism, 322, 329–331
Transcontinental railroads, 395, 396, 461; in Panama, 392
Trans-Mississippi West, 213
Transportation: American System and, 233, 234; in Civil War, 425, 436; after Civil War, 465; colonial, 88; discrimination in public, 479; innovations in, 298–304; main routes West, 303 (map); of raw materials, 290; revolution in, 159, 276, 297, 304; roads in, 233, 234, 238, 298; in South, 70; steamboats in, 236, 238, 298–299; in West, 303. *See also* Railroad(s); specific forms
Travel: by immigrants, 282; to Pacific Coast, 395. *See also* Transportation
Travels of Marco Polo, The, 12
Travis, W. B., 268
Treason: Burr and, 216; Civil War and, 453, 472
Treasury Department: in Civil War, 434; Gallatin as secretary of, 210
Treaties: for Louisiana, 214; between Mexico and Texas, 269; with Native Americans, 3, 56, 152, 258; for Oregon, 368, 371; by Texas, 366; U.S./New Granada, 392. *See also* specific treaties
Treaty ports, in China, 393
Trent affair, 430
Trenton, Battle of, 133, 138 (map), 146
Triangular trade, 86
Tribes (Native American), 6. *See also* Native Americans; specific groups
Tripolitan War, 212–213, 212 (map)
Trist, Nicholas P., 375
Trollope, Frances, 364
Troops. *See* Armed forces; Military; Soldiers
Troy (New York) Female Seminary, 315
Trumbull, John, 94, 136, 185, 257, 327
Truth, Sojourner, 353, 355
Tubman, Harriet, 385, 411
Tuckerman, Henry Theodore, 330
Tudor dynasty (England), 26
Tupac Amaru II, 130, 131
Turgot, Anne Robert Jacques, 182
Turks, Greeks and, 326
Turner, Frederick Jackson, 275
Turner, Nat, 350, 355, 410
Turnpikes, 298. *See also* Roads and highways
Tuscarora Indians, 151
Tuscarora War, 37
Twain, Mark, 303, 303 (map), 341
Tweed, William Marcy ("Boss"), 479
Twenty-second Amendment, 195
Two-party system, 188, 200, 210, 248, 253, 273–274
Tye, Colonel, 144
Tyler, John: cabinet of, 364; China and, 393; election of 1840 and, 171, 272, 363; election of 1844 and, 366; Texas and, 366–367, 370; Whig party and, 363, 364
Typhoid, 428

WASHINGTON
1889

OREGON COUNTRY
(By Agreement
with Britain, 1846)

OREGON
1859

IDAHO
1890

MONTANA
1889

NORTH DAKOTA
1889

SOUTH DAKOTA
1889

WYOMING
1890

NEVADA
1864

UTAH
1896

NEBRASKA
1867

MEXICAN CESSION
(1848)

COLORADO
1876

LOUISIANA
PURCHASE
(From France, 18__)

CALIFORNIA
1850

KANSAS
1861

ARIZONA
1912

NEW MEXICO
1912

OKLAHO__
1907

GADSDEN PURCHASE
(From Mexico, 1853)

TEXAS
(Independent Republic,
Annexed 1845)

TEXAS
1845

Great
Salt
Lake

Columbia R.

Missouri R.

Colorado R.

Rio Grande

Nueces R.

PACIFIC
OCEAN

PACIFIC OCEAN

HAWAI'I
(Annexed 1898)

HAWAI'I
1959

0   50 100 Km.
0   50 100 Mi.

RUSSIA

ALASKA
1959

CANADA

MEXICO

ALASKA PURCHASE
(From Russia, 1867)

PACIFIC OCEAN

0   200   400 Km.
0   250   400 Mi.

CANADA

Lake Superior

Lake Michigan

Lake Huron

Lake Ontario

Lake Erie

St. Lawrence R.

MAINE
1820

VT.
1791

N.H.

MASS.

CONN.

R.I.

**WISCONSIN
1848**

ESOTA
858

**MICHIGAN
1837**

NEW YORK

**IOWA
1846**

**ILLINOIS
1818**

**INDIANA
1816**

**OHIO
1803**

PENNSYLVANIA

NEW
JERSEY

1790

DELAWARE

MARYLAND

COLONIES

THIRTEEN

MASON-DIXON LINE

**WEST
VIRGINIA
1863**

VIRGINIA

**MISSOURI
1821**

2010

**KENTUCKY
1792**

**THE ORIGINAL UNITED STATES
(By Treaty with Britain, 1783)**

THE ORIGINAL

36°30'N
**MISSOURI
COMPROMISE
LINE**

**ARKANSAS
1836**

**TENNESSEE
1796**

**NORTH
CAROLINA**

**SOUTH
CAROLINA**

Mississippi R.

**MISSISSIPPI
1817**

**ALABAMA
1819**

GEORGIA

**LOUISIANA
1812**

**(Seized from Spain,
1810, 1813)**

**FLORIDA
(By Treaty with
Spain, 1819)**

**FLORIDA
1845**

Gulf of Mexico

BAHAMAS

Territorial Growth
of the
United States

1820 Date of states admission to the Union

● Geographic center of population by decade

ATLANTIC

OCEAN

N

0   150   300 Km.

0   150   300 Mi.

CUBA

DOMINICAN
REPUBLIC

HAITI

PUERTO RICO
(Acquired from
Spain, 1898)

VIRGIN IS.
(Acquired from
Denmark, 1916–1917)

19°N

PUERTO RICO

VIRGIN
ISLANDS

18°N

68°W

67°W

66°W

65°W

0   25   50 Km.

0   25   50 Mi.

GREENLAND
(DENMARK)

ICELAND

IREL

PORTUGA

Azores
(Port.)

M

ALASKA
(U.S.)

CANADA

80°N

60°N

40°N

UNITED STATES

Bermuda
(U.K.)

ATLANTIC OCEAN

WESTERN
SAHARA
(MOROCCO)

Midway Is.
(U.S.)

Hawaiian Is.
(U.S.)

MEXICO

BAHAMAS

CUBA
JAMAICA
BELIZE
HONDURAS

DOMINICAN REP.
Virgin Is.
(U.S.)
HAITI
Puerto Rico
(U.S.)

ST. KITTS AND NEVIS
ANTIGUA AND BARBUDA
DOMINICA
BARBADOS
ST. LUCIA
ST. VINCENT AND
GRENADA
THE GRENADINES

20°N

MAURIT

CAPE
VERDE

SENEGAL
GAMBIA

GUINEA-BISSAU

GUINEA

PACIFIC OCEAN

GUATEMALA
EL SALVADOR

NICARAGUA

COSTA RICA

PANAMA

VENEZUELA

TRINIDAD AND TOBAGO
GUYANA

SIERRA
LEONE

LIBERIA

COLOMBIA

FR. GUIANA
(FRANCE)

E

SURINAM

SÃO TO

Equator

Galapagos Is.
(Ecuador)

ECUADOR

PERU

0°

BRAZIL

SAMOA

French Polynesia
(France)

BOLIVIA

TONGA

20°S

PARAGUAY

CHILE

Easter Is.
(Chile)

URUGUAY

ARGENTINA

| 0 | 1,000 | 2,000 Km. |
| 0 | 1,000 | 2,000 Mi. |

40°S

Falkland Is.
(U.K.)

160°W   140°W   120°W   100°W   80°W   60°W   40°W   20°W

60°S

80°S

C OCEAN

WAY
FINLAND
SWEDEN ESTONIA
N.
LATVIA
LITHUANIA
BELARUS
RMANY POLAND
CZ.
SLK.
AUS. HUNG.
SLN. CR.
B. H. SE.
ITALY
MO.
K. BULGARIA
MAC.
ALBANIA
GREECE
TUNISIA
MALTA

RUSSIA

KAZAKHSTAN

MONGOLIA

N. KOREA

JAPAN
S. KOREA

PACIFIC OCEAN

UKRAINE
MOLDOVA
ROMANIA

GEORGIA

UZBEKISTAN

TURKEY
ARMENIA
CYPRUS
LEBANON
ISRAEL
SYRIA

AZERBAIJAN
IRAQ
IRAN

TURKMENISTAN

KYRGYZSTAN
TAJIKISTAN

AFGHANISTAN

PEOPLE'S REPUBLIC OF CHINA

TAIWAN

LIBYA
EGYPT
JORDAN
KUWAIT
SAUDI
ARABIA
BAHRAIN
QATAR
UNITED
ARAB EMIRATES
OMAN

PAKISTAN

NEPAL
BHUTAN

BANGLADESH

INDIA

MYANMAR
(BURMA)
LAOS

Mariana
Islands
(U.S.)

Wake I.
(U.S.)

IGER
CHAD
SUDAN
ERITREA
YEMEN

THAILAND
VIETNAM

CAMBODIA
(KAMPUCHEA)

PHILIPPINES

Guam
(U.S.)

MARSHALL
ISLANDS

IN
ERIA

DJIBOUTI

SRI LANKA

BRUNEI
DARUSSALAM

PALAU

FEDERATED STATES
OF MICRONESIA

KIRIBATI

CAMEROON
CENTRAL
AFRICAN REP.
SOUTH
SUDAN
ETHIOPIA

SOMALIA

MALDIVES

MALAYSIA

GABON
NGO
RWANDA
DEM. REP.
OF CONGO
BURUNDI
UGANDA
KENYA
TANZANIA

SEYCHELLES

INDIAN OCEAN

SINGAPORE

INDONESIA

PAPUA
NEW
GUINEA

SOLOMON IS.

NAURU

TUVALU

ANGOLA
ZAMBIA
MALAWI
COMOROS

TIMOR LESTE

VANUATU

FIJI

NAMIBIA
ZIMBABWE
MADAGASCAR

BOTSWANA
MAURITIUS

MOZAMBIQUE
SWAZILAND
SOUTH
AFRICA
LESOTHO

New Caledonia
(France)

AUSTRALIA

NEW
ZEALAND

ABBREVIATIONS

AUS.	AUSTRIA
BEL.	BELGIUM
B. H.	BOSNIA AND HERZEGOVINA
CR.	CROATIA
CZ.	CZECH REPUBLIC
DEN.	DENMARK
HUNG.	HUNGARY
K.	KOSOVO
LUX.	LUXEMBOURG
MAC.	MACEDONIA
MO.	MONTENEGRO
NETH.	NETHERLANDS
SE.	SERBIA
SLK.	SLOVAKIA
SLN.	SLOVENIA
SWITZ.	SWITZERLAND

20°E   40°E   60°E   80°E   100°E   120°E   140°E   160°E